Order
from
Confusion Sprung

for Elliott
with best wishes
Claude

Order
from
Confusion Sprung

Studies in
Eighteenth-Century Literature
from Swift to Cowper

CLAUDE RAWSON

Humanities Press
New Jersey ▼ London

First published in 1985
by George Allen & Unwin (Publishers) Ltd.

©1985 by Claude Rawson

This paperback edition first published
in 1992 by
Humanities Press International, Inc.
Atlantic Highlands, NJ 07716, and
3 Henrietta Street, Covent Garden, London WC2E 8LU

Library of Congress Cataloging-in-Publication Data
Rawson, Claude Julien.
Order from confusion sprung : studies in eighteenth-century
literature from Swift to Cowper / Claude Rawson.
p.   cm.
"First published in 1985 by George Allen & Unwin, Ltd."—T.p.
verso.
Includes index.
ISBN 0-391-03745-5 (pbk.)
1. English literature—18th century—History and criticism.
2. Swift, Jonathan, 1667–1745—Criticism and interpretation.
3. Pope, Alexander, 1688–1744—Criticism and interpretation.
4. Fielding, Henry, 1707–1754—Criticism and interpretation.
I. Title.
[PR442.R36   1992]
820.9'005—dc20

92–5336
CIP

A CIP record for this book is available from the British Library.

Printed in the United States of America

for Judy, Hugh, Tim,
Mark, Harriet and
Annabel Rawson

Contents

Preface

The title of this book may suggest to some an optimism or confidence often associated with eighteenth-century authors. But the words are from the closing couplet of Swift's *Lady's Dressing Room*,

> Such Order from Confusion sprung,
> Such gaudy Tulips rais'd from Dung,

and my concern is as much with the ironic energies contained in assertions of order as with the assertion itself. The interplay between them, which has always interested me, is no simple thing, neither tidy nor consistent, even within the work of individual authors. The ironic energies do not cancel the aspirations to order. But neither do the perceptions of order subdue the reservations and uneasinesses which, in one form or another, show themselves in the work of every author of the period who is still read today. Swift's couplet, with its mixture of festive insolence and tart undercutting, of celebration vitalised as well as tarnished by the recognition of squalor, is only one manifestation, particularly striking and characteristic, of the interplay explored in these pages. In several of my other authors, urbanity and order are seen in combination with, or under pressure from, forces of disorder, the lures of introspection and self-exposure, the ambiguous attractions of 'low' or demotic styles. Hogarth's *Southwark Fair*, reproduced on the cover, is a pictorial evocation of some of the themes and art-forms with which Augustan authors and their ideas of order were compelled, willingly or reluctantly, to come to terms.

As in my earlier books, I have worked on the assumption that eighteenth-century authors are not only rooted in their own time and culture, but exist in an older and continuously evolving tradition. Their attitudes, themes and styles derive from the past and look forward to the future. The continuities and interactions (as well as the discontinuities) of eighteenth-century writers both with their predecessors (notably classical predecessors in satire and epic) and with writers of our own century are frequently under scrutiny in these pages. This is not because I have any wish to see eighteenth-century authors as, in some modish sense, 'our contemporaries'. It is a fact of history that certain themes, preoccupations, images, forms reappear in widely different periods, in imitation or allusion or reaction, by design or coincidence, in recurrent cultural contexts or personal circumstances, or in response to the challenges of particular literary media or genres. An understanding of both resemblance and difference, of continuity and transformation, may sharpen our focus on past and present. That has been a subsidiary ambition of this book: not as a topic of systematic enquiry or formal argument, but as a matter of local awarenesses and exploratory glimpses where the texts under discussion seemed to me naturally to invite connection with others of different date.

There is a vulgar philistinism which holds that to bring a later writer into the discussion of an earlier one is somehow 'unhistorical'. This view seems to me as much a denial of history as are the opposite pedantries of those who insist on reading texts in rigorous abstraction from their original contexts, and perhaps more dangerous because it sports an appearance of academic piety. The idea that literary periods are sealed units, and that to believe this is in some sense more historical than to register movement and interaction and variety between and within different times, dies hard. One of its corollaries is that 'periods' or centuries have thoughts, opinions and outlooks, often remarkably simple, consistent and apparently unanimous: on the villainy of Augustus, for example, or on neo-classical literary 'doctrine' or the workings of Providence. It would seem that the past, unlike the present, was of one mighty mind, and that the notion that different people felt differently is a modern invention. Selective quotation, often at saturation levels, provides the necessary 'historical' credentials, as though a hundred extracts from the *Church Times* or *Morning Star* were presented as a complete epitome of the twentieth-century British mind. In particular, the pseudo-historical operations of neo-Christian and history-of-ideas interpreters have been moving into eighteenth-century studies in some force. As I argue in my final chapter or Appendix such approaches make a parade of what inexpert readers will readily mistake for historical learning, while the very nature of their methods and assumptions falsifies and perhaps precludes the act of historical recovery the critics believe themselves to be engaged in. For better or worse, the essays in this book are written in the belief that writers in any period resist assimilation to official world-pictures, real or imagined, and may well resemble writers of other periods in ways that repay study.

Preface

The volume brings together, in a revised form, some uncollect-ed studies of eighteenth-century authors, chiefly Swift, Pope and Fielding. Most belong to the last twelve years, though one or two are earlier. In selecting them, I have systematically excluded certain essays on Swift which are designed as chapters of a separate book on that author, and some discussions of the canni-bal theme in literature which are also intended for a separate study. A number of review-essays have been included, where these deal substantially with an eighteenth-century author or topic and not predominantly with the recent publication under review. Partial exceptions are the three pieces which make up chapter 8, and also and more especially the Appendix entitled 'More Providence than Wit: Some Recent Approaches to Eighteenth-Century Literature', which are concerned with some of the larger issues of method or approach I have mentioned, and indeed with some current or prevailing conceptions of the period. The questions raised there, and the tendencies discussed, are common to many more writings than those immediately under review. Even in this group of review-essays, the reader will, I hope, find some extensive discussion of primary and not merely of secondary topics. Except in the Appendix, I have tried wherever possible to remove or abbreviate comments mainly concerned with the book under review, unless these were inextricably bound up with the larger discussion.

I have revised or updated material and where appropriate have added or extended the annotation and documentation. Excep-tions are 12, one of the very earliest pieces, which expresses views I no longer hold in every detail, but which seemed worth reprint-ing as a perspective on seldom discussed material; 15, which although it is concerned with critical issues of wider import had as its occasion the publication of particular volumes at a particular moment; and some of the pieces from the *Times Literary Sup-plement*, the *London Review of Books* or the *Sewanee Review*, where the addition of notes and references would have been out of keeping with the general character of the piece. Each piece is dated by first publication of its various parts, whether or not I have introduced subsequent revisions or additions: thus Chapter 9, which is given the dates of first publication of its two parts (1971 and 1974), has been extensively revised for this volume, and contains references to works published after these two dates. The slightly surreal effect this may sometimes produce seemed a price worth paying for the sake of clear indications of dates of origin. I have changed the titles of some of the pieces.

The chapters in this book are made up of one or more previously published pieces, sometimes merged into one another and sometimes in separate sections. They were written as separate pieces, not as 'chapters' of a single unfolding argument, and the word 'chapters' is used merely as a convenient shorthand. There is inevitably some overlap and repetition, which I have tried to minimise but which could not be removed altogether without weakening the argument or impairing the integrity of individual pieces. I have sometimes explored the same theme or passage in different contexts of argument, or in a learned as well as a non-specialist publication. Where each of two or more related pieces had something to say which was not in the others and which seemed worth preserving, I have brought them together within the same chapter. Some chapters will thus consist both of a fully documented article and of an unannotated essay originally addressed to a more general readership.

Acknowledgements

I am grateful to the editors and/or publishers of the books and journals in which these essays (most of them now more or less extensively revised) have previously appeared:

1 Claude Rawson (ed.), *The Character of Swift's Satire*, Associated University Presses, 1983: the essay is composed of material from *Focus: Swift*, Sphere, 1971, and *Sewanee Review*, LXXXVIII (Winter, 1980), University of the South;

2 (i) *Dutch Quarterly Review*, XIII, 3–4 (1983); (ii) and (iii), *London Review of Books*, 18 November–1 December 1982 and 16 September–5 October 1983;

3 J. C. Hilson, M. M. B. Jones and J. R. Watson (eds.), *Augustan Worlds: Essays in Honour of A. R. Humphreys*, University of Leicester Press, 1978;

4 (i) *Times Literary Supplement*, 4 September 1981 and 10 February 1978; (ii) Maximillian E. Novak (ed.), *English Literature in the Age of Disguise*, University of California Press, 1977;

5 *London Review of Books*, 6–19 November 1980;

6 *Essays and Studies*, XXXV (1982), John Murray for the English Association;

7 (i) *Times Literary Supplement*, 30 December 1977; (ii) Broadcast as Open University lecture A204/03, BBC Radio 3 and 4, 1980; and *Uttar Pradesh Studies in English*, I (1980);

8 (i) and (iii) *London Review of Books*, 18 September–1 October 1980 and 18 February–3 March 1982; (ii) *Times Literary Supplement*, 12 August 1983;

9 (i) *Durham University Journal*, XXXIII (1971); (ii) Larry S. Champion (ed.), *Quick Springs of Sense: Studies in the Eighteenth Century*, University of Georgia Press, 1974;

10 Introduction to Henry Fielding, *A Journey from this World to the Next*, Everyman's Library, Dent, 1973;

11 *Notes and Queries*, CCIV (1959), Oxford University Press;

12 *Journal of English and Germanic Philology*, LXI (1962), University of Illinois Press;

13 *Sewanee Review*, LXXXVIII (Winter, 1980) and XCI (Spring, 1983), University of the South;

14 *Times Literary Supplement*, 2 January 1981 and 9 November 1984;

15   *ELH*, XLII (1975), The Johns Hopkins University Press.

I owe gratitude to many friends, colleagues and students, at universities and learned societies in Britain, the United States and other countries, where I have taught or have delivered papers. They are too many to name, in itself a reflection of the size of the debt. Particular mention, however, must be made of G. K. Hunter, Jenny Mezciems and Judy Rawson for continuous and detailed help on many points over many years. I am also indebted to the editors who provided the stimulus for most of this book by encouraging me to contribute to the journals or collections of essays in their care. In particular, Karl Miller, editor of the *London Review of Books*, and two successive editors of the *Times Literary Supplement*, John Gross and Jeremy Treglown, each created the occasion for several pieces in this volume.

Texts and Editions Used

Swift. Unless otherwise noted quotations are from Herbert Davis and others (eds.), *Prose Works*, Oxford, Blackwell, 1939–1974, 16 volumes (abbreviated as *Works*); Harold Williams (ed.), *Poems*, 2nd edn., Oxford, Clarendon Press, 1958, 3 volumes, and *Correspondence*, Oxford, Clarendon Press, 1963–1965, 5 volumes.

Pope. Quotations from Pope, unless otherwise noted, are from John Butt, Maynard Mack and others (eds.), *Twickenham Edition of the Poems of Alexander Pope*, London, Methuen, 1939–1969, 11 volumes in 12.

Fielding. W. B. Coley, Martin C. Battestin and others (eds.), *The Wesleyan Edition of the Works of Henry Fielding*, Oxford, Clarendon Press, 1967 – (in progress), for *Miscellanies I, Joseph Andrews, The Jacobite's Journal, Tom Jones* and *Amelia*; Douglas Brooks (ed.), *Joseph Andrews and Shamela*, London, Oxford University Press, 1970, for *Shamela*; Claude Rawson (ed.), *A Journey from this World to the Next*, London, Dent, 1973; *Jonathan Wild*, World's Classics edition, London, Oxford University Press, 1961 reprint; Harold E. Pagliaro (ed.), *Journal of a Voyage to Lisbon*, New York, Nardon Press, 1963. Where there are modern scholarly editions of individual plays, these have been used. For other works, including plays, I cite from W. E. Henley (ed.), *Complete Works*, London, Heinemann, 1903, 16 volumes (abbreviated as *Works*).

PART I

Swift

1

The Character of Swift's Satire

Reflections on Swift, Johnson, and Human Restlessness

Restlessness and Doubt

Swift's satire rests on a traditional assumption (especially common perhaps among conservative and authoritarian thinkers) about the human condition: that it is a prey to subversion and unhappiness from within, that men are by mental constitution restless, irrational and unsatisfied, congenitally prone to false needs and driven to supererogatory and destructive satisfactions. Samuel Johnson was later, and more compassionately than Swift, to speak of this universal mental predicament as 'that hunger of imagination which preys incessantly upon life', relentlessly craving new satisfactions:

> Those who have already all that they can enjoy, must enlarge their desires. He that has built for use, till use is supplied, must begin to build for vanity, and extend his plan to the utmost power of human performance, that he may not be soon reduced to form another wish.
>
> (*Rasselas*, 1759, ch. 31 [32])

'Vanity' means both pride and emptiness, and man aptly emerges as both guilty and trapped in a kind of suffering emptiness or unreality, self-inflicted, and incurable:

> There is no man whose imagination does not sometimes predominate over his reason, who can regulate his attention wholly by his will, and whose ideas will come and go at his command. No man will be found in whose mind airy notions do not sometimes tyrannise, and force him to hope or fear beyond the limits of sober probability. All power of fancy over reason is a degree of insanity.
>
> (*Rasselas*, ch. 43 [44])

3

The last few words bring to mind Swift's description of madness, in the famous 'digression' in *A Tale of a Tub*, as the state that occurs 'when a Man's Fancy gets *astride* on his Reason, when Imagination is at Cuffs with the Senses, and common Understanding, as well as common Sense, is Kickt out of Doors' (*Tale*, sec. 9). The differences may seem more apparent than the similarities, since all that ostensibly links the two passages is a commonplace notion of madness as a state where reason is subdued by fantasy. Swift's words have a zany violence absent in Johnson's definition. Swift's emphasis is satirical, rather than soberly and compassionately descriptive. And Swift is castigating certain groups of men, rather than generalising about all mankind.

These differences are real, but not as great as they seem, especially the last. The digression on madness has a strange universalising tendency that somehow (by an irrational feat of irony, rather than by open argument) turns the specific types Swift is castigating, the tyrants, system-builders, occultists, nonconformist sectarians, free-thinkers and the rest, into examples of a radical human perversity, common to all. The sense of the culpable and compulsive unreality of men's pursuits, the insatiable, self-complicating play of ever-renewed need, is, in the *Tale* as in other works of Swift, not unlike Johnson's. The notion of a radical restlessness is itself common enough: Swift could find it in Hobbes, whom he disliked but with whom he shared many ideas, or in his own patron, Temple, whose essay 'Of Popular Discontents', which Swift saw through the press, defined 'restlessness of mind' as distinguishing men from beasts.

The latter distinction was not in fact always felt to be very strong. Both Swift and Johnson were deeply impregnated with the old homiletic notion that men very readily lapsed into living 'like beasts'. Swift's most extreme version of this are the Yahoos. Johnson once, in a more casual context, varied the formula when replying to a lady's complaint about excessive drinkers who made 'beasts of themselves': 'I wonder, Madam, . . . that you have not penetration enough to see the strong inducement to the excess; for he who makes a *beast* of himself gets rid of the pain of being a man' (G. B. Hill (ed.), *Johnsonian Miscellanies*, Oxford, 1897, 2:333). In a way, Johnson is even saying that 'being a man' is worse than being a beast. Swift might have said the same, comparing real mankind with the Yahoos to its disadvantage. Johnson's 'worse' in this case partly means more unhappy and Swift's mainly means more evil. Both would regard bestial reversion not only as squalid in itself, but (whether 'better' or 'worse' than the human state) as entailing a radically damaging reflection on that human state. Johnson's compassion does not deny the hard fact, but Swift tends to cut off any possibility of compassion.

For Johnson is under no sentimental illusion about the bestiality of man, and critics have pointed out that his view of man's nature is in some ways that of Hobbes, Swift or Mandeville. Bate and others have cited from Boswell's Hebridean *Tour* the episode in which 'Lady MacLeod asked if no man was naturally good'. When Johnson (varying the old adage, also found, incidentally, in Hobbes and Mandeville, about man being a wolf to man) replied 'no more than a wolf', the lady commented, 'This is worse than Swift' (Boswell, *Journal of a Tour to the Hebrides with Samuel Johnson*, Yale Edition, New York, 1963, 170; W. Jackson Bate, *Samuel Johnson*, New York, 1977, 196, 493). It is Swift who is normally 'worse' in the sense intended by Lady MacLeod, however, although the difference in their respective treatments of men who make beasts of themselves is superimposed on a common perception in both that the process is lamentably natural.

But the main traditional emphasis which Swift shares with Johnson has to do with man's unregenerate restlessness of spirit, rather than with primitive savagery of the Hobbesian or the Yahoo kind, though these were not, in Swift's imagination, unconnected. For both Swift and Johnson the restlessness was a radical perversity of the human mind. Because the condition was mental rather than circumstantial, they felt it to be incurable, and because it was universal they understood that its reach extended to themselves. Both men had the same self-implicating fear of the human mind left to its own spontaneous motions, with its natural tendency to 'free-thinking', which meant not only political and religious subversiveness, and immorality, but intellectual disorder and clinical insanity. Both men dreaded madness in themselves and tended to equate the mad with the bad.

Both also felt compassion for the clinically mad. Swift's was a gruff and dismissive compassion, solidly demonstrated in the financial legacy that he insultingly left for the Irish 'To build a House for Fools and Mad' (*Poems*, 2:572). In the imaginative as distinct from the practical dimension, madness in Swift's satire is the viciousness and squalor of the Academy of Modern Bedlam or the Legion Club. Johnson, on the other hand, is notable for a continuously sustained tenderness towards the mentally afflicted in his writings as well as in his personal life. The common factor in the writings of both men on folly and on vice is a feeling, never far from the surface, of 'there but for the grace of God go I'. Johnson's satirical impulse tends to be contained by this reflection and quickly turns benign, whereas Swift's is exacerbated into added urgencies of rejection. Thus mad scientists serve in both authors as examples of the dangers of free-wheeling unregulated intellect, but the treatment of the Academicians of Lagado, as we shall see, is very different from that of the mad astronomer in *Rasselas*.

Swift shared with Johnson an unusually active and personalised conception of mankind's restlessness. Both were not only quick to feel that their view of a universal 'madness' implicated themselves also, but that the dividing-line between the universal malady in which they shared by definition and an individual pathological insanity was very narrow. It is not just that both men happened at times to feel menaced by insanity in themselves, and that Johnson's Imlac could say, poignantly, that 'Of the uncertainties of our present state, the most dreadful and alarming is the uncertain continuance of reason' (*Rasselas*, ch. 42 [43]). Less dramatically, and perhaps more importantly, both men felt that even states of ordinary sanity are in a sense precarious and momentary victories of 'reason' over 'fancy', victories of a vigilance needing constant renewal, perhaps at times a matter not even of 'control' or 'repression' (the latter word is used idiomatically, of course, and without the technical colouring of Freudian terminology), but of show:

> All power of fancy over reason is a degree of insanity; but while this power is such as we can controul and repress, it is not visible to others, nor considered as any depravation of the mental faculties: it is not pronounced madness but when it comes ungovernable, and apparently influences speech or action.
>
> (*Rasselas*, ch. 43 [44])

Similarly Swift, in a short undated piece, 'Some Thoughts on Free-Thinking', describes 'free-thinking' as an undirected flow of consciousness, of a kind to which all men are subject but which only madmen fail to regulate. He quotes with approval an Irish prelate who

> said, that the difference betwixt a mad-man and one in his wits, in what related to speech, consisted in this: That the former spoke out whatever came into his mind, and just in

the confused manner as his imagination presented the ideas. The latter only expressed such thoughts, as his judgment directed him to chuse, leaving the rest to die away in his memory. And that if the wisest man would at any time utter his thoughts, in the crude indigested manner, as they come into his head, he would be looked upon as raving mad.

(*Works*, 4:49)

In Swift's approval of the prelate's analysis (Johnson would have endorsed it too) one senses the conscious reasoning behind Swift's exposure of the 'author' of *A Tale of a Tub*, that compound of intellectual and religious deviation, and of disordered thought, compulsively confessional and wildly digressive. That 'author', and the parodied energies of his stream-of-consciousness, anticipate a powerful mode of the 'modern' imagination, those heroes of the wandering mind in Sterne or Beckett whose 'repertory of permitted attitudes has never ceased to grow', who have 'to overflowing, the exasperated good-will of the over-anxious' (*Molloy, Malone Dies, The Unnamable*, London, 1959, 25), and whose mentalities are restlessly indecorous, digressive, disordered. Swift's official attitude is one of uncompromising censure. He would have abhorred Tristram Shandy and seen Molloy, who is for Beckett a pained and witty embodiment of the human condition, as merely another mad modern to be savaged. But if Swift parodied both Sterne and Beckett in advance, they, in turn, were able to assimilate the parody and then to transcend it into primary creations, and Swift may be said to have prepared the way for these creations by a prophetic and imaginative feat of repudiation. The fact suggests an intuitive understanding of the fragmentation of 'modern' sensibility and of the literary modes this was to call forth. And Swift's diagnosis seems to have proceeded not merely from the protesting reasonings of a satirist, but also from a kind of sympathetic involvement. At all events, Swift enlarges the bishop's notions in 'Some Thoughts on Free-Thinking' by a self-implicating generalisation that is almost Johnsonian in its literalness, its moral determination, and its reductive practicality:

And indeed, when we consider our thoughts, as they are the seeds of words and actions, we cannot but agree, that they ought to be kept under the strictest regulation. And that in the great multiplicity of ideas, which ones mind is apt to form, there is nothing more difficult than to select those, which are most proper for the conduct of life.

7

This cool glimpse of the psychological constitution of human-kind leads straight to the risks of sectarianism and free-thinking:

> So that I cannot imagine what is meant by the mighty zeal in some people, for asserting the freedom of thinking: Because, if such thinkers keep their thoughts within their own breasts, they can be of no consequence, further than to themselves. If they publish them to the world, they ought to be answerable for the effects their thoughts produce upon others.

The pun on 'free-thinking', sliding tacitly between a general meaning of 'unrestricted flow of thought' and the more usual technical sense of 'free exercise of reason in matters of religious belief' (the latter definition is the Oxford English Dictionary's) is not merely disingenuous: sectarian folly, like other kinds (described most exhaustively in *A Tale of a Tub*), is not only 'disease' as well as vice, but the product of elementary mental instincts common to us all. Hence the 'realistic' acceptance that these instincts cannot be eradicated, but can and must be regulated: by concealment, discretion, discipline, practical sanctions concerned with 'the conduct of life'. Men's 'answerability', not for their thoughts but 'for the effect their thoughts produce upon others', entails, says Swift, a need for political restrictions on religious free-thinkers (and sectarians) similar to the restrictions that governments employ against those who openly propose 'innovations in government'. The King of Brobdingnag, after noting 'the several Sects among us in Religion and Politicks . . . said, he knew no Reason, why those who entertain Opinions prejudicial to the Publick, should be obliged to change, or should not be obliged to conceal them' (*Gulliver's Travels*, 2:6). The political treatment of the sectarian is exactly parallel to the personal discipline a man must impose on his subversive inner thoughts:

> The want of belief is a defect that ought to be concealed when it cannot be overcome. . . .
> I am not answerable to God for the doubts that arise in my own breast, since they are the consequence of that reason which he hath planted in me, if I take care to conceal those doubts from others, if I use my best endeavours to subdue them, and if they have no influence on the conduct of my life.

> ('Thoughts on Religion', *Works*, 9:261–62)

The practical stress on the conduct of life, the conception of the limits of 'answerability', are the same, down to the use of the same phrases, as in 'Some Thoughts on Free-Thinking'. The same language and the same patterns of thought apply to political government and to mental self-government, and the King of Brobdingnag's views (often repeated in Swift's own name) on how to treat religious and political sectarians, echo exactly Swift's views on how to treat his own doubts and subversive thoughts.

One notices in both spheres a recognition of the fact of unceasing tension, of radical 'incurability'. Because the subversions are *psychologically* determined (as distinct from being seen as bad *behaviour* or unhappy *circumstance*, both of which would have seemed easier to put right than a congenital cast of mind), there can be no question of any solution. Swift, in such places as the loaded pun on free-thinking, characteristically carries a greater attribution of guilt, not just to free-thinkers, but to mankind, than Johnson would normally be inclined to emphasise. But Swift's two 'thoughts on religion' may be compared with Johnson's prayer of 12 August 1784:

> teach me by thy Holy Spirit to withdraw my mind from unprofitable and dangerous enquiries, from difficulties vainly curious, and doubts impossible to be solved.
>
> (*Diaries, Prayers, and Annals*, Yale Edition, 383–84)

Because neither Swift nor Johnson entertains the possibility that the doubts can be resolved or the 'dangerous enquiries' answered, they speak of concealing or trying to subdue them, of preventing their influence upon action or of withdrawing the mind from them, of disciplines rather than solutions. This does not mean that Swift lacked faith or positive values, any more than Johnson did (though Swift, as we shall see, often shied from proclaiming his positives directly). The moral vision of both men rests, with an authoritarian solidity, on some great commonplaces of Christian and humanist thought. Nor does their great complexity of character allow these positives to be refined away in casuistical subtlety ('refinement' is one of Swift's favourite terms of abuse), or to evaporate in a luxurious indulgence of Victorian 'honest doubt'. 'The Grand points of Christianity ought to be taken as infallible Revelations', Swift said (*Correspondence*, 4:7). The attitude reaches out to that area of simplification where controversy is silenced, and the great truths stand in unassailable and uncomplicated authority. If neither Swift nor Johnson envisages the inner peace of a full reconciliation between man and the beliefs by which he lives, they do assert the practical possibility (however strenuous), and the moral necessity, of living under the rule of these beliefs. Just as in the private mind, doubts and difficulties must be neutralised, not solved, so also in the public teaching of religion. In his *Letter to a Young Gentleman, Lately Entered into Holy Orders* (1720), Swift advocates the disarming of the controversial and arcane, either by an uppish refusal to busy oneself 'with philosophical Terms, and Notions of the metaphysical or abstracted Kind', or by unquestioning assent:

> I do not find that you are any where directed in the Canons, or Articles, to attempt explaining the Mysteries of the Christian Religion. And, indeed, since Providence intended there should be Mysteries; I do not see how it can be agreeable to *Piety, Orthodoxy*, or good *Sense*, to go about such a Work. For, to me there seems to be a manifest Dilemma in the Case: If you explain them, they are Mysteries no longer; if you fail, you have laboured to no Purpose.
>
> (*Works*, 9:77)

The *reductio ad absurdum* comes with a characteristic bossiness. Free-thinkers who clamour against the mysteries are like the pedants who 'explain' them: arrogant, obfuscating, divisive – and low, a kind of mob. The proper alternative for a clergyman 'is upon solemn Days to deliver the Doctrine as the Church holds it'. Swift's *hauteur* is schoolmasterly, but there is moral (and political) urgency in its simplifying force. It is perhaps unfair to say that the tenets of 'the Christian Religion' seemed to Swift less interesting for their ideological content or especially for any theological nicety than for their power to provide imperatives by which behaviour can be regulated and the restless mind sustained. But there is a little of this tendency at a certain level of thought. A few pages earlier (p. 73), Swift warns the young gentleman against 'the common unsufferable Cant' by which some clergymen disparage the ancient 'Heathen *Philosophers*' for not knowing certain matters of faith concerning the Christian God, which had not yet been revealed. No person with ordinary human faculties can in any case be expected to grasp inaccessible concepts like 'the Nature of God'. The ancient philosophers preached a very good morality, and their real lack, 'the true Misery of the Heathen World', was 'the Want of a

Divine *Sanction*; without which, the Dictates of the Philosophers failed in the Point of *Authority*' (my italics).

The instruction to deliver doctrine 'as the Church holds it' readily connects with phrases like 'received Doctrine' and 'what is generally believed', and ultimately with the authority of the Religion of the State. Emphasis on this authority goes back, as Swift knew, to some of the ancient philosophers themselves, notably Plato, though it also had many (and varied) modern exponents. Swift was arguing in some detail in favour of this authority at least as early as 1704, when the *Sentiments of a Church-of-England Man* were probably written. It is clear there that the Religion of the State had for Swift this primary feature, that it offered a pragmatic principle of cohesion, a simplifying and official restraint on the anarchic proclivities of the human mind:

> When a *Schism* is once spread in a Nation, there grows, at length, a Dispute which are the Schismaticks. Without entering on the Arguments, used by both Sides among us, to fix the Guilt on each other; it is certain, that in the Sense of the Law, the *Schism* lies on that Side which opposeth itself to the Religion of the State. I leave it among *Divines* to dilate upon the Danger of *Schism*, as a Spiritual Evil; but I would consider it only as a Temporal one. And I think it clear, that any great Separation from the established Worship, although to a new one that is more pure and perfect, may be an Occasion of endangering the publick Peace; because, it will compose a Body always in Reverse, prepared to follow any discontented heads.
>
> (*Works*, 2:11)

One need not question Swift's devotion to the Church of England, or the sincerity of his belief that it is, of all churches, 'most agreeable to primitive Institution'. But he immediately adds that it is 'fittest, of all others for preserving Order and Purity, and under its present Regulations, best calculated for our Civil State' (*Works*, 2:5). And it is clear that Anglicanism would be schismatic, and therefore of subversive tendency, in, say, France. On schism, Swift's speaker confessedly limits his discussion to the *temporal* aspect, but Swift, though seldom patient with the speculations of divines, would endorse the notion that schism, as such, was a 'Spiritual Evil' too. The whole issue, in Swift, is not only readily secularised, but psychologised. The 'discontented Heads' who lead schismatic movements or who

11

turn to sectarianism and free-thinking, are, to a large extent, social nuisances with secular motives, venal and ambitious self-seekers (*Works*, 2:12) or miscellaneous riff-raff on the fringes of society (one notices again Swift's dismissive *hauteur*):

> Where then are these Kind of People to be found? Amongst the worst Part of the Soldiery, made up of Pages, younger Brothers of obscure Families, and others of desperate Fortunes; or else among idle Town-Fops; and now and then a drunken 'Squire of the Country'.
>
> (Letter to a Young Gentleman, Works, 9:78)

But 'these Kind of People' cannot be completely accounted for by such merely external explanations, or any similar simplified categorising of moral or sociological types. Sectarianism and free-thinking would be disruptive enough even if seen merely thus, but in fact Swift frequently presents them as a strange amalgam not only of profit-motive, ambition, mechanical operation, and the like, but of more fundamental mental disruptiveness, an innate mental perversity which might be, or might become, very sincere in its schismatic attitudes. The problem, in other words, is not merely a moral one, implicating only bad men, but a psychological feature of the human condition, implicating all men, including ultimately Swift.

Madness, Badness, and Politics
Free-thinkers, Dissenters, and Schismatics are an example of the anarchic folly of man in its corporate, institutional, or political form. In this, they resemble other group-manifestations of man's wilful disputatiousness, notably those of secular politics and those of learned debate. That there is analogy and interpenetration between the private and the public aspects of the universal psychological condition (that *donnée* of Swift's outlook), we have already seen. A special danger of the public aspect is that it tends to be worse than the mere sum of its private elements, for a reason upon which Swift is often insistent, namely that public groupings,

> besides that they are composed of Men with all their Infirmities about them ... have also the ill Fortune to be generally led and influenced by the very worst among themselves; I mean, *Popular Orators, Tribunes*, or, as they are now stiled, *Great Speakers, Leading Men*, and the like.
>
> (Works, 1:227)

This statement, from Swift's first political publication, *A Discourse of the Contests and Dissensions in Athens and Rome* (1701; ch. 4), refers to popular political assemblies (parliaments or bodies 'of Commons either collective or represented'), but it extends in Swift's mind to many of the other situations in which men attempt to subdue multitudes to their power, their reasons, or their visions (*Tale of a Tub*, sec. 9), especially perhaps to sectarian proselytising in religion. Many of Swift's arguments for limiting the toleration of Dissenters, in sober discourses like the *Sentiments of a Church-of-England Man* as well as in ironic fantastications like the Digression on Madness and the *Mechanical Operation of the Spirit*, emphasise the snowballing threat posed by sectarian leaders. Swift parodied a Free-Thinker's thoughts in 1713: 'It is the indispensable Duty of a *Free Thinker*, to endeavour *forcing* all the World to think as he does, and by that means make them *Free Thinkers* too' (*Works*, 4:36). In secular politics, this process translates itself into a rule that Swift often enunciated, that popular or anarchic governments lead straight to tyranny by 'a single Person': the example of Cromwell, in the *Contests and Dissensions*, emphasises not only the analogy but the interaction between political subversiveness and religious nonconformism (ch. 5; *Works*, 1:230, 231).

The notion that the 'rude, passionate, and mistaken Results' emanating from even the best political assemblies arise 'from the Influence of private Persons upon great Numbers', provides Swift with the basis for a queer, backhanded compliment to the anarchic and contentious nature of man:

> when we sometimes meet a *few Words* put together, which is called the *Vote*, or *Resolution* of an Assembly, and which we cannot possibly reconcile to *Prudence*, or *publick Good*; it is most charitable to conjecture, that such a Vote hath been conceived, and born, and bred in a private Brain; afterwards raised and supported by an obsequious Party; and then, with usual Methods confirmed by an *artificial* Majority. For, let us suppose five Hundred Men, mixed, in Point of Sense and Honesty, as usually Assemblies are; and let us suppose these Men proposing, debating, resolving, voting, according to the meer natural Motions of their own little, or much Reason and Understanding; I do allow, that Abundance of indigested and abortive, many pernicious and foolish Overtures would arise, and float a few Minutes; but then they would die, and disappear. Because, this must be said in Behalf of

human Kind; that common Sense, and plain Reason, while
Men are disengaged from acquired Opinions, will ever have
some general Influence upon their Minds; Whereas, the
Species of Folly and Vice are infinite, and so different in
every Individual, that they could never procure a Majority, if
other Corruptions did not enter to pervert Mens Under-
standings, and misguide their Wills.

(*Works*, 1:231–32)

In these effects of political leaders or influential 'private Brains' we
sense the same strange psychological laws that govern the dis-
semination of folly in the Digression on Madness, supported no
doubt by 'mechanical operation' and the forces of material self-
interest (the 'Corruptions', one supposes, of jobbing, bribery,
and the like). If Swift does not here concede anything so positive
as the Digression's statement that

the Brain, in its natural Position and State of Serenity,
disposeth its Owner to pass his Life in the common Forms,
without any Thought of subduing Multitudes to his own
Power, his *Reasons* or his *Visions*

(*Tale,* sec. 9)

neither does he dramatise as vividly and painfully as in the
Digression those destructive energies that are let loose 'when a
man's Fancy gets *astride* on his Reason . . . and common Understanding, as well as common Sense, is Kickt out of Doors' (*Tale,*
sec. 9). And if the individual 'brain' of the private man is not seen
in the *Contests* as naturally inclined to conformity (see also two
pages further, *Works,* 1:234), nevertheless the pamphlet tells of a
self-regulating quality in man's anarchy that Swift does not
always concede elsewhere. For, Swift argues here, the individual
variations of folly and vice are so 'infinite' that unless men are
artificially unified by a perverse leadership, they will find their
only principle of cohesion in 'common Sense, and plain Reason'.
If any 'publick Conventions' are exempt from the effect of 'all the
Infirmities, Follies, and Vices of private Men' (compounded by
bad leadership), it can only be those which

act by *universal Concert, upon publick Principles, and for publick
Ends;* such as proceed upon Debates without *unbecoming
Warmths,* or *Influence from particular Leaders and Inflamers;* such
whose Members, instead *of canvassing to procure Majorities for*

14

their private Opinions, are ready to comply with general sober Results, although contrary to their own Sentiments. Whatever Assemblies act by these, and other Methods of the like Nature, must be allowed to be exempt from several Imperfections, to which particular Men are subjected.

(*Works*, 1:231–32)

The appeal to public principles and public ends is firm and simplifying. It is not that their content will necessarily be able to *persuade*, for Swift expects them to be contrary to the sentiments of some of their supporters, but that they are somehow identified with '*general sober Results*'. Swift is, of course, attacking party-factionalism in general theoretical terms, so that specific and detailed examples of the public principles and ends are not at this moment called for, but there is no doubt that the largeness of the conception as such, and especially its power to override (rather than settle) disagreement, are what really excite Swift's imagination.

Behind this conception, however remotely, stands a vision of an ideal society which Swift, many years later, was to fashion into the Houyhnhnmland of *Gulliver's Travels*. Or rather, Swift's notions in the earlier work of what can take place in political assemblies at their best are recognisably embodied in the later Utopian vision of creatures whose political (and other) behaviour is *always* at its best. It is not just that a phrase like '*without unbecoming Warmths*' evokes the same aspirations as the picture of the Houyhnhnms conversing without 'Interruption, Tediousness, Heat, or Difference of Sentiments' (*Gulliver's Travels*, 4:10), or that the Houyhnhnms are notable for what the earlier passage calls '*universal Concert, upon publick Principles, and for publick Ends*' (see *Gulliver's Travels*, 4:8, for their public-spirited benevolence towards their 'whole Species', and 4:10 for their political assembly). It is much more that the Houyhnhnms are permanently actuated by criteria that are absolute and simple enough to neutralise the possibility of serious individual disagreement. Swift was always somewhat inclined to see individual disagreement from a general consensus as psychologically rather than rationally motivated, and as tending therefore to the perverse. The Houyhnhnms are not immune from disagreement, as their uncertainty over the proper way to treat Gulliver at the end indicates; and if such disagreements are rare, their theoretical possibility is assumed in the fact, for example,

15

that a Decree of the general Assembly in this Country, is expressed by the word *Hnhloayn*, which signifies an *Exhortation*; as near as I can render it: For they have no Conception how a rational Creature can be *compelled*, but only advised, or *exhorted*; because no Person can disobey Reason, without giving up his Claim to be a rational creature.

(*Gulliver's Travels*, 4:10)

At the same time, the last clause makes clear that no disagreement can be sustained for very long, and Swift had earlier emphasised that 'opinions' and 'controversies' are impossible among the Houyhnhnms, because it stands to 'reason' that there is only one truth:

Neither is *Reason* among them a Point problematical as with us, where Men can argue with Plausibility on both Sides of a Question; but strikes you with immediate Conviction; as it must needs do where it is not mingled, obscured, or discoloured by Passion and Interest. I remember it was with extreme Difficulty that I could bring my Master to understand the Meaning of the word *Opinion*, or how a Point could be disputable; because *Reason* taught us to affirm or deny only where we are certain; and beyond our Knowledge we cannot do either. So that Controversies, Wranglings, Disputes, and Positiveness in false or dubious Propositions, are Evils unknown among the *Houyhnhnms*. In the like Manner when I used to explain to him our several Systems of *Natural Philosophy*, he would laugh that a Creature pretending to *Reason*, should value itself upon the Knowledge of other Peoples Conjectures, and in Things, where that Knowledge, if it were certain, could be of no Use. Wherein he agreed entirely with the Sentiments of *Socrates*, as *Plato* delivers them.

(*Gulliver's Travels*, 4:8)

Obviously there are not, among them, any of those '*unbecoming Warmths*' mentioned in the *Contests*. The Houyhnhnms embody an ideal of social and political health that goes far beyond the modest and pragmatic hope of the *Contests*, that men, in a real world, might be '*ready to comply with general sober Results, although contrary to their own Sentiments*'. Despite the possibility of disagreements among the Houyhnhnms, they somehow seem to have no individual sentiments contrary to general sober results, their unifying 'reason' being a spontaneous thing operating unerringly through 'immediate Conviction'. If there is an inconsistency in this, between an absolute reason without disagreements and the theoretical possibility of at least provisional disagreement on some points, it is at most a minor and technical one, and the whole emphasis of the book is on the Houyhnhnms' cool and righteous cohesion. This cohesion is unthinkable in the real world, where other and more terrible spontaneities, those of 'Passion and Interest', inevitably hold sway. But Swift's invention of Houyhnhnm society, where a secure and absolute reason exercises so much control over disruptive impulses that these impulses hardly appear at all and the control itself becomes effortless and spontaneous, represents a powerful yearning for a state protected from the tyrant-passions. Orwell saw a 'totalitarian tendency' in the Houyhnhnm myth, adding: 'In a Society in which there is no law, and in theory no compulsion, the only arbiter of behaviour is public opinion', and that, Orwell adds, 'is less tolerant than any system of law' (*Selected Essays*, Harmondsworth, 1957, 132). Martin Price is right to point out that Houyhnhnm conformity is spontaneous rather than enforced, so that, in the fiction, 'what, for us, would be defects of liberty' do not arise (*To the Palace of Wisdom*, Garden City, N.Y., 1965, 200). But the fact remains that Swift created the fiction, and it might be argued that such a fiction embodies authoritarian leanings even more radically than a Utopia of socially enforced conformity would have done, as though Swift were saying that the ideal conformism is total and unproblematic.

Not that Swift was opposed to a degree of enforced conformity, especially in religion and politics, as we have seen. The absence of enforcement among the Houyhnhnms depends precisely on the fact that they do not exist in the real world, and that their systematic conformity is only possible in a world whose creatures are reasonable enough to need no sanctions. One of the bleakest implications of the Fourth Book (bleaker perhaps than the Yahoos, or than Gulliver's onslaught upon man, or than our tendency to dislike the Houyhnhnms for their supposed coldness or their 'defects of liberty') is that the most thorough-going positive in the entire fiction is tartly established as outside human possibility. If Houyhnhnm cohesion is more complete and better than the limited harmony envisaged in the passage from the *Contests*, it is by the same token much less hopeful. But even in the passage from the *Contests*, in the very place where Swift asserts 'that common Sense, and plain Reason, while Men are disengaged from acquired Opinions, will ever have some general Influence

17

upon their Minds', we feel that the infinite 'Species of Folly and Vice', like Leavis's Yahoos, 'have all the life'.

This teeming perversity was for Swift, as we have seen, a psychological condition of the human race. He shared the notion of a radical restlessness with earlier thinkers like Hobbes or Temple, and more profoundly (because in a more poignantly personalised way) with a later individualistic conservative, Samuel Johnson. Swift differs from Johnson, and perhaps comes closer to the earlier writers, however, in the emphasis he placed on the political and social implications of restlessness. Not only did Swift feel more acutely than Johnson the analogy between mental and political states, and therefore between psychological and political government. He was also more frequently given to portraying the universal madness in its collective rather than its private manifestations, and, partly as a result of this, likelier to equate mad with bad.

A relatively lighthearted passage from *Gulliver*, 3:2, illustrates the point. The Laputians have a collective insane anxiety about the supposed threat of great astronomical disasters: they fear, for example, the swallowing up of the earth into the sun, the sun's gradual loss of all its heat, the eventual annihilation of both sun and earth. This echoes some fairly widespread speculations among scientists and divines in the seventeenth and eighteenth centuries. Swift makes exquisite comedy of this Laputian folly: 'When they meet an Acquaintance in the Morning, the first Question is about the Sun's Health; how he looked at his Setting and Rising'. Laputian folly readily turns very grim, as parts of the Academy of Lagado (*Gulliver's Travels*, 3:5–6) show, and I shall return to some of the grimmer side. What I wish to note now is that even when the fun is real and disarming, the absurdity is presented as collective to a whole society, and at the same time emphasised as a deviation from the common forms, a fussy and self-disturbing nonconformism:

> These People are under continual Disquietudes, never enjoying a Minute's Peace of Mind; and their Disturbances proceed from Causes which very little affect the rest of Mortals . . .
> They are so perpetually alarmed with the Apprehensions of these and the like impending Dangers, that they can neither sleep quietly in their Beds, nor have any Relish for the common Pleasures or Amusements of Life.
>
> (*Gulliver's Travels*, 3:2)

A passage in Johnson's *Idler*, No. 3, 29 April 1758, mocks a similar intellectual folly:

> Many philosophers imagine that the elements themselves may be in time exhausted. That the sun, by shining long, will effuse all its light; and that, by the continual waste of aqueous particles, the whole earth will at last become a sandy desert.

Johnson mentions this absurdity in passing, in an essay not primarily concerned with philosophical vagaries, and it is doubtless largely fortuitous that where Swift converted a particular learned folly into a mad society, Johnson more literal-mindedly confined himself to mentioning 'many philosophers'. Nor should too much be made of the fact that where Swift signposted a deviation from common ways, Johnson contented himself with noting an irrational absurdity without emphasising a wilful self-isolation from normality. But even if fortuitous, these slight distinctions do sketch out a larger difference that is very real.

Johnson is much readier to sympathise and to withhold blame. As he proceeds, amusingly, to reassure his readers that anxieties about the end of the world are premature, his irony acquires an unSwiftian avuncularity, a note of compassion or sympathy for states of mind afflicted by such worries:

> I would not advise my readers to disturb themselves by contriving how they shall live without light and water. For the days of universal thirst and perpetual darkness are at a great distance. The ocean and the sun will last our time.

He talks as one would comfort a child about some improbable or remote calamity, a show of confident derision mingling with sympathetic reassurance. When Swift (elsewhere: for example, above, p. 10) treats his reader as a child, his tone suggests not a comforting avuncularity but a pedagogue's bossiness. Here, however, Swift mocks with sharply playful exposure what Johnson treats (almost) tenderly.

For, although the notions of the 'philosophers' seemed as absurd to Johnson as to Swift, and although both might see them as symptoms of an illness from which no man is strictly free, Swift's focus on the social dangers of folly yields no possibility of the kind of compassion that Johnson's passage holds in reserve for individual sufferers. Behind Johnson's astronomer cranks is to be

19

discerned the pathos of such a figure as the mad astronomer in *Rasselas* (written less than a year after the *Idler* paper), a learned man 'who has spent forty years in unwearied attention to the motions and appearances of the celestial bodies, and has drawn out his soul in endless calculations' (ch. 39 [40]), and whose real skill as a scientist has curdled into the delusion that he possesses 'the regulation of the weather' (ch. 40 [41]). Ironically, and sadly, he is denied the pleasures of this delusion:

> If the task of a king be considered as difficult, who has the care only of a few millions, to whom he cannot do much good or harm, what must be the anxiety of him, on whom depend the action of the elements, and the great gifts of light and heat! ... I have sometimes turned aside the axis of the earth, and sometimes varied the ecliptick of the sun: but I have found it impossible to make a disposition by which the world may be advantaged; what one region gains, another loses by any imaginable alteration, even without considering the distant parts of the solar system with which we are unacquainted. ... The memory of mischief is no desirable fame.
>
> (*Rasselas*, ch. 42 [43])

Swift would have placed this astronomer in his rogues' gallery of crazed projectors. Johnson presents him as a morally and intellectually admirable man, whose derangement proceeds from the nature and the solitude of his professional calling, and who exemplifies that 'most dreadful and alarming' uncertainty of life, 'the uncertain continuance of reason' (ch. 42 [43]). He is the subject of a tenderly self-involving tragi-comedy on Johnson's part. His delusion of omnipotence is quite free from the self-congratulation of Swift's hack, as the latter announces that his 'Imaginations are hard-mouth'd, and exceedingly disposed to run away with his *Reason*', and *a fortiori* free also from the power-mania which in Swift's same Digression on Madness makes conquerors and other madmen dream of 'subduing Multitudes' (*Tale*, sec. 9). In Swift's vision, moreover, fantasy has a dangerous way of spilling into reality. Ambitions of universal conquest, though they start as mental vapours and anal fistulas, turn into a Louis XIV raising 'mighty Armies' (*Tale*, sec. 9). Swift's most exact parallel to Johnson's astronomer, who imagines that he can control the weather, is the King of Laputa, who *really can* (with his flying island) do just this:

as it is in the Power of the Monarch to raise the Island above the Region of Clouds and Vapours, he can prevent the falling of Dews and Rains whenever he pleases.

(Gulliver's Travels, 3:3)

This is no mere science-fiction extravagance, for it turns out that this manoeuvrability of the flying island is the direct instrument of political tyranny (in particular England's, over the Irish):

If any Town should engage in Rebellion or Mutiny, fall into violent Factions, or refuse to pay the usual Tribute; the King hath two Methods of reducing them to Obedience. The first and the mildest Course is by keeping the Island hovering over such a Town, and the Lands about it; whereby he can deprive them of the Benefit of the Sun and the Rain, and consequently afflict the Inhabitants with Dearth and Diseases. And if the Crime deserve it, they are at the same time pelted from above with great Stones, against which they have no Defence, but by creeping into Cellars or Caves, while the Roofs of their Houses are beaten to Pieces. But if they still continue obstinate, or offer to raise Insurrections; he proceeds to the last Remedy, by letting the Island drop directly upon their Heads, which makes a universal Destruction both of Houses and Men. However, this is an Extremity to which the Prince is seldom driven.

The last phrase, of course, softens nothing. Nor is it meant to: for as we read on, we discover that the reasons for holding back, normally, from 'a universal Destruction', are cynical reasons of expediency. Johnson's moral writing normally rejects examples of great national catastrophes because he feels that they are easily exaggerated and remote from the experience of most readers. 'I cannot bear that querelous eloquence which threatens every city with a siege like that of Jerusalem', says Rasselas to his sister, for such things are usually 'found in books rather than in the world' (ch. 28); and in his own voice Johnson said that 'histories of the downfall of kingdoms, and revolutions of empires, are read with great tranquillity', since the happiness of private men is seldom affected by great events (*Rambler*, No. 60, 13 October 1750; see also Nos. 17 and 68, and *Idler*, No. 84). Even when he is himself writing specifically about the cruelties of war, as in *Thoughts on . . . Falkland's Islands* (1771), he will remind us that 'war is not the whole business of life; it happens but seldom . . . '. He once or

21

twice describes carnage with something like a Swiftian generality, but without the more spectacular details and with a stress on
the drabness of its miseries, as a realistic reminder to readers
deluded by 'heroick fiction'. The 'generality' itself escapes Rasselas's objections, for it has a precise factual validation: Johnson is
referring to specific events of the recent past.

The literal-minded insistence that personal distresses are more
common than large-scale disasters, or that, among acts of personal wrong-doing, violence and bloodshed occur more seldom
than acts of 'concupiscible' sin, runs through all his thought. It is a
theme of sermon 18 in the Yale Edition of Johnson's *Sermons*. The
belief that the more spectacular evils are more uncommon goes
hand in hand with a view that they are more remote and therefore
less effective as moral examples. The fact that they usually occur
'in books rather than in the world' is a warning to the writer to
keep them out of *his* books; it confirms Johnson in his preference
for factual over fictional genres, his special predilection for biography, and his stress on minute personal detail in biography as
more instructively revealing and more moving than public deeds
or occurrences.

Related to this is an important difference in satiric style, which
is more than merely a difference between Swiftian repudiation
and Johnsonian tolerance. That temperamental defensiveness
which built a restless indirection into Swift's most casual utterances, and made his writing bristle with aggressive mystifications
and the concealments of ironic obliquity, is far removed from the
almost compulsively vulnerable, open, literal-minded truthfulness of Johnson. Irony not only tends towards disguise and
indirection. Since it says something different from what it really
means, it is also by definition *literally untrue*; and Johnson often
shows an instinctive impulse to confute or resist its implied
fictions and its distortions of sheer fact. Some of his talking for
victory consists of literalising into nonsense the more figured,
oblique or 'witty' observations of his friends. Johnson shrank
from irony as Swift shrank from plain statement.

Bate notes that *Marmor Norfolciense* failed because 'indirect and
drawn-out irony was never . . . Johnson's forte', and that much
Johnsonian irony resembles that of Hardy rather than that of the
Augustan ironists. He says this is because Johnson's 'vision [is]
more essentially tragic than comic' (Bate, *Samuel Johnson*, 201,
279–80), but Swift's irony or that of Pope's *Dunciad* could plaus-
ibly be described as 'tragic' too. The crucial difference is surely
between an irony that is situational and one that is mainly verbal,

and it is this that gives the analogy with Hardy its pregnant rightness. Johnson is full of pained instances of the cruel turns of life, life's little (and not-so-little) ironies, but the relative absence of Bate's 'Augustan' irony comes not mainly from 'tragic' vision, but from the peculiar literal-mindedness of Johnson's nature. It is the product of a rectitude so open and so doggedly committed to plain palpable fact that it cannot lightly allow itself the distorting obliquities of verbal wit and satiric fantasy.

It is partly for this reason that Johnsonian satire 'misses' (not of course misfires), turning into something else. Johnson will, for example, refuse a satiric exaggeration or distortion simply because it is not factually true, or not so commonly or widely true as the plain occurrences of private domestic existence. His peculiarly literal-minded style, by contrast with the ironic negations and fantastications of Swift, is almost in itself a medium of accommodation and acceptance.

Bate's well-known, acute (and ungrammatical) conception of Johnson's 'satire *manqué*' rightly sees it as 'a form in which protest and satire, ridicule and even anger, are essential ingredients at the start but then, caught up in a larger context of charity, begin to turn into something else' (*Samuel Johnson*, 295). It explains a great deal. The merely formal aspect of the difference from Swift which I have been sketching should not, however, be exaggerated. For just as Swift, in some of his lesser works, and less often than has been claimed, sometimes wrote in a plain style devoid of ironic indirection, so Johnson occasionally did the opposite. Two of his early works were conscious exercises in 'Swiftian' irony: *Marmor Norfolciense* and the *Complete Vindication of the Licensers of the Stage*. This early fixation on Swift was also playfully sustained by the parliamentary reports that he concocted for the *Gentleman's Magazine* under the title 'Debates in the Senate of Magna Lilliputia', and there were examples of 'sarcasm and "sophistry"' among the political writings of his later years. But these works are exceptional, and the few overt Swiftian imitations may be taken as among the more superficial instances of that deep similarity with Swift that Johnson seems uneasily to have sensed in himself. His dislike of Swift, as Bate observed in an earlier book, may have been partly due to the fact that 'he was in some ways temperamentally akin' (*The Achievement of Samuel Johnson*, New York, 1961, 126). The scarcity of sustained irony and of severe satiric exposure in his mature work may also have been due to a desire to minimise this resemblance to Swift, who certainly became (even if Bate overstates in saying that he 'always' was)

23

'a frightening example for Johnson of what not to be' (*Samuel Johnson*, p. 498).

Misfortune, then, seems real for Johnson the less public, the more domestic, it is, and the more literal-mindedly it is described. Swift, on the other hand, makes one feel that huge misfortunes and turpitudes, however extensively spread and however fantasticated in his description, are immediate and indeed almost domestically relevant: think of Ireland beneath the Laputian island, or in the *Modest Proposal*, or the brilliant universalised portrayals in *Gulliver's Travels* of the depravities and devastations of war. What Johnson will describe as a pitiful fantasy of the mind, Swift actualises as totalitarian terror. If the Laputians are at times charmingly mad, with their abstracted air, their flappers, their substitution of things for words, they are no mere unreal society of harmless academics: their school of political projectors is at times mad with the terrible reality of modern research establishments, of obscenely prying secret services, and of other horrors (*Gulliver's Travels*, 3:6). These tyrannical products of the universal madness are a grotesquely concrete version of that 'free-thinking' which Swift imaged in the parody, already cited, of a free-thinker's mind: '*forcing* all the World to think as he does, and by that means make them *Free Thinkers* too' (above, p. 13).

It is not surprising, in view of this, to find that in Swift's satire the notion of madness as something to be punished is expressed with particular vividness. Talking of some of the world's 'Grand Innovators', subduers of multitudes, the Digression on Madness remarks

> that several of the chief among them, both *Antient* and *Modern*, were usually mistaken by their Adversaries, and indeed, by all, except their own Followers, to have been Persons Crazed, or out of their Wits, having generally proceeded in the common Course of their Words and Actions, by a Method very different from the vulgar Dictates of *unrefined* Reason: agreeing for the most Part in their several Models, with their present undoubted Successors in the *Academy* of *Modern Bedlam*.
>
> (*Tale*, sec. 9)

Swift then makes his 'author' add, in a way that emphasises both the fitness of severe punishment for madness and the tyrannical bent of the mad 'Innovators':

24

The Character of Swift's Satire

Of this Kind were *Epicurus, Diogenes, Apollonius, Lucretius, Paracelsus, Des Cartes,* and others; who, if they were now in the World, tied fast, and separate from their Followers, would in this our undistinguishing Age, incur manifest Danger of *Phlebotomy,* and *Whips,* and *Chains,* and *dark Chambers,* and *Straw.* For, what Man in the natural State, or Course of Thinking, did ever conceive it in his Power, to reduce the Notions of all Mankind, exactly to the same Length, and Breadth, and Heighth of his own?

Mad is bad, and a modern reader is struck by the undifferentiated mingling of medical (phlebotomy, or blood–letting) and punitive (whips, etc.) treatments. When, especially in *Gulliver's Travels,* Reason is spoken of as a *moral* faculty, sins and vices come to be seen as deviations from Reason, and therefore, by a familiar buried pun, as forms of *un*reason. The 'natural State ... of Thinking' to which the Digression on Madness refers, means 'normal state' in at least three leading (and interpenetrating) senses: 1, fitting, proper, healthy, the state in which all minds ought to be; and therefore, 2, the state in which the mind naturally or spontaneously exists when not interfered with; and 3, the common, usual, ordinary state of men's minds. A large part of the satiric enterprise of *Gulliver's Travels* consists of exposing radical incongruities in the human character; in which these various senses of 'nature' and 'natural' fail to dovetail: vice is unnatural in sense 1, but man is perversely given to vice, which comes naturally to him in senses 2 and 3. This paradox is elaborated in coil upon coil of painful ironic refinement in *Gulliver's Travels,* reinforcing in endless unpredictable ways the grotesque connection between folly and vice, universalising its reach to the whole of mankind. The passage from the Digression is ostensibly less universalising, since its point is to distinguish sane minds in their 'natural State' from those that are mad-and-bad. The Digression also, however, has some irrational tendencies, in its style rather than its statements, towards a universal applicability to all men, one minor example of which is that '*Academy of Modern Bedlam*' whose inmates are turned into types of the various classes and professions of men.[1]

This literal Madhouse reinforces, by an extra ironic twist, the equation of mad-and-bad: for it says not only the conventional thing, that badness is unnatural, perverse, or mad in a *moral* sense, but also that this equation is so deeply true that typical badnesses may be inferred from the literally mad (in a *medical* sense). This

25

added twist is a rhetorical flourish, not a sober truth, and the equation of mad-and-bad, not rare in satire, is part of a satiric fiction or joke. But the readiness (not facility) with which Swift oscillates between mad and bad, the depth of his imaginative commitment to aspects of the equation in the *Tale* and in *Gulliver's Travels*, and his insistent politicisation of the notion of 'universal madness' (in 'straight' political arguments as well as in ironic fantasies), show that more is at work than a formulaic exercise.

The tendency to see madness as culpable is perhaps one to which highly tradition-conscious and cohesive societies (in which outsiders are neither pitied very much, nor glorified in a Romantic way) are prone, even if, or especially if, the society's values and cohesiveness are felt to be threatened by the pressures of social change. Swift's was a highly conservative temperament, in an age when conservative temperaments (Pope's was another example) felt particularly acutely that their traditions and culture were in grave jeopardy from 'modern' upstart encroachments, notably of arrogant individualists, 'innovators', sectarians. They might have felt that their fears had been fulfilled in the sense that, in the eighty or so years after the death of Pope and Swift, the figure of the outsider, the rebel, the man of feeling, the high soul charged with noble frenzy, acquired an increasing and unprecedented respectability and indeed glamour in European society. It is also in roughly the same period that more compassionate and philanthropic attitudes to social outcasts (the insane, fallen women, and others) established themselves with a new, widespread, and institutionalised effectiveness. Swift was, in a sense, part of both movements himself. It is a curious irony, and perhaps not an entirely inappropriate one, that a powerful later tradition should think of him as a heroic outsider (demonic misanthrope, or Byronic rebel, or Promethean protester): on this paradoxical feature of Swift's self-implication in the objects of his own attack I shall have more to say. Here I wish to note the part he played in the second and less dramatic of the two movements, the growth of philanthropic sentiments and institutions.

For if Swift equated mad with bad in certain ways, and if his satiric fictions (as well as contemporary social fact, in some instances) interchangeably inflict upon their victims phlebotomy and whips, there is another side to the matter. Swift left money to found a mental hospital in Ireland (showing 'by one satyric Touch,/No Nation wanted it so much', as he wryly commented at the end of the *Verses* on his own death), and had liberal and farsighted views about the treatment of mental illness.[2] The ambiguity that this implies existed also in Johnson, though in a less starkly polarised form. If Johnson's notion of the 'universal madness' was by no means free of attribution of sin, he was (though never smug) more compassionate and more self-tolerant about it. He differed from Swift not only in feeling less intensely the analogy between private and political madness, but in being much less concerned (not unconcerned) to make satiric judgments on men's failures to submit energy to rule.

Bate reminds us that Johnson had many of the primary characteristics of a satirist: a quickness to sense incongruity and pretence, a well-developed aggressiveness, a temperamental irritability and dissatisfaction aggravated by personal suffering, an instinctive reductionist talent not unlike Swift's, and one might add, a certain violence or immoderation of character combined with a desperate attachment to the disciplines of moderation and good sense (*Samuel Johnson*, 489–90, 495). Unlike Swift's however, Johnson's reductions do not *leave* their victim humiliated and crushed: instead they readily open into afterthoughts that tend to explain and even defend. The differences are mainly personal, but they have a chronological aptness. For if both men saw 'restlessness' as universal and incurable, and as implicating themselves, it was the earlier of the two who punished himself and others most uncompromisingly for it, and who most explicitly and systematically proposed measures to deal with it on the social and political, as well as the private and introspective planes.

Law, Morals and Hypocrisy

Swift opposed tyranny, whether of the One, the Few, or the Many. We have seen that some of his leanings were authoritarian and that he has sometimes been accused of tyrannical or totalitarian implications. Perhaps this suggests yet another instance of Swift's paradoxical assimilation to the things he attacks. But part of the reason why some modern readers emphasise the totalitarian implications may be that we are more suspicious today of applying a psychological analysis of the human condition too directly in the service of political or social action. Fears of such a direct application would seem less pressingly urgent then than they do to us, with our technologised media of mass-persuasion and our highly developed techniques of individual brainwashing. Psychological accounts of man's nature and condition that have an actual or potential bearing on political programmes or ideals

are not lacking in our time, although it is less easy in our culture to
propose simple direct connections between the morally good and
the politically enforceable; or to say as literally as Swift sometimes
says that because personal and public 'restlessness' are parallel and
interpenetrating, therefore the sanctions dressed against both are
or should be, at a certain level, the same. Swift's equation
sometimes implies greater and more direct legal control over
private morals and personal feelings than we are prepared to
accept in principle, perhaps because we are less able today to
count on rough agreement about the moral standards themselves.
In *The Publick Spirit of the Whigs* (1714), Swift jeered at Steele's
assertion that '*Men's Beings are degraded when their Passions are no
longer governed by the Dictates of their own Mind*', as

> directly contrary to the Lessons of all Moralists and Legisla-
> tors; who agree unanimously, that the Passions of Men
> must be under the Government of Reason and Law; neither
> are Laws of any other Use than to correct the Irregularity of
> our Affections.
>
> (*Works*, 8:46–47)

The statement is, in itself, a commonplace. But it shows the
readiness with which Swift sees Reason and the Law, the inner
and the outer sanctions, as parallel and mutually reinforcing
regulators of the culpable madness to which all men are prone,
and which sects and free-thinkers threaten to institutionalise.

Hence Swift's feeling that laws ought not only to be keepers of
public order, but guardians of private morals. The authority of
princes, Swift says in *A Project for the Advancement of Religion, and
the Reformation of Manners* (1709), must be vigorously exercised
towards 'making it every Man's Interest and Honour to cultivate
Religion and Virtue', by insisting on moral virtue as a pre-
condition of professional preferment, and by appointing censors
to watch over the moral behaviour of public officials, the morality of plays, and the religious orthodoxy of published writings
(*Works*, 2:47 ff., 49, 56, 60). In this *Project* (quite wrongly but
understandably considered by some critics to be ironical), Swift is
almost more concerned with psychological effects, with the
control of mental predispositions, than with legal enforcement as
such. This concern does not make his insistence on authority or
on legal sanctions any less, but the assurance of enforcement is
partly seen as a form of character-management. Most legal or
institutional arrangements have partly a psychological function,

as deterrents to bad actions or incentives to good ones, but Swift insists on this function with particular force, and focuses part of his discussion, with an unusually literal-minded practicality, on the mental operations involved.

A notorious example of this is to be found in Swift's handling of the objection that his project is likely to encourage hypocrisy rather than virtue. He does not deny the charge, but claims pragmatically not only that hypocrisy is better than open vice, but that it can be put to psychological use in support of virtue:

> Neither am I aware of any Objections to be raised against what I have advanced; unless it should be thought, that the making Religion a necessary Step to Interest and Favour, might encrease Hypocrisy among us: And I readily believe it would. But if One in Twenty should be brought over to true Piety by this, or the like Methods, and the other Nineteen be only Hypocrites, the Advantage would still be great. Besides, Hypocrisy is much more eligible than open Infidelity and Vice: It wears the Livery of Religion, it acknowledgeth her Authority, and is cautious of giving Scandal. Nay, a long continued Disguise is too great a Constraint upon human Nature, especially an *English* Disposition. Men would leave off their Vices out of meer Weariness, rather than undergo the Toil and Hazard, and perhaps Expence of practising them perpetually in private. And, I believe, it is often with Religion as it is with Love; which, by much Dissembling, at last grows real.
>
> (*Works*, 2:56–57)

It is possible to be shocked at this apparently cynical pragmatism. Irvin Ehrenpreis says of it: 'As threadbare cynicism or as muddled psychology, it is equally deplorable and naïve' (*Swift: The Man, His Works, and the Age*, vol. 2: *Dr Swift*, London, 1967, 293–94). The reaction is understandable, especially if one emphasises, as Ehrenpreis (at a certain level quite correctly) does, the element of practical political exhortation in the *Project*, its place in a tradition of political thought, and its immediate historical context, at a moment when Queen Anne actually issued 'a royal proclamation "for the encouragement of piety and virtue, and for the preventing and punishing vice"' (Ehrenpreis, 2:289, ff., 293). But the passage can also properly be viewed in the context of Swift's pessimistic sense of the relentless pressure of vicious impulses, where any stratagem that saved a bit of ground for virtue might seem justified. Perhaps the sentiments seem less shocking when expressed by Johnson, no friend to hypocrites (any more, for that matter, than Swift was):

> With the hypocrite it is not at present my intention to expostulate, though even he might be taught the excellency of virtue, by the necessity of seeming to be virtuous; but the man of affectation may, perhaps, be reclaimed, by finding how little he is likely to gain by perpetual constraint, and incessant vigilance, and how much more securely he might make his way to esteem, by cultivating real, than displaying counterfeit qualities.
>
> (*Rambler*, No. 20, 26 May 1750)

Johnson is not advocating a political programme, but his 'psychology' is similar (his distinction between hypocrisy and affectation is marginal to the present discussion), and it does not seem muddled, deplorable or naïve. It belongs with that same literal-minded acknowledgement of human frailty, and the same practical acceptance of less than absolute remedies, which lead Johnson to say elsewhere, for example, that one should not too readily condemn the hypocrisy of authors who fail, in life, to live up to the principles that they honestly advocate in their writings (e.g., *Rambler*, No. 14, 5 May 1750).

When Johnson makes Imlac tell Rasselas not to be too hasty to admire 'the teachers of morality: they discourse like angels, but they live like men' (*Rasselas*, ch. 18), he is engaging in no *mere* stripping of pretences. Living 'like men' is in the end no more than men can do, and Johnson frequently stresses that moralists and men of letters have a duty to 'discourse like angels' and to advocate virtue, even if as men they cannot live up to their precepts; a position ultimately close to that from which Swift, in the *Project*, asserted the social value of some such kinds of 'hypocrisy', though Swift did so with more dry distaste than charitable understanding. In his satire, the yawning failure of men to live like angels or even Houyhnhnms is hardly palliated by the beastly and uncompromising reality known as living 'like men'. Johnson said in a sermon that repentant sinners 'are not to be excluded from commemorating the sufferings of our Saviour, in a Christian congregation, who would not be shut from heaven . . . and the choirs of angels'. The Yale editors (who believe this sermon to be by Johnson despite an element of doubt) cite Johnson's defence to Boswell of the right of a repentant fornicator to be ordained: 'A man who is good enough to go to heaven, is good enough to be a clergyman' (*Sermons*, Yale Edition, 97–98 nn). This may seem to contrast with Swift's emphasis in the *Project* on banning profligates even from *secular* preferments. But both men *begin* with the same literal-minded acknowledgement of a radically peccant world: there is no benign underplaying or softening of that harsh initial fact, as there might be in Chaucer or Dickens, only a partially different response to the fact once noted.

Though no unqualified admirer of Swift, Johnson significantly praised the *Project*, objecting only

> that, like many projects, it is, if not generally impracticable, yet evidently hopeless, as it supposes more zeal, concord, and perseverance than a view of mankind gives reason for expecting.
>
> (G. B. Hill (ed.), *Lives of the Poets*, Oxford, 1905, 3:13)

Swift would, in fact, certainly accept most of this 'objection'. He was at bottom no more optimistic than Johnson, and no more given to viewing mankind in any sort of moral 'concord', actual or potential. It is precisely because of this that he will settle, like Johnson, for *ad hoc* and pragmatic checks on human unruliness, rather than envisaging total or wholly satisfying solutions: 'he that would keep his House in Repair, must attend every little Breach or Flaw, and supply it immediately, else Time alone will bring all to Ruin; how much more the common Accidents of Storms and Rain?' (*Project, Works*, 2:63). The tone is hardly buoyant. If the *Project* is not as 'hopeless' as Johnson feels the facts warrant, this is only because its formal business is to *propose* a few of the needed repairs. Swift sardonically confines his proposals within the reach of existing administrative and legal powers: 'All other Projects . . . have proved hitherto ineffectual. Laws against Immorality have not been executed', and as to any notions of 'introducing new Laws for the Amendment of Mankind', they are just 'airy Imaginations' (*Works*, 2:57, 61). In this most literal Swiftian ruefulness, we recognise a sober echo of the crazed accents of those later, *fictional* reformers of mankind, Gulliver and the modest proposer; just as the *Project*'s confidence in its genuinely limited and 'modest' programme,

> Neither am I aware of any Objections to be raised against what I have advanced
>
> (*Works*, 2:56)

31

anticipates not only the modest proposer's calm assurance, but Gulliver's testy certainty of being

> an Author perfectly blameless; against whom the Tribes of Answerers, Considerers, Observers, Reflecters, Detecters, Remarkers, will never be able to find Matter for exercising their Talents.
>
> (*Gulliver's Travels*, 4:12)

These resemblances do not 'prove' that the *Project* is radically ironical, like the *Modest Proposal*. If anything they rather emphasise the closeness of Swift's relation to the rhetorical postures he assumed through his fictional *personae*, a relation that oscillates between direct congruence and the kind of intimate mirror-opposition where self and anti-self complete one another. Irvin Ehrenpreis compares the ironic advocacy of nominal rather than real Christianity in the *Argument Against Abolishing Christianity* ('Written in the year 1708', about the same time as the *Project*, though not actually published until 1711), with the *Project*'s literal tolerance of a degree of 'hypocrisy'.

> It is one thing for Swift in the *Argument* barely to admit Tartufe as a despicable *pis aller*; it is another thing for him in the *Project* to hold up false godliness as second only to true.
>
> (Ehrenpreis, *Swift*, 2:294)

Ehrenpreis's judgment of the *Project* may, as I suggested, seem unduly unsympathetic; but the parallel, as such, is important.

Properly speaking, the *Argument Against Abolishing Christianity* has two principal ironies at the expense of a hypocritical 'nominal christianity', both of which enter into a teasing relationship with the literal acceptance of 'hypocrisy' in the *Project*. The first is more absolute, and more immediately obvious to the uninstructed modern reader. It says that things have become so bad that the speaker can blandly take for granted that nobody wants real christianity, insisting modestly on the nominal kind as the only one likely to be accepted, and for the crudest reasons of expediency at that: that stocks and shares might otherwise drop, for example (*Works*, 2:38–39). The suggestion at this level is that irreligion – the notion, for Swift, unites atheists and nonconformists indiscriminately – is bad, but a society where irreligion assumes a hypocritical appearance of religion to further its irreligious purposes is worse.

The second and more specific irony is that described by Ehrenpreis. It runs somewhat across the other (no unfamiliar thing in Swiftian satire, which always tends to attack on more than one front, with the victim losing either way), admitting 'hypocrisy' as an unworthy second best, or *pis aller*. Swift dislikes 'nominal christianity' while writing in defence of the Test Act, which imposed a nominal communion on sectarians and free-thinkers in public office. Ehrenpreis (2:284) puts it very well: 'occasional conformists are hypocrites; but ... the true church will be stronger if men are forced into hypocrisy than if they are released into unlimited freedom of worship'. Where Dissenters are concerned, some forms of restraint or disguise of 'natural' impulses seemed to Swift called for. Moreover, the unillusioned (or 'muddled' and 'naïve') psychology which claims that sincerity can supervene on a prolonged or determined or externally induced hypocrisy, does not entail an automatic approval of sincerity as such. Puritans may be scorned as mechanical operators of the spirit, but Swift's point, said to be an original contribution to anti-Puritan satire (see Ehrenpreis, *Swift: The Man, His Works, and The Age*, London, 1962, 1:246), that some of their 'enthusiasm' is 'an Effect grown from *Art* into *Nature*', hardly creates respect for their sincerity (*Mechanical Operation of the Spirit*, 1704, *Works*, 1:176). Swift's graphic vision of their grotesque passionate spontaneities adds a further dimension to the *Project*'s tolerance of hypocrisy.

It is clear that the antithesis between the *Project*'s advocacy of 'hypocrisy' and that side of the *Argument* which ironically praises but actually deplores it, holds together what in fact are closely connected attitudes – as indeed the *other* implication of the *Argument*, that 'occasional conformity' must be enforced, demonstrates. The co-existence in the *Argument* of an attack that both intensifies the distaste for 'hypocrisy' and at the same time asserts a practical if contemptuous preference for it, should not surprise us unduly. For it is precisely because Swift felt that an absolute principle or ideal standard was being violated that he was pained into sarcastic (but not unmeaning) praises of an otherwise unacceptable compromise. No man is more tartly and doggedly 'realistic' than a certain type of disillusioned idealist, and none more likely to insist that unacceptable compromises are what, in the practical politics of life, one must, finally, settle for. Not only is the 'realism' a protest against the betrayal of more absolute expectations, a haughty rubbing-in of the meanness of things: it is also a limiting of moral demands to a scale small enough to satisfy an absolutist temperament instead of oppressing him with dispiriting loose ends. The ideal of perfection embodied in the Houyhnhnms is presented on the assumption that no one can achieve it, and at the same time as a matter of plain utilitarian common sense. It is clear that, in Swift's case at least, the relation between pragmatism and absolutism, between the man who advocates balances of power (*Contests and Dissensions*), middle ways (*Sentiments of a Church-of-England Man*), and specific economic expedients (Irish tracts), and the man who invents Houyhnhnmland, is very close.

The *Project* provides a vivid glimpse not only of the pragmatist who will be content with half-measures that support virtue by preserving appearances, but also of the absolute moralist who recoils from compromise. There is, for example, a strong passage denouncing polite society's tolerance of 'Women of tainted Reputations', as a sign that 'Regard for Reputation' is at a low ebb:

> If this be not so; how comes it to pass, that Women of tainted Reputations find the same Countenance and Reception in all publick Places, with those of the nicest Virtue, who pay, and receive Visits from them, without any Manner of Scruple? Which Proceeding, as it is not very old among us, so I take it to be of most pernicious Consequence. It looks like a Sort of compounding between Virtue and Vice; as if a Woman were allowed to be vicious, provided she be not profligate: As if there were a certain Point where Gallantry ends, and Infamy begins; or that an Hundred criminal Amours were not as pardonable as Half a Score.
>
> (*Works*, 2:46)

There is nothing surprising in the fact that Swift deplored female immorality and the polite world's tolerance of it. The gap between good manners and good morals that the situation exposes exercised many courtesy-writers who, like Swift, wished to insist, more or less emphatically, on the moral basis and the moral function of manners. That it was possible to do this and to value chastity without applying a totally dismissive rigour to 'criminal Amours' is variously shown by, for example, Fielding and Chesterfield. Fielding felt that there were many vices worse than lewdness, and that the *Beau Monde* might profitably be humanised by a certain amount of love, even though 'criminal' (*Tom Jones*, 14:1), at least where a generosity and mutuality of feeling and a benevolent expansiveness were involved. Chesterfield spoke, in a more 'libertine' and less morally concerned way than Fielding, of the civilising properties of fashionable women, the importance to best companies of 'Women of fashion and character (I do not mean absolutely unblemished)' (letter to his godson, 4 December 1765, *Letters*, ed. Bonamy Dobrée, London, 1932, 6:2688); and one might feel that Chesterfield is perhaps close to being an exponent of the kind of attitude Swift had castigated. Even so, Swift's complaint of a gap between morals and the code of manners would not seem surprising or unacceptable to either Fielding or Chesterfield. But what is notable in Swift's passage is the vividness with which he is shocked at the notion of a social compromise with morality ('a Sort of compounding between Virtue and Vice'), and the way the writing kindles into a sense of absolute vacuous absurdity: 'as if there were a certain Point where Gallantry ends, and Infamy begins'. Where Fielding and Chesterfield both seek to narrow the gap between morals and manners, Swift makes use of a logic that inexorably widens this gap until the whole social basis of the compromise is reduced to nullity. In an absolute morality, there can be no chartable point where gallantry ends and infamy begins. One may be sure that for Fielding 'an Hundred criminal Amours' were indeed 'not as pardonable as Half a Score'. Yet it is Swift, the more absolute moralist of the two, who proposes *ad hoc* and practical remedies to patch up the situation, and who, refusing to envisage total changes of heart, recommends the enlisting of hypocrisy and the use of job incentives as viable and not unacceptable aids to morality.

Sound and Moderate Men
From the notion of job incentives for the virtuous to the notion that it is better to employ virtuous than able men is a fairly short step. If state employees were appointed with a regard to their piety and virtue and remained

> exemplary in the Conduct of their Lives, Things would soon take a new Face, and Religion receive a mighty Encouragement: Nor would the publick Weal be less advanced; since of nine Offices in ten that are ill executed, the Defect is not in Capacity or Understanding, but in common Honesty.
>
> (*Project, Works*, 2:48–49)

The matter is taken up in *Gulliver's Travels*. In describing the state of Lilliput in its original Utopian purity (as against the 'scandalous Corruptions' it has since fallen into) Gulliver says:

> In chusing Persons for all Employments, they have more
> Regard to good Morals than to great Abilities: For, since
> Government is necessary to Mankind, they believe that the
> common Size of human Understandings, is fitted to some
> Station or other; and that Providence never intended to make
> the Management of publick Affairs a Mystery, to be com-
> prehended only by a few Persons of sublime Genius, of which
> there seldom are three born in an Age: But, they suppose
> Truth, Justice, Temperance, and the like, to be in every
> Man's Power; the Practice of which Virtues, assisted by
> Experience and a good Intention, would qualify any Man for
> the Service of his Country, except where a Course of Study is
> required. But they thought the Want of Moral Virtues was so
> far from being supplied by superior Endowments of the
> Mind, that Employments could never be put into such
> dangerous Hands as those of Persons so qualified; and at least,
> that the Mistakes committed by Ignorance in a virtuous Dis-
> position, would never be of such fatal Consequence to the
> Publick Weal, as the Practices of a Man, whose Inclinations
> led him to be corrupt, and had great Abilities to manage, to
> multiply, and defend his Corruptions.
>
> (*Gulliver's Travels*, 1:6)

The King of Brobdingnag took a plain moral view of
government, in which a similar preference for sound moral principles over the refinements of expertise is rooted simultaneously
in an uncomplicated rectitude and a simplifying utilitarianism:

> He confined the Knowledge of governing within very *narrow
> Bounds*; to common Sense and Reason, to Justice and Lenity,
> to the Speedy Determination of Civil and criminal Causes;
> with some other obvious Topicks which are not worth con-
> sidering. And, he gave it for his Opinion; that whoever could
> make two Ears of Corn, or two Blades of Grass to grow upon
> a Spot of Ground where only one grew before; would deserve
> better of Mankind, and do more essential Service to his
> Country, than the whole Race of Politicians put together.
>
> (*Gulliver's Travels*, 2:7)

One recognises here the familiar lineaments of an aristocratic contempt for the professional, and also of that distantly related and
rather British cult of the sound mediocre all-round man in preference to the highly trained specialist (Even the 'Course of Study'

required for certain jobs in Lilliput sounds more like a requirement of basic competence in those fields where such competence involves study than any emphasis on a highly developed specialist skill.) Swift's fear is clearly not only of the superior danger of an able rogue 'to manage, to multiply, and defend his Corruptions'. There is too the conception of the expert as a pedant, a fussy distorter of plain central truths and traditional ways, a multiplier of false needs and complications. Mystery, refinement, and similar restless invitations to intellectual and moral perversion are not the exclusive preserve of sects, nor of learned moderns, but extend to those who think of politics as a science or art (*Gulliver's Travels*, 2:7). The expert advisers of monarchs are frequently mocked (*Gulliver's Travels*, 1:2 and 2:3). By contrast, free-minded men like Swift may quite properly advise the great, who, however, will not take advice, for an amusing reason which Swift explained in *A Letter from Dr. Swift to Mr. Pope*, dated 10 January 1721:

> this pedantry ariseth from a maxim themselves do not believe at the same time they practice by it, that there is something profound in politicks, which men of plain honest sense cannot arrive to.
>
> (*Works*, 9:28)

Even good politicians and courtiers, like the Earl of Oxford, are caught up in a pretence which is not only false, but in which they disbelieve. Swift's role in offering advice is that of the man 'of plain honest sense', not that of the professional adviser: 'I have formerly delivered my thoughts very freely, whether I were asked or no, but never affected to be a Councellor, to which I had no manner of call' (loc. cit.). Swift adds in explanation:

> I was humbled enough to see my self so far out-done by the Earl of Oxford in my own trade as a Scholar, and too good a Courtier not to discover his contempt of those who would be men of importance out of their sphere. (loc. cit.)

These lines must not be taken as a celebration of specialist expertise. Their main force is to say, negatively, that men should not meddle in what they know nothing about. 'My own trade as a Scholar', is a mock-modest reference to his liberal education, and to what is expected of a civilised clergyman and man of letters: no pedantry, nothing which a gentleman should lack, as witness the

Earl's outdoing Swift in this sphere (part of the phrasing, of course, is accounted for by the wish to speak handsomely of the former chief minister).

Outside specialist departments of government, where mastery of a 'Course of Studies' is required, Swift's inclination is, then, to insist on a general soundness of character rather than specialist skill or even brilliant ability in general (although he does praise that in Lord Oxford and others). His ideal is perhaps one in which ability and expertise merge with a larger wisdom and with virtue. This passage about the political projectors in Lagado suggests a reluctance to distinguish too closely between moral and intellectual qualifications, seeming instead to take for granted an ideal in which the two are interfused:

> These unhappy People were proposing Schemes for persuading Monarchs to chuse Favourites upon the Score of their Wisdom, Capacity and Virtue; of teaching Ministers to consult the publick Good; of rewarding Merit, great Abilities, and eminent Services; of instructing Princes to know their true Interest, by placing it on the same Foundation with that of their People: Of chusing for Employments Persons qualified to exercise them; with many other wild impossible Chimaeras, that never entered before into the Heart of Man to conceive.
>
> (*Gulliver's Travels*, 3:6)

The list is deliberately headlong, its brisk summarising irony playing down any separation of morality from talent in good politics. But a passage like this easily shades into a protest against the way talented men remain unrewarded while cautious mediocrities prosper:

> There is no *Talent* so useful towards rising in the World, or which puts Men more out of the Reach of Fortune, than that Quality generally possessed by the dullest Sort of People, in common Speech called *Discretion*; a Species of lower Prudence, by the Assistance of which, People of the meanest Intellectuals, without any other Qualification, pass through the World in great Tranquility, and with universal good Treatment, neither giving nor taking Offence. ... And, indeed, as Regularity and Forms are of great Use in carrying on the Business of the World, so it is very convenient, that Persons endued with this Kind of Discretion, should have

38

the Share which is proper to their Talents, in the Conduct of
Affairs; but, by no Means, meddle in Matters which require
*Genius, Learning, strong Comprehension, Quickness of Concep-
tion, Magnanimity, Generosity, Sagacity,* or any other superior
Gift of human minds.

(*Intelligencer*, No. 5, 1728, *Works*, 12:38)

The discussion slightly later notes that many 'Men of eminent
Parts and Abilities, as well as Virtues' in many countries have
been

disgraced, or *banished,* or *suffered Death,* merely in Envy to
their Virtues and superior *Genius,* which emboldened them
in great Exigencies and Distresses of State (wanting a
reasonable Infusion of this Aldermanly Discretion) to
attempt the Service of their Prince and Country, out of the
common Forms.

(*Works*, 12:39)

One recognises here the contempt of the man of great talent
towards the mediocre, and the 'common Forms'. But it is precisely because Swift recognised in himself a subversiveness that
would throw out the 'common Forms' along with their bath-
water of mediocrity, and because he saw in a certain kind of
rule-bound mediocrity a protection against this subversiveness,
that he insisted so often elsewhere on the common forms as a
civilised bastion against individualist misrule. Thus Lord
Munodi stands out from the mad originals of Gulliver's third
voyage in that

being not of an enterprizing Spirit, he was content to go on
in the old Forms; to live in the Houses his Ancestors had
built, and act as they did in every Part of Life without
Innovation;

(*Gulliver's Travels*, 3:4)

and the sane, traditionalist man of sense in the Digression on
Madness is defined as passing

his Life in the common Forms, without any Thought of
subduing Multitudes to his own *Power,* his *Reasons* or his
Visions; and the more he shapes his Understanding by the

Pattern of Human Learning, the less he is inclined to form
Parties after his particular Notions.

(*Tale*, sec. 9)

The paradox behind this has been well described by Robert
M. Adams, in an important essay on Swift and Kafka:

> One could look for no better example of the placid, adjusted
> man than Swift's great enemy William Wotton, whose
> reaction to the *Tale of a Tub* was one of unqualified horror.
> Although Swift's theological blasphemies may have been
> exaggerated, his raging contempt for the whole race of
> moderns can scarcely be overstated; and surely this implies,
> on the face of it, a considerable contempt for the 'common
> forms'. Indeed, a treatise so fantastic, sardonic, and derisive
> as *A Tale of a Tub* could scarcely culminate in a calm
> conformity; the expenditure of so much nervous ingenuity
> merely to endorse the 'common forms' would be at the least
> a paradox, akin to that by which the fourth book of *Gulliver*
> may be read as the most passionate denunciation of passion
> ever penned.
>
> (*Strains of Discord: Studies in Literary Openness*, Ithaca,
> N.Y., 1958, 154)

The point is fairly taken, even though Swift might claim that it
was the essence of modernism to subvert the common forms:
doubtless Wotton would lose either way, since whatever adherence to the common forms one would attribute to him would be
described by Swift as 'Aldermanly Discretion'. In a sense, the
distinction could resolve itself into 'common forms' explicitly
identified with old and solid tradition, as against the cheap
simulacrum of conventionality with which modern mediocrities
disguise their viciousness. But we return to a familiar circularity.
All established states are good, and what subverts them are not
constitutional defects but 'the Corruption of Manners'. Thus the
Church-of-England Man does not 'think any one regular Species
of Government, more acceptable to God than another . . . few
States are ruined by any Defect in their Institution, but generally
by the Corruption of Manners' (*Sentiments, Works*, 2:14; see also
Project, Works, 2:44, 57, 63). If the Church-of-England Man is a
little gloomy over the fact that even 'the best Institution is no long
Security' (2:14) against corruptions of manners, his point is not
that established institutions need to be changed, but that they

must constantly guard against the relentless subversions of human viciousness. The old and established is *as such*, pragmatically, the best available if imperfect protection, needing constant *ad hoc* repairs, but not revolution or reconstitution, which merely (the principle is dear to British conservatism, and has links with the preference for the sound over the brilliant public servant) replaces the old with something 'which may neither be so safe nor so convenient'. Thus the final, somewhat Burkeian, words of the *Project for the Advancement of Religion* demand (in the name of a 'Reformation of Manners' rather than of institutions) great vigilance,

> because the Nature of Things is such, that if Abuses be not remedied, they will certainly encrease, nor ever stop till they end in the Subversion of a Common-Wealth. As there must always of Necessity be some Corruptions; so in a well-instituted State, the executive Power will be always contending against them, by *reducing Things* (as *Machiavel* speaks) *to their first Principles*; never letting Abuses grow inveterate, or multiply so far that it will be hard to find Remedies, and perhaps impossible to apply them. As he that would keep his House in Repair, must attend every little Breach or Flaw, and supply it immediately, else Time alone will bring it all to Ruin; how much more the common Accidents of Storms and Rain? He must live in perpetual Danger of his House falling about his Ears; and will find it cheaper to throw it quite down, and build it again from the Ground, perhaps upon a new Foundation, or at least in a new Form, which may neither be so safe nor so convenient as the old.
>
> (*Works*, 2:63)

We may note the fatalistic concept of human subversiveness, which is identified in the metaphor of the endangered house not only with 'the common Accidents of Storms and Rain', but with something so ineluctable as Time itself.

Abuses in Religion
The threats posed by 'modernism' (sects, factious pedants and their 'speculations', politicians, lechers, etc.) are the threats posed by human nature itself. They reside in that relentless pressure of misdirected intensities which the *Tale of a Tub* dramatises: the frenzies of religious sado-masochism in Peter and Jack, the hack's obsessional feats of pseudo-logic and the dazzlingly imaged per-

versity of his system-making. The outrageous coruscations of the *Tale* have a vitality well beyond the scope of mere parody; it is almost fair to think of it as the greatest of all the bad books it mocks, in the real, not just the mock-sense. Swift's repudiating mimicry of the subversive intensities of the human mind clearly proceeded from a certain inwardness of understanding. The moderation and the traditional centrality of the standards he sets up against these intensities have an avowedly precarious or a resolutely self-protective quality or both. Hence a tendency to subvert his own positives by irony, and (as we saw with the common forms) both to praise and to attack the same things, or things for which he uses uncannily similar language. Many readers of *A Tale of a Tub* have found it difficult to choose between their instinct to read the work as an attack on religion and Swift's official claim that it attacked only 'Abuses in Religion' – namely, Popery and Nonconformism, or, more broadly, '*Abuses . . . such as all Church of* England *Men agree in*' (*Tale*, Apology). Martin's Anglican middle way between the excesses of Peter (the Roman Church) and Jack (Puritanism), and his ecumenical moderation are, however, put forward somewhat ambiguously. Here is his moderate position at its best (a clause is for the moment omitted near the beginning), in the famous passage where Martin tries to restrain Jack's frenzy, as he tears his coat to make it seem least like Peter's:

> But *Martin . . . begged his Brother of all Love, not to damage his Coat by any Means; for he never would get such another*: Desired him *to consider, that it was not their Business to form their Actions by any Reflection upon* Peter's, *but by observing the Rules prescribed in their Father's* Will. That *he should remember*, Peter *was still their Brother, whatever Faults or Injuries he had committed; and therefore they should by all means avoid such a Thought, as that of taking Measures for Good and Evil, from no other Rule, than of Opposition to him*. That *it was true, the Testament of their good Father was very exact in what related to the wearing of their* Coats; *yet was it no less penal and strict in prescribing Agreement, and Friendship, and Affection between them. And therefore, if straining a Point were at all dispensable, it would certainly be so, rather to the Advance of Unity, than Increase of Contradiction*.
>
> (*Tale*, sec. 6)

This is probably the most straightforwardly sensible thing that anyone says in the entire *Tale*, and comes close to the Church-of-England Man's sentiment about Christian unity:

As to Rites and Ceremonies, and Forms of Prayer, he allows there might be some useful Alterations; and more, which in the Prospect of uniting Christians might be very supportable, as Things declared in their own Nature indifferent;

(Sentiments, Works, 2:5)

Even in the *Sentiments*, however, Swift hedges the allowability of 'Alterations' with heavy reservations; and the proposal easily turns into its repudiated Whiggish counterpart, which urges Protestant unity (against Papists) in language very close to Martin's or the Church-of-England Man's. Here is the position ironically summarised in the *Argument Against Abolishing Christianity*:

... It is proposed as a singular Advantage, that the Abolishing of Christianity, will very much contribute to the uniting of *Protestants*, by enlarging the Terms of Communion, so as to take in all Sorts of *Dissenters*; who are now shut out of the Pale upon Account of a few Ceremonies, which all Sides confess to be Things indifferent.

(Works, 2:34)

or again, years later, in the *Intelligencer*'s attack on the Whiggish, time-serving clergyman of 'Aldermanly Discretion' and

his dreadful Apprehensions of *Popery*: his great Moderation towards Dissenters of all Denominations; with hearty Wishes, that by yielding somewhat on both Sides, there might be a general Union among Protestants

(Works, 12:44)

The contradictions would not, on a plane of ideological discourse, be difficult to reconcile. The interesting thing is the similarity in the language, and in the configuration of attitudes, between Martin's correct position, and its Whiggish 'Abuse'. It is not altogether surprising that Martin's speech comes to us slightly subverted in advance, as may be seen by supplying the clause I omitted in the first sentence of the quotation, which actually begins thus:

But *Martin*, who at this Time happened to be extremely flegmatick and sedate, *begged* . . .

Martin is still further subverted by the words that follow his speech:

> *Martin* had still proceeded as gravely as he began; and doubt-less, would have delivered an admirable Lecture of Morality, which might have exceedingly contributed to my Reader's *Repose, both of Body and Mind*: (the true ultimate end of *Ethicks*;) But *Jack* was already gone a Flight-shot beyond his Patience.

The 'admirable Lecture of Morality' and its predicted soporific effect on the reader tend to deflate Martin. The damage should not be exaggerated. Mild ironic underminings of serious statements are common in Augustan writers, as not very damaging (indeed sometimes affectionate) jokes at the speaker's expense, which at the same time release the (real) *author* from too solemn a posture of endorsement. Parson Adams falls asleep during a speech by Joseph Andrews on charity (*Joseph Andrews*, 3:6); Adams himself launches on 'a long Discourse' in contempt of gold, which the author omits 'as most which he said occurs among many Authors who have treated this Subject' (ibid., 3:8); serious words by Allworthy are followed by 'Here Allworthy concluded his Sermon' (*Tom Jones*, 1:12 *ad fin.*); Johnson caps Imlac's famous speech on poetry with 'Imlac now felt the enthusiastic fit, and was proceeding to aggrandize his own profession, when the prince cried out, "Enough ... " ' (*Rasselas*, ch. 11). Such irony came easily to eighteenth-century writers, and its mere presence need not be made much of. In the passages from Fielding and Johnson, however, it is genial and avuncular. Swift's passage, on the other hand, strikes a tart, flattening note: a real sarcasm takes shape at the expense of 'modern' laziness of mind and morals, not just because moral discourse puts moderns to sleep, but because they require their '*Ethicks*' to be, above all, *restful*. The apparent escape, that the comment is made not, as in Fielding or Johnson, by an authorial figure, but by one who is himself under constant parody by Swift, does not really exist as we read. For if part of the ostensible or official sting is directed at the silly speaker (or 'author') and at bad modern readers, Swift's interinvolvement with the speakers he derides is always close and intimate, and the intensities and acerbities that proceed from them have a way of being closer to Swift than the comments of the more directly authorial narrators of *Joseph Andrews*, *Tom Jones*, and *Rasselas* are to Fielding and Johnson. There is in the *Tale* no vivid alternative presence that we can hang on to, which will assure us that things are really more sane than the speaker makes out, and the presupposition (so prominent in the satire of Pope or of Fielding) that writer and reader are in healthy and honest complicity against vice and folly is here totally blocked. If the mad speaker assumes that the reader will be lax, complacent, and lazy, we are somehow forced, in part, to take that insult to ourselves.

In a similar way, it is hard in the reading to feel that Swift is not somehow participating in the deflation of Martin: if the reader is made to feel too shallow to attend to Martin's sensible words, it is Swift who not only put the suggestion in his speaker's mouth, but who also generated the ironic slur of 'an admirable Lecture of Morality' in the first place. That slur, incidentally, is no sudden shock, no simple and clear-cut betrayal of the reader such as critics are fond of attributing to Swift. Martin's speech, as we saw, is also undermined in advance, and what we feel is no merely momentary cancellation or revision of his creditability after the event, but a more continuous and indefinite uneasiness over how to take all his good sense throughout.

This subversive indefiniteness does not merely depend on hints of moral reservation or on simple stylistic deflations. It is compounded by a tendency to dissolve in an exuberance of zany comedy, occasionally quickened by brief eruptions of violence:

> But *Jack* was already gone a Flight-shot beyond his Patience. And as in Scholastick Disputes, nothing serves to rouze the Spleen of him that *Opposes*, so much as a kind of Pedantick affected Calmness in the *Respondent*; Disputants being for the most part like unequal Scales, where the *Gravity* of one Side advances the *Lightness* of the Other, and causes it to fly up and kick the Beam; So it happened here, that the *Weight* of *Martin's* Arguments exalted *Jack's Levity*, and made him fly out and spurn against his Brother's Moderation. In short, *Martin's Patience* put *Jack* in a *Rage*.

It is not so much that the 'weight' of Martin's sensible arguments is morally subverted by the familiar satiric play on 'gravity' and 'lightness' as that it is comically dissipated in a pseudo-scientific description of weird mechanical interchange. The descriptive device of rendering action in such abstracting terms is old in comic narrative and looks forward to Beckett and the French new novelists. The image of a pair of scales in a mental conflict is also commonplace (see, for example, *Joseph Andrews*, 1:9). But although what Swift creates (not merely mental processes allegorised in physical terms, but a ragged mental disagreement elaborately enacting the geometrical predictability of a precision-instrument) is commonplace in a way, his passage has a ghoulish vitality special to itself. And just as the reader's sleepiness is forgotten in the sudden eruption of Jack 'gone a Flight-shot beyond his Patience' and the decorous movement of the scales quickens at the unseemly violence of Jack's rage, so the disembodied ballet of inner feelings goes richly physical as the narrative returns to Jack's ravaged coat, and the populous world of images which it reminds the 'author' of:

> but that which most afflicted [Jack] was, to observe his Brother's Coat so well reduced into the State of Innocence; while his own was either wholly rent to his Shirt; or those Places which had scaped his cruel Clutches, were still in *Peter's* Livery. So that he looked like a drunken *Beau*, half rifled by *Bullies*; Or like a fresh Tenant of *Newgate*, when he has refused the Payment of *Garnish*; Or like a discovered *Shoplifter*, left to the Mercy of *Exchange-Women*; Or like a *Bawd* in her old Velvet-Petticoat, resign'd into the secular Hands of the *Mobile*. Like any, or like all of these, a Meddley of *Rags*, and *Lace*, and *Rents*, and *Fringes*, unfortunate Jack did now appear.

Allegory and satire (of the self-indulgent austerities and destructiveness of Puritan 'enthusiasm', of Puritanism's paradoxical kinship with Popery, of the individual social types in the similes, of pompously elaborate or learnedly garrulous similes as such) are maintained throughout, but they operate well below the vitality of the passage at its varied and animated *face value*. After this, further narrative of Jack's feelings and behaviour, and with it a comparatively unruffled thread of allegorical implication, proceed relatively soberly to the end of a longish paragraph. Even there, however, narrative and allegory are from time to time sparked with momentary finalities of wildness, glimpses of crazed intensity on Jack's part which certainly make narrative and allegorical sense, but which arrest us by an energy that spills over the overt and official functions:

> He would have been extremely glad to see his Coat in the Condition of *Martin's*, but infinitely gladder to find that of

Martin's in the same Predicament with his. However, since neither of these was likely to come to pass, he thought fit to lend the whole Business another Turn, and to dress up Necessity into a Virtue. Therefore, after as many of the *Fox's* Arguments, as he could muster up, for bringing *Martin* to *Reason*, as he called it; or, as he meant it, into his own ragged, bobtail'd Condition; and observing he said all to little purpose; what, alas, was left for the forlorn *Jack* to do, but after a Million of Scurrilities against his Brother, to run mad with Spleen, and Spight, and Contradiction.

This emotional rhythm, of narrative sobriety concluding in a momentary explosive wildness, is repeated in the rephrasing ('To be short') that immediately follows:

To be short, here began a mortal Breach between these two. *Jack* went immediately to *New Lodgings*, and in a few Days it was for certain reported, that he had run out of his Wits. In a short time after, he appeared abroad, and confirmed the Report, by falling into the oddest Whimsies that ever a sick Brain conceived.

By now, Martin has regained most of the strictly *moral* status that he had lost in the earlier deflation. He is more straight-forwardly the sensible and virtuous foil to Jack's mad antics. But he recovers this dignity only by withdrawing from the centre of the stage. If his words are not undercut again by phrases like 'an admirable Lecture of Morality', it is because he is given no more words to speak.

But the problem of Martin's presentation in the *Tale* is not, as we have seen, mainly one of moral deflation of an open and straightforward kind. He is much more radically subverted not by direct slurs but by the tearaway energies of the fictional world he is made to inhabit (or, if one prefers, by the strange unpredict-able autonomy of Swift's irony, which sometimes simply forgets its positive standards and even momentarily ignores its official enemies). The *Tale* is of a kind that does not easily accommodate positives. Even when Martin is no longer directly implicated in the bad doings of his two brothers (as he had been in the early part of their story, in Section 2), their folly illogically rubs off on him. As Wotton said in his *Observations* (1705) on the *Tale*: 'let *Peter* be mad one way, and *Jack* another, and let *Martin* be sober ... Yet still this is all Part of a *Tale of a Tub*' (*Tale*, ed. A. C. Guthkelch and D. Nichol Smith, Oxford, 2nd edn., 1958, 322). Wotton, and many others, felt that religion itself, not just opponents of the Church of England, was affected by the satire:

> that he might shelter himself the better from any Censure here in *England*, he falls most unmercifully upon *Peter* and *Jack*, *i.e.* upon *Popery* and *Fanaticism*, and gives *Martin*, who represents the *Church of England*, extream good Quarter. I confess, Sir, I abhor making Sport with any way of worshipping God, and he that diverts himself too much at the Expense of the *Roman Catholics* and the *Protestant Dissenters*, may lose his own Religion e're he is aware of it, at least the Power of it in his Heart.
>
> (Ibid., 318)

There was little danger of Swift losing 'his own Religion', though one knows what Wotton means. Wotton was understandably pained (ibid., 321, 323) by the description of the Cross as 'an old *Sign-Post* that belonged to his *Father*, with Nails and Timber enough on it, to build sixteen large Men of War' (*Tale*, sec. 4, *Works*, 1:74 and n.) and by the assertion that 'the Fumes issuing from a Jakes, will furnish as comely and useful a Vapor, as Incense from an Altar' (*Tale*, sec. 9). Wotton would not be disarmed by Swift's modern defenders, who might point out quite correctly (as Swift himself might have pointed out) that the first passage refers to the Papist claim to possess relics of the true cross,[3] and is spoken by Peter in a fit of megalomaniac exaggeration; and that the second passage is part of a Digression on Madness. But in refusing to be disarmed, Wotton would, I feel, be right, though for slightly different reasons. If Swift cannot be accused of losing his religion or endorsing the language of his speakers, that language does have energies which resist being neutralised by Swift's mockery of these speakers. Whether or not Swift was always clearly conscious that the firm authoritarianism of his religious admonitions was partly self-protective, he seems as an artist to have sensed that his style, at its highest pitch of creative expression, not only tended to subversiveness but was not easily given to positive affirmations. Martin's speech is such an affirmation, but it is almost unique in the book. It placed Swift in an impasse which he may or may not have acknowledged, but which was nonetheless real. He had either to omit the direct moral deflation and neutralise the centrifugal vitalities of the immediate context, so as to let the speech stand on the dignity of its naked assertion, thus becoming untrue to the book's real manner; or to sustain that manner, thus subverting Martin and, with him, the Church of England and, to some extent, religion and God themselves. Swift took, on this occasion, the artist's choice, not the divine's. But he normally evaded the dilemma. Martin appears less circumstantially, for the most part, than his two brothers, and, unlike them, has no separate section devoted to his particular 'history' (a spurious abstract of this unwritten history was printed in the edition of 1720, by what Guthkelch and Nichol Smith, ed. cit., lxii, call 'an imitator of Swift who was hostile to the Church of England'). The reasons for this seem both religious and artistic, the book being one where positive norms, of any sort, are out of place.

Authority and Truth
The ironic subversions of the *Tale* are so universal that they become self-subversions; and the implied appeal to a simplifying authority is itself subverted by that fact. In other writings also, close relationships exist between attitudes that Swift repudiated through ironic mimicry and attitudes that he held literally, and these relationships extend, for example, to the question of 'authority' itself. The cynical proponent of the *Argument Against Abolishing Christianity* grants that

> it may perhaps admit a Controversy, whether the Banishing all Notions of Religion whatsoever, would be convenient for the Vulgar. Not that I am in the least of Opinion with those, who hold Religion to have been the Invention of Politicians, to keep the lower Part of the World in Awe, by the Fear of invisible Powers; unless Mankind were then very different from what it is now: For I look upon the Mass, or Body of our People here in *England*, to be Free-Thinkers, that is to say, as stanch Unbelievers, as any of the highest Rank. But I conceive some scattered Notions about a superior Power to be of singular Use for the common People, as furnishing excellent Materials to keep Children quiet, when they grow peevish.
>
> (*Works*, 2:34)

The irony of this has many coils, and the speaker puts himself variously in the wrong. But his pondered refusal to accept that Religion is a political instrument 'to keep the lower Part of the World in Awe' and his cautious assertion that there is nevertheless

49

something in such a view do not mirror any Swiftian rejection of a political and disciplinarian conception of the role of religion. If anything can be described as the principal target of Swift's attack in this paragraph, it is the fact that the English are nowadays too free-thinking for religion to fulfil this role satisfactorily. It is free-thinkers themselves who oppose such a disciplinarian conception, and in *Mr. Collins's Discourse of Free-Thinking, Put into plain English, by Way of Abstract, for the Use of the Poor*, 1713, Swift mimics them pointedly:

> It is objected (by Priests no doubt, but I have forgot their Names) that false Speculations are necessary to be imposed upon Men, in order to assist the Magistrate in keeping the Peace, and that Men ought therefore to be deceived like Children, for their own Good. I answer, that Zeal for imposing Speculations, whether true or false (under which Name of Speculations I include all Opinions of Religion, as the Belief of a God, Providence, Immortality of the Soul, future Rewards and Punishments, &c.) has done more hurt than it is possible for Religion to do good.
>
> (*Works*, 4:40)[4]

Mr Collins's mimicked absurdities do not, nowadays, always seem as absurd as Swift meant, and some passages may, as J. M. Bullitt says, 'fail to evoke contempt' (*Jonathan Swift and the Anatomy of Satire*, Cambridge, Mass., 1961, 102). But the passage is as ironical as the *Project for the Advancement of Religion* was literal. Swift's position on the peace-keeping functions of religion might well seem to us a more outrageous invitation to parody than Mr Collins's, for he would have agreed with Bolingbroke's view of free-thinkers as

> Men whom I look upon to be the Pests of Society, because their endeavours are directed to losen the bands of it, & to take att least one curb out of the mouth of that wild Beast Man when it would be well if he was check'd by half a score others. (To Swift, 12 September 1724, *Correspondence*, 3:27; Bolingbroke was protesting against Swift's imputation of free-thinking to him.)

If the scintillating indirections of the *Argument Against Abolishing Christianity* tempt us to feel superior to the speaker's boneheaded statesmanliness as he concedes the uses of religion

'for the common People', we cannot dissociate Swift himself
from some non-ridiculed version of the same view. The proponent of the *Argument* clearly perceives that the proposed
abolishing of Christianity rests not on any doctrinal objections to
particular religious beliefs, but to the status, as a controlling force,
of any religion as such:

> And therefore, if, notwithstanding all I have said, it shall
> still be thought necessary to have a Bill brought in for
> repealing Christianity; I would humbly offer an Amend-
> ment, that instead of the word *Christianity*, may be put
> *Religion* in general; which I conceive, will much better
> answer all the good Ends proposed by the Projectors of it.
> For, as long as we leave in Being a God, and his Providence,
> with all the necessary Consequences, which curious and
> inquisitive Men will be apt to draw from such Premises; we
> do not strike at the Root of the Evil, although we should ever
> so effectually annihilate the present Scheme of the Gospel.
> For, of what Use is Freedom of Thought, if it will not
> produce Freedom of Action; which is the sole End, how
> remote soever, in Appearance, of all Objections against
> Christianity? And therefore, the Free-Thinkers consider it as
> a Sort of Edifice, wherein all the Parts have such a mutual
> Dependance on each other, that if you happen to pull out one
> single Nail, the whole Fabrick must fall to the Ground. This
> was happily expressed by him, who had heard of a Text
> brought for Proof of the Trinity, which in an antient Manu-
> script was differently read; he thereupon immediately took
> the Hint, and by a sudden Deduction of a long *Sorites*, most
> logically concluded; Why, if it be as you say, I may safely
> whore and drink on, and defy the Parson. From which, and
> many the like Instances easy to be produced, I think nothing
> can be more manifest, than that the Quarrel is not against any
> particular Points of hard Digestion in the Christian System;
> but against Religion in general; which, by laying Restraints
> on human Nature, is supposed the great Enemy to the
> Freedom of Thought and Action.
>
> (*Works*, 2:37–38)

If the politic speaker, in the complacency of his moderation,
plays fast and loose with all distinction between one creed and the
next, so to some extent does Swift himself literally, in so far as he
supports religion more as a 'curb' (political and psychological) to

human subversiveness than as a specific body of doctrine, and in so far as he insists on the overriding authority of established national religions in their respective countries. The anarchic 'Freedom of Thought and Action' which (by a familiar paradox) leads straight to tyranny is clearly perceived by Mr Collins to be most threatened by the state religions. In a passage already quoted in part, he is made to say:

> It is the indispensable Duty of a *Free Thinker*, to endeavour *forcing* all the World to think as he does, and by that means make them *Free Thinkers* too. You are also to understand, that I allow no Man to be a *Free Thinker*, any further than as he differs from the received Doctrines of Religion. Where a Man falls in, though by perfect Chance, with what is generally believed, he is in that Point a confined and limited Thinker; and you shall see by and by, that I celebrate those for the noblest *Free Thinkers* in every Age, who differed from the Religion of their Countries in the most fundamental Points, and especially in those which bear any Analogy to the chief Fundamentals of Religion among us.
>
> (*Mr. Collins's Discourse, Works*, 4:36–37)

The wild arbitrariness of Mr Collins's logic, the glimpse it provides of a mental bottomlessness turning into bossy despotism, are a perfect and inventive emblem of the favourite Swiftian paradox, that anarchy leads to tyranny. The particular intellectual nightmare created by Mr Collins's words proceeds partly from the free-thinking claim that, because there are in the world many religions and many scriptures, every man is free to range among them, and 'a great deal of *Free-thinking* will at last set us all right, and every one will adhere to the *Scripture* he likes best' (*Works*, 4:32–33). It will not surprise us to see Swift repudiating a religious relativism that proceeds from the singularity of individuals, while, as champion of state religions, defending one that tends to the cohesiveness of separate national communities. But Swift's own position as a Church-of-England Man, not only upholding state religions as such but personally believing in the superiority of what Mr Collins calls 'the chief Fundamentals of Religion among us' (for the 'straight' version see *Works*, 2:5), seems in some ways an example of the very situation from which Mr Collins's derided reasoning flows:

> Here are perhaps twenty Sorts of *Scriptures* in the several Parts of the World, and every Sett of Priests contends that their *Scripture* is the true One.

The reasoning becomes actively disreputable, presumably, at the point where Mr Collins argues that, since only one of the scriptures can be right and no one can know which that is without '*thinking freely*, every one of us for ourselves',

> The Parliament ought to be at the Charge of finding a sufficient number of these *Scriptures* for every one of Her Majesty's Subjects, for there are Twenty to One against us, that we may be in the wrong: But a great deal of *Free-thinking* will at last set us all right.
>
> (*Works*, 4:32)

My object is not to expose any 'contradictions' in Swift's implied position. There is probably no contradiction that cannot be resolved by logical or theological means, and none of which Swift himself was not, in a high-handed way, aware. If, for example, free-thinking leads ultimately to tyranny, the free-thinker may justly argue that an organised religious conformity does so too. Swift mockingly puts the argument into Mr Collins's mouth, and evades answering it, in a style reminiscent of *A Tale of a Tub*:

> Besides, if all People were of the same Opinion, the Remedy would be worse than the Disease; I will tell you the Reason some other time.
>
> (*Works*, 4:39)[5]

If Swift is mocking muddled and evasive authors, as often in the *Tale* (e.g., sec. 9, *Works*, 1:107 and 113, where the manuscript fails just when a 'knotty Point' is to be unravelled, or the 'author' simply announces that he will 'not farther enlarge' on this or that), the evasion lets Swift out too.

It will not do to conclude too readily that Swift is unconsciously silencing a doubt of his own, since the practice occurs frequently and Swift is not ashamed to signpost it. But in those schoolmasterly bossinesses and arbitrarinesses of his foolish speakers, Mr Collins haughtily dismissing a knotty problem or Gulliver asserting that no critic can impugn what he has disclosed (*Gulliver's Travels* 4:12), Swift not infrequently indulges an hauteur of his own, transferred to fools but not exorcised by the parody. Behind Mr Collins's shoddy laxity stands Swift's uppish refusal to get tangled up in an ungentlemanly and subversive complexity of argument, on a matter best solved by a brisk reduction to practicalities: not only are 'doubts' best concealed and subdued (*Works*, 9:261, 262) and metaphysical fussiness likely to do more harm than good, but 'Violent zeal for truth hath an hundred to one odds to be either petulancy, ambition, or pride' (ibid., 261). This is doubtless aimed at Dissenters, but Swift's own 'zeal for truth' and (for that matter) no lack of 'petulancy, ambition, or pride' turns the sarcasm into one of those self-implicating paradoxes that exemplify the moral impasse underlying Swift's cravings for, and his sense of the urgent importance of, 'authority' (even in preference to 'truth').

In this light, bossy uppishness (whether it silences an argument or diminishes an enemy) ceases to seem merely funny, and becomes, beyond the joke, a primary display of rule. The wittiest, most buoyantly managed hauteurs transcend their element as semi-playful debating points. Consider the celebrated epigram against Steele in *The Importance of the Guardian Considered* (1713):

> What Bailiff would venture to Arrest Mr. *Steele*, now he has the Honour to be your Representative? and what Bailiff ever scrupled it before?
>
> (*Works*, 8:14)

This indeed shows Swift at a very high level of inventive play (Leavis quotes it, a shade solemnly, as an example of the way 'surprise is a perpetually varied accompaniment of the grave, dispassionate, matter-of-fact tone in which Swift delivers his intensities' (*The Common Pursuit*, Harmondsworth, 1962, 76). The dazzling epigrammatic turn escapes no one, nor the imputation that Steele had sought election to Parliament as a means of 'escaping arrest for debt' (Ehrenpreis, *Swift*, 2:690, and *Works*, 8:21). But what is sometimes overlooked is that the epigram is also a brilliant deflection *ad hominem* of an argument more than half-seriously maintained, that the bailiff might be right in both cases, for official status really deserves special respect: 'that supposing the Persons on both Sides to be of equal Intrinsick Worth, it is more Impudent, Immoral, and Criminal to reflect on a *Majority* in Power, than a *Minority* out of Power' (*Works*, 8:14); and that whatever doctrines of his own Swift was contradicting here for polemical purposes (Ehrenpreis, *Swift*, 2:691–92) and

whatever qualifications, in political theory, surround the 'Maxim
. . . that the Prince can do no wrong' (*Works*, 8:23), there is more
than a satiric commitment in Swift's rebuke to Steele for attacking

> those Persons, whom Her Majesty has thought fit to place in
> the highest Stations of the Kingdom, and to trust them with
> the Management of Her most weighty Affairs: And this is
> the Gentleman who cries out, *Where is Honour? Where is
> Government? Where is Prerogative?* Because the *Examiner* has
> sometimes dealt freely with those, whom the Queen has
> thought fit to *Discard*, and the Parliament to *Censure*.
> (*Works*, 8:15)

Swift, an anti-Hobbesian with a Hobbesian view of human nature
and a Hobbesian conception of some of the functions of
government (on this, see for example Martin Price, *To the Palace
of Wisdom*, Garden City, N.J., 1965, 186), opposes Hobbesian and
other tyranny, famously and unquestionably. But his irony, even
when he is at his most explicit on this point, leaves us unsure that
an authoritarian undertone is not present in some form:

> It is a Remark of *Hobbes*, that the Youth of *England* are
> corrupted in their Principles of Government, by reading the
> Authors of *Greece* and *Rome*, who writ under Common-
> wealths. But it might have been more fairly offered for the
> Honour of Liberty, that while the rest of the known World
> was over-run with the Arbitrary Government of single
> Persons; *Arts* and *Sciences* took their Rise, and flourished only
> in those few small Territories where the People were *free*.
> And although *Learning* may continue after *Liberty* is lost, as it
> did in *Rome*, . . . yet it hardly ever began under a *Tyranny* in
> any Nation: Because *Slavery* is of all Things the greatest Clog
> and Obstacle to *Speculation*.
> (*Sentiments of a Church-of-England Man, Works*, 2:17–18)

Although in context these words lead to an eloquent plea for
'limited Monarchy', arguing that as 'Arbitrary Power is but the
first natural Step from *Anarchy* or the *Savage Life*', so a maturer
process leads to a proper 'adjusting *Power* and *Freedom*', they do
not leave us unambiguously convinced that the matter ends here.
Can the word 'Speculation' ever escape altogether the tentacles of
Swift's irony? What reader of *A Tale of a Tub*, whose 'author'
vents his 'Speculations . . . for the universal Benefit of Human

55

kind' (*Tale*, sec. 9) in every possible mad and bad way, will be confident that clogs and obstacles to speculation are altogether wrong? And what reader who then comes upon the dead kings in Glubbdubdrib showing

> with great Strength of Reason, that the Royal Throne could not be supported without Corruption; because, that positive, confident, restive Temper, which Virtue infused into Man, was a perpetual Clog to publick Business,
>
> (*Gulliver's Travels*, 3:8)

can be absolutely certain that the sentiments are as utterly discredited as Swift's irony is meant to suggest; or that Virtue's 'positive, confident, restive Temper' does not tend to the same condition as the 'violent zeal for truth' of the aphorism?

It may be that what Irvin Ehrenpreis said of Swift's conversation applies well to many of his writings:

> Commonplace though his views tended to be, he had to display them as his very own . . . he liked to sound publicly witty, daringly unconventional, even if his moral principles were the most hidebound. Actually, it is just because his substance was orthodox that his style grew iconoclastic.
>
> (Swift, 2:211)

This hints fruitfully at a possible relation of Swift to the moderation and orthodoxy of, for example, Martin in the *Tale*: a refusal to settle unguardedly for the ordinary, while asserting it with genuine commitment. If the style grew subversive because the ideological substance was orthodox, there may yet be a further loop to the spiral: perhaps the ideological substance was orthodox because beneath it lay a temperament (reflected in the style!) that knew itself to be subversive. The sense of his own recalcitrance to the orthodox may have driven Swift to assert it with a passion both overemphatic and undermining in its sheer unruliness. Or rather, not so much *assert* it as castigate its opposite. The positive norms, those standards of central and self-evident human value,

> Anglicanism, humane letters, reason . . . limited monarchy, classical literary standards, and rational judgment . . . the virtue of cultivation of Graeco-Roman antiquity, improved by Christian ethics and a cheering hope of salvation . . . the

doctrines of the Church of England and the political constitution of 1688

(Ehrenpreis, *Swift*, 1:202–3)

in so far as they purport to be central and self-evident, are difficult
to present except in terms of the deviations that the *Tale* superbly
dramatises. This is only partly because of the hoary principle
according to which vice is easier to make interesting than virtue,
especially *ordinary* virtue: this principle has not deterred such
authors as Spenser or Bunyan, for example, from undertaking a
direct presentation of virtue in their most ambitious imaginative
works (nor has it led them necessarily to undercut that presentation with irony). There are, on Swift's part, reasons also that
may be called 'rhetorical': since his claim is that his positive
standards are obvious and in the widest sense normal, restating
them in detail merely concedes that they are not, whereas exposing deviations from what is assumed to be taken for granted by
everyone strengthens the emphasis on the sheer unreason and
perversity of vice. Moreover, Swift's positive standards hold
together a great number of things, 'Anglicanism, humane letters,
reason . . . limited monarchy . . . Graeco-Roman antiquity . . . the
political constitution of 1688', whose coherence (short of elaborate feats of ideological synthesis that would have been not only
rebarbative to Swift's temperament but unsuited to the satire and
fiction he was writing) can only be asserted through generalised
concepts of centrality, moderation, authority, freedom, reason,
common sense, and by confident appeals 'to the Lessons of all
Moralists and Legislators' (*Works*, 8:47) – the last phrase, from
The Publick Spirit of the Whigs, 1714, so typically joining together
the notions of tradition and of rule. In the same work (p. 44),
Swift mocks Steele for using the phrase '*reasonable to common
Sense*; that is . . . *reasonable to Reason*'. The passage is, really, a
piece of trivial polemical word-splitting. But the kind of inclusive
term that united virtue and sense with the plainly obvious and
with the agreed opinion of good men in all ages had a particular
appeal for Swift. He was not, of course, the only man of his age to
be fond of such terms, and it is doubtless true that such a
generalised ethical terminology might be more precisely intelligi-
ble in his time than in ours. But it is also true that terms like *reason*
had a multitude of meanings, that Swift knew this, and that he
nevertheless, while fully exploiting the variety in such crucial
places as the fourth book of *Gulliver*, liked at the same time
bossily to insist that only one real meaning existed, inclusive of all

virtue and sense, yet obvious and unhighfalutin. This Reason, as we have seen, is not

> a Point problematical as with us, where Men can argue with Plausibility upon both Sides of a Question; but strikes you with immediate Conviction; as it must needs do where it is not mingled, obscured, or discoloured by Passion and Interest.
>
> *(Gulliver's Travels*, 4:8)

There may be a jokey quixotism, as of the satirist satirised, in the visionary absurdity of proposing to a fallen humanity the notion that argument is improper because there is never more than one truth, or that lying is a mad perversion of speech, since the only function of speech is to communicate the truth. And there is no suggestion that because Reason's imperatives are few, luminously plain, and absolute, its paths will therefore be easy to follow, since, in a non-Houyhnhnm world, vice and folly are always tending to subvert its rule. But the insistence nevertheless is that the concept is simple and easy to grasp, and thus, though in one sense impossible to abide by, nevertheless not too far-fetched or ambitious for the moralist to proclaim. It permits Swift, in other words, to demand the absolute while sounding moderate, realistic, and low-pitched. It permits a large abstraction to remain earthbound and pragmatic, unimplicated in 'mysteries' of religion or politics, clearly separate from the obscurantism of theology and metaphsyics, from 'Ideas, Entities, Abstractions and Transcendentals' of which, to Gulliver's chagrin, the sensible and practical Brobdingnagians could not grasp 'the least Conception' *(Gulliver's Travels*, 2:7). And it is consonant with the fact that in rejecting abstractions and 'mysterious' terms, Swift is also rejecting the grandiose.

Lofty Style and Ridiculous Tragedy
For, when Swift told the young gentleman lately entered into holy orders:

> I defy the greatest Divine, to produce any Law either of God or Man, which obliges me to comprehend the Meaning of *Omniscience, Omnipresence, Ubiquity, Attribute, Beatifick Vision*, with a Thousand others so frequent in Pulpits; any more than that of *Excentrick, Idiosyncracy, Entity*, and the like
>
> *(Works*, 9:66)

he was ostensibly only recoiling from 'obscure Terms' and 'mysterious' concepts, but the terms he rejects in the first list are also, with only one exception, terms of sublime, transcendent or ecstatic import. This 'distrust of the celebrative and the sublime,' as Martin Price calls it (*To the Palace of Wisdom*, p. 196) goes also with a dislike of grandiose overstatement and of a highly emotional rhetoric. Swift told the young clergyman, approvingly, the comment of a certain 'great Person' upon a sermon he had heard by a preacher of his acquaintance:

> A Lady asked him, coming out of Church, whether it were not a very moving Discourse? *Yes*, said he, *I was extremely sorry, for the Man is my Friend.*
>
> (*Works*, 9:70)

Swift is talking specifically about sermons, and the ideal of a plain sermon style was common among Anglican clergymen from the middle of the seventeenth century, partly in reaction to a highly ornamented 'metaphysical' style, and partly in avoidance of the nonconformists' '*Fanatick* or *Enthusiastick* Strain' (*Works*, 9:68). Both in the *Letter to a Young Gentleman*, and in the sermon 'Upon sleeping in Church,' he stresses that 'plain convincing Reason' is more lastingly effective and generally more satisfactory than 'the Art of wetting the Handkerchiefs of a whole Congregation' (*Works*, 9:70, 217), part of the reason being, as we might expect, the sheer day-to-day practicality of a sermon's function: 'to tell the People what is their Duty; and then to convince them that it is so' (*Works*, 9:70). If the reference is specifically to sermons, however, the preference for practicality over high talk is central and characteristic. It extends beyond sermons, as when he refers to the eloquence of Demosthenes and Cicero, concedes that their case is different because their task was to speak in the immediacy of a political or legal situation, yet prefers Demosthenes as the less 'rhetorical' of the two, finally returning to a preference for English sermons not only because steady reminders of duty do not need rhetoric, but because phlegmatic Englishmen are unlikely to be stirred by it anyway: 'I do not see how this Talent of moving the Passions, can be of any great Use towards directing Christian Men in the Conduct of their Lives, at least in these *Northern* Climates' (*Works*, 9:69). There is something in this affectionate sarcasm not restricted to sermons as a genre, a preference for the placid English above the emotional foreigners of southern Europe (see also the backhanded

compliment to the phlegmatic English, above p. 29), an uppishness far removed in its low intensity from Swift's distaste for
'enthusiastic' dissenters, yet not, one feels, entirely unrelated.
There is, too, about all this, a familiar note of hauteur, again not
restricted to sermon styles: 'I know a Gentleman, who made it a
Rule in Reading, to skip over all Sentences where he spied a Note
of Admiration at the End' (*Works*, 9:69).

Nil admirari, then, joins not only with recent sermon-tradition,
but with Swift's temperamental predilection for the practical and
low-pitched. As further illustration of the latter, consider Gulliver's praise of the poetry of the Houyhnhnms, where the criteria
are justness, exactitude, and moral usefulness, rather than poetic
fire:

> In *Poetry* they must be allowed to excel all other Mortals;
> wherein the Justness of their Similes, and the Minuteness, as
> well as Exactness of their Descriptions, are indeed inimit-
> able. Their Verses abound very much in both of these; and
> usually contain either some exalted Notions of Friendship
> and Benevolence, or the Praises of those who were Victors in
> Races, and other bodily Exercises.
>
> (*Gulliver's Travels*, 4:9)

('exalted Notions of Friendship and Benevolence' may seem to
sort ill with an avoidance of emotional grandeur; the words,
however, imply not grandiose utterance but high moral tone).

Swift is often described, in praise and blame, as speaking in
accents of angry majesty. Yeats, in 'Blood and the Moon',
celebrates him as 'beating on his breast in Sibylline frenzy blind'
(*Collected Poems*, London, 1952, 268), while F. R. Leavis scornfully reminds us that

> *saeva indignatio* is an indulgence that solicits us all, and the use
> of literature by readers and critics for the projection of nobly
> suffering selves is familiar.
>
> (*The Common Pursuit*, p. 86)

Both seem wrong, not because Swift was not, in his way, both
passionate and self-dramatising, but because the comments are so
ill-applied to Swift's persistent refusal of the 'lofty Stile' and
'Heroick Strain' as being 'against my nat'ral Vein' (*Epistle to a
Lady*, 1733, ll. 140, 218, 135–6; *Poems* 2:634, 637). It seems almost

permissible to say (the exaggeration would be slight) that *saeva indignatio* was only openly claimed by Swift in his epitaph.

When Swift claimed that the misanthropy of *Gulliver* was not in Timon's manner, he may have been refusing a *manner* only, and not Timon-like feelings (letter to Pope, 29 September 1725, *Correspondence*, 3:103). More widely, Swift's avoidance of other grand manners hardly precluded intense or passionate feelings. The refusal of the manner is, however, very important. Swift offers some explanations, notably the commonplace that in satire raillery is more effective than railing ('Switches better guide than Cudgels'), but also the more intimate fact that in a 'lofty Stile . . . I Shou'd make a Figure scurvy' (*Epistle to a Lady*, ll. 202, 218–19). The tone is bantering, but Swift's feelings of vulnerability are seriously involved: to imputations of solemnity, of self-importance, of emotional indiscipline, and, above all, of conceding by a lofty manner that high demands have any viability in a bad world.[6] The 'high stilts' that Yeats stood on, Swift from the start rejected in all modern mechanic inventions to rise above the crowd: Dissenters' pulpit, gallows, stage-itinerant (*Tale*, sec. 1). Yeats's stilts may be a come-down from the heroic days of his great-granddad: only 'fifteen foot, no modern stalks upon higher'. But this self-undercutting gives nothing away. If Yeats seems prepared, as the price for 'High Talk', to court a certain ridicule, that is because he makes sure of the clown's closeness to sublimity:

Malachi Stilt-Jack am I, whatever I learned has run wild . . .
I, through the terrible novelty of light, stalk on, stalk on.
(*Collected Poems*, 385–86)

Swift shied from such claims. Stilt-Jack was sinking too low, and the rest talking too high: claim and counter-claim merge at that familiar point where the deepest drop and the highest flight come together, in heroic epiphany for Yeats, climax of folly for Swift.

Swift's refusal of grand manner and high talk cuts, we might say, very deep: deep enough, for example, to extend to serious mock-heroic, that province of the grandiose where other Augustan writers felt sufficiently protected by the built-in irony of the form. There is nothing, in Swift, like *The Dunciad*, nor even like *Le Lutrin*, *The Dispensary*, or *The Rape of the Lock*, but only some octosyllabic burlesques, and that prose foolery, *The Battle of the Books*, where mock-epic is desolemnified not only by the prose medium, but by an admixture of mock-journalese. It is as

61

though Swift shrank from whatever high talk survived in the parody to proclaim positives of lost or betrayed grandeur.

Swift's undercutting of grand satiric rages, postures of Juvenalian majesty, noble self-projections, is thus more radical than that of Pope, whose mock-heroic by its very nature strove, as Pound was to say, 'to maintain "the sublime"/In the old sense', and that of Yeats, who, out of clown and beggar, made the sublime new. High self-praise comes much seldomer in Swift than in the other two and takes itself less seriously. It has recently been suggested (by Barry Slepian, *Review of English Studies*, N. S. 14 (1963): esp. 254–56) that even the self-celebration towards the end of the *Verses on the Death of Dr. Swift*, in lines like

> Fair LIBERTY was all his Cry;
> For her he stood prepar'd to die,
>   (ll. 347–48)

or

> Yet, Malice never was his Aim;
> He lash'd the Vice but spar'd the Name,
>   (ll. 459–60)

is radically self-mocking and ironical. The suggestion, as Mr Slepian makes it, seems improbable, even though he is able to point out that some of the things Swift says about himself were (like the last two lines quoted) perhaps untrue. But even if we do not accept that such strong self-discounting takes place in the poem, the self-celebration is qualified both by the lightly chatty Hudibrastic metre, and by the pleasant joke of the author inventing an 'impartial' (l. 306) obituarist to say these things for himself. There is, at the very least, the friendly undercutting of a coy leg-pull, and certainly none of the glow of Pope's claim to be actuated by 'The strong Antipathy of Good to Bad', or his pride 'to see/Men not afraid of God, afraid of me' (*Epilogue to the Satires*, Dial. 2, ll. 198, 208–9).

If such grandeurs of self-praise in Swift are less than *radically* modified by irony, however, the great denunciations are almost totally removed from their own potential sublimity. When this happens, the strength of feeling is, I believe, greater, not less. The disturbing intensities increase in proportion with Swift's success in devising formulas that release him from direct commitment to a majestic role. In the *Modest Proposal*, for example, the emotional pressure is enormous, and it is reflected in the monstrousness of the fable: but its intensity proceeds largely from a cunning divorce between the monstrous fable and its formal semblance as an economic tract (flat statistical style, calm display of concern for the public good). The mad proposer of cannibal horrors had in the past, he tells us, proposed 'other Expedients', sound measures for Ireland's benefit that we recognise as those Swift himself had fought for in the 1720s, in vain. The proposer's present blandness and assurance of success derive from the fact that his new scheme is so evil that a morally mad world must accept it as good. His crazed lucidity is a Swiftian intensity posing as weary sarcasm. Swift is autobiographically implicated, and the cannibal fiction registers the violence of his protest: but the proposer's new-found worldliness frees Swift from the sentimental risks of posing as a lonely defiant protester, and rant is eschewed without loss of intensity because the violence of Swift's feelings can be melted into the proposer's calm.

Gulliver too had hoped to mend the world, and got nowhere. He, however, is allowed to rant, and Swift's commitment to Gulliver's strident denunciation of man in 4:12 is more teasingly oblique than his relationship of total ironic opposition to the speaker in the *Proposal*. Gulliver's outburst is too petulant, too fraught with a kind of wilful hysteria, for us to be able simply to identify his voice as Swift's; nor are we accustomed to accord Gulliver our whole-hearted respect. But the volume as a whole has been establishing, bleakly and massively, the grounds for an attack on man; and we as readers are left alone with Gulliver's voice at the end, for Swift has taken care to provide no competing point of view to help us towards a more comforting perspective. Swift is readily dissociated from Gulliver's rant, but hardly from the indictment it embodies. Again, there seems no loss, but rather increase of intensity, for the satirist allows us to discount nothing while remaining protected against our dismissal of the rant. Or rather, we are left uncertain how much to discount. Similar uncertainties occur even when Swift himself is talking: 'I hate and detest that animal called man', 'I would hang them if I cou'd' (to Pope, 29 September 1725, *Correspondence*, 3:103; *Epistle to a Lady*, l. 170). Flattened and made elusive by sarcastic overstatement, the denunciation becomes unanswerable by literal denial, because we do not know how to take it: instead of the clearcut remoteness of the satirist on high stilts, the uncertainty creates an uneasy intimacy, a sniping aggression on the reader at close quarters.

Swift's relations with his reader depend, then, not on lofty denunciations from above, but on the strange haughtinesses of a low-pitched intimacy. Gulliver tells the reader, 'my principal Design was to inform, and not to amuse thee' (4:12), echoing Swift's own declared aim 'to vex the world rather then divert it' (to Pope, 29 September 1725, *Correspondence*, 3:102), but using a personal and familiar *thee*, aimed directly at the reader in familiarity and contempt. Compare Pope's use of the contemptuous thee,

> Has God, thou fool! work'd solely for thy good . . . .
> Is it for thee the lark ascends and sings?
>
> > (*Essay on Man*, 3:27ff.),

which is aimed not at the reader, but at Man. Nothing illustrates more clearly the difference between the two men's satire, Pope's grandly decorous, public, and resting on a decent relationship with the reader in which intimacy is held in check by a sense of public agreement, a feeling that both are gentlemen and men of the world; Swift's satire operating at close quarters, creating a relationship with the reader that is intimate but (paradoxically) hardly friendly. A good example both of the low-pitched schoolmasterly haughtiness, and of the intimacy of comic and unpleasant involvement with his satiric victims (and, by the extension that is always felt in Swift, with his readers), are these lines from the *Epistle to a Lady*:

> Let me, tho' the Smell be Noisom,
> Strip their Bums; let CALEB hoyse 'em;
> Then, apply ALECTO's Whip,
> Till they wriggle, howl, and skip.
>
> > (ll. 177–80)

Pope spoke of Swift as 'an Avenging Angel of wrath' (letter to Swift, 15 October 1725), and the words are tempting to critics too literally stirred by notions of *saeva indignatio* and Sibylline frenzy blind. But Pope's reference was playful also, and included an image of farce:

> . . . I find you would rather be employ'd as an Avenging Angel of wrath, to break your Vial of Indignation over the heads of the wretched pityful creatures of this World; nay would make them *Eat your Book*, which you have made as bitter a pill for them as possible.
>
> > (*Correspondence*, 3:108)

The spirit of this remark, in which noble angers are made to turn
into a farcical spectacle of vials broken on heads, captures well
Swift's refusal of a thoroughgoing tragic role. It is true that Swift
once wrote in a letter that 'Life is a Tragedy, wherein we sit as
Spectators awhile, and then act our own Part in it' (to Mrs Moore,
7 December 1727, *Correspondence*, 3:254). He was consoling a
mother on the death of her child, and the occasion dictated a
special solemnity. His more characteristic and more famous
remark to Pope, that

> The common saying of life being a Farce is true in every sense
> but the most important one, for it is a ridiculous tragedy,
> which is the worst kind of composition
> (20 April 1731, *Correspondence*, 3:456)

suggests all the tart pessimism, but plays down the majesty. It is
an important remark, synthesising that desperate gaiety (*vive la
bagatelle*) so vivid in Swift's feats of anarchic mimicry (in the *Tale*
and in some horrible exuberances in *Gulliver's Travels*), with a
tight-lipped severity over the offended decorum. If the remark
looks back to an old tradition of Democritean laughter,

> Like the ever-laughing Sage,
> In a Jest I spend my Rage,
> (*Epistle to a Lady*, ll. 167–68)

it also looks forward to an absurdism which says, with Ionesco,
that 'the comic . . . is another aspect of the tragic' (*Notes and
Counter-Notes*, London: 1964, 123). To Ionesco, this complete
interpenetration is a fact of the human condition, its old faiths
lost, and with them the viability of fixed categories, of decorums
of feeling or style. Ionesco describes his experience of certain
moments of alienation:

> Then the universe seems to me infinitely strange and foreign.
> At such a moment I gaze upon it with a mixture of anguish
> and euphoria; separate from the universe, as though placed at
> a certain distance outside it; I look and I see pictures,
> creatures that move in a kind of timeless time and spaceless
> space, emitting sounds that are a kind of language I no longer
> understand or ever register. "What is all this?" I wonder,
> "what does it all mean?," and out of this state of mind, which
> seems to spring from the most fundamental part of my

65

nature, is strangely born at times a feeling that everything is comic and derisory, at others a feeling of despair that the world should be so utterly ephemeral and precarious, as if it all existed and did not exist at one and the same time, as if it lay somewhere between being and not being: and that is the origin of my tragic farces, *Les Chaises*, for example.

(Notes and Counter-Notes, p. 141)

Swift recognised the condition, and refused it. Life is a 'ridiculous tragedy', but that 'worst kind of composition' is forbidden by the dramatic canons of his day. Swift's response to the absurd is to hang on to the rules. And although he would have understood modern conceptions of the absurd as a gap between aspiration and bodily fact, between what is and what ought to be, between man's desires and a world that disappoints, he would have concealed, suppressed, disciplined, but not accepted or yielded to, the 'doubts' of God and order that these disconnections aroused. For a philosopher of the absurd, like the Camus of the *Myth of Sisyphus*, the absurd is sin without God. For Swift, it resides in man's nature, fallen through disobedience to God. The myths of Sisyphus and of Tantalus, condemned to eternally-repeated torments of effort and desire, are for Camus emblems of an inexplicable universe. For Swift, the restlessness of ever-renewed needs is the price for original sin. Free-thinking, in this light, is punningly but aptly seen as part universal madness, part wilful vice. And this attribution of sin, while in one sense it settles nothing and can seldom calm the restless struggle, yet remains fixed in an overriding faith and an uncompromising morality, asserting obligations not of the individual conscience, but of tradition and rule.

1971–1983

Notes

1 For amplification of these comments on *Gulliver* and on the *Tale*'s Digression, see my *Gulliver and the Gentle Reader*, especially pp. 18ff., 33ff.

2 See the account of 'Swift's Philanthropy' by J. N. P. Moore, the director of the hospital Swift founded, in Roger McHugh and Philip Edwards (eds.), *Jonathan Swift 1667–1967. A Dublin Tercentenary Tribute* (Dublin, 1967), esp. pp. 140 ff.

3 Calvin remarked that if all the claimed fragments of the true cross were put together, they would fill a large ship (see *Traité des Reliques* (1543), in Jean Calvin, *Three French Treatises*, Francis M. Higman (ed.), London, 1970, p. 61). This seems to be a specific part of the background to Swift's joke.

4 The real Anthony Collins, in the *Discourse of Free-Thinking* (1713) which is the object of Swift's parody, had strongly resisted the notion '*That certain Speculations (tho false) are necessary to be impos'd on Men, in order to assist the Magistrate in*

preserving the Peace of Society: And *that it is therefore as reasonable to deceive Men into Opinions for their own Good, as it is in certain cases to deceive Children*' (pp. 111 ff.).

5   The real Collins had said:

'It is objected, *That to allow and encourage Men to think freely, will produce endless Divisions in Opinion, and by consequence Disorder in Society*. To which I answer,

1 Let any Man lay down a Rule to prevent Diversity of Opinions, which will not be as fertile of Diversity of Opinions as *Free-Thinking*; or if it prevents Diversity of Opinions, will not be a Remedy worse than the Disease; and I will yield up the Question.

2 Mere Diversity of Opinions has no tendency in nature to Confusion in Society' (p. 101).

He also said: '... it is evident Matter of Fact, that a *Restraint upon Thinking* is the cause of all the Confusion which is pretended to arise from Diversity of Opinions, and that *Liberty of Thinking* is the Remedy for all the Disorders which are pretended to arise from Diversity of Opinions' (p. 103).

On pp. 123ff. Collins had spoken of the folly of a slavish adherence to state religions.

6 For fuller discussion of these lines from the *Epistle to a Lady*, and their importance to an understanding of Swift's poetic manner, see below chapter 4 (ii), pp. 175ff.

2

Gulliver's Travels *and Some Modern Fictions*

*(i) Gulliver, Marlow and the Flat-Nosed People:
Colonial Oppression and Race in Satire and Fiction*

Gulliver described the Yahoos as having 'the Face ... flat and broad, the Nose depressed, the Lips large, and the Mouth wide', an amalgam of features 'common to all savage Nations' (IV.ii; 230).[1] The stereotype comes from books of travel and exploration and colonial conquest, and includes a customary suggestion of animal (especially simian) features. Flat noses appear in descriptions of Amerindians, Africans and other remote peoples, in Léry, in Hakluyt's travellers, in Sir Thomas Herbert and Dampier and other writers, including many whose books were well-known to Swift.[2]

Flat noses are evidently used as a criterion of racial identity in South Africa at the present time: a woman with 'pale skin, blue eyes and blonde hair' was recently forbidden, because of her flat nose, high cheekbones and mode of speech, to live in a white area. She claimed 'that her flat nose was caused by a car accident' and two Supreme Court judges subsequently reversed the Johannesburg magistrate's ruling and awarded white status to the aggrieved lady.[3] The flat nose is a standard image throughout the history of racial oppression. In his celebrated essay, 'Niggers', R. B. Cunninghame Graham spoke sarcastically of the flat-nosed peoples of 'Africa, Australia, ... America', and 'all the myriad islands of the southern seas' as having been made by God to serve Englishmen.[4]

In 1899, the year when 'Niggers' (originally 'Bloody Niggers') was published in book form in *The Ipané*, Graham's friend Joseph Conrad was serialising *Heart of Darkness* in *Blackwood's Magazine*. His narrator Marlow expressed an introspective disquiet whose basis goes back at least as far as that sixteenth-century

68

questioning of Amerindian conquest to which Montaigne gave classic expression and which runs through the liberal conscience of Europe in ensuing centuries: a disquiet at oppressions carried out in the name of Christianity and at the thought that the bringers of civilisation may be as savage as the savage, or more. Marlow probes further:

> The conquest of the earth, which mostly means the taking it away from those who have a different complexion or slightly flatter noses than ourselves, is not a pretty thing when you look into it too much. What redeems it is the idea only. An idea at the back of it; not a sentimental pretence but an idea; and an unselfish belief in the idea – something you can set up, and bow down before, and offer a sacrifice to.
>
> (50–51)

It is a passage which is of a piece with Marlow's (and Conrad's) celebrations of 'efficiency' and of that discipline of work which is not only a conquest but also an evasion of the savagery in ourselves as well as in savages, leaving no time 'to peer into our creepy thoughts' (98.) Likewise the brutalism ('not a pretty thing when you look into it too much') involved in the white man's enterprises of colonial conquest has to be controlled, that is to say partially restrained, and partially overlooked, by a curious combination of 'efficiency' and of a form of disciplined self-deception: not a 'sentimental pretence' (for that deceives only others) but an 'idea' and positive *belief* in that idea, analogous to a religious faith. It is a matter of silencing both one's inner savage pressures and one's civilised doubts and is common among unillusioned conservative thinkers of a certain kind. It is for example similar to that emphasis on the no-nonsense discharge of practical duty, combined with a rigorous self-suppression both of disruptive instinctual impulses and of 'rational' doubts, which (as I argued in chapter 1) is found in Swift's personal introspections and in his more public religious and political thought:

> The want of belief is a defect that ought to be concealed when it cannot be overcome.

> I am not answerable to God for the doubts that arise in my own breast, since they are the consequence of that reason which he hath planted in me, if I take care to conceal those doubts from others, if I use my best endeavours to subdue

them, and if they have no influence on the conduct of my life.

(*Works*, IX: 261, 262)

Such reflections come naturally to thinkers who believe that the human mind in its unregulated state is a dangerous and self-destructive force. Samuel Johnson, though no admirer of Swift, wrote in a very similar way about the need to silence or allay subversive instincts by resolute acts of faith and by practical activity. (By definition, no question arises of eliminating these instincts, as distinct from silencing or allaying them: they are part of our radical nature, and indeed are what made such insistence on practical disciplines seem necessary in the first place.) Conrad would have understood the peculiar practicality with which Swift asserted the need for his 'belief' even when a total inner conviction was impossible to him. It was for Swift, almost independently of specific doctrinal content or theological nicety, a foundation for the conduct of life, helping to regulate behaviour and to give stability to restless minds.

In that sense a degree of practical self-deception was involved, in the interests of virtue, sanity and order. The 'belief' is both a lid and a covering, which not only conceals the unruliness within but also prevents its eruption. This unillusioned acceptance of the need for a protective mask is accompanied by a stark and opposite distaste for the deception: the moralist who knows the need for a mask is also the satirist who advocates unmasking, an uncompromising recognition of the horror within, exposure of the disturbing reality of flayed woman or gutted beau. The fool who dislikes looking 'into the Depth of Things' is precisely the same as the one who ordered the gutting of the beau, and who had earlier 'dissected the Carcass of *Humane Nature* . . . till at last it *smelt* so strong, I could preserve it no longer' (*Tale of a Tub*, secs. IX and V; *Works*, I: 109–10, 77). He is in one sense, therefore, his own lunatic opposite, equally committed to remaining complacently on the surface and to probing restlessly into the ugliness beneath. He is also the mirror-opposite of Swift himself, who looks starkly 'into the Depth', enjoining us to contemplate the horror, and at the same time insists that the lid must be kept on, preferring at times even hypocrisy to open vice or infidelity.

Conrad explores the same opposites. The Marlow of *Heart of Darkness*, as Eloise Knapp Hay points out, 'believes . . . that dangerous knowledge must be suppressed'. In some ways, as she says, this Marlow differs from the Marlow of *Lord Jim*, who believes 'that even dangerous knowledge' should be examined.[5]

But the Marlow of *Heart of Darkness* also responds with a kind of admiration to Kurtz's 'victory' in seeing the horror within, and (before that 'final burst of sincerity') even to his delirious injunction to 'Exterminate all the brutes' (151, 145, 118). Conrad himself could respect the naked truth of such an outburst,[6] and it seems certain that he upholds Marlow's speculation that 'perhaps all the wisdom, and all truth, and all sincerity, are just compressed into that inappreciable moment of time in which we step over the threshold of the invisible'(151). But this is what Kurtz did, while Marlow was 'permitted to draw back my hesitating foot', and Conrad's sympathy with Marlow is clearly greater than the real respect which both of them express for Kurtz.

Swift, as we shall see, could both entertain and suppress glimpses of 'the horror' and impulses to 'exterminate'; but we never see Swift drawing back a hesitating foot. His opposites interact in their total state, where Conrad's merge into one another in tentative and continuously shifting relations. The Swift who insists on frank unmasking of the horror, or on the disciplines of self-suppression, or who expresses an exasperated wish to exterminate the foolish or the vicious, does so totally and absolutely; the Swiftian fools or villains who poke 'into the Depth', or recognise that 'the Surface' is preferable, or advocate extermination and mass-cannibalism, are totally and absolutely repudiated as fools or villains. Conrad and Marlow experience the same opposites but also the entire spectrum of intermediate states, and neither, at any stage, thinks of himself or is thought of by the reader as a fool or villain, any more than he is thought of as unquestioningly or unquestionably right.

This distinction applies particularly strongly to the question of 'belief'. The 'belief' in Swift's case was a religious faith, and in Conrad's merely analogous to religion: 'an unselfish belief in the idea – something you can set up, and bow down before, and offer a sacrifice to'. Swift sought to sustain his 'belief' at a level of total unquestioning conviction, and doubtless succeeded more often than not, despite those underminings from within which he recognised as radical to man, and which in his view threatened chaos if not resolutely suppressed. Conrad, for reasons which he considered personal to his temperament and circumstances, found such unquestioning conviction much more difficult to achieve. But he admired those who did, whether they were anti-colonial activists like R. B. Cunninghame Graham, or the practical colonial administrators who did an honest job of improving the conquered territories, those whom Marlow praises for their 'unselfish belief in the idea' and whom Conrad meant when he expressed respect for some colonial activities, especially those of the British.

The 'belief' or 'idea' is for Conrad as for Swift something simpler and more reductive. Its power to allay the 'gnawing' doubt though not to resolve it, and to prevent the destructive release of 'the inner truth' but not to eliminate this truth ('the inner truth is hidden – luckily, luckily. But I felt it all the same'), has a great deal to do with the simplifying injunctions of unhighfalutin duty and the power of practical work (93). More specifically, in Conrad's case, it is the kind of discipline of the mind which sees through the common cant about bringing light to dark places, and yet knows in a no-nonsense way that 'light', and even (in a characteristic phrase, from *Lord Jim*) 'electric light', need bringing.[7] The words are full of irony, but they have at bottom a good deal of the spirit of the King of Brobdingnag's comment (which is not specifically concerned with colonial improvements) 'that whoever could make two Ears of Corn, or two Blades of Grass to grow . . . where only one grew before' was preferable to all purveyors of political systems, mysteries and refinements, and indeed to 'the whole Race of Politicians put together' (II. vii; 135–36).

The 'belief', for both Conrad and Swift, is thus distinguished from abstract systems, theological or political, whether of the left or of the right. Swift argued that no single system of government was intrinsically better or worse than another, as long as a necessary balance existed in practice between the One, the Few, and the Many. His Platonic insistence on the obligation to observe the religion of the state, whatever its doctrinal colouring, requires a 'belief' and loyalty which are 'total' in practical effect rather than in spiritual or ideological completeness or in systematic metaphysical coherence. He advised the young clergyman that his duty was not to explain 'the Mysteries of the Christian Religion' but 'upon solemn Days to deliver the Doctrine as the Church holds it, and confirm it by Scripture' (*Works*, IX: 77). The insistence is on practical instruction, supported by 'authority', and undisturbed by the kind of abstract intellection which impairs the practical understanding and performance of duty by encouraging speculative self-indulgence, divisive or enervating doubts and introspective indiscipline.

Conrad allowed himself the freedom to doubt on every front, while Swift required of himself as well as of others certain kinds of simplifying allegiance. That is an important difference between them. It is a difference of moral style in the deepest sense, and emerges in radical differences of literary manner. But it springs in both men from the same deep scepticism of abstract ideologies as such, notably in the political domain. Thus Conrad, even in his expressions of sympathy with liberal or radical causes, had no truck with revolutionary doctrines of liberty or fraternity, any more than Swift had with such versions of these doctrines as existed in his day (Swift would surely have agreed with Conrad's remark to R. B. Cunninghame Graham that 'Fraternity means nothing unless the Cain-Abel business').[8] By the same token both men despised the sanctimonious ideological pretensions with which oppressors justified their exploitation of others. Just as Conrad was sickened by the show of lofty ideals and the self-proclaimed sense of Christian mission with which colonial powers sought to justify their murderous profiteering enterprises, so Swift makes Gulliver give this sketch of how 'a new Dominion' is 'acquired with a Title by *Divine Right*':

> Ships are sent with the first Opportunity; the Natives driven out or destroyed, their Princes tortured to discover their Gold; a free Licence given to all Acts of Inhumanity and Lust; the Earth reeking with the Blood of its Inhabitants; And this execrable Crew of Butchers employed in so pious an Expedition, is a *modern Colony* sent to convert and civilize an idolatrous and barbarous People.
>
> (IV. xii; 294)

Gulliver's sarcasm expresses the paradox made familiar by Montaigne (though not invented by him), that savages and even cannibals are less savage than their conquerors, a paradox also eloquently invoked by those liberal churchmen who in the sixteenth and seventeenth centuries challenged the self-justifying arguments of the conquerors of America. It is an apt and eloquent coincidence that Conrad's friend Cunninghame Graham, who shared Conrad's loathing of the Congo affair and corresponded with him about *Heart of Darkness*, should have extolled the work of these liberal missionaries, and indeed of the more humane conquistadors in general, contrasting them with the present-day excesses of British imperialism, and that Conrad read and praised his writings on the subject.[9] Ironically, Gulliver's words precede a famous paragraph in which Gulliver excepts the British from his sweeping condemnation of colonial activity:

But this Description, I confess, doth by no means affect the *British* Nation, who may be an Example to the whole World for their Wisdom, Care, and Justice in planting Colonies; their liberal Endowments for the Advancement of Religion and Learning; their Choice of devout and able Pastors to propagate *Christianity*; their Caution in stocking their Provinces with People of sober Lives and Conversations from this the Mother Kingdom . . .[10]

This redirection of Swift's irony is very characteristic. Gulliver's immediately preceding attack on colonial exploitation was directly and totally Swift's. Gulliver's praise of British colonists is a sudden and complete reversal of his previous cynical disillusion, and expresses the total opposite of Swift's own view. Unless we regard Gulliver himself as an ironist, his view lurches from utter recognition of 'the horror' to an equally complete acceptance of the sanctimonious pretensions commonly invoked to disguise it. Intelligent readers do not talk about this as an inconsistency of character, because they do not regard Gulliver as a 'character' or *Gulliver's Travels* as a novel. What they witness is a tactical shift in the manner of Swift's irony, while the *matter* remains constant: in both paragraphs, Swift's condemnation of colonial oppressors, British and other, is absolute.

Gulliver's transition is of particular interest here, because both Conrad and Marlow are also on record in praise of British colonial administrations whilst disliking those of other European powers.[11] But whereas Gulliver's praise has to be translated into a sarcasm of absolute repudiation on Swift's part, Marlow's comparison with the Roman colonists and others reflects a view which Conrad often expressed in his own name, and which shows (both in Marlow, and in Conrad's own non-fictional statements) a free and open play of mixed feelings, of ambiguous and sceptical reservations mingled with a pragmatic respect. Lionel Trilling has noted that Conrad's preference of English imperialism will seem difficult to read 'without irony' today: 'The present state of opinion does not countenance the making of discriminations among imperialisms, . . . and the idea that more virtue might be claimed for one nation than another is given scant credence'.[12]

Swift, for different reasons, would have been out of sympathy with any such relativism, or at least with the sceptical openness with which it is ready to concede certain virtues, in certain cases, to the despoiling of 'those who have a different complexion or slightly flatter noses'. Gulliver's singling out of the British above others is Swift's way of saying that the British are as bad, if not worse, than the others. The nearest Swift comes to what Trilling calls 'the idea that more virtue might be claimed for one nation than another' is that some have *less* virtue than others. Conrad and some of his contemporaries sometimes singled out the Dutch as worse colonisers than others, and Swift's detestation of the Dutch would make him a ready recruit to such a view.[13] But Swift would not allow the comparison to become a matter of fine distinctions. Dutch iniquities (the venality, cruelty and impiety noted in *Gulliver's Travels*, for example) may call for a greater intensity of loathing because they happen to be Dutch (III.i, xi; 154–55, 216–17). But the denunciation of their venality, cruelty and impiety is no more and no less absolute than that of the same iniquities as found elsewhere.

Conrad's respect for certain kinds of colonial activity, his reservations in denouncing what he admits to be 'not a pretty thing when you look into it too much', are the direct counterpart to his and Marlow's mixed feelings about the 'savagery' of savages, a matter on which Swift's feelings are opposite and unmixed. In *Heart of Darkness* and elsewhere in Conrad, there is a sense that 'savagery' is no more absolute than 'civilisation', that it differs from individual to individual and depends on circumstance, that it is capable of being corrupted as well as improved by 'civilised' intervention, and that it may have virtues lacking in the civilised even as its barbaric brutalities are being literal-mindedly conceded. When Swift portrays 'savages', in the shape of Yahoos, his repudiating portrayal is as absolute and uncompromising as that of the so-called civilised colonialists of Europe. There are no Yahoos like Marlow's skilled fireman, no Yahoo fine fellows, and no sign of the decency or restraint Marlow notices in the cannibal crew. Even when he plays with the primitivist idea that the Yahoos, in their state of nature, lack some of the refinements of evil which their European counterparts have acquired through civilisation, Swift's point is not so much to palliate his portrait of the Yahoos as to cast additional discredit on Englishmen or Europeans. Swift's notion of the right way to treat the Yahoos is by absolute subjection, although he also denounced colonial subjection, as well as domestic tyranny, totally.

It is the Yahoos who, in Conrad's compassionate yet patronising phrase about subject races, have 'flatter noses than ourselves', as we have seen. Yet when Swift is denouncing colonial conquest no reference to flat noses, large lips or likeness to monkeys is allowed to enter into the mention of subject races. Description remains unspecific, neutralising all opportunities for distaste or scorn, and allowing only such information as will arouse compassion for the victims and, even more important, anger against the oppressor. Instead of the fully depicted Yahoos, we read of a generalised 'harmless People', who treat their invaders 'with Kindness' and are murdered and despoiled in return. Conrad's blend of deep compassion and mildly contemptuous patronage exists in Swift in an unmingled form, radically separated into distinct components. The contempt, intensified to stark detestation, is applied to the Yahoos, and the compassion, equally starkly, to some generalised or typical category of oppressed 'harmless People'.

This radical separation, in another sense, is only apparent, a satirical convenience which may also have had a certain emotional usefulness for Swift. It is partly, but only partly, a difference between the stark rhetoric of satire, and that modulated idiom, open to shadings and discriminations, which we associate with the novel-form as it was practised by Conrad or James. The oppositions are also temperamental, in Swift. In his normal political thinking, a stark co-existence of opposite feelings is often evident, notably in his attitude to the 'savage' Irish natives, whom he despised as a species of sub-human animal and for whom he nevertheless felt a kind of fierce compassion. Indeed, it has more than once been observed that the Yahoos, a literary product of the years when Swift was most actively and passionately involved in Irish affairs, have many of the features which Swift ascribed to the Irish poor.[14] Swift's contempt for the latter, as expressed in the *Modest Proposal* and elsewhere, is as absolute as, and simultaneous with, his pity, and coexists with it in no finely blended Conradian interplay, but an uncompromising and explosive collocation. The culpability of the oppressed Irish, rich or poor, is very explicit.[15] In the *Modest Proposal*, indeed, they are shown ready to eat one another. A justified anger against them needed to be protected from an equally justified pity, and vice-versa. Both feelings needed equally to be expressed, but the pity for the oppressed was also in some measure required in order to give voice to Swift's other justified anger, against the external (i.e. English) oppressor. In that sense the preservation of strong feelings, contending yet distinct, was both emotionally necessary to Swift, with his highly ambiguous attitude to Ireland and indeed his mixed feelings about 'liberty', and tactically necessary for the full release of his satire, at maximum intensity, on all its fronts.

In *Gulliver's Travels* these matters are, in some ways, even more firmly partitioned. The Yahoos are formally distinct from the 'harmless People', and this enables the contempt and the compassion to emerge with an even greater sense of separate intensity than in the Irish writings, where they are simultaneously directed at the same whole Irish people. It is moreover possible to feel that part of the compassion for the 'harmless People', like the pity for the Irish, exists in order to highlight Swift's loathing for the oppressor rather than as a sign of tenderness for the oppressed, and that this emphasis is experienced even more clearly in the passage from the last chapter of *Gulliver's Travels* than in the Irish tracts.

The 'harmless People' are not only referred to in non-specific and indeed non-descriptive terms, and quite briefly, but they are shown mainly in an abstract role of passive victim. They show nothing of the proud ferocious courage of Montaigne's Amerindians, who are undoubtedly present in the background to this passage.[16] The stress is almost entirely on what is done to them by their conquerors rather than on their own actions or even on their own sufferings. The whole focus of the narrative, indeed of the syntax itself, is on the nature and deeds of the invaders, and we experience a much more forceful sense of them than of their victims despite the fact that Gulliver's account of both together is a generalised and contemptuously summarising one, as though concerned with wearisomely 'typical' rather than specific situations:

> For Instance, A Crew of Pyrates are driven by a Storm they know not whither; at length a Boy discovers Land from the Top-mast; they go on Shore to rob and plunder; they see an harmless People, are entertained with Kindness, they give the Country a new Name, they take formal Possession of it for the King, they set up a rotten Plank or a Stone for a Memorial, they murder two or three Dozen of the Natives...
>
> (IV. xii; 294)

Even when the 'harmless People' actually are referred to as performing actions instead of being acted upon, as when they entertain the invaders 'with Kindness', the syntax diverts attention from them to those who 'are entertained'. The savage Yahoos, by contrast, are not only more graphically described as well as more important and more elaborately dwelt on throughout the work, but display more active energies: we constantly see them in the performance of their dirty or evil actions, and relatively seldom as the recipients of actions committed upon or against them.

The 'oppressors' of the Yahoos are Houyhnhnms, and from time to time the Houyhnhnms debate the question of doing to the Yahoos what Conrad's Kurtz in his delirious postscript wanted to do to his 'natives': 'Exterminate all the brutes' (118).[17] The Houyhnhnms use similar language: 'The Question to be debated was, Whether the *Yahoos* should be exterminated from the Face of the Earth', and even the word 'Brutes' is used of the Yahoos in the debate, and elsewhere in Book IV (IV. ix, x; 271 ff., 279; also 'Letter to Sympson', 8). Those who question Swift's endorsement of such sentiments as inconsistent with his Christianity might ponder the fact that the Houyhnhnms are contemplating no more than the fate which God proposed for mankind in *Genesis*, 6, 7: 'I will destroy man whom I have created from the face of the earth'.[18] The idea that Swift is putting such thoughts into the mouths of the Houyhnhnms in order to discredit them, or that Swift himself would never speak thus in his own name, is further contradicted by occasional statements like the one from *A Proposal for Giving Badges to the Beggars* (1737) that strolling beggars (in this case) are 'fitter to be rooted out off the Face of the Earth, than suffered to levy a vast annual Tax upon the City' (*Works*, XIII: 139). The point in such cases is not that God, or the Houyhnhnms, or Swift are murderous psychopaths, but that their intended victims deserve to be punished. The extermination project, or velleity, is meant to throw light not on the exterminator but on the exterminee. And accordingly, as Gulliver summarises the argument in favour of extermination, the focus naturally shifts to the character and actions of the Yahoos, not that of their rulers, the exact reverse of what happens in the case of the harmless natives of Gulliver's account of colonial conquest. A partisan of extermination argues

That, as the *Yahoos* were the most filthy, noisome, and deformed Animal which Nature ever produced, so they were the most restive and indocible, mischievous and malicious: They would privately suck the Teats of the *Houyhnhnms* Cows; kill and devour their Cats, trample down their Oats and Grass . . .

(IV. ix; 271)

The passage is not without comedy, and it may help to disarm in laughter whatever sense of shock or embarrassment we may feel at the idea of the Houyhnhnms as potential exterminators. At this moment, for a strategic instant, the Yahoos, sucking the teats of cows and eating cats, appear more as a species of comically obscene beast than as the fundamentally human creatures they are normally presented as being. Far from showing, as is sometimes suggested, that Swift is disowning the Houyhnhnms for proposing mass-murder, this passage shows an effort to prevent or reduce any shocked repudiation of the Houyhnhnms on the reader's part. The procedure enables Swift to indulge an extermination-fantasy against mankind without arousing such a revulsion against the proposers as would diminish the unsettling force of the fantasy itself. We note too that, probably for the same reasons, the Houyhnhnms are not shown implementing the proposal, but only debating it. It is a characteristic example of having it both ways. The proposal is not rejected, and we assume that it might some day be activated. Meanwhile, an alternative solution, castration, also enters into the debate. Swift has some fun with this too. It will, as he points out, have the same result in a generation.[19] It is a joking reversal of what men do to horses, and carries a frisson of black humour. That it is also what, in 1719, the Irish Privy Council suggested doing to unregistered Catholic priests (the English Privy Council restrained them in this case, preferring an alternative suggestion of branding on the cheek 'with a large P') is probably no more than a grim coincidence.[20] Swift had no great liking for Catholic priests, though he might have found this treatment for them inappropriate, as mass-extermination is inappropriate, in real life.

As we have seen, the Houyhnhnms' impulse to perform one or other of these 'final solutions' on the fictional Yahoos means less that Swift is disowning the Houyhnhnms, than that anger on this scale against the Yahoos is fully deserved. They are the fictional counterpart, or the allegorical crystallisation, of Swift's own outbursts of murderous exasperation against the human race or whole sections of it in other works or in his correspondence. The rhetoric which expresses such anger, whether in exclamatory hyperbole or in more extended fictional parables of extermination, obviously amounts to something less than a firm practical proposal on Swift's part. But it certainly does not imply that such extreme anger is not called for. Even the *Modest Proposal*, whose formula appears to come closest to a simple irony of reversal, has been shown to carry a considerable animus against the very people in whose defence it was written; and as I argue in chapter 3, the irony of reversal is itself at times reversed, as when it is said of the plump Irish girls whose expensive habits are ruining Ireland that 'the Kingdom would not be the worse' if they really were eaten up (*Works*, XII: 114).

The Houyhnhnms who favoured extermination argued that the Yahoos were less acceptable as beasts of burden than asses were. This possibly contains an allusion to the recent introduction of asses into Ireland,[21] and may tell us something about the teasing connection between the Yahoos and Ireland. But ultimately the difference between fiction and life is decisive. What is good for the Yahoos must not *actually* be done to the Irish or to other real people. But what the Houyhnhnms propose to do with the Yahoos is presented as a measure of Yahoo depravity rather than as an example of Houyhnhnm cruelty. In real life, the reverse would be true, and Swift knows it. In this case, *Gulliver's Travels* makes a concession to real life, in that neither the extermination nor the castration is actually shown to take place. Swift is thus able to make his point that the Yahoos are fit for extermination or castration without, as I have suggested, risking that alienated recoil from the Houyhnhnms which the reader might feel if they were shown implementing either scheme. Swift, as so often, extracts the maximum rhetorical effect on every front, exploiting the difference between fiction and life, and (within the fiction itself) between the rightness of monstrous proposals and the possible discredit of their implementation.

In any event, Gulliver does not complain of the projects as unjust. He does complain of lesser horrors performed by Europeans on their colonial subjects, and Swift, broadly, agrees with Gulliver on both questions. Whatever the comedy and whatever the horrific frissons, the Houyhnhnm account of Yahoo noisomeness is accurate, and neither Gulliver nor Swift suggests that the Houyhnhnms deserve any blame for this or any other act of 'oppression' on the Yahoos. Nor, until modern times, have any readers supposed that they did.[22] This is another example of that greater partitioning of things in *Gulliver's Travels* to which I have referred. The oppressors of the 'harmless People', unlike the Houyhnhnms, are evil men, whose greedy and aggressive behaviour shows how much they partake of the savage degeneracy of Yahoos. Leavis's saying that 'the Houyhnhnms . . . may have all the reason, but the Yahoos have all the life'[23] is applicable in small, and in reverse, to the pattern which exists between the 'harmless People' and their rulers. It is the latter, at all events, who have 'all the life', like the Yahoos, although their political role in relation to the savage 'Natives' is more like that of the Houyhnhnms.

Within the fiction, the 'harmless People' of conquered colonies share with the Irish of the political pamphlets the fact that, unlike the Yahoos, they belong to the 'real' world, rather than to a fantastic allegory. Their idealised presentation was, as we have seen, a device to highlight the wickedness of their oppressors, not to demonstrate the virtues of any unspoilt 'noble savagery'. When such a purpose is absent, 'Savages' or 'Natives' have their full share of Yahoo viciousness. There is as it happens another passage about 'real' savages, 'stark naked ... round a Fire', whom Gulliver comes upon soon after leaving Houyhnhnmland, who attack him with their possibly poisoned arrows and wound him in the knee.[24] No idealisation of them is offered, although, at the prospect of rescue by a European ship, Gulliver chooses, after 'some Doubt ... rather to trust my self among these *Barbarians*, than live with *European Yahoos*' (IX. xi; 284–85). That these particular European Yahoos turn out to be the crew of the good Portuguese captain does not alter the savagery of the 'Savages', any more than it contradicts the savagery of those other civilised Europeans who conquer 'harmless People'. It merely shows Swift separating his allegorical types according to the demands of satiric expediency, showing 'harmless' savages when European Yahoos need to be denounced, and bad ones when, within a page of Gulliver's leaving Houyhnhnmland, he wants to show primitive humanity to be little better than Yahoos. Both belong to the 'real' world, as distinct from the Houyhnhnm utopia, within the fiction. In that other 'real' world, outside the fiction, the Irish are shown in both guises, as 'harmless' victims and also as noxious and contemptible pests.

These rhetorical separations are, in the total effect of the work, more apparent than real. Both types of savage, the passive victims of Gulliver's onslaught on colonial conquest and the actively murderous ones who shoot Gulliver with their arrows, are equally Yahoo, as are the European conquerors and even the good Don Pedro. In his introductory letter to his cousin Sympson, Gulliver sets the tone by insisting, as Marlow so much more tentatively insisted, on the kinship between the savage Yahoo and the European city-dweller: 'there are so many Thousands in this City, who only differ from their Brother Brutes in *Houyhnhnmland*, because they use a Sort of *Jabber*, and do not go naked' (8). What for Marlow is matter for a tentative and humble apprehension is for Gulliver a harsh, clear, uncompromising truth.

In so far as the Yahoos are an allegory of man, notable for their humiliating resemblance to European mankind as Gulliver knows it, they carry not only the degrading ape-like animalism of 'all savage Nations' but the vicious greed and cruelty of the conquerors of 'harmless Peoples', as well as the 'harmless People' themselves in their capacity as humans. The fact that Gulliver and Swift are not the same person does not permit us to discount this fact. The fundamental likeness between men and their apelike Yahoo prototypes is supported by 'objective' evidence which Swift has deliberately planted at various points in the work. It is not without significance that, before we ever meet the Yahoos, Gulliver should have been mistaken by a Brodingnagian monkey for 'a young one of his own Species' (II. v; 122). This cannot be taken as a simple reflection of Gulliver's distorted vision. It is an actual incident in the narrative, a 'fact' consciously introduced by Swift, and paralleled later by that other objective 'fact' of the female Yahoo who demonstrates kinship in the most spontaneous and practical way, by being 'inflamed by Desire' for Gulliver (IV. viii; 266–67).

These identifications are in their way absolute. But opportunistic separations exist, for purposes of satirical strategy, between various categories of human creature: 'real' persons and allegorical Yahoos, 'harmless' savages and noxious ones, vile Europeans whose vileness is set off by instances of innocent persecuted 'Natives', good Europeans like the Portuguese Captain setting off in their turn the nastiness of a murderous tribe of 'Natives', as well as demonstrating (by their smell, for example) that even good Yahoos are Yahoos.[25] The separations tend towards a certain kind of tense totality, enabling Swift to establish the natural depravity of the human animal in its pre-civilised state, as well as to show the 'civilised' encroachments on the savage as a manifestation of the same depravity.

This totality is of the kind we observe in a narrower compass in the Irish writings, where total distaste for conqueror and conquered alike is so often given its head. Just as *Gulliver's Travels* alludes to many of the particular themes of the Irish tracts, and is in its way one of them, so the Irish tracts are partly, like *Gulliver's Travels*, a wider-reaching anatomy of human perversity or satire on man. The mad and suffering condition of Ireland is a specific and specialised instance of that human predicament of which Swift gave a more generalised account in *Gulliver's Travels*. It is a condition self-inflicted and deserved yet full of cruelty and injustice, the product of wicked exploitation from without and also of a mad self-destructiveness from within, each aspect totally vivid and totally active, each sometimes concealing the other for satirical emphasis.

To put it differently, the satire of *Gulliver's Travels* includes Ireland, but extends away from specific examples of human turpitude or folly to the radical nature of 'that animal called man', including such deviant particular cases as the Portuguese captain or those individual types of the logic textbooks, 'John, Peter, Thomas' (*Correspondence*, III: 103). There oppressor and oppressed, whatever the specific culpabilities of each, are both ultimately Yahoo. As in the Irish writings, Swift ultimately wishes a plague on both their houses, and his feelings on this point are total and absolute in each case. The savagery of savages may have to be toned down, kept brief or even concealed in order to highlight the cruelty of their conquerors, but only to be asserted with even greater power in another part of the book. The totality which the separate feelings form is one which holds them together in a unified but in many ways unresolved state. Throughout, as always, a sense of irreconcilable opposition between two absolutes is generated, whereas Conrad's opposed feelings are mixed on both sides, merging into and out of one another across the whole field of intermediate possibilities.

If an element of contradiction is implied in the strict logic of Swift's position, this is not uncommon. There are many places in his writings, including *Gulliver's Travels*, where an intensity of satirical insight transcends such logical complications as may make themselves felt when paraphrasable content is extrapolated from the total context of a work. In this particular case, moreover, contradiction is in a sense side-stepped or prevented from arising in too literal a form. It is not Europeans, or men, but horse-shaped Houyhnhnms who rightfully hold the Yahoos in subjection, and when Gulliver attacks colonialism he is not contemplating the conquest of the Yahoos, but discussing the pros and cons of invading the Houyhnhnms. Gulliver rejects the idea because he does not like European conquests, because the Houyhnhnms would in any case foil any attempt, and because they are better than Europeans and ought instead to be civilising *them* (IV. xii; 293–94). As to the Yahoos, it is lucky that the Houyhnhnms are in charge, since civilised men are no better than Yahoos and in some ways worse. At the same time Swift knew that however close we might be to the Yahoos, there were no

Houyhnhnms in real life, and therefore that the oppositions he set up were those of a country of the mind, the only kind of place in which ideal perfections can exist. To that extent, the presentation in *Gulliver's Travels* of absolute and contradictory feelings about the subjection of 'savages' side-steps, as well as transcends, the particularities of actual colonial activity which Conrad made it his business to 'make us see'.

Marlow's preference for British rule over that of other European powers has much to do with the idea of 'work'. On the map in the Company's office in the European capital he remembers noticing the 'vast amount of red – good to see at any time, because one knows that some real work is done in there' (55). The saving 'efficiency' ('What saves us is efficiency') and the saving 'idea' ('What redeems [colonial conquest] is the idea only') exist in a relationship which is both inextricable and strangely blurred. The vagueness of the link is part of its potency, since the object is to still any disabling introspection. Its logic does not bear looking 'into . . . too much', any more than those dark motives of colonial conquest which it is meant both to disguise and to transcend (50–51).

It is this blend of proclaimed evasion and severe practicality which makes the colonial enterprise acceptable. That is an important truth which Conrad knows and Marlow gropes towards. The civilised lie is partly a saving self-obfuscation and partly a matter of real self-silencing *work*, both necessary. And so the brilliant comedy of the skilled fireman, or the white accountant whose books 'were in apple-pie order' and who taught a black woman to clean his linen, are also an unillusioned defence of the colonial appropriation, even though, in the particular case, it happens not to be wholly British (97–98, 68). One might say that the skilled fireman is a small British achievement, a ray of genuine light in the general darkness of a foreign 'scramble for loot',[26] since he is at least partly Marlow-trained; while the comic accountant, who is presumably not British, constitutes an acknowledgement that foreign enterprises sometimes contain, in sporadic or imperfect forms, those virtues of creative 'efficiency' which the British empire supposedly had in much greater share.

If so, the peculiar quality of affectionate, respectful derision ('I respected the fellow') with which the accountant is presented, though he looked like a 'hairdresser's dummy', differs from Gulliver's apparently total praise for British as distinct from foreign conquests, as it differs from Swift's equal and opposite denunciation of both.[27] At all events, although both Marlow in the tale, and Conrad in real life, expressed preference for the British way, there is a frequent tendency to blur the edges of demarcation, though not to remove the distinction. There is often a sense in which all European colonising is implicated, as, with an almost allegorical explicitness, it is implicated in the figure of Kurtz, that employee of a Belgian company and bearer of a German name, of whom we learn that he

> had been educated partly in England, and – as he was good enough to say himself – his sympathies were in the right place. His mother was half-English, his father was half-French. All Europe contributed to the making of Kurtz . . .
>
> (117)

Characteristically, the passage contains an ironic undercutting of the English boast. Marlow is amusing about it, though Kurtz pays it a foreigner's or part-foreigner's tribute. But the truth or half-truth of the boast is probably one of the things which makes Kurtz preferable to the manager and his gang, these wholly non-British colonisers who are inspired by no animating 'idea' and who lack 'efficiency' too. The virtue of the British way, ironically yet feelingly asserted, opens possibilities for a wider defence of colonial exploitation, not confined to the British, especially in cases where British virtue rubs off, a little, on others. The matter is not given a clear ideological formulation. It comes through in hints, impressions and significant inconsistencies, alongside a powerful and bitter exposure.

This defence, and the scepticism which yet questions it, are equally Marlow's and Conrad's. But there is also the curious truth that the colonial appropriation, though existing in an obvious realm of fact, somehow remains an extension of those mental appropriations of Marlow's, those little acts of verbal imperialism contained in the phrases about fine chaps and good fellows – self-protecting and partly rooted in fantasy. This Marlow probably does not fully understand, and Conrad's comedy reveals to us. For although Marlow does grasp part of the strange farcical unreality of conquest, as when he observes the 'lugubrious drollery' of the French ship with the six-inch guns, 'incomprehensible, firing into a continent',

> a small flame would dart and vanish, a little white smoke would disappear, a tiny projectile would give a feeble screech

– and nothing happened. Nothing could happen. There was a touch of insanity in the proceeding,

(62)

his understanding is less than his author's, and subtly different. The word 'incomprehensible' is his, not Conrad's: or rather, it conveys honest bafflement from Marlow, and a knowing sense of absurdity from Conrad.[28]

If, however, Marlow understands less about his own attitudes than Conrad does, some uncertainty nevertheless exists as to how much comedy comes directly from Marlow's view of things, and how much from a Conrad who includes Marlow in the comedy. When Marlow's language turns the blacks into music-hall jokes (61, 96), or when he domesticates the savage drums by likening them to church bells (71), we may suspect that Conrad knows more than Marlow; but we cannot be sure, and it may be that Conrad 'makes us *see*'[29] more than he knows. But there are occasions where a profoundly Conradian comic sense establishes itself over what from Marlow seems no more than a form of high-spirited patronising. When Marlow notes the fact that the cannibal crew whose hippo-meat had gone rotten 'did not eat each other before my face' (94) or exclaims:

Why in the name of all the gnawing devils of hunger they didn't go for us – they were thirty to five – and have a good tuck in for once, amazes me now when I think of it,

(104)

certain questions arise which Marlow can only partially articulate and to which he does not know the answers.[30] H. R. Collins puts some of these questions well, and knows which answers, however interesting, 'take us outside of the story':

Perhaps it would help if we could identify the tribe to which the cannibals belonged. Although the letters to Marguerite Poradowska, George Jean-Aubry's *Joseph Conrad in the Congo*, and Conrad's *Congo Diary* do not mention the cannibals, Marlow tells us that they were recruited 800 miles from Stanley Falls and that they wear their hair in 'oily ringlets'. The Bayanzi about Bolobo would seem to be plausible candidates. Might we not consult the ethnological studies published by the Institut Royal Colonial Belge of Brussels and the Musée du Congo of Tervueran, Belgium, and determine just what kept the man-eaters from having that 'tuck in'? Have the Bayanzi ever dared to eat white men? After all, when Stanley first came down the Congo the natives below Stanley Falls pursued him yelling, *nyama, nyama* (meat!). Did the Bayanzi eat only slaves and prisoners of war, or did they, like the Basoko, eat even their own dead, except their chiefs and those dying of infectious diseases? Were they fairly fastidious, or did they, like the Manyema, eat diseased bodies and enjoy their meat 'high'?

This research might be a pleasant game. The trouble is, it would take us outside of the story. No matter what we may happen to know about the eating habits of Congo cannibals, no matter which tribe Conrad's cannibals belonged to – the Bayanzi, Bateke, and Bangala are a few of the possibilities – we must simply take Marlow's word for it: the restraint was a mystery. And wouldn't we do well to admit that the motives of human conduct are often inexplicable?[31]

But 'Marlow's word for it' is 'one of those human secrets that baffle probability' (104), and the statement is hardly the kind of flat invitation to acknowledge the inexplicable that Collins implies. It carries a rich flavour of Marlovian bafflement, a touch of Marlow's uncomprehending irony, and more than a touch of (undoubtedly affectionate) Conradian irony at Marlow's expense. As with the 'incomprehensible' gunfire, an element of sharp knowingness is generated, which implies not that Conrad knows the answers but that he has a wide sceptical awareness of the nature of the question. Conrad himself is not above this kind of mystifying rhetoric, and some of Marlow's abuses of it undoubtedly rub off on his author. But the element of dissociation here seems evident, and is beautifully under control. It is what saves *Heart of Darkness* from the crudity of *Falk*. Whatever Conrad's other blind spots he understands his Marlow, and another sense in which the questions raised by Collins are not the appropriate ones is that Marlow does seem to have his theory at least as to why the cannibals did not eat each other in front of the whites.

Or rather, Marlow chooses, as we saw, to interpret it as a delicacy, a natural considerateness that brings to mind those vaguely 'British' codes of solidarity, honour, decency, fair-play which are an instinctive part of Marlow's outlook, and to which he is quick to assimilate the behaviour of any 'savages' who earn his affection or respect. Conrad viewed these 'British' qualities with an outsider's or foreigner's self-consciousness, which may explain why they are both more vaguely apprehended, and also cherished with a greater and more sentimental tenacity, than one finds in other writers. On the other side, they are more tentatively rendered than Kipling's version of similar things. In Marlow's eyes, the natives act out modes of social organisation which are those of a well-run ship's crew ('They were men one could work with'), or evoke a schoolboy world of cheeky daring checked by an odd decency, or impish adventure by a rather specialised form of honour (the 'good tuck-in' resisted out of 'some kind of primitive honour' and an 'inborn strength' of somewhat Kiplingesque complexion) (94, 104–5). Marlow's speculative interpretations on such matters are not those of the historian or anthropologist, asking the questions listed by Collins, but nor are they after all the simple refusal to explain the inexplicable which Collins prefers to emphasise. They are the views of a self-implicated introspective narrator, with his social and political preferences, prejudices and blind spots, the combined product of baffled brooding, an instinctive readiness to scale down the 'incomprehensible' to domestic or even home-counties size, and a capacity for human sympathy which is incomplete yet in its way perceptive and humble.

It is difficult to know how much Conrad is parodying, through Marlow, some old European habits of thought, patronising and affectionate. The ancient idea of the savage as a child, whose primitive state is an early stage or 'infancy' in the evolutionary history of man, who requires the 'adult' protection of the civilized European, but who also arouses protective affection and even has the virtues that naturally belong to the innocent and childlike, could easily shade into the more specialised view of him as a rather English kind of schoolboy. The process is clearly visible in the writings of Rider Haggard, G. A. Henty, Kipling and others, as Brian V. Street brings out in *The Savage in Literature*.[32] In Henty's *With Kitchener in the Sudan*, for example, some Sudanese troops are described as being '"as full of fun or life as a party of school boys"'; when punished or disciplined by the white man, Kipling's Bhil natives, like several of their analogues in other writers, 'respect British rule and accept their punishment with the wise stoicism of the English public school boy'; Haggard's Umslopogaas, whose 'idea of sport may be a trifle bloodier than that of the Victorian public school [but] stems from the same sense of honour and dignity', is yet another variant of a pervasive pattern of analogy.[33] All are predecessors or near-contemporaries of Marlow's natives.

In Ballantyne's *Coral Island* the child-like natives showed a 'kindly nature' in some cases, but their sport is more than 'a trifle bloodier' than anything known to the English boys who see them, full of cruel carnage and cannibalism and 'foul deeds of darkness of which man may not speak' which may be compared with Kurtz's 'unspeakable rites'.[34] Ballantyne's pattern is more concerned with the savagery of savages than with their schoolboy honour, and while their 'unspeakable rites' are performed directly by blacks instead of by Conrad's white man 'gone native',[35] the boy heroes (not schoolboys themselves, but cut of schoolboy cloth and made up for schoolboy readers) of *Coral Island* are English and not blacks tarred, in reverse, with a white brush. *Coral Island* and later the Tarzan books belong to a common and presumably earlier variant of the tradition I am describing, in which it is the white coloniser who is identified with the honour and prowess of public schools, while the South Sea island or African bush is thought of as a place 'for character training and physical toughness, an idea of which modern "outward bound" courses are perhaps a survival'.[36] In Kipling's *Stalky & Co.*, a series of tales of English schoolboy life published as a book in 1899, the year in which *Heart of Darkness* was serialised in *Blackwood's Magazine*, schoolboy adventure and prowess are occasionally extended or transplanted to the world of imperial activity in India ('India's full of Stalkies – Cheltenham and Haileybury and Marlborough chaps . . .'), while a simultaneous airing is also given to the alternative notion of the 'native' as, at his best, likewise imbued with schoolboy honour, whether as honest foe ('an awf'ly sportin' old card . . . angry with his own side for their cowardice') or faithful ally ('Sikhs don't understand fightin' against the Government after you've served it honestly'). In this last story of the series, 'Slaves of the Lamp, Part II', Stalky, serving in the Indian army, saves his men from ambush by means of a trick first used in his schooldays in Part I.[37]

Conrad must have known Kipling's story. It had first been serialised in *Cosmopolis* in April and May 1897, 'immediately followed, in the issues for June and July', by the serialisation of the other of Conrad's two Congo stories, 'An Outpost of Progress'.[38] *Heart of Darkness* was begun late in the following year. Conrad had some respect for Kipling, and shared some of his attitudes about, for example, the discipline and comradeship of a ship's crew, and the ethic of work and its power to preserve sanity in a lonely and demoralising colonial wilderness. He defended Kipling, though less than wholeheartedly, against Cunninghame

Graham's dislike.[39] He would have recoiled from some of the callousness of the schoolboy ethics of *Stalky & Co.*, especially as applied to empire, and Marlow's patronising praise of black natives in terms which imply schoolboy standards is an altogether gentler and kindlier thing. He would not himself have written stories extolling the cruder aspects of schoolboy adventure,[40] but *Heart of Darkness* has moments in which Marlow consciously sees himself as engaged in a situation which calls such adventure to mind:

> I kept to the track . . . then stopped to listen. . . . I was strangely cocksure of everything that night . . . I was circumventing Kurtz as though it had been a boyish game.
>
> I came upon him, and, if he had not heard me coming, I would have fallen over him, too, but he got up in time.
>
> . . . If he makes a row we are lost, I thought to myself. This clearly was not a case for fisticuffs . . .
>
> (142–43)

A satirical element is present here, an ironic detachment in which Marlow views his own adventure, a serious and disturbing one, on a reduced schoolboy plane, and notes, with a self-conscious or self-critical exhilaration, that he was 'strangely cocksure . . . that night'. Conrad probably played both his schoolboy themes (that of the white man as schoolboy, as well as that of the native as schoolboy) with a touch of satire at the expense of certain aspects of imperialist fiction and imperialist modes of thought. Schoolboy decencies and honour are respected, with an attendant note of mildly superior adult awareness. This hint of a satiric colouring (which may be contrasted with the unredeemed contempt with which Swift applies schoolboy analogies to adult doings in his satire)[41] extends to Marlow's other and related acts of mental or linguistic domestication, like calling cannibals fine chaps and fine fellows (97, 94). Such language is not unusual in white writings about blacks.[42] Sometimes the 'good fellows' are contrasted with the 'fiendish' cannibals, who actually practise their cannibalism. In Melville's *Typee*, for example, cannibals are said tentatively to be 'good fellows' in so far as it is assumed that they might not after all be cannibals: 'It is impossible that the inhabitants of such a lovely place as we saw can be anything else but good fellows'.[43] In W. H. Bentley's *Pioneering on the Congo*, 1900, the 'fine, bright, intelligent fellow' Bapulula is an example of the 'free and lovable' wild man, in contrast to his fiendish brother, who had no 'restraint' and exclaimed, 'Ah! I wish I could eat everybody on earth'.[44]

In Ballantyne's *Coral Island*, the references to 'black fellows', 'black critters', 'black chaps' are always a little harsh, in comparison with those of *Heart of Darkness*, just as Kipling's way of reducing the native to schoolboy dimensions lacks the gentleness and friendly irony of Marlow's. For Ballantyne, the old irony that civilised whites are sometimes worse than black savages means only that whites are guiltier 'inasmuch as they know better', and not because, as in the traditional paradox associated with Montaigne's essay on cannibals, the things they do are actually worse.[45] As we might expect from such an unquestioning apology for white civilisation and especially its Bible-bearing missions, the 'kindly nature' of cannibals in *Coral Island* is conceded largely to the extent that their activities are restrainable by whites.[46]

The comedy of Marlow's perception of the cannibals' restraint, the manner in which he notes that they held back from eating the white men, or even other blacks in front of whites, thus shows more than a merely personal instinct on his part to domesticate the wilderness by means of schoolboy or comradely analogies. Such domestications had become in some degree part of the natural rhetoric of Europeans, including the special use of them in cases where the cannibal behaves or was thought to behave less cannibalistically than the speaker might have expected. Indeed, the 'restraint' of cannibals seems to have become a stock situation, and also the registering of such restraint by the white man, whether as author, narrator or character, with varying degrees of satisfaction or approval. An element of parody and of knowing allusion is undoubtedly present, although its extent is hard to measure exactly, because it merges with a primary concern to show us Marlow's personal propensity for putting things in this way, and also the particular and individual humanity with which he does so.

There is thus a complicated interplay of satire at typical attitudes and situations in colonial literature with a humaner and subtler enactment of these same attitudes and situations. The elements of satire are included, and transcended, in an exploration which must allow them a voice but in which they cannot become the only or the main point. It is not that Marlow merely embodies attitudes which Conrad satirises, since Marlow's is a richer and finer version of such attitudes than is common in the literature of colonial adventure. If Conrad is a much more finely articulate commentator on the human mind, hardly to be identified with Marlow's blunt and comic perceptions, Marlow himself, for all his bluntness, shows a more sensitive consciousness than the narrators of Ballantyne or Kipling. Conrad may impress on us a sense of Marlow's difference from the man who created the wry comedy which Marlow describes and also the comedy of Marlow's commentary upon it. But the humane rectitude with which Marlow contemplates both the 'restraint' of the savages, and the notion that it may well be a satisfactory product of an otherwise ugly colonial influence, gives a status to Marlow's perceptions which we are invited to respect, even where we sense that they are less sophisticated than his author's.

Conrad does not merely show an extraordinary delicacy of moral judgement in rendering Marlow's richly tentative state of mind, and in suggesting a delicacy of feeling in Marlow himself in the midst of uncertain or blundering perceptions. There is also a potential alignment on Conrad's part with Marlow's views, as well as with his hesitations and equivocations. The interest of Conrad's style in much of *Heart of Darkness* lies not in a detachment from Marlow which would indicate that Marlow's analyses are wrong, but in its ability to suggest that, for all Marlow's naive puzzlements and his hefty jokes, Marlow might be right. Swift's relationship with Gulliver is of a different order, oscillating between total congruence (as when Gulliver attacks colonial exploitation) and total separation (as when Gulliver praises the discreditable doings of his own dear country). Swift's manner induces an unsettling bewilderment, as the reader is forced to negotiate radical redirections of irony, but no hesitation as to where Swift stands on the immediate substantive issue in hand. Conrad's style, on the other hand, with its deliberately indistinct demarcations from the narrator's voice, registers and shares uncertainty on the substantive questions. It casts an openminded and exploratory scepticism over the whole relationship between savage vitality and civilised lie, acknowledging the savage appeal and the 'untruth' of the lie, but also the dangers and brutalities of savagery and the lie's possible ability to subdue them, and yet casting doubt on this also, as an explanation, because Marlow's theorising is tentative and Marlow himself hardly the shrewdest-seeming or most articulate theorist. This, moreover, is not merely a matter of tone, in the limited sense of being an interplay between Marlow's voice and an authorial consciousness tacitly present. It is partly a matter of Conrad's arrangement of the incidents. For Marlow to discuss the cannibals' restraint, Conrad must have invented or selected or decided to emphasise this restraint just as Swift had to invent the story of the Brobdingnagian ape or the Yahoo female, 'planting' it as an objective 'fact' independent of any interpretative bias of Gulliver. The effect in Swift is to remove uncertainty as to Gulliver's basic resemblance to the monkey-race or to Yahoos. In Conrad it does not remove uncertainty but gives the uncertainty itself a factual basis.

The restraint is a fact, and so are the questions it gives rise to in Marlow's mind, and his sense of its incomprehensibility. We are encouraged to wonder whether some deeper delicacy of feeling than can be accounted for by the fellowship or discipline of work animates these savages, who, as Marlow says, have 'not much capacity to weigh the consequences'; or whether it is entirely from some primitive or some conditioned awe of the white man and his authority that they not only do not eat their white companions, but virtually ask the white men's permission to eat blacks (103–4). Such questions are not fruitless, though they may have no conclusive answer. It is in the nature of a work like *Heart of Darkness* that they can be asked without irrelevance and that they should be complicated by certain countertruths. It is in the end not a black, but Kurtz, a white man partly gone native, who abandons 'restraint' in murderous lusts which probably include cannibalism. His behaviour too is an 'inconceivable mystery' to Marlow (145), and at the same time it suggests to him and probably to Conrad the achievement of what Lionel Trilling calls 'authenticity'.[47] The inexplicability of the 'mystery' is important in itself. Despite the Conradian, as well as the Marlovian, penchant for the occasional grandiloquent evasion, Conrad's strategy does not mainly seek either to evade, or for that matter to resolve, but to explore a play of possibilities, inconstant and provisional and subtle in their own right, and also interacting with the shifting and tentative subjectivities of the observer's or commentator's mind.

Applied to the political issues at hand, the method reflects, or translates itself into, the special kind of clear-sighted non-commitment (not lack of interest nor of strong feelings) which is Conrad's most characteristic political attitude: 'I feel deeply what happens in the world – a genuine sentiment qualified by irony'.[48] The 'irony' in question is exactly that 'ironie sceptique' which André Breton considered inimical to the black humour of which Swift, in his view, was the 'véritable initiateur'.[49] It is also uncongenial to the kind of uncompromising satirical commitment with which, on another level, Swift is also naturally identified. If black humour operates 'beyond' satire in one sense, it has had to travel along satire's path in order to transcend it,[50] and is itself an extremist or radical gesture akin to some of the absolute moral positions adopted by Swift against a universe of cosy accommodations or easy slippages. The 'irony' which is pervasive in Conrad's political fictions is neither mainly satiric, nor emancipated from or 'beyond' satire as Sade or Genet (or Swift as read by Breton) might be thought to be. It includes the satirical viewpoint as one which enters naturally into a situation. The 'irony' is one which *qualifies*, multiplying possible points of view instead of intensifying and concentrating a single dominant one, as in Swift or, in a different way, in modern authors of violent radical fictions. Nor does it seek to resolve these points of view into a tightly refocused and inclusive 'totalisation', or stark paradox: they remain open, a play of possibilities, and for Conrad the preservation of intellectual integrity in the face of these entails a withholding of simplifying commitment.[51] He had to warn a radical friend like R. B. Cunninghame Graham that, passionately as he felt about the Congo scandal, *Heart of Darkness* would be more ambiguous than a committed political radical might expect. In a famous letter of 8 February 1899, Conrad warns Graham, who had seen and liked the first instalment of the tale in *Blackwood's*, that 'There are two more instalments in which the idea is so wrapped up in secondary notions that You – even You! – may miss it'. Conrad goes on to say that 'So far the note struck chimes in with your convictions – mais après? There is an après.' Graham will find 'the right intention' at bottom but 'nothing that is practically effective'.[52]

The two related points to be stressed are the presence of 'secondary notions', qualifying any simple anti-colonial message, and the absence of any simplifying 'practical' commitment. In the same letter, and in the same spirit, he describes himself as unlikely to sympathise with a 'peace meeting' of the Social Democratic Federation, at which Graham, Jaurès and others were to speak (he did, however, go, and Graham reported: 'Conrad was I think revolted a little'). In his first letter to Graham, on 5 August 1897, Conrad had written ambiguous praise of Kipling, whom Graham detested for his imperialist attitudes, but whom Conrad praises not only for 'impeccable form' as an artist, but also for a 'squint' which 'sees round the corner', and which may be the equivalent to those 'secondary notions' in the later letter: 'It is a beautiful squint; it is an useful squint. And – after all – perhaps he sees round the corner? And suppose Truth is just round the corner like the elusive and useless loafer it is?'.[53]

The artist concerned with 'the whole matter' must be aware of the 'secondary notions', the complications 'round the corner', which tend to be missed when simple ideological positions are asserted, whether these are of the anti-imperial sort, as in *Heart of Darkness* in the main, or of the opposite tendency, as in Kipling. Conrad seems to have valued a recognition of this in Kipling, against Graham's doctrinaire expectations on one side and his simple repudiation of Kipling on the other. A revealing passage about Kipling occurs on 14 October 1899, some months after the letter about 'secondary notions' in *Heart of Darkness*, when Conrad wrote to Graham expressing, somewhat vehemently, views on the Boer war and on Kipling's attitude to it which Graham would find broadly sympathetic, and then allowing an odd qualification:

> There is an appalling fatuity in this business. If I am to believe Kipling this is a war undertaken for the cause of democracy. C'est a crever de rire. However, now the fun has com-menced, I trust British successes will be crushing from the first – on the same principle that if there's murder being done in the next room and you can't stop it you wish the head of the victim to be bashed in forthwith and the whole thing over for the sake of your own feelings.[54]

We may suspect that 'I trust British successes will be crushing from the first' has at least something to do with a residual loyalty to British imperial activities, of a kind we have already seen Conrad to have. The more disenchanted or cynically world-weary reason which Conrad actually gives for this hope is one which Graham would doubtless not have approved of, and by an odd and ironic coincidence it resembles some reflections of the narrator of *Coral Island*, watching a horrible fight among black natives. The losers are bound and about to be roasted for a cannibal feast:

> Next moment one of the savages raised his club, and frac-tured the wretched creature's skull. He must have died instantly; and strange though it may seem, I confess to a feeling of relief when the deed was done, because I now knew that the poor savage could not be burned alive.[55]

Conrad would have found an analogy between his feelings about internecine struggles among whites, and those of Ballantyne's hero about murderous combats among blacks, not without piquancy. Ballantyne writes as an apologist for white civilisation, with a feeling of humanitarian revulsion against murderous tribal practices; Conrad writes, nominally, as an opponent of imperial exploitation, yet wanting the British to win, even cruelly, in order to get it over with. But the convergence of the two is in accord with the Conradian instinct to cover the 'whole matter', with all its 'secondary notions' and its sense of unexpected and complicating truths 'round the corner'.

But Conrad shows what for very different reasons Ballantyne and Graham do not, and that is a quality of deep sceptical disenchantment. While Ballantyne is full of missionary fervour and Graham angrily rejects the wickedness of imperial adventure, Conrad speaks, almost as an aesthete, not only of the desire to have his feelings spared, but also of the 'fatuity' rather than primarily 'wickedness' of the anti-Boer enterprise: 'idiotic war', 'war inanities', 'inexpressibly stupid', 'positively imbecile'. In *Heart of Darkness*, 'imbecility' as well as 'cruelty' comes through, even when cruelty is a major aspect: Ford reports that while writing the tale 'Conrad would declaim passionately about the gloomy imbecility and cruelty of the Belgians in the Congo Free State'.[56]

Conrad's reaction to distasteful political situations is sometimes to suggest that they defy emotional reactions, and deserve at best a sour and disenchanted laugh, and the contemptuously unconcerned response due to a bad play. In a letter to Edward Garnett in March 1899, Cunninghame Graham called life 'A dingy farce played by fools & harlots, on a poor stage, with an incompetent stage manager, & the only laugh in it, being at one's own antics & folly for continuing to act'. The words are almost more characteristic of Conrad than of Graham except that for Conrad even the scornful laugh might be too much 'action'. Writing to Graham on 14 January 1898 about the final scene in his other Congo story, 'An Outpost of Progress', in which the hanged Kayerts is seen with his tongue sticking out at his Managing Director, Conrad says:

'Put the tongue out' why not? One ought to really. And the machine will run on all the same. The question is, whether the fatigue of the muscular exertion is worth the transient pleasure of indulged scorn . . . The fate of a humanity condemned ultimately to perish from cold is not worth troubling about. If you take it to heart it becomes an unendurable tragedy.[57]

The two passages have something of the spirit of Swift's much-quoted remark that 'The common saying of life being a Farce is true in every sense but the most important one, for it is a ridiculous tragedy, which is the worst kind of composition' (*Correspondence*, III: 456). Conrad's advocacy of inaction may seem at odds with Swift's emphasis on constant vigilance and piecemeal improvement. But the latter finds its pragmatic and literal-minded counterpart in Conrad's ethic of work, while Conrad's mood of deep disenchantment ('The attitude of cold unconcern is the only reasonable one ... If you believe in improvement you must weep ...') is undoubtedly matched by Swift's other mood of profound disbelief in human perfectibility, in the efficacy of any solution as such.

Conrad's next letter to Graham (23 January 1898) says that even the 'noblest cause' is tainted by 'something of [the] baseness' common to all men, so that the same evil is present both in those causes which Graham calls evil and those he calls good.

> I am more in sympathy with you than words can express yet if I had a grain of belief left in me I would believe you misguided. You are misguided by the desire of the impossible – and I envy you. Alas! what you want to reform are not institutions – it is human nature.[58]

All this is part of the background to the remarks in the letter of 8 February 1899 about the 'secondary notions' in *Heart of Darkness*, and about that tale's studied lack of anything 'that is practically effective', despite what Graham will sense as the 'right intention' of its general tendency. This assertion of practical inapplicability goes with an explicit refusal to 'start with an abstract notion': a refusal, quite specifically, of abstract libertarian principles which is very much in that tradition of English conservative pragmatism propounded by Swift and later by Burke against the political radicals of their day.[59] The paradox of denying both 'practical effect' and 'abstract notions' is only apparent, since the essence of the outlook I am describing is that abstract principles are bad guides to practical politics, and since, as has been said, Conrad, like Swift, asserts in *Heart of Darkness* and elsewhere the simple, limited but real practical (and indeed moral) value of useful work.

Conrad goes on in the letter to express his lukewarm feelings about attending the socialist 'peace meeting' and about 'l'idée democratique' (he shared with Swift a feeling that the rule of the

Many quickly turned itself into a one-man dictatorship or tyranny of the One),[60] and to disavow those political sentiments – 'abstract notions'? – with which his attack on the exploitation of the Congo might be thought by Graham to have aligned him: 'Fraternity means nothing unless the Cain-Abel business'.[61]

Then follows a famous long passage, in not wholly correct French, which begins:

> L'homme est un animal méchant. Sa mechanceté doit être organisée. Le crime est une condition nécéssaire de l'existence organisée. La société est essentielment criminelle – ou elle n'existerait pas. C'est l'égoisme qui sauve tout – absolument tout – tout ce que nous abhorrons tout ce que nous aimons. Et tout se tient. Voilà pourquoi je respecte les êxtremes anarchistes. – 'Je souhaite l'extermination generale' – Très bien. C'est juste et ce qui est plus c'est clair.[62]

These words read like an amalgam of Hobbes and Sade. Sade, or Genet, would understand the social analysis ('La société est essentielment [*sic*] criminelle') and its logical consequence for Conrad's extreme anarchist ('Je souhaite l'extermination generale'). Hobbes, or Mandeville, or Swift would have agreed about the 'animal méchant' and understood the opposite logical consequence, that this 'mechanceté doit être organisée'.

It is, in a way, characteristic of Conrad to formulate an outlook ironically sympathetic to opposing sides. But at first sight, the formulation may seem to suggest the kind of polarising or 'dialectical' outlook which I have been suggesting is deeply alien to Conrad. There is something of that bold confrontation of opposites, that sense of their mirror-resemblance and their mutually complementary logic, which we associate rather with more absolutist temperaments like Swift or, at an opposite extreme, some modern writers in the 'radical' tradition of Sade. There is the same readiness to strip political issues to their bare and most starkly uncompromising essentials, and an apparent leaning towards forms of highly definite political commitment which are uncharacteristic of Conrad's scrupulous and almost morbidly discriminating and sceptical vision. The wording seems to align Conrad with the extreme conservative (say Hobbesian or Swiftian) view of man's vicious nature and of the consequent need for an authoritarian 'organising' of this viciousness; and it expresses 'respect' for the equal and opposite absolutism of the 'extreme anarchist', and his frank and clear acknowledgement of the urge to exterminate.

All the evidence, however, suggests that these impressions are misleading. On the matter of 'extermination', something has already been said about the differences between Swift's and Conrad's parallel treatments of this theme. Certainly Conrad's writings do not normally evince much 'respect' for 'extreme anarchists': he normally speaks of them with contempt, a fascinated and somewhat gingerly loathing. And on the matter of man as 'un animal méchant', Conrad is on record, notably in other letters to Cunninghame Graham, as not really believing this in the starkest sense. About a year before, he is explicitly anxious to qualify any such suggestion: 'Not that I think mankind intrinsically bad. It is only silly and cowardly'. In a weary way, he accepts that this is depressing, but that society and civilisation, even in the good and necessary sense, depend on this depressing truth: 'Now *You* know that in cowardice is every evil – especially that cruelty so characteristic of our civilisation. But without it mankind would vanish'.[63]

Swift could never show such a tolerant acceptance of the fact that the survival of society depends on 'evil', suitably 'organised', although he might agree as to the fact. In one of his best-known letters, he too, like Conrad, made a show of qualifying or softening an extreme statement about man's depravity by expressing a form of cynical, world-weary 'acceptance': he does not 'hate Mankind'; is not angry at man's lack of 'reason' because, expecting nothing, he is not disappointed; no more angry, that is, than at the kite which stole one of his chickens, though glad when the kite was shot (*Correspondence*, III: 118). If the conservative pessimism is the same as Conrad's, and the world-weary cynicism seems similar, the difference is that Swift lives in uncompromising recalcitrance towards this ineluctable evil, while Conrad accepts it as a source, albeit the only source we have, of partial good.

This should prepare us to see the stark paradoxes of the French statement in the letter to Graham not as the tense confrontation of polarised opposites which it might seem, but rather as an unresolved co-existence of attitudes or sympathies, less clear and less extreme than their face-value. We should recall that the discussion is partly touched off by the publication of the first section of *Heart of Darkness*, a sceptical and ambiguous work with a mainly liberal bias, and that Conrad has just been trying explicitly to allay a radical friend's expectation that the tale will show an unwaveringly *radical* partisanship. Since the tale in fact explores intermediate, unresolved and indeed hesitant positions, and since Conrad actually protests its ambiguity, the presence of 'secondary notions', we may feel that the extreme play of opposites in the French passage is more an expression of ambiguity and tentativeness than it would have been in Swift or, say, in Mailer; that the extremeness of the formulation is *in itself* ironically and self-consciously exaggerated and thus self-undercutting; and even that the absurdity of the contradiction, taken literally, not only expresses unresolved or ambiguous feelings but undercuts the ambiguity itself, as though Conrad were refusing to commit himself even to a relative non-commitment. As Irving Howe has said: 'Conrad is finally unable to sustain either commitment or scepticism'.[64] The harsh and cynical knowingness is doubtless no more total than Conrad's frequent and shoulder-shrugging expressions, in fiction as in direct statements, of incomprehension at the world's inscrutable ways. Both are self-conscious postures, pretending complete knowledge or complete ignorance, but hardly able to disguise the fact that Conrad's interest in the world's ways, and in the nature of man, is both active and exploratory, combining an urge to exhaustive subtlety of understanding with an acknowledgement that insight will remain in the end incomplete.

Extreme knowingness, and sweeping declarations of incomprehension, are thus to be seen as simplifying and provisional gestures adopted as a temporary refuge from complexities of which the author is all too sensitively aware even as he recognises their inexhaustibility. Conrad's bewilderments are real, but they are neither unspecific nor total, and the crude clear-sightedness of the French statement, with its 'respect' for exterminators and the rest, is a way of disguising, and also of expressing, partial bewilderment in a show of provocative and outrageous clarity. It does not, as in Swift on the shooting of the kite, suggest an impulse to share in those homicidal velleities which both authors elsewhere denounced or derided in evil men. And it seems possible that Conrad's slipping into French at this point represents an impulse to remove such extreme talk to the safer distance of a language foreign to both correspondents.

1983

Notes

1 References to *Gulliver's Travels* in this form give the book and chapter, followed by the page reference in volume XI of Swift's *Works*. *Heart of Darkness* is cited throughout from the relevant volume in the Dent Collected

Gulliver's Travels *and Some Modern Fictions*

Edition, *Youth, Heart of Darkness. The End of the Tether* (London, 1946, rptd. 1956) and the page references in the text are to that edition. Conrad's other works are also quoted from this Collected Edition.

2 For example, Henry Hawks, *A Relation of the Commodities of Nova Hispania*, 1572, in R. Hakluyt, *Principal Navigations*, Everyman edn., London, n.d., VI. 286; Jean de Léry, *Histoire d'un Voyage fait en la Terre du Brésil*, 1580, ed. J.-C. Morisot (Geneva, 1975), 98; 'Extracts of a Tractate, Written by Nicholas Withington, which was left in the Mogols Countrey' *c.* 1612, in Samuel Purchas, *Hakluytus Posthumus or Purchas His Pilgrimes*, IV (Glasgow, 1905), 162; Sir Thomas Herbert, *Some Yeares Travels into Africa and Asia*, 3rd edn., 1665, 29; Sir Matthew Hale, *The Primitive Origination of Mankind*, 1677, 200; William Dampier, *A New Voyage Round the World* (1697), ed. Sir Albert Gray (London, 1937), 31, 358; see also Locke, *Essay Concerning Human Understanding*, 1690, IV. iv. 16 ('Make . . . the Nose a little flatter . . . Add still more and more of the likeness of a Brute . . .'; see above p. 78 and n. 17 for the use of 'brute' in Swift and Conrad). For the general resemblance between the Yahoos and 'accounts in travel-books of savage tribes' see Paul Turner (ed.), *Gulliver's Travels* (London, 1971), 363nn.13–17, and R. W. Frantz, 'Swift's Yahoos and the Voyagers', *Modern Philology*, XXIX (1931), 49–57, esp. 53. The most recent study of Swift's relation to travel-writers is Arthur Sherbo, 'Swift and Travel Literature', *Modern Language Studies*, IX (1979), 114–27. For information on books Swift possessed, see Harold Williams, *Dean Swift's Library* (Cambridge, 1932) and the Sale Catalogue reprinted there.

3 *The Times*, 27 May 1982, 8.

4 R. B. Cunninghame Graham, *Thirty Tales and Sketches* (London, 1929), 12. The essay, originally entitled 'Bloody Niggers', was published in 1897 in the *Social Democrat* and reprinted as 'Niggers' in Graham's book, *The Ipané* (1899).

5 Eloise Knapp Hay, *The Political Novels of Joseph Conrad* (Chicago, 1963), 129.

6 See C. T. Watts (ed.), *Joseph Conrad's Letters to R. B. Cunninghame Graham* (Cambridge, 1969), 117 (8 February 1899).

7 *Lord Jim*, chapter 21, 219.

8 *Letters to R. B. Cunninghame Graham*, 117, 8 February 1899; see also 94, 97nn., 30 July 1898; and a letter to S. Kliszczewski, 19 December 1885, Frederick R. Karl and Laurence Davies (eds.), *Collected Letters of Joseph Conrad. Volume I, 1861–1897* (Cambridge, 1983), 16, 'Socialism must inevitably end in Cæsarism'.

9 *Letters to R. B. Cunninghame Graham*, 138–9, 141, 149, 152, 192–93 (31 December 1901, 19 March and 26 December 1903, 28 June 1922).

10 In this passage Swift may be parodying assertions of British pre-eminence as explorers and colonisers, of the kind typified in the 'Epistle Dedicatorie' to the first edition of Hakluyt's *Principal Navigations*, where Englishmen are said to 'have excelled all the nations and people of the earth' (Everyman edition, I.3), cited by Howard Mumford Jones, *O Strange New World. American Culture: The Formative Years* (London, 1965), 183–84.

11 See, for example, 'An Observer in Malaya' (1898), *Notes on Life and Letters*, 58–9; and a letter of 25 December 1899 in Zdzislaw Najder (ed.), *Conrad's Polish Background* (London, 1964), 232: 'liberty . . . can only be found under the English flag all over the world'; see also 242–43, 242n.3, where Conrad is forced to defend himself against accusations of pro-English bias, 16 December 1903. Probably the best discussion of Conrad's complex feelings about imperialism is in Ian Watt, *Conrad in the Nineteenth Century* (London, 1980), 155–61; see also Avrom Fleishman, *Conrad's Politics* (Baltimore, 1967),

79–125, esp. 97–8, 115, 124–25. The most recent book on the subject is Benita Parry, *Conrad and Imperialism* (London, 1983). Marlow praises British imperial rule by contrast with others in *Heart of Darkness*, 50, 55.

12   Lionel Trilling, *Sincerity and Authenticity* (Cambridge, Mass., 1973), 110.

13   For Conrad on the Dutch as colonial rulers, see *Conrad's Polish Background*, 232, and (in fictional treatments) Fleishman, *Conrad's Politics* 85ff., 100ff., 118–19. For Swift, see Ellen Douglass Leyburn, 'Swift's View of the Dutch', *Publications of the Modern Language Association of America*, LXVI (1951), 734–45; J. Kent Clark, 'Swift and the Dutch', *Huntington Library Quarterly*, XVII (1954), 345–56; William J. Brown, 'Gulliver's Passage on the Dutch *Amboyna*', *English Language Notes*, I (1964), 262–64; John A. Dussinger '"Christian" vs. "Hollander": Swift's Satire on the Dutch East India Traders', *Notes and Queries*, CCXI (1966), 209–12. For a number of recent items on more specific aspects of Gulliver's or Swift's view of the Dutch, see Richard H. Rodino, *Swift Studies, 1965–1980: An Annotated Bibliography* (New York, 1984), Nos. 908, 1047, 1059 etc. For the background to popular British dislike of the Dutch in Swift's time, see John Arbuthnot, *The History of John Bull*, ed. Alan W. Bower and Robert A. Erickson (Oxford, 1976), lix–lxvi; and Douglas Coombs, *The Conduct of the Dutch: British Opinion and the Dutch Alliance During the War of Spanish Succession* (The Hague, 1958).

14   See Donald T. Torchiana, 'Jonathan Swift, the Irish, and the Yahoos: The Case Reconsidered,' *Philological Quarterly*, LIV (1975), 195–212 (special number also published separately as *From Chaucer to Gibbon: Essays in Memory of Curt A. Zimansky*, ed. William Kupersmith (Iowa City: U. of Iowa Press, 1975)). As Torchiana notes, the resemblances between the Yahoos and the savage Irish described in Swift's Irish tracts had been remarked on by Sir Charles Firth, 'The Political Significance of *Gulliver's Travels*,' reprinted in Firth's *Essays Historical and Literary* (Oxford: Clarendon Press, 1968), 227 ff. For a perverse interpretation of these resemblances, which sees *Gulliver's Travels* as an anti-slavery tract against the Houyhnhnm treatment of the Yahoos, symbolising England's treatment of the Irish, see Ann Cline Kelly, 'Swift's Explorations of Slavery in Houyhnhnmland and Ireland,' *Publications of the Modern Language Association of America*, XCI (1976), 846–55. For other analogies between Ireland and *Gulliver's Travels*, see Claude Rawson, 'The Injured Lady and the Drapier: A Reading of Swift's Irish Tracts', *Prose Studies*, III (1980), 22 ff.

15   For a fuller discussion of *A Modest Proposal* from this point of view, see below, chapter 3.

16   Montaigne's two most important statements about Amerindians are *Essais*, I. xxxi ('Des Cannibales') and III. vi ('Des Coches').

17   A similar vocabulary of 'brutes', extermination, etc., occurs in Conrad's other Congo story, 'An Outpost of Progress', *Tales of Unrest*, 93, 108 etc.

18   If the language resembles that of Genesis, the situation has also been thought to be reminiscent of the slaughter of helots by the Spartan *krupteia*: see W. H. Halewood, 'Plutarch in Houyhnhnmland: A Neglected Source for Gulliver's Fourth Voyage', *Philological Quarterly*, XLIV (1965), 191; Ian Higgins, 'Swift and Sparta: the Nostalgia of *Gulliver's Travels*', *Modern Language Review*, LXXVIII (1983), 517.

19   Richard Wright, in 'The Ethics of Living Jim Crow', tells of a black boy who was 'castrated and run out of town' and who was to be considered lucky because he was not killed (*Uncle Tom's Children*, New York, 1965, 12). The irony, however, is closer to that of the 'gentle indulgent Manner' of the King of Luggnagg's punishments (III,ix; 205) than to the castration project of the

Houyhnhnms, which Swift is portraying as appropriate to the Yahoos rather than as a Houyhnhnm cruelty. Wright was no stranger to Swiftian irony: he wrote an unpublished pastiche of *A Modest Proposal*, in the form of a letter to President Roosevelt, in 1935, beginning 'Let's eat the Negroes', a copy of which has kindly been made available to me by his widow, Mrs. Ellen Wright, and Professor Michel Fabre.

20   Oliver W. Ferguson, *Jonathan Swift and Ireland* (Urbana, Illinois, 1962), 16. Torchiana, 'Jonathan Swift, the Irish, and the Yahoos' (see n.14 above), 204, points out that Shane Leslie saw a connection in Swift's mind between the passage about castrating the Yahoos and the fact that 'the castration of priests had actually been included in the English penal laws' (*The Skull of Swift*, London, 1928, 263).

21   See Paul Turner (ed.), *Gulliver's Travels*, 373n.6.

22   The following interpret the Fourth Book as an exposure of totalitarian slavery: Michael Wilding, 'The Politics of *Gulliver's Travels*', in R. F. Brissenden (ed.), *Studies in the Eighteenth Century, II* (Canberra, 1973), esp. 313–22; Ann Cline Kelly, 'Swift's Explorations of Slavery' [see n. 14 above].

23   F. R. Leavis, *The Common Pursuit* (Harmondsworth, 1962), 84.

24   Scenes of savages round a fire, as often as not engaged in some cannibal feast, are a staple feature of novels set in primitive lands, from *Robinson Crusoe* (ed. J. Donald Crowley, London, 1976, 164–65, 182 etc.) to the boys' adventure novels of Ballantyne (e.g. *Coral Island*, chapter 19) and others. The model reappears in a modified or ironic form in the primitive or neo-primitive fictions of Golding or of Genet. It seems still to be sufficiently common to come up for playful treatment, which the knowing reader recognises as a fictional stereotype, in children's books of a kind not normally associated with such things. Thus in Mary Norton's *Bedknob and Broomstick* (1945–47), there is an episode in which the three children protagonists and the good witch Miss Price are transported by magic bed to the remote island of Ueepe, where they experience a replay of the classic adventure story situation of being captured by cannibals, blacks with thick lips and flat noses who dance round a fire, with 'flashing teeth, gleaming eyes', and who put Miss Price in the middle of the circle, in order to eat her. (Mary Norton, *Bedknob and Broomstick*, I. viii, Harmondsworth, rev. 1970, rptd 1972, 69–71; a 1982 reprint of the same Puffin edition omits the mention of thick lips, flat noses, flashing teeth and gleaming eyes).

25   This point is more fully discussed in my *Gulliver and the Gentle Reader* (London, 1973), 21–32.

26   The phrase is from 'Geography and Some Explorers', *Last Essays*, 17.

27   For some important reservations about the accountant, see Ian Watt, *Conrad in the Nineteenth Century*, 221: these do not in my view cancel the respect which is shown for the piece-meal achievement.

28   In spite of this passage and the information in n.11 above, Conrad sometimes admired the French as imperialists: see Fleishman, *Conrad's Politics*, 115.

29   Preface, *The Nigger of the 'Narcissus'*, x.

30   The rotten hippo-meat may be compared with the Yahoo diet of putrefied ass's flesh and other disgusting meats (IV, ii, vii, ix; 230, 261, 271). The contrast between Swift's starkly alienating use of this information and Conrad's Marlovian blend of revulsion and puzzled and almost affectionate tolerance will be obvious: the 'Mangeurs-de-choses-immondes' or 'Unclean-Eaters' in Flaubert's *Salammbô* occupy an intermediate position of disgust stripped of moral judgment.

On stinking hippo-meat, see Gide's two African travel-journals, written under the influence of *Heart of Darkness: Voyage au Congo* (1927; dedicated to the memory of Joseph Conrad) and *Le Retour du Tchad* (1928), in *Journal 1939–1949. Souvenirs* (Paris, 1954), 705, 904ff, 909, 913–14. See also Laurens van der Post, *The Lost World of the Kalahari* (Harmondsworth, 1978), 17–18.

On the cannibals' restraint, see Céline's reversal of Conrad's episode in the African part of *Voyage au Bout de la Nuit* (1932). Like Marlow, Céline's Bardamu reports that the blacks could have eaten him but did not, and the reason for this relative decency towards him turns out to be 'crapuleuse': they wanted to sell him as a galley-slave (Livre de Poche edn., Paris, 1952, 179–85). Céline speaks of his cannibals as 'braves gens' (179) in a sarcastic variant of Conrad's 'good fellows'. Céline's novel, like Gide's travel-books, is deeply impregnated with elements from *Heart of Darkness*, though these are refashioned into a harsher and more uncompromising vision, closer in some ways to Swift's.

For some remarks on the theme of 'restraint' in *Heart of Darkness*, see Cedric Watts, *Conrad's Heart of Darkness: A Critical and Contextual Discussion* (Milan, 1977), 98, 104–06.

31 Harold R. Collins, 'Kurtz, the Cannibals, and the Second-Rate Helmsman' (1954), in Leonard F. Dean (ed.), *Joseph Conrad's Heart of Darkness: Backgrounds and Criticisms* (Englewood Cliffs, 1963), 154–55.

32 See Brian V. Street, *The Savage in Literature: Representations of 'Primitive' Society in English Fiction 1858–1920* (London, 1975), 56–59; 68 ff, 136, 173; see also John A. McClure, *Kipling and Conrad* (Cambridge, Mass., 1981), 23–24. For an eighteenth-century view (Kant's, in 1764), rather more unfriendly, of the African Black as childish, see Sander L. Gilman, 'The Figure of the Black in German Aesthetic Theory', *Eighteenth-Century Studies*, VIII (1975), 388–89. The contemptuous view is doubtless the most common; for a nineteenth-century example, see Alan Moorehead, *The White Nile* (Harmondsworth, 1973), 44.

33 Cited in *The Savage in Literature*, 59, 136, 56–57.

34 R. M. Ballantyne, *Coral Island*, Chapters 21, 30; new edn. (London, 1896), 188, 294–95.

35 For some evidence of the special disrepute of 'going native', see McClure, *Kipling and Conrad*, 30, 38, 41–42, 45 ff, 57–58, particularly in relation to Kipling's India.

36 *The Savage in Literature*, 30, 38.

37 Rudyard Kipling, *Stalky & Co.* (London, 1929), 271, 263.

38 See Watts's Introduction to Conrad's *Letters to R. B. Cunninghame Graham*, 19–20; see 19–24 for a good account of Conrad's attitude to Kipling. See also Ian Watt, *Conrad in the Nineteenth Century*, 157–59. McClure's *Kipling and Conrad* is of more limited value.

39 *Letters to R. B. Cunninghame Graham*, 45, 47, and (a somewhat harsher passage), 126 and 127 nn. Conrad wrote an unsigned article, apparently unprinted or lost, defending Kipling (and himself) from some criticisms by Arthur Symons. It is mistakenly said to have appeared in the *Outlook*, 2 April 1898, by Frederick R. Karl, *Joseph Conrad: The Three Lives* (London, 1979), 422, 940n. Professor Karl has kindly informed me of this error.

40 See for example a letter to Frederick Watson of 24 May 1912, responding to a suggestion that he should write a boy's adventure story: 'inventing adventures would not amuse me' (G. Jean-Aubry, *Joseph Conrad: Life and Letters* (London, 1927), II: 139).

41 On Swift's schoolboy analogies, and the figure of the schoolboy in satire,

see my *Henry Fielding and the Augustan Ideal Under Stress* (London, 1972), 175, 171 ff.; and below chapter 5.

42 It is used with various tonalities, from the affectionate to the contemptuous. See John Buchan, *Prester John* (1910; London, 1946), 123, 167, 172, 206; Saul Bellow, *Henderson the Rain King* (1959; Harmondsworth, 1966), 53–54, 55, 56, 93, 122, 123, 162, 226 etc. See also Harriet Beecher Stowe, *Uncle Tom's Cabin* (New York, 1966), 113, 128, 130, 254–55, 384–94.

43 Herman Melville, *Typee*, chapter 8, ed. H. Hayford, H. Parker and G. T. Tanselle (Evanston, 1968), 56.

44 Cited by H. R. Collins (see note 31 above), p. 152, and Norman Sherry, *Conrad's Western World* (Cambridge, 1980), 60, 402 nn.

45 *Coral Island*, chapters 26, 31: 242, 299–300. On relative savageries, see also Street, *The Savage in Literature*, 72.

46 *Coral Island*, chapters 20, 21: 184, 187–88; cf. Street, *The Savage in Literature*, 70–1.

47 Trilling, *Sincerity and Authenticity*, 106–10 (esp 106, 108), 133.

48 Richard Curle, *The Last Twelve Years of Joseph Conrad* (Garden City, N. Y., 1928), 23–24.

49 André Breton, *Anthologie de l'Humour Noir*, new edn. (Paris, 1966), 21, 25.

50 I have discussed aspects of Breton's comment on Swift in *Gulliver and the Gentle Reader*, 34–35.

51 Cf. *Under Western Eyes*, III, iv, where Sophia Antonova says: 'Remember, Razumov, that women, children, and revolutionists hate irony, which is the negation of all saving instincts, of all faith, of all devotion, of all action' (279).

52 *Letters to R. B. Cunninghame Graham*, 116. For Conrad's indignation about the Congo scandal, see 150–51n., and Ford Madox Ford, *Joseph Conrad: A Personal Remembrance* (London, 1924), 95–96, 122, 133–34. On Conrad's general dislike of simplified or absolute attitudes, see the Familiar Preface to *A Personal Record*, xvii–xx.

53 *Letters to R. B. Cunninghame Graham*, 120 nn., 20, 45. Frederick R. Karl thinks this praise of Kipling is contemptuously ironical, *Joseph Conrad: The Three Lives*, 395, but this view seems to me mistaken.

54 *Letters to R. B. Cunninghame Graham*, 126. On Conrad's loyalty to the British in the Boer War, see 127 nn.

55 *Coral Island*, chapter 19: 176.

56 *Letters to R. B. Cunninghame Graham*, 126; Ford, *Joseph Conrad*, 122.

57 *Letters to R. B. Cunninghame Graham*, 27, 65. See also Conrad's letter of 29 August 1908 to Arthur Symons, in G. Jean-Aubry, *Life and Letters*, II. 83.

58 *Letters to R. B. Cunninghame Graham*, 68.

59 For another account of the 'Burke tradition' and Conrad's relation to it, see Fleishman, *Conrad's Politics*, 55–77. See also McClure, *Kipling and Conrad*, 95–96.

60 Cf. 'Socialism must inevitably end in Caesarism' (see above, n. 8).

61 *Letters to R. B. Cunninghame Graham*, 117.

62 Compare Conrad's remarks to Graham (170) on 7 October 1907 about the Professor in *The Secret Agent*: 'every extremist is respectable'. The quality of Conrad's 'respect' is in both letters almost aesthetic, as though the clarity and singlemindedness of attitude took precedence over substance and as though Conrad were taking a playfully cynical holiday from his usual view of extremists, anarchists or revolutionists. See Irving Howe, *Politics and the Novel* (London, 1961), 98.

63 *Letters to R. B. Cunninghame Graham*, 68. For some interesting comments on

this letter, see Karl, *Joseph Conrad: The Three Lives*, 48–50. For a brief statement of differences between Conrad and Hobbes, see Hay, *Political Novels*, 24.
64   Howe, *Politics and the Novel*, 82.

(ii)   Gulliver and Crusoe in Malamudland

In Genesis 6 God said: 'I will destroy man whom I have created from the face of the earth'. He was behaving like a certain kind of satirist, and an untutored reader might even suppose that a satirical author was speaking through Him. The Houyhnhnm Assembly in *Gulliver's Travels* was similarly given to debating 'Whether the *Yahoos* should be exterminated from the Face of the Earth' (a type of proposition Swift entertained in his own name from time to time) or whether they should merely be castrated, a more humanely gradualist project that would achieve the same result in a generation. The gist of these texts, as I argued in the preceding section of this chapter, is that mankind deserves extermination, and they are wholesale extensions of what may once have been the satirist's principal urge and perhaps his magical power: to kill his enemies or, in the sublimated version, to punish the world's malefactors.

There is a de- (or pre-) sublimated version, in which extermination proceeds at the mere whim of the Gods, or the tyrant-satirist. So the Mesopotamian gods of the *Gilgamesh* epic bring down the Flood because men are so noisy that the gods can't sleep, and a Kurtzian character in Céline's *Voyage au bout de la nuit* wishes to exterminate all the 'niggers' because they too keep him awake, adding that he would do so if he weren't so tired.

In *God's Grace*, Bernard Malamud's post–nuclear fabulation, there is a Second Flood, the one which God promised Noah there wouldn't be. It supervenes on the second or terminal Big Bang of nuclear destruction, and it mops up those who escaped that event, on some variation of the principle that he who was born to be drowned shall never be banged. But Malamud's Noah, a paleologist called Calvin Cohn (he changed his first name from Seymour, to the disapproval of his rabbi father), escapes both fates, having 'of all men . . . miraculously survived in a battered oceanography vessel'. The book opens with God patiently explaining that this was a minor error, which He proposes to rectify. For Cohn's survival is not, like Noah's, a reprieve for the virtuous: it 'has nothing to do with your once having studied for the rabbinate, or for that matter, having given it up'. But nor, in intending his elimination, does God have a wish to torment him: it's a question of keeping the system in order, taken as a whole. The Supreme Bureaucrat of this modern theodicy retains something of Jehovah the righteous exterminator, though the offences for which he arranges retribution are less against the old moral law than against the zealous pieties of our post-Romantic, post-Freudian, ecological era. Man is faulted for 'failing to use to a sufficient purpose his possibilities', for 'self-betrayal' and inauthenticity, for his death-wish, and for sins against the environment ('They tore apart my ozone, carbonized my oxygen, acidified my refreshing rain'). God is not unmoved by 'violence, corruption, blasphemy, beastliness, sin beyond belief', but wants them greened out of existence (almost literally: like John Hersey's Hiroshima, Cohn's island's vegetation has vivid accesses of post-nuclear lushness). The old Thunderer has turned ecologist and technocrat, and his vendetta against man retains some of that insouciance which impels some deities old and new to regard a good night's sleep, or tidy book-keeping, as more important than human life.

He knows Himself to be the non-personal God of the new theologians ('Don't presume on Me a visible face . . . I am not that kind'), and the fact is cunningly adapted to highlight the suggestion of *im*personality or unfeelingness. He is the pointed opposite of Crusoe's God, a source of perpetual discomfort rather than reassurance. There is a Big Brotherish side to him, and Cohn feels he'd 'better stay out of his ESP and/or Knowing Eye'. He also has about him a certain aestheticism of the sort that goes with tyrannical fantasy or totalitarian rule, the sort which has sometimes given rise among authors of the last two centuries to intellectual cults of the more depraved Roman emperors, or which animates the Célinian pamphlets of the *Bagatelles pour un massacre* group: Cohn's God 'enjoys performance, spectacle . . . He loves sad stories, with casts of thousands'. There is a link between Céline's Kurtzian exterminator in the *Voyage* and the crazed (and autobiographical) aesthete of the 'pamphlets' just as there is a link between Kurtz's 'Exterminate all the brutes' and the fact that he (like Hitler after him) was a failed artist. Cohn's God is a Being of that kidney, though undercut and made cosy, as much in Malamud is undercut and made cosy, by His creator's irony.

The God of *God's Grace* is an Author, as He has often been of old. But in the manner of our time, He is an academic author, who knows His way around Comparative Religion ('I am not a tribal God; I am Master of the Universe'), who 'liked beginnings and endings' and perhaps has read Edward Said and Frank

Kermode. And in this He is also in the image of His maker, for Malamud's book has its own academic accoutrements, including a Preface which (like that of any learned monograph) acknowledges the Center for Advanced Study in the Behavioral Sciences for institutional support and sundry other persons (including authors and typists) for other help. The very ship in which his Noah-Crusoe survives the Flood is a research institution. His second protagonist Buz, an educated chimpanzee roughly corresponding to Crusoe's Friday, was once a scientist's research specimen. The hero Cohn is himself an academic who, having left his typewriter on the abandoned ship (thinking only, Crusoe-like, to write up his adventures by hand), lives to regret it because he wants to 'knock out an article or two' about the bones and fossils of his island. As further monkeys come to light, adding themselves to Buz-Friday, he founds what is in effect a Simian University, with courses in Scripture, theology, literature and evolution. Cohn's island, it might be said, is a campused-up version of Crusoe's.

The plot follows *Crusoe* closely (uninhabited island, self-reliance in inhospitable surroundings, lesser breeds patiently taught civilised ways), but with all the purposeful optimism finally put into a Gulliverian or Goldingesque reverse. From *Gulliver's Travels*, itself sometimes thought of as a *Crusoe* parody, Malamud borrows a few stylistic flourishes (straightfaced enumerations, a bit of scatological comedy here and there), some Yahoo behaviour, and a number of specific episodes, including one or two which play on man's kinship to near-resembling brutes. The Brobdingnagian monkey who takes Gulliver for a baby of its own kind, and 'held me as a Nurse doth a Child she is going to suckle', is a model for some scenes in which Buz 'mounted Cohn's lap and attempted to suckle him' (as far as I can make out from the tangle of transgeneric intimacy, in which both pairs of participants are male, Malamud differs from Swift in using 'suckle' to mean what the child does to the nurse and not vice versa). A second and parallel Gulliverian episode, in which a female Yahoo makes amorous advances to the hero, is elaborated by Malamud into the story of Mary Madelyn, the female chimp whose love-affair with her teacher Cohn is a main part of the action.

It all begins when Mary Madelyn, in heat, runs away from pursuing male chimps, putting this unnatural coyness down to the learning of human speech. It might appear that speech confers shame as part of the human inheritance, but she is eager to mate with teacher Cohn, as if aspiring to raise herself from a low racial group. Esau the Alpha Ape thinks of her as a kind of uppity nigger and tells Cohn 'your stupid schooltree has made her too proud to dip her butt for friends'. The burgeoning love between professor and student has the lineaments of a college romance. They walk together holding hands amid the campus palm trees. 'When they rested she groomed his balding head. In turn, he groomed her breasts and belly. They talked as friends'. Buz complains that she's not Cohn's kind, and Cohn of course replies that there's 'only one kind'. '"We're sort of affectionately in love," he told Buz, "or something close to it."'

Connoisseurs of that archetypal figure of modern American fiction known as the WISP (White Intellectual Sublimated Professor) will recognise here a less than wholeheartedly sensuous response. Certainly the idea of actually mounting the lovelorn lady is at first repellent to the Gulliver in him. He responds to her advances by citing biblical interdictions against cross-breeding of all kinds, and human mating with beasts in particular. But she stumps him by asking whether he thinks of her as a beast, and he is forced, in all intellectual consistency, to back down with a pondered 'not really'.

Meanwhile, it is poor Buz who has to practise the sublimation Cohn has taught him the meaning of, collecting rare stones and shells and taking up algebra, while the balding professor follows the classic scenario, eventually dipping his phallus into the hot flower of the fair co-ed. It is only right to add, however, that the latter's female wiles do not seem to have been motivated by any ambition for improved grades, and that she does not subsequently accuse the professor of sexual harassment. Malamud's universe is more innocent than the modern university by at least a generation.

The mating is done swiftly and without foreplay or afterplay. 'There was an instant electric connection and Cohn parted with his seed'. Mary Madelyn 'waited . . . for more to happen, but when nothing more did, she chewed up a fig and fell asleep in his bed'. Human capability has been measured against simian expectation. Later, when the apes have reverted to full apehood, Buz (whose human voice-box has been symbolically disconnected by Cohn a page or two earlier) gratifies Mary Madelyn with multiple penetration, displacing the arrogant Esau as Alpha Ape. Esau, like Cohn, only 'pumped once', eating a bruised banana before and after, so it is not after all a mere difference of species: both man and monkey come over in a subdued glow of Malamudian feeling for the pathos of the spent phallus.

'Bananas!' image-sleuths will exclaim knowingly, as well they might. There are bananas everywhere. When we first meet Esau the Alpha Ape, he devours the basketful of bananas with which Cohn decides to win over (Malamud's word is 'woo') the small gang of chimps to which he belongs. Bananas are Cohn's chief instrument of persuasion and the first weapon in the armoury of his benevolent despotism. He even serves 'bananas flambé' at his seder of Thanksgiving 'for our own personal escape from the Second Flood'. Everywhere in the book we see apes eating bananas and getting drunk on banana beer. They hunt for them and fight over them. Banana-eating accompanies couplings, and sometimes a chimp like little Saul of Tarsus, faced with a girl-monkey and a banana, 'felt amorous and . . . felt hungry, yet not at all sure which desire grabbed him most'.

But do not jump to conclusions, reader. A bunch of bananas is not just an image-cluster, not even of the phallic sort. It is food and drink to most monkeys, though Calvin Cohn and Sigmund Freud have other ideas. When Cohn holds a little tutorial on the subject of metaphor, 'Like when a banana is conceived to symbolize a man's phallus', Buz (who was taught to speak by a German-born scientist) replies 'I don't believe it. I don't think a phollus is a bonona. I eat bononas, I don't eat pholluses'. Cohn might have disabused him with a Gulliverian disclosure that such 'politer Pleasures' did indeed exist 'on our Side of the Globe', but perhaps he hadn't read the report of a learned francophone Freudian symposium on cannibals which recently spoke of 'cette forme tendre du cannibalisme qu'est la fellation'. But Buz knows what's for eating and what not, and even Saul of Tarsus knows, though he doesn't know which to prefer.

After trying to teach Buz all about metaphor, Cohn proceeds to intertextuality and perhaps to some primitive form of the anxiety of influence ('He wanted to know where stories came from. Cohn said from other stories'). Buz hasn't a lot of time for the logos of the old scriptures, preferring Jesus of Nozoreth who 'preached to the chimponzees' in some word-transcending idiom ('"In what language?" "I don't know thot. We heard His voice in our ears"'). Talmudic commentators ('who told stories about stories') leave him cold and, disliking violence, he generally prefers the New Testament to the Old. He 'liked happy endings' rather than senses of endings: '"God is love," he said', with half a thought on that 'intercourse' which he is told Adam and Eve had together ('When will I get some of it?') and no thought at all on the bossy Jehovah whom Cohn has been encountering uneasily throughout. The Thunderer not surprisingly thunders at this point ('Is thot bod?', asks Buz). All this time Cohn is explaining Abraham and Isaac to him, and promising to wheel in Kierkegaard and Freud before much longer ('Do I hov to know everything?'). Cohn keeps on retelling the Abraham–Isaac story 'though it seemed to get more involved every time he retold it. Buz said he thought it was a pretty simple story'. Cohn's reward for this at the end is that Buz will re-enact the story in reverse, leaving his 'dod' Cohn to what will be his extinction, and that of the human race, without benefit of sacrificial ram, in a final rite that puts God's books in order. It is the 'Dying Whimper of man' which Cohn intertextually predicted in his schooltree lectures on the cosmos.

Cohn's ambition is to restart civilisation on a more ethical base than the last, and he pins his hopes on an evolutionary development of the island's chimpanzees. This he expects to help along not only by education (including accounts of evolution from the great apes to man, and cautionary warnings about the human instinct for overkill and self-destruction), but, when he comes to mate with Mary Madelyn, by genetic means. The thought fills him with a kind of punning awe: 'monkey with evolution? That much chutzpah?' (Malamud's punning itch is rather furious. Cohn wonders whether to call his island the Chimpan Zee, and when he is treacherously assaulted by his ape-subjects exclaims 'Et tu, Buz?'). But he goes ahead with it, and the humanoid product looks as if she might become an effective instrument for the fresh evolutionary start. (Hermeneutically disposed readers will be pleased to know that she is called Rebekah, which by a happy coincidence was also the name of the oceanographic boat on which Cohn survived the Flood.)

But just as Cohn's programme begins to look hopeful, there is a Goldingesque savage reversion. Led by Esau, the chimps capture and eat Sara, a girl baboon. The cannibal act is of a gastronomic rather than ritual nature, so some anthropologists will find the book full of improbable lies and won't believe a word of it. It is also racially aggressive, the baboons being of another racial type: Esau says monkeys should look like monkeys and not have dog faces. Cohn is outraged, because the act is committed by rather advanced apes, unlike 'the naive chimpanzees of the past, many of whose recent progenitors had performed as comedians in vaudeville, television, zoos'. The words hint winkingly at the recent social evolution of guess who, and we recall that the monkeys on Cohn's island take the place of the human cannibals on Crusoe's, with Buz in the role of Friday. No doubt it is awkward for Malamud, as it wasn't for Defoe, to ascribe cannibalism to humans of other races, but it might occur to some readers that a monkey-allegory was not perhaps the most graceful way out of that particular difficulty.

Crusoe's Friday is converted from his cannibal ways, while Cohn's subjects 'revert' to them. It is arguable that both processes are the result of the White Man's educational project. The chimps' reversion not only occurs at an advanced stage of the programme, but Esau protests that it is a reaction against the unnatural restraints it imposes, including 'that horseass sublimation you are trying to trick on us'. Buz once protested to Cohn, a vegetarian by ecological conviction, that 'I'm on onimol and hov always been a vegetorion', though he will readily swallow every fish in a Portuguese sardine-tin. Esau, 'sick and tired of eating so much goddam fruit', says that chimps in the old days hunted small baboons: 'The hunt was stimulating and the flesh delicious'. So a teasing question-mark hovers over whether the cannibal acts are mainly to be seen as features of their human or their simian nature.

In Golding's *Lord of the Flies* and *The Inheritors*, which the later parts of this novel call to mind, there is no falling back on an animal allegory and therefore no doubt that whatever 'unspeakable rites' are perpetrated, they are unequivocally human. Only, in Golding, the 'unspeakable' remains unspoken: for all the relentless intimations in both novels, I do not think there is a single phrase actually naming a cannibal act outright. Conrad, who coined the phrase 'unspeakable rites' from the sensationalising vocabulary of adventure-stories like *Coral Island* (Golding's main source), applied it to the doings of Kurtz, also presumably cannibal and also never defined: the only outright references to cannibalism in *Heart of Darkness* involve black Africans who, in the story, actually refrain from any cannibal act. The irony of that is that the word 'cannibal' is used of black men who don't do it and not of the white man who evidently does.

Such reticences are a common feature of modern fiction in its often obsessive encounters with the cannibal theme. In Genet's *Pompes funèbres* and Monique Wittig's *Le Corps lesbien* cannibal acts of a homosexual character are indeed explicitly and graphically described: what remains uncertain in these books is not the nature of the act but the extent to which it 'happened', if at all, as distinct from being a fantasy in the characters' minds. We know what it is but not whether they did it, whereas in Kurtz's case we know that he did it but not what it was.[1]

112

In Malamud's novel there is another variation on this manoeuvre. We know what was done and we know that it happened, not only with poor Sara but with other baboons and then with baby Rebekah. But it is done by creatures not in every way human, and secondary uncertainties are introduced as to whether or not it is the humanoid or the bestial element in them which is chiefly responsible. If it is the bestial, a large part of the allegory becomes flaccid, but the full harsh truth which would make this allegory as bitter as the one similarly intended by Golding's novels is, as in Golding, not wholeheartedly proffered. Like much else in Malamud's book, the result is schmaltzy and fudged, as fudged and more schmaltzy than the books of other modern masters who have flirted with the cannibal theme, not knowing how to deal with it but unable to leave it alone. Crusoe's old-fashioned directness, which furnishes one of Malamud's epigraphs, might seem to do it better: 'I came upon the horrible remains of a cannibal feast'.

1982

Notes

1   Such reticences are discussed more fully in my study 'Cannibalism and Fiction, Part II: Love and Eating in Fielding, Mailer, Genet, and Wittig', *Genre*, XI (1978), 227–313, esp. 276 ff, 287 ff, and 290 ff.

(iii)   Little People: Mary Norton and Lilliputian Stories

'When once you have thought of big men and little men, it is very easy to do all the rest', said Dr Johnson of *Gulliver's Travels*. This might do for a put-down of Swift, whom Johnson disliked, perhaps from a sense of likeness. But big men and little men have old folkloric origins, so the idea in itself was not new: as more than one character says in Mary Norton's *Borrower* books, 'our ancestors spoke openly about "the little people"'. *Gulliver's Travels* bears an intriguing relation to children's books. It is not 'for nothing that, suitably abbreviated, it has become a classic for children': Leavis's oracular utterance, like Johnson's, was intended as a put-down. And 'suitable abbreviation' has tended to mean the removal of Books 3 and 4, which leaves 'big men and little men', usually stripped of the more stinging harshnesses of Books 1 and 2.

This involves a separation of 'satire' from 'story' which serious readers might consider deeply untrue to *Gulliver's Travels*. It

113

'works', since there's no doubt of the success of the children's adaptations. But I suspect that the separation, which sentimental-ises children, is equally untrue to the idea of what a good children's book might be. The severity of Swift's disenchanted wisdom is doubtless something children are unlikely to be able to grasp. Perhaps they even need protecting from its full force. It's arguable that *Gulliver's Travels*, read with a sensitive awareness of its full implications, might be more disturbing to a young mind than much of the insignificant twaddle that gets banned for 'pornography' and 'obscenity'. But what seems certain is that the simple distinction implied by Leavis and by the bowdlerisers alike, and the mechanical scissors-and-paste surgery which would leave you with a story about little or big people stripped of 'satirical' elements, involves a misconception about what some good children's books are like.

Mary Norton's Borrowers are 'little people' and, as may become evident, the books about them have lots of Gulliverian elements, whether 'borrowed' directly or absorbed as a gen-eralised influence. Borrowers aren't nasty like some Lilliputians, and tend to be victims rather than villains. They have their vices (petty snobberies, for example), as Lilliputians do, and home truths about them are truths about human beings, transposed. Such alternative humanoid species, whether in children's fiction or in moral allegories, always carry a potential for satirical conversion or for stinging recognitions of likeness. Though by no means primarily satirical, the Borrower books occasionally erupt into severities that would not be out of place in the harshest satire. In *The Borrowers Avenged* it is said of Mr and Mrs Platter, the wicked full-sized humans who wish to capture the Borrowers and exhibit them for profit, that, as part-time undertakers by trade, they regretted that 'people were not dying as often as they used to'. These are the accents of Swift's Modest Proposer, satisfied that people are 'every Day *dying*, and *rotting*, . . . as fast as can be reasonably expected'. The resemblance, whether coincidental or otherwise (a similar thing is said, by the way, in *Uncle Tom's Cabin*), momentarily shows the Platters not as the fairy-tale ogres they partly are, nor as cardboard villains who bring a note of menace to a nursery idyll, but as nasty specimens viewed from a knowing and sophisticated adult perspective. The fact that this sarcastic eruption seems neither unbalancing nor discordant tells us something about what children's books can absorb without strain, and suggests that the schematic demarcations between satire and children's classic which sometimes get into discussions

114

of *Gulliver's Travels* lack insight into children as well as into satire. If *Gulliver's Travels* became a formative influence on the way children's books treat 'little people', this is not confined to the use of an allegorical formula nor necessarily a matter of mere playful fancy.

I mean 'little people' in the precise Lilliputian sense of one twelfth of human height, as in the books by T. H. White or Mary Norton. Borrowers are about 'five or six inches'. Little people can come in various other sizes, small as a thumb or smaller (Andersen's Thumbelina fits into a walnut-shell), or, in the case of full-sized dwarfs or midgets, two or three feet, which is the usual range in real life. Bruno Bettelheim, whose book on fairy tales reads like the work of a Laputian philosopher, says dwarfs symbolise a phallic existence. It's lucky that he didn't take in Lilliputians, whose size is actually that of a human phallus, for he would have been less amusing about the implications than Swift was, and a good deal less brief. Children's books about Lilliputians are not explicit about such things, and if a darker theme attaches to their dimensions, it has more to do with fears of extinction than with subterranean sexuality. They are easily crushed underfoot and otherwise at the mercy of forces which to full-sized humans are normal unmenacing features of daily life. The extraordinary and sustained pathos of the Borrower books comes largely from this.

In this special sense of 'little people', ordinary dwarfs don't count, nor that Tom Thumb who (we are told in *The Borrowers*), being 'nearly two feet high, would seem a giant to a Borrower': this may refer to some real-life dwarf to whom the name was attached, like the famous Charles Stratton, 'General Tom Thumb', for the Tom Thumb of early ballad or folk-tradition was sometimes literally 'but an inch in height'. It's essential for little people not to be 'real-life', though fully 'human' within their alternative world. Dwarfs are within the range of quotidian experience, while Lilliputians and Borrowers are totally outside it. Where dwarfs are merely unnaturally small, and can be called freaks, the others are a separate form of life. The philosophers of Brobdingnag (where Gulliver himself is a 'Lilliputian') come in for scorn when they solemnly opine that Gulliver is a *lusus naturae*, though they rightly 'would not allow me to be a Dwarf, because my Littleness was beyond all Degrees of Comparison'. As if to make the point, Swift gives us a Brobdingnagian dwarf who, like Tom Thumb to Borrowers, is a giant to Gulliver. One of the themes of 'little people' books, especially prominent in *The*

Borrowers Avenged, is the exceptional wrongness, beyond ordinary cruelty or insensitivity, of displaying such creatures in circuses and shows, as men do with dwarfs. Lilliputians and Borrowers are, on their terms, 'normal': it's important that they are never misshapen or misproportioned as dwarfs are often supposed to be, but perfect replicas of human form and psyche, on an alternative scale. They are at once totally like us, 'as like to humans as makes no matter', and totally other. That otherness is so absolute that it argues impossibility. The greater the human likeness and the more 'realistic' the portrayal, the greater the disbelief we are invited (or challenged) to suspend. Teasing uncertainties about their existence, even within the stories in which they are principal actors, as it were *given*, attend upon their appearances. It is never fully clear whether they have been really 'seen'. The curious play of affirmation and doubt which so often surrounds their presentation exemplifies some of the ploys and defences with which fiction (not just in children's books and allegorical fantasies) manipulates our credulity, and acknowledges or half-admits the limits on its power to do so.

The freak-show theme turns up with some insistence. In the first two books of *Gulliver's Travels* it is prominent but in a sense desultory. It provides some narrative interest without being very strongly integrated into the satire, beyond sparking off a number of reflections on the natural malignity of man. Swift knew quite a bit about the shows. Plenty of dwarfs were exhibited in his day, but no Lilliputians. Fiction's explanation of the lack is that Gulliver was forbidden by the Emperor of Blefuscu to bring any away, though he took with him some tiny sheep and cattle, which he was able to show to 'many Persons of Quality' for 'a considerable Profit', as well as to sell and breed successfully in England. That these were therefore 'seen' is part of the authenticating tease ('real life' got its own back when later circus-masters developed a habit of giving to ordinary dwarfs the name of Lilliputians). Captain John Biddel, who brought Gulliver back from Lilliput in his ship, was apparently not so scrupulous as Gulliver. According to T. H. White, he brought away quantities of Blefuscan and Lilliputian people for exhibition 'among the Fair Grounds of the Kingdom', but they escaped from his drunken custody and settled on a small island in the grounds of the Palace of Malplaquet in Northamptonshire known as *Mistress Masham's Repose*, where their descendants are living to this day.

T. H. White's book of that name came out in 1947, and tells of a dastardly plot by the wicked Miss Brown and the Reverend Hater to get rich by capturing and exhibiting them for profit, as Captain Biddel did with their ancestors. They are protected by the young ducal heiress Maria, who is a giantess to them, as Gulliver is cared for by the young giantess Glumdalclitch (though *he* doesn't escape the freak shows). *Mistress Masham's Repose* appeared five years before *The Borrowers* (1952) and is a kind of intermediary between *Gulliver's Travels* and the Borrower series: *The Borrowers Afield* (1955), *The Borrowers Afloat* (1959), *The Borrowers Aloft* (1961), and now, after 21 years, *The Borrowers Avenged*. Borrowers live in small family groups, mostly 'under the floors and behind the wainscots' of old houses, and subsist on scraps of food and equipment 'borrowed' from the human occupants. The threat of capture for profit occasionally raises its head in the earlier volumes, but first becomes prominent in *The Borrowers Aloft*, where the wicked Platters abduct little Pod and his family in order to exhibit them. They escape through the air in a basket attached to a balloon, as Gulliver in his box was flown out of Brobdingnag by a large bird, a standard folk-tale or tall-tale adventure also experienced by Tom Thumb and Cyrano de Bergerac.

In *The Borrowers Avenged*, a fresh attempt by the Platters to capture and exhibit the Borrowers becomes the main concern of the plot, as in *Mistress Masham's Repose*, and they are similarly foiled in a bustling and eventful climax. The role of Maria/ Glumdalclitch is played by the kindly Miss Menzies, who, like Gulliver's giant protectress, makes clothes for them and provides them with the comforts of a doll's house. Miss Menzies has 'Gulliver-like strides', and the perspective of the Borrower books is largely Lilliputian, unlike that of *Mistress Masham's Repose* or Swift's Lilliput, where things are seen through the giant eyes of Maria or Gulliver. But it is Brobdingnag which is closer to Mary Norton's story, and it is in Brobdingnag, where Gulliver is the only little person, that the angle of vision is Borrower-like, both because it is the small person's and because of Gulliver's solitary vulnerability.

In T. H. White, as in Swift, the Lilliputians are populous communities, advanced nations: 'the Lilliputians were not toys. They were grown up ... and they were civilized. Lilliput and Blefuscu had been countries of high civilization'. The Borrowers are a few scattered families, not nations. There is no original Borrowerland where everything is to scale, no Borrower-sized sheep or cattle, only an alien 'human' environment: Arrietty reflects 'how many millions of human beings there were in the world, and how few borrowers'. We see them in tiny groups,

117

struggling to survive, with an extraordinary loneliness about them. The predicament of Gulliver in the giant grass, or confronting a Brobdingnagian rat, is closer to them in spirit than the elaborate imperial concerns of the Lilliputians, whose dimensions they share in actual as distinct from relative arithmetic. Their survival is correspondingly more precarious. In novel after novel, Pod and his family have to uproot just because some apparently harmless sighting has occurred. No story about them is ever finally resolved, with the tidy closure we might expect from children's stories. Some event remains unexplained, someone's fate uncertain or their whereabouts untraced. Villains remain unpunished and menacing. The titles (*Afield, Afloat, Aloft*) suggest thrusting movement and an open end. The new book is unusual in the participial finality of its *Avenged*, which suggests both closure and poetic justice. The Platters seem at last to have been caught and brought to book. But in fact 'the borrowers never discovered *exactly*' what happened to them. Arrietty longs to let Miss Menzies know the Borrowers are safe, but Peagreen, 'smiling his quizzical, one-sided smile', says ' "Are we? Ever?" ' I hope this means there'll be more Borrowers books, but it's likely that none is going to end happily ever after.

Extinction is a more urgent fear than that 'Indignity . . . to be exposed for Money as a publick Spectacle' which afflicts Gulliver. Protestations that they're grown-up, civilised, 'not toys', are less to the fore. They would in fact like nothing better than a doll's-house existence, and the one Miss Menzies strives to give them in good Mr Pott's model village would be a dream, or at least an Ideal Homes Exhibition, come true. For Borrowers the main thing wrong with exhibition is not the indignity but the fact that it's a public and formalised extension of being 'seen', and as Miss Menzies tells Mr Pomfret the policeman, 'to be seen by a human being might be the death of their race'. He says she says she has seen them and she replies: 'I have been very privileged'.

The term comes over with a quasi-technical flavour, an inadvertent whiff of litcritspeak. It evokes a special grace or magical access within the strict rules of a fictional game. Only a few very special children are privileged, and one or two grown-ups like Miss Menzies, a 'kind of overgrown schoolgirl' who believed in fairies. The rules serve to explain why *you're* not going to see them. Borrowers don't, for example, stay 'where there are careless people, unruly children', so if you aren't privileged it's probably because you don't live up to certain standards, a species of realistic cover which exploits that mild guilt-inducing element on which children's books thrive. But there's a sort of reverse magic, the obverse of 'privilege', by which a few deep villains, like the Platters, can see and even touch a Borrower, as though the mystery were accessible only to the very innocent or the very vicious, at moral extremes which bypass normal adult vision.

Non-privileged persons who 'see' Borrowers, like gipsy Mild Eye and Mrs Whitlace, who believed in fairies, can't confirm it or are never really sure. Great Aunt Sophy speaks to Pod nightly but only after her third glass of Madeira, because after that she 'never believed in anything she saw'. She looks forward to these talks, which she believes to be fictive, and Pod consents to take part only because she'll never think they're for real. Arrietty once complained that it's sad 'to belong to a race that no sane person believes in', but that's a maverick view since the Borrowers know they wouldn't survive if people knew about them. The words are also a doubt-defying ploy, and it is a condition of the story that doubts should both be conceded or even humoured *and* also cunningly allayed. On the one hand, the narration is hearsay and often at two or three removes from the speaker; privileged narrators like Tom Goodenough are known liars; Mrs May, who is the main narrator, 'never saw' a Borrower and says her brother told her the story or 'made it up. If it was made up'. On the other hand, there are moments of what seems to be authorial reassurance. And there is 'objective' evidence, like that of Arrietty's notebook, 'not quite' conclusive, but tending that way. There are all those missing small objects, 'safety-pins, needles, pencils', the drawer 'never found ... quite as you left it', the slightly diminished stock of tea or sugar, which can only be accounted for by 'borrowing'. And Borrowers are good at doing things which look like something else, open to the 'natural cause' explanations akin to what an older litcritspeak called the *surnaturel expliqué*. Pod chips out some footholes which 'for years after ... were considered by naturalists to be the work of the greater spotted woodpecker', a fact which may remind us of the learned explanations of the Gulliver phenomenon by the scientists of Lilliput and Brobdingnag.

The toing and froing between 'it's true' and 'it's only a story' is essential to the more 'incredible' kind of story, and perhaps to all fiction. *Ce livre est vrai et c'est une blague*: Genet's words resemble the oscillations of Mrs May, and the refusal to distinguish in his novels between what 'really happened' and what happened only in the mind are in one sense a self-conscious replay of the same narrative impulse, remote as these novels are from the gentle

119

world of Arrietty and Pod. The Gulliverian tall story similarly oscillates between a cheeky flaunting of improbability and protestations of veracity backed by 'objective' evidence. And it 'worked', sometimes better than Swift meant, since the satire depends on your not taking the book straight. Some readers took out their map, or claimed to know Gulliver. But the prize gull was the Irish bishop who thought 'that Book was full of improbable lies, and . . . hardly believed a word of it', for he was a true product of the uncertainty principle, taken in precisely as he preened himself on not having been.

The Borrowers, like other 'improbable' fictions, thrive on the same curious bid to keep disbelief in suspension at the very moment when they most invite that disbelief. The danger of being 'seen' not only menaces the Borrowers' existence but also the story's. They depend on an odd fictional contract which ensures that we 'believe' in them only as long as we are allowed to doubt them. If there were no rules preventing our world from seeing theirs, their existence would be either disproved or demystified: the tale would then have no truth, or else no strangeness worth the telling. After his return from Houyhnhnmland, Gulliver considers his 'Duty as a Subject of *England*' to report its location 'to a Secretary of State'. He decides not to, because any attempt to take over the Houyhnhnms as a crown colony would simply make them destroy us. One lesson of this is anti-imperialist. The other is that when an 'alternative' fictional world is fully exposed to ours, it seems that one or the other must die: if all of us could see the Borrowers, they would be exterminated, as we should be if we saw the Houyhnhnms. The secrecy which protects the survival of both sides is the one which protects the fiction. If everybody saw the Lilliputians, or the Houyhnhnms, or the Borrowers, it would be the same as if nobody did, so we may as well leave such sightings to Gulliver, and Maria, and Tom Goodenough, and take their word for it.

1983

3

A Reading of A Modest Proposal

The title is famous, but still bears examination: *A Modest Proposal for Preventing the Children of Poor People from Being a Burthen to their Parents, or the Country, and for Making them Beneficial to the Publick.*[1] The form of title is that of many 'modest proposals' and 'humble petitions' which appeared in the seventeenth and eighteenth centuries, 'dealing with economic problems, particularly with problems concerning population, labor, unemployment, and poverty'.[2] It captures accurately the conventional postures: concern for the public good, profitability, the air of planned or scientific management of human material. It is hard for the modern reader, more familiar with the gruesome irony of Swift's *Modest Proposal* than with conventional formulas of pamphleteering, to realise that the title would be taken quite straight and give no hint of shocks to follow. At the same time, it would be wrong to infer, when the shocks do come, that what is at work in any important sense is 'a burlesque on projects concerning the poor' or 'on the titles of certain types of economic tracts'.[3] If there is a poker-faced mimicry of these things, it is only a seasoning, not the main point. And to suggest that Swift was radically attacking the notion of economic planning of human affairs, or even that his attitude on certain central questions (poverty, beggars, the care of children) was 'humane' or 'liberal' in a sense which a modern reader would understand or assent to, is misleading.

A crucial part of the title speaks of preventing the children of the poor 'from Being a Burthen to their Parents, or the Country'. Swift himself used this sort of phrase unironically and (some readers might feel) quite callously when, for example, he noted that society ought to be protected from strolling beggars, and proposed schemes for reducing the 'burden' to the community (IX: 191, 209; XIII: 132, 137).[4] Wittkowsky has shown that behind such a phrase, in the social thinking of the day, lay a

121

hard-headed distinction between the 'able' and the 'impotent', or unproductive, poor.[5] The latter (including the sick, beggars, vagrants etc.), unable to work for their keep, are, in the words of Charles Davenant in 1699, 'nourish'd at the Cost of Others; and are a Yearly Burthen to the Publick'. The seventeenth-century economist, Sir William Petty, commenting on losses from the plague, regretted that the plague made no distinction between 'the bees and the drones', but killed 'promiscuously'.[6]

More recently, an Irish law of George I's reign 'classified unemployable children as impotent poor', declaring that there were many children who had to beg and who thus risked becoming ' "*not only unprofitable but dangerous to their country*" '. The act empowered 'the ministers to bind out these children to tradesmen, provision being made to prevent cruel treatment'. Wittkowsky also cites a work of 1695–6, *A Modest Proposal for the More Certain and yet More Easie Provision for the Poor. And Likewise for the Better Suppression of Thieves. . . . Tending Much to the Advancement of Trade, Especially in the most Profitable Part of it.*[7] This plan advocates the setting up of workhouse-hospitals and workhouse-prisons, and answers the objection 'that the plan will be a needless burden on the public, "in loading it with the Charge of so many children" ' by saying that ' " . . . it is a fault not to encourage the increase of Lawful Children, especially when they are likely to be train'd up in all Frugality and Industry" '. This training will be inexpensive, and ' "a mighty Advantage to the Public" '.

It is tempting to think of Swift's *Modest Proposal* as a parody of this kind of thing. But there is no reason to suppose that his own attitude was radically different, or to attribute to him a Dickensian protest about child-labour. He was no exception to Dorothy Marshall's statement that 'Despite the growth of the Charity School movement, charity to children in the seventeenth and eighteenth centuries meant enabling them to earn their own living at the earliest possible moment, no matter how laborious their life might be'.[8] In his sermon on the 'Causes of the Wretched Condition of Ireland' he gave qualified support to Charity Schools, agreeing, as Louis Landa has pointed out, with those criticisms of the schools which said that they had failed in their purpose of supplying cheap labour, and had over-educated their pupils, making them unfit for menial work (IX: 130, 202ff.).[9] He argued in particular that the schools ought to instil in their pupils a 'teachable Disposition' (a phrase, as it happens, which calls to mind the Houyhnhnm master's patronising praise of the Yahoo Gulliver, IV: iii; *Works*, XI: 234) in order to make of them good household servants, since the common run of servants were, in Swift's view, an idle and vicious lot (IX: 204–5, 203ff.). He made it clear that pupils must 'be severely punished for every Neglect' in study, religion, cleanliness, honesty, industry and thrift. After this training, they should be 'bound Apprentices in the Families of Gentlemen and Citizens, (for which a late Law giveth great Encouragement)' – the late law being the one cited by Wittkowsky presumably as an instance of what Swift would be inclined to deplore.[10] They would thus be learning useful things while being at the same time 'very useful in a Family, as far as their Age and Strength would allow' (IX: 205). In such a passage, Swift gets close to the flat economic utilitarianism which the *Modest Proposal* is alleged to be attacking.

Swift's comments on Charity Schools in the sermon have yet more light to throw on the *Proposal*. He argued that the children admitted to these schools should be those of 'honest Parents' struck by misfortune, rather than

> the Brood of wicked Strolers; for it is by no means reasonable, that the Charity of well-inclined People should be applied to encourage the Lewdness of those profligate, abandoned Women, who croud our Streets with their borrowed or spurious Issue.
>
> (IX: 202)

(Cf. Swift's distinction in the *Modest Proposal* between 'Beggars by Profession' and those worthy persons who have become 'Beggars in Effect' because of the wretched condition of Ireland, XII: 117.) It was also wrong, except in the bigger well-endowed schools, to train poor children to anything but 'the very meanest Trades':

> otherwise the poor honest Citizen who is just able to bring up his Child, and pay a small Sum of Money with him to a good Master, is wholly defeated, and the Bastard Issue, perhaps, of some Beggar, preferred before him. And hence we come to be so over-stocked with 'Prentices and Journeymen, more than our discouraged Country can employ; and, I fear, the greatest Part of our Thieves, Pickpockets, and other Vagabonds are of this Number.
>
> (IX: 203)

Against the background of such passages, the opening paragraphs of the *Modest Proposal* acquire an irony a good deal less simple than is normally thought:

It is a melancholly Object to those, who walk through this great Town, or travel in the Country; when they see the *Streets*, the *Roads*, and *Cabbin-doors* crowded with *Beggars* of the Female Sex, followed by three, four, or six Children, *all in Rags*, and importuning every Passenger for an Alms. These *Mothers*, instead of being able to work for their honest Livelyhood, are forced to employ all their Time in stroling to beg Sustenance for their *helpless Infants*; who, as they grow up, either turn *Thieves* for want of Work; or leave their *dear Native Country, to fight for the Pretender in* Spain, or sell themselves to the *Barbadoes*.

I think it is agreed by all Parties, that this prodigious Number of Children in the Arms, or on the Backs, or at the *Heels* of their *Mothers*, and frequently of their *Fathers*, is *in the present deplorable State of the Kingdom*, a very great additional Grievance; and therefore, whoever could find out a fair, cheap, and easy Method of making these Children sound and useful Members of the Commonwealth, would deserve so well of the Publick, as to have his Statue set up for a Preserver of the Nation.

(XII: 109)

If there is compassion in this passage, it is no straightforward feeling. Swift was intensely hostile to beggars. 'There is not a more undeserving vicious Race of human Kind than the Bulk of those who are reduced to Beggary, even in this beggarly Country', he wrote in 1737, in a serious sociological tract, the *Proposal for Giving Badges to the Beggars* (XIII: 135). This explosive irritation recalls the King of Brobdingnag's 'little odious Vermin' speech (*Gulliver's Travels*, II: vi, *Works*, XI: 132). But Swift went further, in the same late tract, making his own Modest Proposer seem modest indeed by comparison, when he added that the strolling beggars from the country were 'fitter to be rooted out off the Face of the Earth, than suffered to levy a vast annual Tax upon the City' (XIII: 139): the Gulliverian analogy here, as we have seen, is with the Houyhnhnms who debate 'Whether the *Yahoos* should be exterminated from the Face of the Earth' (*Gulliver's Travels*, IV: ix; XI: 271). This is, no doubt, a rhetoric of exasperation and not an advocacy of massacre. But we should recognise squarely that this exasperation is present also in the *Modest Proposal*, and that ridding society of its beggarly 'burdens' was not a notion which Swift identified exclusively with the cant of the profiteering and the inhumane. If Yeats was right that Swift

A *Reading of* A Modest Proposal

'understood that wisdom comes of beggary' ('The Seven Sages'), Swift would not have understood what Yeats meant. The beggars were usually poor through their own fault.[11] The notion runs through the whole pamphlet, and had been strongly expressed in the sermon on the 'Wretched Condition of Ireland': 'there is hardly one in twenty of those miserable Objects who do not owe their present Poverty to their own Faults; to their present Sloth and Negligence; to their indiscreet Marriage without the least Prospect of supporting a Family, to their foolish Expensiveness, to their Drunkenness, and other Vices . . .' (IX: 206).[12] Family relations among the Irish poor are part of the whole 'anti-nature' of the state of Ireland:

> In all other Nations, that are not absolutely barbarous, Parents think themselves bound by the Law of Nature and Reason to make some Provision for their Children; but the Reason offered by the Inhabitants of *Ireland* for marrying, is, that they may have Children to maintain them when they grow old and unable to work.
>
> (XIII: 136)

Thus the *Proposal for Giving Badges to the Beggars* in non-ironic analysis. It gives an edge to the Modest Proposer's sixth argument in support of his cannibal scheme:

> This would be a great Inducement to Marriage, which all wise Nations have either encouraged by Rewards, or enforced by Laws and Penalties. It would encrease the Care and Tenderness of Mothers towards their Children, when they were sure of a Settlement for Life, to the poor Babes, provided in some Sort by the Publick, to their annual Profit instead of Expence. We should soon see an honest Emulation among the married Women, *which of them could bring the fattest Child to the Market.* Men would become as *fond* of their Wives, during the Time of their Pregnancy, as they are now of their *Mares* in Foal, their *Cows* in Calf, or *Sows* when they are ready to farrow; nor offer to beat or kick them, (as it is too *frequent* a Practice) for fear of a Miscarriage.
>
> (XII: 115)

There is about this a fierce, angry compassion. But it is hardly a flattering glimpse of the domestic mores of the Irish poor.[13] The Proposer is, of course, writing *de haut en bas*, as a Protestant member of the ruling class (as, in his own different way, is Swift). When he coolly protests his own disinterestedness, and his absence of family-inducements to profit, he begins squarely as a solid, patriotic and profit-minded economist:

> I profess, in the Sincerity of my Heart, that I have not the least personal Interest, in endeavouring to promote this necessary Work; having no other Motive than the *publick Good of my Country, by advancing our Trade, providing for Infants, relieving the Poor, and giving some Pleasure to the Rich.*
>
> (XII: 118)

But he comes in his next (and final) sentence to be queerly identified with the values of the Papist poor:

> I have no Children, by which I can propose to get a single Penny; the youngest being nine Years old, and my Wife past Child-bearing.

It is all much more decorous, of course, than the glimpse of Papist family life. Conveniently, the Proposer has not the same temptations. But this convenience was set up by Swift, and is very double-edged. For it confirms our strong instinctive tendency to separate the cool Proposer from the messy and intimate sub-humanities of the Papist poor, while at the same time establishing a profound link. The mindless brute with his base family life, and the soundly calculating Whig planner, unite in their commercial priorities, with Swift wishing a plague on both their houses.

This charged, quizzical note is very important. Swift chose to end the tract with it. The Papists' profit-motive was largely the result of conditions brought about by the Whig planner and his like (the governing Anglo-Irish, and the English), as Swift knew. But his emphasis in the *Modest Proposal* is not 'judicial', and his intense exasperation lurches throughout the tract from one side to the other. The gibe in the opening paragraph about the Irish Catholics who 'leave their *dear Native Country, to fight for the Pretender in* Spain' (XII: 109) contains protest at real Irish 'disloyalty', as well as at the cruelties of economic circumstance which force them into the armies of Catholic princes.[14] There may also be anger at the apparent tolerance of this situation by the government, and the following year, in the 'Answer to the Craftsman' (1730 but published posthumously; XII: 171ff.), Swift found himself using his Modest Proposer's voice to satirise an arrangement between George II and the French to allow French recruiting-officers in Ireland. And running in a sense against both these feelings was a third, in which Swift complains of exaggerated anti-Papist fears, and a Whiggish cant always ready, at the drop of a hat, to accuse anyone (Swift was not excepted) of Jacobitism. It is this kind of scaremongering which is parodied in the Modest Proposer's 'first' argument:

> [the cannibal scheme] would greatly lessen the *Number of Papists*, with whom we are yearly over-run; being the principal Breeders of the Nation, as well as our most dangerous Enemies; and who stay at home on Purpose, with a Design to *deliver the Kingdom to the Pretender*; hoping to take their Advantage by the Absence *of so many good Protestants*, who have chosen rather to leave their Country, than stay at home, and pay Tithes against their Conscience, to an idolatrous *Episcopal Curate.*
>
> (XII: 114)[15]

Here, moreover, the Papist pauper comes into yet another surprising proximity, this time with Protestant Dissenters who emigrated to America, and who, like Catholic defectors to foreign armies, betray Ireland by going away. (Swift hated these most of all: the sarcasm about clergymen's tithes is a sure additional sign of angry Swiftian grievance.) Both groups of underprivileged defectors might, in an essential respect, be likened to that other, by no means underprivileged, category, the Anglo-Irish landlords whose economically ruinous absenteeism from Ireland is complained of in the *Proposal* and elsewhere (XII: 116, 126 etc.).

These comparisons do not raise the Papist poor in estimation. The compassion Swift feels for them is real. But at some of the places where a modern reader senses this compassion (in the opening paragraphs about the beggars and vagrants, and in the many exposures of family cruelty) Swift is partly exposing to derision his modest proposer's sentimental show of tenderness where it is not due. When the proposer says of 'that horrid Practice of *Women murdering their Bastard Children*' that it 'would move Tears and Pity in the most Savage and inhuman Breast' (XII: 110); or when he protests that cruelty 'hath always been with me the strongest Objection against any Project, how well soever intended' (XII: 113), Swift is only partly exposing the hypocrisy of profiteering do-gooders. He is also, and importantly, guying a lazy-minded (and mainly Whiggish) benevolism, given to indiscriminate tolerance, misguided charities and that whole sentimental euphoria which drives moderns to write books like those projected long ago by Swift's first mad 'author': *A Panegyrick upon the World*, for example, or, *A Modest Defence of the Proceedings of the Rabble in all Ages* (*Tale of a Tub*, Preface; I: 32).

The complicated interplay of compassion and contempt is not to be taken as a finely textured, sensitively judicial blend, a mellowly pondered product of the liberal imagination. It is an explosive mixture, and Swift's feelings oscillate starkly among extreme positions. When he discloses that it is not only the English but also (and at times especially) the Irish and, among the Irish, not only the ruling classes but the ruled, who are to blame for the state of Ireland, fierce convergences of anger take place which make the rational lucidities of the most subtle and comprehensive political analysis seem irrelevant. These convergences gain a particular edge from the fact that Swift was always insisting to himself and to others on the *differences* between the English and the Irish, and between the Anglo-Irish and the Catholic natives; and that it was frequently important to him to identify himself now with the English, now with the Anglo-Irish Protestant establishment, even at moments when his most heartfelt compassion was directed towards the Papist poor whom he despised. To some extent, these complexities were due to factors inherent in the Irish situation itself.[16] But Swift's intensely individual charge of feeling was very strong. He wrote in 1734 in 'A Letter on the Fishery':

> As to my Native Country, (as you call it) I happened indeed by a perfect Accident to be born here ... thus I am a *Teague*, or an *Irishman*, or what People please, although the best Part of my Life was in *England*. What I did for this Country was from perfect Hatred of Tyranny and Oppression ... I have done some small Services to this Kingdom, but I can do no more ...
>
> (XIII: 111–2)

There is here something of the self-righteous hauteur that we find in the *Verses on the Death*, and the presumably unconscious echo of Othello's 'I have done the state some service' (V. ii. 341) is not without an element of valedictory self-indulgence. But Swift understood the risks and temptations of such luxurious postures, and usually shied from them, to assert more low-pitched and untidy motives. He said to Pope on 1 June 1728: 'I do profess without affectation, that your kind opinion of me as a Patriot ... is what I do not deserve; because what I do is owing to perfect rage and resentment, and the mortifying sight of slavery, folly, and baseness about me, among which I am forced to live' (*Correspondence*, III: 289). If the denial of 'affectation' has itself a touch of affectation, and if the denial of higher motives is hardly altogether fair to himself, the passage conveys well the enforced emotional raggedness, the self-conscious impossibility for Swift of any clear self-ennobling stand. English tyranny was vicious, but the 'Letter on the Fishery' is quick to say that 'corrupt as *England* is, it is an Habitation of Saints in Comparison of *Ireland*. We are all Slaves, and Knaves, and Fools, and all but Bishops and People in Employments, Beggars' (XIII: 112).[17] The last word thrusts the Anglo-Irish (Members of Parliament and others) into the familiar sarcastic identification with 'the vulgar Folks of *Ireland*', 'so lazy and so knavish' that any economic scheme is doomed to founder among them. But 'Oppressed Beggars are always Knaves' (XIII: 113), and the 'Letter on the Fishery' comes quickly to all the giddy circularities of guilt which make it so hard and so absurd to apportion blame clearly, or to hope for a remedy. It is not surprising that the targets of Swift's Irish satires cannot always, and are not always meant to, be clearly distinguished from one another, nor that Swift's allegiances as between the English, the Anglo-Irish and the natives, are blurred and irrationally fluctuating things, whose very confusions provide the essential energies of his style.

Thus the sarcasms of the 'Answer to the Craftsman' aim at England, and simultaneously at the Anglo-Irish and Ireland's original native rulers:

> For, as to *England*, they have a just Claim to the Balance of Trade on their Side with the whole World; and therefore our Ancestors and we, who conquered this Kingdom for them, ought, in Duty and Gratitude, to let them have the whole Benefit of that Conquest to themselves; especially, when the Conquest was amicably made, without Bloodshed, by a Stipulation between the *Irish* Princes and *Henry* II. by which they paid him, indeed, not equal Homage with what the Electors of *Germany* do to the Emperor, but very near the same that he did to the King of *France* for his *French* Dominions.

(XII: 177)

Behind this are various further ironies. The speaker is ostensibly expressing that Anglo-Irish point of view with which, among the three alternatives, Swift himself was most closely identified. The speaker here, however, is the Modest Proposer himself, Swift's Whiggish opposite, selling Ireland out to England as (it would seem to be implied) the native Irish rulers had before. But what Molyneux had called the 'Intire and Voluntary Submission' of the Irish to Henry II was one of the bases of that constitutional doctrine of Ireland's status as a kingdom rather than a conquered or colonial territory which Swift himself accepted.[18] That submission Swift recognised to have been somewhat qualified. In *The Story of the Injured Lady*, Ireland is made to say that she was won 'half by Force, and half by Consent' (IX:5). When the speaker of the 'Answer to the Craftsman' says it is 'our Ancestors and we' who 'conquered' Ireland, he is speaking not only of conquests as distinct from free compacts, but of more *recent* conquests, including those of William III, which fell within Swift's lifetime and to which Swift himself felt loyal, though not without ambiguity. And since the Irish have continuously needed subduing in spite of their 'Intire and Voluntary Submission', there may even be some kind of exasperated hint that that submission was not only less than 'Voluntary' but also less than 'Intire', and therefore also unreliable and insincere.[19] To make things seem still more confused, Swift was mocking a Whiggish supporter of the English government for defending a scheme by the present King of England which was clearly to England's disadvantage, since it encouraged disaffected Irish Catholics to enlist in the armies of a potential enemy. And it seems clear at the same time that the Irish mercenaries who did so enlist are (as in the opening of the *Modest Proposal*) viewed by Swift as traitors. The follies are viciously intermerged, and so are the turpitudes.

This is notably true in the cannibal theme, and in other elaborations of the *mythe animal*. England *'would be glad to eat up our whole Nation'* (without salt!; XII:117), but the Whig proposer expects his scheme to commend itself to his own profit-minded Irish fellow-Protestants, while (as we have seen) the Papist poor are assumed to be likely not only to embrace it heartily, but to improve their family relationships as a result. The fact that at previous and historically recorded times of famine, actual instances of cannibalism, including child-eating, had occurred in Ireland (about which Swift certainly knew), adds hideous and tragic overtones to the insinuation.[20] Swift's compassion would certainly have been mixed with a very uppish revulsion, for the fact was clearly in accord with his notions of the barbaric squalor of 'the poor Popish Natives' (IX: 209). In *An Answer to ... A Memorial* (1728) Swift noted, from a certain ironic distance, 'that our Ancestors, the *Scythians*, and their Posterity our Kinsmen the *Tartars*, lived upon the Blood and Milk, and raw Flesh of their Cattle; without one Grain of *Corn*; but I confess myself so degenerate, that I am not easy without *Bread* to my Victuals' (XII: 19). In 1729, newspaper reports were saying that the unemployed Dublin weavers were forced to feed 'on Grains, and Blood from the Slaughter-Houses'.[21] In 1730, in the 'Answer to the Craftsman', Swift returns to the modern Irish descendants of the Scythians, and their diet, as '*Virgil* describeth it':

> *Et lac concretum cum sanguine bibit equino.*
> Which, in *English*, is Bonnyclabber, mingled with the Blood of Horses, as they formerly did, until about the Beginning of the last Century Luxury, under the Form of Politeness, began to creep in, they changed the Blood of Horses for that of their black Cattle; and, by Consequence, became less warlike than their Ancestors.
>
> (XII: 17?)

Behind the pained compassion of such passages lies a whole tradition of contempt for the Irish and their barbarous ways. The link between the Irish and the Scythians was a popular tradition,[22] and many authors (notably Spenser) noted the diet of boiled blood, sometimes adding to this some cannibal variants. Spenser and others noted not only that the Irish in times of famine nourished themselves on human bodies, but that like the Scythians they were given (for various ritual reasons) to drinking human blood.[23] Long before, Strabo[24] had spoken of both the Irish and the Scythians as cannibals or reputed cannibals. There was also a tradition that the Scythians made mantles out of the skins of their enemies,[25] which gives a doubtless fortuitous additional irony to the *Modest Proposal*'s notion that the skins of cannibalised babies 'will make admirable *Gloves for Ladies*, and *Summer Boots for fine Gentlemen*' (XII: 112).

There are also, in the background to Swift's Scythian parallel, Swift's own frequent references to the Scythians in the *Tale of a Tub*, the 'Mechanical Operation of the Spirit' and elsewhere, as prototypes of the many 'modern' madnesses of Britain: a reverence for asses and '*True Criticks*' (*Tale* III, I: 60–1) and allied zaninesses in the domain both of 'Learning' (VII, I: 93–4), and of

religion, notably Roundhead or Puritan enthusiasm, and 'artificial Extasies' ('Mechanical Operation'; I: 175–6, 178).[26] The
Scythians were often thought of as a generalised type of barbarian, rather than as a very precisely defined race.[27] For Swift, in
particular, they clearly meant not only barbarism, but certain
archetypal forms of human folly which he felt to be very close at
hand. Such radical folly, for Swift, is both 'modern' and atavistic,
and thus poses a perennially immediate threat of disruption, in
which man, either by simple primitive reversion, or (as in the
Tale) through excesses of arrogant intellect, brings himself back
to an animal state. The descriptions of Scythian barbarisms
among the Irish in the tracts of the late 1720s are shot through
with pity, but the pity is an angry one, mixed with many kinds of
resentment and contempt. And the same inextricable amalgam of
fierce compassion and contemptuous fury lies behind Swift's
description of himself in 1732 as soured and dispirited by 'fighting
with Beasts like St. Paul, not at Ephesus, but in Ireland' (*Correspondence*, IV: 79).[28] As Ferguson says of the *Modest Proposal*:
'Swift is saying to the Irish, in effect, "You have acted like beasts;
hence you no longer deserve the title of men." '[29]

Swift's ways of animalising Ireland and the Irish are clearly not
ironic in that simple compassionate sense presupposed by many
readers of the *Modest Proposal*. In an essay of the same date, 'A
Proposal that All the Ladies and Women of Ireland should appear
constantly in Irish Manufactures', Swift wrote:

> the three seasons wherein our corn hath miscarried, did no
> more contribute to our present misery, than one spoonful of
> water thrown upon a rat already drowned would contribute
> to his death; ... the present plentiful harvest, although it
> should be followed by a dozen ensuing, would no more
> restore us, than it would the rat aforesaid to put him near the
> fire, which might indeed warm his fur-coat, but never bring
> him back to life.
>
> (XII: 122)

In the following year, on 21 March 1730, Swift wrote to
Bolingbroke: 'I would if I could get into a better [world than
Ireland] before I was called into the best, and not die here in a rage,
like a poisoned rat in a hole' (*Correspondence*, III: 383). In the
Drapier's second letter, it is William Wood, exploiter of the Irish,
who is described as a rat: 'It is no Loss of Honour to submit to the
Lion: But who, with the Figure of a *Man*, can think with Patience

of being devoured alive by a *Rat*?' (X: 20). The latter usage is close to Pope's in a note of 1729 to *Dunciad* A, III: 337, warning us not to underestimate the power of the dunces: 'the *Dutch* stories somewhere relate, that a great part of their Provinces was once overflow'd, by a small opening made in one of their dykes by a single *Water-Rat*'. In 'A Proposal that All the Ladies . . .' it is Ireland herself that is a dead rat, and it is a characteristically teasing coincidence that he should on separate occasions have used the same image to describe a victimised Ireland, one of her more contemptible oppressors, and himself to boot. The drowned rat which is Ireland evokes a mixture of feelings. If the passage includes exasperation at the Irish, it also angrily mimics the contemptuous way in which the condition of Ireland is normally spoken of, and it contains an obvious gruff compassion on Swift's part, itself partly contemptuous.

The same compassion is clearly present in 'An Answer to Several Letters', also of 1729. Swift angrily answers those who explain or justify Ireland's troubles by the primitive and vicious squalor of the 'poor native Irish': 'supposing the size of a native's understanding just equal to that of a dog or a horse, I have often seen those two animals to be civilized by rewards, at least as much as by punishments' (XII: 88). Swift hints eloquently here at 'how easily those people may be brought to a less savage manner of life'. But Swift was often as pessimistic as any of his objectors about the prospects of any improvement in Ireland through practical expedients; and if his Modest Proposer is mimicked as referring to the native Irish as '*our Savages*' (XII: 111), Swift himself spoke without irony of 'the savage old Irish' (*Correspondence*, V: 58), and often thought of them as sub-human Yahoos.[30] Ferguson quotes a mid-century Lord Chancellor of Ireland as saying ' "The law does not suppose any such person to exist as an Irish Roman Catholic" ', and adds that 'In 1709, Swift could write of them with an easy callousness, "We look upon them to be altogether as inconsiderable as the Women and Children" '.[31] Ferguson later points out that it was in the late 1720s that Swift's sympathies and commitment were extended beyond the Anglo-Irish interest to ' "the whole People of Ireland" '.[32] It is, however, sometimes held that this last phrase applies only to the Protestant Irish.[33] Oddly, moreover, Swift's point in the passage of 1709, from the *Letter . . . Concerning the Sacramental Test* (II: 120), was actually to minimise the supposed dangerousness of the Irish Catholics, compared with that of Protestant Dissenters, whilst in the tracts of the 1720s and after we find many expressions by

Swift of the kind of harsh contempt which he was at the same time, as in 'An Answer to Several Letters', quick to resent in others.

Swift's celebrated, proto-Malthusian use of dehumanised economic jargon must be seen in the light of these complexities. It is not simply, perhaps not even mainly, an ironic protest at the statistical reduction of human beings, in the manner of, say, Auden's 'The Unknown Citizen'.[34] The statistician's hard depersonalising vocabulary, 'males', 'females', 'couples', 'breeders', 'souls', is mimicked with a kind of aggressive playfulness, as though Swift were flaunting his ability to play the statisticians' game with the best:

> The Number of Souls in *Ireland* being usually reckoned one Million and a half; of these I calculate there may be about Two hundred Thousand Couple whose Wives are Breeders...
>
> (XII: 110)

It is very like Swift, consciously or otherwise, to seize on the incongruous fact that the incorporeal term 'Soul' should be making the same point as the solidly animal 'Breeders', and the whole passage tingles with an unsettling, deadpan humour. But Swift had no disrespect for economic surveys as such, and his over-riding concern here is in any case well beyond parody. The warm, direct ballad protest of Auden's displaced person:

Say this city has ten million souls,
Some are living in mansions, some are living in holes:
Yet there's no place for us, my dear, yet there's no place for us,
('Twelve Songs', I)[35]

is far removed from Swift's hard cold note. If there is, in Swift as in Auden, a complaint about inhumane attitudes as expressed through language, it has relatively less place in Swift's total effect. And his tendency to talk of the Irish Catholics as 'things' and 'beasts' is almost as great in his direct utterances as in the parodied voice of the Modest Proposer. Dehumanised terminology ('Females', 'Couples' etc...) and an insulting use of animal terms occur plentifully, for example, in the *Proposal for Giving Badges to the Beggars*. Thus Swift says of the beggar who stays within his own parish:

If he be not quite maimed, he and his Trull, and Litter of
Brats (if he hath any) may get half their Support by doing
some Kind of Work in their Power, and thereby be less
burthensome to the People.

(XIII: 133)

When a resident beggar becomes a strolling beggar, he becomes a
still greater object of distaste:

But, when the Spirit of wandring takes him, attended by
his Female, and their Equipage of Children, he becomes a
Nuisance to the whole Country: He and his Female are
Thieves, and teach the Trade of stealing to their Brood at
four Years old . . .

(XIII: 134)

A little later, Swift says about the marriage-customs of the
Catholic poor:

many thousand Couples are yearly married, whose whole
united Fortunes, bating the Rags on their Backs, would not
be sufficient to purchase a Pint of Butter-milk for their
Wedding Supper, nor have any Prospect of supporting their
honourable State but by Service, or Labour, or Thievery.
Nay, their *Happiness* is often deferred until they find Credit
to borrow, or cunning to steal a Shilling to pay their Popish
Priest, or infamous Couple-Beggar.

(XIII: 136)

But Swift is equally harsh about the English Protestant Beggars
whom England exports to Ireland – in 'large Cargoes'
(XIII: 136–7). And as to the wealthier, ruling Protestant Interest
(the section of Ireland with which Swift, in the last analysis,
identified himself) they are no more spared than the poorer
classes. All the insulting exploitations of the *mythe animal* may
occur just as fiercely when Swift has reason to complain of them.
The 'Answer to Several Letters' says of Swift's favourite bugbear,
the women who use foreign rather than Irish manufactures, that
they are

a kind of animal suffered for our sins to be sent into the world
for the Destruction of Familyes, Societyes, and Kingdoms;
and whose whole study seems directed to be as expensive as

they possibly can in every useless article of living, who by long practice can reconcile the most pernicious forein Drugs to their health and pleasure, provided they are but expensive; as Starlings grow fat with henbane: who contract a Robustness by meer practice of Sloth and Luxury: who can play deep severall hours after midnight, sleep beyond noon, revel upon Indian poisons, and spend the revenue of a moderate family to adorn a nauseous unwholesom living Carcase.

(XII: 80)

(One grotesque piquancy of the *Modest Proposal*, it may be noted in passing, is that it is a perverse application of Swift's insistently reiterated view that the Irish should consume their own, rather than imported, products.)

The famous onslaught on the dead Lord Chief Justice Whitshed in *An Answer to . . . A Memorial* justifies itself by saying that though the memories of people like him 'will *rot*, there may be some Benefit for their Survivers, to smell it while it is *rotting*' (XII: 25). In the *Vindication of . . . Lord Carteret* (1730), Swift describes himself as a 'political *Surgeon*' opening up the carcase of Lord Allen before his death and displaying his noisome innards (XII: 157–8). The same Lord Allen (nicknamed Traulus) is the subject of some of Swift's angriest verse:

> Traulus of amphibious Breed,
> Motly Fruit of Mungril Seed:
> By the *Dam* from Lordlings sprung,
> By the *Sire* exhal'd from Dung.
> (*Poems*, III: 799)

The Modest Proposer, who thinks of the Irish as part statistical objects and part beasts, who speaks of children dropped from their dam, of carcases, of couples and breeders and the rest, is not mainly parodying other pamphleteers, so much as giving vent to a certain side of Swift himself. Part of what parody there was would have, characteristically, to turn on himself, and on acts of verbal aggression of which he was as guilty as any real statistician, and which he shows no evidence of wanting to recant. There is a further coil of self-mockery which is never far from the surface, a wry sense (not always allowed to become fully conscious) that the predicament of those unhappy Irishmen he most pitied and despised was an image of his own. The *Modest Proposal*'s 'Child, *just dropt from its Dam'* who might later regret that he had been allowed to live on in wretched Ireland instead of being 'sold for Food at a Year old' (XII: 110, 117) may not seem much like the Dean of St Patrick's. But was Swift half-remembering these phrases from the *Proposal* when he wrote to the Earl of Oxford in 1737 of his personal feelings about the 'wretched Kingdom' of his birth: 'I happened to be dropped here, and was a Year old before I left it, and to my Sorrow did not dye before I came back to it again' (*Correspondence*, V: 46–7)?

The 'other Expedients' passage in the *Modest Proposal* (XII: 116–7) and similar passages elsewhere confirm, as Ferguson has shown, that Swift was 'not concerned with satirizing the proposals of other writers on Irish affairs', many of whose schemes he had himself championed.[36] The genuinely sane and practical suggestions included in the list of 'other Expedients' divert whatever mockery of economic projectors there may have been, wrily back to Swift himself. The self-mockery is here one of Swift's ways of emphasising not the culpability of economists but the hopeless incurability of the human material whose lot they are trying against odds to improve. The 'malicious Pleasure' he is half-tempted to feel, in *An Answer to . . . A Memorial* (XII: 22), at the dire realisation of all his past warnings, is part of the same charge of hostility which makes him so ready to talk of the Irish as mere *material*, economists' fodder, cattle. But even such element of protest as there nevertheless was, on Swift's part, at the fact that people were being treated, or thought of, as animals, or as mere economic commodities, certainly does not mean (as Wittkowsky thought) that he was objecting to such specifically reifying doctrines of the economists as that 'people are the riches of a nation'.[37] Louis Landa has made it clear that Swift does not 'attack' this maxim 'because he thinks it false', but because the Irish situation is so unnatural that even such a universally valid economic law 'does not apply to Ireland'.[38] Nor is there evidence to suppose that he rejected such hard-headed mercantilist corollaries of the maxim as that large dense populations kept wages low and manufacture cheap, provided that the people were made productive and that idleness or beggary were kept to the minimum. Nor was he in favour of depopulation (e.g. through emigration).[39] Some statements in support of this are in fact bitter upside-down ironies, expressing a deep dismay at how Ireland's unnatural economy made it a grimly special case. This irony he expressed very clearly in the 'Letter . . . Concerning the Weavers':

I am not in the least sorry to hear of the great Numbers going to America, though very much so for the Causes that drive them from us, since the uncontrolled Maxim that People are the Riches of a Nation is no maxim here under our Circumstances. We have neither [manufactures] to employ them about, nor food to support them.

(XII: 66–7)

Actually, Swift is very 'sorry' indeed. Again, in 'Maxims Controlled' he felt driven to say that the poverty and unemployment in Ireland had

made me often wish, for some years past, that, instead of discouraging our people from seeking foreign soil, the public would rather pay for transporting all our unnecessary mortals, whether Papists or Protestants, to America, as drawbacks are sometimes allowed for exporting commodities where a nation is over-stocked.

(XII: 136)

And yet there is another irony than the obvious one. Many of the emigrants to America were Ulster Presbyterians who 'found the enforced payment of tithes to an Anglican clergyman not only an economic burden but something that went against their consciences'.[40] Swift would be no friend to them, and part of him, for reasons which cut across any economic maxims about population, would not be sorry to see them go. The recruitment of Papists by foreign armies introduced further complexities still. Swift opposed the idea, which he ironically made his Modest Proposer advocate in the 'Answer to the Craftsman'. But again it seems possible to feel that he was not wholly and unequivocally dissociated from his callous Whig spokesman. The latter produces the following piece of political arithmetic based on the supposition, first, that the kings of France and Spain take away for their armies six thousand 'Bodies of healthy, young, living Men' from Ireland:

by computing the Maintenance of a tall, hungry, *Irish* Man, in Food and Cloaths, to be only at Five Pounds a Head, here will be Thirty Thousand Pounds *per Annum* saved clear to the Nation, for they can find no other Employment at Home beside begging, robbing, or stealing.

(XII: 174)

He then contemplates a more large-scale project:

> But, if Thirty, Forty, or Fifty Thousand, (which we could
> gladly spare) were sent on the same Errand, what an
> immense Benefit must it be to us; and, if the two Princes, in
> whose Service they were, should happen to be at War with
> each other, how soon would those Recruits be destroyed,
> then what a Number of Friends would the Pretender lose,
> and what a Number of Popish Enemies all true Protestants
> get rid of.

The glimpse of Papist hordes of Irishmen destroying each other
abroad is three parts mimicry of cynical Whigs, but also one part
Swiftian animus. (The Papists in question would, after all, be
allowing themselves, and had in the past illegally allowed themselves, to be bought, like cattle, into the service of potential
enemies of Protestant Britain.)[41] It is one of a whole series of black
jokes in which a mock-cynical compassion shades unsettlingly
into a certain exasperated velleity for 'final solutions',[42] a velleity
which encompasses Papist slave and Protestant ruler alike. The
country-beggars in Dublin are 'fitter to be rooted out off the Face
of the Earth, than suffered to levy a vast annual Tax upon the
City', he was to say in *A Proposal for Giving Badges to the Beggars*
(XIII: 139), having first made the point that shopkeepers ought to
order the whipping of 'every Beggar from the Shop, who is not of
the Parish, and doth not wear the Badge of that Parish on his
Shoulder', a practice which would quickly get rid of all the
'sturdy Vagrants' from other parishes.[43] 'As for the Aged and
Infirm, it would be sufficient to give them nothing, and then they
must starve or follow their Brethren' (XIII: 138).

Similar outbursts occur against the ruling Protestant society,
notably, as we should expect, against the women who do not use
Irish manufactures. The Modest Proposer's extension of the
cannibal project to include them is much more literal, and carries a
much simpler hostile animus, than the rest of the work's exploitation of the cannibal formula. Indeed, the irony momentarily
ceases to work *in reverse*, according to the formula, and moves
instead in some kind of direct parallel with Swift's own feelings:

> Neither indeed can I deny, that if the same Use were made of
> several plump young girls in this Town, who, without one
> single Groat to their Fortunes, cannot stir Abroad without a
> Chair, and appear at the *Play-house*, and *Assemblies* in foreign

Fineries, which they never will pay for; the Kingdom would not be the worse.

(XII: 114)

To this may be added this outburst against Bankers in the *Short View*: 'I have often wished, that a Law were enacted to hang up half a Dozen *Bankers* every Year; and thereby interpose at least some short Delay, to the further Ruin of *Ireland*' (XII: 11), and a similar passage in the 'Answer to the Craftsman' (XII: 177).

The 'malicious Pleasure' at Ireland's plight in the *Answer to . . . A Memorial* (XII: 22) is surely also one of the ingredients of that later, eloquent and compassionate sarcasm in 'Maxims Controlled', when, immediately after expressing a wry approval of the emigration of Papists and Protestants to America, Swift continues:

> I confess myself to be touched with a very sensible pleasure, when I hear of a mortality in any country-parish or village, where the wretches are forced to pay for a filthy cabin and two ridges of potatoes treble the worth, brought up to steal or beg, for want of work, to whom death would be the best thing to be wished for, on account both of themselves and the public.

(XII: 136)

1978

Notes

1 For a further treatment of some of the themes in this essay, extended to Swift's other Irish tracts, see my article 'The Injured Lady and the Drapier: A Reading of Swift's Irish Tracts', *Prose Studies*, III (1980), 15–43.

2 George Wittkowsky, 'Swift's *Modest Proposal*: the biography of an early Georgian pamphlet', *Journal of the History of Ideas*, IV (1943), 88–9. This important article is full of valuable information on which I have drawn, whilst not always agreeing with its conclusions. It is referred to as Wittkowsky throughout.

3 Wittkowsky, loc. cit.

4 The notion that beggars and vagabonds were above all a social nuisance was widespread; see Christopher Hill, *Puritanism and Revolution. Studies in Interpretation of the English Revolution of the 17th Century* (1968), 218, 222–30; *Society and Puritanism in Pre-Revolutionary England* (1969), 251, 258, 262–87 *passim* (the whole chapter on 'The Poor and the Parish', 251–87, surveys the sixteenth- and seventeenth-century debate on the duty of charity and the opposite need for severity towards beggars. Hostility to beggars was a feature of Puritanism but it was by no means confined to the Puritans.)

5 Wittkowsky, 83–4. See also R. H. Tawney, *Religion and the Rise of Capitalism*

(1948), 193; Hill, *Puritanism and Revolution*, 218, 226–30, *Society and Puritanism*, 264–87, *passim*.

6 Wittkowsky, 84.

7 Wittkowsky, 88n.

8 Cited Wittkowsky, 84n. See Dorothy Marshall, *The English Poor in the Eighteenth Century* (1926), 24.

9 Swift's qualified advocacy of charity schools (he 'actively assisted in founding a charity school', IX: 129n) distinguishes him from the much more hostile attitude which Mandeville expressed in his 'Essay on Charity and Charity-Schools', printed in the 1723 edition of the *Fable of the Bees*. But there are many similarities between Swift's and Mandeville's thinking, and some of Mandeville's harshness will also be found in Swift.

10 On the possible date of the sermon, see IX: 136, where Louis Landa suggests various possibilities, and inclines to 1724–5.

11 On the common notion that poverty and beggary are evidence of unrighteousness, and deserve harsh treatment, see Tawney, op. cit., 262–5; Hill, *Puritanism and Revolution*, 215, 218–19, 225, *Society and Puritanism*, 276–7 and 251–87 *passim*. Max Weber identified this attitude with the Puritan ethic (*The Protestant Ethic and the Spirit of Capitalism*, trs. Talcott Parsons, 1971, 163, 177–8, 268nn), but it was by no means confined to Puritans or to dissenting sects. For some similar views to mine on the question of Swift's attitude, see David Nokes, 'Swift and the beggars', *Essays in Criticism*, XXVI (1976), 218–35, which appeared after this essay was sent to press.

12 See also the sermon 'On the Poor Man's Contentment': 'there is hardly one in a hundred who doth not owe his Misfortunes to his own Laziness or Drunkenness, or worse Vices' (IX: 191).

13 Oliver W. Ferguson, *Jonathan Swift and Ireland* (Urbana, 1962; hereafter Ferguson), p. 174, shows that actual cruelty to children, among the Irish poor, was a known fact of the time, reported on by non-ironic observers. More generally, the Irish seem to have had a reputation for outlandish family life and marriage customs, including unusually early disposal of daughters in marriage, the eating of their dead parents' flesh, the feeding of male infants on the point of a sword, incest, easy dissolution of the marriage-bond and intense enmities arising from unhappy marriages (see, for example, William Camden, *Britannia*, facsimile of 1695 edn, 1971, cols 965, 1041, 1046).

14 In a letter dated July–2 August 1732, however, Swift wrote to Charles Wogan, an Irish Catholic Jacobite exile who had served in Dillon's regiment in France and later took service with the Spanish army:

> Although I have no great Regard for your Trade, from the Judgment I make of those who profess it in these Kingdoms, yet I cannot but highly esteem those Gentlemen of *Ireland*, who, with all the Disadvantages of being Exiles and Strangers, have been able to distinguish themselves by their Valour and Conduct in so many Parts of *Europe*. I think above all other Nations, which ought to make the *English* ashamed of the Reproaches they cast on the Ignorance, the Dulness, and the Want of Courage, in the Irish Natives; those Defects, wherever they happen, arising only from the Poverty and Slavery they suffer from their inhuman Neighbours, and the base corrupt Spirits of too many of the chief Gentry, &c.

He goes on to say that 'the poor Cottagers' of Ireland 'have much better natural Taste for good Sense, Humour and Raillery' than their English counterparts, although 'the Millions of Oppressions they lye under, the Tyranny of their Landlords, the ridiculous Zeal of their Priests, and the general Misery of the whole Nation, have been enough to damp the best Spirits under the Sun' (*Correspondence*, IV: 51). Allowance must be made for Swift's desire to compliment his addressee. But the letter also shows the tendency to ambiguity and to fluctuation of emphasis in Swift's feelings about Ireland.

15 An official letter to the Duke of Dorset, who became Lord Lieutenant of Ireland in 1730, argued that in view of Protestant emigration, the scheme to permit recruiting of Irish Catholics for the French army 'might have the appearance of right policy, to diminish, on that account, the Number of the Popish Inhabitants' (cited by Ferguson, 177).

16 On this, see Ferguson, 19–23.

17 Calling England 'an Habitation of Saints in Comparison of *Ireland*' seems to be a pointed irony. See Camden's *Britannia*, col. 969: 'St *Patrick*'s disciples in Ireland were such great proficients in the Christian Religion, that in the age following, Ireland was term'd *Sanctorum Patria*, i.e. the Country of Saints'.

18 · Ferguson, 21. For a summary of the historical facts about Henry II's intervention in Ireland, see J. C. Beckett, *A Short History of Ireland* (1952), 17ff, and, for a more detailed treatment, A. J. Otway-Ruthven, *A History of Medieval Ireland* (London and New York, 1968), 42–65, esp. 48ff. The 'Voluntary Submission' was not unmixed with military conquest, of course. In his by no means original account of Henry's reign in the 'Fragment of the History [of England] from William Rufus', Swift notes that Henry II requested the Pope's 'licence for reducing the savage people of *Ireland* from their brutish way of living, and subjecting them to the crown of *England*' (V: 76: see V: 73–8 for Swift's overall account of Henry II). In his 'Essay upon the Advancement of Trade in Ireland', Temple had spoken of Henry II's 'conquest' of Ireland (*Works of Sir William Temple*, 1770, III: 7).

19 I am indebted to Professor J. C. Beckett for some valuable comments on this whole question.

20 Wittkowsky, 91–3, and Thomas B. Gilmore, Jr., '*A Modest Proposal* and *Intelligencer* Number XVIII', *The Scriblerian*, II, i (Autumn 1969), 28–9, draw attention to the fact that Thomas Sheridan had in 1728 cited in *The Intelligencer*, No. XVIII, an account from Fynes Moryson's *Itinerary* (1617), of Irish women eating children, and in one case children eating the flesh of their dead mother (see *The Intelligencer*, 1729, 195–6). Several numbers of *The Intelligencer*, including one by Swift himself (No. XIX), dealt with the condition of Ireland. No. XV contained a reprint of Swift's *Short View of the State of Ireland*. See also Spenser's *View of the Present State of Ireland*, in Rudolf Gottfried (ed.), *Spenser's Prose Works*, Variorum Edition (Baltimore, 1949), 158, and (for other sources) annotation, 382. Spenser is advocating measures for subduing the Irish so that they will 'quicklye Consume themselues and devour one another', having already displayed their cannibal propensities anyway. Critics differ as to whether this is 'a terrible proposal, uttered with cold deliberateness', or more neutral or compassionate (381).

In Swift's own time, cannibal jokes and associated ironies about, for example, flaying the Irish and selling their skins, were evidently not uncommon, whether in a contemptuous or a compassionate or other context: see the examples cited in Clayton D. Lein, 'Jonathan Swift and the population of Ireland', *Eighteenth-Century Studies*, VIII (1975), 436 (also cited in *Works*, IX: xx) and 452.

21 Ferguson, 170.

22 Spenser alludes to this throughout much of his *View*, and for other authorities see the Variorum Edition, 309–11, 320 etc. Sir William Temple devoted a

whole section of his essay 'Of Heroic Virtue' to a (not altogether unfavourable) account of the Scythians, noting that those who conquered Scotland and Ireland 'retained more of the ancient Scythians . . . both in their language and habit' (*Works of Sir William Temple*, 1770, III: 347–68, 351; also III: 78–80, a passage from *An Introduction to the History of England*, which notes the habit of 'eating blood they brew from living cattle'). For hostile analogies, see Donald T. Torchiana, 'Jonathan Swift, the Irish, and the Yahoos: the case reconsidered', *Philological Quarterly*, LIV (1975), 195–212, esp. 197 (special number published separately as *From Chaucer to Gibbon. Essays in Memory of Curt A. Zimansky*, ed. William Kupersmith, Iowa City, 1975). Strabo reports that the Scythians used to castrate their horses like English Yahoos (Strabo, *Geography*, VII. iv. 8, Loeb edn, III, 249; *Gulliver's Travels*, IV: ix, *Works*, XI: 272–3).

23 Spenser, Variorum Edition, 108, 112, and annotation, 340, 343–4. On the Scythians, see Herodotus, IV. lxiv, lxx.

24 Strabo, *Geography*, IV. v. 4; VII. iii. 6–7 (Loeb edn, II, 259–61; III, 189, 195, 199).

25 Noted by Johannes Boemus (1571), and cited in annotation to Spenser, Variorum Edition, 328. For the manufacture by the Scythians of various objects out of the parts of human bodies, see Herodotus, IV, lxiv, lxv; Strabo, *Geography*, VII. iii. 6–7 (Loeb edn, III, 189, 197). Cf. the passage of 1716 by Archbishop William King, adapting these motifs to the sad predicament of the Irish poor: 'I cannot See how any more can be got from them, except we take away their potatoes and buttermilk or flay them and Sell their Skins' (cited Lein, op. cit., 452).

26 At I: 178 it is also said that the 'noble [Irish] Nation, hath of all others . . . degenerated least from the Purity of the Old *Tartars*'. On Tartars and Irishmen see also XII: 19 and the quotations from Berkeley in Torchiana, op. cit., 197.

27 E.g. as 'a vague "northern nation"' (annotation to Spenser, Variorum Edition, 327). It is presumably as generalised Barbarians that the Scythians and Tartars are referred to in Blackmore's *Satyr Against Wit* (1699), ll. 277–8, Frank H. Ellis (ed.), *Poems on Affairs of State*, VI, New Haven and London, 1970, 149.

28 For scriptural echoes and allusions in Swift's Irish writings, see C. A. Beaumont, *Swift's Use of the Bible* (Athens, Georgia, 1965), 36–52. Beaumont, p. 66, says that the *Modest Proposal* 'ignores the Bible' because Biblical allusions would be inappropriate in a work purportedly written by 'a modern economic projector', but Robert A. Greenberg has suggested in a persuasive note that a source of the cannibal formula might have been the frequent and 'almost conventional Old Testament admonition that unless the Hebrews mend their ways they will be reduced (amongst other extremities) to the eating of their children' ('*A Modest Proposal* and the Bible', *Modern Language Review*, LV (1960), 568–9). For Swift's sarcastic exploitation of the cannibal formula, there may also have been a patristic model in Tertullian's *Apology* (see Donald C. Baker, 'Tertullian and Swift's *A Modest Proposal*', *Classical Journal*, LII (1957), 219–20, and J. W. Johnson, 'Tertullian and *A Modest Proposal*', *Modern Language Notes*, LXXIII (1958), 561–3).

29 Ferguson, 173.

30 For a fuller recent discussion of this point, see Torchiana, op. cit. For the widespread view of the Irish as savages, see especially ibid., 196–202.

31 Ferguson, 17. See *Works*, II: 120, and cf. X: 104. I think Ferguson may here be exaggerating the 'easy callousness', which, in so far as it is evident, is partly

ironic. But the general point that Swift often took a harsh view of the native Irish is undoubtedly right.

32 Ferguson, 150.

33 J. C. Beckett, 'Swift and the Anglo-Irish tradition', in Claude Rawson (ed.), *The Character of Swift's Satire: A Revised Focus* (Newark, De, London and Toronto, 1983), 157–8.

34 W. H. Auden, *Collected Shorter Poems 1927–1957* (1966), 146–7.

35 Ibid., 157. Compare with the first line a late eighteenth-century prose usage in John Howard's *State of the Prisons*, about Amsterdam: 'In this city they compute 250,000 souls . . . . ' (Everyman edn, London and New York, 1929, 54). Both the cold statistical and the compassionate usages were common long before Swift and remained common long after (see *Oxford English Dictionary*, Soul 12 and 13; for some examples with a close bearing on Swift see Andrew Carpenter (ed.), *Letters to and from Persons of Quality. Being the Third Volume of Irish Writings from the Age of Swift* (Dublin, 1974), 18, and passages cited in Lein, op. cit., 435, 441). Howard and Auden are perhaps merging the two usages, creating compassionate connotations by charging the statistical usage with bitterness or irony in varying degrees. Perhaps to some extent Swift does so too. For a specialised irony, exploited in Gogol's *Dead Souls*, see T. E. Little, 'Dead Souls', in Christine J. Whitbourn (ed.), *Knaves and Swindlers. Essays on the Picaresque Novel in Europe* (London, New York and Toronto, 1974), 115.

36 Ferguson, 175.

37 Wittkowsky, 90ff. It has been suggested that an immediate source for Swift's reference to this maxim might have been Sir William Temple's essays 'Upon the Advancement of Trade in Ireland' and 'Of Popular Discontents' (F. V. Bernard, 'Swift's maxim on populousness: a possible source', *Notes and Queries*, CCX (1965), 18). The first of these essays has also been suggested as a possible source of the *Modest Proposal* in other respects (Thomas B. Gilmore, Jr, 'Swift's *Modest Proposal*: a possible source', *Philological Quarterly*, XLVII (1968), 590–2).

38 Louis Landa, reviewing Wittkowsky in *Philological Quarterly*, XXIII (1944), 179. See also Landa's '*A Modest Proposal* and populousness', *Modern Philology*, XL (1942), 161–70, and (for the larger question of Swift's general attitude to mercantilism) 'Swift's economic views and mercantilism', *ELH: A Journal of English Literary History*, X (1943), 310–35.

39 Landa, review of Wittkowsky, 179, and the more complex discussions of the question of emigration in '*A Modest Proposal* and populousness', *passim*, and Ferguson, 161ff. For two discussions of emigration by Swift himself, see XII: 58–61 and 75–7.

40 Ferguson, 162. For Swift's concern 'about the danger of depopulation' and useful accounts of his attitude to the question of emigration, see Ferguson, 161–4, and Lein, op. cit., 431–53, esp. 443–5 (on emigration).

41 See Ferguson, 176–7.

42 It was not unprecedented for writers on Irish affairs to toy more or less ambiguously with notions of large-scale extermination. See n. 20 above, and 'A Brief Note of Ireland', possibly also by Spenser, Variorum Edition, 240, 244, and cross-references at 439, n. 328–9.

43 On the legal basis, developed in the preceding century and a half in England, for whipping beggars back to their own parish, see John Wilders (ed.), *Hudibras* (1967), 377 (note to II.i.817), and Hill, *Society and Puritanism*, 261.

PART II

Swift, Pope and Augustan Verse Satire

4

Swift's Poems

(i)   The Poet Swift

Swift's poems, after long neglect, have become a growth industry. For a long time, the only adequate introduction to them in
book form was Maurice Johnson's *The Sin of Wit* (1950). Now
there are at least six books published in the last few years.

Writing poems was no small part of Swift's activity. In sheer
bulk, his poetic output was not far short of Pope's, if one excludes
Pope's Homer. The poems have suffered neglect because Swift's
great prose satires naturally command the lion's share of attention, and because they have not been easy to accommodate within
the Pope-centred conception of Augustan poetry which has
served as the working model for the academic revaluation of
eighteenth-century literature in the last fifty years. The Pope-
centred view is itself much older, of course, and goes back to Pope
himself. Swift was infected with it. His self-depreciating claim to
have been 'only a Man of Rhimes', and the tendency of his own
contemporaries to grant full poetic status only to the more
elevated styles, have also helped to keep the standing of his poems
low among critics. But practising poets from Byron to Eliot and
Auden and James Reeves have known the value of his flat 'low'
styles. His place in that 'colloquial tradition' which runs from
Skelton and Cotton and Butler is a strong one and his example
contributed creatively to the reinstatement of 'light verse' as a
self-respecting poetic idiom in this century.[1] He himself made no
great claims. But his modest disavowal of 'serious Couplets' was
accompanied by an insistence that his 'Rhimes' had their own
special seriousness, 'never without a moral View'.

The study of Swift's writings in general has often been
bedevilled by an excessive emphasis on themes and on structure:
on the ideological coherence of his beliefs and the supposed
orderly arrangement of his compositions. In a writer so elusively
ironic and so given to unsettling and aggressive mimicries of

disorder, such treatments have been especially reductive, and some recent discussions of the poems have imported from studies of the prose works the same limiting habits. The more enlightening commentators, however, have sensed that beyond ideology or form, important as these are, lies a more difficult and in Swift's case an almost always more important question: that of his characteristic *tone*, in a deep sense of that term which implies a whole style of feeling and thought.

Swift's poems are his most personal works, if by 'personal' one means something like 'confessional' or 'autobiographical'. The major prose satires (*A Tale of a Tub, Gulliver's Travels, A Modest Proposal*) show him in states of intensity which are highpoints of self-realisation, and thus 'personal' in another, perhaps stronger, sense. They display combinations of tearaway playfulness and contemptuous fury, of cool distance and unsettling intimacy, of uppish certainty and an occasional almost nihilistic doubt, of moral purposiveness and destructive impulse, which are largely outside the scope of the poems. Deep urges of self-display and of self-disguise are simultaneously given their head, so that even in the most vivid passages of anger or delight, the author is not allowed to appear openly. Swift's 'presence' is always felt and never witnessed, and this passionate guardedness is paradoxically his most characteristic and self-expressive quality.

In the poems, it is otherwise. Among them are found self-portraits, semi-fictionalised accounts of his personal relationships and of his friendships with women, and some essays in autobiography. He speaks as his own 'I' more often than elsewhere, tells us more facts about himself, addresses his friends and enemies 'directly'. Indirections continue to exist, mock-playfulnesses and real ones, self-deflations and conscious self-inflations, but they fictionalise or modify, without seeking to conceal or destroy, a self-expression which retains a basic minimum of superficial overtness.

It was thus appropriate that when Maurice Johnson published the first modern critical book on Swift's poems nearly thirty-five years ago, he should have chosen for his title a phrase from Swift's own self-description in 'The Author Upon Himself':

S — had the Sin of Wit no venial Crime;
Nay, 'twas affirm'd, he sometimes dealt in Rhime.

The lines illustrate Swift's conscious sense of himself as a poet, as well as his tendency to write apologies for himself in verse and to undercut them by coy self-depreciating gestures. But the poem actually begins without indirection, in a raw explosive outburst against personal enemies which has the force of a ritual curse. Nora Jaffe, whose book *The Poet Swift* (1977) was the first (and remains one of the best) of the recent spate of studies, dislikes this as 'aggressive, self-pitying, and intensely righteous', but it has some of the primitive power of those later hate-poems of which *The Legion Club* is the best known example. And when the poet moves away from direct attacks on enemies to 'indirect' praises of himself, Jaffe seems to desire more 'indirection' and not less. She would actually prefer a 'persona', some 'outside observer to comment on the power of his satire and the nobility of his goals' like the one offered in the *Verses on the Death*, to the frankly explosive self-exposure of the opening of 'The Author upon Himself', or the limited ironic distancing of that poem's self-praise.

Here, I think, she lacks the courage of her own convictions, and comes closest to some recent orthodoxies with which she otherwise disagrees. Like other critics, she seems too ready to take at face-value Swift's retreats, in parts of the *Verses*, into an archly protective use of the third person. As contemporaries of Norman Mailer, we know to our considerable cost in boredom and embarrassment, that third-person narration about an author's own self is hardly a guarantee against solipsism, any more than coy self-ironies are. When Swift put his closing self-eulogy into the mouth of the supposed impartial observer, he was not seeking ironically to discount the claims made on his behalf. Jaffe rightly asserts that 'those parts of the eulogy which deal with his political career' are 'straightforward', and knows from 'The Author upon Himself' that Swift was capable 'of at least slightly heavy-handed self-praise'. But she justifies the eulogy on the grounds that 'Swift really did feel, and rightly, that he had been of use to friends and countrymen'. Fair LIBERTY really *had* been all his Cry. This is true, and grounds for pride: but in that case, self-praise by means of an 'impartial' commentator invented for the purpose, is an unworthy subterfuge, betraying loss of nerve, false modesty or worse, and one turns with relief to the frankly self-glorying magniloquence of Pope or of Yeats.

The *Verses on the Death* open with La Rochefoucauld's maxim about how we find private satisfaction in the 'Distresses of our Friends,' and goes on to the well-known (and *first*-person) confession that Swift himself is not free of envious impulses:

149

> In POPE, I cannot read a Line,
> But with a Sigh, I wish it mine:
> When he can in one Couplet fix
> More Sense than I can do in Six:
> It gives me such a jealous Fit,
> I cry, Pox take him, and his Wit.

Similar compliments are paid to Gay, Arbuthnot, St John and Pulteney. It is a delightful coterie-celebration, whose satisfactions are partly those which we derive from Yeats's 'In Memory of Major Robert Gregory' or 'The Municipal Gallery Revisited': the sense of a brilliant company of gifted friends, each potentially or actually admired by us in their own right, being given fit celebration by one of their number. And yet it is not in the overtly self-mythologising grandiloquence of Yeats, but in the transparent humilities of Swift, that we sense a calculated and egocentric refocusing of praise back on the author himself. I mean not only the labyrinthine self-applause, disguised as self-depreciation, where satire at his own expense serves to mitigate the force of naked self-compliment:

> ARBUTHNOT is no more my Friend,
> Who dares to Irony pretend;
> Which I was born to introduce,
> Refin'd it first, and shew'd its Use;

but also and especially the display of 'envy' calculated to 'prove' that he is free of envy: 'If with such Talents Heav'n hath blest 'em/Have I not Reason to detest 'em.'

The application of La Rochefoucauld's maxim to himself aims to display Swift's toughmindedly perspicacious frankness about his own motives as well as being a second-time-round demonstration that he isn't like that really. I find this embarrassing. I have no difficulty in thinking of Swift as a greater figure than all his friends, including Pope, just as Yeats stands head and shoulders above John Synge, Lionel Johnson, Augusta Gregory and the other assorted notables of his own coterie poems. But I prefer Yeats's way of saying 'my glory was I had such friends' to Swift's doubtless better founded but more oblique bids to derive glory from his friendships with the gifted and the great.

Swift was a merciless scourge of solipsism. The mockeries of *A Tale of a Tub* reverberate through those long historic corridors of 'modern' self-importance which stretch all the way from Dryden through Sterne and Lamb and Thackeray to those amplified echo-chambers of our time where Mailer lives. He parodied Dryden straight, and the rest in anticipation. But the *Tale*'s brilliance resides partly in the inwardness of its mimicry, and the coy self-regard which Swift mocked in the *Tale* is perhaps what he himself lapsed into in such poems as *Cadenus and Vanessa* or the *Verses on the Death*. Talking about himself was, for Swift, a problematic thing, and to the extent that the poems do it more than the prose they are open to special risks. This may be partly why almost all his poems are undercut by an element of parody, as though Swift were determined to indicate that he knew how often poets displayed self-absorption or self-importance, and that *he* would not fall into this trap. But he was not proof against the subtler trap, in which the guard against self-absorption becomes itself a form of self-absorption.

The normal solemnities of the 'lofty Stile' were easier to guard against, and indeed he avoided them even in their ironically undercut forms: there is virtually no mock-*heroic* among Swift's poems, although all of them mock *something*. His explanation for avoiding loftiness is that in that style 'I Shou'd make a Figure scurvy', and the point is seldom understood. Jaffe oversimplifies when she says that Swift professed to prefer a gentle Horatian indirection while really drawn to Juvenalian indignations. His phrase about the savage indignation lacerating his breast was coined for posthumous use, when all such grand feelings could be said to be over, and with all the protective distance and formality of a Latin epitaph: its English form we owe to Yeats, himself no enemy to lofty styles. Very few of the poems (*The Legion Club* is the sole major example) conform to the 'Juvenalian' stereotype, even in a loose sense. And, as discerning readers have always sensed, it is Pope, the celebrated Imitator of Horace, who is really given to postures of Juvenalian majesty. What Jaffe does capture well about the refusal of loftiness in Swift's *Epistle to a Lady*, and that poem's definition of the aims of satire, is the fact that 'the reader is left to believe, perhaps as Swift himself believes, that satire can torture better than it can correct': this is no more a matter of Horatian urbanity than of Juvenalian denunciation, it is pure Swift.

Parody of the idealisations of conventional love-poetry carried less risk of 'a Figure scurvy', because Swift was less likely to betray a residual attachment to the derided original. The famous 'excremental' poems are nowadays well-recognised as upside-down versions of the routines of conventional love-poetry. Swift

151

seems to offer larger quantities of erotic 'anti-poetry' than of
other mock-loftiness not because he needed to guard more against
the primary impulse but perhaps because he needed to guard *less*.
The lighter poems in the group (*Strephon and Chloe, Cassinus and
Peter*) suggest a freedom from any sense of emotional risk which is
unusual in Swift, while the grimmer examples (*The Progress of
Beauty*, *A Beautiful Young Nymph*) hardly give the impression that
what Swift needed to guard against was an undue predilection for
the celebratory forms against which they are played off.

In the Stella poems, however, the parody of amorous poeticisms does coexist with a primary impulse of deep and tender
affection. The point is neither to mock the absurdities of others,
nor even to deny or protect his own vulnerable feelings, so much
as to give these a more precise and vivid definition. When he
signposts his avoidance of '*Cupid*'s Darts' and the rest, he brings
to mind the 'anti-rhetoric' of Shakespeare's 'My mistress' eyes are
nothing like the sun', as Jaffe rightly notes. But Shakespeare's
sonnet depends more than Swift's poems on the serious survival
of the primary convention, and Shakespeare himself wrote
'straight' if less extreme examples. Secondly, Shakespeare's
sonnet carries a strong and very sophisticated erotic charge, a
sharply sensuous fascination with even the uglinesses of the
mistress, a vivid blend of *odi et amo* which belongs to the world of
Catullus and Baudelaire rather than of Swift.

But the most interesting difference is that whereas Shakespeare
declares his love to be as rare as any she belied with false compare,
Swift ultimately maintains that the repudiated traditions of 'false
compare' may well, in Stella's case, be not far from the sober
truth. Swift insists that Stella in her youth was indeed as beautiful
as poets usually say and that this beauty is matched by her virtue.
What middle-age has done is slightly to crack the 'Angel's Face'
without damaging the 'Angel's Mind'. The tenderness contained
in this gruff humour is obvious. What sometimes escapes notice is
the extent to which the hyperbolic routines of love-poetry are
allowed here to survive, not undercut but revalidated by the frank
acknowledgement of unromantic middle-aged realities. In her
youth, Stella's beauty was not only unquestionable, but reminiscent of poetic or romance-heroines, and Swift says so, not only
in poems but in the private memorandum which he wrote to
relieve his grief on the night of her death. The hint of parody, the
seeming realistic deflation, actually help to emphasise the portrait's substantial truth: she 'was looked upon as one of the most
beautiful, graceful, and agreeable young women in London,

only a little too fat. Her hair was blacker than a raven, and every feature of her face in perfection'.[2]

The Stella poems are unique. The parodic compulsion survives as much as elsewhere, but here it is transmuted to serve positive, not negative, ends. Its purpose, paradoxically, is celebration. The phenomenon shows how deep the guardedness was in Swift, as well as the remarkable nature of the readiness to drop it in this case: Swift preserves the stylistic shell while standing the mockery on its head.

As everyone knows, Stella is repeatedly praised for the durable virtues which, unlike physical beauty, survive the ravages of time and are therefore more solid foundations for 'friendship' (including marital friendship), whatever the sex of the persons. This is also one of the themes of the excremental poems. Swift refers to the necessary virtues as masculine ones, but his point is that they are so not because women are incapable of them, but because society educates women to be ornamental idiots or objects of idealised worship. Swift wanted this changed, and despite his alleged misogyny is closer to 'modern' thinking than those contemporaries of his whose friendliness to women took the customary patronising form of gallant poetic compliments.

But even this freedom from misogyny should not be simplified. Jaffe is particularly subtle, eloquent and just when she observes that even the good-humoured raillery to Stella contains certain hints of withdrawal and a potential flicker of aggression:

> Teasing implies the withholding of something besides commitment. Raillery, however affectionate, is a form of suspended aggression. Stella must always have felt, in reading the poems, that Swift could hurt her if he wanted to. In one sense he was dangling a carrot. In another, he was arresting the downward swing of an axe. These darker aspects do not obscure the primary impression of genuine love. They do reveal the complexity, and perhaps the ambivalence, of his feelings in his most significant relationship with a woman. Swift was entirely capable of desiring to hurt women.

A critic earns the right to report this only when the depth of Swift's feelings for Stella has first been adequately realised, and this critic's credentials are good.

1978–1981

Notes

1 This and several other points touched on here are treated in fuller detail in the second section of this chapter, entitled 'The Nightmares of Strephon'.

2 These and ensuing points about the Stella poems are more fully elaborated at the end of the next section, below pp. 178ff.

(ii) The Nightmares of Strephon: Nymphs of the City in the Poems of Swift, Baudelaire, Eliot

This discussion is partly concerned to explore some aspects of Swift's poetic treatment of cities, and of those typical inhabitants of cities, the whore and the fine lady. Two other city poets, Baudelaire and Eliot, belong, so to speak, to the subplot. They are there to illustrate, by similarity or difference, certain features of Swift's writing, and of a poetic tradition to which he made some memorable contributions.[1]

I begin with the 'Description of the Morning' ([1709] *Poems*, I: 123 ff.), a parody of poetical descriptions of dawn, as well as a 'realistic' description of a town scene. It is one of Swift's relatively few poems in the heroic couplet, and puts it to subheroic use. The form is here not only parodied, but (perhaps more important) pointedly reduced to a banal flatness:

> Now hardly here and there an Hackney-Coach
> Appearing, show'd the Ruddy Morn's Approach.
> Now *Betty* from her Masters Bed had flown,
> And softly stole to discompose her own.
>
> (ll. 1–4)

This poem and its companion piece, the 'Description of a City Shower', belong to a proud tradition of city poems which includes Juvenal's third and Boileau's sixth satires (Boileau's satire is rather close to Swift's poems in several details, and has a vivid account of a 'city shower'), Baudelaire's 'Tableaux Parisiens', and Eliot's 'Preludes' and 'Morning at the Window'. But Swift strikes a more sober and deadpan note than any of the others. There is no Juvenalian indignation, and none of Boileau's irritated grandiloquence. Nor is there the Baudelairian note of suffering self-involvement, the touch of self-glamorising eloquence, the fascinated wonder at the 'Fourmillante cité, cité pleine de rêves'.[2]

Eliot's laconic notation of city squalors is perhaps closest to

Swift's. He is known to have been deeply interested in Swift. He once intended to write an essay on Swift as a poet, among other studies of seventeenth- and eighteenth-century poets. This intention was not fulfilled. But he made, over the years, a number of memorable comments upon him. His imagination was impregnated with Swiftian presences and echoes.[3] It was Yeats and not Eliot who said in so many words that he was 'haunted' by Swift,[4] but Eliot has revealed that Swift, in combination with Yeats, was a principal element in that 'familiar compound ghost' who appears to Eliot in *Little Gidding*.[5]

Both poets, especially in their earlier works, in the 'Description of a City Shower' or parts of the *Waste Land*, display a strongly localised sense of London, a rhetorical as well as a topographical feeling, mixed with irony, for its street-names and place-names, and also a sense that the decays of London evoke the fall of other great cities, notably Troy. And it is Eliot, in the 'Preludes' and 'Morning at the Window', who, of all the poets I have mentioned, most nearly approached the flat descriptive idiom of the 'Description of the Morning'. But even Eliot departs fairly readily from this flatness, dramatising the comic scene into a sweeping mock-cynical pathos ('the damp souls of housemaids', the 'aimless smile that hovers in the air'),[6] and allowing himself an unSwiftian release of lyric impulse and meditative luxury:

> I am moved by fancies that are curled
> Around these images, and cling:
> The notion of some infinitely gentle
> Infinitely suffering thing.[7]

The disciplines of parody help Swift to keep clear of such self-commitment and its sentimentalising risks. But parody, and especially mock-heroic, often preserves a perverted residue of original grandeurs. Swift's mock-*descriptio* of Dawn, however, has the effect not so much of inflating or deflating, as of *levelling*. The commonplace of Aurora rising from Tithonus's bed gives way to an unfussily earthbound glimpse of Betty stealing from her master's bed to discompose her own. An almost novelistic episode, something out of Scarron or Fielding, is sketched out, passingly, with a graceful, laconic completeness.[8] Baudelaire's 'Crépuscule du Matin' and Eliot's 'Preludes' also evoke episodes that might, in a sense, be developed into fictions beyond the limits of the descriptive set piece: see Baudelaire's 'bruns adolescents' tormented by unhealthy dreams, for example, or the suggestions in Eliot of an element of narrated activity ('You tossed a blanket from the bed, . . .' 'His soul stretched tight across the skies . . .'). But there is nothing in either Eliot or Baudelaire of Swift's take-it-or-leave-it factuality. Eliot's shadowy and unnamed figures, and Baudelaire's generalised adolescents, both come charged with an authorial fervour of romantic agony.

But Swift's Betty should most strongly be contrasted with those solitary fallen women who appear in such post-Baudelairian city poems of Night and Dawn as Wilde's 'Impression du Matin'. There 'one pale woman all alone', standing under a gaslight, is set against Whistlerian colours of fog and river, the central figure in a sentimental set piece. Betty is neither a central figure, nor sentimentalised. Swift's poem has no Wildeian luxuries of fascination or recoil, just as it preserves no grandeurs of mock-heroic (a later poem, 'A Beautiful Young Nymph Going to Bed' [1731], is, like Wilde's, about a whore at the end of her night's work, and has some celebrated anatomical squalors which may call Baudelaire to mind, and to which I shall return). In the 'Description of the Morning', Betty takes her place in a flat but animated world which includes a 'Slipshod Prentice', Moll whirling her mop, a loud chimney sweep, turnkeys, bailiffs, proverbial 'School-Boys . . . with Satchels in their Hands', and other citizens.[9] Introducing the poem in *Tatler*, No. 9, Steele said that Swift 'described things exactly as they happen: he never forms fields, or nymphs, or groves, where they are not . . . .' This catches the mixture of realism and parody well because it suggests the resolute avoidance, rather than the derisive elaboration or exploitation, of traditional poeticisms. Roger Savage has said that, in this poem,

> Warbling larks and tuneful linnets become coalmen and chimney-sweeps; the shepherd-swain about to wake and sound his jovial pipe becomes the turnkey counting his flock of thieves as they come in from night-pasture.[10]

But these parodic patterns, though inescapable, are relatively uninsistent. They are a token of certain stylistic refusals, but they are transcended into a primary idiom of sober description. For many Augustans, mock-heroic routines, and other stylisations, acted as a strongly visible 'dress of thought', covering (or distancing or modifying) the unsettling nakedness of fact. Swift was less concerned than some with such signposted disguises, but he shared the impulse, and it may be that for him also a dash of parody seemed a desirable stylistic protection against, and even a condition of release for, the rowdy indecorum of fact. But, if so, the 'dress' is very plain, and Swift clearly felt it even more important to avoid the excesses of *over*-dress (heroic and mock-heroic alike) than the vulnerabilities of nudity.

By the late 1690s, as is well known, Swift had abandoned Cowleyan pindarics and 'serious Couplets'. He did not often return to the less 'serious' couplets of the 'Description' poems either. He experimented with various lighter, more deflating, or more 'popular' verse forms. In 'The Discovery' ([1699] *Poems*, I: 61 ff.) and 'A Ballad on the Game of Traffick' ([1702] *Poems*, I: 74–75), he explored variant kinds of witty quatrain, a stanza which he was later to develop into a style anticipating or resembling some of T. S. Eliot's early *vers de société*. For example, the satiric quatrains on financiers in 'The Run upon the Bankers' ([1720] *Poems*, I: 239):

> Money, the Life-blood of the Nation,
> Corrupts and stagnates in the Veins,
> Unless a proper Circulation
> Its Motion and its Heat maintains,
> (ll. 9–12)

are comparable, in metre as well as in tone and atmosphere, with the stanzas about dividends and Exchequer Bonds in Eliot's 'The Hippopotamus' or 'A Cooking Egg'.[11]

Among his other metrical experiments were the sprawling garrulous rhythms of 'Mrs Harris's Petition' ([1701] *Poems*, I: 68 ff.), which anticipate Ogden Nash rather than Eliot:

> So next Morning we told *Whittle*, and he fell a Swearing;
> Then my Dame *Wadgar* came, and she, you know, is
>   thick of Hearing;
> *Dame*, said I, as loud as I could bawl, do you know what
>   a Loss I have had?
> Nay, said she, my Lord *Collway*'s Folks are all very sad.
> (ll. 24–27)

But the 'Petition' is also the first of several brilliant mimicries of servant-talk, looking forward not only to 'Mary the Cook-Maid's Letter' ([1718] III: 985 ff.), but to famous feats of cliché-anthologising, of demotic as well as of polite speech, in prose.[12] It is a talent which Eliot displayed very memorably at least once, in the second half of 'A Game of Chess' in the *Waste Land*.[13]

Over the years, Swift became one of the masters in a great English tradition of serious light verse which includes Skelton, Butler, Prior, Byron and Auden. Byron said, Swift 'beats us all hollow, his rhymes are wonderful'.[14] Swift recognised as much as the others that light verse could be made a vehicle of serious commentary, and that an avoidance of the more officially recognised 'serious' styles did not necessarily imply triviality. 'I have been only a Man of Rhimes, and that upon Trifles, never having written serious Couplets in my Life; yet never any without a moral View,' he wrote in 1732 (*Correspondence*, IV: 52). Among the forms of light verse which he adopted instead, the principal one was the Hudibrastic,[15] which he developed into that sinewy, flexible style, with its conversational manner, its controlled digressiveness and its cheeky rhyming, so admired by Byron.

Swift's abandonment of the decasyllabic or 'heroic' couplet (he used it less than Byron, for example) extended even to those satiric or mock-heroic or informally colloquial contexts to which Pope and other contemporaries were able triumphantly to adapt the form. In the 1730s, both Swift and Pope wrote apologias for their own satire, in imitation of Horace, *Sat.*, II: i, and their respective kinds of informality may usefully be contrasted. Swift's poem begins:

> Since there are persons who complain
> There's too much satire in my vein . . .
> ([1730] *Poems*, II: 489)

Pope's begins:

> There are (I scarce can think it, but am told)
> There are to whom my Satire seems too bold . . .[16]

Both are informal, easy, colloquial. But Swift's colloquial ease is that of brisk, dry chatter, whereas Pope's has a proud witty sweep, a formalised freedom and a kind of excited grandeur not unlike that of Yeats (Yeats's deep regard for Swift, and his dislike of Pope, may be paradoxically connected with this: did Yeats shy, in Pope, from an arrogant fervour too like his own?).[17] Pope's poem, though imitating Horace, is full of Juvenalian majesties of self-projection: 'To VIRTUE ONLY and HER FRIENDS, A FRIEND', 'Scriblers or Peers, alike are *Mob* to me' (ll. 121,

140).[18] Swift, on the other hand, though often called Juvenalian, keeps the attack in a low key ('Must I commend against my conscience / Such stupid blasphemy and nonsense?' [ll. 37–38]), shortening his Horatian original so as to evade some high gestures, with a short dry angry boast coming only at the end (and through the mouth of his 'adversary' or interlocutor at that). The metrical difference has much to do with these differences of tone, Pope's couplets preserving, within the informal idiom, much of their 'heroic' flavour, Swift's Hudibrastics waiving all such claims from the start. Metre is, of course, only one contributory factor in the total effect, but it is fair to say that the initial choice of metre was already, in both poets, an expression of personality.

The Hudibrastic metre was not only a guard against 'heroic' pretension in a limited sense. The fluent finalities of the high couplet gave it a certain tendency to orderly containment which Swift's temperament repudiated (although, as the ending of the 'City Shower' or the lines on Walpole in 'To Mr Gay' show, he could himself transcend this tendency in order to do justice to the vitality of disorderly fact). In the face of life's teeming disorders, the order of art seemed to Swift a falsifying thing, and the confident accents of priests of the muses a kind of misplaced rhetoric. In a satire on Vanbrugh ([1703] *Poems*, I: 80) he wrote:

> And now he spreads his little Fans,
> (For all the Muses Geese are Swans)
> And borne on fancy's Pinions, thinks,
> He soars sublimest when he Sinks.
>
> (ll. 49–52)

This manuscript of 'Vanbrug's House', like its fuller printed version (*Poems*, I: 105 ff.),[19] is full of characteristic Swiftian jokes against the republic of bad poets: garrets, castles in the air, poverty, soaring-and-sinking, a maggotlike destructiveness of ancient edifices of sweetness and light. The little parenthetic mock-courtesy of '(For all the Muses Geese are Swans)' is instructive. Its ironic point is, of course, that swans like Vanbrugh are actually geese, and there is no Yeatsian glow at the thought that swans might grow out of ugly ducklings: 'For even daughters of the swan can share / Something of every paddler's heritage'.[20] It seems possible that Swift's line mingled with Hans Andersen's story in Yeats's mind, to be sublimed not only by a grand reversal of valuations (openly soaring 'sublimest when he Sinks'), but by Yeats's bold and somewhat Popeian decasyllabic sweep.

Swift made no Yeatsian claims for farmyard birds, but he did recurrently compare poets to them. In 'The Progress of Poetry' ([1720] *Poems*, I: 230 f.), a poet is again compared to a farmer's goose who, if in funds, is too fat to fly, and if hungry, 'singing flies, and flying sings, / While from below all *Grub-street* rings'.[21] The sublime counterpart of Swift's goose is Baudelaire's albatross, proud and beautiful in the air, but unable to walk on the ground: the poet as a high lonely figure, ill adapted to society's earthbound ways. Baudelaire would not have shared Swift's contempt for that high place of poets, the garret, but that is a matter of period and of differing cultural attitudes. Swift resists high-flying *as such*, and part of him instinctively thought of poetry as high-flying. The Hudibrastic metre is a stylistic declaration of this resistance.

But Swift's most notorious poetic deflations are those which are directed against the idealisations of conventional love poetry, or which make use of excremental imagery as a comically or harshly degrading reminder of the animal facts; and there is an important group of poems which, like some of the city poems, have a signposted mock-pastoral element. Just as the city squalors are played off against poetic inventions of Arcadian innocence and peace, so the physical realities of the human animal are played off against the erotic idealism, and the stylised plangencies, of the pastoral universe of Strephons, Chloes, Celias and their like. And as in the city poems, more is usually at work than a simple parody of idealising poeticisms.

'The Progress of Beauty' ([1719] *Poems*, I: 225 ff.) is the first of the Strephon-Celia poems. It is a piece of neo-metaphysical *vers de société*, some of whose language and cadence seems to look back to Marvell ('Twixt earthly Femals and the Moon / All Parallells exactly run,' [ll. 9–10]), but which seems even closer in feeling to T. S. Eliot:

> When first Diana leaves her Bed
> Vapors and Steams her Looks disgrace,
> A frouzy dirty colour'd red
> Sits on her cloudy wrinckled Face.
>
> But by degrees when mounted high
> Her artificiall Face appears
> Down from her Window in the Sky,
> Her Spots are gone, her Visage clears.
>
> (ll. 1–8)

Until the last line and a half, which makes it clear that Diana is the Moon, not a woman, she seems a figure from the world of Sweeney or Grishkin. The parallel between the moon and the unchaste woman (a reversal of 'the conventional comparison of the chaste lady with the pure Diana')[22] is found again in Eliot's 'Rhapsody on a Windy Night', where the moon and the street-walker are made to blur into one another:

> The lamp hummed:
> 'Regard the moon,
> La lune ne garde aucune rancune,
> She winks a feeble eye,
> She smiles into corners.
> She smooths the hair of the grass.
> The moon has lost her memory.
> A washed-out smallpox cracks her face, . . . '

The main and overt influences are Laforguian, and the haunting and ambiguous fluidities of interpenetration are far removed from the ruthless, clipped Marvellian logic of Swift's analogy. But the subject matter of the analogy in both poets is the same, and Eliot's last line has a certain imaginative kinship with the cracked face of the Diana-Celia of Swift's poem ('The Paint by Perspiration cracks, / And falls in Rivulets of Sweat, . . . Each Night a Bit drops off her Face' [ll. 37–38, 87]).[23]

Swift's poem elaborates its parallel between 'earthly Femals and the Moon', so that all it says about Diana is applicable to Strephon's Celia. Its theme, a recurrent one in the whole group to which this poem belongs, is that if Strephon could see Celia as she got out of bed, 'All reeking in a cloudy Steam, / Crackt Lips, foul Teeth, and gummy Eyes' (ll. 14–15), he would be horrified. Luckily, Celia can restore herself with cosmetics, so that 'after four important Hours / Celia's the Wonder of her Sex' (ll. 53–54). But there comes a time when nothing is left for the cosmetic art to work on, and 'The best Mechanick Hand must fayl' (l. 79).

At this point, Celia is like the waning moon, and the waning is seen as a mechanical disintegration (parts dropping off each night):

> And this is fair Diana's Case
> For, all Astrologers maintain
> Each Night a Bit drops off her Face
> When Mortals say she's in her Wain.
> (ll. 85–88)

This not only reverses the preceding image of mechanical or cosmetic patching up, but is in turn reversed by tentative but finally unfulfilled notions of a new mechanical reassembly. As, ashamed to be seen in her growing ugliness, 'rotting Celia stroles the Street / When sober Folks are all a-bed' (ll.103–104), she starts to decompose, and cosmetics are not enough:

> No Painting can restore a Nose,
> Nor will her Teeth return again.
>
> Two Balls of Glass may serve for Eyes,
> White Lead can plaister up a Cleft,
> But these alas, are poor Supplyes
> If neither Cheeks, nor Lips be left.
>
> (ll.111–116)[24]

This has a kind of horrific jauntiness, and the poem closes with a gay mock-gallant appeal to the gods of love to 'Send us new Nymphs with each new Moon'. The jauntiness is not present in a more famous poem of twelve years later, 'A Beautiful Young Nymph Going to Bed' ([1731] *Poems*, II: 580 ff.). Here also a decaying whore is held together in working hours by means of artificial hair, eye, eyebrows, teeth, breasts, etc., which conceal 'Her Shankers, Issues, running Sores' (l.30), and she is also heavily cosmeticised. Before retiring to sleep, she takes off her artificial parts one by one, revealing the real presence beneath the patchwork. The flayed woman of the *Tale* is brought to mind; but the poem, though more circumstantial, is, as I have argued elsewhere,[25] less shocking because it is a leisurely formulaic elaboration, working out a clearly spelled out moral theme, rather than generating a sudden 'gratuitous' shock.

Nevertheless, the details are horrific, and the poem is often instanced as an example of unhealthy intensity and morbid body-hatred on Swift's part. Ehrenpreis counters this view by citing several parallels which show that the main formula of an apparently beautiful woman (or handsome man) held together by artificial parts was a literary commonplace before and after Swift.[26] Swift's description possibly outdoes most of the others in scabrous detail; but this might be partly due to a desire to play the gimmick for all it is worth, outdoing the competitors with a cheeky perfectionist bravura. Such bravura would not be inconsistent with the dry, poker-faced quality of Swift's enumeration.

On the other hand, Swift adds elements that do not seem to

exist in the analogues. He has his heroine wake up to find that during the night

> A wicked Rat her Plaister stole,
> Half eat, and dragg'd it to his Hole.
> The Crystal Eye, alas, was miss't;
> And *Puss* had on her Plumpers p – st. . . .
> (ll.59–62)

And while poor Corinna labours every morning to 'recollect the scatter'd Parts' (1.68), the poet's 'bashful Muse' turns away,[27] and the poem ends with a dry abruptness which surely subdues any previous overtones of playful fantastication:

> *Corinna* in the Morning dizen'd,
> Who sees, will spew; who smells, be poison'd.
> (ll.73–74)

This extreme dryness, and the tart *literalness* of the outburst, are relatively rare in Swift's verse. Even in the 'Beautiful Young Nymph', the eruption is very brief, a spasm of irritation (real or rhetorical or both) as the cumulative force of the whole scabrous enumeration gathers in the poet's mind in the conclusion. 'Strephon and Chloe' and 'Cassinus and Peter' ([both 1731, and published as a pamphlet with the 'Beautiful Young Nymph' in 1734] *Poems*, II: 584 ff.) are, almost throughout, much more animated in manner and feeling. In the first, Strephon (along with many other swains) woos the beautiful Chloe. Modern courtship is described with a brisk headlong grace which calls to mind the Byron of *Beppo* or *Don Juan*:

> Think what a Case all Men are now in,
> What ogling, sighing, toasting, vowing!
> What powder'd Wigs! What Flames and Darts!
> What Hampers full of bleeding Hearts!
> (ll.33–36)

But the principal purpose of 'Strephon and Chloe' is to expose the foolish idealism of Strephon, who does not expect, and cannot bear, to find a human reality behind his wife's fine clothes. Chloe, unlike the heroines of 'The Progress of Beauty' and the 'Beautiful Young Nymph', is not a withered hag, but only a normal girl, who, after the eating and drinking of her wedding day, will naturally have some unromantic bodily needs. Strephon had been shy of touching this goddess, but he now

> Cry'd out, ye Gods, what Sound is this?
> Can *Chloe*, heav'nly *Chloe* —— ?
> (ll. 177–178)

As the smell grows and he recognises that she is 'As *mortal* as himself at least' (l. 186), he is himself emboldened 'To reach the Pot on t'other Side' (l. 190). The result is a situation out of slapstick farce:

> And as he fill'd the reeking Vase,
> Let fly a Rouzer in her Face.
> (ll. 191–192)

This devolution into farce marks a decisive and vigorous change. The 'little *Cupids*' who had attended on the lovers with an aerial delicacy out of *The Rape of the Lock*, now vanish forever, taking with them the brittle idealisms of the polite world (ll. 193 ff.). (Their feelings of shame reappear, much transformed, in the two golden Cupidons of the *Waste Land*, [ll. 80–81].) The marriage is vulgarised, not improved. If there is some dubious gain in the fact that the couple 'learn to call a Spade, a Spade,'[28] the advantages of seeing them freed 'from all Constraint' are hardly seductive (ll. 203 ff.). Smelly intimacies, coarse words, and free farting replace decency as well as pretence:

> For, Beauty, like supreme Dominion,
> Is best supported by Opinion;
> If Decency brings no Supplies,
> Opinion falls, and Beauty dies.
> (ll. 223–226)

But if 'Decency' itself is a mere social fiction, Swift would nevertheless not do without it. The ambiguity, or impasse, is characteristic. Between the civilised lie and the beastly truth, the middle way is hard to find. The poem may seem to warn the Strephons against poetic fictions which impute aethereality to the fair sex. But the moral is not quite as cosy as the commonsense critics would have it. If Strephon had known the bodily facts beforehand, the marriage, far from being started on a sounder basis, would probably not have occurred at all:

O *Strephon*, e'er that fatal Day
When *Chloe* stole your Heart away,
Had you but through a Cranny spy'd
On House of Ease your future Bride,
In all the Postures of her Face,
Which Nature gives in such a Case;
Distortions, Groanings, Strainings, Heavings;
'Twere better you had lickt her Leavings,
Than from Experience find too late
Your Goddess grown a filthy Mate.
Your Fancy then had always dwelt
On what you saw, and what you smelt;
Would still the same Ideas give ye,
As when you spy'd her on the Privy.
And, spight of *Chloe*'s Charms divine,
Your Heart had been as whole as mine.

(ll. 235–250)

When Swift asks near the end of the poem, 'What Edifice can long endure, / Rais'd on a Basis unsecure?' (ll. 299–300), he does not primarily mean a more clearheaded acceptance of the facts of the body. He means that the body must take second place to Sense, Wit, Decency, Prudence, Good Nature (ll. 307–309). The 'Decency' which was earlier identified with sentimental or truth-evading conventions (ll. 225, 252), is now identified with a good decorum which must surely keep the cloacal necessities just as firmly out of sight.

Reality and artifice, in other words, are at their usual tug of war. We must in some sense face the reality of the flayed woman and the gutted beau, but decency and civilisation demand that they also be kept out of sight. It is sentimental of the critics to say that Swift resolved the dilemma by some kind of 'compromise' or middle way; it is the fact that he never resolved it at all which gives his work its particular urgency and truth. The imbecile 'author' of the 'Digression concerning Madness', extolling 'the Assistance of Artificial *Mediums*, false Lights, refracted Angles, Varnish, and Tinsel', is the very same who, in the next sentence, speaks more than he knows for his satirist-creator when he says that the art 'of *Unmasking* . . . has never been allowed fair Usage, either in the *World* or the *Play-House*' (*Works*, I: 109).

In some ways Swift's foolish 'author' resembles the Baudelaire of 'L'Amour du mensonge':

> Mais ne suffit-il pas que tu sois l'apparence,
> Pour réjouir un coeur qui fuit la vérité?
> Qu' importe ta bêtise ou ton indifférence?
> Masque ou décor, salut! J'adore ta beauté.

Such outrageous paradoxes are for 'moderns' to wallow in. Baudelaire in other moods, like Swift's 'author', enjoyed digging beneath surfaces to the squalors within. The famous prefatory poem addressed to the *hypocrite lecteur* speaks of our fondness for the repugnant realities of life's Satanic puppet show:

> C'est le Diable qui tient les fils qui nous remuent!
> Aux objets répugnants nous trouvons des appas.

But where Baudelaire embraces with eloquent sensuousness the visceral squalors of flayed women and decaying nymphs, Swift's 'author' cannot take more than a limited dose of such pungent realities. When he tries to dissect 'the Carcass of *Humane Nature*', he quickly finds that it '*smelt* so strong, I could preserve it no longer' (*Works*, I: 77). The Baudelairian cherishing of our uglinesses of mind and body, 'Comme les mendiants nourrissent leur vermine', is not for him. But nor is it for Swift himself, who would not deny the existence of the vermin or the beggars (and offers some grim descriptions of both), but would not encourage anything that increased their visibility in everyday life or allowed their open presence to impair the hard-won decencies of civilised living.

Like Baudelaire, Swift thought of life as a shoddy spectacle, puppet show or bad play, full of falsehood and disguise, yet all too wretchedly real. The blurring of world and playhouse into unexpected interpenetrations occurs in 'Strephon and Chloe', as in the *Tale of a Tub*, but in a lower and frankly more farcical key. The awakening to an ugly reality (Strephon farting in Chloe's face as he fills the pot) happens paradoxically through a stylised chamberpot accident which comes straight out of slapstick comedy. When Pope called Swift 'an Avenging Angel of wrath', he spoke at the same time of Swift's breaking his 'Vial of Indignation over the heads of the wretched pityful creatures of this World' (*Correspondence*, III: 108).[29] Sublimities of punitive fury were aptly seen as going hand in hand with a farcical indignity. Swift's own saying that life was 'a Farce ... in every sense but the most important one, for it is a ridiculous tragedy, which is the worst kind of composition' (*Correspondence*, III: 456), similarly contains other elements than the grandiose poignancy we tend to see in it, as I suggested in chapter 1. If truth is painful, and indecorous, like a play in bad taste, it is also 'ridiculous', funny – and, in some paradoxical ways, just as artificial.

If the chamberpot farce in 'Strephon and Chloe', like the satirist's vials of indignation broken on the heads of mankind, is a means of awakening us to reality, that particular reality, in the poem at least, is rejected by Swift. Its faecal intimacies are not much better than the glamorised vacuities which they replace, though clearly more physical or 'organic'. But later in the poem, as sometimes in Baudelaire, it is to the 'mechanisms' of the puppet show that life (disguise *and innards* both) is compared:

> Why is a handsome Wife ador'd
> By ev'ry Coxcomb, but her Lord?
> From yonder Puppet-Man inquire,
> Who wisely hides his Wood and Wire;
> Shews *Sheba*'s Queen completely drest,
> And *Solomon* in Royal Vest;
> But, view them litter'd on the Floor,
> Or strung on Pegs behind the Door;
> *Punch* is exactly of a Piece
> With *Lorraine*'s Duke, and Prince of *Greece*.
> (ll. 283–292)

Tangible excrement and the idiot void, human viscera and bits of string are closer to one another in this vision than we think, or than Swift might openly claim. Appearance and Reality (those sturdy handmaids of the critic) are locked in an unnatural embrace, and Swift finally knows (unlike the critics) that he cannot separate them. Still less can he decide which to prefer, for Appearance is not only 'false Lights' but 'Decency', and Reality is frank 'unmasking' *and* the Yahoo beast.

If it seems complacent to see in this a simple fondness for middle ways and golden means, it is also facile to overemphasise morbidity and disgust. The verse of 'Strephon and Chloe' has a witty *élan*, which stops well short of Rabelaisian expansiveness, but which neither seems frozen to a morbid constraint, nor buried in indulgent sensualities of squalor. A live, intelligent and not unjoyful vitality animates the portrayals, not only of vacuous courting rituals ('ogling, sighing, toasting, vowing!' [l. 34]), but also of excremental fact ('Distortions, Groanings, Strainings, Heavings' [l. 241]).

A similar degree (if not quite the same kind) of animation occurs in 'Cassinus and Peter' ([1731] *Poems*, II: 593 ff.). In this lighthearted amalgam of mock-pastoral and undergraduate fun (the two heroes are 'Two College Sophs of *Cambridge* Growth' (l.1]), the ironic contrast between erotic idealisation and excremental fact is established more crudely or formulaically. Peter visits Cassinus and finds him dejected, a dejection connected with his beloved Caelia, but whose exact cause neither Peter nor we can discover for over a hundred lines. After a protracted mock-suspense, as Cassinus grows more and more frantic and Peter more and more curious, the famous pay-off line occurs at the close:

> Nor wonder how I lost my Wits;
> Oh! *Caelia, Caelia, Caelia* sh—.
> (ll.117–118)

As in 'Strephon and Chloe', the verse has a Byronic lightness, playful rhyming, a brisk animation of movement. It lacks the more many-sided sharpness of 'Strephon and Chloe', however, and much of its vigour lies in the zany elaboration of mystery and the comic drop of the final revelation. The last line has become famous because it shocked Lawrence, Huxley and others into healthy-minded denunciations of Swift's bowel-hatred and misogyny.[30] The verve, and the formulaic arrangement itself, of this poem make very clear not only Swift's fun, but the exposure of Cassinus as a bit of an ass. The irony spells out not bowel-hatred, but the fatuous naivety of the bowel-hater.

But Huxley and others were talking not only of this poem, but of its more famous predecessor, 'The Lady's Dressing Room' ([1730] *Poems*, II: 524 ff.), where the offending line also occurs (l.118). Strephon steals into Celia's room and discovers the detritus of her toilette, 'various Combs for various Uses, / Fill'd up with Dirt' (ll.20–21), a paste composed of 'Sweat, Dandriff, Powder, Lead and Hair' (l.24),[31] 'Ointments good for scabby Chops' (l.36), a basin for spitting and spewing, dirty towels, petticoats, handkerchiefs, stockings, tweezers. These things are enumerated with a headlong exuberance which, despite the squalor of the material, is prevented in various ways from acquiring the aggressive disturbance of some satiric enumerations in *Gulliver's Travels*, where catalogues of abundance tend to suggest, or to mimic, irrepressible energies of evil. Here, on the other hand, an urbane elegance of descriptive notation, a lively

168

exactitude of reportage, the metrical lightness, the early sign-posting of the parody of idealistic inflation and gallant compliment ('Strephon ... / ... swears how damnably the Men lie, / In calling *Celia* sweet and cleanly' [ll.16–18]) keep any undue intensities at bay.

A Gulliverian image in the poem helps to define its essential difference from Gulliverian acerbity:

> The Virtues we must not let pass,
> Of *Celia*'s magnifying Glass.
> When frighted *Strephon* cast his Eye on't
> It shew'd the Visage of a Gyant.
> A Glass that can to Sight disclose,
> The smallest Worm in *Celia*'s Nose,
> And faithfully direct her Nail
> To squeeze it out from Head to Tail;
> For catch it nicely by the Head,
> It must come out alive or dead.
>
> (ll.59–68)

This repeats a joke which occurs several times in *Gulliver*, where the relative sizes of Lilliputians, Brobdingnagians, and Gulliver himself enforce some ironies of visual perspective:[32] Brobdingnagian women drive home to Gulliver how human ladies would look to a Lilliputian eye: the Nurse with her 'monstrous Breast ... The Nipple ... half the Bigness of my Head ... the Dug so varified with Spots, Pimples and Freckles, that nothing could appear more nauseous' (*Works*, XI: 91); the Beggar 'with a Cancer in her Breast, swelled to a monstrous Size, full of Holes, in two or three of which I could have easily crept, and covered my whole Body', and the lice of the Beggars, with their limbs distinctly visible, 'and their Snouts with which they rooted like Swine' (*Works*, XI: 112–113), etc. ... There is comedy here too. Gulliver the projector would have done some dissecting of one of these lice 'if I had proper Instruments (which I unluckily left behind me in the Ship) although indeed the Sight was so nauseous, that it perfectly turned my Stomach' (*Works*, XI: 113). But the last words show how quickly the comedy blackens. Grotesqueries like that of the Maid of Honour who used to set Gulliver 'astride upon one of her Nipples' (*Works*, XI: 119) have a Rabelaisian extravagance, but it is Rabelais, as Coleridge said, 'in a dry place',[33] and charged with astringency and revulsion. (It is interesting that Baudelaire, so much more often than Swift given to indulgences of revulsion, has, in 'La Géante', a similar erotic fantasy involving a young giantess, but full of a genial, tender and undisgusted longing to enjoy and explore the magnificent geography of her body.) And Swift's humour on this theme in *Gulliver's Travels* is closely related to some Kafkaesque horrors, like that of the huge rat in the first chapter of book II which might have torn Gulliver to pieces (*Works*, XI: 93).

The metaphorical worms in Celia's nose are hardly to be compared with the lurid nausea of the Beggar's breast, or even with the tart disgust of the Nurse's 'Spots, Pimples and Freckles'. They belong much more closely to a world of Hudibrastic fun.[34] The passage from the poem is something of a set piece, with (surprisingly) a quality of light, almost balletic, animation:

> And faithfully direct her Nail
> To squeeze it out from Head to Tail;
> For catch it nicely by the Head,
> It must come out alive or dead.
>
> (ll. 65–68)

This animation is quite special. The worms have neither the energetic bestiality of the Gulliverian lice, nor for example the teeming and deathly splendours of the 'noirs bataillons / De larves' which come out of the stomach of Baudelaire's 'Charogne', that 'carcasse superbe' which opens up like a filthy-smelling flower. Here, as the poet compares the carrion by the wayside to the fate of his mistress, the serenities of 'La Géante' are wholly absent.

The theme of worms doing their business on the dead is one to which Baudelaire often returned, sometimes with surprising self-identifications, often with a queer tenderness, and always with a special and vivid intensity. In 'Je t'adore à l'égal de la voûte nocturne', Baudelaire compares his pursuit of his cold mistress to worms attacking a corpse; in 'Remords Posthume', the guiltlike worm will eat away at the skin of the mistress's corpse; in 'Le Mort Joyeux', the poet invites the worms, 'noirs compagnons, ... Philosophes viveurs, fils de la pourriture', to take him freely; in 'La servante au grand coeur', the lovely passage beginning, 'Les morts, les pauvres morts, ont de grandes douleurs', which speaks of the dead with an almost sensuous nostalgic compassion, has a vivid line about their 'Vieux squelettes gelés travaillés par le ver'.

Swift's animation in the passage about Celia's nose is that of deadpan humour. Baudelaire's is of horrified enchantment. The difference of subject matter accounts for much of the difference. The special dryness with which Swift can play with a metaphorical fantasy of worms eating away at the human frame is something of which Baudelaire would have been incapable. In *A Full and True Account of the Solemn Procession to the Gallows, at the Execution of William Wood, Esquire and Hard-ware-man, Written in the Year 1724*, we read:

> We hear the Body is not yet interred; which occasions many Speculations. But what is more wonderful, it is positively assured by many who pretend to have been Eye-witnesses; that there does not appear the least Alteration in any one Lineament or Feature of his Countenance, nor visible Decay in his whole Frame, further than what had been made by Worms long before his Execution. The Solution of which Difficulty, I shall leave among Naturalists.
>
> *(Works, X: 149)*

Swift delights in this 'antinatural' problem for 'Naturalists': its 'Solution' is, of course, that the dead 'Wood' is a wooden effigy. Swift the joker and Wood the victim aptly share the wooden or deadpan expression of the stage comic.

There are, in Swift, both worms and carcasses which, unlike those of Wood's effigy, or of Celia's nose in 'The Lady's Dressing Room', *are* charged with a special intensity: '*Wisdom* is . . . a *Nut*, which . . . may cost you a Tooth, and pay you with nothing but a *Worm*' (*Works*, I: 40); the dissected 'Carcass of *Humane Nature*', which '*smelt* so strong, I could preserve it no longer' (*Works*, I: 77); the flayed woman and stripped beau in the 'Digression concerning Madness' (*Works*, I: 109–110). These things, however, are not only partly controlled in each case by a note of parodic playfulness, but also (insofar as, very powerfully, they transcend the parody) have a vitality of harsh sudden shock rather than of protracted indulgence.[35] And the shock is largely conceptual, with relatively little visual elaboration. In the 'Beautiful Young Nymph', where elaboration of visual detail *does* exist, it exists largely, as we have seen, as a formulaic accumulation, where most of the effects are predictable in principle, and where super-charged intensities based on *surprise* are therefore rare. Perhaps the only such intensity of suddenness is the laconic eruption which brings all contemplation of the carcass, and indeed the poem itself, to an end ('Who sees, will spew; who smells, be poison'd').

The 'Beautiful Young Nymph' may be contrasted with one of

Baudelaire's poems about the 'affreuse Juive', Sara. The poem, 'Je n'ai pas pour maîtresse une lionne illustre', resembles Shakespeare's 'My mistress' eyes are nothing like the sun' both in the rhetorical reversal of its opening line, and in its peculiar combination of erotic tenderness and sensual recoil or disgust. Like Swift's poem, it is about a whore who strolls the streets, suffers from hunger, diseases and tormented dreams, is heavily covered in make-up, wears 'artificial Hair' and has 'flabby Dugs' (Swift, *Poems*, II: 581–583; Baudelaire, *Oeuvres Complètes*, 196–198). But where Swift coolly recoils from the squalor, Baudelaire lavishes a rich, erotically charged devotion on the woman ('ma reine, ma duchesse, / . . . qui dans ses deux mains a réchauffé mon coeur'), showering kisses on her balding brow (more peeled than a leper) and sucking and biting her sagging breasts. The poem illustrates closely Baudelaire's famous statement in 'Au Lecteur' about our fateful sensuous fascination with such 'objets répugnants' in their most specifically sexual manifestations ('Ainsi qu'un débauché pauvre qui baise et mange / Le sein martyrisé d'une antique catin').

There is no *fascination* of hate in Swift's portrayal of the crippled old hag in the 'Beautiful Young Nymph', but none also of the queer fascinated tenderness with which Baudelaire writes of the misshapen hags (once beautiful women, mothers, courtesans, or saints) in 'Les Petites Vieilles', for example when he notes their shrivelled smallness in old age and death:

> Avez-vous observé que maints cercueils de vieilles
> Sont presqu'aussi petits que celui d'un enfant?

This tenderness is not unconnected with the more positively erotic charge of feeling in 'Une Charogne', where the poet tells his mistress that one day she will resemble the putrefying carcass, and especially when the carcass itself is seen with its legs in the air, 'comme une femme lubrique'. The 'Shankers, Issues, running Sores' of the 'Beautiful Young Nymph' are cool by comparison.

Baudelaire responded to such things with a warmth of self-involvement, and a quality of entranced sensuousness unthinkable in Swift:

> Dans les plis sinueux des vieilles capitales,
> Où tout, même l'horreur, tourne aux enchantements . . .

This grand opening of 'Les Petites Vieilles' shows that in Baudelaire's vision, as in Swift's, the teeming squalors of great cities,

172

and those of the decaying human body, were closely related. But Swift refused the *enchantments*, whether of cities or of carcasses. Baudelaire, not surprisingly, thought of Swift as a 'farceur froid';[36] and Swift might have scorned not only these grandeurs, but some of the humourless dandy rigidities of Baudelaire, dismissing him as a 'modern' and a beau. Swift's self-implication in the frailties and corruptions revealed by his own satire is insistent and profound, like Baudelaire's: but it differs greatly from Baudelaire's in its character. Swift would certainly recognise, wryly, that if 'his *Brain*, his *Heart*, and his *Spleen*' were 'laid open', like those of the Beau in the 'Digression concerning Madness' (*Works*, I: 110), the operation would likewise alter his appearance for the worse. But when Baudelaire proclaims his identity with the hanged man in 'Un Voyage à Cythère' (with his innards, opened by birds of prey, pouring out into his thighs), he indulges in quite unSwiftian luxuries of self-immolation:

> Ridicule pendu, tes douleurs sont les miennes! . . .
>
> Dans ton île, o Venus! je n'ai trouvé debout
> Qu'un gibet symbolique où pendait mon image . . . .

Later critical tradition has sometimes seen Swift as a Byronic or Baudelairian hero, taking to himself, like Byron's Prometheus, 'the sufferings of mortality', lonely and proud as the vulture devours his innards.[37] In *his* poem *Prometheus* ([1724] *Poems*, I: 343 ff.), Swift treats that hero not as a noble rebel, but as a squalid thief, alias William Wood, for whom he recommends an updated form of Promethean torment, the gallows (the fate, oddly, of Baudelaire's hero),

> Where, if we find his *Liver* grows,
> For want of *Vultures*, we have *Crows*[38]
> (ll. 75–76)

(When Byron wrote on Ireland's oppression in 'The Irish Avatar' [ll. 45 ff.], it was one of Ireland's champions, Grattan, and not an oppressor like Wood, whom he identified with Prometheus.)[39] Characteristically, Swift's lines show him not only steering clear of those Romantic grandeurs of the suffering self which Yeats and others imputed to him ('Swift beating on his breast in sibylline frenzy blind / Because the heart in his blood-sodden breast had dragged him down into mankind'),[40] but also rewriting the old Titanic myth in a very low key.

Even in mock-heroic, Swift shied from those grandeurs which might rub off on the mockery. He seldom wrote sustained mock-heroic, on the model of *The Dunciad*, and his rare and sporadic moments of mock-heroic inflation are rigorously prevented from disturbing the radical flatness of his manner. When Strephon, in 'The Lady's Dressing Room',[41] wishes that Celia may

> better learn to keep
> 'Those Secrets of the hoary deep!',
> (ll. 97–98)

a stately Miltonic enjambment (*Paradise Lost*, II: 891) is wittily assimilated into Swift's light octosyllabic measure, while Milton's 'dark/Illimitable Ocean without bound' (II: 891–892) shrinks to the mysteries of a girl's chamberpot. The buoyant mock-heroic inflations of Pope's Miltonising 'vast profound'[42] are completely absent, just as '*Fleet-Ditch*'s oozy Brinks, / Surrounded with a Hundred Stinks' in the 'Beautiful Young Nymph' (ll. 47–48) lack the rolling amplitude of Pope's riverine pageant, in the *Dunciad* (II: 271–272),

> ... where Fleet-ditch with disemboguing streams
> Rolls the large tribute of dead dogs to Thames.[43]

Fleet-ditch is part of the mock-heroic geography of London,[44] and its 'oozy Brinks' serve Augustan poets as a polluted modern version of great mythological waters, archetypal rivers and seas. In Swift, such waters easily shrink, as he made Milton's illimitable ocean shrink, to the size of a privy. The poet in 'The Lady's Dressing Room' compares Celia to Venus rising from the sea:

> Should I the Queen of Love refuse,
> Because she rose from stinking Ooze?
> (ll. 131–132)

The poet's taunt to Strephon acquires its quasi-heroic colouring by imagining the heroic or mythological prototype as itself containing modern squalors, not as a grandeur from which we have lapsed (contrast Baudelaire's Cythère, which preserves in its modern degradation not only the 'superbe fantôme' of ancient

Venus, but also the splendours and miseries, the ironic or paradoxical sublimities, of the hanged young man).[45] Swift's couplet
(one of several witty perversions of the Venus story)[46] has,
however, a special bracing quality: Venus remains Venus, though
she rises from the privy each day.

The whole question of misogyny, body-hatred, obscenity
must be viewed in the context of Swift's temperamental dislike of
'lofty' writing. Virtually all the examples we have examined
occur in contexts of parody, and there may be a correlation
between Swift's insistence on the 'low' bodily functions, and the
deflations or self-deflations of parody. This correlation is doubtless not a simple one, just as Swift's parody and the motives
behind it are seldom simple. But it is an apt coincidence that the
same friend who elicited the playful denials of misogyny in 'The
Journal of a Modern Lady' also inspired the poem in which Swift
most fully repudiates the 'lofty Stile'. In 'An Epistle to a Lady,
Who Desired the Author to make Verses on her, in the Heroick
Stile' ([1733] *Poems*, II: 628 ff.), Lady Acheson begs Swift to
suspend his 'paultry *Burlesque* Stile ... Turning all to Ridicule'
(ll.50–52) and to 'Sing my Praise in Strain sublime' (l.57).
Swift's reply begins with a few bantering compliments, conceding her social and domestic qualities, but also saying (the theme is
familiar in Swift's serious writing about women) that she must
also learn 'With good sense to entertain us' (l.114). He then enters
into a long account of his unfitness in 'a Stile sublime' (l.258),
concluding on a characteristic note of cheeky friendliness about
her intellectual deficiencies. Towards Lady Acheson, the tone, as
George P. Mayhew has said, is 'one of *raillery*, which turns
seeming blame to praise sincerely meant'.[47]

The second half of the poem (ll.133 ff.) deals with Swift's
rejection of the 'lofty Stile' (ll.140, 218). It contains at the same
time a strong attack on Walpole and his ministry which is
somewhat out of keeping with the genial levity of the first half,
and is believed to have been written at a different time
(1732–1733, as against 1728–1730).[48] Walpole was reputedly so
angered by this poem and by 'On Poetry: A Rapsody' (1733) that
he contemplated arresting Swift.[49] The intensities of the second
half are not only at variance with the first half, but also with the
more bantering portions within the second half itself – notably the
poem's concluding lines, with their renewed 'raillery' of Lady
Acheson, which may perhaps have been drafted earlier, together
with the first half. Moreover, the corrosive political attack is
woven into the parade of lighthearted self-analysis in a way which

175

further complicates or confuses the tone, and which is not altogether free of the lofty postures that Swift pretends to decline. From one of the opening couplets of the second half, 'I, as all the Parish knows, / Hardly can be grave in Prose' (ll. 137–138), to the next couplet, 'Still to lash, and lashing Smile, / Ill befits a lofty Stile' (ll. 139–140), a small tightening of feeling occurs. And very soon, the lightheartedness which Swift boasts of turns into a harsh and jeering scorn: 'I can easier scorn than hate' (l. 144); 'All their Madness makes me merry' (l. 164); 'Like the ever-laughing Sage, / In a Jest I spend my Rage' (ll. 167–168); 'I would hang them if I cou'd' (l. 170); 'Not by Anger, but a Sneer' (l. 228). It is as though the chatty Byron of *Beppo* or *Don Juan* had turned, within the same poem, into the graver and more sinister Byronic hero of *Lara*, that 'hater of his kind' whose gay smile, 'if oft observed and near, / Waned in its mirth, and wither'd to a sneer' (I: xvii).

Unlike Byron, Swift was not temperamentally able to sustain romantic self-projections of the *Lara* type. He must have sensed that he was coming dangerously close to such a posture, and that the urbane banter to Lady Acheson was not sufficient to undercut it. Accordingly, there are some more decisive drops into quasi-farcical or knockabout humour ('Switches better guide than Cudgels'; 'a little gentle Jerking / Sets the Spirits all a working', (ll. 202, 205–206), often charged with coarseness:

> Let me, tho' the Smell be Noisom,
> Strip their Bums; let CALEB hoyse 'em;
> Then, apply ALECTO's Whip,
> Till they wriggle, howl, and skip.
>
> (ll. 177–180)

The scourge of infamy yields to the humbler role of muckraker, a reduction of dignity without reduction of anger. A queer intimacy is established, in which satirist, victim, and reader all partake, the teasing, harsh intimacy of an enclosed, fetid atmosphere.

This intimacy exists also in *Gulliver's Travels*, where a 'lofty Stile', or at least a Swiftian commitment to 'Timons manner' (*Correspondence*, III: 103), is also avoided, and where scatological play and exposure also take place at close quarters. For example, Gulliver's explanation in I: ii that he has given us an unimportant detail about his bodily functions because his maligners have attacked his character 'in Point of Cleanliness' alludes to accusations against Swift of excessive scatological indecency. But, in fact, Swift is cheekily doing the very thing he is denying against the critics, and saying that this proves that he isn't like that really.[50] There is about this kind of joke an aggressive defiance of the reader, an invitation to embarrassment in case the mere scatology on its own failed to shock. Much of the excremental element in *Gulliver*, as well as related passages of so-called body-disgust or sexual revulsion, and the celebration of what the 'Panegyric' called 'The *Horse's Countenance Divine*' (l.176), suggests not so much an excremental obsession as a concern with shaking us out of our 'healthy' sensibilities. *Hypocrite lecteur.*

Swift's scatology is undoubtedly aggressive. But the aggression, fierce as it sometimes is, may, in other words, be less against the bowels or the sexual parts than against that highly personalised representative of mankind, the reader: against his squeamishness, his complacent normality, his shoddy idealisms and self-deceptions, his attachment to the human form divine, and his belief in the rationality of the human mind, in short, against all those serene peaceful states that Swift wants to 'vex' the world out of.

I do not mean by this merely a conscious or official didacticism. Critics remind us that dung is a time-honoured element not only in satiric but in homiletic tradition; that Swift as a churchman wished to instil in us a proper humility, and warn us against sins of the flesh; that he wished us to see truth clearly and without delusion; that he was exhorting us to a middle course between this and that form of excess; or advocating hygiene; or playing with scientific notions of the relativity of vision (e.g., à propos of the huge cancers in the breasts of the Brobdingnagian ladies); or parodying some foolish literary conventions. It would be difficult to say that these views do not all contain some truth. But one sometimes feels that the hysterias of revulsion displayed against Swift by Thackeray or Lawrence, or the equally dispiriting pedantries of the psychoanalysts, are preferable to the calmer but more obstinate scholastic nervosities of present-day 'golden mean' fetishists and other commmon-sense explainers-away.

These current academic explanations of alleged conscious or 'official' purposes always ignore the peculiar energies of Swift's manner, the sudden intensities, the redirections of irony, the needling intimacy, the unsettling exuberance, the laconic asperities. Certainly, Swift took seriously the didactic obligations of the satirist, but when he made Gulliver say to the reader 'my principal Design was to inform, and not to amuse thee', he introduced a special tease into the old Horatian tag about pleasure and instruction. For Gulliver is here protesting not his (undoubted) reformative leanings, but his factual truth, 'plain Matter of Fact' as opposed to wild travellers' tales (*Works*, XI: 291): and by the end of *Gulliver's Travels*, such a joke has a dry disturbing ring. Critics often shy from the exact implications of another of Swift's variations, this time in his own name, on Horace's tag: 'the chief end I propose to my self in all my labors is to *vex* the world rather then divert it' (*Correspondence* III: 102; my italics). *Vex* relates closely to the mood of the 'Epistle to a Lady': 'Till they wriggle, howl, and skip' (l.180), 'a little gentle Jerking / Sets the Spirits all a working' (ll.205–206). We should not be misled by 'gentle'. The word carries a touch of sadistic glee insofar as it is not simply a contrast to the 'Bastings heavy' (l.203) of a more pretentious loftiness of denunciation.[51]

Many of Swift's scatological poems are more lighthearted in manner than the 'Epistle to a Lady', or than *Gulliver's Travels*. Poems like 'The Lady's Dressing Room' and 'Cassinus and Peter' are said by Huxley to be a childish bowel-hating 'refusal . . . to accept the physical reality of the world'.[52] These poems are actually pleas for seeing reality straight, rather than through a rosy film of false poeticising. But Huxley's real mistake, it seems to me, lies in giving a melodramatic gloss to an issue which Swift almost always kept in a low key. The point about '*Celia, Celia, Celia* shits' is not so much that Swift is entirely unmoved, but that any Huxleyan revulsion Swift may have felt is disguised in the comedy of Strephon's or Cassinus's plaintiveness, or undercut by the witty *élan* of the verse. But this *élan*, this lightheartedness, not only parodies solemnity. It also serves to shield Swift from seeming solemn, even in his mockery of solemnity. Like other forms of ironic indirection, it is partly a playing for victory (flinging dung more because it shocks the reader than obsesses Swift), and partly a concealment or defence against the vulnerabilities of an over-exposed sincerity as well as against the risks of self-importance. One of the final objections to a 'lofty Stile' made in the 'Epistle to a Lady' was that 'I Shou'd make a Figure scurvy' (l.219), and perhaps this playful admission should be taken as seriously as the purpose (also playfully expressed) of vexing rather than diverting the world.

A dimension of stylistic undercutting, chiefly through parody, exists even in Swift's most personal poems, those which he wrote to Esther Johnson (Stella) on her birthdays and at other times, between 1719 and her death in 1728. In 'To Stella, Who

Collected and Transcribed his Poems' ([1720] *Poems*, II: 727 ff.), he wrote:

> Thou *Stella*, wert no longer young,
> When first for thee my Harp I strung:
> Without one Word of *Cupid*'s Darts,
> Of killing Eyes, or bleeding Hearts:
> With Friendship and Esteem possesst,
> I ne'er admitted Love a Guest.
>
> (ll. 9–14)

How true the last line is, nobody knows. Swift's relationship with Stella, whom he probably first met in Temple's household in 1689 when she was very young, has never been satisfactorily understood. The mystery surrounding it (which, like the larger questions about Swift's sexual character, has been much sensationalised) seems partly the result of the same temperamental guardedness which produced the protective obliquities of parody, and the self-concealing deflations of Swift's whole ironic manner. The signposted disavowal of '*Cupid*'s darts' and other gestures of love-poetry is part of an exercise which began when, in 1719, he first gave Esther Johnson her poetic name of Stella, in a half-mocking allusion to the heroine of Sidney's poems. The joke could disengage Swift from some vulnerabilities of high sentiment, while not impairing the deep tenderness he clearly felt. As Herbert Davis said, 'paradoxically it could at the same time hide and flaunt the truth that she was "the star whereby his course was only directed"'.[53]

An important theme of these poems, along with the denial of romantic love, is that of a 'Friendship and Esteem' based on mutual respect for moral and intellectual qualities. Swift believed profoundly that these were the only sure basis for a durable relationship between men and women, within or outside marriage. He argued that for this purpose women must cultivate the same intellectual interests as men, meeting them on terms of intelligent conversation and of mutual respect,[54] and abandoning the mindless seductions of female affectation. This doctrine, most fully stated in the prose 'Letter to a Young Lady, on her Marriage, Written in the Year 1723' (*Works*, IX: 83–94), occurs again and again in his writings to and about Stella, as well as in the earlier *Cadenus and Vanessa* (1713). His relationship with both Stella and Vanessa involved a 'tutorial' role on his part. Some of his most moving praise of Stella deals with her success in living up to these exacting 'male' standards (*Poems*, II: 725–726, 734–736; *Works*, V: 228 ff.).

There is nothing unique or necessarily abnormal in this praise of a woman for her 'male' qualities. At a time when women were conventionally expected to be social ornaments rather than intelligent beings, Swift was speaking not of virtues which women necessarily lacked (his point was to assert the opposite), but which society pretended they lacked or discouraged them from possessing. Occasionally, as in 'To Stella, Visiting me in my Sickness', ([1720] *Poems*, II: 722 ff.), he allows a formulaic distinction, in order to praise Stella for combining the best of both sexes:

> Say, *Stella*, was *Prometheus* blind,
> And forming you, mistook your Kind?
> No: 'Twas for you alone he stole
> The Fire that forms a manly Soul;
> Then to compleat it ev'ry way,
> He molded it with Female Clay:
> To that you owe the nobler Flame.
> To this, the Beauty of your Frame.
>
> (ll. 85–92)

The light and chatty compliment is perhaps, at worst, less patronising than Pope's compliment to Martha Blount (was it modelled on Swift's lines?):

> Heav'n, when it strives to polish all it can
> Its last best work, but forms a softer Man.[55]

It is possible that these backhanded gallantries to Stella, together with the disavowal of romantic love and the celebration of intellectual companionship, were Swift's way of saying to Stella *not* that he did not love her, but only that his love was deeper, more soundly based, and freer of cant, than poems normally say. Like the parodic elements, they disengage Swift from the foolishness of cant, and from the vulnerabilities of naked disclosure. We cannot tell exactly what flavour the romantic appellation of Stella had for them both, but the joke would have no point, or might seem merely cruel, if they were not lovers, or at least in love, in some (still puzzling) sense.[56] The Stella poems have this distinctive feature, that the anti–romantic elements are often not denials of the conventions of love poetry, so much as revalidations by means of a saving 'realism'. Even when, as in the

180

birthday poem of 1721 (*Poems*, II: 734 ff.), he asserts that Stella's intellectual qualities will outlast the prettiness of poetic heroines, a gruff tenderness gives literal value to the mock-romantic talk of Stella's angel face and mind:

> Now, this is Stella's Case in Fact;
> An Angel's Face, a little crack't;
> (Could Poets or could Painters fix
> How Angels look at thirty six)
> This drew us in at first to find
> In such a Form an Angel's Mind
> And ev'ry Virtue now supplyes
> The fainting Rays of Stella's Eyes . . .
>
> (ll. 15–22)

Behind this lies a lightly sketched mock-mythology, in which Stella, young, was a pastoral heroine, 'The brightest Virgin of the Green' (*Poems*, II: 721), or perhaps 'Beauty's Queen', whom some youthful poet might have 'sweetly sung' (*Poems*, II: 757). These last words are from the very moving birthday poem of 1725, in which Swift says that age has given her wrinkles, but dimmed his sight so that he cannot see the change:

> No Length of Time can make you quit
> Honour and Virtue, Sense and Wit,
> Thus you may still be young to me,
> While I can better *hear* than *see*;
> Oh, ne'er may Fortune shew her Spight,
> To make me *deaf*, and mend my *Sight*.
>
> (ll. 49–54)

In his copy of the volume in which this poem appeared, Swift wrote fifteen years later, against the last line: 'now deaf 1740'.

Stella died in 1728. Swift gave release to his grief in a prose piece 'On the Death of Mrs. Johnson', begun the night of her death. It is one of the most moving things he ever wrote:

> This day, being Sunday, January 28th, 1727–8, about eight o'clock at night, a servant brought me a note, with an account of the death of the truest, most virtuous, and valuable friend, that I, or perhaps any other person ever was blessed with. She expired about six in the evening of this day; and, as soon as I am left alone, which is about eleven at night,

I resolve, for my own satisfaction, to say something of her life and character.

She was born at Richmond in Surrey on the thirteenth day of March, in the year 1681. Her father was a younger brother of a good family in Nottinghamshire, her mother of a lower degree; and indeed she had little to boast of her birth. I knew her from six years old, and had some share in her education, by directing what books she should read, and perpetually instructing her in the principles of honour and virtue; from which she never swerved in any one action or moment of her life. She was sickly from her childhood until about the age of fifteen: But then grew into perfect health, and was looked upon as one of the most beautiful, graceful, and agreeable young women in London, only a little too fat. Her hair was blacker than a raven, and every feature of her face in perfection . . . .

(Works, V, 227)

There is no question, in such a passage, of tricks of style. The writing has the flat dignity of pain, a brokenhearted matter-of-factness, giving each meticulous detail (the time of death, the date of birth) a kind of stunned significance. But this profound, unguarded genuineness preserves all the lineaments of Swift's parodic manner. The factuality of 'Her father was a younger brother of a good family in Nottinghamshire' is very close to the poker-faced idiom of the opening of *Gulliver*: 'My Father had a small Estate in *Nottinghamshire*; I was the Third of five Sons.' The sentences of heartfelt praise are laced with literal-minded admissions that seem the nonsatiric counterpart to the deflations in the burlesque poems: 'indeed she had little to boast of her birth',[57] 'only a little too fat'.

The latter may be compared with the affectionate quasi-parodic literalness with which Fielding describes Sophia Western: 'a middle-sized Woman; but rather inclining to tall', etc. (*Tom Jones*, IV: ii). The parallel is reinforced by the fact that Fielding tells us that Sophia resembled a now dead woman very dear to him (actually his late wife). Fielding's heavyheartedness on this point is distanced by time, and by a comic context. He sets off his fresh realistic portrait against the blowsy extravagance of a burlesque preamble which mocks the 'sublime' introductions of heroines in romances. Though he makes it clear that Sophia (like Stella in Swift's account) is very beautiful, the drop into the real is the climax of a stylistic deflation as decisive as any in Swift's burlesque poems, though doubtless more genial. It differs from these poems in that their heroines do not necessarily remain beautiful after the rant has been punctured. But it differs from the account of Stella, not because that account is free of hyperboles of celebration, but because these remain wholly unpunctured. The touch of romance jargon in '[she] was looked upon as one of the most beautiful, graceful, and agreeable young women in London .... Her hair was blacker than a raven, and every feature of her face in perfection' is not at all devalued by the insertion of 'only a little too fat' in the middle. The example illustrates the force of his commitment to literal truth, and his guardedness even with those stylistic sublimities to which he wants to give literal value. It shows also how deep a part of his personality is involved in the more stylised undercuttings of the burlesque poetry.

Again, the hyperbole of 'truest, most virtuous' is not undercut but *revalidated* by its context, so that we are disposed to think of it as nothing but the sober truth. The same effect was already present in the earliest poems to Stella, for example 'To Stella, Visiting me in my Sickness' ([1720] *Poems*, II: 722 ff.):

> Ten thousand Oaths upon Record,
> Are not so sacred as her Word:
> The World shall in its Atoms end,
> E'er *Stella* can deceive a Friend.
> (ll. 55–58)

In these deeply felt passages all impulse to parody is waived, or transcended. The fact that the potential, or the raw material, for parody is so freely proffered suggests the extent of Swift's readiness, where Stella is concerned, to drop his ironic guard. There are, of course, several lighthearted poems, like the birthday poem of 1723 or the same year's 'Stella at Wood-Park' (*Poems*, II: 748 ff.). The latter is a banter on Stella getting used to high living at Wood-Park (Charles Ford's house), and then returning to Dublin and homelier fare, with Swift for company. But at the end, the poem takes an uncharacteristic turn, not into deflation, but to a cancellation of the mockery (ll. 73 ff.). The final witty twist is a tender compliment (very different from the satiric mock-gallantries of the burlesques or even the friendly ones to Lady Acheson) in which Swift says that for him, although 'my Raillery were true, / A Cottage is *Wood-Park* with you' (ll. 91–92). Conversely, when Swift warns Stella of certain faults in her character, as in 'To Stella, Who Collected and Transcribed his Poems' (ll. 83 ff.), there is a frank, tender firmness which, though lightly carried, differs radically from the witty badinage to Lady Acheson in the 'Epistle to a Lady' and other Market Hill poems.

In his tributes to Stella's selfless nursing of him in his illness (*Poems*, II: 722 ff. and, especially, II: 754–755), affectionate humour modulates into an unusual, soberly introspective gravity. Even more moving are the poems in which he expresses anxiety for her in her last illness. The verses written while his crossing to Ireland was delayed at 'Holyhead. Sept. 25. 1727' (*Poems*, II: 420–421) have an unusual self-exposing starkness:

> I never was in hast before
> To reach that slavish hateful shore
> Before, I always found the wind
> To me was most malicious kind
> But now, the danger of a friend
> On whom my fears and hopes depend
> Absent from whom all Clymes are curst
> With whom I'm happy in the worst
> With rage impatient makes me wait
> A passage to the land I hate.
>
> (ll. 19–28)

In the last of the birthday poems ([1727] *Poems*, II: 763 ff.), written a few months before the Holyhead verses, the opening badinage strikes a note of tender, mock-cantankerous desperation:

> This Day, whate'er the Fates decree,
> Shall still be kept with Joy by me:
> This Day then, let us not be told,
> That you are sick, and I grown old,
> Nor think on our approaching Ills,
> And talk of Spectacles and Pills;
> To morrow will be Time enough
> To hear such mortifying Stuff.
>
> (ll. 1–8)

Swift then announces a new-found sobriety:

> From not the gravest of Divines,
> Accept for once some serious Lines.
>
> (ll. 13–14)

The poem proceeds to some serious meditations on past and future, on Stella's virtue and her 'Life well spent' (l. 36). There is a spare eloquence about this which is paradoxically heightened, not reduced, by the light octosyllabic metre. But it is at the end of the poem, where a final complimentary turn occurs, that the most poignant effect is achieved. A hint of neatly executed gallantry is transfigured into the most soberly and urgently truthful praise of all:

> O then, whatever Heav'n intends,
> Take Pity on your pitying Friends;
> Nor let your Ills affect your Mind,
> To fancy they can be unkind.
> Me, surely me, you ought to spare,
> Who gladly would your Suff'rings share;
> Or give me Scrap of Life to you,
> And think it far beneath your Due;
> You, to whose Care so oft I owe,
> That I'm alive to tell you so.
>
> (ll. 79–88)

Stella was the only person who drew from Swift such stark unembarrassed sincerities.

1977

Notes

1 Swift's writings are cited in the editions used throughout this volume. The dates given for each poem are dates of composition as suggested by Harold Williams and may or may not be the same as the dates of publication.

   Quotations from Pope's poems use the text and lineation of the Twickenham edition. Page references are not supplied for these, nor for the poems by Baudelaire and Eliot, all of which are easy to find in any collected edition. Texts of Baudelaire are from *Oeuvres Complètes*, ed. Y.-G. Le Dantec, revised by Claude Pichois (Paris: Pléiade, 1961); texts of poems by Eliot are from *Collected Poems 1909–1935* (London: Faber and Faber, 1951), and *Four Quartets* (London: Faber and Faber, 1950).

2 'Les Sept Vieillards'.

3 See Maurice Johnson, 'T. S. Eliot on Satire, Swift, and Disgust', *Papers on Language and Literature*, 5 (1969), 310–315. Some of Eliot's statements are reprinted in *Jonathan Swift. A Critical Anthology*, ed. Denis Donoghue (Harmondsworth: Penguin, 1971), 128–135. For some parallels and resemblances between Eliot and Swift, see above pp. 155–8, 160–1, and nn. 5, 11, 13, 23.

4 'Swift haunts me; he is always just round the next corner.' Introduction to *The Words upon the Window-Pane*, in *Explorations*, ed. Mrs W. B. Yeats (London: Macmillan, 1962), 345.

5   In a letter to Maurice Johnson, 27 June 1947: see Johnson, 'The Ghost of Swift in Eliot's *Four Quartets*', *Modern Language Notes*, 64 (1949), 273; *The Sin of Wit. Jonathan Swift as a Poet* (Syracuse: Syracuse University Press, 1950), 130–131. See also Grover Smith, *T. S. Eliot's Poetry and Plays* (Chicago: University of Chicago Press, 1962), 290, 328n. Eliot seems to have put a different emphasis on the importance of the Swiftian presence in speaking or writing to different persons. Richard Ellmann, *Eminent Domain* (New York: Oxford University Press, 1967), 94, 144n, reports that Eliot told Kristian Smidt that although 'the figure blends various writers, especially Yeats and Swift, it is primarily and recognizably Yeats'. Kristian Smidt's recent book, *The Importance of Recognition: Six Chapters on T. S. Eliot* (Tromsø: A. S. Peder Norbye, 1973), 44, 46n, 81, suggests a still firmer emphasis on Yeats.

6   'Morning at the Window'.

7   'Preludes'.

8   And compare the burlesque night piece which opens *Tom Jones*, X, ii, where Susan the chambermaid is about to retire 'to the Arms of the fond, expecting Ostler'.

9   For an earlier example of lines about morning, in which elements of formal *descriptio* mingle comically with scenes of everyday unromantic activity, and in which several characters similar to Swift's appear (including the slow-paced schoolboy with his satchel), see Charles Cotton's 'Morning Qua-trains', in *Poems*, ed. John Buxton (London: Routledge, 1958), 1–5, cited by Maurice Johnson, *The Sin of Wit*, 14–15.

10 Roger Savage, 'Swift's Fallen City: "A Description of the Morning"', in Brian Vickers (ed.), *The World of Jonathan Swift* (Oxford: Blackwell, 1968), 177.

11 Maurice Johnson, *The Sin of Wit*, 111–112, notes that the line '*Carminative* and *Diuretick*', in 'Strephon and Chloe' ([1731] *Poems*, II: 588, l.133) has an affinity with 'the polysyllabic "Mr Eliot's Sunday Morning Service"'. For another suggested parallel, see Richard C. Turner, 'Burbank and Grub-Street: A Note on T. S. Eliot and Swift', *English Studies*, 52 (1971), 347–348.

12 Swift began collecting materials for the *Complete Collection of Genteel and Ingenious Conversation* ([1738] *Works*, IV: 97 ff.) in 1704 or earlier. On this work, and on Swift's interest in linguistic fashions and affectations, see Herbert Davis's introduction in *Works*, IV: xxviii ff. See also *A Full and True Account of the Solemn Procession to the Gallows, at the Execution of William Wood, Esquire, and Hard-ware-man* ([1724] *Works*, X: 143 ff.).

13 According to the second Mrs Eliot, 'Eliot said this passage was "pure Ellen Kellond", a maid employed by the Eliots, who recounted it to them'. Valerie Eliot (ed.), *The Waste Land: A Facsimile and Transcript of the Original Drafts, Including the Annotations of Ezra Pound* (London: Faber and Faber, 1971), 127n.

14 Ernest J. Lovell, Jr. (ed.), *His Very Self and Voice. Collected Conversations of Lord Byron* (New York: Macmillan, 1954), 268.

15 For some qualifications on the extent of Butler's influence on Swift, see C. L. Kulisheck, 'Swift's Octosyllabics and the Hudibrastic Tradition', *Journal of English and Germanic Philology*, 53 (1954), 361–368.

16 Pope, *The First Satire of the Second Book of Horace Imitated* (1733), ll.1–2. I make a brief comparison of these two poems in 'The Proper Study of Pope', *Times Literary Supplement*, 14 March 1975, p. 275. The discussion goes on more fully to compare Swift, Pope, and Yeats as poets.

17 On 7 April 1930. Yeats wrote to Lady Gregory: 'I am reading Swift, the *Diary to Stella*, and his correspondence with Pope and Bolingbroke; these men

fascinate me, in Bolingbroke the last pose and in Swift the last passion of the Renaissance, in Pope, whom I dislike, an imitation both of pose and passion'. Allan Wade (ed.), *Letters* (London: R. Hart-Davis, 1954), 773. In a manuscript book of 1921, referred to in Donald T. Torchiana's *W. B. Yeats and Georgian Ireland* (Evanston: Northwestern University Press, 1966), 114, Yeats deplored the rigid Roman influence introduced into English letters by Milton, Dryden, and Pope. In his Introduction to *The Oxford Book of Modern Verse 1892–1935* (Oxford: Clarendon Press, 1936), xxi-xxii, Yeats speaks of the early T. S. Eliot as 'an Alexander Pope, working without apparent imagination . . . satirist rather than poet'. See also *A Vision* (London: Macmillan, 1961), 296. There are some excellent brief remarks about 'the arrogance of formal mastery' in the late poems of Pope and of Yeats in Martin Price, *To the Palace of Wisdom* (Garden City, N.Y.: Doubleday, 1965), 166–168.

18 The first of these lines translates l.70 of Horace's poem. Horace is talking about Lucilius, Pope about himself. On this question, and on the Juvenalian qualities of Pope's Horatian imitation, see G. K. Hunter, 'The "Romanticism" of Pope's Horace', *Essays in Criticism*, 10 (1960), 390–404.

19 A third satirical piece on Vanbrugh is 'The History of Vanbrug's House' ([1706] *Poems*, I: 85 ff.).

20 Yeats, 'Among School Children', *Collected Poems* (London: Macmillan, 1952), 243.

21 For a variant of this fable, see the 'Poet, starving in a Garret', in 'To Stella, Who Collected and Transcribed his Poems', ll.25 ff. (*Poems*, II: 728–729), written in the same year as 'The Progress of Poetry'.

22 Kathleen Williams, *Jonathan Swift and the Age of Compromise* (Lawrence: University of Kansas Press, 1958), 149. See also Christine Rees, 'Gay, Swift, and the Nymphs of Drury-Lane', *Essays in Criticism*, 23 (1973), 17. This essay has an enlightening discussion of several of the poems and themes with which I am concerned (esp. 14–20).

23 Eliot's 'Rhapsody' (Swift, incidentally, also used this word for the ironic title of one of his best-known poems) continues with references to 'female smells in shuttered rooms' and other sleazy properties which would not be out of place in Swift's poems. Cf. also the passage about the 'hearty female stench' in Eliot's cancelled pastiche of Pope in the typescript of the *Waste Land*'s 'Fire Sermon', *The Waste Land. A Facsimile and Transcript of the Original Drafts*, 23, 39. The 'passage was written in imitation of *The Rape of the Lock*', as Mrs Eliot says (127n.). Pound told Eliot to scrap it (127n. cited from Eliot's Introduction to Pound's *Selected Poems* [London: Faber and Faber, 1948], 18; see also Eliot's *Paris Review* interview, in Van Wyck Brooks (ed.), *Writers at Work, Second Series* [London: Secker & Warburg, 1963], 83. For Yeats's comment that Eliot was 'an Alexander Pope . . . satirist rather than poet', see above, n. 17). And in the verse-paragraph which includes the 'hearty female stench', Pound objected to a particular coupleteering 'trick of Pope' (39). But much that disappeared at Pound's insistence, though written in 'Popeian' couplets, was more like Swift than Pope. The 'brisk Amanda' with her 'coarsened hand, and hard plebeian tread', who attends on the heroine Fresca's awakening, would be at least as much at home in the 'Description of the Morning' as in Pope's *Rape* (23, 39).

In ensuing lines about Fresca herself, various details of scene or atmosphere take us back to Swift's satires of female polite conversation or to his Celia poems almost as much as to Pope's Belinda (pp. 23, 27, 39–41). Then, in the scene of the typist and the 'young man carbuncular', a draft passage about 'drying combinations ... stockings, dirty camisoles, and stays', from which Pound urged the deletion of the last two words (45) and which nevertheless survived in the finished poem as 'drying combinations ... Stockings, slippers, camisoles, and stays'. (ll. 225–227), likewise has more in common with some items in the 'Inventory' of 'The Lady's Dressing Room' (ll. 10 ff.) than with, say, the 'Puffs, Powders, Patches, Bibles, Billet-doux' of *Rape of the Lock*, I: 138. 'The Lady's Dressing Room' and related poems by Swift have of course their own ironic relationship with the *Rape*, as Murray Krieger has shown in *The Classic Vision: The Retreat from Extremity in Modern Literature* (Baltimore and London: The Johns Hopkins Press, 1971), 260–268; and see above, 164, 168–9. After the seduction of the typist, the young man went on to 'urinate, and spit' before Pound removed the detail as 'proba[b]ly over the mark' (*Waste Land Facsimile*, 47). Pound's deletion of the Fresca passage and of other lines in the original 'Fire Sermon' were in nearly all cases for the better, but he threw out a certain amount of Swift in the course of eliminating Pope, whether he knew it or not.

24 Lines 113–116 and some earlier passages in the poem were omitted when the poem was first printed in the Pope-Swift *Miscellanies, The Last Volume*, 1727. See *Poems*, I: 221–222, and textual commentary, *Poems* I: 226–229.

25 *Gulliver and the Gentle Reader. Studies in Swift and our Time*, 34–35.

26 Irvin Ehrenpreis, *The Personality of Jonathan Swift* (London: Methuen, 1958), 43–46.

27 Cf. Spenser, *Faerie Queene*, I: viii, 48: 'My chaster Muse for shame doth blush to write.' This occurs in the horrific portrait of Duessa, at I: viii, 46–48, which has a number of details in common with Swift's poem, and shares its theme of a fair exterior revealed as being a cover for appalling ugliness.

28 The phrase is used not only in 'Strephon and Chloe', l. 204, but in a short prose piece, probably by Swift, defending a related poem, 'The Lady's Dressing Room'. See *Works*, V: 340.

29 Two months later, on 14 December 1725, in the same celebrated series of letters alluding to the composition of *Gulliver's Travels*, the 'misanthropy' of Swift, and the kind of satire which 'vexes', Pope returned to a similar image: 'Not that I have much Anger against the Great, my Spleen is at the little rogues .... It would vexe one more to be knockt o' the Head by a Pisspot, than by a Thunderbolt. As to great Oppressors (as you say) they are like Kites or Eagles, one expects mischief from them: But to be Squirted to death (as poor Wycherley said to me on his deathbed) by *Potecaries Prentices*, by the under Strappers of Under Secretaries, to Secretaries, who were no Secretaries — this would provoke as dull a dog as Ph[ilip]s himself' (*Correspondence*, III: 120). Pope is voicing to Swift sentiments which were probably more characteristic of Swift than of Pope himself: that satire had more to do with undignified exposure than with grand denunciation; that the most effective kind of 'vexing' came from pettier rather than grander sources, etc. The *hauteur* which grants greater nuisance-value to 'the under Strappers of Under Secretaries, to Secretaries, who were no Secretaries' than to the truly powerful is only part of the significance of Pope's letter for the student of Swift. It conveys indirectly a point which Swift was to make himself in his 'Epistle to a Lady' ([1733] *Poems*, II: 634–638, ll. 137–248), that needling and humbling irritations are more vexing than more openly angry onslaughts, and perhaps by implication that the 'great Oppressors' are best attacked by means which concede no 'greatness' to them. A peculiar identity develops in the two passages from Pope's letters between the satirist who breaks vials on the heads of his victims, and satiric victims who annoy the satirist more by

dropping pisspots on his head than do 'the Great' by their 'greater' misdeeds.

30 D. H. Lawrence, Introduction to *Pansies*, in *A Propos of Lady Chatterley's Lover and other Essays* (Harmondsworth: Penguin, 1961), 10–11, and the account of Lawrence's views in Burton S. Kendle, 'D. H. Lawrence: The Man Who Misunderstood Gulliver', *English Language Notes*, 2 (1964), 42–46; Aldous Huxley, 'Swift', in *Do What You Will* (London: Chatto and Windus, 1939), 93–106. See also Milton Voigt, *Swift and the Twentieth Century* (Detroit: Wayne State University Press, 1964), 126 ff; and Athar Murtuza, 'Twentieth-Century Critical Response to Swift's "Scatalogical [*sic*] Verse". A Checklist', *Bulletin of Bibliography*, 30 (1973), 18–19 (an incomplete listing of this inexhaustibly tedious and inescapable topic). The most recent significant discussions of the scatological elements in Swift are Jae Num Lee, *Swift and Scatological Satire* (Albuquerque: University of New Mexico Press, 1971), and Thomas B. Gilmore, Jr., 'The Comedy of Swift's Scatological Poems', *PMLA*, 91 (1976), 33–43 and 464–467 (the latter an exchange of views between Donald Greene, Peter J. Schakel and Gilmore).

31 Contrast the 'Puffs, Powders, Patches, Bibles, Billet-doux' of Belinda's toilet in *Rape of the Lock*, I: 138, which show satire without the ingredient of revulsion, however comic; and see the whole scene in *Rape*, I: 121 ff. See also above, n. 23.

32 On the scientific background to this, see Marjorie Nicolson's study, 'The Microscope and English Imagination', in her *Science and Imagination* (Ithaca: Cornell University Press, 1956), 155–234, especially 193–199.

33 S. T. Coleridge, *Table Talk*, 15 June 1830.

34 Cf. *Hudibras*, II: iii, 317–320, 377–378.

35 See above p. 162 and n. 25.

36 Baudelaire, 'Mon Coeur Mis à Nu', *Oeuvres Complètes*, 1296 (xl). In 'Yeats and the Rhetoric of Defilement', *Review of English Literature*, 6, no. 3 (July 1965), 48–49, Jean Alexander distinguishes interestingly between Swift, Baudelaire, and the Marvell of 'To His Coy Mistress'. In 'Une charogne', she argues, Baudelaire 'uses putrefaction both as a refinement of sensuous pleasure and as an instrument of sexual power .... Marvell snatched the beloved back from the tomb and its worms, but Baudelaire thrusts her body prematurely into dissolution. One might say that Baudelaire is as destructive as Swift, were it not for his perverse sensuous pleasure in the sight and smell of rot and the grotesque, obscene posture of death. In Swift's use of defilement in the second and especially the fourth books of *Gulliver's Travels*, the sexual indignities and smearing with excrement are intended to destroy every idealisation of the human body and its functions; further, they are intended to destroy the erotic impulse itself. In contrast, the erotic impulse is violently displaced in Baudelaire's poetry: instead of desire shrivelling before the image of love defiled, the desirable object ("une femme lubrique / Brûlante ...") lends its excitement to the image which would defile it. Thus desire is not destroyed, but the natural order of desires is shattered and the poet replaces it with his own perverse constructions.'

37 E.g., Thackeray, *English Humourists of the Eighteenth Century* (London: Macmillan, 1910), 19: 'what a vulture that tore the heart of that giant!' Thackeray is not, of course, being wholly friendly to Swift.

38 That such neo-Promethean immolations did not in Swift's eyes dignify a victim is confirmed by an angry marginal note on Henry VIII: '... I wish he had been Flead, his skin stuffed and hangd on a Gibbet, His bulky guts and Flesh left to be devoured by Birds and Beasts ...' (*Works*, V: 251). For other

references to Prometheus in Swift's poems, see *Poems*, I: 266; II: 659, 726. For a seventeenth-century satirical allusion in which Prometheus is thought of primarily as a thief, see the attack on Dryden, *A Panegyric on the Author of Absalom and Achitophel*, 1681, l.54: 'Thy soaring heights Prometheus' thefts excel,' *Poems on Affairs of State, vol. 2: 1678–1681*, ed. Elias F. Mengel, Jr. (New Haven and London: Yale University Press, 1965), 503.

39 I owe the reference to Raymond Trousson, *Le Thème de Promethée dans la Littérature Européenne* (Geneva: Droz, 1964), II: 344. On the Romantic development in which Prometheus 'incarne le poète paria et préfigure ainsi l'albatros' of Baudelaire, see Trousson, II: 300. Baudelaire himself sometimes mocked the Promethean pretensions of others (Trousson, II: 299n, 378; Baudelaire, *Oeuvres Complètes*, 596–598, 1262), but was attracted to the myth, and returned with a particular fascination and self-involvement to images of devouring by birds of prey, not only in 'Un Voyage à Cythère', but in 'Le Mort Joyeux'.

40 Yeats, 'Blood and the Moon', *Collected Poems*, 268.

41 The poem is not without its own Promethean flippancies: Celia's closestool is compared with '*Pandora*'s Box' (l.83).

42 *Dunciad*, I: 118. Pope's note to the passage as a whole refers us to the devil's progress through Chaos (*Paradise Lost*, II: 927 ff.). See also the 'vast profunditie' of *Paradise Lost*, VII: 229. A significant fact is that Pope also uses 'vast profound' in serious heroic contexts in *Iliad*, VIII: 162 and *Odyssey*, IV: 777; VIII: 34; and XIII: 185. See Arthur Sherbo, 'No Single Scholiast: Pope's *The Dunciad*', *Modern Language Review*, 65 (1970), 505. The example adds confirmation of the closeness of Pope's mock-heroic to those primary heroic grandeurs which it mimics.

43 Again Pope also wrote a straight heroic version, in *Odyssey*, IV, 480: 'the deep roar of disemboguing Nile'. The whole passage from *The Dunciad* (II: 271 ff.) may also be contrasted with the closing lines of the 'City Shower'. It is true that Swift talks of a 'huge Confluent' (l.59), but his overriding effect is not of a large majestic movement but of an animated crowd of little things: 'Drown'd Puppies, stinking Sprats, . . . Dead Cats and Turnip-Tops' (ll.62–63). Where Swift's parody of pompous versifying reduces the subject-matter to its actual chaotic 'lowness', Pope's mock-heroic elevates his (here very similar) subject-matter with an almost Baudelairian delight in putrescent majesty. Part of this topsy-turvy loftiness derives (as Johnson, Reynolds and others have said of the *true* grand style) from an economy of detail, the 'large tribute of dead dogs' moving as a single mass in stately progress. Swift's passage, by contrast, derives its vitality from the gusto with which Swift threw himself into the *particularities* of the scene.

44 Cf. Garth, *Dispensary*, III: 125–126, and Gay, *Trivia*, II: 168 ff. On Fleet-ditch and its literary associations and significance, see Pat Rogers, *Grub Street: Studies in a Subculture* (London: Methuen, 1972), 142–174. See also Ian Donaldson, 'The Satirists' London', *Essays in Criticism*, 25 (1975), 116, 122n.

45 The theme of the modern degradation of the island of Venus to a barren British colony is to be found in Baudelaire's source, Nerval's article 'Voyage à Cythère', published in *l'Artiste*, 30 June and 11 August 1844 and subsequently absorbed into his *Voyage en Orient*; and also in Victor Hugo's 'Cérigo', a poem inspired by Baudelaire's. But it is in Baudelaire that the memory of Venus's 'superbe fantôme' is at its richest, and (although the episode of the hanged man was probably invented by Nerval) it is only in Baudelaire that the poet's self-identification with the 'Ridicule pendu' occurs. See Baudelaire, *Oeuvres Complètes*, p. 1555; Nerval, *Oeuvres*, ed. Albert Béguin and Jean

Richer (Paris: Pléiade, 1961), II: 63–72, 1292–1296; Hugo, *Oeuvres Poétiques*, ed. Pierre Albouy (Paris: Pléiade, 1967), II: 704–706, 1587–1589; Paul Maury, 'Cérigo ou Un Épisode de l'Hellénisme en France', *Mercure de France*, 183 (1925), 392–400; Georges Collas, 'Victor Hugo et Baudelaire', *Revue d'Histoire Littéraire de la France*, 36 (1929), 268–269.

46 See 'The Progress of Marriage' ([1722] *Poems*, I: 289 ff., lines 107 ff.), for a different one. And see *The Bubble* ([1720] *Poems*, I: 248 ff., ll. 93–96), where Venus dives *into* the sea for pearls and coral – a jibe at female investors in the South Sea Bubble.

47 George P. Mayhew, *Rage or Raillery. The Swift Manuscripts at the Huntington Library* (San Marino: Huntington Library, 1967), 95, 111.

48 See Williams in *Poems*, II: 629, Mayhew, 111–112, and Pat Rogers (ed.), *Jonathan Swift: The Complete Poems* (Harmondsworth: Penguin, 1983), 867.

49 *Poems*, II: 629. The printer, bookseller and others were actually taken into custody (*Poems*, II: 629, 640).

50 I discuss the passage more fully in *Gulliver and the Gentle Reader*, 6–7. For another reference to attacks on Swift's 'Cleanliness', see also the verse 'Panegyric on the Reverend D — n S — t' ([1730]; *Poems*, II: 491 ff.), sometimes attributed to Swift but more probably by James Arbuckle (Rogers, ed., *Complete Poems*, 810–811).

51 Swift's appeal to Horace's view that 'Ridicule has greater Pow'r / To reform the World, than Sour' (ll. 199–200) should not mislead us into thinking that Swift's own forms of ridicule are often of an urbane Horatian sort. It is true that elsewhere, notably in his praise of the *Beggar's Opera* in *Intelligencer*, No. III, Swift similarly celebrates humour, which is 'the best Ingredient towards that Kind of Satyr, which is most useful, and gives the least Offence; which, instead of lashing, laughs Men out of their Follies, and Vices; and is the Character that gives *Horace* the Preference to *Juvenal*' (*Works*, XII: 33). Such an emphasis would doubtless seem particularly appropriate in a friendly celebration of a relatively genial work like the *Beggar's Opera*, but there is no reason to suppose that Swift was not sincere in voicing his allegiance to some official pieties about the satirist's art. Some important passages of the 'Epistle to a Lady', however, as well as *Gulliver's Travels* and the great Irish tracts, lack this note of easy and inoffensive laughter and are truer to Swift, revealing him in a more total creative engagement of his whole personality. The *Intelligencer*'s reference to the satirist's *'publick Spirit'* which prompts 'Men of *Genius* and Virtue, to mend the World as far as they are able' (XII: 34), likewise expresses a conventional piety sincerely. But it similarly bears a less than total relationship to Swift's more sombre satiric energies and motivations and to his many ironies (themselves hard to evaluate exactly) about the world's unmendability.

52 Aldous Huxley, *Do What You Will*, 99.

53 Herbert Davis, *Jonathan Swift. Essays on his Satire and Other Studies* (New York: Oxford University Press, 1964), 37.

54 For some predecessors in this attitude to women, see James W. Johnson, *The Formation of English Neo-Classical Thought* (Princeton: Princeton University Press, 1967), 119. See also Irvin Ehrenpreis, 'Letters of Advice to Young Spinsters', in Earl Miner (ed.), *Stuart and Georgian Moments* (Berkeley, Los Angeles, London: University of California Press, 1972), 245–269, which compares Swift's attitude with earlier and later attitudes.

55 *Of the Characters of Women: An Epistle to a Lady* (1735), ll. 271–272. Pope knew the Stella poems, most of which were first printed in the joint Pope-Swift *Miscellanies, The Last Volume*, 1727. A few lines later in his own poem, he

equivocates on Martha Blount's age in a way which recalls another of the Stella poems (l.283, and Twickenham note). For a recent discussion of Pope's lines, and a brief comparison with Swift, see Felicity A. Nussbaum, 'Pope's "To a Lady" and the Eighteenth-Century Woman', *Philological Quarterly*, 54 (1975), 451–454.

56   Writing to the Rev. James Stopford on 20 July 1726, Swift expressed his deep anxiety about Stella's health, adding: 'believe me that violent friendship is much more lasting, and as much engaging, as violent love' (*Correspondence*, III: 145). The word 'love' is not conceded, but what Swift meant by 'violent friendship' is not clear and probably never will be. Theories of a secret marriage between Swift and Stella have often been entertained, and much gossip about their relationship plagued them in their own lifetime.

57   Swift speaks of his own birth much as he does of Stella's (and of Gulliver's) in a letter to Bolingbroke, 31 October 1729: 'My Birth although from a Family not undistinguished in its time is many degrees inferior to Yours ... a Younger Son of younger Sons' (*Correspondence*, III: 354).

5

Slaughtering Satire

You wouldn't guess it from *The Oxford Book of Satirical Verse*, but satire was once a deadly activity. It literally killed, or was believed to, which sometimes had the same result. Robert C. Elliott's classic study of *The Power of Satire* tells us that poems were used as weapons of war in pre-Islamic Arabia, and it is not only there, or in the curses of primitive tribesmen remote from our literary tradition, that this 'power' showed itself. It existed in the Greece of Archilochus and his descendants, and among Irish bards whose reputed ability to rhyme enemies or rats to death still excited the imagination of poets in the age of Ben Jonson or Swift.

Sometimes the enemy destroyed was a rival poet, and perhaps this is what the tradition eventually narrowed down to. Jonson and more recently Roy Campbell are on record as threatening to destroy some fellow-poets, in the latter case better ones, who all survived. Geoffrey Grigson, the editor of the *Oxford Book*, does not print any of this, but his anthology reveals, a bit depressingly, how much the satire of poets has been concerned with other poets. Perhaps this marks a minor decadent track in that progress from 'magic' to 'art' which Elliott has written about. The 'art' itself has declined, or so it will seem if one compares the reciprocal barbs of Grigson's contemporaries with the corresponding performances of Pope or Byron. Grigson has modestly left himself out. But his own scatterings of spleen are among the richer moments of an art in decline, and in one or two poems ('Committed, or Mr Yeats and Mr Logue', or 'Birth of Criticism') he has preserved some traces of the old ritual imprecation, at times scaled down to a stylish nagging.

Perhaps Grigson has mellowed, or perhaps he dislikes the invective of others, especially the earlier and robuster sort. He omits Marston 'because he uses words like a rumbling bully', and he is 'not too happy' about Skelton, though he quotes a pungent example in his Preface and gives him a few pages in the book. The Skeltonic heaping of graphic scatological or animal insults is a descendant of the old magical shamings, which struck men dead, or drove them to suicide, or caused blisters (the Irish satirists were good at causing blisters, and we still speak of 'blistering attacks'). It has remained part of the satirist's armoury, though otherwise unrepresented in this book. There is a fair sprinkling of it in the later Irish satires of Swift, in *Traulus* or *The Legion Club*:

> Traulus of amphibious Breed,
> Motly Fruit of Mungril Seed:
> By the *Dam* from Lordlings sprung,
> By the *Sire* exhal'd from Dung:
> Think on ev'ry Vice in both,
> Look on him and see their Growth.

The nearest we get to this aspect of Swift in this anthology is an altogether lighter affair called 'On the Irish Club'. Even the curse on Traulus is in any case no simple replay of the primitive bardic imprecation, but a sophisticated thing, conscious of its own excess, playing the game for all it is worth. Nor do its intensities, fierce as they are in their way, place Swift at the Juvenalian pole of what Grigson calls 'those ancestral antipodes in satire, Horace and Juvenal'. There is little that is identifiably Juvenalian in Swift, though the myth to the contrary dies hard. Swift's temperamental dislike of 'lofty stiles' was too well-developed to tempt him often into the majesties of 'tragical satire'. It is Pope, the official Imitator of Horace, who is given to Juvenalian postures. Swift 'imitated' Horace too and preferred him to Juvenal, not the Yeatsian Horace invented by Pope, aglow with egocentric fervours of 'urbanity', but a drier, low-key, scurrilous and self-undercutting figure (perhaps equally unlike the real Horace) whose 'laughing satire' unsettles and undermines instead of issuing defiant self-assertions. This, for the most part, is the Swift who is represented here, though the particular choice of poems is a little drab.

Perhaps the nearest thing to a survival of the old magical cursing in its naked form is to be found nowadays in the lore and language of schoolchildren. 'Drop dead', the curtest and most essential boiling down of the bardic imprecation, is an idiom which we may or may not owe to the playing fields of wherever, but the Opies have collected many an example of the death-dealing taunt, with savagely loving elaborations of humiliating incantation. 'Guy, Guy, Guy, / Poke him in the eye, / Put him on the fire / And there let him die' is addressed to the safely and famously dead, but it differs little from pleasantries addressed to living schoolmates: 'When he's dead / Lay him on a bed / And bake his head with gingerbread' or (a Scottish variant):

> Oor *Leebie* is a fule,
> And a donkey at the skule.
> If she had a langer tail,
> I would hang her up for sale.

Even these raw modern incarnations of the noble primitive mostly exist between inverted commas. Their enabling factor is that they aren't normally for real, however near the bone. One suspects that in most cases there is a more or less sophisticated awareness that it's only a game, that we're only kids, protected from any commitment to practical follow-through, though tragic exceptions sometimes occur. Perhaps 'I would hang her up for sale' is after all not so very different from Swift's saying about the nation's representers that 'I would hang them if I cou'd'. The thing is said largely because he knows he can't: Swift doesn't 'mean it', though he doesn't *not* mean it either. The old bards apparently both meant it, and *could*.

Satire has often had a schoolboy dimension, both in its horrors and in its fun, not least where murders, hangings and extermination are involved: think of Fielding's Jonathan Wild, who was once a schoolboy thug and retains his bully-boy oafishness in his later role of gangster and political boss; of Ubu Roi, whose original was an unfortunate pedagogue pilloried in schoolboy sketches by Jarry and his friends; or of Alan Coren's Idi Amin, who amid his slaughtering pranks sends up 'fo' de *Boys' Own Paper* Giant Packet o' One Hunnerd Top Worl' Stamps fo' A Mere Shillin''', orders his radio equipment from Hamleys, and wants a cowboy suit for his 'birfday'.

The schoolboy tyrant is often a mock-heroic figure, Wild proclaiming that the more nefarious trickeries of Homeric and Virgilian heroes, read in schoolboy cribs, confirmed him in his high opinion of the wisdom of the ancients (see below, chapter 6), or Ubu taking on the features of Shakespearean kings. Satirists have more than once compared the practical jokes of schoolboys with the cruel whims of tyrant-emperors and the 'tricks played . . . by ministers and statesmen'. Schoolboys have been taught the heroic poems since Greek and Roman times, and Yeats was later to reflect that the great warrior kings eventually survived only in classroom recitation. The epic spirit has tended through the

195

centuries to shrink to schoolboy size, whether by way of the classroom, or through the deep analogy, identified by Auden and Isherwood and others before and since, between what Horace Walpole called the 'mimic republic' of schoolboys and the worlds of epic and saga, with their fighting, games and conspiracies, their codes of honour and leadership, and indeed (in Auden's phrase) their 'gangster virtues'.

In this mythology, the classroom, playground and OTC shade into one another, and so do the figures of master and boy. Boy bully readily turns into tyrannical pedagogue and vice versa. It is hard to tell whether Ubu has more of one than of the other. And satirists have many times, more or less self-mockingly, adopted the figure of the punitive pedagogue to describe their own operations. Swift repeatedly described his satire as a flogging of his victims' backsides, noting in one place that 'there is not, through all Nature, another so callous and insensible a Member as the *World's Posteriors*, whether you apply to it the *Toe* or the *Birch*', as if all the world had become an intractable schoolboy.

There is also a more genial side to the schoolboy dimension. Emrys Jones pointed out in a brilliant British Academy lecture how Pope's dunces disport themselves like 'children at play', shouting, chattering, having peeing competitions and the rest, though none of this appears in Grigson's extracts. An analogous feeling comes through in a poem Grigson does print, Henry Carey's *Namby-Pamby*, which is in fact directed at one of Pope's dunces ('Namby-Pamby, pilly-piss, /Rhimy-pimed on Missy Miss'). The whole poem is an exuberant orchestration of the nagging sing-song of mocking children. It is blended with some shrewd literary criticism, but its masterly mimicry is less of Ambrose Philips's poems than of the schoolboy's hectoring taunts.

Such 'childishness' is, in Jones's words, 'viewed with the distance and distaste of the Augustan adult'. *The Dunciad*'s sympathies take in more than the satirical intention suggests and are in some ways subversive of it. And such elements in satire, when they became too visible, have tended to arouse disapproval. Dryden looked down on the burlesque verse of Butler's *Hudibras* for its 'boyish kind of pleasure', and indeed in the time of Dryden and Pope satire was already making a big point of being grown-up. Swift's poems (which used the same Hudibrastic verse-form as Butler's) would have seemed 'boyish' to Dryden, and Swift in some moods disparaged his own poems for being on the trivial side. It is at about this time too that the serious epic finally went out of business. Those good poets who paid tribute to it wrote mock-heroics instead, while the direct celebrations of 'heroic' deeds which excited Juvenal's schoolboys retreated more and more exclusively into the classroom, until Yeats could point to them as having dwindled to a classroom chore:

> Where are now the warring kings?
> An idle word is now their glory,
> By the stammering schoolboy said . . .

Perhaps the epic and satire, on the face of it so incompatible, have in common a deep underlying childishness. Certainly the two have never shown a greater need for each other than when both became subjected to the uneasiness of a world which thought itself too polite and grown-up for the cruelties and scurrilities of either. Some of the greatest poems of the age of Dryden and Pope (as never before or since) mixed the two together in the form of mock-heroic. It is not a case of the one being brought in at the expense of the other. Whatever mock-heroic satirises, it is usually not the grandeurs of epic. Some mock-heroics, like *Jonathan Wild*, brought into juxtaposition the oafish murderousness of heroes and the strutting of the school thug. Others, like *The Dunciad*, touched other features of a common childishness but studiously avoided bringing to mind the most damaging of heroic properties, the killings of the battlefield. The grandeurs, in rational terms inseparable from these killings, were somehow kept separate in poetic fact, and remained largely protected from satiric damage. The loyalty of mock-heroic is to some notional ideal of an older and nobler time, from which moderns have lapsed. And it is a truism too that, at least until recent times, the greatest satires have usually been culturally and politically conservative, looking back to old models, older standards of virtue. Even the most apparently alienated of outsider-satirists, Juvenal or Swift, is really recalling his countrymen to ancient values now neglected, not calling for a new order.

If epics celebrate slaughter and the earliest satire actually killed, perhaps it is as well that society has slowly grown out of them. Augustan sensibilities were well aware that heroic times were good to write of but bad to live in. It is also not surprising that that most direct-of poetic utterances, the bardic curse, has steadily grown more oblique. Its progress from magic to art has been marked by an increasing indirection of tone and point of view, by accretions of 'allusion' and learned wit and coterie-humour, and by a versatile talent for wrapping itself up in the protective covering of satirical fictions.

The schoolboy metaphor is one such fiction. It has been a means of preserving for satire some of its original vigour and also of domesticating it by building-in an accompanying note of grown-up superiority. It is largely by such lofty disengagement that Pope and his best contemporaries were able to take on board both the scurrilities of satire and some of the awkward majesties of the heroic.

The increasing attenuation of satire's primitive aggressions was attended for a time by a corresponding elaboration of formal structure. The design of the neo-Horatian epistle or the epic plots of Augustan satire are intricate pieces of rhetorical and narrative management. This largely escapes from view in the *Oxford Book*, which prints hardly any of the most finely articulated examples in full. Not a single poem by Pope is given complete, for example. We seem to have lost the taste for such things, as well as for the more primitive simplicities, preferring briefer and more manageable compositions, as Grigson prefers his Pope broken up into gobbets entitled 'Plain Fools', 'The Bookful Blockhead', or 'The Patron'.

I do not know the reason (perhaps that unceasing and all-purpose historical process known as the Rise of the Middle Classes should be invoked at this point), but there is hardly a single distinguished modern poem which amounts to an extended satiric composition on the scale of *The Rape of the Lock* or *The Dunciad*. Eliot's *Waste Land* seems to have begun as an attempt at such a poem. *The Dunciad* had in a sense been Pope's *Waste Land*. The subject of both poems is a modern cultural decline, played off against an ambiguous sense of ancient grandeurs, and a substantial part of Eliot's cancelled draft is an outright pastiche of *The Rape of the Lock*, heavily impregnated with elements of Swift in whom Eliot was deeply interested. Mock-heroic is not likely to have much point if the heroic itself no longer seems important enough for lapses from it to matter. Nor can one imagine any poet since Pope investing his whole imaginative being in a massively sustained composition which went in at much length for calling people dunces (a word which, by the way, in the course of its own history has been steadily transferring itself from school*men* to school*boys*). We have doubtless become even more grown-up than our Augustan ancestors.

When Pound got Eliot to discard the Popeian couplets he

explained: 'you cannot parody Pope unless you can write better verse than Pope – and you can't'. The satirical couplet in its high Popeian form seems also to have become increasingly hard to write with conviction. The twentieth-century examples collected by Grigson usually have the cutting edge of a rolling pin. The best succeed by subverting and ostentatiously coarsening the form, as Wyndham Lewis did:

> So there you have (in this political age)
> The secret of the dishonour of the sage –
> The one that's young enough to have some teeth,
> The one that's suspected honest underneath.

Lewis's own teeth were all on display. Their power came less from their intrinsic sharpness than from the muscles of his jaw. It is in any case in blasting and not in coupleteering that Lewis put his best tooth forward, while Roy Campbell's copious couplets are like an outsize set of flashing dentures.

The naturalness and force of the Popeian couplet presumably rested on some kind of live assumption that a sufficient degree of order and certainty existed to make patterned summations possible without patness or falsity. Pound, who excised Eliot's couplets, is represented here by some intermittent couplets of his own, although his greatest triumphs of satirical observation are surely to be found in such free-verse sketches as 'The Garden' and 'The Social Order', which operate more by a kind of quasi-novelistic or short-story portraiture than through the buoyant certainties of summary judgment to which the couplet tends. Eliot's best satiric writing, outside the special sense in which *The Waste Land* is satire, is perhaps to be found in a similar kind of short-story sketch, of which the finest example is 'Aunt Helen'. Eliot, whom Yeats had spoken of as 'an Alexander Pope ... satirist rather than poet', is not represented in this volume at all, not even by those early descriptions of city mornings or the witty quatrain poems which very largely derive from Swift and from Marvell.

It is in general a relief, in the later sections of this volume, to turn from the strident coupleteering patnesses of Campbell and others to the fondly nurtured exactitudes of spite of Lawrence's vers libre, to its precisions of mimicry and its rich flow of superlatively placed contempt (it is as though the Middle Classes, having Risen at Satire's expense, were being put back in their place in 'How Beastly the Bourgeois Is'); or to Stevie Smith's

'Lord Barrenstock', a poem of strange moral and metrical turns and counterturns, comparable in some ways to Pope's lines on Sporus, but making its point through the full elaboration of a highly specific case rather than through an assured reliance on a pre-existing sense of fitness or the high and unwavering aplomb of Popeian virtuosities of definition.

1980

6

Pope's Waste Land: *Reflections on Mock-Heroic*

'An Epic Poem, the Criticks agree, is the greatest Work Human Nature is capable of.'[1] So said Martinus Scriblerus in Pope's *'Receipt to make an* Epic Poem'. The words are cited verbatim in Pope's Scriblerian gloss on *Dunciad*, IV: 174. The critics did indeed 'agree'. The thing was a commonplace, and like other commonplaces it was much repeated by Dryden, most ringingly when he ushered in his translation of the *Aeneid* with words which differ from those of Pope's boorish and undisciplined pedant mainly in their avoidance of the unmannerly final preposition: 'A heroic poem, truly such, is undoubtedly the greatest work which the soul of man is capable to perform.'[2]

Pope's 'capable of', used on both occasions, is a tell-tale sign, for although the words occur in an *Art of Sinking in Poetry* or the mock-commentary to a mock-epic, Pope is mocking neither the sentiment, nor Dryden, nor epics. He was not given, like his friend Swift, to jeering at Dryden. If Dryden was in his mind at all, it was probably as the best-known recent authority against the barbarism of ending sentences with 'of'. Dryden had spoken in 1672 of such final prepositions as an example of the unpolished nature of Elizabethan English, unworthy of a more refined age.[3] It is likely, however, that Pope just used the rather crude example as a self-evident solecism, signalling the character of his speaker rather than questioning the intrinsic truth of the statement.[4] The targets of his ridicule are vulgar pedants uttering sacred truths by rote, without literacy or comprehension, and poetical hacks like Blackmore, scaling heroic heights, according to receipt, *'without a Genius,* nay without Learning or much Reading'.[5] The proposition itself, that an epic was the noblest product of the human mind, was accepted by Pope as unreservedly as by Dryden. It was indeed so securely taken for granted that he could afford to put it in the mouth of a foolish and derided speaker without fear of being misunderstood.

A century or so later, as is well-known, Mill and Poe and others were saying that an epic poem, 'in so far as it is epic . . . is not poetry at all', that a long poem was 'simply a flat contra-diction in terms', that 'no long poem was ever written; the finest long poem in the world being but a series of short poems linked together by prose'.[6] The notion that poetry can only be sustained in brief charged moments is still our normal assumption, and we forget that the short poem has not always been regarded as the principal or most characteristic vehicle of poetic expression. Dryden tended to reserve the word 'poem' for grander things than 'a paper of verses' or 'ordinary sonnet'.[7] The French, 'light and trifling' in both language and genius, are more fitted 'for sonnets, madrigals, and elegies than heroic poetry',[8] and Boileau's famous line, 'Un sonnet sans défauts vaut seul un long Poëme' (*Art Poétique*, II: 94), might seem to confirm Dryden's view of this frivolity.[9] But the assertion is less whole-hearted than it sounds, and Boileau says that no one has yet achieved such a sonnet anyway ('cet heureux Phénix est encore à trouver'). He is not asserting the superiority of sonnet to epic, but preferring a small-scale per-fection to the long and tedious, or to work more ambitious but botched. He mocked the failure of modern French attempts at epic, as Dryden noted 'the failings of many great wits amongst the Moderns, who have attempted to write an epic poem',[10] or as Pope ridiculed Blackmore and others in the 'Receipt', the *Dunciad* and elsewhere.

A well-known paradoxical aspect of this was that epics on classical models were often written by those who seemed least committed, and scorned by those most committed, to the values of the classical past. This commitment, for Pope, was no mere abstraction. The vitality of his reverence for ancient epic is visible not only in his critical writings on Homer, but also whenever he engages with the epic masterpieces in his own poems. In the *Essay on Criticism*, Pope imagines the young Virgil, at first unconcerned with rules or models, scorning the critic's law and drawing only from nature's fountains:

> But when t'examine every Part he came,
> *Nature* and *Homer* were, he found, the *same*.
>   (ll. 134–35)

The last line is much cited as a pithy formulation, and Pope repeated its substance in critical prose.[11] But the real force of the passage is in the spare vibrant finality, the feeling of excited recognition, as of an old truth suddenly become vivid. It would be hard to imagine anything further removed from mere critical lip-service to an ideal which had lost its creative force.

There is a second paradoxical fact, also familiar. The high view of epic survived, with greater or less vitality, throughout the lifetimes of Dryden, Pope and Fielding, and indeed beyond. Perhaps it has never fully disappeared. And yet there is no major epic in English nor perhaps in any of the main West European languages after *Paradise Lost*. Both Dryden and Pope planned, as Milton had deliberately planned from an early stage, to write epics of their own. Pope in particular began his poetic career by publishing the *Pastorals*, thus signalling a Virgilian promise of greater things. But neither Dryden nor Pope achieved their epics. Part of the epic impulse, adulterated by romance elements and generally coarsened, was diverted, by Dryden and others, into the heroic play, a genre which was quickly seen by many as a further example of the failure of the heroic mode to animate genuinely good writing. It became a target for parody from *The Rehearsal* to Fielding's *Tragedy of Tragedies*, much as many modern epics were parodied and derided. Some recent critics believe that Dryden himself was subverting certain features of the heroic outlook in his plays.[12]

Dryden's one completed and successful attempt at epic was the translation of Virgil, as Pope's was the translation of Homer. It was as though they could only do it by proxy, or through a filter of irony. Boileau said he wished someone would write a new *Aeneid* to celebrate French triumphs in war, and that he sometimes toyed with the idea himself, but found he could not because his own bent was satirical (*A.P.*, IV: 203–36; *Ep.*, VIII: 1–12). But Blackmore did what Dryden had merely talked of doing, and produced not one but two Arthurian epics. Dryden said 'I will deal the more civilly with his two poems, because nothing ill is to be spoken of the dead', but Blackmore continued undeterred.[13] Pope was to refer to him as one 'whose indefatigable Muse produced no less than six Epic poems' (*Dunciad* II: 268n.). Bad poets writing epics were an upstart modern arrogance, a desecration of ancient altars, and above all an awful warning of dangers amusingly codified in Pope's 'Receipt'; while good poets, like Boileau or Pope, unable to write epic straight nor yet to leave it alone, wrote mock-epics.

The unease to which this testifies was, in this period, a creative force. It animates the great mock-heroic poems of the Augustan age, and underlies the prose style of Fielding and others. But it begins in England with *Paradise Lost*, not a mock-heroic in any ordinary sense. This last great classical epic bears no direct relation to any 'heroic age', any more than the *Aeneid* does. But unlike those nineteenth-century poems by Tennyson or Morris whose evocation of the heroic was largely a matter of nostalgia for 'a world that no longer exists and . . . values that have passed away',[14] *Paradise Lost* retains a live (though 'secondary' or 'literary') relation to the epic tradition. The imaginative grandeurs embodied in the great epics were for Milton, as they had been for Virgil, a focus of aspiration sufficiently rich and active to provide a form for expressing some high preoccupations and ideals of their own time: for Virgil's sense of Roman destiny or Milton's project of vindicating the ways of God to man in a great English poem.

But although Milton's poem is in an important sense the *Aeneid* of his age and nation, and vividly projects its loyalty and its debt to its predecessor, it also turns its back on Virgilian (and Homeric) themes, 'the wrauth / Of stern *Achilles* . . . or rage / Of *Turnus* for *Lavinia* disespous'd' (IX: 13 ff.). He even claims that his subject is 'Not less but more Heroic' than these and adds a list of typical epic and romance elements (itself verging on a kind of mock-heroic derision) which he had no wish to emulate, though he had once considered such things: battles, races, games and 'gorgious Knights'. His point here is not the abandonment of a classical for a 'national' theme (though like Dryden he had toyed with the idea of an Arthurian epic poem), but a radical retreat from the principal subject-matter of the epic, including many Biblical or Christian epics: 'Warrs, hitherto the onely Argument / Heroic deemd' (IX: 28–29).[15]

Such language, within the poem, puts Milton into an adversary relation with the epic tradition which is in some ways ambiguous as the relation of mock-heroic to the epic was ambiguous. It retains Milton's reverence for the classical models, whose form and structure and whose elevation of style and perspective he 'imitated', while conveying that neither he nor his age was in tune with their ethos. Like Pope and so many others, he was openly disturbed by epic morality, the cruelty and bloodshed and the exaltation of war, and he fell back, as others did, on a partial separation of that morality itself from the larger totality of the great heroic poems in which it is contained.[16]

The successors to Milton whose tribute to epic took the form of mock-heroic poems, but who like Milton had no wish to convey any radically hostile imputation against the epic originals, effected the separation by the method, though not in the manner, which he appeared to propose: by largely avoiding the subject-matter of war. It is seldom remarked that when we speak of mock-heroic, we almost always refer to stylistic or rhetorical parody, and hardly ever to the characteristic subject-matter of epic poems. But the fact reflects a characteristic emphasis in the mock-heroic works themselves. *Mac Flecknoe* and *The Dunciad* leave battles out altogether, though *The Dunciad* has everything else: a Virgilian 'progress', games, hell, prophecy and the rest, while Boileau's *Lutrin*, Garth's *Dispensary* and *The Rape of the Lock* contain mock-battles of a trifling and ludicrously unmilitary or unsanguinary kind. A glance in the Pope Concordance at the words *blood*, *bleed* and their derivatives reveals virtually no significant instances in either of the mock-heroic poems, but many dozens in the translation of Homer: *The Dunciad*'s action is in this regard epitomised by 'Pomps without guilt, of bloodless swords and maces' (I:87). The only thing approaching Homeric bloodshed in *The Dispensary* occurs in a ridiculed recitation of Blackmore's 'straight' Arthurian pieces, rather than in the main mock-heroic idiom through which the poem articulates its allusions to ancient epics and conducts its own narrative business.[17] It is a bookish joke within a bookish joke. It is striking that the mock-battles are frequently 'battles of books', whether in the strictly physical sense in which opponents hurl romances and other volumes at each other in *Le Lutrin* (V:123–216), or in an allegorised sense even further removed from physical contact, as in Swift's prose *Battle*, where what is spilled is ink or some parody of ichor or 'nectarous' fluid and where (in one of epic's more genial moods) severed bodies 'soon unite again' or are restored or metamorphosed by divine intervention.[18]

The unsanguinary wound has a tiny source in *Iliad*, V:339–40, where a wounded immortal sheds ichor or (as Byron rhymingly put it, perhaps in mockery of Hobbes's translation of Homer) 'some such other spiritual liquor'.[19] The original Homeric episode, so unlike his gory battle-scenes, seems tailor-made for genial mock-heroic imitation, as Swift and Pope and Byron showed, but it is interesting that it is also used in *Paradise Lost*, in a passage which also includes an example of that instant celestial healing in which airy substance soon unites again:

th' Ethereal substance clos'd
Not long divisible, and from the gash
A stream of Nectarous humor issuing flowd
Sanguin, such as Celestial Spirits may bleed,
And all his Armour staind erewhile so bright.
                                    (*P.L.*, VI: 330–34)

Milton (whom Pope cites in his note to his translation of the Homeric passage,[20] as well as at *Dunciad*, II: 92, and refers to without quoting at the corresponding passage in *The Rape of the Lock*) is not being 'mock-heroic'. The nectarous bleeding of Satan is not genial but spectacular. The fact that it is Satan who is wounded ensures that no great distress need be felt at the thought of his suffering, and the brio of 'Armour staind' has a touch of jeering triumph. Even so a saving suggestion is created that the wound is not for real in human terms, as well as healing instantly anyway. This is a central feature of the War in Heaven whereas the episode of divine bloodshed in Homer is incidental. Milton rejected the theme of heroic warfare not by simply bypassing it (in the manner of *The Dunciad*), but by transferring it wholly from the human to the celestial domain. The epic's traditional preoccupation with war is preserved on a plane which escapes the censures of a human morality. War in the disreputable human sense is sublimated as well as 'derealised'. The War in Heaven is too high to arouse our disapproval of war, much as the mock-battles of *Le Lutrin* or *The Rape of the Lock* are too low.

Where Milton attacks war outright in the poem, or declares against the epic view that it is the only argument heroic deemed, he might be seen as making a more radical critique of the epic tradition than ever the mock-heroic did. It is perhaps only because he includes this critique that he was able to achieve success in a 'straight' as distinct from a *mock*-epic. But the War in Heaven, as the poem's counterpart of epic wars, is not directly implicated in Milton's condemnation of secular warfare, and the epic models remain essentially undamaged by this particular imitation of them. The War in Heaven is righteous as no other war can be, as well as incapable of killing anyone. There is a degree of separation of the anti-war morality from the admired epics which are said at one level to offend against it. Where many other Biblical or Christian epics necessarily retained the traditional elements of human warfare, Milton overcame the problem partly by placing his celestial war outside the normal range of criticism, and partly by shifting his main focus onto non-martial themes traditionally forbidden by epic theorists: Brower has said well that while Renaissance critics asked for a Christian colouring which yet excluded the 'central mysteries of the faith', Milton boldly 'chose the prohibited subject and wrote the most successful heroic poem of the Renaissance'.[21]

The mock-heroic poems of the next generation generally side-stepped the issue of battle altogether. Pope indeed softened or excised some of the grimmer Homeric cruelties even from his translation of the *Iliad*. Goriness on anything approaching the Homeric scale seems to have been the property of Bartholomew Fair spectacles like Settle's *Siege of Troy*, widely despised as the kind of demotic rubbish where 'Farce and Epic get a jumbled race' (*Dunciad*, I: 70: Settle is prominent in the poem, playing Anchises to Theobald-Cibber's Aeneas).[22] It is as though Pope and the other mock-heroic poets were determined to protect the epic originals from the disrepute which might accrue to them from any serious reminder of bloody deeds.

Swift went further. I have argued elsewhere that this most unremittingly parodic of eighteenth-century writers hardly ever attempted mock-*epic* (though he mocked most other forms of poetic inflation), as though anxious to avoid damaging the originals through any unintended energies of his irony, or contaminating them by exposure to parody, however innocent of anti-epic purposes. *The Battle of the Books*, the only sustained exception, is in prose and offers itself simultaneously as mock-journalese in a way which draws some potential disapproval from the alternative or epic model. It is also only a paper fight. It is notable that whenever Swift attacks war, it is in contexts conspicuously free of epic associations.

Procedures designed to shield the epic from the risks of both moral disapproval and parodic ridicule could take various forms. A late example is the mock-heroic of Fielding's *Jonathan Wild*, which operates at two removes from epic originals. The first remove is effected by Fielding's use of the terms 'heroic' and 'great' to convey certain moral turpitudes as such, and in abstraction from any pressing reminder of the doings of particular epic heroes: the words, so harpingly reiterated, ask to be translated directly into some obvious moral opposite ('wicked', 'murderous', 'thieving'), rather than related to any heroic personage or episode in an epic orginal. (Similarly, Pope's 'serious' epic on Brutus looks as if it would have become a didactic or philosophical poem, largely focused on moral and social questions in abstraction from any typically epic action). Secondly, where famous 'heroes' are referred to, the book insinuates a distinction between those from 'real life', past (Alexander, Caesar) or present (Walpole), and those from revered heroic poems. The latter seldom appear, and when they do distinctions quickly establish themselves. Fireblood is ironically described as Wild's *fidus Achates*, but the first time this happens Fielding takes care to separate epic from history by adding immediately 'or rather the Hephaestion of our Alexander' (III: iv).[23] He is thus promptly redefined as the henchman of a historical conqueror whom Fielding despises, rather than the faithful friend of an admired epic hero. Since Fireblood is usually called faithful when he is being pointedly *un*faithful, a two-fold irony comes into being which suggests that he is all too unlike the one, and all too like the other.

A similar ironic doubling or split-level allusiveness, pointedly distinguishing between poetic and historical parallels, underlies the Virgilian 'progress' of *The Dunciad*. The westward removal of Dulness's empire 'from the City to the polite World', Scriblerus tells us, replicates the *Aeneid*'s westward displacement of 'the empire of Troy . . . to Latium'.[24] It also involves comic extensions of the legend that Britain was founded by a further stepping westward, that of Aeneas's descendant Brutus (the subject of Pope's projected late epic), and the consequent idea of London as a new Troy and new Rome. The court and polite world were to the west of the City, and the poem's brooding sense is of unlettered and aldermanic hordes pressing upon it from the easterly regions of trade and Grub Street: a local replay, if Pope but knew it, of a westward drift which has been said to be a recurrent characteristic of the growth of great cities.[25] Set against Aeneas's voyages, it becomes matter for a simple mock-heroic put-down. But another westward movement is also brought into play, that of the invasions of the Roman empire and 'all the western world' (III: 100) by barbarians from the East and North, whose resemblance to the encroachments on Pope's London is a direct rather than a reverse one. As in *Jonathan Wild* a disreputable phenomenon is shown up against both a Virgilian and a 'historical' model, the parallels with epic registering an unheroic decline, and those with history a disreputable continuity.

Such separations of fact from artefact were a necessary manoeuvre, if the idealised reverence for the ancient past was to survive the evidence, abundant in every kind of classical text, that older times were as rich in human depravity as more recent ones. The suggestion that historical precedents are likely to be uglier than epic ones also reflects old assumptions that poetry (and especially heroic poetry) reaches 'above the life' and expresses a higher truth than that of mere phenomena. The famous Aristotelian distinction between the truth of poetry and the truth of history might even, in the hands of some of the lordlier theorists, imply a sarcastic downgrading of the 'historian' to a mere peddler of facts, or journalist. The mock-epic of *The Battle of the Books* is as I said also mock-journalese ('A Full and True Account of the Battel Fought last Friday . . . '), and Fielding's scorn of low-grade fact-mongers is well known.[26] Pope's note on Caxton, one of 'The Classics of an Age that heard of none' at *Dunciad*, I: 147 ff., identifies him as 'a Printer [who] . . . translated into prose Virgil's Aeneis, as a history; of which he speaks, in his Proeme, in a very singular manner, as of a book hardly known'. Caxton's trade, his 'rude' old-spelt English (always an easy victim of Augustan mirth) gloatingly reproduced by Pope, his imputed ignorance of humane letters are typical targets of anti-duncic artillery. The fact, which had aroused mockery since the early sixteenth century, that he translated Virgil from a French translation, placed him on a par with Welsted, one of Pope's dunces, whose Longinus was described in Swift's *On Poetry: A Rapsody*, l. 261, as 'Translated from *Boileau*'s Translation'.[27] But it is Caxton's double degrading of Virgil, into prose and into *history*, which is of interest to the present argument, because it is evidently represented as an illiterate error and especially as a gross trivialising of Virgil's poem. Caxton, as quoted, speaks praisingly of 'historyes' and 'historye', in a sense which seems to slide between history and story (cf. French *histoire*), as Fielding was often to do with ironic playfulness. It may be part of Pope's point that the *Aeneid* had been degraded not only to mere history, but to false history or 'low' fiction. The business of epic is *high* fiction, and it seemed necessary at this time, though this was not always deliberately acknowledged, to stress the extra-factuality (in the sense of their being somehow outside the factual domain) or superfactuality ('above the life') of epic doings as much as their loftiness as such: Caxton had certainly not altogether overlooked the latter, even in the remarks Pope quotes.

This helps to explain a further feature of Pope's two-way parallel for the dunces' westward progress. Fielding's Fireblood and Wild are the equivalents in viciousness to Hephaestion and Alexander, but they are small-time scoundrels who reduce these ancient historical counterparts, men of imperial scope and power, to their own shoddy level. The process is doubtless assisted by the flattening medium of prose. Their *epic* counterparts, Achates and

Aeneas, being opposites rather than direct likenesses, are morally undiminished, though the prose medium and the small-time sleaziness of the *Jonathan Wild* scene may leave them, 'poetically' speaking, somewhat flattened too. This effect is the reverse of what normally happens in *The Dunciad*, where moral reduction and contempt are accompanied by a poetic *aggrandisement*, a sense of grandeur however polluted: 'Great Cibber's brazen, brainless brothers', 'Slow rose a form, in majesty of Mud' (I: 32, II: 326).

A similar majesty, even more richly orchestrated, is conveyed in the famous account of barbarian invasions:

> Soon as they dawn, from Hyperborean skies
> Embody'd dark, what clouds of Vandals rise!
> Lo! where Maeotis sleeps, and hardly flows
> The freezing Tanais thro' a waste of snows,
> The North by myriads pours her mighty sons,
> Great nurse of Goths, of Alans, and of Huns!
> See Alaric's stern port! the martial frame
> Of Genseric! and Attila's dread name!
> See the bold Ostrogoths on Latium fall;
> See the fierce Visigoths on Spain and Gaul . . .
> (III: 85 ff.)

This leads to cultural catastrophe, but the lights go out with a certain splendour. If the dunces are the modern avatars of these invading hordes, the fact confers on them an importance richly at odds with the contemptible character we know them to have in the 'prose sense' of the poem. And their historical originals, instead of being wholly distinguished from alternative epic models in the manner we have already observed elsewhere, are themselves given some epic associations. The passage derives from Milton:

> A multitude, like which the populous North
> Pour'd never from her frozen loins, to pass
> *Rhene* or the *Danaw*, when her barbarous Sons
> Came like a Deluge . . .
> (*P.L.*, I: 351 ff.)

a sure sign of highly deliberate elevation in Pope.[28] (In the 'Postscript to the *Odyssey*' Pope suggests that he has made 'some use . . . of the style of *Milton*' in order to 'dignify and solemnize' the 'plainer parts' of Homer himself).[29]

Johnson reports that the Tanais couplet was the one in all Pope's works by which Pope 'declared his own ear to be most gratified'. He added drily that he could not discover 'the reason of this preference'.[30] But the *fact*, if it is one, is consistent with the bravura of the passage, its almost festive grandeur. Its curious elevation of deplorable events into a species of neo-Miltonic gorgeousness is, in particular, comparable to a striking feature of the much-discussed 'Mob of Metaphors' sequence (I: 55–78), with its topsy-turvy splendours:

> In cold December fragrant chaplets blow,
> And heavy harvests nod beneath the snow.

This is an official rebuke, in the manner of *Peri Bathous*, to Grub Street poetasters who get things wrong.[31] But readers keep finding in such passages a 'surrealist' loveliness of a kind which (like his pleasure in the Tanais lines) might suggest a more direct imaginative surrender on the poet's part to the beauty he creates out of rejected ugliness.

Pope was assisted in this by the fact that the images he scorned in one sense as 'Figures ill pair'd, and Similies unlike', could be indulged in another as legitimate instances of the figure *adynaton*, 'impossibility', in its commonest 'world upside down' form ('Realms shift their place, and Ocean turns to land'), practised since ancient times in certain rhetorical situations by Theocritus, Virgil, Horace, Ovid and many others. (Indeed Pope had Horace's own precedent for condemning such muddles in critical precept, mimicking their extravagance, and using them straight.)[32] In Pope's December chaplets and snow–clad harvests, an unacknowledged loveliness, superficially at odds with the ostensible argument, is thus reintegrated into a mainstream of classically sanctioned poetical 'beauties',[33] as the passage about the barbarian hordes is unexpectedly naturalised into a tradition of epic grandeur by means of its Miltonic mimicry. Whenever, as with the hordes, the ugliness so insolently transfigured tends specifically towards heroic rather than Horatian or Ovidian models, a feeling arises that *The Dunciad*, as the last of the great mock-heroic poems, is close to turning back into some form of epic in its own right; much as *Paradise Lost*, the last of the classical epics, occasionally seemed poised on the edge of mock-heroic.[34]

This tends in *The Dunciad* against that separation between epic and history which I have been discussing, but it does so by casting an epic grace over squalid doings rather than by an opposite effect

sometimes found in *Jonathan Wild*. It also differs conspicuously
from the great modern counterpart of Pope's passage, the lines
about 'hooded hordes swarming / Over endless plains, stumbling
in cracked earth', in *The Waste Land* (ll. 368 ff.). There is a
technical difference, which is perhaps only a matter of local
emphasis. Pope's hordes are in the historical past, but bear on the
present, Eliot's belong to the present but are linked to all the
crumbling civilisations of the past,

> Falling towers
> Jerusalem Athens Alexandria
> Vienna London
> Unreal

In both cases past and present reflect ill on one another, and we
should remember that *The Waste Land* has a Popeian ancestry. It
began life containing satirical couplets modelled on *The Rape of
the Lock*, with a Swiftian admixture. Its method of playing off a
decaying present against an ambiguously noble past derives
partly from Augustan techniques of ironic literary allusion; and it
shares with *The Dunciad* especially its great theme of cultural
disintegration.

But the passing in view of history's fallen empires in Eliot's
lines is dry, fragmented, pinched: a bare list, its ancient splendours picked clean, as it were, by the passage of time and
successions of hooded hordes. There is nothing of the blowsy
amplitude of Pope's invading barbarians, also relentlessly defeat-
ing each successive portion of the civilised world, but doing so
with a steady conquering march which belies the disintegration, a
gaudy stateliness which holds the broken pieces together in its
single onward sweep. The destruction itself is apprehended with a
nobility and a coherence which derive largely from Pope's ability
to measure it against the normative background of an epic
tradition still majestic and stable enough to provide a kind of
ordering focus even to the vision of disaster. The order is
experienced not conceptually (for at that level it is mainly a
disappointed aspiration) but stylistically, in that special feeling
evoked throughout the poem's vast network of allusion that the
heroic imagination from Homer to Milton is a single continuously flowering thing. It is, ironically, and in a more restricted sense
than Eliot intended, that very 'tradition' which Eliot described as
a 'feeling that the whole of the literature of Europe from Homer
... has a simultaneous existence and composes a simultaneous

order', and the absence of which *The Waste Land*, with its frenetic, dislocated and eclectic allusiveness, so poignantly registers. 'The existing monuments form an ideal order among themselves', but what their presence in the poem reveals is the 'heap of broken images . . . fragments . . . shored against my ruins'.[35]

The terms of Eliot's discourse are different from mine and his argument is that each 'really new' work of art modifies and rearranges the tradition. This would properly presuppose that in *The Waste Land* the 'fragments' *are* the 'order'. But the sense in which this is eloquently true does not remove the vivid differences between *The Waste Land* and Pope's presentations of the fragmented, the chaotic, the 'uncreating'. Pope's poem is full of embryos and abortions, images unfinished or twisted or broken-backed. They are, however, contained within the larger visible stabilities of the Popeian universe, and sometimes display their own miniature order: 'Maggots half-form'd in rhyme exactly meet' (I:61). The line occurs in the sequence which includes the *adynata*, and like them is caught in some odd self-vitalising circularities. The perverse 'anti-order' of maggots rhyming 'exactly' is noted as a poor parody of good rhyming verse. But it is parodied in reverse, or 'upwards', in a poem which not only mimics such things, but itself also 'in rhyme exactly meets' in its own *full*-formed state.

Pope's own triumphant command of couplet-styles, even as he plays at bad couplets, is part of that bravura expression of normative harmonies and coherences which distinguishes his mock-heroic from Eliot's. As I noted in the previous chapter, Eliot too attempted couplets in 'The Fire Sermon' until Pound told him to remove them because 'you cannot parody Pope unless you can write better verse than Pope'.[36] These miniature coherences, like the larger ones, were it seems not for him, even at that doubly protective distance of *mock*-mock-heroic which his 'imitation' of *The Rape of the Lock* had set out to be. For a mock-heroic in couplets in Eliot's time, we have to look to Roy Campbell, roughly the Blackmore of the day. Traditional mock-heroic was as impossible in Eliot's day as the straight epic had become in Pope's. As Pope could not complete his epic, but wrote a *Dunciad*, Eliot did not complete his mock-heroic, but achieved *The Waste Land*, while the Blackmores who once wrote *King Arthurs* were now turning their hand to 'satirical' *Georgiads*.

The scrambling of parallel and contrast in both *The Dunciad* and *The Waste Land* is a version of that 'perception, not only of the pastness of the past, but of its presence' of which Eliot wrote in

'Tradition and the Individual Talent'.[37] Eliot's own poem provides an essentially negative model for this. It offers a much more insecure assertion that ancient grandeurs were as noble as a mock-heroic insistence on later decay might make them out to be, and sees them indeed as containing the germ of present sickness. Indeed its effect, much more than we ever feel in Pope's poem, is to show the past as contaminated by the present: a negative version, in some ways, of Eliot's sense of the way 'tradition' and its past triumphs may be retroactively modified and enriched by the new. Pope was as unlikely to give voice to such a 'modern' presumption as to the negative obverse. The nearest he comes to it is a protest at the undervaluing of the best living poets, which is anyway Horatian in origin and has an ancient '*Precedent* to plead': the undervaluation is itself ironically conceived in Pope's or Swift's eyes as a paradoxical form of perennial 'modernism'. And it was easier for Pope than for Eliot to suspend scepticism of heroic models. He could retain sufficient confidence in their validity to feel that the modern failure to match their standard was culpable or contemptible. Eliot proposed something like the same decline from high to low, but he could only sustain the comparison by extending his scepticism to the past, conferring upon it some of his contempt for the present as Pope conferred on the contemptible present a residual sense of heroic value from the past.

That value was of course notional, indirect and 'fictive'. It rested on heroic poems rather than heroic deeds, and the separation in Pope's *Dunciad* between the grandeurs of ancient utterance and the doings of historical villains, like the sheer omission from it of the chief epic subject-matter of carnage and war, emphasises this in a way in which Eliot's poem does not. Eliot's poem (whose allusions to earlier grandeurs are no longer 'epic' in any strict or dominant sense anyway) tends persistently to collapse that distinction between past facts and past artefacts which provided some Augustan poets with an unspoken saving clause. The meannesses and depravities of the present are continually referred back to painful precedents both in poems and in life, in Ovid or Webster as well as in the historical lives of Elizabeth and Leicester.

In this, as I suggested elsewhere, *The Waste Land* finds a rudimentary Augustan predecessor not in *The Dunciad* but in *Jonathan Wild*, in occasional passages which breach the work's usual attempt to insulate epic precedents from the discredit which can freely be lavished on Alexander and Caesar.[38] Thus the schoolboy Wild was not only 'a passionate admirer of heroes, particularly of Alexander the Great', but (though unwilling 'to acquire a competent sufficiency in the learned languages') also expressed a high regard for certain episodes in both *Iliad* and *Aeneid*, as he heard them translated at school. For example, 'He was wonderfully pleased with that passage in the eleventh Iliad where Achilles is said to have bound two sons of Priam upon a mountain, and afterwards to have released them for a sum of money. This was, he said, alone sufficient to refute those who affected a contempt for the wisdom of the ancients' (I: iii). It is a small effect, easily discountable, up to a point, by its comic context of schoolboy oafishness, and by the character of the speaker: Wild is no more an authority on 'the wisdom of the ancients' than Martinus Scriblerus was on the status of epic poems as 'the greatest Work Human Nature is capable of'.

But an ambiguous complication of the mock-heroic contrast nevertheless makes itself felt, implying on the one hand that the heroic norm is better or nobler than the modern reality, but suggesting at the same time that there may not have been much to choose between them after all. The absurd tendentiousness of Wild's conception of Homeric epic connects uneasily with the common recognition that Homeric times were, as Pope himself put it, an age of 'Rapine and Robbery',[39] and that this was reflected in the poems, though distinguishable from their total greatness as imaginative achievements. It is consistent with the hope, which had been recently expressed in Thomas Blackwell's *Enquiry into the Life and Writings of Homer* (1735), '*That we may never be a proper Subject of an* Heroic Poem', which in turn goes back to a line of thinking most memorably formulated by Cowley in 1656: 'a warlike, various, and a tragical age is best to *write of*, but worst to *write in*'.[40] If such constatations, as we have seen throughout, left enough imaginative leeway for a deep and flourishing devotion to what Fielding, in a famous passage at the end of his life, referred to as 'those noble poems that have so justly collected the praise of all ages', it should be remembered that these very words occur in a strange late act of revisionism: 'I must confess I should have honoured and loved Homer more had he written a true history of his own times in humble prose'.[41]

Jonathan Wild's schoolboy celebration of the gangster-virtues of Homeric and Virgilian heroes is a version of an old connection, made especially familiar in our time in several formulations by Auden and Isherwood, between the ethics of heroes, gangsters and schoolboy toughs.[42] If it has, in the case of Wild, a certain backhanded geniality, this geniality is of a rather different order from that of the epic 'games' in Book II of *The Dunciad*, with their races and their 'urinating, tickling, shouting, and diving competitions', about whose childlike character Emrys Jones has written tellingly.[43]

In both the poem and the novel, an almost affectionate humour is allowed to compete occasionally with the serious business of scorning dangerous enemies. But where the schoolboy antics of the dunces exist in a holiday mood of gleeful irresponsible play, Wild's schoolboy enthusiasms, like his occasional displays of adult childishness, are all concerned with joyless projects of plunder and bullying. If a soft spot is nevertheless to be entertained for Wild, contrary to some conventional or 'face-value' readings of him as a figure of dark unrelieved diabolism, it is because of his boorish effrontery, the hapless automatism of his thieving instinct, the clownish failure of his projects. Of playground innocence, of carefree bustle and happy noises and cheerful smut, there is no trace.

Fielding's sympathies were in many ways more relaxed and easy-going than Pope's. But he was readier to see a sinister connection between the childish forms of supposedly harmless mirth or 'practical Jests', and the 'little jocose Mischiefs' of Roman emperors and other tormentors of mankind: Domitian torturing flies, Phalaris and his bull, or (for an epic-related example) Nero, whose 'comical Humours' doubtless included his singing the 'Sack of Ilium' while Rome burned.[44] For Fielding the link between schoolboy viciousness and murderous tyranny was as immediate as it is in Jarry's Ubu or Alan Coren's Amin: as 'comical' and as brutally horrifying.

When by contrast Pope speaks of 'Domitian . . . killing flies' (*Dunciad*, I: 15 n.) is it not in order to imply that this activity, though apparently trivial, leads to more dreadful things; but on the contrary that he the poet, in satirising dunces, is doing much more than 'killing flies'. The larger-scale cruelties of Domitian are evidently viewed (if viewed at all) with some detachment: Pope leaves them unmentioned, much as epic carnage is left out of view in the body of the poem. This is all the more striking because Pope's argument is that his own attack on the apparently trivial is really concerned with a bigger menace, so that the example of Domitian might have provided an analogy rather than a contrast. Dulness, he says, is

> not to be taken contractedly for mere Stupidity, but in the enlarged sense of the word, for all Slowness of Apprehension,

Shortness of Sight, or imperfect Sense of things. It includes
... Labour, Industry, and some degree of Activity and
Boldness: a ruling principle not inert, but turning topsy-
turvy the Understanding, and inducing an Anarchy or confused State of Mind.

The point of this 'Bentleian' note is the same as that of Scriblerus's reminder at III: 333 of 'what the Dutch stories somewhere
relate, that a great part of their Provinces was once overflowed,
by a small opening made in one of their dykes by a single
Water-Rat'.

The point is made here with a certain Swiftian urgency,
perhaps for once outdoing Swift in shocking formulation (cf.
Swift's sermon on 'Doing Good': 'The weakest hand can open a
floodgate to drown a country, which a thousand of the strongest
cannot stop').[45] *The Dunciad's* theme of engulfing disorder is
pressingly apprehended, and the sense of a total cultural black-out
proceeding from small origins is everywhere apparent. But it is
conveyed in images of 'Universal Darkness' and a large sleepiness, not with strongly particularised scenes of disruption and
certainly without sanguinary elements. The very convulsions are
stately, and from the style which creates such effects it is possible
to derive a feeling of reassurance and even stability which we do
not find in *Jonathan Wild*, even if we read that work (as I think we
should) as a milder or more genial satire than it is often taken to
be.

Pope separates the sinister aspects of his theme from the playful
ones more completely than Fielding does. For all its menacing
features, 'gentle Dulness ever loves a joke' (II: 34), and unlike the
merry pranks of Jonathan Wild the 'games' in Book II, with all
their allegorical imputations of filth and foolishness, attain 'a
mock solemnity that is too deeply humorous to be finally cruel'.
'*The Dunciad*', Wilson Knight has said, 'is Pope's *Inferno*, his
Macbeth. That it refuses any violent evil is characteristic, for he
writes from a mental horizon where such depths are not of
primary importance: he feels ... "letters" taking the place of
"lances" ... '[46] *The Dunciad* begins, in its first version, by signposting precisely that shift from lances to letters, from 'Arms, and
the Man' to 'Books and the Man I sing'. When he later changed
this to 'The Mighty Mother, and her Son', it was not in order to
return to epic lances, but in some ways to move the poem another
step away from epic's ancient matter.[47]

1982

Order From Confusion Sprung

Notes

1 E. L. Steeves (ed.), *The Art of Sinking in Poetry (Peri Bathous)* (New York: Russell & Russell, 1968), 80. The 'Receipt' had first appeared, in a slightly different form, in *Guardian*, No. 78, 10 June 1713. Quotations from Pope's poems use the Twickenham Edition (TE) text throughout, except in the case of the mock-editorial paraphernalia of *The Dunciad*'s four-book or B version of 1743 (the one normally cited here), which is from the *Poetical Works*, ed. Herbert Davis, introd. Pat Rogers (Oxford: Oxford University Press, 1978). This is because TE does not give a full continuous text of this editorial material in the form in which it appeared in 1743. This essay is in part an attempt further to develop some notions in my book *Henry Fielding and the Augustan Ideal Under Stress* (London: Routledge, 1972), where fuller documentation on some points touched on here is to be found.

2 George Watson (ed.), *Of Dramatic Poesy and other Critical Essays* (London: Dent, 1962), II: 223; also I: 198, II: 96 (hereafter cited as Watson). For Rapin's expressions of this view, see W. P. Ker (ed.), *Essays of John Dryden* (Oxford: Clarendon Press, 1900), I: 313; for others, see William K. Wimsatt and Cleanth Brooks, *Literary Criticism. A Short History* (New York: Knopf, 1957), 197–98.

3 Dryden admits having committed the fault himself (Watson I: 174). He took steps to correct it in the second edition of the *Essay of Dramatic Poesy* (Watson, I: 174 n.4 and see I: 13 n.3, I: 23 n.4: for many further examples, see the footnotes to the *Essay, passim*, in the California Dryden, vol. XVII). H. W. Fowler, *Dictionary of Modern English Usage*, 2nd ed., rev. Sir Ernest Gowers (Oxford: Clarendon Press, 1965), 473–74, cites Dryden as the chief authority, with Gibbon, for the objection to final prepositions.

4 In practice and especially in informal contexts Pope, like most speakers of English (including Dryden), himself committed the supposed solecism, e.g. *Correspondence*, ed. George Sherburn (Oxford: Clarendon Press, 1956), I: 57, 108 (the first, oddly, from a letter which contains one of Pope's rare censures of Dryden).

5 *Art of Sinking*, 80.

6 M. H. Abrams, *The Mirror and the Lamp* (London: Oxford University Press, 1960), 23–4, 136–7; Arthur Symons, citing Poe's authority, *The Symbolist Movement* (London: Constable, 1911), 134. The chief texts are Mill's 'What Is Poetry?' and Poe's 'The Poetic Principle'. One of Mill's formulations gets the older valuation of epic in by a side door: 'an epic poem, though in so far as it is epic (*i.e.* narrative) it is not poetry at all, is yet esteemed the greatest effort of poetic genius, because there is no kind whatever of poetry which may not appropriately find a place in it' (Edward Alexander (ed.), *Literary Essays* (New York: Bobbs-Merrill, 1967), 60).

7 Watson, I: 87. Sonnet, for Dryden, is likely to have meant any short poem.

8 Watson, II: 238. Mill also, for different but not unrelated reasons, thought the French were 'the least poetical of all great and intellectual nations' (*Literary Essays*, 57).

9 Boileau's 'long Poëme' seems to refer mainly to bad epics. In the nineteenth-century discussions, 'epic' and 'long poem' were also sometimes interchangeable, and in a sense what was deemed by Poe to be wrong with epic is precisely that it was extended. The older opposition to epic by certain authors in Hellenistic and Roman times (Callimachus, Martial, Juvenal) sometimes involved considerations of length, though on different grounds.

10 Gordon Pocock, *Boileau and the Nature of Neo-Classicism* (Cambridge: Cambridge University Press, 1980), 109 ff.; Watson, II: 85.

11 'Postscript to the *Odyssey*', TE, X: 389. For a fuller discussion of this passage, see below, chapter 8 (i).

12 See Derek Hughes, *Dryden's Heroic Plays* (London: Macmillan, 1981), viii and 168–9 n.3, for a convenient listing of such views.

13 Watson, II: 292–93. Dryden accused Blackmore of stealing the idea from him. Milton had considered an Arthurian epic before Dryden.

14 Graham Hough, *The Last Romantics* (London: Methuen, 1961), 132.

15 See also *P.L.*, XI: 689ff., for scornful comments on the martial values called heroic.

16 On this, see *Henry Fielding and the Augustan Ideal Under Stress*, 158–9, 168–9 nn.25–6; Pope, Preface to *Iliad* and note to *Iliad* XIII: 471 (TE, VII: li, 14; VIII: 129). See also the comment in *Spectator*, No. 548, 28 November 1712, on Homer's Achilles as 'Morally Vicious, and only Poetically Good'.

17 *Dispensary*, 2nd edn., 1699, IV: 178ff., in *Poems on Affairs of State, . . . Volume 6: 1697–1704*, ed. Frank H. Ellis (New Haven: Yale University Press, 1970), 101.

18 For the spilling of ink, and divine repair-work, see *Battle of the Books*, in Swift's *Works*, I: 143, 155, 159. For airy substance uniting again, see *Rape of the Lock*, III: 152; for ichor used as divine ink, see *Dunciad*, II: 92.

19 *Vision of Judgment*, xxv; cf. Hobbes's *Iliads*, 1676, 68, where what is shed is not human blood, 'but *Ichor*. /For Gods . . . / Have in their Veins another kind of Liquor'. Spence reported Pope as saying that there were several passages from Hobbes's translation which 'if they had been writ on purpose to ridicule that poet, would have done very well', and instancing 'the Ichor' among them (James M. Osborn (ed.), *Observations, Anecdotes*, etc. (Oxford: Clarendon Press, 1966), No. 451; S. W. Singer, (ed.), *Anecdotes* (London: W. H. Carpenter, 1820), 210; Edmund Malone (ed.), *Observations, Anecdotes* (London: John Murray, 1820), 285). The two earliest editions of Spence appeared in 1820, the year before Byron's poem was written. Byron was reading Spence early in 1821 (Leslie A. Marchand (ed.), *Letters and Journals* (London: John Murray, 1973–81), VIII: 14, 16, 21, 61). See *Byron Journal*, XI (1983), 48–51.

20 Pope's *Iliad*, V: 422, 424 nn.; cf Pope's *Iliad*, V: 1009ff. (Homer, V: 899ff.) and note, for an example of quick-healing divine wounds (TE, VII: 287–9, 320–1).

21 R. A. Brower, *Alexander Pope. The Poetry of Allusion* (London: Oxford University Press, 1968), 102.

22 See *Henry Fielding and the Augustan Ideal Under Stress*, 213, 226nn.; and Pat Rogers, 'Pope, Settle, and The Fall of Troy', *Studies in English Literature*, XV (1975), 447–58.

23 *Henry Fielding and the Augustan Ideal Under Stress*, 153–4.

24 'Martinus Scriblerus of the Poem'. The fullest discussion of this aspect of the poem is Aubrey L. Williams, *Pope's Dunciad. A Study of its Meaning* (London: Methuen, 1955).

25 Claude Lévi-Strauss, *Tristes Tropiques* (Paris: Plon, 1955), 136–7.

26 The most recent discussion, whose emphases differ from mine, is Brian McCrea, 'Romances, Newspapers, and the Style of Fielding's True History', *Studies in English Literature*, XXI (1981), 471–80.

27 On Caxton's Virgil and early attacks on it, see N. F. Blake, *Caxton and his World* (London: Deutsch, 1969), 195–6, 202; C. S. Lewis, *English Literature in the Sixteenth Century* (Oxford: Clarendon Press, 1954), 81. Pope evidently had not read Caxton's work, but obtained the text of 'CAXTON's *Preface to his Translation of* VIRGIL' from Lord Oxford in 1728 (*Correspondence*, II: 498), printing it as an Appendix to the editions of 1729 to score a point against

Theobald. From 1735, when the Appendix was dropped, Pope quoted from the Preface in his note to the Caxton reference in the poem (TE, V: xxivn., 79–80, 213–16, 281). Caxton's *Eneydos* (1490) has been published as Early English Text Society Extra Series, No. 57, 1890, rptd. 1962.

28 For other verbal sources of Pope's passage, see TE, V: 156–7n.

29 TE, X: 390.

30 G. Birkbeck Hill (ed.), *Lives of the English Poets* (Oxford: Clarendon Press, 1905), III: 250.

31 E.g. *Art of Sinking in Poetry*, 48–9, including an instance involving Blackmore, and 19–24, several cases of 'this happy and antinatural way of thinking'. See the good discussion by Howard Erskine-Hill, *Pope: The Dunciad* (London: Arnold, 1972), 28–31.

32 See the important recent discussion of these lines and the *adynaton*-tradition by A. D. Nuttall, 'Fishes in the Trees', *Essays in Criticism*, XXIV (1974), 20–38, esp. 27 ff. For references to studies and lists of *adynata*, see my note 'Rabelais and Horace: A Contact in *Tiers Livre*, ch. III', *French Studies*, XIX (1965), 376–8 and nn. 8–12.

33 There are also some Shakespearean precedents for specific elements in Pope's couplet: 'At Christmas I no more desire a rose / Than wish a snow in May's new fangled shows' (*LLL*, I. i. 105–06); 'hoary-headed frosts / Fall in the fresh lap of the crimson rose; / And on old Hiems' thin and icy crown, / An odorous chaplet of sweet summer buds / Is, as in mockery, set' (*MND*, II. i. 107–11).

34 See above pp. 204 ff. For an effect of contemptuous comedy in *Paradise Lost*, itself verging on mock-heroic and drawn upon by Pope in the Dunciadic games, see II: 947 ff.: 'So eagerly the Fiend / O'er bog or steep, through strait, rough, dense or rare, / With head, hands, wings or feet persues his way, / And swims or sinks, or wades, or creeps, or flies'. Pope imitated and cited these lines at *Dunciad*, II: 63 ff.

35 'Tradition and the Individual Talent', *Selected Essays* (London: Faber, 1953), 14, 15; *Waste Land*, ll. 22, 430. For other recent discussions of *The Dunciad* and *The Waste Land*, see Patricia Meyer Spacks, *An Argument of Images* (Cambridge, Mass.: Harvard, 1971), 96–104, 125–32; J. S. Cunningham, 'Pope, Eliot, and "The Mind of Europe"', in A. D. Moody (ed.), *The Waste Land In Different Voices* (London: Arnold, 1974), 67–85.

36 Valerie Eliot (ed.), *The Waste Land. A Facsimile and Transcript of the Original Drafts* (London: Faber, 1971), 127n., cited from Eliot's Introduction to Pound's *Selected Poems* (London: Faber, 1948), 18.

37 *Selected Essays*, 14.

38 *Henry Fielding and the Augustan Ideal Under Stress*, 156–8.

39 Preface to *Iliad*, TE, VII: 14.

40 Blackwell, 28; Cowley, *Poems*, ed., A. R. Waller (Cambridge: Cambridge University Press, 1905), 7. It is in this same Preface of 1656 that Cowley discusses his failure to complete his two epics, *The Civil War* and the *Davideis* (9, 11–12).

41 Preface to Harold E. Pagliaro (ed.), *Journal of a Voyage to Lisbon* (New York: Nardon Press, 1963), 26.

42 On Auden and Isherwood, and schoolboy analogies, see *Henry Fielding and the Augustan Ideal Under Stress*, 172ff.

43 'Pope and Dulness', *Proceedings of the British Academy*, LIV (1968), 253–4.

44 See *Henry Fielding and the Augustan Ideal Under Stress*, 192–3, 220–21 nn.

45 *Works*, IX: 235.

46 G. Wilson Knight, *The Poetry of Pope, Laureate of Peace* (London: Routledge,

1965), 60, 62. The phrase about letters and lances is from Lyly's *Campaspe*, I. i. 82: Alexander is speaking to Hephaestion.

47 The opening words respectively of Dryden's translation of the *Aeneid* (*arma virumque cano*), and of the A and B texts of *The Dunciad*. On *The Dunciad* as a poem tending away from the epic tradition, see John E. Sitter, *The Poetry of Pope's Dunciad* (Minneapolis: University of Minnesota Press, 1971).

7

Pope's 'Opus Magnum' and An Essay on Man

(i) The 'Opus Magnum' and the Epic

Pope never wrote the epic poem which had been his particular ambition from early adolescence, when he made his abortive attempt on *Alcander*. This early work, which Pope destroyed, may have been jumping the gun. But there were certainly thoughts of that Virgilian progress from pastoral to epic which Renaissance poets liked to follow and which is implicit in Pope's ostentatiously 'modest' publication of four *Pastorals* at the start of his career. Like Dryden before him, still believing that 'A heroic poem, truly such, is undoubtedly the greatest work which the soul of man is capable to perform', he could only write epics as it were by proxy: by translating Homer as Dryden had translated Virgil, or by paying to epic the oblique tribute of ironic imitation in poems which, together with one or two by Dryden and others, constitute the small handful of *mock*-heroic masterpieces in the language.

The old reverence for epic had survived, in an age which knew instinctively that the heroic could no longer be for it a natural medium of self-expression. Epics went on being written by Blackmore and his like, which merely proved the point. To the best sensibilities of the age, the Blackmores were a hideous example of 'modern' overreaching, an upstart defilement of ancient altars, and above all an example of what to avoid. The sudden short-lived flowering of mock-heroic as a major idiom of literary expression during the lifetimes of Boileau, Dryden and Pope is the product of this survival of epic loyalties, which remained strong in principle but no longer capable of being sustained in poetic practice: the great poets of the day could only write epic through a filter of irony.

Mock-epic forms existed before and after, of course, but as

222

literary jokes or as pedantic anachronisms. The urgency and power of the *Dunciad* are unprecedented and unrepeatable. They are those of a great primary poetic vision, transcending mere parody while of course preserving its pleasures. They deflect a live epic aspiration into a paradoxical and negative form, as the Homer translations (and Dryden's Virgil) provided a positive outlet by proxy.

Nevertheless Pope persisted in the idea of writing an epic himself, and near the end of his life declared that 'If I had not undertaken [the Homer translation] I should certainly have writ an epic'. At about the time of this remark, he was making plans for an epic on *Brutus*, the Trojan founder of Britain. The late Miriam Leranbaum dates the early planning in 1742 (rather than 1739–40, as implied by Warburton), and in April 1744, a few weeks before his death, Pope told Spence that *Brutus* is 'all planned already, and even some of the most material speeches writ in prose'. It is clear from the surviving plans that *Brutus* would have contained discourses on civil and ecclesiastical government, which would have been more prominent in the poem than any traditional epic action. Indeed the poem was to absorb the material on government which had originally been planned for the third book of the celebrated *opus magnum*, that 'ethic work', also unfinished, with which Pope was preoccupied in his last fifteen years. In the same way, some material on education from the 'ethic work' found its way into the fourth book of the *Dunciad* in 1742, in a negative or satirical form. If, as Miriam Leranbaum says in her important study, *Alexander Pope's 'Opus Magnum', 1729–1744*, 1977, the four-book *Dunciad* of 1743 and the *Brutus* are linked as negative and positive forms of epic, dwelling respectively on disorder and restoration, the fact remains, whether fortuitously or otherwise, that it is only the negative or 'anti-epic' poem which was written. How precariously close to one another the positive and negative forms might be in Pope's imagination, how ready they were to interpenetrate, may be sensed also from the fact that Pope's other (admittedly earlier) recorded references to the legend of Brutus seem tinged with derision, whereas the poem he finally planned was on the contrary to be a rather solemn and humourless treatment of a Benevolent Man.

Leranbaum gives one of the few good accounts we have of the *Brutus* scheme, and of its relation to the projected philosophical poem which is the main subject of her book. But she is no more interested in the reasons why this 'ethic work' was not finished than in why Pope never wrote an epic. It is possible that these are related: that a secure and widely shared sense of the world's comprehensibility, which makes possible the writing of coherent and convincing poems about man's nature and place in the universe, may also be necessary to the expression of high ideals and aspirations in a heroic mode.

For this secure sense, the 'optimistic' theodicy of the *Essay on Man* was no substitute. That poem, the largest self-contained relic of the unfinished *opus magnum*, often reads like a buoyant piece of ideological coat-trailing, a *tour de force* of poetic summation rather than an expression of urgent philosophical convictions. Pope did not wholly understand, and was not in the first place greatly interested in, the divisive philosophical and theological issues which touched off so much controversy after the poem appeared. I do not mean that the poem is intellectually trivial, but (as the second section of this chapter will argue) that its central poetic excitement resides in Pope's delight in the creation or staging of harmonious and orderly systems, and not in any active literal belief in Great Chains of Being or other such articles of pseudo-faith. The small-scale completeness of the *Essay* itself is among other things a tribute to the pleasures of the conclusive and the ship-shape, while the non-completion of the scheme as a whole may be due to a sense that such a ship-shape conception of man and of the world could not be sustained on any large or com-prehensive scale.

The poem invites comparison with Lucretius, one of its acknowledged sources, and Dr Leranbaum (who is, with Bern-hard Fabian, one of the two most interesting recent students of the question) devotes a useful chapter to this. She notes how Pope deliberately reverses certain negative patterns in the Lucretian model. Lucretius emphasised a falling movement, from creation to destruction, while Pope offered an opposite scenario. Lucretius spoke of indifferent gods and of the disorders and eventual disintegration of the universe; Pope stressed a watchful Provi-dence and a 'universal order'. Leranbaum skilfully discusses structural affinities between the two poems which were precisely adapted by Pope to this reverse relationship. And yet it is the more negative, darker Lucretius who feels able to enunciate a comprehensive cosmology with a massive and unforced feeling of poetic conviction, even though he must have known that his Epicurean philosophy and cosmology would not as such meet with the universal assent of his readers. The confidence comes not from doctrinal solidarity, but from a natural sense that the universe was still amenable to intellectual and imaginative comprehension. (It is interesting that even at the planning stage Pope's *opus magnum* was not going to include the wider cosmological material which Lucretius took in his stride).

Pope wrote to Swift in 1734: 'Whether I can proceed in the same grave march like Lucretius, or must descend to the gayeties of Horace, I know not, or whether I can do either.' (All four parts of the *Essay* itself had already appeared when Pope said this). Leranbaum chooses to pursue the Lucretian emphasis, and there is much to be said for this, if only to restore a balance tilted the other way by many critics. But the difference between Lucretius and Horace is not merely a matter of 'gravity' and 'gaiety'. Lucretius's poem is a sustained and systematic treatment in a single long poem. The Horatian *oeuvre*, on the other hand, consists of shorter works on miscellaneous and often 'informally' explored themes: its reflections on the nature of man and on the universe inevitably emerge in a more piecemeal and fragmentary way. The attraction of Horace was not only his 'gaiety', but the sanction which he provided for not sustaining the 'grave march' beyond the point where a felt conviction about the universal order was no longer there to validate it. The division of the *Essay* into 'Epistles' rather than 'Books' has more than an obvious and vague Horatian flavour: it offers the protective suggestion of informal miscellaneous discourse, a suggestion not wholly true to the poem as we have it, but serving to disarm equally unfounded expectations of a genuinely universal coherence and reach. The jostling between Lucretian and Horatian elements in the poem is very active. A revealing small sign is that the opening words, in the manuscript version, are 'Awake my Memmius'. In early printed editions, Memmius (the addressee of Lucretius) became Laelius, a Horatian figure. Horace prevailed over Lucretius, until both addressees were supplanted by Pope's own friend St John, whose name opens the poem in the version which we know best. The significance of this tug of war between Lucretius and Horace to an understanding of Pope's *Essay* deserves to be more fully looked into.

Leranbaum also discusses those other 'completed' portions of the *opus magnum*, the four *Moral Essays*. She is extremely good in sorting out the tangled question of the relation of each of them to the others, to the *Essay on Man*, and to what can be reconstructed of the scheme of the 'ethic work' as a whole. She is inclined to accord more philosophical seriousness to the doctrine of the Ruling Passion than I think it deserves, and overlooks the inconsistencies, the pseudo–logic and the curious displays of bravura with which it is asserted in the poems: 'This clue once found, unravels all the rest,/The prospect clears, and Wharton stands confest'. As with the wider coherences of the *Essay on Man*, what comes through is the delight of their setting–up, an excited patness rather than a sense of deep intrinsic conviction. In the *Epistle to Cobham* and its companion, the *Epistle to a Lady*, the factitious certainties about the Ruling Passion provide a convenient framework for other certainties *not* factitious: the subtle, unerring exactitudes of the individual portraits which they frame, the vivid sense of human contradictions grasped. Pope's attempt to generalise these brilliant *aperçus* into a comprehensive theory of the human mind is perfunctory and shallow, although Pope could derive *some* poetic energy from almost any bravura assertion of his ordering powers. But it is the small–scale finalities of each portrait which carry conviction, not the pseudo–system in which they are enclosed.

Leranbaum's book does not in the main address itself to these questions. But her lucid and methodical study of the *opus magnum* which Pope did not write, but which occupied his thoughts in the last fifteen years of his life, makes it possible to enquire into them in a more informed way than before. The poems Pope did not write claim our attention more than those which Blackmore did. The fact that a book has been written about them will doubtless seem to some a further absurd triumph of what James Reeves attacked, in a mildly notorious recent book, as Pope's self-publicising enterprise. But the subject of Leranbaum's book is in fact very real. It haunts every aspect of Pope's later work. It has never before been thoroughly and systematically examined. We owe her a considerable debt.

1977

(ii) Pope's Essay on Man

The most famous passage from the *Essay on Man* is the opening of Epistle II:

> Know then thyself, presume not God to scan;
> The proper study of Mankind is Man.
> Plac'd on this isthmus of a middle state,
> A being darkly wise, and rudely great:

With too much knowledge for the Sceptic side,
With too much weakness for the Stoic's pride,
He hangs between; in doubt to act, or rest,
In doubt to deem himself a God, or Beast;
In doubt his Mind or Body to prefer,
Born but to die, and reas'ning but to err;
Alike in ignorance, his reason such,
Whether he thinks too little, or too much:
Chaos of Thought and Passion, all confus'd;
Still by himself abus'd, or disabus'd;
Created half to rise, and half to fall;
Great lord of all things, yet a prey to all;
Sole judge of Truth, in endless Error hurl'd:
The glory, jest, and riddle of the world!

(II: 1–18).

The doctrine expressed here is that of the Great Chain of Being, a traditional idea in classical antiquity which was widely adapted to Christian conceptions of world harmony. It is arguable that in Pope's day it was no longer widely believed in in its simple literal sense, but survived as a metaphorical expression of the aspiration for order, a 'supreme fiction'. Certainly Pope's lines have the air of reflecting not so much a solid faith taken for granted as a tense triumph of poetic containment. The attachment to 'correctness', to couplet-symmetries, to sharp lucidities of definition in individual lines and half-lines, the unerring command of climax and anti-climax, the absolute mastery of tone: these stylistic accoutrements of Augustan confidence, in such a passage, imply no easy serenities or insipid poise, but the excitements of a verbal conquest. The notional regularities of the metre are not crudely metronomic but exist in live tension with the natural rhythms of speech, the shifting cadences dictated by sense and feeling. The play of conflict and antithesis is controlled not only by its own local tensions but by a rhetorical progression in the passage as a whole, in which triumphs of summation mingle with lofty displays of scorn, and heaving energies settle at the bidding of what sometimes looks like sheer poetic muscle.

The balances and symmetries are of a kind also suggested in the other arts, in the patterned elaborations of a formal dance, in the proportions of a neo-Palladian building, in musical compositions strongly dominated by the certainties of closure. It may be that the verbal arts are better adapted than others to conveying both the sense of pattern *and* the turbulences which challenge it, because words have meanings and are capable of suggesting subversive undercurrents more directly than is possible in some non-verbal media. But in Pope there is perhaps a special feeling that both pattern and turbulence are not so much *given* facts of a pre-existing equilibrium, as assertions of a balance freshly re-discovered or re-created by the poet's personal fiat.

Much earlier, in *Windsor-Forest*, Pope first displayed his delight in those larger-scale arrangements in nature, 'Where Order in Variety we see,/And where, tho' all things differ, all agree'. The forest landscape is 'as the World, harmoniously confus'd'. This looks forward to the Universe of the *Essay* not only in its main idea, but also in giving the feeling that Pope delights in the confusion for the sake of the harmony; that he has, in a certain sense, staged both; and that he is expressing his own high imaginative delight in ideas of order at least as much as expressing a shared and settled faith in an ordered universe. In the *Essay*'s 'mighty maze! but not without a plan' (I: 6) the maze seems partly set up in order to bring into being the triumphs of the 'plan' and the 'plan' asserts a prior cosmic order less vividly than it reflects the poet's imaginative victories in setting it forth.

The rendering of the order thus has the air of a personal assertion, but the order itself is not of course a private one. It consists of traditional notions of world harmony common among both classical and Christian authors. The idea that life subsists through a conflict of opposing elements and passions ('ALL subsists by elemental strife; / And Passions are the elements of Life', I: 169–70), and the idea that these vital clashes are held within a firm cosmic arrangement, are both very ancient. Pope's way with these ideas is individual not in its content but in its tone. Pope differs from some older poets, and from his own blander contemporaries, in the particular charge of tension, and the special vibrancies of resolution, with which he renders them. He differs, conversely, from a more disenchanted or more anguished contemporary like Swift in that his vision of the 'elemental strife' is never allowed to generate a feeling of radically disruptive forces, nor even of a taut but merely precarious equilibrium. A necessary *tension* is constantly suggested, but it does not become unbalancing. At the same time, the verse hardly ever settles to a flaccid and unearned optimism, even where a note of calm composition is struck:

> Passions, like Elements, tho' born to fight,
> Yet, mix'd and soften'd, in his work unite:
> ....
> Love, Hope, and Joy, fair pleasure's smiling train,
> Hate, Fear, and Grief, the family of pain;
> These mix'd with art, and to due bounds confin'd,
> Make and maintain the balance of the mind:
> The lights and shades, whose well accorded strife,
> Gives all the strength and colour of our life.
>
> (II: 111–22)

'Mix'd and soften'd' may suggest the cosier complacencies of Addison or Thomson. But much of the language, from 'born to fight' to 'all the strength and colour', suggests energy both enjoyed and controlled.

This pattern of release and containment thus reveals itself simultaneously in themes or visions of order (the universal harmony, the ruling passion as organising principle) and in triumphs of poetic definition. The poet both proclaims and enacts it, both in the generalising statement of Book II about man's place in the universe, and in the vibrant finalities of the character-portraits in the *Moral Essays*. It may manifest itself in the composed dignity of the last passage, or in a piece of poetic bullying like the famous knockdown argument about why man has been denied certain powers which animals possess:

> The bliss of Man (could Pride that blessing find)
> Is not to act or think beyond mankind;
> No pow'rs of body or of soul to share,
> But what his nature and his state can bear.
> Why has not Man a microscopic eye?
> For this plain reason, Man is not a Fly.
> Say what the use, were finer optics giv'n,
> T'inspect a mite, not comprehend the heav'n?
> Or touch, if tremblingly alive all o'er,
> To smart and agonize at ev'ry pore?
> Or quick effluvia darting thro' the brain,
> Die of a rose in aromatic pain?
>
> (I: 189–200)

Patness is a crude term to describe the rich modulations of certainty, the derision enriched by a vivid sensuousness of apprehension, the commanding play of impassioned wit, of this passage. But it suggests itself because there is here a relentless pressure of victorious argumentation, which makes its points not through an unanswerable logic, but through the imposition on the reader of a barrage of inspired debating points. We witness a shameless oversimplification of philosophical issues, but submit to the authoritative energies of an extraordinary feat of stylistic containment.

There is a related containment of human absurdities which consists, not (as here) of refutation but of a peculiar kind of indulgence. The poet gives folly its head, but makes it seem oddly self-regulating and self-comforting, each case a little pseudo-system so self-enclosed that it can hardly disrupt our larger world. We think of the Cave of Spleen in *The Rape of the Lock*, or of this passage from Epistle II:

> Whate'er the Passion, knowledge, fame, or pelf,
> Not one will change his neighbor with himself.
> The learn'd is happy nature to explore,
> The fool is happy that he knows no more;
> The rich is happy in the plenty giv'n,
> The poor contents him with the care of Heav'n.
> See the blind beggar dance, the cripple sing,
> The sot a hero, lunatic a king;
> The starving chemist in his golden views
> Supremely blest, the poet in his muse.
> See some strange comfort ev'ry state attend,
> And Pride bestow'd on all, a common friend;
> See some fit Passion ev'ry age supply,
> Hope travels thro', nor quits us when we die.
>
> (II: 261–74)

The word 'strange' somehow has the effect of implying not that the poet is puzzled, but rather that he has taken the measure of the whole thing and found the word 'strange' to be the right one.

In such passages, we move from vividly imaged examples to maxims ('Hope travels thro', nor quits us when we die') and back. The poem is full of maxims that have passed into the language, a measure not only of eloquence and insight, but of a kind of memorable and ringing certainty: 'Hope springs eternal in the human breast' (I: 95), 'The proper study of Mankind is Man' (II: 2). In two of the Epistles, the first and the last, Pope picks up some of these and introduces new ones in a fugal display of hammer-blow abstractions:

All Nature is but Art, unknown to thee;
All Chance, Direction, which thou canst not see;
All Discord, Harmony, not understood;
All partial Evil, universal Good:
And, spite of Pride, in erring Reason's spite,
One truth is clear, 'Whatever IS, is RIGHT'
(I: 289–94)

Here, some will feel, patness has become damaging. Readers often react against the supposed smugness of 'Whatever IS, is RIGHT,' aggravated in print by block capitals. Pope is not, of course, asserting that there is no evil and that all is cheerful. He is saying that in a divinely ordained universe, evil and misery (though ugly and painful) have an ultimate purpose which may be invisible to us. This is 'optimism' in a special philosophical sense, not in the usual colloquial one. Johnson, Voltaire and others who derided such 'optimism' understood the point perfectly well, but pretended for satiric reasons not to. The miseries portrayed in *Candide* are no logical refutation: the traditional scheme of 'optimistic' philosophies allows for misery from the start. What Voltaire is getting at *behind* his reductive and ostensibly irrelevant objection is the foolish inappropriateness of such philosophies, however fool*proof* their self-enclosed logic. It is ultimately a complaint about tone, tone not as mere style or vocal inflexion but as moral texture, way of looking, *life*-style.

A modern reader might concur, but may be repelled even more by the deadening array of abstract propositions as such. We do not, nowadays, take kindly to argument in poetry, and the philosophical poem (as practised in the past by Lucretius or Dante) has no place among us. Such objections would have less force in Pope's time, and readers from Dryden's day to Wordsworth's were accustomed to the practice and prepared to respect it. At the same time, the period produced no Lucretius and no Dante. There was sufficient expectation of the world's amenability to comprehensive definition for the idea of a poem on the nature of man or of the universe to seem appropriate, without the deep spiritual confidence which animated Lucretius's or Dante's great poems. Such a confidence might be pagan or Christian, sectarian (like Lucretius's epicureanism) or confidently universal (like Dante's catholicism), irradiated with faith, as Dante was, or even shot through with dark apprehensions of disorder like Lucretius. What both poets had in

231

common was a deeply *enabling* sense that poems of cosmic reach and global summation were meaningful and possible enterprises.

It is this sense which Pope lacked, perhaps without knowing it. He modelled himself on Lucretius, and even consciously reversed Lucretian pessimism in his emphasis on a watchful and beneficent providence (on this, see the preceding section of this chapter). But he abandoned the form of Lucretius's large-scale philosophic poem and retreated behind the less ambitious atmosphere of the Horatian *Epistle*, the more fragmentary and unsystematic causerie in a letter to a friend (the *Essay on Man* is divided into four Epistles, not Books or Cantos, just as the companion *Moral Essays*, as we now refer to them, are all called Epistles and were commonly grouped as 'Epistles' in lifetime collected editions of Pope's *Works*).

Even more revealing is the fact that the great philosophical *opus magnum* which Pope planned to write, to which the *Essay on Man* was to be an introduction and which was to include the *Moral Essays* and other works of Pope's later years, was never finished, just as Wordsworth's 'philosophical Poem, containing views of Man, Nature, and Society' was never finished, though one of its surviving elements is the 'introductory' poem we know as *The Prelude*, which eventually took on a separate existence. The *Essay on Man* is Pope's prelude to an uncompleted long poem.

Wordsworth's stage in the process I am talking about is a late one, in which it is assumed that universal truth can only be arrived at privately, through an intensely personal self-exploratory experience. Pope's way is not in this sense private. It has none of Wordsworth's introspective character, and Pope would indeed have regarded that as improperly intimate. The tone which Pope strikes is a social or public one, even when he addresses the personal friend, Bolingbroke, who inspired the poem:

> Come then, my Friend, my Genius, come along,
> Oh master of the poet, and the song!
> And while the Muse now stoops, or now ascends,
> To Man's low passions, or their glorious ends,
> Teach me, like thee, in various nature wise,
> To fall with dignity, with temper rise;
> Form'd by thy converse, happily to steer
> From grave to gay, from lively to severe;
> Correct with spirit, eloquent with ease,
> Intent to reason, or polite to please.
> Oh! while along the stream of Time thy name

Expanded flies, and gathers all its fame,
Say, shall my little bark attendant sail,
Pursue the triumph, and partake the gale?
When statesmen, heroes, kings, in dust repose,
Whose sons shall blush their fathers were thy foes,
Shall then this verse to future age pretend
Thou wert my guide, philosopher, and friend?
That urg'd by thee, I turn'd the tuneful art
From sounds to things, from fancy to the heart;
For Wit's false mirror held up Nature's light;
Shew'd erring Pride, WHATEVER IS, IS RIGHT;
That REASON, PASSION, answer one great aim;
That true SELF-LOVE and SOCIAL are the same;
That VIRTUE only makes our Bliss below;
And all our Knowledge is, OURSELVES TO KNOW.

(IV: 373–98)

The address to Bolingbroke, and the broad sketch of Pope's own poetic progress towards an increasing seriousness, 'from fancy to the heart', have about them a public posture: 'the guide, philosopher, and friend' appears only in his role of mentor, a wise and gentlemanly Horatian adviser, the poet's autobiography only in its broadest, least intimate outline. We are a long way from Wordsworth's addresses to Dorothy or to Coleridge; from his vividly autobiographical progress from youthful rapture to mature wisdom and his highly specific and introspective scrutiny of 'the growth of a poet's mind'. Through a rhetoric of gentlemanly solidarity, rather than through the deep insights of a solitary inward quest, Pope moves to the excited finalities of that closing series of universal maxims. (Note that here, 'WHATEVER IS, IS RIGHT', and 'true SELF-LOVE and SOCIAL are the same', which formed the stirring closures of earlier statements, are only individual parts of the final closure, of an excited summation of summations.)

The argument retains its universalising claims, then, and the discourse is public. We are given general propositions about man, not disclosures of private feeling, and they belong to a larger order, traditionally recognised. Nevertheless, this order, as we have seen, is revealed to us through what we feel to be the intensities of a personal re-creation, the privately experienced reassertion of 'a rage for order' rather than the deep security of large beliefs taken for granted. In a way, Pope has provided a paradigm, in much that goes before, of how self-love widens to

233

social and the part to the whole. The immediately preceding passage reads:

> God loves from Whole to Parts: but human soul
> Must rise from Individual to the Whole.
> Self-love but serves the virtuous mind to wake,
> As the small pebble stirs the peaceful lake;
> The centre mov'd, a circle strait succeeds,
> Another still, and still another spreads,
> Friend, parent, neighbour, first it will embrace,
> His country next, and next all human race,
> Wide and more wide, th'o'erflowings of the mind
> Take ev'ry creature in, of ev'ry kind;
> Earth smiles around, with boundless bounty blest,
> And Heav'n beholds its image in his breast.
>
> (IV: 361–72)

The paradigm of a movement from self to whole, presented as a general law, oddly comes through as the satisfying conclusion of an individual drama of discovery. The widening vistas that open out not, as in Swift or Johnson, into the terrors of limitlessness, but to a more generous inclusiveness ('Take ev'ry creature in, of ev'ry kind'), are deeply and characteristically Popeian, and not as is sometimes supposed, the common property of eighteenth-century men. If it is in the nature of these 'certainties' to seem, unlike Wordsworth's, the easy common property of all, it is because it is a necessity of Pope's temperament and of his culture that they should *seem* so: certainties more privately limited would not be considered worth having. But if the idiom and the materials of these proclaimed beliefs were in a sense widespread, traditional, they have had to be reactivated in a highly special way, for they were no longer, as they are sometimes thought to be, matters of received and settled conviction securely entrenched in their time.

1980

8

'Neo-classic' and 'Augustan'

(i)   Boileau, Pope and Neo-classicism

Was there such a thing as 'neo-classicism', outside the special sense of the term which art historians apply to a later period than the one students of literature lose so much of their composure over? It seems to have existed sufficiently strongly in French studies to have produced a body of revisionist denials. The term 'neo-classic' has largely dropped out of the corridors of Englitbiz, usually to be replaced by 'Augustan', though there have been attempts in recent English studies to dislodge 'Augustan' too, on the grounds that some eighteenth-century authors took a dim view of Augustus Caesar.

Gordon Pocock, in his book on *Boileau and the Nature of Neo-classicism*, 1980, is untroubled by problems of nomenclature, ignoring (I suppose in the French as well as the English sense of ignoring) the existence of this particular non-problem. He uses 'Augustan' of English poets as readily as he uses 'neo-classic' of the French, though with a more refreshing air of prelapsarian innocence. For he knows that in France the value of the word, and even the existence of the thing, have been questioned, and Pocock intends to assert both. Not for him, however, the convenient imprecision of approximate labels, which are serviceable largely because they identify a broadly recognised set of common features (as one might use Augustan to refer to Swift, Pope or Fielding and not to Defoe, Richardson or Blake) without claiming to force every individual case into a tight and elaborate fit. For him 'neo-classicism' means the rules codified by Renaissance pedagogues, the Horatian injunction to instruct and to please, and a few other things which are either (like the former) so specific and limiting as to raise the question of how the system survived for more than five minutes among authors of intelligence and talent if they understood it as Pocock does; or (like the latter) so unspecific as to be applicable in his hands to almost any text in almost any way. An endearingly bizarre example is this passage on the continuity between the Middle Ages and neo-classic times: 'A well-known device of mediaeval poetry is allegory, by which moral truths can be taught delightfully. This doctrine also flourishes in neo-classicism'.

'Doctrine' is a favourite word, though the usage here is more than usually loose, and it seems curious that a volume devoted to the expounding and rehabilitation of neo-classicism should lay quite so much stress on the 'doctrinal' channels of transmission and very little on the imaginative ones. The two, in any live culture, are not easily separable. But the idea that the classical tradition was more securely passed on from great poet to great poet than through the repetition of precepts might have seemed better calculated to win over the supposedly resistant modern reader, as well as being what Boileau or Pope tended to think anyway.

It is certainly how English Augustans often looked on Boileau himself. When Spence recorded Pope's remarks on the subject, that was the visible emphasis: 'Boileau the first poet of the French in the same manner as Virgil of all the Latin. Malherbe (*longo intervallo*) the second'. Malherbe was the one who introduced correctness, or Augustanised French verse, much as Waller and Denham were felt to have done for English. 'Enfin Malherbe vint' is Boileau's celebration of his impact on the progress of French poetry in the *Art Poétique*. The correctness he brought was, in reality, no very classical thing *per se*, in the sense that it had nothing much in common with the Greek or Latin poets. But it was felt, in an obscure but potent sense, to be an integral part of the 'neo-classical' enterprise: thus also 'Augustanism' often refers to those features in English writers which are least like the Roman poets (the couplet, for example, or 'wit' or the drawing-room ethos), yet insists by name on the Roman connection.

Boileau was something else. Dryden called him 'a living Horace and a Juvenal,' and credited him with the perfecting of a new idiom, that of serious mock-heroic, the 'most noble kind of satire' in which 'the majesty of the heroic' is 'finely mixed with the venom of the other'. Dryden is said to have thought he had invented this himself in *Mac Flecknoe*, and had to be reminded that he'd got it from *Le Lutrin*, Boileau's mock-epic about a clerical squabble which also helped to make possible Pope's *Rape of the Lock*. That is a literally *neo*-classical thing. It derived from and presupposed an awareness of ancient epic, but in a new ironic way, not as mere parody (there had always been plenty of that) but as primary creative idiom, the edgy product of an age that could no longer, as I have argued, imitate epic directly.

It is in these senses that Boileau was, for Dryden as for Pope, 'a living Horace and a Juvenal' as well as the first of the French in the manner in which Virgil was 'of all the Latin'. What *Le Lutrin* did to link the serious epic with the satires of a later day the *Art Poétique* achieved more directly for the line of poems about poetry which runs from Horace's *Ars Poetica* to Pope's *Essay on Criticism*. Part of his impact was as a poetic model, but he was of course also regarded as an authority, and it is in the nature of arts of poetry to hand down precepts. Pope values (and practises) this too, but the praise of Boileau on this point in the *Essay on Criticism* is notoriously double-edged:

> But *Critic Learning* flourish'd most in *France*.
> The *Rules*, a Nation born to serve, obeys,
> And Boileau still in Right of *Horace* sways.

Pope's main sarcasm is at the expense of traditional British complacencies about the servility of the French and means that the vaunted English freedom is really an anarchic barbarism, '*unconquer'd*, and *unciviliz'd*'. But the compliment is elaborately back-handed. Empson's famous gloss that 'while Pope despises the English for breaking the rules he contrives still more firmly to despise the French for keeping them' may sound a little bald, but he has got Pope roughly right: a sarcasm about a sarcasm doesn't comfortably cancel out into whole-hearted approval.

If Pope welcomed Boileau's authority, and even 'the Critick's Law' it partly rested on, he was more insistent and more eloquent than most in his reminders that the 'rules' were distilled from poems and not invented for them ('*discover'd*, not *devis'd*'), that they had a creative and ordering rather than a restricting relation to 'Nature,' that they were means and not ends and should be interpreted humanely. There is about his writing on the subject something of that immediacy of practical concern of a writer for his craft which we sense in Ben Jonson when he says that a writer might find in Aristotle 'not only ... the way not to err, but the short way we should take not to err'. The idea was common, and Jonson is in fact translating from the Latin of the Dutchman Heinsius. The Latin lacks the fervour of practicality which Jonson made largely his own, but that fervour is even further removed from Chapelain's version of the commonplace that the rules were short-cuts to composition, which speaks of

> des préceptes invariables, des dogmes d'éternelle vérité, qui convainquent l'esprit, qui lui épargnent des recherches douteuses, et qui l'informent en un moment de ce qu'un homme n'aurait pu découvrir tout seul qu'en plusieurs centaines d'années . . .

Chapelain's notion of invariable precepts and dogmas eternally true, which remove the need for uncertain searches and teach us in a moment what no single man could arrive at by himself in less than several centuries, superficially resembles the words of Heinsius and Jonson. But the short-cuts are contemplated at a level of abstraction which is even more ghoulishly striking than the peremptory insistence on the *préceptes invariables* and the *dogmes d'éternelle vérité*. Those imagined centuries which a man might take without the rules removes the contemplation of the rules themselves to a domain of remote hyperbole, a long way away in practice from 'the short way we should take not to err'. What is chiefly left out of sight on this plane of rhetorical fantasy is any vivid sense of a real author considering the practicalities of his craft, though the short-cuts in question purport to be for his use more than anybody's.

Pocock speaks of Chapelain's awkward prose stumbling into life at this point, but if there is any life it is that of a self-intoxicating pedantry rehearsing the ghostly pleasures of a mental closed system. It is against this kind of thing that the half-concealed anti-Gallicanism which Empson identified in Pope's lines about critic learning flourishing most in France was mainly directed. 'Neo-classicism', in this uglier form, is neither of one time nor of one place. The type is always with us, with its fondness for formalist methodologies, the comforts of systematic procedure, the self-validations of centralising precept, and other assorted mechanical operations of the spirit. There may be something in the view that France is where this 'flourishes most'. Its classroom descendant of yesterday is the *explication de texte*, and a glossier reincarnation wears smart Parisian clothes in the deconstructive carnivals of the international conference circuit. But who shall 'scape whipping? The thing is indeed international, and so was its older version, and it would be hard to claim that all Frenchmen were in its grip, whether then or now. The 'neo-classicism' which Mr Pocock attributes to Boileau comes near to this older version, although he would doubtless have us think otherwise. Pope knew that Boileau himself bore little resemblance to that atrophy of classicism which sturdy Britons were quick to attribute to the slavish French. Boileau is not really being blamed for this in Pope's lines on the subject but the disturbing thing is that he is being praised for it by Mr Pocock.

The little fable about Virgil in the *Essay on Criticism* I noted in chapter 6 illustrates a different neo-classicism. Virgil is first imagined as a young poet, scorning 'the Critick's Law' and drawing only 'from *Nature's Fountains*'. But later, says the next couplet,

> when t'examine ev'ry Part he came,
> *Nature* and *Homer* were, he found, the *same*.

There is a tacit transition in the narrative from critic's law to Homeric poem, as though they too were much the same. The rules were Nature too: 'To copy *Nature* is to copy *Them*'. The sliding, whether cunning or instinctive, is typical of Pope's easy sense of the closeness of 'just *Precepts*' and 'great *Examples*' to one another. But they are not substitutes. Their relationship is a *working* one, as in Jonson's 'short way we should take not to err'. The 'great *Examples*' come first and last, and in the line about Nature and Homer he knows exactly where he wants his final emphasis to rest. The energy of the passage comes mainly from that last line. It has little to do with the truth or plausibility of the account of Virgil, or with any status or immediacy it may have as a piece of transferred autobiography on the part of a self-idealising Pope. The sentiment, paraphrased, might seem banal, and the compliment to Homer would be a mere paradoxical turn or elegancy if it were not for the glow of excited recognition contained in that triumph of vivid closure: Virgil's discovery about Homer is also Pope's own, not in any sense which relates to the biographical progress of either poet, but in the poetic *now* of its setting down. The declared pieties of neo-classical doctrine, the roll-call of revered masters, the sketch of Virgil's career act as a mere catalyst for the real point, which is that of an exhilarated personal recapturing of the whole classical tradition.

Such moments of fervour, where the penny suddenly drops, irradiating all the assertions of loyalty with an urgency of freshly re-experienced conviction, may be found in most of the great neo-classic poets, in Milton and in Dryden and of course in Boileau. In particular, Pope's line about Nature and Homer compares in force and resonance with that other memorable declaration of European neo-classicism, Boileau's 'Enfin Malherbe vint'. Boileau was here celebrating a modern end-product of classicism, Pope its origin and earliest full-fledged triumph. But both passages achieve their distinction by transcending the bits of literary history which they are ostensibly offering. The merits of Malherbe, or the accuracy of Boileau's account of the progress of French poetry, are secondary to the sense of excited appropriation of a tradition whose liberating vitality has become manifest. Mr Pocock is right that Ronsard and Malherbe, like Horace and other classical authors named in Boileau's poem, 'appear as representatives of particular positions rather than as historical figures'. He seems to mean this in a somewhat deadening 'allegorical' sense, and certainly not one which directs our attention away from the 'historical' Malherbe to Boileau's felt sense of the liberation of poetry in the new correctness, in just cadence and the power of the well-placed word.

The *Art Poétique* is an 'imitation' of Horace's *Ars Poetica*, which stands behind Boileau's poem as both stand behind Pope's: as richly pervasive presences even more than as repositories of precepts, which of course they also are. The later poem in each case includes a signposted awareness and a sense of the active survival of its predecessors. What Boileau would call the 'commerce' between them enacts a chain of 'imitation' which is itself one of the great pathways of the classical tradition.

Mr Pocock has little to say about 'imitation', and in a discussion of the *Art Poétique* which takes up more than a third of his book, Horace is mentioned only on a handful of perfunctory occasions, and at best only as a local 'source' in a strictly limited sense. *His* pathway to Boileau runs from the prefaces of Chapelain rather than from the poems of Horace. This may explain why he finds it so difficult to get past the 'doctrine'. He claims at one point to transcend this by reading the *Art Poétique* as a 'dramatic event', but this turns out to mean mainly that the poem was partly designed to be read aloud. There is despite some perfunctory motions no serious intention to come to terms with the question of whether the greatness of the *Art Poétique* (or the *Ars Poetica* or *Essay on Criticism*) can fully be accounted for by the precepts which they enunciate, or whether they observe these precepts, or formulate them in ways which ask in particular places if not in all to be taken at other than face value. There is little awareness that the neo-classic system, if it existed as a live system, must have done so more as a habit of mind, a set of velleities and aspirations, of loyalties and spiritual kinships, of questionings and hesitancies and contradictions, even more than as an elaborate and conformist structure of formal belief.

Mr Pocock is clearly more interested in the works of the seventeenth-century critics than in those of classical or Renaissance poets. He can register every turn and counterturn in the debate over the dramatic unities, every hint of a blend of low and lofty styles, every reassertion of the old prescription about mixing pleasure and instruction, and every occasion when Boileau's poems achieve this mixture or either component of it. But he shows a pronounced tendency to interpret as particular to Boileau attitudes or stylistic features which are recognised commonplaces of classical and neo-classic satire. He says of a passage denouncing Alexander the Great as a conquering madman that 'this seems to represent Boileau's personal view, as it recurs in other works and is not a seventeenth-century commonplace', although attacks on Alexander as a type of the folly and immorality of conquest were common from classical times (Lucan, Juvenal) through the Renaissance (Rabelais) to the English Augustans (Pope, Young, Fielding).

A larger case involves a set of early satires in which Boileau portrays himself as comically besieged by the discomforts and nuisances of the town, unable to sleep for these and other irritations, and driven compulsively to write his angry satires in spite of worldly advice to the contrary from a temporising inner voice or a prudent friend. This set of predicaments is a common routine of self-portraiture in the satires of Horace and Juvenal, as well as in later satirists from Régnier to Pope and beyond, who write with a richly conscious and allusive sense of being engaged in a recognisably traditional enterprise. The last item, involving a debate between the righteous satirist and some kind of moderating adversary, was particularly standard in satiric self-apologies, a fact not only evident in the poets but much discussed by later (including recent) scholarship. But Mr Pocock takes it all as a matter of anguished self-division, personal to Boileau: 'I can only describe it as self-contradiction, or the division of an attitude against itself'.

The case of the satirist's self-portraiture is a small example of how a literary tradition perpetuates itself through signposted commonplaces, scenes or attitudes or situations which acquire a kind of standardised significance, expected in advance or instantly recognised when encountered. They come charged with past history, and signal their relation to it with whatever allusive flavour of witty surprise or tacit familiarity. This hardly rules out a personal dimension, though to see only the personal dimension is to falsify even that.

Such commonplaces, where they are part of a live tradition, tend to establish themselves as 'classic' in more than the specifically Graeco-Roman sense. They become norms of utterance, things one says and ways of saying them which are called for or generated by certain occasions. They may be absorbed unconsciously and even turned to ugly or inhumane uses. Readers of Céline will not instinctively think of him as belonging to a tradition which includes Horace and Boileau. He would have abhorred this, and it him (although the notion that he assumes some of the accents of Juvenalian denunciation and some ancient postures of righteous madness need not, I think, cause surprise). But several of his works, including *Mort à Crédit* and the notorious series of anti-semitic 'pamphlets' beginning with *Bagatelles pour un massacre*, set up the traditional kind of half-comic self-mythologising portrait of the besieged satirist, surrounded by noisy nuisances and syco-phants, unable to sleep for all the noise and wickedness, protesting his beleaguered virtue, incapable of *not* writing his angry denun-ciations or of softening his attacks on the powerful, though urged to do so by a prudent and temporising friend, an *adversarius* in the mould of Horace's Trebatius or Pope's Fortescue. That 'friend' is Gustin in *Mort à Crédit* and also in *Bagatelles*, where he later turns into Gutman the Jew. The temporising friend, the noisy nui-sances, the powerful establishment whom Céline has the integrity to attack, and the other traditional targets of the older satirists, all become Jews in *Bagatelles*, a somewhat specialised narrowing of the customary satiric spectrum as Céline's one-track obsessiveness is a narrowing and a curdling of the large humanity of the satiric masters. But the forms and the detailed particularities of self-mythologising are the classic ones, though this is hardly the most agreeable example of that transmission of the classical tradition through poems or poetic moments rather than through precepts which I have been talking about. Perhaps its very availability to unexpected, perverse and evil uses is itself a sign of the potency of its survival. Or perhaps, in this as in its more formalistic aspects, neo-classicism is, or was not long ago, alive and sick and living in Paris.   *1980*

(ii) 'The Augustan Idea'

In 1978 Howard Weinbrot published a book which argued that Augustus, far from being thought in the eighteenth century or at other times a paragon of political virtue and a model of enlightened cultural patronage, was frequently regarded as a cruel and sexually depraved tyrant whose atrocities resembled those of Tiberius, Caligula and Nero, and whose poets were either syco-phants like Virgil and Horace, or driven into exile like Ovid. It was a highly informative book, but less than even-handed in its presentation of evidence: you would not learn from it, as you do from Howard Erskine-Hill's *The Augustan Idea in English Litera-ture*, that when Gilbert Burnet praised Charles II he compared him to Augustus, but when he later attacked him he compared him to Nero.

One of Weinbrot's purposes was to discredit the word 'Augustan' as it is used of certain eighteenth-century authors, and if anyone ever supposed that these authors had an uncritical admiration for the darker episodes of imperial Roman history, they have no business to think so any longer. But the term has long ceased to rest on any detailed awareness of Augustan Rome, with or without its grimmer aspects. Such awareness would only get in the way: as someone pointed out, we don't think of white togas whenever we use the word 'candidate'. 'Augustan' remains serviceable largely because of its near-meaninglessness. It doesn't even mean 'eighteenth-century', which it can't therefore be replaced by. We use it of Dryden, who did not live in that century, and not of Defoe or Richardson, who did. It points loosely to features common to some writers (Dryden, Swift, Pope, Fielding) and not others. Like 'Romantic' or 'Victorian', it suggests broad categories, not fine distinctions. It should not be abused: but to give it up is to limit discourse by reduction of options.

Nomenclature is a passionate matter. 'Augustan' brings in letters to the Editor faster than you can say Doctor Johnson, and as surely. One of the merits of Erskine-Hill's richly elaborate and liberating book is that it is more preoccupied with the history of Augustus's reputation and of the imperial idea than it is with the jargon of the trade. Its theme is not confined to the eighteenth century but pervades our intellectual history since Roman times.

Augustus has always had his detractors. The most distin-guished and influential of these were probably Tacitus and Machi-avelli, who felt that the Augustan settlement had destroyed the values and freedoms of Republican Rome. An alternative view is that of the Virgilian and Horatian eulogies, which have ensured the transmission of a favourable Augustan myth in later times. A third version is 'the Christian providential view' of Origen,

Eusebius and Orosius, which derived ultimately from the second chapter of St Luke's gospel. It saw in Augustus's pacification of the world and in the fact that Christ was born within Augustus's reign the fulfilment of a great providential purpose. Out of this Dante and others developed their conception of Augustus as the proleptic ruler of a Holy Roman Empire descended in direct succession from the Rome of the Caesars. A syncretic Christianised view of Augustus, and by extension of later rulers who came to be eulogised as new Augustuses, recurs through the ages in a variety of forms: in Jean Bodin on Augustus, in Ariosto on Charles V, in Jonson, Joseph Hall and James Montagu praising James I, in Restoration panegyrics on Charles II, in various rhapsodic poems, echoing Virgil's Fourth Eclogue and Isaiah, in the late seventeenth and early eighteenth centuries.

The hostile Tacitean perspective was available to those writers who chose nevertheless to see Augustus as a great ruler, a unifier of the empire, a bringer of peace, and a patron of the arts. Erskine-Hill says Bodin's *Six Livres de la République* (1576) was the first work by a Renaissance political thinker to give 'full weight to the whole range of classical sources and viewpoints on Augustus and to have formed from them a highly complex but . . . unified account'. Lipsius contrived to press Tacitus 'into the service of a favourable view'. Among poets, Ariosto had earlier shown awareness of a mixed view. One of the most interesting things in this book is Erskine-Hill's rich exposition of the ambiguous play of the Augustan idea in treatments of English rulers from Elizabeth to Charles II (including Cromwell). James spoke in 1603 of Elizabeth as a ruler unparalleled 'since the dayes of the Romane Emperour *Augustus*'. Erskine-Hill describes this as 'a public affirmation, by the queen's probable successor, of some of his own political values'. It was in fact James who became the first royal object of Augustan compliment on a large scale, and the compliment to Elizabeth masked an uneasy picture.

Elizabeth was usually Astraea, not Augustus, although there is a natural association between the idea of Astraea's return to earth in a new golden age, and the great regeneration which Virgil's Fourth Eclogue was often taken to have celebrated as the product of Augustus's peace (W. V. Clausen reminds us that when Virgil's poem was written Octavian was not yet Augustus, and Antony was the dominant figure). Virgil's Virgin Astraea was an apter emblem for the Virgin Queen than was Augustus, not least because the Augustan idea of expanding empire did not really match that 'defensive rather than expansive' state which was the

Fortress England of her reign. It was James who brought peace at home and abroad, and enlarged the nation by uniting the kingdoms of Scotland and England. Elizabeth's unpeaceful reign had not been happy for poets, few of whom experienced Astraea's age as golden, for few then 'found support, security, or freedom of speech'. 'Mecoenas is yclad in claye, / And great *Augustus* long ygoe is dead': the author of these lines, the poet of Gloriana, was to die poor, as Jonson and Joseph Hall noted, and his grave in Westminster Abbey had no monument. After Elizabeth's death, Shakespeare, Chapman, and Jonson ('our English *Horace*') were rebuked in Chettle's *England's Mourning Garment* for not praising her memory.

Elizabeth was thus a good candidate for the more ambiguous kind of Augustan analogy, which questioned among other things his vaunted role as a patron of poets. But explicit analogies with Augustus are rare. In such anti-courtier poems as Donne's Fourth Satire the Augustan allusion is implicit only because the poem is a loose adaptation of Horace's *Sat.* I: ix. The main feeling was that the modern reality fell appallingly short of the 'Augustan standard'. Of 'the remarkable outburst of formal satire' in the 1590s, in the work of Donne, Hall and Marston, Erskine-Hill notes how much of this writing, though actively aware of Horace's example, was nevertheless 'closer to the models of Juvenal and Persius'. Juvenal's seventh satire laments that there is no Maecenas in his day as there had been in Horace's, a complaint explicitly echoed by Hall and others. In so far, indeed, as Juvenalian accents may more generally be detected in Horatian satires from this period, as later in Pope's own, it is arguable that they reflect not so much a distaste for the alleged suavities of Horace's praise of Augustus as a feeling that modern England is less like Augustus's Rome than Domitian's, the altogether grimmer emperor under whom Juvenal suffered (though Juvenal's seventh satire was addressed to Hadrian, in eulogistic terms). As Juvenalian majesties of indignation erupt from an ostensibly Horatian imitation, is there a suggestion that modern times are so degraded as to call more for Juvenalian than for Horatian protest?

In Jonson's *Poetaster* (1601), Augustus is identified with a flourishing of the arts, and is again *not* a 'paralel' to Elizabeth. But the play does incorporate elements of the Tacitean Augustus and is in its own special way an expression of the mixed or ambiguous conception, which had developed so markedly in the sixteenth century, and which in this case freed Jonson 'from the difficulty of expressing simultaneous praise and criticism of his own ruler'.

Augustus's punishment of a Marlovian Ovid, an adversary figure with a 'daring and iconoclastic career', is seen as just. But Horace's defence of Ovid in the play is respected. Horace stands up strongly to Augustus, the very antithesis of that time-serving figure whose sycophancy has been an exaggerated element in recent revisionist views of Augustus's reputation. Augustus usually responds appreciatively to Horace's plain-speaking, behaving 'as the ideal ruler of Prince literature' (a genre whose pertinence to the Augustan idea is sketched with great sureness in this book).

When on the other hand Jonson came to deal with James I, notably in his contributions to *The King's Entertainment* of 1604, he was able to offer a direct and wholehearted parallel between Augustus and the king, viewed in the full Christianised perspective of Augustus's providential role as peacemaker. James emerges as *Augustus Novus*, in an elaborate orchestration of visual design, Horatian and Virgilian allusion and Jonsonian verse. It was the first time the Augustan (as distinct from the Astraean) parallel had featured in a British royal entry, and Jonson's spectacular use of it seems to have inaugurated the tradition among English poets of writing about their monarchs in Augustan terms. If the tradition was to emerge, as it did, beyond the stage of simple compliment, it needed to accommodate the political and cultural realities of an imperfect world. The most interesting works in this mode are those which carry within them 'the subtle blend of independence and respect to be found in Horace's Epistle to Augustus', though neither Jonson nor any of the Tribe of Ben seems to have attempted a direct imitation of that poem. James I's well-known relish for flattery became a source of discomfort, and Jonson developed a humorous non-Horatian way of conveying criticism without causing offence. Erskine-Hill says finely that he achieved in *The Gypsies Metamorphos'd* (1621) what 'Dryden was to do in *Absalom and Achitophel*: first he gives us the King as a man, then the King as a king'.

It is not in Jonson's or Carew's or Herrick's poems to James or to Charles I that the 'dark side' of Augustus is allowed to enter significantly in a nevertheless laudatory context, but in Thomas May (1595–1650), the translator of Lucan (1627) and member of the Tribe of Ben, and in Andrew Marvell. Lucan did not at first infect May with anti-Caesarism, though May became anti-Royalist in the Civil War. In his own *Continuation* (1630) of Lucan, fulsomely dedicated to Charles I, he managed to make an anti-Augustan point in the support of an ultra-Royalist sentiment. Augustus is reviled for the murder of Caesarion, the son of Julius Caesar and Cleopatra: since Caesar was the founder of a monarchy, Caesarion might be his heir and Augustus a usurper! As the *Continuation* proceeds, however, Augustus redeems past crimes, establishes a 'happy Monarchy', and becomes a fit subject for the Muses, 'Whose stately layes shall keep thy deathlesse fame'. It's a garbled embodiment of Bodin's scenario. May openly incorporates 'the dark side of Augustus's rise to power' in order to assert, not deny, that breakthrough into divinely sanctioned monarchy which has so often to be achieved by bloody and evil means.

Tom May's progress was unedifying. When Charles was losing the Civil War, May was a parliamentarian, and in his *History of the Parliament of England* (1647) he described as a 'Tyranny' what he had earlier celebrated as 'great *Augustus* happy Monarchy'. In *Tom May's Death* Marvell treats his political changeability with comic contempt. May meets his old master Jonson in Elysium, and is fiercely rebuked. Jonson's sentiments are taken as Marvell's by most commentators, but Erskine-Hill's view is that while Marvell has admiration for the old poet's angry integrity, he is expressing his own properly ambiguous feelings as between Charles and Cromwell. Marvell's *Horatian Ode Upon Cromwell's Return* is closely related in time, in language, and in its awareness of Lucan and of May's Lucan, to *Tom May's Death*, and it is suggested that similarly complex sympathies surround Marvell's treatment of May.

The examples of Marvell and even of May illustrate an interesting fact about the 'dark side' of the Augustan idea. It not only co-existed with an ultimately pro-Augustan view at a level of coherent political analysis, but might readily enter, as in May's *Continuation*, into poetic celebrations of Augustus. If the combination, at the lowest valuation, seems preferable to the crudest sort of panegyric, there is also a more ambitious point to be made. The discreditable elements of Augustus's traditional reputation, so far from being mainly fuel for anti-Augustan sentiments, were themselves a positive strength where panegyric needed to carry a latent reservation or monitory note, or where a high political idealism needed to be checked by a recognition of harsher realities. It may be, in particular, that this 'dark side' entered creatively into those situations where better poets than May (Marvell, Waller, Dryden) wrote from mixed or fluctuating loyalties, and not always from the most honourable motives, both about Cromwell and about one or both of the Charleses. (Cromwell warmed to the quasi-monarchical Augustan parallel of Waller's *Panegyrick to My Lord Protector*, but seems to have been cooler about the *Oceana* of Harrington, who thought the Caesars had betrayed liberty and wanted Cromwell to establish a lasting republic).

Conscious Augustanising in English literature began with Jonson on James I, not with Dryden on Charles II. By the time of *Astraea Redux* (1660), saluting a new monarch as a new Augustus was nothing new. Of the many literary welcomes to Charles, it seems that only five compared him to Augustus: Charles was more often compared to David, a comparison which in *Absalom and Achitophel* was later to produce a finer poetic expression than any Augustan analogy. (Charles came also to be imagined as resembling Antony rather than Augustus, a king of pleasure rather than of policy: in a very fine earlier chapter on 'Shakespeare and the Emperors', Erskine-Hill examines the Antony-Augustus opposition, which was traditional.)

It was sometime after the Restoration that 'Augustan' began to be used of specific periods of English culture, and in a mainly literary rather than political sense. In 1690, Atterbury (probably), praising Waller, wondered 'whether in Charles II's reign English did not come to its full perfection; and whether it has not had its Augustan age as well as the Latin'. Erskine-Hill makes much of this statement, citing it repeatedly and protesting a little too much that it refers to more than linguistic refinement. (Weinbrot, by contrast, doesn't mention it at all.) The praise of Waller as the first of the 'refiners' calls to mind Boileau's 'Enfin Malherbe vint', and might suggest a wider emphasis. Erskine-Hill surprisingly does not mention this. Waller had become the English equivalent for that liberating surge of 'refinement', that poetic revival through correctness, which Boileau had credited to Malherbe. When in 1683 Dryden supplied the corresponding English poets for Soame's translation of the *Art Poétique*, Malherbe became Waller:

> *Waller* came last, but was the first whose Art
> Just Weight and Measure did to Verse impart.

Nevertheless, Atterbury's Preface is remarkably specific in its linguistic emphasis, and for less 'narrow' conceptions of an English Augustan age one must turn elsewhere: to Oldmixon and Bevil Higgons for Charles II's reign, to Prior and Rowe and Joseph Warton for William's and Anne's. Warton defines

248

'Augustan Age' as the time 'when the arts and polite literature, were at their height in this nation'. He and Hume thought it 'excessively false', 'preposterous', to speak thus of Charles's reign, perhaps echoing Swift, who said it was 'reckoned, although very absurdly, our *Augustan* age'.

Swift may be glancing back to Atterbury. Both have (rather dissimilar) Epicurean allusions, and Swift spoke elsewhere of Charles's reign as a time when the *language* was corrupted. Swift does not deny the *first* Augustan Age, though his picture of it is sometimes downbeat, and he could be less than flattering about Augustus himself. It is clear that he saw it as a moment of rare cultural achievement, whatever he thought of the monarch. He wrote to Pope on 20 September 1723: 'I have often endeavoured to establish a Friendship among all Men of Genius, and would fain have it done. they are seldom above three or four Cotemporaries and if they could be united would drive the world before them; I think it was so among the Poets in the time of Augustus, but Envy and party and pride have hindred it among us'. He had a noble idea of Augustus's poets. In 'Of Mean and Great Figures Made by Several Persons', a kind of prose adumbration of Yeats's 'Beautiful Lofty Things', Swift lists 'Virgil, when at Rome the whole Audience rose up, out of Veneration, as he entred the Theatre'. The credit is Virgil's, but as in the letter it rubs off on and enhances his society and his age, very unlike the present. So also the noble figure of Virgil shows up the ludicrously pretentious Dryden in the *Battle of the Books*. Swift himself cultivated Horatian loyalties. If the Horatian Pope adopted a Juvenalian voice, the supposedly Juvenalian Swift of *saeva indignatio* always avoided lofty utterance, preferring Horace to Juvenal and citing him many times more often.

Swift gets short treatment from Erskine-Hill (his *On Poetry: A Rapsody*, an important companion-piece to Pope's *Epistle to Augustus*, is not discussed, for example). Swift offers a striking example of nasty historical realities being distinguished from great poetic achievements. Others made the distinction less starkly, by emphasising or extolling the admired poets more than the dubious monarch. A parallel strategy sometimes appears in discussions of epic, where an admiration for great poems coexists with uneasiness about the cruelties of battle celebrated within them. Achilles was described in the *Spectator* as 'Morally Vicious, and only Poetically Good'. Alternatively, as I argued in chapter 6, heroic discredit might be shifted away from epic heroes (Achilles, Aeneas) towards historical conquerors (Alexander, Caesar), as in

Fielding's *Jonathan Wild*. In one place he describes Fireblood as *fidus Achates* to Wild's Aeneas, and corrects himself by adding 'or rather the Hephaestion of our Alexander'. Epic heroes and historical villains resembled each other in ways which were uneasily and ambiguously recognised.

Thomas Blackwell, whose *Enquiry into the Life and Writings of Homer* (1735) expressed the wish '*That we may never be a proper Subject of an* Heroic Poem', also wrote some *Memoirs of the Court of Augustus* (1753–1763). This provided an 'influential argument' for detaching 'a literary Augustan Age' from Augustus himself, whom Blackwell on balance admired, and whose career he divided into three phases: patriot-republican, then tyrant-triumvir, then father of his people. Blackwell's point about the poets was that they were 'not *formed* under *Augustus* ... [but] under the Common-Wealth, during the high struggles for Liberty'. Virgil and Horace were not '*courtbred* Poets under *Augustus*: no more than Milton, Waller and Cowley were under Charles II'. The argument reappears in Gibbon and others. It is an attempt to give a historical basis for distinctions which were necessary to the survival of a myth, at a time when, as it happens, most historians (including Gibbon) were hostile to Augustus. You could evidently have an Augustan age, ancient or modern, even if you repudiated its ruler.

The outspoken, independent Horace was not a recent invention, however, and Erskine-Hill powerfully argues that this is the Horace of Pope's *Imitations*. The first of the series, the famous *Sat.* II:i, was urged upon him by Bolingbroke, whose view of Augustus was the Tacitean one and whose attacks on the English Augustus, alias George II, and his Whig henchmen, exploited the negative analogy. Erskine-Hill observes that Bolingbroke 'did not think Horace, by this token, a sycophantic court poet', or he would scarcely have urged Pope to adopt a Horatian persona, least of all from '*this* poem of Horace, which happens to focus on the relation of poet and prince'. Erskine-Hill writes well on Pope's Horatian (or 'Horatian-Lucilian') self-image, 'as plain / As downright *Shippen*, or as old *Montagne*', but oddly overlooks the fact that Pope's statement a few lines later, 'Tories call me Whig, and Whigs a Tory', itself derives more closely from Montaigne's 'au Gibelin i'estois Guelphe, au Guelphe Gibelin' (*Essais*, III: xii) than from the corresponding lines of Horace. This omission leads (I think) to a slightly impoverished account of 'old *Montagne*'s' role in the passage. But Pope's free-speaking Horace, as expounded here, was at least as traditional as his opposite, the urbane

250

sycophant described by the Friend in the *Epilogue to the Satires*, in a portrayal of which Erskine-Hill gives a particularly subtle account.

There was a strand in eighteenth-century thought, from Berkeley to Horace Walpole, that expected any new Augustan age to arise in America or in some other new world. In 1792 Pitt imagined a Roman senator contemplating the ancient Britons, 'little superior . . . to the rude inhabitants of the coast of Guinea'. Britain would then have seemed as unlikely to 'rise to civilization' as Africa did in 1792. Pitt's speech was quoted by Stanley in 1892 and thence may have found its way into the opening of Conrad's *Heart of Darkness*, which it resembles. Erskine-Hill pauses, in his suggestive Epilogue, on this unwritten chapter of the Augustan idea, with its view of Conrad's agents of empire 'bearing the sword, and often the torch' into the dark places of the earth. Civilisation was, and had to be, paid for by blood and servitude, and the evil deeds of Augustus were part of that price, just as the vicious conquerors of later times brought light, including 'electric light', into the heart of darkness.

The Kurtz of *Heart of Darkness*, to the making of whom 'all Europe had contributed', is not only an instrument of that imperial enterprise of the nineteenth century which Conrad compares with the Roman original. He became, as a monarch of the bush, the embodiment of a kind of absolute personal power which made possible a total gratification of all his desires. This had the lineaments of a type of 'Caesarism' which fascinated Sade, Flaubert, Wilde and Artaud, and against which Max Nordau fulminated as a sign of degeneration. Kurtz's Caesarian features include tyranny, mass-slaughter, the satisfaction of unbridled and 'unspeakable' lusts, and an assumption of god-like status (Flaubert said Augustus 'se fait appeler Dieu par ses poètes').

This is a parallel not glimpsed in Erskine-Hill's concluding panorama. But it involves an essential part of the history of the 'Augustan idea'. The dark side of Augustus's reputation seems from earliest times to have included the cruelties and the perverse lusts with which the more infamous of his successors were particularly identified. But the image of unbridled self-indulgence was balanced by the reputation for prudence which made people say (according to Suetonius) that even his adulteries had political rather than passionate motives. De Quincey said that 'the cruelties of Augustus were perhaps equal in atrocity to any which are recorded', though 'they were not prompted by a ferocious nature, but by calculating policy'.

It would be interesting to know how this affected the reputation of Augustus among those later writers, from Sade to Artaud and after, who admired rather than reprobated the post-Augustan Emperors as types of total self-realisation in cruelty. Was he assimilated to the Nero whose memory is venerated in Sade and whom Flaubert affected to admire, or was he distinguished from his successors? Sade mentions an Augustan atrocity from time to time, but in the speech about virtuous and vicious rulers in *Aline et Valcour* he is listed with Trajan and the Antonines rather than with Nero and Tiberius. In Flaubert's youthful 'Rome et les Césars', some homage is paid to Augustus, but it is only after his reign that the Caesars are seen as coming into their own: 'Avec Tibère commence l'ère nouvelle, voluptueuse . . .'. If his correspondence is anything to go by, Flaubert seems thereafter to have lost interest in Augustus. Where, if at all, did Augustus stand, in that late chapter of the imperial myth? Was the Tacitean scoundrel revalued upwards, like his successors, into a lordly master of libertine, romantic or anarchic heroism, or was the alternative Augustus, the wise and politic prince, revalued downwards, as an embodiment of dull prudence, corrupt compromise and a colourless officialdom? Or did he simply drop out of view?

1983

(iii)   Lordly Accents

In Fielding's *Journey from this World to the Next* the author comes upon Shakespeare in Elysium, standing between the actors Betterton and Booth, who are disputing about the exact emphasis of a line from *Othello*. Shakespeare is very lofty about it all: 'it is so long since I wrote the line, I have forgot my meaning', but if any of their conjectures is right 'it doth me very little honour'. He is then asked about 'some other ambiguous passages in his works' and, as is proper for an author talking to critics, deals even more haughtily with those who 'gird themselves at discovering obscure beauties in an author':

> the greatest and most pregnant beauties are ever the plainest and most evidently striking; and when two meanings of a passage can in the least ballance our judgments which to prefer, I hold it a matter of unquestionable certainty that neither of them is worth a farthing.

252

Two features of this are interesting. First is the assumption that authors express plain meanings, and that 'ambiguous passages' are faulty as such. The statement is doubtless more reductive than the real Shakespeare, or Fielding himself, would have thought appropriate to the full facts, but it highlights an emphasis we no longer take for granted. We nowadays assume that poetry is 'ambiguous', that this is a source of its value, and even that the ability to generate multiple suggestions is what distinguishes literary from practical discourse. For at least a century before the polysemic text was found germinating in the gaudy rubble of the deconstruction site, poets have been telling us that explicitness destroys three-quarters of a poem's 'jouissance', that a poet who explains or interprets his poem 'limits its suggestibility', that poems are 'ambiguous or uncertain' because emotions are. When Stevens (or Yeats or Eliot) said 'poets do not like to explain', it was because poems have and should have many 'meanings' and not as in Fielding's parable because they should have only one. And if having many meanings means having none, so that poems do not mean but are, that would have seemed equally absurd to Fielding.

The second point in the parable is the lordly treatment of those who think otherwise. They are not, as in Mallarmé or Valéry or Yeats, the true poets and creators, but wretched hacks and pedants. The Shakespeare of Fielding's invention is so contemptuous of their disputes that he finds the loftiest put-down of all: 'I have forgot my meaning'. He would rather give up his line than listen to any more of their wrangling. Shakespeare's behaviour here is Fielding's lordliness by proxy, an unremarked but not unprecedented trick in the rhetorical armoury of Augustan satirists. When Swift sent Gulliver on a visit to the afterworld of Glubbdubdrib, one of the sights was that of Homer and Aristotle among their innumerable mob of commentators, both of them 'perfect Strangers to the rest of the Company'. There are people one does not know, just as there are things beneath one's notice. As Pope said in *An Essay on Criticism*, combining both senses of not knowing, '*not* to know some Trifles, is a Praise'.

It is, then, a feature of certain *hauteurs* to imply that things are plainer than captious little minds make out, and at the same time to hint at insights and values which only the chosen few will be able to share or even decode. The irony of the Augustan masters was a sign-system of privileged implication, operating beneath a deceptive surface. The two passages I have cited are not discussed in Irvin Ehrenpreis's good book, *Acts of Implication*, but they are germane to it. In an earlier book of essays, *Literary Meaning and Augustan Values* (see below, chapter 15), Ehrenpreis was concerned to correct certain excesses of recent criticism by reminding us that Augustan literature is a literature which addresses readers by way of 'meaning'. But he believes that his insistence was taken as suggesting that this was 'all the poem had to offer', so he now wants to show that 'explicit meaning' is as capable of 'implication' as any flower of the doctrine that 'a poem should not mean but be'. This is what Fielding's Shakespeare did not go on explicitly to say, and as Ehrenpreis notes Augustan authors complicate his argument by often pretending to be merely simple and lucid. But the type of 'implication' with which he is especially concerned is one which Fielding's parable exemplifies, and which differs greatly from what is normally associated with modern notions of poetic suggestiveness. In a provocative opening chapter, Ehrenpreis notes the frequency with which eighteenth-century writers harp on the idea of innuendo or covert meaning, coyly denying and cheekily flaunting the fact that their discourse is ironic, using irony in their very protestations of plain statement. 'Clarity and explicitness were not the only virtues to which Pope aspired'. And when Swift, or writers in *The Craftsman*, needled the reader with hints of a concealed element of personal attack, 'the appeal to clarity' became 'a method of teasing the reader into thinking dangerously'.

Linked to this theme is one which involves attitudes to rank, and the styles called forth by such attitudes. His four authors, Dryden, Swift, Pope and Jane Austen (representing the broadest chronological stretch of the tradition sometimes called Augustan) all 'share an acquiescent view of the social order and a distrust of courtiers and courtly aristocrats', and the book is concerned with the styles which express and control such contrary tendencies. In Pope especially, Ehrenpreis enumerates with acumen the formal manifestations, the devices and strategies which tend in various ways to establish 'two realms of implication in his satires – one, conventionally didactic; the other, boldly subversive'. 'Subversiveness' is too stark a term, perhaps, for the play of crackling resentments, the virtuosities of insolence, which give Pope's essentially loyal traditionalist eloquence its peculiar energy. The word smacks a little of that easy revisionism with which critics sometimes attribute to authors characteristics deemed admirable in the critic's own intellectual climate. If Pope is 'subversive', what word shall we use for Swift? Ehrenpreis's summarising formulation seems unsatisfactory, but not his detailed exposition.

He is particularly strong and specific in his account of Pope's 'habit of setting up the moral and social values traditionally belonging to the country house as vastly superior to those traditionally assigned to a royal court'. Not, as Ehrenpreis freely points out, a new idea, but brought vividly to life with the brevity and sureness with which he discussed some years ago the social assumptions of a chapter of *Tom Jones* and their stylistic expression.

Pope wrote in a famous couplet:

> And who unknown defame me, let them be
> Scriblers or Peers, alike are *Mob* to me.

The lines are more than a pointed scrambling of high and low ranks, like the juxtaposition of 'Pimps, Poets, Wits, Lord Fanny's, Lady Mary's', and I think they indicate more than 'Pope's special tendency . . . to cast into doubt the proper association of rank with merit, virtue, or even good manners . . .' They are a matter of putting lords down in lordly language, though in the name of high moral standards which would themselves be expected to prohibit contemptuous uppishness. Swift and Fielding pushed the paradox even further, exposing the uppishness itself in uppish language, dismissing it as 'low', a pedantry of manners characteristic of and worthy of social inferiors. We see them do it in their essays and letters, and not merely through the mouths of fictional narrators. But it happens with additional and revealing piquancy when Swift expresses himself through the mouth of spokesmen like the Examiner and especially the Drapier whose commercial values and social rank are ostentatiously less than lordly.

It is these two figures who are the subject of Ehrenpreis's chapter on Swift. And it is surprising that he should hardly pause over the fact that the Drapier, though much given to recognising and protesting his own low condition as a mean, illiterate shopkeeper, has an even more pronounced habit of despising the notorious financier William Wood in the lordliest manner as an obscure nobody, 'one Mr. WOOD, *a mean ordinary Man, a Hard-Ware Dealer*', 'one *William Wood*, now or late of *London*, Hard-ware-man', and so on. This, as I once pointed out elsewhere, is very like the tone in which, a few years later, Lord Hervey referred to the *Beggar's Opera*, a phenomenon at least as familiar or notorious as that of Wood's halfpence: 'One Gay, a poet, had written a ballad opera'.

Here it is not simply that Swift, like Pope, speaks in tones of lofty grandeur. It is that he does so in the very act of impersonating a humble shopkeeper, the last person from whom such accents would seem pertinent or expected. And not a 'snobbish' shopkeeper either (if the anachronistic usage may be permitted), nor, as we have seen, one who seeks to disguise his own humble origins. There is a gap between the Drapier's voice and his impersonator, not necessarily because Swift would not have admitted to humble origins, but because he would hardly have made such an unctuous display of them as he sometimes foists on the Drapier; and a further gap between the Drapier's lowlinesses and his *hauteurs*. But the striking gap is between the righteous moral denunciation which lies at the centre of the case against Wood, and the surface of *social* contempt through which the moral denunciation is expressed. This is something which transcends the 'contradictions' in Swift's feelings on all matters concerning rank: the mixture of respect and resentment, of regard for high birth and withering contempt for many lords, of loathing for upstarts and some upstart cravings of his own. It is true that in a period when an aristocratic temper still set the pattern for speech and social manner, we are likely to find elements of lordly idiom in notably unlordly speakers: not only in imperious personalities deeply attached to old standards of 'politeness', but in Grub Street authors whose origins or allegiances showed no sign of such an attachment. This fact may contribute its mite of 'realism' to the Drapier's uppishnesses, but it doesn't explain their explosive force, which is hardly felt to be issuing from the mercantile dummy set up by Swift's rudimentary fiction, and clearly belongs to the animating voice behind it.

This explosive feeling suggests the exasperations of defeated aspiration, an aspiration not primarily personal (to do with individual pretension to or cravings for rank) but cultural (to do with the society's ability to live up to a noble ideal). The burden of these angry *hauteurs* is the pained perception, shared also by Pope and Fielding, that moral nobility and nobility of social rank were not congruent. The bare fact was too obvious to cause surprise. But the gap was nevertheless deeply disillusioning to authors whose model of the good life was an aristocratic one in a way that derived not from high social rank (which they themselves as individuals for the most part lacked), but from an ideal extending to all areas of mind, morality and manners: an ideal which bestowed on the word 'noble' its moral as well as its social sense and ultimately aspired to a perfect order in which those who were noble in one sense were noble in the other, what Fielding and others sometimes spoke of as 'the great and good'. The lordly accents of Augustan satirists who make no pretence of being lords proceed from an attachment to a standard which remains live even as reality violates it at every turn. They accepted the aristocratic model as essentially valid, despising lords not because the model was lacking but because the lords were. Thus peers, like scribblers, became mob to Pope if, and only if, their moral nobility didn't match the title. Scribblers who had moral nobility were not scribblers but poets, a status which Pope is not slow to call noble. But the important thing is not that the moral nobility is better than the social, though of course it is: it is that the social nobility and its idiom and pretensions are adopted as the appropriate badge for it.

This should not be sentimentalised. Swift and Pope despised the pride of social rank, but they were not altogether without hankerings or affectations that way. Their *hauteurs* have a fervour not unlike those of Yeats, and very different from the cool confident lordliness of a Chesterfield: a fervour which may derive from a commitment to aristocratic values, shot through with an anxiety of not belonging. The Yeats of those great poems which evoke the ceremonious country-house civilisation which he associated with the century of Swift and Burke was also the Yeats who made silly attempts to prove a noble lineage for himself. His claims to be descended from 'the *real* Butlers' of the noble Ormonde line sound very much like those of Swift's patron Harley, who claimed a connection with the de Veres and Mortimers. Swift thought Harley overvalued such things even though Swift didn't disclose and perhaps didn't know that the claim was unfounded; but there is evidence that in a smaller way both Swift and Pope would have welcomed a grander lineage for themselves. The signs of this perhaps melted more readily into a context in which aristocratic assumptions were more widely taken for granted than in Yeats's time. Yeats needed in a sense to recreate a lordly ethos where this was no longer dominant, and to do so largely by force of individual aspiration and fantasy.

Like Yeats, Swift had oscillating feelings about the 'common people', amusingly epitomised in his emending of 'the *Rabble*' to 'my faithful Friends the Common People' in the 1735 revised edition of the fifth Drapier's Letter. And he had something of Yeats's habit of valuing the highest and the lowest ranks at the expense of the money-minded middle to which the Drapier, ambiguously, both does and does not belong. Swift was indeed

257

mythologised by Yeats into a Yeatsian hero. Yeats may have invented part of the likeness, but one learns much about Swift through Yeats's many vivid evocations of him. Pope, on the other hand, Yeats disliked: but (as is suggested in chapter 4 (ii) above) the arrogant decasyllabic sweep of some of Yeats's most imperious grandee poems is much closer to the later style of Pope than to anything in his beloved Swift, and it is not farfetched to surmise that Yeats's feelings about Pope contained something of the antipathy of unadmitted resemblance.

Ehrenpreis is strongest on Pope. With Swift, on whom he is one of the small handful of very good critics now writing, this book is less happy. The exclusive concentration on the *Examiner* and the *Drapier's Letters* has the slightly magisterial self-consciousness of the expert bestowing his attention on the lesser works of an author he knows too well. These writings are important, but they are not Swift's most important or most characteristic works, even in relation to Ehrenpreis's chosen theme. Ehrenpreis is good on the blend of 'impersonation' and 'irony' in the two quasi-authorial speakers, but the role of the Drapier especially was one which didn't sit easily on Swift – perhaps because the figure of a tradesman was the least likely to arouse his genuine unforced respect. This is itself matter for the argument of the book, but the fact is not really faced, and Ehrenpreis writes below his usual perceptiveness when he presents the Drapier's awkward overemphasis on his ignorance or social meanness as a Socratic naïveté and a finely achieved mastery of tone on Swift's part.

1982

PART III

Fielding

9

Dialogue and Authorial Presence in Fielding's Novels and Plays

(i) Part I

That Fielding is an intrusive narrator has always been known. Despite his early training in the theatre, his novels seldom attempt a 'dramatic' rendering of character or situation, with a minimum of authorial commentary, as in Richardson. Fielding's debt to his playwriting experience normally tended away from unmediated rendering, and towards stylisations which hold naked reality at arm's length: 'well-made' plots, carefully patterned scenes with a certain quality of self-containment, the gallery of strongly sketched comic characters, set-pieces of repartee, elements of burlesque or farce. This is not surprising, since his plays themselves belonged to stylised genres: wit-comedies in which pointed exchanges of dialogue played a primary part, *Rehearsal*-plays with a play-within-the-play, parodies, farces. In the novels, the narrator has more open ways of establishing a sense of his controlling presence than in plays, and his stylisations (for example) can be, for various purposes, drawn attention to, as well as merely taking place. One purpose of this discussion is to examine some implications of this in the field of dialogue, where the novelist is closest to the playwright, since most of the talking, by definition, is left to the characters.

I begin with an example from *Shamela*, where Fielding is (for once) not even the official narrator. Shamela writes:

O Madam, I have strange Things to tell you! As I was reading in that charming Book about the Dealings, in comes my Master – to be sure he is a precious One. *Pamela*, says he, what Book is that, I warrant you *Rochester's* Poems. – No,

261

forsooth, says I, as pertly as I could; why how now Saucy
Chops, Boldface, says he – Mighty pretty Words, says I, pert
again. – Yes (says he) you are a d—d, impudent, stinking,
cursed, confounded Jade, and I have a great Mind to kick
your A—. You, kiss — says I. A-gad, says he, and so I will;
with that he caught me in his Arms, and kissed me till he
made my Face all over Fire. Now this served purely you
know, to put upon the Fool for Anger. O! What precious
Fools Men are! And so I flung from him in a mighty Rage,
and pretended as how I would go out at the Door; but when I
came to the End of the Room, I stood still, and my Master
cryed out, Hussy, Slut, Saucebox, Boldface, come hither –
Yes to be sure, says I; why don't you come, says he; what
should I come for, says I; if you don't come to me, I'll come
to you, says he; I shan't come to you I assure you, says I.
Upon which he run up, caught me in his Arms, and flung me
upon a Chair, and began to offer to touch my Under-
Petticoat. Sir, says I, you had better not offer to be rude;
well, says he, no more I won't then; and away he went out of
the Room. I was so mad to be sure I could have cry'd.[1]

(*Shamela*, Letter VI)

This is parody of Richardson (especially Letters XI and XV of
Pamela), but its vitality is thoroughly Fielding's. The characters
come through with a crude vigour which does not depend on the
Richardsonian originals, but on Fielding's sense of the comic
possibilities of his own version of the story. Nor can one really
say that, as sometimes happens in parodic genres (when, for
example, mock-heroic acquires a certain heroic grandeur of its
own), any essential quality of the original has here rubbed off on
the parody. Shamela, with her crude relish in the narration, her
unabashed little glosses ('says I, pert again'), and her hard,
hoydenish energy, is much more than a sham Pamela. There is
about the passage a metallic exuberance worthy of some of the
best moments in *Jonathan Wild*. Squire Booby, the impetuous
lover easily cooled ('began to offer to touch my Under-Petticoat'
is at four removes from doing anything to the girl),[2] also at
times seems less a parody of Mr B. than a Fielding character in
his own right, related to the spindle-shanked beaux of the plays
and looking forward perhaps to Beau Didapper.[3]

The passage, however, does not merely show the comic novelist's energies overwhelming mere parodic objectives. It also has a
special kind of vitality, which partly derives from stylised

reminders of drama, but which Fielding never achieved in his plays. A strong farce element competes with the parody. Booby's invective, 'Hussy, Slut, Saucebox, Boldface', consists entirely of words used by Mr B. in the relevant letters of *Pamela*, but their headlong succession here turns them into a clownish routine of a sort which depends on extended mechanical repetition, excessive to the ostensible purpose. This excess is distinctly evident, but so are its limits. There is a suggestion of control, by author or performer (as distinct from speaker), which distinguishes it from the rhetoric of those expansive lists of insults which one finds in Rabelais or Swift, where ideas of abundance and of limitlessness (whether contemptuously registered or cheerfully indulged) are actively in play. The two kinds of routine are not unrelated, and both may be found close together especially in authors who are equally steeped in traditions of Rabelaisian wit and of popular farce. Here is an example from Jarry's Ubu cycle:

LE ROI
Lâche, gueux, sacripant, mécréant, musulman!
PÈRE UBU
Tiens, pochard, soûlard, bâtard, hussard, tartare, calard, cafard, mouchard, savoyard, polognard![4]

You might say that the king's words, where enumeration is in excess of normal vituperative utterance but remains relatively short, resemble Fielding's 'Hussy, Slut, Saucebox, Boldface'. Père Ubu's reply, on the other hand, has the whole-hearted Rabelaisian commitment to an enumeration which need never stop. Both are 'routines', but one advertises its limits, pointing to excess as something which will be checked by some automatic regulator or will itself run out of steam; the other hints at infinities of reiteration. The first notation is the one which concerns us here. It presupposes a non-excessive norm ('hussy' or 'slut' or whatever appearing in ones or twos, not fours, as in Richardson or in 'real life'), whose recognisability as ordinary discourse is retained even as it is made absurd by a comic overdoing. This overdoing is circumscribed by its own stylish inner laws (of rhythmic timing, balanced repartee, or pointed disproportion). The words of Jarry's king come from old farce conventions, and I believe Fielding is in his own way playing with such conventions too. The formula is one which attracted Scriblerian satirists, as a satirical way of rendering demotic speech *de haut en bas*. Arbuthnot's *History of John Bull* has several examples: 'Fool, Puppy, and

Blockhead was the best Words they gave', 'traducing them . . . as Drunkards, Thieves and Whore-masters', 'Blockhead, Dunce, Ass, Coxcomb, were the best Epithets he gave' (III: viii; IV: i; V: i). Here, as often in Fielding, some layerings of oblique or reported speech add an effect of lofty distancing, as of energetic lownesses being glimpsed from above, and create also a comic uncertainty as to whether the words all came together in one, or were singly or collectively habitual. I shall return to this feature in Fielding's writings.

Arbuthnot, like Fielding, is openly conscious of 'Clownish' (i.e. boorish, but also verging on stage-knockabout) elements in his characters, who are given to 'Belching and Calling of Names', and who leap like 'Tumblers or Rope dancers' and indulge in slapstick brawls (V:iv, vii). Like his fellow-Scriblerians, Swift and Pope, he has his own versions (e.g. III: x; V: v) of *Shamela*'s 'kick your A—. You, kiss —' formula, well-recognised in word and deed as a farce-ritual, noted as such, for example, in *Mac Flecknoe*, ll.181–2, and featured in the satirical puppet-show of Jonson's *Bartholomew Fair* (V. iv. 131–2, 322–5).[5] The stylisation of demotic speech, or evocation of farce and slapstick (which comes to the same thing in such cases), is a way of rendering demotic energies with a wholehearted mimicry but without any suggestion that the author has surrendered or been engulfed by them. In the passage from *Shamela*, the verbal horseplay helps Fielding to suggest that the author of *Pamela*, being no gentleman, would naturally mistake this boorish yokel for one. But this classic Scriblerian put-down is enriched by the knowing and stylised vulgarism of the reminders of 'low' stage-humour.

This too is an accredited effect, accentuated by the quick-time reflex-nature of insult and retort and by the clockwork alternations of 'says I' and 'says he'. These are found in Arbuthnot and others, but they are particularly important in Fielding. In Shamela's letter, they have the accelerated automatism and the precision timing of farce-tempos, generating a comic opera raciness in place of Richardson's slow hot-house crisis. The stepped-up and slightly frantic rhythm is accepted as normal, and all reactions become absurdly cut-and-dried, as in the clockwork perfunctoriness of 'Sir, says I, you had better not offer to be rude; well, says he, no more I won't then; and away he went . . .'. (One is reminded of the comedy of instant fainting-fits and other simplified and accelerated emotion in Jane Austen's early burlesques).

The passage from *Shamela* may be compared with the following, from *Moll Flanders*:

She was no sooner gone; but comes a Wench and a Child, puffing and sweating, and asks for the *Barnet* Coach, I answer'd presently *Here*, do you belong to the *Barnet* Coach, *says she*? yes Sweetheart, *said I*, what do ye want? I want Room, for two Passengers *says she*, Where are they Sweetheart, *said I*? Here's this Girl, pray let her go into the Coach, *says she*, and I'll go and fetch my Mistress, make hast then Sweetheart, *says I*, for we may be full else; the Maid had a great Bundle under Arm; so she put the Child into the Coach, and *I said*, you had best put your Bundle into the Coach too; No, *says she*, I am afraid some body should slip it away from the Child, give it me then, *said I*, and I'll take care of it; do then, *says she*, and be sure you take care of it, I'll answer for it, *said I*, if it were for Twenty Pound value. There take it then, *says she*, and away she goes.[6]

The business of '*says she*' and '*said I*' is on a similar scale to Shamela's, but differs in conveying the headlong breathlessness of Moll's narration rather than the mechanical interchange of farce-repartee. Both passages are related by a non-authorial (and female) speaker, but the peculiarly pointed quality of Fielding's passage causes us to be more conscious of a manipulating author behind the speaker than of the speaker herself (this remains true even if the author's identity is unknown: *Shamela* was published pseudonymously). The notation of *says she/said I* in Defoe is much more 'neutral', stylistically: it has colloquial truth and is suited to the speaker's natural idiom and character, rather than enlisted in the service of an authorial irony.

There are times in Defoe when the neutrality of the formula appears to be absolute, serving merely to give the identity of the speaker. A recent statistical study by Helmut Bonheim of the 'inquit' (Latin for 'he says') in a wide range of English fiction reveals that in extended conversations in Defoe the inquit is sometimes dropped in favour of the playwriting device of simply prefixing the speaker's name to his speech.[7] This practice is not unknown in Fielding, but it is rare and (once again) never neutral. *Jonathan Wild*, III: viii and IV: xiv, for example, are in 'dramatic' form, and have lengthy headings which begin respectively '*A Dialogue matrimonial*' and '*A Dialogue between the* Ordinary of Newgate *and Mr* Jonathan Wild the Great'. These indicate at the outset that what follows are set-pieces or compositions rather than slices of life, and what is suggested is a sottisier rather than a play. Each dialogue is a satirical anthology of usages and attitudes, tending towards the genre of Swift's *Complete Collection of Genteel and Ingenious Conversation*, which is likewise in dramatic form, and also of such non-dramatic anthologising passages in the novels as the dialogue about 'some People' and 'some Folks' or '*A Dissertation concerning high People and low People*' (*Joseph Andrews*, II: v, xiii):

> A dialogue matrimonial, which passed between JONA-THAN WILD *Esquire, and* LAETITIA *his Wife, on the Morning of the Day Fortnight on which his Nuptials were celebrated; which concluded more amicably than those Debates generally do.*
>
> (*Jonathan Wild*, III: viii)

Such a title, prefixed to an ostensibly dramatic dialogue, is obviously itself a strongly marked authorial statement, whose assertions of typicality, as well as of exceptions to the typical, actually stamp the passage as tendentious rather than lifelike: the manner is very characteristic of the novels, and (as I indicate below) Fielding had indeed tried clumsily to introduce it even into the plays themselves.

Fielding's practice is far removed from Defoe's as reported by Bonheim. When Defoe adopts the dramatic form, it is in order to give the identity of the speaker without fuss. Moreover, although Defoe uses many more inquits than we should normally find in some twentieth-century writers, they often seem 'rather a luxury than a necessity', so that their removal might make little difference to the tone of a passage. Bonheim is at this point concerned with two features other than tone: the informative function and 'the scale of immediacy' according to which, roughly speaking, 'immediacy' increases in inverse ratio to the frequency of the inquit, which is an interventionist or mediating device.[8] This observation would not apply in any simple way to the passage I quoted from *Moll Flanders*, where Moll's own use of inquits contributed strongly to the character and tone of her narration, and where the inquits are as frequent as in the passage from *Shamela*. But the *authorial* 'neutrality' of the inquit in Defoe remains strong even in that passage and contrasts with the highly manipulative exploitation of it in *Shamela*: 'immediacy' is not what Fielding is after, in any of his fiction.

At least one of Defoe's narrators, not cited by Bonheim, went so far as to say that inquits were a bit of a nuisance, which it would be nice to be able to avoid:

I shall no longer trouble the story with a relation in the first person, which will put me to the expense of ten thousand said I's, and said he's, and he told me's, and I told him's, and the like; but I shall collect the facts historically as near as I can gather them out of my memory from what they related to me, and from what I met with in my conversing with them, and with the place.[9]

This passage from the *Farther Adventures of Robinson Crusoe* predates *Moll Flanders* and cannot be taken as a bald statement of authorial intention. Defoe did not share in any far-reaching way the distaste Cowper was later to express for narratives which 'echo conversations dull and dry,/Embellished with, *he said*, and *so said I*': Cowper is anyway talking about boring speakers who report conversations in conversation, not about novels (*Conversation*, ll. 211–12). But Defoe was more likely to think of the inquit as a potentially tiresome consequence of certain modes of narrative than as an active stylistic device to be exploited and savoured in its own right and beyond its ostensible functions.

A similar sentiment to Crusoe's is expressed by one of Richardson's principal narrators, Harriet Byron, in *Sir Charles Grandison*:

By the way, Lucy, you are fond of plays; and it is come into my head, that, to avoid all *says-I's* and *says-she's*, I will henceforth, in all dialogues, write names in the margin: So fansy, my dear, that you are reading in one of your favourite volumes.[10]

(II: v.)

It is interesting that this simple interventionist device should be thus commented upon by narrators of both the novelists whose modes of realism are commonly recognised to be the antithesis of Fielding's manner. Harriet Byron offers dialogue in the style of plays, and this might be seen as an extension to dialogue of a basic principle of epistolary fiction, which, in the words of Mrs Barbauld in 1804, makes the narrative itself 'dramatic, since all the characters speak in their own persons'. Early commentators on Richardson's 'dramatic' manner saw in it weaknesses (including a certain artificiality) as well as strengths, but what was emphasised for both good and ill was what Bonheim calls 'immediacy'. Mrs Barbauld, following Richardson himself, spoke of its giving 'the feelings of the moment as the writers felt them *at* the moment', and a still earlier critic spoke of the special risks of Richardson's

'strictly dramatical' narratives, which necessarily 'exert themselves with a stronger influence on the minds of those who are
affected by them'.[11] Fielding's first response to this species of
immediacy was scornful: Shamela says 'You see I write in the
present Tense' (Letter VI).

But as George Sherburn has said, 'Richardson can hardly have
believed that printing a conversation in dialogue form made it
really dramatic', even though 'it did perhaps bring us closer to
the moment'. Perhaps it was 'a sort of economic literary shorthand which chiefly saved words', like the economy which
Bonheim says Defoe sought.[12] More recent students of Richardson's 'dramatic' style have emphasised his elaborate awareness of
the stage, of dramatic structure, of particular plays, and his
strong predilection for coy stage-directions (*'Enter my Rascal'*,
'Exit Landlord. Re-enter with two great-coats') and related features
of epistolary *mise-en-scène*:

> And here, supposing my narrative of the dramatic kind,
> ends Act the first. And now begins
> ACT II
> SCENE – *Hampstead Heath, continued.*[13]

Again, it is often not Richardson but his characters who speak or
write thus (Lovelace, in the last cited instances), but this self-
consciously allusive manner is scattered about the novels and
suggests that Richardson's notations of dialogue are hardly less
stylised in their way than Fielding's, and are indeed as deeply-
rooted in stage conventions. Even the 'to the *Moment*' immediacy lacks some of the air of innocence which characterises the
reporting voice of Defoe's narrators.[14]

Modern readers coming upon such things might feel there
was more dramatic allusion than *illusion* in Richardson's style.
Even so, Richardson's dialogues do not show anything resembling Fielding's positive determination to create an illusion-
breaking artifice, a determination as much motivated by anti-
Richardsonian parodic purposes as by Fielding's own energetic
recoil from the merely immediate and pressing. Fielding's
reminders of plays are as interventionist in a self-projecting way
as are his openly non-dramatic exploitations of the narrator's
says he/ says I. Bonheim's study of inquits does not discuss
Fielding much, but *Tom Jones* appears in a statistical table of
sixteen narrative works from 1485 to 1975 as the novel with the
highest incidence of 'medial' inquits, i.e. those where 'he said' is

sandwiched inside the quoted speech, as distinct from the beginning or end.[15]

This may or may not reflect contemporaneous usage. No comparable figures are cited for Defoe or other eighteenth-century writers, but the two authors nearest in time (Aphra Behn and Jane Austen) do not show a comparable frequency. The medial inquit is arguably the most interventionist, the one in which the narrator is least self-effacing and most able to control the impact and emphasis of the words in the dialogue. The initial or final inquit is naturally better adapted to a neutral or informative role, the initial form being especially close to the play-script notation which Defoe and Richardson sometimes used. The most inconspicuous is usually what Bonheim calls the 'zero-stage' form, where 'he said' is understood or implied, not stated. A strongly self-projecting author like Fielding might well turn even play-script zero-stage notations to self-displaying purposes as we have seen. But the fact is that in Bonheim's table *Tom Jones* shows the lowest proportion of zero-stage instances among nearly all works tested, from all periods; in a hundred speeches examined from *Tom Jones*, there were twenty-three initial, sixty-nine medial, seven final and only one zero-stage instances (two cases, from works by Caxton and Behn, showed no zero-stage occurrences in passages tested, and no final ones either, as it happens).

One should be cautious in making inferences from bare statistics, especially when the actual passages tested are not cited. But the evidence tends to reinforce the observation from *Shamela* and elsewhere that even so modest a narrative intervention as the bare 'he says' actively serves Fielding's purposes in a way which would be denied him in his plays. The clockwork alternations of Shamela's speech act not merely as information in the way notionally aimed at in Defoe or Richardson, but as a signal of narrative management. Fielding's exploitation of the inquit shows no urge to abandon or transcend the device in pursuit of a more effectively anti-interventionist idiom. On the contrary, the bravura show of ostensibly unadorned demotic vulgarism acts as a signpost of artifice. In a play, the characters would just speak, not be said to be speaking. Paradoxically, stage-farce in the passage from *Shamela* is brought to mind partly by a device in itself undramatic. On the stage, the brisk automatism would be conveyed by actors and producers, rather than *wholly* supplied by the text, and the rudimentary *narrative* intrusion here takes the place of these external middlemen. It is characteristic of Fielding to want to manage the whole operation himself, and the narrative more effectively cuts off the element of control by others to which stage-productions are subject.[16] In this particular passage there is also a further paradox that, although Fielding is not reporting the dialogue in his own person, Shamela's 'says I' and 'says he' become part of Fielding's managerial self-display.

This witty control is remarkable in the degree to which it prevents the naked reality of the scene from acquiring an unbalancing vitality. The dialogue is direct, unimpeachably demotic, alive with the racy cadences of the vulgar tongue, rendered with great gifts of mimicry. But we are not for all that invited to respond to the passage with the illusion that it is a real-life scene. The Richardsonian originals have less immediate vitality, but their power to create an absorbing illusion is a matter of record, among early readers at least. This is no doubt partly because Richardson has established the character of Pamela in considerable depth, so that the action comes through her terrified consciousness with what, from the author, is an easy narrative assurance. We are not formally conscious of Richardson's presence as, through the lively two-dimensional caricature that Shamela is, we are, and are meant to be, conscious of Fielding's. The formal fact of parody is important here. Despite the passage's tendency to bulge out into autonomous life, we are always in context aware that the Shamela story does not exist for its own sake but to score off *Pamela*, and that the hidden author's combination of contempt and high spirits palpably controls the overall atmosphere.

An effect of this is to create a curious interplay between the vigorous life of the action and a certain urbane reassurance that reality, however vivid or coarse, will not get out of hand. There is no contradiction in the notion of an urbane stylisation which depends partly on overtones of crude popular farce. Fielding easily combines a hearty sense of fun with the necessary element of saving detachment. The combination is peculiarly appropriate to *Shamela*, where one of the purposes is precisely to indicate, from a position of lofty and high-spirited superiority, that the author of *Pamela* is a canting vulgarian. Such an uppish posture is familiar in Augustan satire. One recalls Swift's treatment of Grub Street in the *Tale of a Tub*, or Pope's treatment of the dunces.[17] But the joyful élan with which Fielding throws himself into crude demotic styles while maintaining an uppish presence is special to himself. And this quality in *Shamela* provides a primitive model of the way Fielding's presence makes itself felt in the maturer fiction, whether he

270

explicitly 'intrudes' or not, and whether or not burlesque is involved.

This presence vitalises Fielding's best writing in the novels. Though it is something which the plays largely lack, they helped to make available to the novelist some of the technical means towards it. Plays do not normally accommodate the open presence of a narrator or author. The *Rehearsal*-plays (*The Author's Farce, Pasquin, The Historical Register, Eurydice*, etc.) are partly an exception, since they contain authors-within-the-play who stand outside their own play (the play-within-the-play), planning its production or commenting upon the text, and to this extent creating a skeletal model for that more plastic interplay between the teller and the tale which we find in the novels. But these 'authors' have very limited scope. In one sense, they are mere characters of the larger play we are watching, reduced to equal status with other characters. Often, moreover, they are rather foolish figures, whose power to transmit any impulse of self-expression from Fielding is very limited.[18] Thus when Trapwit (*Pasquin*, II.i) announces at one point during the performance of his comedy, 'Now, sir, you shall see some scenes of politeness and fine conversation among the ladies',[19] the remark has the somewhat limited energy of a well-tried satiric routine, common to *Rehearsal*-plays and mocking incompetent writers without seriously transcending the (perfectly legitimate) element of parody. But when Fielding footnotes an unpleasant dialogue in *Joseph Andrews* (IV: ix) with the words: 'Lest this should appear unnatural to some Readers, we think proper to acquaint them, that it is taken verbatim from very polite Conversation', the effect is to re-emphasise Fielding's knowledgeable, morally reliable and controlling presence at a moment when the rawness of the scene threatens to acquire an unbalancing vitality. A vividly specific incident becomes framed inside the author's knowing grasp of the world's ways, its uncouth factuality (while remaining undiminished and alive) brought under the ordering influence of the firm and steady values implicit in the comedy. The note generalises the situation, satisfying both neo-classic predilection and a certain gentlemanly refusal to get embroiled in the *merely* specific. These effects depend on the words being Fielding's own, rather than those of a character in a play. The comment acquires not only a greater moral fervour, but a more central satiric pertinence: the silly Trapwit's comment does reflect on social usage, but its burlesque context makes it primarily a literary joke on the way plays are written.[20]

271

Now consider the scene from *Joseph Andrews* to which the note refers. Lady Booby and others, including the effeminate Beau Didapper, who had recently tried to rape Fanny, are visiting Parson Adams's house. Fanny and Joseph are also there:

> The Parson and his Company retreated from the Chimneyside, where they had been seated, to give room to the Lady and hers. Instead of returning any of the Curt'sies or extraordinary Civility of Mrs. *Adams*, the Lady turning to Mr. *Booby*, cried out, '*Quelle Bête! Quel Animal!*' And presently after discovering *Fanny* (for she did not need the Circumstance of her standing by *Joseph* to assure the Identity of her Person) she asked the Beau, 'whether he did not think her a pretty Girl?' – 'Begad, Madam,' answered he, ''tis the very same I met.' 'I did not imagine', replied the Lady, 'you had so good a Taste.' 'Because I never liked you, I warrant,' cries the Beau. 'Ridiculous!' said she, 'you know you was always my Aversion.' 'I would never mention Aversion,' answered the Beau, 'with that Face★; dear Lady *Booby*, wash your Face before you mention Aversion, I beseech you.' He then laughed and turned about to coquette it with *Fanny*.

The dialogue, though part of a continuous action, has that semi-autonomous quality of a set piece which resembles certain individual scenes in stage-comedy.[21] Moreover, while vividly true to colloquial speech, it maintains a self-contained and faintly fantasticated absurdity, almost balletic in its quality of routine interchange and shapely self-completion. It may be compared with a scene from an early play, *The Temple Beau* (1730; I. i), which likewise presents the vacuously haughty acidities of a 'polite' quarrel, and likewise (though too long to quote in full) has a distinct and self-completing internal rhythm:

> LADY GRAVELY . . . sister, since we are in private, I'll tell you what the world says of you. – In the first place, then, it says that you are both younger and handsomer than you seem.
> LADY LUCY PEDANT Nay, this is flattery, my dear!
> LADY GRAVELY No, indeed, my dear! for that folly and affectation had disguised you all over with an air of dotage and deformity.
> LADY LUCY PEDANT This carries an air of sincerity – thank you, my dear. . . .

LADY GRAVELY ... In every circle you engross the whole conversation, where you say a thousand silly things, and laugh at them all; by both which the world is always convinced, that you háve very fine teeth and very bad sense. ... That you are not restrained from unlawful pleasures by the love of virtue, but variety; and that your husband is not safe from having no rival, but from having a great many; for your heart is like a coffee-house, where the beaus frisk in and out, one after another; and you are as little the worse for them, as the other is the better; for one lover, like one poison, is your antidote against another.

LADY LUCY PEDANT Ha, ha, ha! I like your comparison of love and poison, for I hate them both alike.

LADY GRAVELY ... In short, to end my character, the world gives you the honour of being the most finished coquette in town.[22]

The most evident thing about this dialogue (which belongs to a dramatic type of which the exchange between Célimène and the prude Arsinoé in Molière's *Misanthrope*, III. iv, seems the classic model) is its lifelessness. Lady Gravely's stiff, ponderously barbed harangues and Lady Lucy's flaccid sarcasms lack all edge and conviction, as they answer one another in a kind of elephantine ballet of pique (the dialogue symmetrically balances some immediately preceding and similarly devitalised exchanges in which Lady Lucy makes the speeches and Lady Gravely is at the receiving end). Any sudden freshness ('your heart is like a coffee-house, where the beaus frisk in and out, one after another') is embedded almost beyond recovery in the stale epigrammatic routine. A glance at Congreve would quickly show by comparison the extent to which Fielding fails to catch fire in a conventional mode of Restoration comedy. All suggestion of shapely interchange, both in the style of speech and in the larger organisation of the scene, solidifies into a heavy show of neatly-proportioned petrifaction. The dialogue comes nowhere near to achieving that quality of satiric fantasy where the foolish and nasty speakers become (as in the novels) transposed into a pointedly 'unreal' dimension of disreputability which is one of Fielding's most characteristic and inventive effects.

For one of the uses of patterned artifice, and of a related tendency of individual scenes to seem self-enclosed, is, in Fielding, precisely to set vice and folly in the mad world of their own self-absorption, where they seem disconnected from all humane and rational purposes. In the dialogue from *Joseph Andrews*, Lady Booby and Beau Didapper perform a ritual of social nastiness, staged with clockwork precision, signposted by the author as typical or exemplary, and standing out slightly, in its clean and pointed outlines, from the bustling scene in which it is set. The dialogue is undoubtedly more 'realistic' than that of *The Temple Beau*, though one of its liveliest idiomatic exactitudes ('I would never mention Aversion ... with that Face; dear Lady *Booby*, wash your Face before you mention Aversion') happens to echo stage-comedy as well as real life;[23] and the 'realism' exists in piquant relationship with the suggestion of autonomous artifice, rather than subverting it. This interplay the plays seldom achieve, despite comparable efforts to set certain things into relief through 'self-conscious' announcements of artifice, as when Trapwit advertises his scene of 'fine conversation' or Lady Gravely coyly speaks of her 'character' (i.e. character-sketch) of Lady Lucy. But these stylisations in the plays inhibit Fielding's creative vitality instead of providing a congenial framework for its release. Part of the reason is that the plays belong to genres in themselves highly stylised, where there is no strongly competing note of *vraisemblance*, and where the stylisation (including these slightly externalised reminders) is of a sort that takes itself for granted, not easily permitting the author to use the sheer act of stylisation as a form of self-expression and of commentary.

Another reason is that the externalising has in plays to be done by a character and not by the narrator. This should not be oversimplified. The example from *Shamela* shows that some of the most buoyant suggestions of farcical stylisation, the routine mechanical interchange of 'says I' and 'says he', comes from a narrator who is a character in the story and formally very distinct from Fielding himself. There, as we saw, the special modulations of the parody were partly responsible for establishing the strong sense of authorial direction. But the very nature of the narrative mode had also a great deal to do with this effect, because the strategic placing of the narrative links into pointedly mechanical rhythms gave its own flavour of ironic mastery. Shamela might be doing the talking, but the irony was that of the author (whether one knew him to be Fielding or not), and despite the dialogue's demotic authenticity we are always conscious that Shamela is being mimicked rather than (like Pamela) 'rendered'. Behind her, the voice of the derisive impersonator is vividly, even spectacularly, implied.

In the very different dialogue from *Joseph Andrews*, there is, by contrast, nothing spectacular. The passage relies neither on parodic high spirits, nor on pointed overtones of farcical automatism. Authorial presence asserts itself in relatively sober ways. The rudimentary narrative links, 'she said', 'answered he', and the rest, do not in themselves suggest stylisation, as in *Shamela*. They seem almost to retreat into their bare functional role of identifying the speakers, or to be the merest reminders of the narrator's existence.[24] With a few marginal exceptions, which need not detain us here, dialogue is the only medium in Fielding's novels where the main narrator does not speak in his own voice, so that it imposes on an author of his temperament a special need for such reminders. But even such unemphatic narrative pointers may contribute an element of commentary, helping here and there to modify or heighten an emphasis. '"I would never mention Aversion," answered the Beau, "with that Face . . ."'': the placing of 'answered the Beau' creates a pause exactly timed to give the ensuing insult its ludicrous note of explosive venom.

Such authorial interventions are delicate and, no doubt, are often spontaneous instances of Fielding's natural manner rather than carefully calculated effects. One hesitates to call them stylisations. The author, as an assertive personality, is *almost* absent. But the very nature of the narrative mode permits him, however quietly, to maintain a visible mastery, and it really does look as though the mere fact of narration were in itself enough here to energise Fielding into all the ease, confidence and securely-carried moral passion which the scene from *The Temple Beau* lacks. Not only the dialogue's narrative links, but also the brief narrative preliminaries, do some powerful if unobtrusive work, crisply sketching the unpleasant social atmosphere in which the dialogue takes place: the grandee boorishness of the visitors, the flustered servility of Mrs Adams, the sexual situation somewhat charged by Didapper's recent attempt on Fanny and by Lady Booby's desire that Didapper should win Fanny so that she may have Joseph for herself. On the stage, much of the establishing of such social atmosphere would be done by actors and producer. But the vivid conciseness of this passage (narrative and dialogue together) contrasts with the verbose obviousness of much of Fielding's dramatic dialogue, as though he felt compelled to be sole master even in the plays and to leave as little as possible for anyone else to do. Whatever the reasons, the dialogue, when it comes, completely outclasses – in economy, pungency and authenticity of rendering – the stilted acidities from *The Temple Beau*, and other similar scenes from Fielding's plays.[25]

In *Tom Jones*, VII: iii, Mrs Western tries to get Sophia to marry Blifil:

> 'What Objection can you have to the young Gentleman?'
> 'A very solid Objection, in my Opinion,' says *Sophia*, – 'I hate him.'

But Fielding's interest does not reside in this crisp and lively naturalism for its own sake. His concern is to let the limpid truthfulness and centrality of Sophia's answer erupt in all its freshness from the context of grotesque fantastication which surrounds it:

> 'If I was not as great a Philosopher as *Socrates* himself,' returned Mrs. *Western*, 'you would overcome my Patience. What Objection can you have to the young Gentleman?'
> 'A very solid Objection, in my Opinion,' says *Sophia*, – 'I hate him.'
> 'Will you never learn a proper Use of Words?' answered the Aunt. 'Indeed Child, you should consult *Bailey's Dictionary*. It is impossible you should hate a Man from whom you have received no Injury. By Hatred, therefore, you mean no more than Dislike, which is no sufficient Objection against your marrying of him.

This is a classic illustration of Fielding's tendency to set his 'realistic' effects inside a comically stylised frame. The realistic core of this exchange leaps out of its surroundings with a startling and vivid pertinence, but much of its force depends on the contrast with the aunt's disconnected and almost 'operatic' absurdity.

A more straightforwardly unstylised dialogue from Fielding's play *The Wedding-Day* (1743), where Charlotte, in love with Millamour, rejects her (eventually successful) suitor Heartfort, offers itself for comparison. It contains an almost identical retort to that of Sophia, but the surrounding frame is entirely different.

> CHARLOTTE Well, well, tell the wretch I will see him, to give him another final answer, since he will have it. Poor creature! how little he suspects who is his rival! – Oh! Millamour, thou has given this heart of mine more sighs in one week than it ever felt before – nay, than it hath ever made any other feel. How shall I let him know my passion, or how

avoid this match intended for me by my father! Well, sir,
how often must I tell you, I won't have you, I can't have you?

HEARTFORT Madam, as you have often told me the
contrary, *I think you should give some reason why you will not
have me.*

CHARLOTTE *I tell you a reason – I hate you.*

HEARTFORT I might expect a better reason for that
hate than the violence of my love.

CHARLOTTE Oh! the best reason in the world. I hate
every thing that is ridiculous, and there is nothing so ridiculous as a real lover.

HEARTFORT Methinks, gratitude might produce the
highest affection.

CHARLOTTE Your humble servant, sweet sir – Gratitude! – that implies an obligation; but how am I obliged to
you for loving me? I did not ask you to love me – did I? – I
can't help your loving me; and if one was to have every one
that loves one, one must have the whole town . . .

(*The Wedding-Day*, II. viii)[26]

The dialogue here is in no way fantasticated, and belongs to the
moderately realistic conversational idiom which one finds in
many comedies of the day. Obviously, the particular piquancy of
Sophia's answer, which depends on a contrast of styles, is absent.
But what is especially notable is the lack of vitality of this dialogue
as a whole, from the tired explanatory soliloquizing of the opening
to the faintly factitious sprightliness of the exchanges themselves.
It has a certain mild charm, but totally lacks the vivid pointedness
and thrust of the exchange from *Tom Jones*, where (as in the earlier
and in themselves very different dialogues from *Shamela* and
Joseph Andrews) realistic notation is vitalised by its interplay with
the surrounding artifice.

More is at stake than a local aesthetic effect. The contrast
between Sophia's language and that of her aunt dramatises radical
differences between the two women. Sophia is of the real world
not only because she talks 'realistically', but more profoundly
because she has a normal human contact with the world outside
herself, while Mrs Western flowers in a private, fetid world of
self-nourishing grotesquerie. It is not simply that Sophia is
virtuous and her aunt wicked, but that Sophia is in touch with
central human purposes: concepts like virtue, affection, recipro-
city have a living significance for her, whereas they have no
meaning whatever for her aunt. Mrs Western, of course, is

neither so unreal nor so disconnected from the life around her as to be harmless. She is the grotesque embodiment of a moral turpitude that really exists in a corrupt world. Her private universe is in some ways not unlike that of Swift's *Tale of a Tub*, where mad means bad and a fantasticated self-absorption is by no means merely funny. While her absurdity dissolves much of the moral sting, and prevents her nastiness from toppling the comic novel into an inappropriately sombre (or Swiftian) mood, she nevertheless holds a considerable threat at this moment to the prospects of happiness of Sophia and Tom. She is partly the product of Fielding's slightly superior readiness to regard evil as in some ways ridiculous, and we read the dialogue with a mixture of alarm and amused reassurance which remains just sufficiently uncertain to maintain suspense. The confrontation is finally not between mere alternative points of view, but between a humane decency rooted in the real world, and a zany disconnected nastiness that lives in a world of its own, yet would (and could) turn the real world to its own *Tale of a Tub*-like image. The interplay of contrasting conversational idioms is, in this context, more than a stylistic piquancy, and constitutes a powerful moral notation in its own right.

If it is, therefore, insufficient to say that the exfoliating absurdity of Mrs Western exists merely in order to bring Sophia's sharply sensible reply into relief, that is nevertheless one of its effects – just as, outside the domain of dialogue, Fielding's burlesque absurdities in the famous scene which first introduces Sophia bring into relief the fresh realistic description which eventually emerges: '*Sophia* ... was a middle-sized Woman; but rather inclining to tall ...' (*Tom Jones*, IV: ii). The play of contrasts is variously charged with moral comment and bookish parody, giving a sense that the narrative details are not naked phenomena, but have their place in a wider and more inclusive authorial perspective. It does so with only a limited dependence upon explicit authorial assertion, or formal acts of presence. Some of the liveliest and most characteristic scenes in the novels occur through the importation of elements from some other genre, whether plays, epic poems, history, or even opera. But often these importations are unproclaimed and unofficial, a matter of hinted resonances and semi-concealed jokes, as much the product of habit of mind as of conscious systematic signposting. It seems probable that allusive arrangements of incident or scene often come as naturally and spontaneously to Fielding as the more explicit kinds of authorial self-display (the ironic commentary, the various formal tricks of 'self-conscious narration', etc.).

While Sophia and Mrs Western were arguing about Blifil, Sophia's father has been listening in. As the dialogue rounds itself to its predictable dead-end (the 'scene', as it were, completing itself), we are made aware of the Squire, skulking, with increasing impatience, as though in a half hidden corner of the stage:

> *Western*, who had been within hearing during the greater Part of the preceding Dialogue, had now exhausted all his Patience; he therefore entered the Room in a violent Passion, crying, 'D–n me then if *shatunt* ha' un, d–n me if *shatunt*, that's all – that's all – D–n me if *shatunt*.'

This impression of a stage-arrangement is reinforced in various ways. Squire Western very obviously belongs to a long tradition of stage-squires, a fact which would be sensed particularly forcibly in Fielding's own time, when drama was still a dominant form of literary entertainment, and when Western's stage-predecessors (who include characters like Squire Badger and Sir Gregory Kennel from Fielding's own plays) would be sufficiently well-remembered for Western to be readily identified as a dramatic type.[27] His language, moreover, is as much drawn from stage-Zummerzet as from the real-life region: however authentic, it cannot help bringing to mind the stylised country-speech long associated with stage-rustics, and it exists (like Mr Booby's rather different demotics in *Shamela*) in a quizzical no-man's-land between realistic notation and dramatic routine. Moreover, Squire Western does not speak invariably in dialect (a fact which, as readers, we tend to overlook). This suggests that Fielding reserves the trick for highlighting certain comic effects, or that he confined the mimicry to what seemed sufficient to establish a powerful impression in the reader's mind, without attempting a fully consistent, still less an elaborately lifelike, rendering. In the present passage Western subsides into more or less standard English after the initial outburst in dialect has established his oafish rusticity strongly enough for the immediate purpose of the scene. It is hard to be sure how much we are meant to be conscious in detail of linguistic artifice. But we cannot, and are surely not expected to, avoid a strong generalised sense of such artifice.

Not only is the Squire's entry timed to occur exactly at the point when, in stage-terms, a new person is called for on the 'scene', to inaugurate the next formal phase of the dramatic business, but his dialogue with his sister in Sophia's presence has itself the overall shape, and the tendency to self-containment, of a dramatic scene in its own right. It contains a fresh comic quarrel between two strongly sketched types, and, having begun with an explosive entry, it culminates near the end in an explosive exit (Mrs Western's). The chapter as a whole is thus manifestly constructed as a balanced pair of complementary 'scenes'.

Many acidities pass between the brother and the sister. The dialogue has a driving absurdity, as the two vie with each other in obsessive and self-fantasticating extravagance. Oddly, there is considerable representational exactitude in the way the details of quarrelsome misunderstanding and free-wheeling recrimination are captured. Intemperate rage, injured self-esteem, haughty pique and nagging illogic pass backwards and forwards with an unerring sense of the natural rhythm of such things in real-life quarrels. But it is all bloated to an extravagant, as it were 'operatic', size. By contrast with the brashly limited resonances of the *Shamela* passage, the dialogue here reveals character with a capacious abundance. It not only brings out a wider range of particularised information about the speakers, but also creates a world in which character manifests itself with more than life-like amplitude. Western's driving rage, his superhuman obtuseness, his engaging readiness to sentimentalise his relations with his daughter, his imprisoning political obsessions and their outrageous illogicalities, combine into a heaving amalgam of comic self-realisation. The massive folly of the dialogue becomes almost *literally* operatic when Western answers his sister's taunt that he is a 'boor':

> Boar, ... I am no Boar; no, nor Ass; no, nor Rat neither,
> Madam. Remember that – I am no Rat.

Remarkably, this conveys a recognisable impression of the rhythms of mounting pique, but magnified to a full-throated comic-opera extravagance, a rising baritone frenzy completing itself in a zany, rhyming recapitulation.[28]

Squire Western has a vitality which his fellow squires in Fielding's plays entirely lack. This is no doubt partly due to a natural maturing of Fielding's comic art. But here again it seems that Fielding could give full uninhibited release to his comic energies only when he had at his disposal such formal opportunities of projecting his presence, and at the same time of safeguarding his ironic detachment, as the narrative mode provides. Given these opportunities, however, Fielding's mastery of modulation, even in crude or spectacular contexts, is astonishing. Once the presence and the chosen tone of voice are confidently established, the most ordinary story-telling language becomes edged with extraordinary life. A simple narrator's phrase like 'had now exhausted all his Patience' (as Western is about to burst upon the conversation) evokes a purple-faced indignation which then suffuses all that Western says, and which no speech of Squire Badger, or of his fellow stage-squires, can by itself suggest with the same force. If, on the stage, such things can be supplied by actors, we have already seen that a reliance on actors is hardly liberating to an author who, like Fielding, is at his best only when he can advertise himself as in full control of his effects; and the speeches of the stage-squires are wooden in comparison with any corresponding ones of Western.[29]

The dialogue in this chapter is not only 'externally' sustained by such simple narrative factualities, but is also laced with the periphrastic mock-bewilderments and the authorial archnesses ('I will not determine', 'uttered Phrases improper to be here related', etc.) with which all readers of Fielding are familiar.[30] The confident pretence of fussy indirection amalgamates preposterously with the coarsely forthright oafishness of Western's ways:

> 'Ho! are you come back to your Politics,' cries the Squire, 'as for those I despise them as much as I do a F—t.' Which last Word he accompanied and graced with the very Action, which, of all others, was the most proper to it. And whether it was this Word, or the Contempt exprest for her Politics, which most affected Mrs. *Western*, I will not determine; but she flew into the most violent Rage, uttered Phrases improper to be here related, and instantly burst out of the House.[31]

The archness hardly inhibits the vitality of presentation. But in this interplay of crude vigour and gentlemanly reservation, the reservation provides a necessary setting for the full release of the vigour.[32] The result is one of those bold and delightful effects of abundance (urbanity cheek by jowl with low jests) which the extraordinary inclusiveness of Fielding's irony keeps under buoyant authorial management.

There is also here a pointed reminder of farce. Farting (the blank is Fielding's or his printer's, but the coyness in this seems itself to be offered for enjoyment) is no extraordinary thing, and not confined to farces. But Western's 'Action', at the climax of his invective, is remarkable not so much for its vigour or its truth to character (though it has both) as for its exact timing, worthy of the envy of any professional *pétomane*.[33] Precision-farting, even in novels, is essentially a stage-effect. Novels sometimes imitate it, from *Tom Jones* to *An American Dream*,[34] but whenever the deed is timed to act as a retort or as a comment, clowning is inescapably brought to mind. Stage-treatments differ from novels, however, in that they are bound, almost by definition, to verge on the slapstick. What the plot presents as a digestive disorder in the protagonist inevitably comes over on stage as an actor's peto-manic feat.[35] Playwrights from Aristophanes to the present have exploited the comic potential of this, especially where there has been a readiness to merge comedy and farce.[36] Such a readiness existed in Fielding's day (*The Author's Farce*, like many other plays, includes a puppet-show inside the play itself), but it was severely circumscribed. Like the 'kick your A—. You, kiss —' exchange in *Shamela*, Western's 'Action' is outside the normal decorous boundaries of the contemporary comic stage (one does not find it in Fielding's own plays), and it functions as sophisti-cated evocation of cruder popular entertainments (farces at the London fairs, puppet-shows, and the like).[37] Fielding had an interest in such entertainments. His plays were popular in puppet-show adaptations, and he and Tom Jones both regretted that puppet-shows were nowadays being emasculated by the removal of 'low Wit or Humour, or Jests' and notably of such traditional figures as Mr Punch, whose association with comic farting was particularly explicit[38] (here, as elsewhere in Fielding, there is a touch of that aristocratic attitude which prefers the demotic freedoms of the frankly 'low' to the pseudo-gentilities of the middle ranks).

It is only in the relative freedom of prose-fiction that Fielding felt able openly to give expression to some of his farcical interests. But there is also evidence of some clandestine activity in that direction. It has recently been discovered that in March 1748, at the time he was writing *Tom Jones*, Fielding opened a puppet-theatre of his own.[39] An advertisement, probably written by himself, and which ran for many days, announced one of the performances as:

> ... that Excellent old English Entertainment, call'd A PUPPET-SHEW [.] Every Day this Week will be shewn the lamentable Tragedy of BATEMAN, WHO DIED FOR LOVE. *With the Comical Humours of* PUNCH *and his Wife*

JOAN, With all the Original Jokes, F—rts, Songs, Battles, Kickings, &c.[40]

The specifying of 'F—rts' as a standard part of the show sounds exactly like a self-conscious joke of Fielding's. It throws light on the passage we are considering, where the 'F—rt' is also drawn attention to rather than, so to speak, taken for granted. This suggests in *Tom Jones* a stylisation which not merely borrows from the conventions of popular farce, but which is almost allusive, signposting itself as an imported artifice. (Contemporaries seem incidentally to have recognised an affinity between this novel and the world of puppet-shows, and a hostile critic associated it with the humour of Mr Punch.)[41] Squire Western's fart pointedly exists both inside and outside the expected boundaries of our response to the narrative. It is perfectly in character that he should both use the word and perform the act in the presence of others. But the clockwork timing and finality of the act also make it a sort of victory in his argument with his sister, and the slapstick world in which such things are taken as victories is neither the real world nor that of the quasi-realistic fictional medium to which *Tom Jones* ostensibly claims to belong.[42]

Western's sister, with her compulsive politicking and her preposterous pedantry, matches the Squire's absurdity, and their duet takes place in a zany world of their own creation, where this absurdity can freely flower. Sophia is present throughout, and the discussion is ostensibly about her, but she gets no chance to say a word. Her presence, though now silent, continues to run through the entire chapter as a discreet but unbreakable lifeline to reality. The dialogue is throughout disconnected from the matter in hand (Sophia's choice of husband), and the two speakers perform a ritual of almost pure self-realisation. This of course is true to their highly self-absorbed characters, and the inability of Western and his sister to enter into Sophia's feelings about Blifil is necessary to the advancement of the plot, for it leads to Sophia's escape from home. In this sense, the scene's tendency to a kind of autonomy is itself something which merges intimately into the overall movement of the novel. But this autonomy also stands out as something shaped by an ostentatiously masterful creator, and which we are in a sense meant to see in all its roundedness, as in itself a kind of complete and considered statement from him. It is not simply that the fantastication of Mrs Western and her brother has in itself a quality of sheer performance which, very evidently, contributes to our sense of Fielding's active presence. The feeling of creative abundance which the scene exudes is also held in check by the combination of distancing artifice and of a small hard note of rueful distaste. Amid all the bustle a very exact suggestion is established of *nil admirari* streaked with moral concern. Something not only of the self-completeness of dramatic 'scenes' but also of the delicate integrity of some of Pope's Horatian poems is sensed, transcending the horseplay. This surprising flavour, actually by no means rare in *Tom Jones*, has its own way of disengaging itself, momentarily, from the narrative flow, as perhaps the finest, and the most informal, authorial intrusion of all.

(ii) *Part II*

The dialogues in Fielding's novels, then, are often highly stylised and tend, like many other elements in his writings, towards the self-enclosed autonomy of the set piece. At the same time such highlighting of authorial 'artifice' exists in piquant interplay with an extremely authentic (or 'realistic') sense of the emotional and social overtones of speech, and the dialogues reveal in particular that Fielding had a remarkably sharp ear for the cadences and vocabulary of the actual spoken language. As we might expect, however, it is an ear that specialises in normal usage, the readily recognisable social idiom,[43] including cant phrases and accredited polite slang as well as (in *Shamela*) certain aspects at least of coarse demotic speech. It does not extend to those singular or coined usages in expressive common speech which come from the need to express a particular feeling more exactly, or from a linguistically creative awkwardness, or from an individual's freedom (whether subliterate or sophisticated) from the inhibitions of standard usage. The existence of such 'singular' idiom is normal in the common speech of any social milieu (though there were pressures against it, as against any singularity, in the gentlemanly code of Fielding's day), and it is one of the factors which makes languages develop. But many individual singularities would in themselves seem too remote from normal (let alone 'correct') speech to be acceptable to an author like Fielding for serious literary notation.

The master among eighteenth-century novelists of this more adventurous and subtle linguistic field was of course Richardson. His coinages (whether they are inspired singularities of his own imagining, or current usages caught at an early stage of their career in the actual spoken language) offended many contemporaries, one of whom feared that they might 'become current in common Conversation, be imitated by other writers, or by the laborious industry of some future compiler, transferred into a Dictionary' – in other words, improperly made standard by Richardson's authority.[44] *Meditatingly* and *scrupulosities* are two examples which this critic disliked, but such phrases have the living accent of colloquial speech and several have in fact passed into normal current usage.[45] Chesterfield perceptively recognised that Richardson's coinages admirably expressed the 'little secret movements' of the heart, but this was coupled in his mind with the feeling (also and more viciously expressed by Lady Mary Wortley Montagu, Horace Walpole, and others) that, when Richardson deals with 'high life, he grossly mistakes the modes.'[46]

The gentlemanly avoidance of singularity in all things, preached by Chesterfield and other courtesy-writers, naturally extended to language: 'In *Words*, as *Fashions*, the same Rule will hold; / Alike Fantastick, *if too New*, or *Old*.'[47] Gentlemanly decorum and a neo-classic centrality blend in Pope's couplet and underlie a severe linguistic self-consciousness among many writers of the period. Defensive phrases like 'as they call it' or 'as they say' occur remarkably often, accompanying usages which (however widely accepted) savoured remotely of neologism or of any other form of oddity. Richardson's Sir Charles Grandison, speaking to Sir Hargrave Pollexfen and other gentlemen, says that his father let him go abroad on 'the Grand Tour, as it is called.' The phrase 'Grand Tour' had in fact been in use since the seventeenth century, and one would not expect Sir Charles's friends to be unfamiliar with it or with the fashionable activity which it described. It would be oversimple, however, to take this as an example of Richardson mistaking 'the modes' of 'high life.' Fielding, writing of the squire in *Joseph Andrews* (III: vii), says: 'He made in three Years the Tour of *Europe*, as they term it', and Hogarth, in a rejected passage of the *Analysis of Beauty*, spoke of 'The grand Tour, as its [sic] calld'. It appears that 'grand tour', though widely used over a long period, had not yet become fully naturalised, in itself a measure of extreme linguistic guardedness in the culture as a whole.[48] Phrases like 'as it is called' seem to have been used by most writers, and in particular by both Fielding and Richardson, in essays and personal letters as well as by narrators and characters in their novels.[49] Perhaps the very self-consciousness which this denoted might be thought ungentlemanly by a purist like Chesterfield, for he includes the phrase in an amusing mimicry of typical trite usages of a 'vulgar man': 'If anybody attempts being *smart*, as he calls it, upon him, he gives them *tit for tat*, ay, that he does.'[50]

Thus a phrase used to soften or to excuse singularity is pilloried for its 'commonness', and a gentleman might not want to distinguish too precisely between the excessively singular and the excessively common, singularity being itself a typical symptom of vulgarity. Chesterfield's letters are full of monitory lists of trite phrases, proverbs, vulgarisms, and it is an amusing fact that Richardson's Pamela happens to use many of these. Since the speaker in this case is a servant-girl, an obvious justification can be made on 'dramatic' grounds. But in such matters, there would not always be a readiness to distinguish too precisely between an author's speech and that of his characters.

'Singularity' and trite vulgarisms were almost equally 'low'. 'Lowness' also meant indecorous or gross language. And the literary decorum which prescribed '"accommodation" of style to subject' might well come into conflict with another decorum, which shied from 'low' subjects as such. John Lawlor has written well that such stylistic congruences were felt to have their limits, and that '"lowness" of style . . . offers difficulties to a sensibility that cherishes the ideal of "correctness"'.[51] This easily implied in some cases not only that a writer must not use 'low' language, but that his 'low' characters should not use it either, or even that he should not deal in such characters at all.[52] By Fielding's time gentlemanly standards and the centralising, normative predilections of neo-classicism came to be partly reinforced, and also partly undermined, by an increasingly vocal element of middle-class squeamishness. This created a piquant situation in which the bourgeois Richardson, and the gentleman novelist Fielding, could each think of the other as 'low', Richardson being so taken for his pseudo-genteel awkwardness and his use of idioms both 'singular' and 'common', and Fielding for his interest in a coarser, more popular kind of 'lowness'. Richardson said patronisingly to Sarah Fielding: 'Had your brother . . . been born in a stable, or been a runner at a sponging-house, we should have thought him a genius, and wished he had had the advantage of a liberal education, and of being admitted into better company.'[53] It is a coincidence which Fielding would have relished that in the letter of the following year (1753) in which Chesterfield noted Richardson's genius and his ignorance of 'high life', he also said that Richardson 'would well have deserved a higher education than he has had'![54]

Fielding's notation of the coarser kind of 'low' speech has considerable vigour, although it occurs most freely, perhaps, in *Shamela* and in those places in the novels where it can claim the excuse of parody or of a special comic or satiric need; and Fielding always tends in any case to distance it by various means. Even so, critics not only of Richardson's persuasion accused him of lowness in both matter and manner. Fielding's limited but hearty freedoms with 'low' matter and language doubtless sprang from natural gusto combined with a pointed superiority to the straight-laced middle-class form which the objection (as he would see it in Richardson) sometimes took. His fondness for a popular entertainment like the puppet show, and his dislike of the contemporary tendency to soften popular entertainments by the extrusion of 'low stuff,'[55] suggests an element of that patrician readiness to assert itself on the side of genuine demotic vitality against more bourgeois forms of genteelism.[56] Moreover the coarse 'lowness,' in certain literary kinds, could be defended by an appeal to time-honoured comic tradition (Aristophanes, Lucian, Rabelais). This would satisfy some neo-classical objections, since precedents of such distinction and antiquity in themselves supplied a kind of norm. Fielding was not, however, altogether easy on this whole question, and came, later in life, to repudiate Aristophanes and Rabelais, though not Lucian, for their indecency.[57]

Fielding's dialogue may at times be 'low' (whether coarsely or otherwise) in ways which reproduce actual widespread usage, but it has little or no singularity in the Richardsonian sense. Fielding's interest in spoken language, particularly in the cant phrases which reveal moral and social attitudes, is, on the other hand, enormous; and *this* interest (in the expressive clichés of current informal idiom – of whatever class, though not fully received as part of the polite *standard*) does in fact overlap with Richardson's. But where Richardson treats such 'typical' idiom as part of the vivid flow of spontaneous speech, Fielding stylises it, standing outside, isolating it by some act of ironic distancing, implying that it is regrettably 'normal' (i.e., in general use) rather than mainly 'natural' to the particular, immediate situation. Characteristically he is given to anthologising such usages, in oddly exuberant lists which occur from time to time in the novels.

The fantasticating 'dissertation' on high people and low people in *Joseph Andrews*, for example, notes the refusal of these two orders 'to regard each other as of the same Species' and immediately launches into a linguistic list for proof of this: 'This, the Terms *strange Persons, People one does not know, the Creature,*

Wretches, Beasts, Brutes, and many other Appellations evidently demonstrate.'[58] One recognises here the language of many a dialogue from Fielding's works, but also the sense of sheer generalising pleasure which the list communicates, as if an infinity of particular snobberies were being triumphantly boiled down to their verbal essentials. The point about these phrases is that they are the normal vacuous currency of snobbish contempt. There is not one among them which is original or fresh in itself, yet they kindle into a wittily disembodied life in this abstract catalogue. A more remarkable example of such cataloguing occurs in *Jonathan Wild*, when it is announced that Theodosia Snap has given birth to an illegitimate child. For here there is no frankly generalising 'Dissertation' and the list occurs as sheer narrative of a specific event:

> At this Time an Accident happened, which, though not immediately affecting our Hero, we cannot avoid relating, as it occasioned great Confusion in his Family, as well as in the Family of *Snap*. It is indeed a Calamity highly to be lamented, when it stains untainted Blood, and happens to an honourable House. An Injury never to be repaired. A Blot never to be wiped out. A Sore never to be healed. To detain my Reader no longer: Miss *Theodosia Snap* was now safely delivered of a Male-Infant, the Product of an Amour which that beautiful (O that I could say, virtuous) Creature had with the Count.
>
> (III: xiii)

The cant of moral outrage is catalogued with a similar routine comprehensiveness, comically suggesting that, whenever such things happen, the same phrases all come up. We observe Fielding's familiar procedure of interweaving particular narration with a generalising awareness of the world's ways. The Snap household is in fact very disreputable, which is part of the joke, but the phrases specifically anticipate the reactions of Theodosia's extremely dissolute sister Laetitia, who, in the next paragraph, expresses shock at this 'Dishonour' to her 'chaste Family' and 'Affront to her Virtue.' To this extent, Fielding's amusingly generalised mimicry is partly a projection of the mind of a main character. For while Fielding addresses the reader and proclaims his own share of the joke, he is also entering into Laetitia's outlook, presenting the situation through mental processes which Laetitia is about to adopt in her own name.

Fielding's passage might be compared with a similar cataloguing of the cant of outraged virtue in Cleland's *Memoirs of a Coxcomb* (1751):

> I had opened my attack by some little presents, which she returned me with great dignity and spirit. 'She wondered, that she did, what I meant by it. – She hoped nothing in her conduct had given me any encouragement for bad designs. – She knew she was indeed too mean for me to think of her for a wife, and she was sure she was too good to be a mistress to the highest lord in the land. If she was poor, she was virtuous.' – with all this cant stuff that has so often ruefully taken in many a country booby . . .[59]

The passage is crude by comparison with Fielding's, though one sees in it the same anthologising habit, down to the phrase 'that she did' (which occurs in at least one of Chesterfield's lists, see above, p. 286). In Cleland's case the sequence appears as a report ('indirect' and no doubt modified in some indeterminate way by the narrator's ironic telling) of words actually spoken by the girl. In Fielding, by contrast, there is an active interplay between the consciousness of narrator and character, much more radically indeterminate and fluid: we cannot disentangle character from narrator from authorial mimic, or words spoken from words imputed or thought. Fielding's passage is an especially interesting variant, generalising and proleptic, of what we have learned to call free indirect discourse, though both passages operate in an amusing twilight zone where signposted typicality and the highly specific interpenetrate.[60]

A good modern parallel might be the scene in *Ulysses* where Stephen looks over Mr Deasy's cliché-ridden letter to the press:

> May I trespass on your valuable space. That doctrine of *laissez faire* which so often in our history. Our cattle trade. The way of all our old industries. Liverpool ring which jockeyed the Galway harbour scheme. European conflagration. Grain supplies through the narrow waters of the channel. The pluterperfect imperturbability of the department of agriculture. Pardoned a classical allusion. Cassandra. By a woman who was no better than she should be. To come to the point at issue.[61]

This is presumably how Stephen's mind selects and reacts to what he is reading. But, as in Fielding, the passage conveys a teasing two-way traffic between witty authorial summary and the mental processes of the character; and as in Fielding, a typifying and anthologising satire interpenetrates with the highly specific episode in the novel's action.

Such interpenetration occurs also, in a different way, in the more frankly abstract list from *Joseph Andrews*. The list comes in the middle of a lengthy digression on snobbery, whose ostensible purpose in the narrative is to explain why, in the previous chapter, Mrs Slipslop ignored the greeting of Fanny, whom she knew well, pretending to wonder '*who the Creature was*'. The digression, which proves 'that Mrs. *Slipslop* did not in the least deviate from the common Road in this Behaviour,' is nevertheless a humorous essay in its own right, frankly labelled a 'Dissertation' in the chapter heading. Its relation to the story is formally gone into only at the beginning and end. But at the point where the catalogue occurs, Fielding flashes Mrs Slipslop back into the picture, allowing a quick glimpse of her individual part in the mazy dance of universal snobbery:

> The People of Fashion [and] . . . the People of no Fashion . . . seem scarce to regard each other as of the same Species. This the Terms *strange Persons, People one does not know, the Creature, Wretches, Beasts, Brutes*, and many other Appellations evidently demonstrate; which Mrs. *Slipslop* having often heard her Mistress use, thought she had also a Right to use in her turn: and perhaps she was not mistaken; for these two Parties, especially those bordering nearly on each other, to-wit the lowest of the High, and the highest of the Low, often change their Parties according to Place and Time; for those who are People of Fashion in one place, are often People of no Fashion in another.
>
> (*JA*, II: xiii)

This brief sight of Mrs Slipslop consciously deciding that the entire repertoire of contemptuous phrases is at her disposal shows the snobbery being mechanised to a further degree of clockwork absurdity. It is, as we can see from the quotation, part of a protracted escalation of absurdities which is otherwise conducted in general terms until the formal return, several sentences later, to the story proper. But her momentary emergence in this sea of jargon adds a further reciprocal vitality to both her and the catalogue.

These catalogues of standard usages testify not merely to a

generalising temperament, but to a positive creative delight in viewing specific events through generalising arrangements. They show Fielding not only capturing those cliché phrases which typically reveal certain attitudes, but collecting them in the abstract – that is, outside actual conversations. In such lists vacuous banalities come alive through the sheer enumeration, as well as entering into lively relationships with the individual incidents. This kind of generalising abstraction helps to make the particular typical, but it highlights instead of ironing-out the vividness of the particular itself. Several of Fielding's great set pieces of *actual* dialogue have a similar air of being stylised anthologies of cant phrases, too exactly and exclusively drawn from standard social jargon to be quite credible as realistic rendering, yet preserving in this stylised form both the rhythms of actual speech and the authentic play of disreputable attitudes. The famous quarrel between Mrs Western's maid and Mrs Honour shows phrases like 'their Betters', 'Hoity! toity!', 'Madam is in her Airs,' 'Marry, as good as yourself I hope,' 'Creature! you are below my Anger', in a self-absorbed ballet of highly vivid but formalised absurdity (*TJ*, VII: viii). The dialogue between Mrs Slipslop and Miss Grave-airs about admitting Joseph into the stagecoach likewise concentrates a mass of emotionally charged but utterly commonplace banalities, to a degree almost of ritual: 'Miss *Grave-airs* said, "some Folks, might sometimes give their Tongues a liberty, to some People that were their Betters, which did not become them: for her part, she was not used to converse with Servants." *Slipslop* returned, "some People kept no Servants to converse with"' (*JA*, II: v). The barbed phrases, the pointed use of the third person, are the standard usage of haughty pique. They convincingly suggest low people giving themselves the airs of high people, and they are charged with the crude emotions of the quarrelling women. But sheer ritual concentration makes the dialogue move by way of this realistic-typical notation to a world beyond realism, which derives its moral authenticity, as well as the proper pointing of ridicule, from a brilliant stylisation of the actual. Like other passages considered in this essay, the 'smart Dialogue between some People, and some Folks'[62] is something of a set piece, conspicuously holding the centre of the stage for its appointed length, and halted by further narrative developments only when it has fulfilled itself.[63] Fielding's exploitation of typical spoken usage has much the same function as his other stylisations, modifying the realism, giving the scene a certain air of authorial performance, suffusing it with comic life, yet making it vulnerable to a special kind of moral exposure. The tendency of such passages to the self-sufficiency of the set piece, like the self-feeding absurdity of the characters, gives the snobbery a motiveless, disembodied air, as of an irrepressible moral pedantry existing *in vacuo*.

The 'smart Dialogue' is further formalised by being partly in a form of semi-indirect speech which as we have seen Fielding was fond of exploiting. A more elaborate example is the dialogue between Joseph Andrews and Parson Barnabas (I: xiii). Joseph, after being robbed and beaten, is lying at an inn, where Parson Barnabas visits him:

> Mr. *Barnabas* was again sent for, and with much difficulty prevailed on to make another Visit. As soon as he entered the Room, he told *Joseph*, 'he was come to pray by him, and to prepare him for another World: In the first place therefore, he hoped he had repented of all his Sins?' *Joseph* answered, 'he hoped he had: but there was one thing which he knew not whether he should call a Sin; if it was, he feared he should die in the Commission of it, and that was the Regret of parting with a young Woman, whom he loved as tenderly as he did his Heartstrings?' *Barnabas* bad him be assured, 'that any Repining at the Divine Will, was one of the greatest Sins he could commit; that he ought to forget all carnal Affections, and think of better things.' *Joseph* said, 'that neither in this World nor the next, he could forget his *Fanny*, and that the Thought, however grievous, of parting from her for ever, was not half so tormenting, as the Fear of what she would suffer when she knew his Misfortune.' *Barnabas* said, 'that such Fears argued a Diffidence and Despondence very criminal; that he must divest himself of all human Passion, and fix his Heart above.' *Joseph* answered, 'that was what he desired to do, and should be obliged to him, if he would enable him to accomplish it.' *Barnabas* replied, 'That must be done by Grace.' *Joseph* besought him to discover how he might attain it. *Barnabas* answered, 'By Prayer and Faith.' He then questioned him concerning his Forgiveness of the Thieves. *Joseph* answered, 'he feared, that was more than he could do: for nothing would give him more Pleasure than to hear they were taken.' 'That,' cries *Barnabas*, 'is for the sake of Justice.' 'Yes,' said *Joseph*, 'but if I was to meet them again, I am afraid I should attack them, and kill them too, if I could.' 'Doubt-

less,' answered *Barnabas*, 'it is lawful to kill a Thief: but can you say, you forgive them as a Christian ought?' *Joseph* desired to know what that Forgiveness was. 'That is,' answered *Barnabas*, 'to forgive them as – as – it is to forgive them as – in short, it is to forgive them as a Christian.' *Joseph* reply'd, 'he forgave them as much as he could.' 'Well, well,' said *Barnabas*, 'that will do.' He then demanded of him, 'if he remembered any more Sins unrepented of; and if he did, he desired him to make haste and repent of them as fast as he could: that they might repeat over a few Prayers together.' *Joseph* answered, 'he could not recollect any great Crimes he had been guilty of, and that those he had committed, he was sincerely sorry for.' *Barnabas* said that was enough, and then proceeded to Prayer with all the expedition he was master of: Some Company then waiting for him below in the Parlour, where the Ingredients for Punch were all in Readiness; but no one would squeeze the Oranges till he came.

(I: xiii)

This pseudo-'death bed' dialogue with a bibulous parson may usefully be compared with the scene between Moll Flanders and the Ordinary of Newgate:

The Ordinary of *Newgate* came to me, and talk'd a little in his way, but all his Divinity run upon Confessing my Crime, as he call'd it, (tho' he knew not what I was in for) making a full Discovery, and the like, without which he told me God would never forgive me; and he said so little to the purpose, that I had no manner of Consolation from him; and then to observe the poor Creature preaching Confession and Repentance to me in the Morning, and find him drunk with Brandy and Spirits by Noon; this had something in it so shocking, that I began to Nauseate the Man more, than his Work, and his Work too by degrees for the sake of the Man; so that I desir'd him to trouble me no more.[64]

Moll's reporting of the chaplain's speech, brisk with indignation at its worthlessness, comes in the context of a state of mind so taken up with urgent fears of hanging and of hell that this worthlessness would be bound to strike her forcibly. Immediately before, she had described 'how I was harrass'd, between the dreadful Apprehensions of Death, and the Terror of my Conscience reproaching me with my past horrible Life.' In such a state of mind, the routine pieties of a disreputable parson might well be dismissed with a terse distaste such as the summarising account in indirect speech conveys. There is nothing of the set piece about Moll's paragraph. It describes a shabby episode as something that comes and goes, an event among others in a full factual and emotional context, and its feeling develops from the preceding mood with a complete and self-authenticating inner logic. The emotional charge in her account does not lead to anything resembling Fielding's externalising procedures: the facts remain naked, unclothed by any stylistic business, and intimately near.

When Mrs Barbauld spoke of Defoe's 'minuteness' as being 'more employed about things' than, like Richardson's, 'about persons and sentiments', she was speaking about *Robinson Crusoe* and the *Family Instructor*, not having read the novels proper.[65] But this description of Defoe's manner has sometimes been extended to the novels, and (despite the rough justice of the comparison with Richardson) it seems worth stressing that the entire Newgate sequence in *Moll Flanders* is more vividly concerned with the feelings of Moll than with the mere recording of what she sees and hears.[66] Fielding is normally and correctly described as much less interested in detailed particularities than Defoe. But it is arguable that more 'facts' about the Newgate scene, and especially about the people there, may be acquired from the Newgate chapters of *Amelia* than from *Moll Flanders*, even though Fielding is concerned to present these facts as moral or sociological 'examples', rather than as realistic detail for its own sake.[67] Similarly, as between the two dialogues, we learn a great deal more about what was said in Fielding's than in Defoe's, even though the intimacy with which we enter into the feelings of Fielding's characters and narrator is much less. That our sense of Fielding's implied 'presence' is much greater will surprise no one; but it is interesting to find him more 'particular.'

Thus, where Moll Flanders skimps the details of her parson's preachings because they are 'so little to the purpose' and her anxious feelings leave little time for him, Fielding opens up Barnabas's preachings into an animated ritual of vacuous self-revelation. The energetic particularity with which everything is put down becomes a pointed exposure of the moral nullity. Fielding's use of indirect speech is part of the piquancy of this contrast. Where Moll frankly summarises to get the account over quickly, Fielding dwells on the unabridged entirety of what is said, so that the summarising tendency of indirect speech makes the particularity seem especially absurd and mechanical. Fielding, unlike Moll, is not really, but 'artificially', in a hurry, and the indirect reporting, while preserving all the content of a more direct quotation, speeds the dialogue up just beyond its natural pace to the brisk tempo of a comic routine. As in the dialogues from *Shamela* and elsewhere discussed in the first half of this chapter, the automatic regularity of the narrative links, '*Joseph* said,' '*Barnabas* said,' '*Joseph* answered,' '*Barnabas* replied,' and so on, contributes to the clockwork effect.[68] Authorial domination and a sharp efficient wisdom are strongly established. The automatism conveys a quick and knowing grasp. As with the 'smart Dialogue between some People, and some Folks,' we are made to understand that in similar situations similar persons can invariably be relied upon to go on thus. Barnabas and Joseph, like the quarrelling ladies, become actors in a wildly extravagant collection of stock responses, and the highly circumstantial report is edged with a feeling of endless recurrence, of perpetual re-enactment 'these 4000 Years, and I hope . . . as many yet to come' (III: i).

Fielding's use of the past tense paradoxically supports this feeling. Neither Moll nor Fielding is much given to 'writing in the present Tense,' like Pamela or Shamela.[69] But Moll's past tense is merely part of the normal idiom of her chronicle and places the incident (however typical it may or may not be of Newgate parsons) as a single event in her story. As the syntax of *oratio obliqua* obviously requires, Fielding's past tense highlights itself by entering into the very fabric of what is said in the dialogue: 'he told *Joseph*, "he was come to pray by him, and to prepare him for another World: In the first place therefore, he hoped he had repented of all his Sins?"' But the point about this is not so much that it introduces further layers of remoteness in time, as that (unlike Moll's or Pamela's normally quite unselfconscious use of indirect speech) it reinforces the feeling of mechanical repetition. Fielding's particularity aims neither at the immediacy of present reality, nor at a scrupulous reconstruction of the past. It is a particularity of the typical, celebrated not by the 'naked' truth but with the full honours of authorial 'performance.'

This suggests that the correlation sometimes implied by critics of the early English novel, between a 'naked' or unstylised notation, and circumstantial particularity or even prolixity, is not always justified. The Royal Society scientists had many years before claimed that a 'naked, natural way of speaking' would tend on the contrary to be very concise.[70] Scientific conciseness is not of course the same thing as a detailed novelistic recording of events and feelings; but it does share with the often prolix styles of

Defoe and Richardson a readiness (absent in Fielding) to treat facts 'nakedly', without the distancing veil of stylised interference. 'Nakedness' and 'prolixity' were thought of as going together from an early date. An amusing illustration is Lady Mary Wortley Montagu's famous complaint about Clarissa's habit of 'declaring all she thinks to all the people she sees, without reflecting that in this Mortal state of Imperfection Fig leaves are as necessary for our Minds as our Bodies, and tis as indecent to shew all we think as all we have.'[71] The real point of the 'Fig leaves' is not of course that Clarissa (or Richardson) gave many details that were indecent, but that it was indecent of them to give so many details. Involved in it is a recoil, both gentlemanly and neo-classic, from, as Fielding put it in the Preface to the *Voyage to Lisbon*, 'recording things and facts of so common a kind, that they challenge no other right of being remembered, than as they had the honour of having happened to the author, to whom nothing seems trivial that in any manner happens to himself.' This point is often made by courtesy-writers, in their prescription of conversational good manners, and is often thus extended to literary styles. Fielding's preface says that the only small incidents which his journal records are those which 'naturally' give rise to 'some observations and reflections.'

This distaste for the 'naked' immediacy of fact also motivates many procedures of 'style', which was, after all, the *dress* of thought: procedures of decorous distancing, ironic indirection, and generalising implication (which makes a fact more than a *mere* fact). The traditional metaphor of 'dress' should in this context be understood not primarily in the expected way, as a matter of accommodation of style to subject, but as a stylistic covering for what would otherwise seem a bare circumstantial notation. Provided the stylistic protections were sufficiently firm, the particular and the specific could be allowed a good deal of play. Fielding can turn certain kinds of circumstantiality in themselves into signs of an expansive stylisation. In the dialogue between Joseph and Barnabas the strongly rendered implications of typicality give an edge to the specific exchange, without significantly blurring its individual force. It is remarkable how exactly this style of brisk summarising dispatch captures Barnabas's very special kind of lazy patness, the readiness with which his pedantic legalism peters out in a muddled get-it-over-with laxity when Joseph agrees to forgive 'as much as he could', and the Pickwickian conviviality with which he hurries back to the parlour to 'squeeze the Oranges' for punch.

This delightful detail about squeezing the oranges is in its way more circumstantial than Moll Flanders's bare remark that her parson was 'drunk with Brandy and Spirits by Noon'. But the real difference is that it is flecked with Fielding's sharp but companionable irony. The small detail adds its own animation to the portrait, but not so much because it contributes to a full record, as because of a selective vividness which conveys Fielding's mixed feelings of affection and censure, and his fun. The detail adds to our knowledge of Barnabas, but convivially (that is, at a social distance) rather than intimately. Contrast the closeness of emotional hostility in Moll Flanders's remark; and *a fortiori* in one of Pamela's comments about Mrs Jewkes, 'I dare say she drinks'.[72] Fielding's special use in this dialogue of indirect or semi-indirect speech, and of the past tense, emphasises the kind of controlling and externalising authorial 'presence' which defines his 'realism', in Ian Watt's language, as a 'realism of assessment' rather than of 'presentation.' It is not, however, the mere grammatical forms but a certain witty manipulation that differentiates Fielding from Richardson or Defoe. Richardson's or Defoe's narrators both, after all, use indirect speech and the past tense[73] and can indeed make them convey ironic or indignant commentary rather than mere neutral reporting. But they seldom use it to convey a feeling of distance or superiority in the narrator or author, whereas Fielding is very fond of playing with forms of indirect speech for exactly this and related purposes.

When Mrs Western tries to get her brother the squire, as a magistrate, to punish Mrs Honour for having cast aspersions on her beauty, the magistrate's clerk feels compelled to warn that 'you cannot legally commit anyone to *Bridewell* only for Ill-breeding'. Western knows that a magistrate nevertheless has considerable discretionary powers, but since the offence, not being against the laws of hunting, is of limited gravity, he is prepared to take his clerk's advice. 'The Squire, therefore, putting on a most wise and significant Countenance, after a Preface of several Hum's and Ha's, told his Sister, that upon mature Deliberation, he was of Opinion that "as there was no breaking up of the Peace, such as the Law," says he, "calls breaking open a Door, or breaking a Hedge, or breaking a Head; or any such Sort of Breaking; the Matter did not amount to a felonious Kind of Thing, nor Trespasses nor Damages, and, therefore, there was no Punishment in the Law for it"' (*TJ*, VII: ix). The narrator, in such high spirits, is here almost a raconteur, and any incredulity at Western's headlong absurdity is disarmed by our willingness to share the raconteur's fun rather than question his truth; straight dialogue, unless hedged with other stylisations which we have seen Fielding use, would more readily tend to strain belief. This indirect speech purports to record as completely as any straight dialogue, but does not emulate its impartiality or self-effacement. If the narrator is straight-faced, it is so as to bring out the squire in his full comic splendour. If he is aloof, it is to establish himself as a superior presence.

It may indeed be that, despite the example of Defoe and Richardson, certain kinds of indirect reporting of speech or thought tend towards an effect of authorial superiority, whether intended or not, and this effect is probably accentuated when dialectal or idiosyncratic forms of speech are being reproduced. In Fielding this superiority often emerges as that of the comic artist over a predictably erring humanity, or again that of an urbane and gentlemanly Augustan sage. There is no doubt that Fielding is consciously committed to these attitudes and tones. But compare this passage from Ford Madox Ford, who set great store by authorial self-effacement and who complained of Fielding's gentlemanly posturing.[74]

> Sergeant-Major Cowley, his form blocking the doorway, surveyed the stars. He found it difficult to realize that the same pinpricks of light through black manifolding paper as he looked at, looked down also on his villa and his elderly wife at Isleworth beside the Thames above London. He knew it to be the fact, yet it was difficult to realize. He imagined the trams going along the High Street, his missus in one of them with her supper in a string bag on her stout knees. The trams lit up and shining. He imagined her having kippers for supper: ten to one it would be kippers. Her favourites. His daughter was at the w.a.a.c.'s by now. She had been cashier to Parks's, the big butchers in Brentford, and pretty she had used to look in the glass case. Like as if it might have been the British Museum where they had Pharoahs and others in glass cases.... There were threshing machines droning away all over the night. He always said they were like threshing machines.... Crikey, if only they were! ... But they might be our own planes, of course. A good welsh rarebit he had had for tea.[75]

Ford's narrator in *No More Parades*, unlike Dowell in *The Good Soldier*, is unnamed, and seems to approximate to what Ford called an 'official Author'.[76] He is of course not to be confused with the hero Tietjens. Nevertheless he is sometimes impregnated with Tietjens's romantic squirearchism, and has for this sergeant-major in Tietjens's command something of Tietjens's own affectionate paternalism. This at least is the effect of Ford's attempt to enter into the sergeant's thoughts, while keeping the sergeant's idiom slightly at bay through the narrator's reporting voice. The effort to create a sober particularised illusion of the sergeant's consciousness creates a form of free indirect style which belies any apparent or presupposed neutrality in the narrator's voice. Phrases like 'and pretty she had used to look', 'like as if it might have been the British Museum', and 'a good welsh rarebit he had had for tea' come over with a condescension which the reader cannot help taking, at least in part, as a class-conscious emanation of the authorial voice. The passage is by no means representative of Ford's distinguished best. But Ford often rebuked Fielding for supercilious intrusion, and it is open to us to prefer Fielding's undisguised and morally generous presence to the somewhat mealy-mouthed uppishness of Ford's passage. Fielding does not involve us in illusions of actuality, and thus does not run Ford's particular risks. The mimicry of Western's subliterate demotics belongs so much to fantasticating comedy that any offensiveness is unlikely to arise: nor does this particular scene involve *social* superiority. But it can be said for Fielding's patrician *hauteurs* that they not only have the chance to declare themselves frankly, but that they are at their most stinging when directed at arrogant pride of rank or vulgar pretensions to gentility.

When Fielding says that 'Mrs. *Western's* Maid claimed great Superiority over Mrs. *Honour*' because 'her Birth was higher: For her great Grand-mother by the Mother's Side was a Cousin, not far removed, to an *Irish* Peer,' he is, in a rudimentary way, purporting to render her state of mind (and doing so, once again, through a comic idiom of almost anthologised typicality).[77] What is irony from him is her sober thinking, rather as, in the passage from *Jonathan Wild* about Theodosia Snap, Fielding's irony entered into the mind of canting hypocrites like Laetitia. The irony is in both cases very obvious, because the states of mind are rendered in their full moral outrageousness rather than their realistic form. There is no serious invitation to enter into the characters' consciousness, and every invitation to share Fielding's implied comment. If illusion is lacking, there is no lack either of narrative vitality or of a humanly attractive and centrally relevant moral viewpoint. Ford's passage suggests that a formal practice of self-effacement, or purist ambitions that way, do not, on the other hand, necessarily guard against intrusive impressions of actual authorial attitude; that a high degree of illusion may even intensify such impressions where they occur; and that there may indeed be a special risk of unguarded and damaging self-projections from the author's sheer security in his formal self-effacement. An example from Richardson, whom Ford admired, will illustrate this. Pamela is talking about Mrs Jewkes: 'I was sadly teazed with her impertinence and bold way; but no wonder; she was an inn-keeper's house-keeper, before she came to my master; and those sort of creatures don't want confidence, you know.'[78]

This comes from one of the most brilliant scenes in *Pamela*, showing Mrs Jewkes wielding power over Pamela in her repellently ingratiating way and combining a bullying pandarism with a vivid element of arch Lesbian heartiness. Pamela's words are a masterly, *un*stylised notation of actual usage, without witty interference or any formal shapeliness of sentence or phrase. Even the neatness of 'an inn-keeper's house-keeper' is not a sign of conscious verbal craftsmanship, but an idiomatic form of verbal play, in very common use. The phrase 'gentleman's gentleman' (for a footman or valet) occurs in Steele in 1703, twenty-two years earlier than the *OED*'s first example (from Defoe).[79] Trapwit in Fielding's *Pasquin* speaks of the Mayoress in his play as having 'been Woman to a Woman of Quality'; and Mrs Western's maid haughtily tells Mrs Honour that 'in Town I visit none but the Women of Women of Quality.'[80]

Pamela speaks as a maidservant might well have spoken, both in her idiom and presumably in the sentiment expressed. Richardson's genius to render this with great authenticity and vividness is something Fielding cannot normally match. Only, in order to speak thus, the maidservant would need, whatever her other virtues, to be arrogant, complacent, and mealy-mouthed, like Mrs Western's maid, or more especially perhaps like the sort of person Fielding read into *Pamela* and Richardson never meant.[81] Thus, despite the masterly rendering in a narrow sense, the words reflect a Pamela somewhat other than the one which the novel as a whole invites us to see, and by that fact creates an illusion-breaking shock that diverts attention momentarily to the author. It seems a sign not merely of a technical lapse but of moral obtuseness that Richardson should take such remarks for granted as raising no moral problems and leaving his heroine unscathed. The notion that this is simply dramatic notation without any participation by the author cannot be entertained. Unlike Ford, Richardson did not feel committed to a rigorous theory of self-effacement. The general feeling of his novel, moreover, tends to suggest endorsement of what the heroine says or does. It also induces in us the habit of expecting that anything meant to be taken as reprehensible will be voluminously pointed out. (Pamela is virtually the only narrator, but she quotes what people write and say to her, and plenty of openings for corrective views exist).[82] On a matter like this and in such a context, an absence of authorial disengagement, however lightly hinted, readily turns into an uncomfortable sense of authorial presence. And the personality which imposes itself unavoidably at such moments, however unconsciously and with whatever actual relation to the biographical Richardson, is one which has understandably repelled many of Richardson's readers. The point is not that Fielding would have been incapable of recording sentiments like Pamela's, but that he would normally have felt compelled to present them as repellent. No character of his can get away unscathed with saying 'those sort of creatures' of anyone, and if intrusion is the price to pay for this, it may be felt not to be too high.

1971–1974

Notes

1 Quotations from Fielding use the Wesleyan edition (Oxford, 1967–) for works already published in that edition. *Shamela* is cited from *Joseph Andrews and Shamela*, ed. Douglas Brooks (London, Oxford and New York, 1971); *Jonathan Wild* from the first edition text as reprinted in World's Classics (London, 1961). Other works are from *Works*, ed. W. E. Henley (London, 1903).

2 The Richardsonian original of this particular sentence is 'he offered to take me on his knee, with some force. O now I was terrified!', where 'offered' describes a positive, unhesitant and alarming attempt (*Pamela*, Letter XV, Everyman's Library, 1955, 19–20). Presumably Fielding is mimicking Pamela's habit of detailing events so minutely that even things which did not happen are recorded, as well as reversing the Richardsonian pattern in which it is the heroine who is passive and the hero aggressive. But *mere* parody would be content with inventing a lecherous young booby who gives hot, gauche kisses (i.e. Mr B. made oafish), instead of turning him also into a reluctant rapist: that this refinement is parodically apt enough does not cancel the fact that Mr Booby becomes by way of it something of a primary Fielding type.

3 Thus the unHerculean Booby, whose sexual stirrings are real but easily cooled, seems in some ways a country version, as well as something of a preliminary sketch, of the effeminate Didapper who was 'No Hater of Women; for he always dangled after them; yet so little subject to Lust, that he had . . . the Character of great Moderation in his Pleasures' (*Joseph Andrews*, IV: ix); and who, when he tries to rape Fanny, begins (like Booby) by rapping

301

'out half a dozen Oaths', but is 'soon out of breath' and quickly discouraged (*Joseph Andrews*, IV: vii; cf. also *Shamela*, Letter II, where Booby 'kissed me again, and breathed very short, and looked very silly', but where, however, the breathlessness is not altogether unambiguously due to premature exhaustion. Booby is less purposeful than the 'Jolly Blades' of an older generation, but he does have 'some hot Blood' (Letter VI), and seems to acquit himself 'well enough' on his wedding night, though not up to the standard of Parson Williams (see Shamela's last letter)). It is an apt coincidence that Lord Hervey, the original of Didapper, should (under the name of Miss Fanny) be the mock-dedicatee of *Shamela*.

Perhaps Shamela's 'spindle-shanked young Squire' (Shamela's last letter) should also be linked in a general way with the type of the 'spindle-shanked beau', which earns many a brief mention or sketchy appearance in Fielding's other writings: *Eurydice* (1737; *Works*, ed. Henley, XI: 272 ff.); *The Fathers; Or, The Good-Natured Man* (largely written before 1743, posthumously produced and published 1778), II. i (*Works*, XII: 173); *Joseph Andrews*, III: ii.

Booby's driving oafishness compares more obviously with Jonathan Wild's and Squire Western's; and the amalgam of this quality with a spindle-shanked or Didapperish unmanliness has some piquancy.

4   *Ubu sur la Butte*, I.i, in *Tout Ubu*, ed. Maurice Saillet (Paris, 1962), 462.

5   cf. Swift, *Tale of a Tub*, XI, *Works*, I: 126; Pope, *A Further Account of the Most Deplorable Condition of Mr. Edmund Curll*, 1716, *Prose Works*, ed. Norman Ault, I (Oxford, 1936), 276 (the passage resembles Shamela's letter in more than one detail: 'he . . . *read* Rochester's *bawdy Poems* . . . gave *Oldmixon* a *slap* on the *Chops*, and wou'd have kiss'd Mr *Pemberton's* A— *by Violence*'). All quotations from Arbuthnot are from *The History of John Bull*, ed. A. W. Bower and R. A. Erickson (Oxford, 1976).

6   *Moll Flanders*, ed. G. A. Starr (London and Oxford, 1976), p. 239.

7   Helmut Bonheim, 'Inquits', in *The Narrative Modes* (Cambridge, 1982), 75–90, esp. (on Defoe) 85–9. Bonheim also has interesting observations on the use of past and present tenses in inquits, noting for example that in *Moll Flanders* 'the memoir-writing narrator sometimes prefers the past-tense-inquit for herself, the present-tense-inquit for her interlocutor at the time' (p. 85), though both forms are used of both speakers in the passage I quoted. On this question see the Appendix, 'Narrative Tense and Direct Quotation', in Mark Lambert, *Dickens and the Suspended Quotation* (New Haven and London, 1981), 142–51, 182, esp. 146–8 on *Moll Flanders*.

8   Bonheim, 88–9. Lambert discusses the inquits in a dialogue from *Tom Jones*, principally in terms of their informative function (*Dickens and the Suspended Quotation*, 97–100).

9   *Robinson Crusoe*, ed. G. H. Maynadier (Boston, 1903), II: 38. Compare H. W. Fowler, *A Dictionary of Modern English Usage* (2nd ed., Oxford, 1965), s.v. 'Inversion in Dialogue Machinery', 302 on novelists who are 'unduly worried' by the 'machinery problem' of reporting dialogue.

10 *Sir Charles Grandison*, ed. Jocelyn Harris (London and New York, 1972), I: 273. For similar comments on the nuisance of inquits, and the value of dramatic notation, in French writers of the period, see Vivienne Mylne, 'Dialogue as Narrative in Eighteenth-Century French Fiction', in J. H. Fox, M. H. Waddicor and D. A. Watts (eds), *Studies in Eighteenth-Century French Literature Presented to Robert Niklaus* (Exeter, 1975), 174, 176, 189 n.15. For a checklist of French fiction in dialogue-form, see 190–2.

11 *Correspondence of Samuel Richardson*, ed. A. L. Barbauld (1804), I: xxvi–xxvii; *Critical Remarks on Sir Charles Grandison, Clarissa and Pamela* (1754), 11.

12 George Sherburn, 'Samuel Richardson's Novels and the Theatre: A Theory Sketched', *Philological Quarterly*, XLI (1962), 327–8.

13 *Clarissa*, Everyman's Library (London and New York, 1932), III: 30, 32. These examples are cited by Sherburn, 328, and see 327. The most important recent studies of Richardson's 'dramatic' style (and much else besides) are Mark Kinkead-Weekes, *Samuel Richardson, Dramatic Novelist* (London, 1973), and Margaret Anne Doody, *A Natural Passion. A Study of the Novels of Samuel Richardson* (Oxford, 1974).

14 The phrase 'to the *Moment*' is from Richardson's preface to *Sir Charles Grandison*, I: 4.

15 Bonheim, 77.

16 cf. William Hogarth, *The Analysis of Beauty*, ed. Joseph Burke (Oxford, 1955), 161: 'Action consider'd with regard to assisting the authors meaning, by enforcing the sentiments or raising the passions, must be left entirely to the judgment of the performer . . .'. Fielding, as a playwright, doubtless knew how much 'assisting' and 'enforcing' was inevitably in the hands of performers, but his instinct would be to counteract this as much as possible. Hogarth is distinguishing not between author and performer, but between general principles of stage deportment and the needs of particular performances.

17 cf. Lambert's interesting discussion of the 'suspended quotation' in Dickens as an instrument of antagonism and indeed a form of 'class warfare' against his own characters (*Dickens and the Suspended Quotation*, 70 ff.).

18 I differ from the view expressed by F. W. Bateson, *English Comic Drama 1700–1750* (New York, 1963), 142–3: 'In each of his burlesques (except *Tom Thumb*, where the footnotes take its place) there is a central character, or group of characters, that acts as a commentator upon the play as it progresses. In *The Author's Farce* it is Luckless, the "Master of the Show"; in *Pasquin* it is the trio of Trapwit, Fustian, and Sneerwell; in *Tumble-Down Dick* it is Machine; in *The Historical Register* it is Medley. It is impossible not to see in these characters a device which would permit Fielding to indulge in the same comments and interpolations he was later to employ (with less justification, it seems to me) in the novels. They were a safety valve. In everything but name they were *ipsissimus* Henry Fielding'. My argument is that they are usually rather weak precisely because they cannot be '*ipsissimus* Henry Fielding', whereas the novelistic narrators can, though *ipsissimus* should not imply (in Fielding any more than in other novelists) any simple identity between narrator and real-life author.

19 *Works*, XI: 178.

20 Another difference is that Trapwit speaks in advance, whereas the footnote in *Joseph Andrews* comes after we have experienced most of the dialogue (see also below, n.23). But this is not in itself as important a difference as it might seem. The chapter-heading to *Amelia*, XI: i, 'Containing a very polite Scene', comes, like Trapwit's announcement, before the event. But though its sarcasm falls on duller ground than in *Joseph Andrews*, in the sense that the ensuing scene (as so often in *Amelia*) falls short of Fielding's best work as a novelist, it nevertheless suffuses the scene with a firm authorial acerbity which has Fielding's eloquent stamp.

21 It is also immediately preceded by a formal 'character' of the Beau, which is not only a set piece in a traditional genre but specifically recalls Pope's famous recent portrait of Sporus (*Epistle to Dr Arbuthnot* (1735), ll. 305 ff.) attacking the same historical personage, Lord Hervey. Both Pope and Fielding present Hervey as a sexually ambiguous 'thing', and Fielding, in the sentence

immediately preceding the quoted passage, further fantasticates Didapper into a sort of obscenely effeminate bird (a didapper is a dabchick): 'Such was the little Person or rather Thing that hopped after Lady *Booby* into Mr. *Adams*'s Kitchin'.

22 *Works*, VIII: 106–7.

23 Martin C. Battestin cites Vanbrugh, *A Journey to London* (1728), IV. i, in a note to this passage in his Wesleyan Edition of *Joseph Andrews* (Oxford, 1967), 314. Fielding's footnote about 'very polite Conversation' is keyed to the word 'Face' and refers most directly to that specific insult; but it is hard to resist the feeling that it extends to the whole set-piece in a more general way (see above, n.20 and p. 272).

24 Mark Lambert has noted Fielding's preference for relatively 'neutral' inquits, i.e. straightforward terms like *answer* rather than more 'literary' wordings like *reply* or *return*, by comparison with Dickens's practice (*Dickens and the Suspended Quotation*, 16–17). My argument, however, concerns the *pointedness*, the manifest interventionism, with which even such linguistically 'neutral' inquits are used in Fielding. In that sense, the linguistically neutral is stylistically anything but neutral.

25 Fielding's inferiority as a playwright has from time to time been accounted for in terms similar to these. Scott's illuminating discussion, *Lives of Eminent Novelists, etc.*, Chandos Classics, [n.d.], 421 ff., emphasises a general incompatibility between the arts of the novelist and of the playwright, whereas it seems to me that the major explanation lies in those aspects of Fielding's personality which made a self-effacing medium uncongenial *to him*. I would, however, dissociate this view from Leslie Stephen's shallow and patronising account: 'Fielding will not efface himself; he is always present as chorus; he tells us what moral we ought to draw; he overflows with shrewd remarks, given in their most downright shape, instead of obliquely suggested through the medium of anecdotes; he likes to stop us as we pass through his portrait gallery; to take us by the button-hole and expound his views of life and his criticisms on things in general. His remarks are often so admirable that we prefer the interpolations to the main current of narrative. Whether this plan is the best must depend upon the idiosyncrasy of the author; but it goes some way to explain one problem, over which Scott puzzles himself – namely, why Fielding's plays are so inferior to his novels. There are other reasons, external and internal; but it is at least clear that a man who can never retire behind his puppets is not in the dramatic frame of mind. He is always lecturing where a dramatist must be content to pull the wires. Shakespeare is really as much present in his plays as Fielding in his novels; but he does not let us know it; whereas the excellent Fielding seems to be quite incapable of hiding his broad shoulders and lofty stature behind his little puppet-show' (*Hours in a Library*, London, 1909, II: 169–70). Stephen appears to think that he is, at least partly, praising Fielding, and Ford's frankly hostile attacks on Fielding's 'moustache-twisting, cane-twirling, gold ball juggling' interventions seem preferable in comparison (*The March of Literature*, London, 1947, 532–3).

Stephen was by no means the first to use the puppet image in this way. Scott said that Smollett, unlike Fielding, 'manages his delightful puppet-show without thrusting his head beyond the curtain' (*Lives of Eminent Novelists and Dramatists*, London, n.d. [Chandos Classics], 466). Richard Cumberland used the image in 1795 in his *Henry*, I: i, on the subject of his own management of his novel, suggesting that he will not 'play my puppets after my own fancy' in any wanton way. To be fair to Stephen, the puppet-image was not always in such contexts felt to be derogatory, as A.J.

Hassall points out: 'Fielding's Puppet Image', *Philological Quarterly*, LIII (1974), 71–83, esp. 71–2. The article provides a good general account of Fielding's interest in puppetry and his use of the puppet metaphor. The classic example in fiction of a puppet-show which brings up the question of fictional 'illusion' and the dangers of mistaking art for life is in *Don Quixote*, II: xxvi. I do not know when 'puppet' came to be used in an unequivocally or mainly bad sense in relation to novels: perhaps James's Preface to *The Princess Casamassima* contains an example (*The Art of the Novel*, ed. R. P. Blackmur, New York and London, n.d., p. 74).

26 *Works*, XII: 93–4. My italics. Though produced and published in 1743, the play was written in its original form in 1730.
27 In *Don Quixote in England* (1734), and *The Fathers; Or, The Good-Natured Man*. Such stage squires also appeared in novels by Richardson (see Doody, *A Natural Passion*, 284–85) and Smollett (*Ferdinand Count Fathom*, ch. xxiv). On Western's type of West Country speech, its use in plays and novels, and the attitude of contemporaneous readers to such dialectal forms, see J. M. S. Tompkins, *The Popular Novel in England, 1770–1800* (London, 1932), 188 and n.3; Norman Page, *Speech in the English Novel* (London, 1973), 54–6. See Pope's burlesque composition, as by 'this old *West Country* Bard of ours', a joke at the expense of Ambrose Philips's pastorals, in *Guardian*, no. 40, 27 April 1713.
28 Arbuthnot's series of *John Bull* pamphlets ends with a blowsy operatic finale, including a comic element of choric repetition: '*J. Bull*. Extremely glad? *All*. Extremely glad, Sir' (V: viii). For some suggestive reflections on the 'operatic' element in Fielding, see Michael Bell, 'A Note on Drama and the Novel: Fielding's Contribution', *Novel*, III (1970), 125.
29 Contrast the scenes where Western shows his anger at Sophia's refusal to marry Blifil (e.g. *Tom Jones*, VI: vii, or the chapter now under discussion, VII: iii), with similar situations between Sir Gregory Kennel and his son in *The Fathers; Or, The Good-Natured Man*, III: ii and V: iv (*Works*, XII: 192–3, 223–5).
30 On such reticences and mock-bewilderments, and their somewhat paradoxical gentlemanly flavour, see my *Henry Fielding and the Augustan Ideal Under Stress*, 75, 84–86. Such phrases partly suggest a gentlemanly superiority that will not stop to enquire into small details (while hiding nothing from us in fact) or embarrass us with unseemly language (while giving us all we need to go on).
31 *Tom Jones*, VII: iii.
32 Thus 'F—t' can be uttered by Western, and not so easily by Fielding, and gains part of its special force from the contrast with the author's periphrastic formulation, which describes the action as the very one 'which, of all others, was the most proper' to what Western said.
33 On the *pétomane* (one 'who lets farts! at command!'), see *The Autobiography of William Carlos Williams* (New York, 1967), p. 40; and the account of Pujol, a famous *pétomane*, by Peter Lennon in the *Guardian*, 13 July 1967. For a fine petomanic exploit in an eighteenth-century novel, see the Harlequin episode in *Peregrine Pickle*, ed. James L. Clifford (Oxford English Novels, 1964), ch. lxx, 348–9. There is a display of willed precision-farting by Giton in Petronius, *Satyricon*, 117.
34 Norman Mailer, *An American Dream* (London, 1966), ch. iii, 69: 'The fat detective farted. Abrupt as that', in effect a deflating response to a speech by the main character and narrator Rojack, who seems to take it that way.
35 This is amusingly highlighted in Roger Vitrac's play, *Victor ou les Enfants au*

Pouvoir, II. v, where Ida, a character afflicted with abdominal wind, describes herself as the envy of no one except 'le pétomane de l'Eldorado'. The play was produced by Artaud in the Théâtre Alfred Jarry in 1928.

36 Fart routines in comedy go back at least as far as *The Clouds* of Aristophanes (e.g. ll. 388 ff.). For a twentieth-century example see preceding note.

37 The author of *An Essay on the New Species of Writing Founded by Mr. Fielding*, 1751, 29, noted that the novelist 'may ingraft in his Performance many Characters and Circumstances, which tho' they are entirely natural and very probable, often fall below the Dignity of the Stage.'

38 *Tom Jones*, XII: v. For Punch and farting, see Swift's poem, 'Mad Mullinix and Timothy', ll. 121–2: 'In doleful Scenes, that breaks our heart,/ Punch comes, like you, and lets a F—t' (*Poems*, III: 777; see also III: 783, 784, 788); cf. Garrick to Robert Lloyd, c. May 1761: 'If he has attacked me merely because I am the Punch of the puppet-show, I shall not turn my back upon him, and salute him in Punch's fashion . . .'. (*Letters of David Garrick*, ed. David M. Little and George M. Kahrl (London, 1963), I: 338). I owe these references to George Speaight.

39 Martin C. Battestin, 'Fielding and "Master Punch" in Panton Street', *Philological Quarterly*, XLV (1966), 191–208. The activities of this theatre were in part satirical, and attended by 'unusually distinguished' audiences (194). As we might expect, Fielding's experiments in puppet theatre seem to have been sophisticated.

40 Cited Battestin, *op. cit*, 193, from *The General Advertiser*, 30 March 1748.

41 *An Examen of the History of Tom Jones, a Foundling*, 1750, 34; on p. 82, it is said, with reference to *Tom Jones*, XII: v, that Fielding '*loves a Puppet-shew*' (Cited Battestin, *op. cit.*, 196–7n.).

42 Compare also Fielding's account of Western's use of the 'Kick your a—. You kiss —' vulgarism. In *Shamela*, as we saw, the exchange seems very realistic, though it simultaneously has overtones of stage-farce. In *Tom Jones*, such vulgarisms are sometimes ritualised through all the familiar periphrastic routines of the narrator's style, which turn them into a kind of patterned and habitual verbal ceremony, and yet insist that they are also a simple part of everyday life among country gentlemen. Thus, in VI: ix, Western berates Tom:

> He then bespattered the Youth with Abundance of that Language, which passes between Country Gentlemen who embrace opposite Sides of the Question; with frequent Applications to him to salute that Part which is generally introduced into all Controversies, that arise among the lower Orders of the *English* Gentry, at Horse-races, Cock-matches, and other public Places. Allusions to this Part are likewise often made for the Sake of the Jest. And here, I believe, the Wit is generally misunderstood. In Reality, it lies in desiring another to kiss your A— for having just before threatened to kick his: For I have observed very accurately, that no one ever desires you to kick that which belongs to himself, nor offers to kiss this Part in another.
>
> It may likewise seem surprizing, that in the many thousand kind Invitations of this Sort, which every one who hath conversed with Country Gentlemen, must have heard, no one, I believe, hath ever seen a single Instance where the Desire hath been complied with. A great Instance of their Want of Politeness: For in Town, nothing can be more common than for the finest Gentlemen to perform this Ceremony every Day to their Superiors, without having that Favour once requested of them.

43 For some special aspects of Fielding's pleasure in the habitual phrase, see

Sheridan Baker, 'Henry Fielding and the Cliché', I (1959), 354–61. A good recent treatment of Fielding's interest in language and in the social uses and abuses of language in his day is Glen W. Hatfield, *Henry Fielding and the Language of Irony* (Chicago and London, 1968).

44   *Critical Remarks on Sir Charles Grandison, Clarissa and Pamela* (London, 1754), 4. See Ian Watt, *The Rise of the Novel* (London, 1957), 195. Garrick is said to have told Johnson, soon after his *Dictionary* was published, that people 'objected that he cited authorities which were beneath the dignity of such a work, and mentioned Richardson'. Johnson said he had 'done worse than that' and had cited Garrick himself: see G. B. Hill and L. F. Powell (eds.), *Boswell's Life of Johnson*, IV (Oxford, 1934), 4 and n.3. For praise of Richardson's coinages, see *A Candid Examination of the History of Sir Charles Grandison*, 3rd edn. (London, 1755), 38–9.

45   *O.E.D.* credits Richardson with the first use of *meditatingly*, but *scrupulosity* goes back at least as far as 1526 in the singular and 1600 in the plural.

46   Chesterfield to David Mallet, 5 November 1753, cited in A. D. McKillop, *Samuel Richardson, Printer and Novelist* ([n.p.], 1960), 220. Lady Mary Wortley Montagu to Lady Bute, 20 October 1755, *Complete Letters*, ed. Robert Halsband (Oxford, 1965–67), III: 96–7. Walpole to Sir Horace Mann, 20 December 1764, *Correspondence*, ed. W. S. Lewis *et al.*, XXII (London, 1960), 271. There is an interesting discussion of Lady Mary's view of Richardson by her granddaughter, Lady Louisa Stuart, in her 'Biographical Anecdotes of Lady M. W. Montagu', in *Lady Mary Wortley Montagu, Essays and Poems*, ed. Robert Halsband and Isobel Grundy (Oxford, 1977), 49–50.

47   Pope, *Essay on Criticism*, ll. 333–4.

48   *Sir Charles Grandison*, I: 263; Hogarth, *Analysis of Beauty*, 191.

49   *Champion*, 13 March 1739–40, *Works*, XV: 242; *Amelia*, X: ix; *Pamela*, Everyman's Library (London and New York, 1955), I: 91; Richardson to Astraea and Minerva Hill, 4 August 1749, *Selected Letters of Samuel Richardson*, ed. John Carroll (Oxford, 1964), 128.

50   Chesterfield, *Letters*, ed. B. Dobrée (London, 1932), IV:1407, 27 September 1749. For a fuller survey of notions of 'correctness', and their relation to gentlemanly standards of usage, see S. A. Leonard, *The Doctrine of Correctness in English Usage, 1700–1800* (New York, 1962 [reprint]), esp. chapter X; and see Hatfield, *op. cit.*, 109 ff.

51   John Lawlor, 'Radical Satire and the Realistic Novel', *Essays and Studies*, N.S. VIII (1955), 59.

52   The author of *An Essay on the New Species of Writing Founded by Mr. Fielding* (London, 1751), 29, described a crude form of this: '. . . these very kind of Books I am treating of fall into the Hands of a Set of People who are apt to cry out, on the Sight of any Thing that gives a lively Representation of the Manners of the common People, – Oh! that's cursed low, intolerably vulgar, &c.'. Even Richardson was censured for 'not altogether unexceptionable' language (see A. D. McKillop, *Samuel Richardson*, 48).

53   See Richardson to Lady Bradshaigh, 23 February 1752, *Selected Letters*, 198.

54   McKillop, *Samuel Richardson*, 220. See above, n.46.

55   *Tom Jones*, XII: v. On the anti-low in the theatre, see also *Tom Jones*, V: i and VII: i.

56   The canting puppet-master in *Tom Jones*, XII: v, prides himself on having resisted the wishes of 'some of the Quality at *Bath*, two or three Years ago, [who] wanted mightily to bring *Punch* again upon the Stage'. For some discussion of this passage, see Martin C. Battestin, 'Fielding and "Master Punch" in Panton Street', *Philological Quarterly*, XLV (1966), 194.

57 *Covent-Garden Journal*, No. 10, 4 February 1752, ed. G. E. Jensen (New Haven, 1915), I: 194; No. 52, 30 June 1752, Jensen, II: 47–8.

58 *Joseph Andrews*, II: xiii. See also the list in *Champion*, 26 February 1739–40, *Works*, XV: 218. Fielding dealt, in several other essays, with the jargon of various social classes: *Champion*, 17 January 1739–40, *Works*, XV: 157–61; *Covent-Garden Journal*, No. 4, 14 January 1752, Jensen, I: 153–7; No. 27, 4 April 1752, Jensen, I: 293–8; No. 37, 9 May 1752, Jensen, I: 344–49.

59 John Cleland, *Memoirs of a Coxcomb* (New York, 1974 [facsimile reprint of 1751 edition]), 103–4.

60 For an account of some uses of free indirect style in Fielding, see Alfred McDowell, 'Fielding's Rendering of Speech in *Joseph Andrews* and *Tom Jones*', *Language and Style*, VI (1973), 83–96. See also, with reference to English fiction of the eighteenth century and earlier, Gérard Strauch, 'Problèmes et Méthodes de l'Etude Linguistique du Style Indirect Libre', in *Tradition et Innovation: Littérature et Paralittérature. Actes du Congrès de Nancy (1972)*, Société des Anglicistes de l'Enseignement Supérieur (Paris, 1975), 409–28, esp. 418ff. on Fielding. The phenomenon of *style indirect libre*, formally identified by Charles Bally in 1912 (though some of its features had been observed earlier), has been the subject of extensive discussion in recent years: for useful introductions, see Page, *Speech in the English Novel*, 24–50; Roy Pascal, *The Dual Voice. Free Indirect Speech and its Functioning in the Nineteenth-Century European Novel* (Manchester, 1977); Seymour Chatman, *Story and Discourse. Narrative Structure in Fiction and Film* (Ithaca, 1978, reprinted 1983), 198–209 (cf. also 181ff.); Shlomith Rimmon-Kenan, *Narrative Fiction: Contemporary Poetics* (London, 1983), 106–16. Probably the fullest recent discussion is in Ann Banfield, *Unspeakable Sentences: Narration and Representation in the Language of Fiction* (London, 1982). A very lucid short account for the untutored reader may be found in Graham Hough, *Style and Stylistics* (London, 1969), 34–7. For a few comments on the interplay of direct and indirect reporting, and on the role of summarising abstraction in speech-reporting in a work of eighteenth-century satire, see Robert C. Elliott on *Gulliver's Travels*, in *The Power of Satire: Magic, Ritual, Art* (Princeton, 1960, reprinted 1966), 196, 201.

61 *Ulysses* (London, 1955), 30.

62 *Smart* as mockingly used here seems to have been a current pseudo-genteel vulgarism; the term is mentioned in Chesterfield's admonitory list, *Letters*, IV: 1407, 27 September 1749. See above, n.50.

63 Contrast the scene on the waggon and at the inn in *Roderick Random*, ch. xi, which contains satire of similar haughty usages ('Some people', 'better folks', 'Creature!'), and which may have been partly inspired by the scene from *Joseph Andrews*. Smollett's action shows much less tendency to crystallize momentarily into self-enclosing set-pieces, and flows instead with a boisterous continuity. In ch. liii, Smollett's Roderick gives 'A smart Dialogue between my Mistress and the Captain', but this label is only part of a long chapter-heading, and the dialogue itself (also in a stage-coach, as it happens) once again has no special tendency to self-enclosure. For a snobbish exchange, archly conveyed in indirect speech, see ch. liv; and for '*some people* and *some folks*', see ch. xix.

64 *Moll Flanders*, 277–8.

65 'Life' prefixed to Richardson's *Correspondence* (London, 1804), I: xx.

66 *Moll Flanders*, 273ff. For a particularly good discussion of the way Defoe's style reflects the mind of his protagonist-narrators see G. A. Starr, 'Defoe's Prose Style: 1. The Language of Interpretation', *Modern Philology*, LXXI (1974), 277–94.

67 I discuss more fully these scenes from *Amelia*, and compare them with Defoe, in *Henry Fielding and the Augustan Ideal Under Stress*, 71ff.

68 This method of reporting speech is superficially commonplace, and occurs in Defoe and others, but the special *effect* is Fielding's. Contrast the neutral and unmodified factuality of Moll's lively narration: '. . . After some very kind Expressions he ask'd me, if I would be very honest to him, and give a sincere Answer to one thing he would desire of me? after some little Cavil with him at the word *Sincere*, and asking him if I had ever given him any Answers which were not Sincere, I promis'd him I would; why then his Request was, *he said*, to let him see my Purse; I immediately put my Hand into my Pocket, *and Laughing at him*, pull'd it out, and there was in it three Guineas and a Half; *then he ask'd me*, if there was all the Money I had? I told him no, *Laughing again*, not by a great deal' (*Moll Flanders*, 111–12).

69 *Shamela*, Letter VI. Swift, like Fielding, mocked the foolish use of present-tense narrative, among other aspirations to immediacy and up-to-dateness, in 'modern' writers: see Ronald Paulson, *Theme and Structure in Swift's Tale of a Tub* (New Haven, 1960), 31–2. For a broader discussion of present-tense narrative, see Christian Paul Casparis, *Tense Without Time: The Present Tense in Narration* (Berne, 1975), which has, however, little to say on Fielding or Richardson.

70 Thomas Sprat, *History of the Royal Society*, 1667, Part II, section xx; Jackson I. Cope and Harold Whitmore Jones (eds.) (St Louis and London, 1966), 113, and editors' Introduction, xxv–xxx. See also Christopher Hill, *Intellectual Origins of the English Revolution* (London, 1972), 129–30: the connection between science and the new prose style goes back to the first half of the seventeenth century, and the aspiration to a plain naked style also had Puritan connections, which would contribute to the distaste of authors like Swift and Fielding.

71 To Lady Bute, 20 October [1755], *Complete Letters*, III: 97. See also Robert Halsband, 'Lady Mary Wortley Montagu and Eighteenth-Century Fiction', *Philological Quarterly*, XLV (1966), 153: 'The fig-leaf metaphor occurs elsewhere in Lady Mary's letters; it was a decorum which she, with stoic reticence, generally observed herself'. See also Chesterfield, *Detached Thoughts*, cited in *Letters*, I: 165: 'a man would be as impudent who would exhibit his inside naked, as he would be indecent if he produced his outside so'.

72 *Pamela*, I: 97.

73 E.g., *Moll Flanders*, 80ff.; *Pamela*, I: 90, 319. See also the example in n.68 above.

74 Ford's major attack on Fielding occurs in *The March of Literature* (London, 1947), 552–40. See also his book on *The English Novel* (London, 1930), 89ff.

75 Ford Madox Ford, *No More Parades*, I: i (West Drayton, 1948), 13–14.

76 See Ford's description of the 'official Author', who must limit 'himself to presenting without comment or moralization', in his article, 'Techniques', *Southern Review*, I (1935–36), 33. See also his *Joseph Conrad. A Personal Remembrance* (London, 1924), 194, 208, and the remarks on authorial neutrality in the dedicatory letter to William Bird prefixed to *No More Parades*. Nevertheless, Ford has an interesting letter of October 1900 to Galsworthy suggesting the desirability of a certain authorial superiority to one's characters and even of letting it 'peep out' on occasion (Richard M. Ludwig (ed.), *Letters of Ford Madox Ford* (Princeton, 1965), 12).

77 *Tom Jones*, VII: viii. That such elaborate and fine-spun accounts of ancestry were a well-established comic stereotype is confirmed by the fact that Gray

had composed a parody in a letter to Horace Walpole of 25 February 1735: 'it is well known that your petit[rs] Grandmother's Aunt's Cousin-german had y[e] honour to pull out your honour's great Uncle's Wive's brother's hollow tooth; as also, to go further backwards, your Pet[rs] relation was Physician to King Cadwallader' (Paget Toynbee and Leonard Whibley, eds., *The Correspondence of Thomas Gray*, rev. by H. W. Starr (Oxford, 1971), I. 24). For modern examples, see *Ulysses* (London, 1955), 579, 'it was the daughter of the mother in the washkitchen that was fostersister to the heir of the house or else they were connected through the mother in some way', and see 578–79 *passim*; and Eugène Ionesco, *La Cantatrice Chauve* (*The Bald Prima Donna*), end of scene viii (*Théâtre*, I (Paris, 1954), 46–7).

78 *Pamela*, I: 91.

79 See Tuvia Bloch, '"Gentleman's Gentleman"', *Notes and Queries*, CCXII (1967), 405. I have not seen the recent book by Rosina Harrison, *Gentlemen's Gentlemen*, reviewed by Emma Tennant in the *Sunday Times*, 2 January 1977. For some modern variants, see 'a working girl's working girl' (James M. Cain, *The Institute* (London, 1977), 99; end of chapter 13) and '*cock*sman's cocksman' (John A. Williams, *The Man Who Cried I Am* (New York, 1968), 155 and, for a related phrase, 157; chapter 16). Some of the usages are closer to 'poet's poet' than to 'gentleman's gentleman', however!

80 *Pasquin*, II. i: O. M. Brack, Jr., William Kupersmith, and Curt A. Zimansky (eds.) (Iowa City, 1973), 13 (Trapwit is trying to explain how it is that in his play a 'Country Mayoress' is said, 'out of Character', to have been at a ridotto. Her previous occupation is supposed to account for this, but the main reason for the improbability is that polite conversation in a comedy 'cannot be carried on without these Helps' of uncharacteristic speech); *Tom Jones*, VII: viii.

81 Leslie Fiedler notes in a different connection that Richardson 'knows really what Pamela is after . . . though he does not quite know how he knows it; this happy state of quasi-insight (he never falsifies the hidden motivations of his protagonists) he shares with his heroines and the readers who identify with them' (*Love and Death in the American Novel* (London, 1970), 60). There are weaknesses as well as strengths in this.

82 Despite Ford's view that Richardson 'never intrudes' nor gives himself the opportunity to do so (*March of Literature*, 548, 542), there are ways in which he makes his presence felt (see Kinkead-Weekes, *Samuel Richardson: Dramatic Novelist*, 398–99). Richardson told Warburton on 19 April 1748 that he did not seek a total illusion of life, in which the letters in his novels might be taken for real, but only 'that kind of Historical Faith which Fiction itself is generally read with, tho' we know it to be Fiction' (*Selected Letters*, 85).

10

A Journey From this World to the Next

The *Journey from this World to the Next* first appeared in the second volume of Fielding's *Miscellanies*, in April 1743. Much of it was probably composed in 1741–2 (perhaps drafted before the appearance of *Joseph Andrews* in February 1742, and touched up after it), but some parts may be earlier still. A certain patchwork quality about the work, and the fact that some of its chapters can more or less stand as self-contained set-pieces, make it seem possible that Fielding gathered into it some early sketches, or perhaps drafts of one or two *Champion* essays (the *Champion* for 24 May 1740 contains a Lucianic judgment-piece closely related to *Journey*, I.vii). The *Miscellanies* as a whole contain a variety of uncollected early pieces, including poems, dialogues, essays and plays; and even their most considerable work, *Jonathan Wild*, although more obviously complete and more coherent in its design than the *Journey*, also shows signs of patchwork composition, with certain parts of the Heartfree plot probably imported from drafts of other projects.

The *Journey* is inferior to *Jonathan Wild*, but comes next in importance among the works in the *Miscellanies*. Because of its unfinished quality, it has received less attention than any other of Fielding's more substantial works, and has not been easily available to readers in our own time. It was admired in the eighteenth century, and several editions, and translations into German, French, and other languages, appeared in the first few decades after Fielding's death. Gibbon referred to it as 'the romance of a great master, which may be considered as the history of human nature'; Tom Moore, reading it on a rainy day, wrote in his journal: 'few things so good as the first half of it'; Dickens was greatly moved by an episode in it, and spoke of it as 'a book by one of the greatest English writers'; and Fielding's biographer W. L. Cross claims that it 'surpasses in humour

and irony all other attempts by himself or anyone else to moder-
nize Lucian'.

Fielding was a great admirer of Lucian, the prolific Greek
satirist who lived in the second century AD, and whose satirical
works include several otherworldly journeys (of which the best-
known is the *True History*), many dialogues of the dead, and a
variety of other satiric sketches. The *Miscellanies* contain several
Lucianic imitations, and as far back as the *Author's Farce* (1730),
Act III, there is an underworld scene which looks forward to the
Champion essay of 24 May 1740 and to the *Journey* itself. Near the
end of his life, in the *Covent-Garden Journal* for 4 February 1752,
Fielding named Lucian as a member, with Cervantes and Swift,
of 'that great Triumvirate' of witty moralists whom 'I shall ever
hold in the highest Degree of Esteem', greatly superior in morality to both Aristophanes and Rabelais. And on 30 June 1752,
writing in support of a proposal for a translation of Lucian's
works by himself and the Rev. William Young, he celebrated him
as 'the Father of true Humour', comparable only to his great
English imitator, Swift. In the same essay, he referred to himself
as one 'who hath formed his Stile upon that very Author'. Of all
Fielding's imitations of Lucian, the *Journey* is certainly the most
sustained, and the best.

The *Journey* looks back not only to Lucian, but to more recent
traditions of learned satire, including Swift and the Scriblerus
Club. Although never a member of that group, Fielding had
identified himself with its satiric manner and objectives many
years before the *Journey*. He used the pseudonym Scriblerus
Secundus when he published the *Author's Farce* (1730), the
Tragedy of Tragedies (1731), the *Grub-Street Opera* (1731), and
other plays. Among the targets of the *Journey*'s satire are several
(the Royal Society, the medical profession, etc.) which are part of
the staple repertoire of Augustan satire, and notably of that satire
of the 'learned' and of intellectual folly in which the Scriblerians
specialised. Like several works by Swift, Pope, and others, the
Journey carries a parade of mock-scholarship in which a supposed
'editor' learnedly comments on the text. From the start, this
annotator makes his foolish, interfering presence felt. Against the
opening words, 'On the first day of December, 1741', he notes
'Some doubt whether this should not be rather 1641', goes on to
suggest an argument in favour of this nonsensical subversion of a
date that is obviously correct, and concludes with a fatuous
display of scholarly fair-mindedness: 'To say the truth, there are
difficulties attend either conjecture'.

A Journey From this World to the Next

Like Swift's *Tale of a Tub*, the *Journey* is presented not simply as an argument or narrative, however satirical, but as a learned edition of itself. It gets the weighty treatment normally accorded to classical texts, and like many classical texts it is said to have survived only in a defective manuscript, whose gaps and lack of a conclusive ending give the annotator opportunities to display his talents. The Introduction says that the manuscript came to light when the editor found part of it used as wrapping-paper round a bundle of pens. His stationer told him he had 'about one hundred' further pages left,

> but that the book was originally a huge folio, had been left in his garret by a gentleman who lodged there, and who had left him no other satisfaction for nine months lodging. He proceeded to inform me, that the manuscript had been hawked about (as he phrased it) among all the booksellers who refused to meddle; some alleged that they could not read, others that they could not understand it. Some would have it to be an atheistical book, and some that it was a libel on the government; for one or other of which reasons, they all refused to print it. That it had been likewise shown to the R——l Society, but they shook their heads, saying, there was nothing in it wonderful enough for them.

Many stock jokes and stylistic routines of Augustan satire may be seen here: the manuscript used as, or fit only for, wrapping-paper; the figure of the Grub Street garreteer; the bringing into play of an editor and a bookseller (or in this case a stationer) as figures who come between reader and author, who help to surround the supposed author with flaunted mystification and mocking disclaimers, and help the *real* author to disguise his exact feelings (or even in some cases his identity) by means of a witty indirectness; the implied apology for publication; the hint (true or false) that the work has been found subversive of religion or government (the Preface to the *Miscellanies* further protests that the *Journey* had no design 'to oppose any present System, or to erect a new one of my own').

But if these features are clearly drawn from conventions of Augustan satire, it would be wrong to identify the *Journey* too closely with the works of Swift and Pope in which these conventions play a prominent part. The *Journey* is not, for example, a mock-learned work in the primary and thoroughgoing way in which the *Tale of a Tub* or the *Dunciad* are. In the latter, the

313

mock-learned commentary exists in very close relationship with the main body of the work, because the book as a whole, including the commentary, is concerned with intellectual folly, and because both text and commentary are composed in a broadly similar, and complementary, mode of parody. In Fielding's *Journey*, there is not this close relation. The work does not have that pervasive concern with the state of culture and the forms of 'modern' writing and thought which provides the organising theme of the *Tale* and the *Dunciad*, nor is it at all times parodic or even satirical. There are in it several threads of story, and several passages of autobiographical disclosure, which assume an interest independent of satiric purposes, focusing on the emotional or (as in the novelettish history of Anne Boleyn, possibly written by Fielding's sister Sarah) the 'sentimental' aspects of the situation, or occasionally on the unfolding of the narrative for its own sake. Even where a satiric emphasis predominates, as it does most often, it is not normally of a sort to which mock-learned commentary is particularly relevant, and the pedantic interventions of the annotator tend to appear as witty ornaments rather than as integral parts of the work's whole fabric.

When Swift's *Tale* pretends to be an incomplete work, and uses its commentary to signpost the gaps in the manuscript, or speaks elsewhere of the unfinished nature of the author's project, both text and commentary collaborate to expose the loose ends and the muddle-headed disorderliness of 'modern' writing. The misplaced pedantries of the commentary act as both signposts and symptoms of the same cultural disease. The effect is quite different when the *Journey*'s commentator notes that 'Here part of the manuscript is lost' or that

> Here ends this curious manuscript; the rest being destroyed in rolling up pens, tobacco, etc. It is to be hoped heedless people will henceforth be more cautious what they burn, or use to other vile purposes; especially when they consider the fate which had likely to have befallen the divine Milton; and that the works of Homer were probably discovered in some chandler's shop in Greece.

These footnotes not only lack that close relationship with the main satiric design which we find in Swift. They also strike a note of coy whimsy which looks forward to Sterne more than it looks back to Swift. The satire is more benign, the irony more affectionately self-indulgent than anything in Swift's *Tale*. In Swift,

314

the parody is primarily attacking or derisive: here it tends more towards amiable posturing or playful self-expression than towards aggression. If Swiftian parody is also, in its way, a mode of self-expression, that self-expression is itself primarily aggressive. Moreover, the targets of the parody have changed slightly in Fielding, and more than slightly in Sterne. The pedantries of the learned still figure prominently in both authors, and their writing (especially Sterne's) doubtless includes some affectionate parody not only of learned works but of mock-learned satires of the Swiftian or Scriblerian sort. Sterne, indeed, almost certainly includes not only Swift but also Fielding in his increasingly elaborate and self-conscious parodic enterprise.

Further, it is not only learned works, or mock-learned works of the Scriblerian kind, which have gaps in the manuscript and editorial commentators. New modes of fiction-writing adopted similar conventions straight, either to suggest historical authenticity or else to produce a flavour of endearing fussiness or eccentricity. Richardson's *Pamela* (1740), presented as a series of letters discovered by an editor, was a recent example, and the most famous then known, of an attempt to give the story the appearance of an actual record of real life. Fielding would not be inclined to imitate that, but his whimsical play with the notion that parts of his manuscript were used 'in rolling up pens, tobacco, & c.' looks forward not only to the self-ironic spontaneities of Sterne but also to later, more straightforwardly 'sentimental' works like Mackenzie's *Man of Feeling* (1771). The latter also purports to reproduce 'a bundle of papers' made incomplete because the curate who owned it found that it made 'excellent wadding' on his shooting expeditions. As a result, the novel as we have it is full of pretended gaps. It begins at Chapter xi, proceeds regularly to Chapter xiv, which is then followed by Chapter xix, etc. Similarly Fielding's *Journey* runs uninterruptedly through the first twenty-five chapters of Book I, and then leaps to Book XIX, Chapter vii, the story of Anne Boleyn.

In Mackenzie, the gaps in the manuscript are not mainly satirical. They combine a Richardsonian concern for verisimilitude with a strong touch of poignant or 'sentimental' whimsy in the manner of Sterne. That is designed to signal a freely self-regarding spontaneity of expression, in which self-irony is openly part of the self-regard. These facts help us to see Fielding's 'editorial' signposting of the *Journey*'s incompleteness in another perspective. Fielding's work is not Shandean nor Mackenzie-like, any more than it is Richardsonian. But the mock-editorial coyness tends towards that immediacy of utterance, that intimate nudge of complicity with the reader, which Sterne and Mackenzie carried to far greater lengths, even as they parodied not only 'learned' works and mock-learned satire, but also, perhaps, Richardson's pretence of being the editor rather than the author of the authentic 'to the moment' letters of his characters.

But although the editorial mannerisms of the *Journey* can be seen in relation to two traditions, that of Scriblerian satire and that of a less satiric irony associated with the new novel of 'sentiment', the *Journey* sits uneasily between the two. The editorial fussiness about gaps in the manuscript and the rest comes over neither as part of any sustained parodic programme, nor as an authenticating device, nor yet as 'sentimental' self-expression. The gestures are too sporadic and aimless. When Mackenzie came to use the device of mock-incompleteness, he was able to exploit the supposed gaps in the manuscript with a certain structural finesse, relegating to these gaps elements which we might expect to find in an unliterary reporting of real life, but unnecessary or distracting to the strict economy of his novel. Fielding's highly episodic book has no such purpose, any more than it has Swift's overall parodic design. The uneasiness is compounded by the fact that the mock-indications of incompleteness cover up, as they do not in Swift's *Tale* or in Mackenzie, an *actual* incompleteness. The *Journey* was patched together from a variety of papers, and Fielding did not do much to ease his transitions or to round off his sectional or final conclusions. Pretended manuscript-gaps are used as a bridge between the transmigrations of Julian the Apostate (which are themselves broken off before their expected end) and the quite different story of Anne Boleyn which follows them. They are used again after the Anne Boleyn story, to explain why the entire work abruptly leaves off at that point. These facts suggest that the conventionally assumed device of pseudo-incompleteness is partly an attempt to make a really incomplete work seem to be complete within a genre or convention of pseudo-incompleteness. The trick is only partly successful.

The *Journey* falls into three broadly distinct sections. The first, consisting of the first nine chapters of Book I, deals with the narrator's trip to the next world after his death, and the people he meets on the way to Elysium and in Elysium. It belongs to a popular Lucianic genre of which there is a recent example in Chapter 20 of Kurt Vonnegut's *Jailbird* (1979). The second, which takes up the rest of Book I (Chapters x–xxv) deals with the various transmigrations of Julian the Apostate, before he was allowed into Elysium, where the narrator has met him. A final section, whimsically numbered Book XIX, chapter vii, is the story of Anne Boleyn already referred to.

The first section is the most uniformly successful. Its crisp and efficient narrative has a combination of irony and warmth very characteristic of Fielding at his best. A vivid authorial personality, not unlike that of *Joseph Andrews* and *Tom Jones*, makes itself felt here more consistently than in other parts of the work. This is indeed the only section in which an authorial or quasi-authorial narrator does most of the telling (the rest is mainly told by Julian and by Anne Boleyn) and Fielding is always more at home when he writes in some formalised version of his own person than when he has to speak through other characters. This does not mean that he needs or seeks to establish a close intimacy with his reader. By a paradox which is only apparent, it is Richardson's almost wholly 'dramatic' practice of making the characters rather than the author tell the story which generates a sense of intimate involvement with the narrative. Fielding shied from this, preferring to keep the reader at arm's length, creating an atmosphere of conversational relationship and of rational agreement on important issues, rather than a close sharing of experience. At times the reader is not only kept at a distance but actually put down. Thus in I:ii, speaking of 'seraphic love' as differing from the cruder forms of carnal love, Fielding declares that it is

> an extreme delicacy and tenderness of friendship, of which, my worthy reader, if thou hast no conception, as it is probable thou mayst not, my endeavour to instruct thee would be as fruitless, as it would be to explain the most difficult problems of Sir Isaac Newton to one ignorant of vulgar arithmetic.

The passage looks forward to some famous passages in the later fiction. In *Tom Jones*, VI: i, at the end of an extended definition of the various forms of genuine love, Fielding says:

> Examine your Heart, my good Reader, and resolve whether you do believe these Matters with me. If you do, you may now proceed to their Exemplification in the following Pages; if you do not, you have, I assure you, already read more than you have understood; and it would be wiser to pursue your Business, or your Pleasures (such as they are)

than to throw away any more of your Time in reading what
you can neither taste nor comprehend.

The characteristic take-it-or-leave-it treatment purports to bring
all humane readers on the author's side, wrong-footing any
others, and keeping the author in a superior position, dictating
terms. Disagreement is not likely to make any reader stop reading
the book, as the gesture defies him to do. Instead, Fielding makes
sure that any feeling of disagreement will undermine the reader's
self-esteem and place him on the defensive. This undermining is
not as radical as that experienced from Swift's irony, whose main
energies are continuously directed towards unsettling all complacency or ease of mind in the reader. Fielding projects a
comfortingly strong sense that positive values and decent readers
genuinely exist, and may be set against the others; and the
'superiority' is not resented because the prevailing idiom has
established a readiness to submit to the narrator's righteous and
genially authoritative control.

In a similar passage in *Amelia*, III:i, the tone is rasping and
unfriendly. Fielding tells us that he is placing an account by Booth
of a tender scene with Amelia in a chapter by itself,

> which we desire all our Readers who do not love, or who
> perhaps do not know the Pleasure of Tenderness, to pass
> over; since they may do this without any Prejudice to the
> Thread of the Narrative.

Here, the *hauteur* has become more stridently aggressive. It is in
keeping with the grimmer and less hopeful atmosphere of the
novel as a whole, and indeed of most of Fielding's other late
writings. But both passages show a Fielding whose style depends
on a degree of contact with the reader which is live but not
intimate, and which places the narrator in that position of authority and control which is a necessary part of Fielding's most
authentic voice. The passage from the *Journey* lacks the high-
spirited confidence of *Tom Jones*, as well as the bitterness of
Amelia. But in its smaller and charming way it too asserts a
controlling presence, that open display of authorial power which
Fielding's writing needs for the release of its most vital energies.

These energies are correspondingly less evident in the narratives of Julian the Apostate later in the work. When Fielding
speaks through other persons, his style seldom manages to rise
above what is, at its best, a briskly competent summarising

notation. The easy plasticity, the richly modulated geniality, the knowing broadmindedness of the authorial voice turn into something flatter and more subdued. In *Journey*, I:xviii, Julian reports his discovery that 'a woman will bear the most bitter censures on her morals, easier than the smallest reflection on her beauty', a witty observation which might well have come from Fielding's own voice at any stage in his career, but which is here embedded in a passage of dull summarising narrative:

> I had not the least suspicion of Adelaide: for, besides her being a very good-humoured woman, I had often made severe jests on her reputation, which I had all the reason imaginable to believe had given her no offence. But I soon perceived, that a woman will bear the most bitter censures on her morals, easier that the smallest reflection on her beauty; for she now declared publicly, that I ought to be dismissed from court, as the stupidest of fools, and one in whom there was no diversion; and that she wondered how any person could have so little taste, as to imagine I had any wit.

Compare the passage in *Tom Jones*, I:vi, where Jenny Jones is suspected of being the mother of the foundling Tom, and, like the court-lady of Julian's account, endures 'affronts to her chastity' much better than slurs on her beauty:

> Not a single Female was present, but found some Means of expressing her Abhorrence of poor *Jenny*; who bore all very patiently, except the Malice of one Woman, who reflected upon her Person, and, tossing up her Nose, said, 'The Man must have a good Stomach, who would give Silk Gowns for such Sort of Trumpery.' *Jenny* replied to this, with a Bitterness which might have surprized a judicious Person, who had observed the Tranquility with which she bore all the Affronts to her Chastity; but her Patience was perhaps tired out: For this is a Virtue which is very apt to be fatigued by Exercise

or the passage in *Tom Jones*, VII:ix, where Mrs Western has developed an implacably vindictive resentment against Mrs Honour for calling her ugly, a resentment which Fielding pretends to find unaccountable, because:

319

> Mrs. *Western* was a very good-natured Woman, and ord-
> inarily of a forgiving Temper. She had lately remitted the
> Trespass of a Stage-coach Man, who had overturned her
> Post-chaise into a Ditch; nay, she had even broken the Law in
> refusing to prosecute a High-way-man who had robbed
> her, not only of a Sum of Money, but of her Ear-rings; at the
> same Time d—ning her, and saying, 'such handsome B—s as
> you, don't want Jewels to set them off, and be d—nd to you.'
> But now, so uncertain are our Tempers, and so much do we
> at different Times differ from ourselves, she would hear of
> no Mitigation.

The passages from *Tom Jones* have what Julian's description has
not, a confident, festive, extravagant amplitude. Unlike Julian's
summary reportage, whose flat explicitness combines lifelessly
with the tart cantankerous irony, the narrative reporting in *Tom
Jones* is, for example, vitalised by well-timed eruptions of actual
quoted speech. A deadpan mock-commentary cheekily gives
wrong explanations or suggests a false uncertainty, whilst the
firmly managed irony leaves no *real* doubt of the true nature of the
case. Mock-bewilderment at supposedly unaccountable
behaviour is actually a paradoxical token of confident certainty.
The success of the whole mixture is partly attributable to the
maturity of Fielding's art in *Tom Jones*: the *Journey*, by contrast, is
an early work. But the fact that the narrator in *Tom Jones* is a
quasi-authorial figure, through whom Fielding can manifest his
total grasp of the action he describes, is also relevant to the
difference; and those interpolated stories in *Tom Jones* (or *Joseph
Andrews*) which are told by non-authorial narrators tend to suffer
from a similar flatness.

Nevertheless some of Julian's sarcasm retains a genuine satirical
vigour, and it might be argued that in the course of his long
narrative he becomes himself at times a quasi-authorial figure,
whose tone of voice and whose mode of irony acquire properties
of Fielding's own, as in I:xxv, where Julian describes his incarnation as a dancing-master:

> I do not remember that in any of the characters in which I
> appeared on earth I ever assumed to myself a greater dignity,
> or thought myself of more real importance than now. I
> looked on dancing as the greatest excellence of human nature
> and on myself as the greatest proficient in it. And indeed, this
> seemed to be the general opinion of the whole court; for I was

the chief instructor of the youth of both sexes, whose merit was almost entirely defined by the advances they made in that science which I had the honour to profess. As to myself, I was so fully persuaded of this truth, that I not only slighted and despised those who were ignorant of dancing; but I thought the highest character I could give of any man was that he made a graceful bow . . .

Though so little of my youth had been thrown away in what they call literature, that I could hardly write and read, yet I composed a treatise on education; the first rudiments of which, as I taught, were to instruct a child in the science of coming handsomely into a room. In this I corrected many faults of my predecessors, particularly that of being too much in a hurry, and instituting a child in the sublimer parts of dancing before they are capable of making their honours.

The play of irony is anything but lifeless, and the passage would not be out of place in *Tom Jones* or *Amelia*. Julian is speaking of a past incarnation from which he has now emerged, and he states that 'I have not now the same high opinion of my profession which I had then'. Perhaps the fact that Julian is now in Elysium, and has expiated and indeed disconnected himself from all his foolish lives, gives him a detachment which makes it easier for Fielding to merge his own authorial accents, ventriloquously, into parts of Julian's narrative. The particular target of Julian's sarcasm, the self-importance of dancing-masters, is also very familiar to readers of Fielding. It occurs in his early plays, and in his mature novels. The person chiefly mocked is perhaps a dancing-master called John Essex, who had claimed in *The Young Ladies Conduct: or, Rules for Education* (1722) that, 'altho' other Arts and Sciences have their peculiar Use in Life, and are valuable in Education; yet few, if any, are so Necessary and Advantageous as [dancing], especially under a good Master . . . ' But Fielding is of course placing under ironic scrutiny the whole question of the role, in a 'polite education', of those taught graces of outward bearing on which so much emphasis is placed, not only by dancing-masters but by serious courtesy-writers.

On this question, Fielding is by no means so simply dismissive as Julian's irony might suggest. In both *Tom Jones* and *Amelia*, where he conducts a profound and protracted investigation of 'politeness', his attitude is richly ambiguous. For one thing, a gentleman must be taught to dance by a dancing-master, but must not dance *like* a dancing-master. More important, the taught graces of behaviour which dancing-masters help to instil are there seen as legitimate elements in a progress to 'courtesy' in a high sense, as the art of true gentlemanliness, which softens aggression and teaches us to be tactful, considerate, anxious to avoid displeasing or embarrassing others. And dancing-masters, including Mr Essex, are mocked with an irony which may resemble that of Julian, but which has additional and complicating resonances. Mr Essex, for example, is complimented in a not wholly sarcastic way in *Tom Jones*, XIV:i, and he turns up again in *Amelia*, V:ii, where Fielding describes the slightly awkward carriage of the good sergeant Atkinson, unschooled in dancing, as he enters Mrs Ellison's house (I have discussed this scene in detail in *Henry Fielding and the Augustan Ideal under Stress*, pp. 3ff.). Behind the satire of dancing-masters and their self-importance, and behind the whole class-conscious archness about Atkinson, there is a genuine sense that dancing-masters have their role in a polite education, and that such an education, in turn, has high value as a civilising force, contributing to ease of intercourse and softening our more unkind, unmannerly or cruel natural instincts. The dancing-master is being honestly celebrated, as well as uppishly derided. In the *Journey*, by contrast, Julian expresses only a straight disapproval of the dancing-master's self-importance and affectation. There is no doubt that his feelings are Fielding's. But they are only part of what Fielding felt and was able to reveal in the richer context of *Amelia*, as also in *Tom Jones*. His loyalty to the good aspects of a 'polite education', including its necessary trivialities, was as strong as his dislike of the bad. The mature novels are able to give a fully-developed view which would not be possible nor perhaps appropriate in a brief satirical sketch of the kind provided by Julian. The episodic nature of the *Journey* tends to make each of Julian's narrative chapters seem a separate self-contained sketch, and a medium of thumbnail portraiture is not suited to the large-scale orchestration of an author's attitudes in their full complexity. Fielding may not yet have developed stylistic powers adequate to the full range of his feelings (although parts of the *Journey* must have been contemporary with *Joseph Andrews*, which was published in 1742). And the fact that Fielding is speaking not in his own voice but through Julian probably has something to do with the relatively crude irony of the passage, even though Fielding was here able to identify himself with his speaker more closely than in some other parts of the *Journey*. The passage is nevertheless in its way sharp and eloquent, characteristic of Fielding in its ironic thrust as well as in its subject-matter, and it is by no means unworthy of its author.

On his way to the next world, the main or quasi-authorial narrator passes through the City of Diseases, which enables Fielding to write satirically of the medical profession; and the Palace of Death, an edifice both 'gothic' in style and fraught with the atmospherics of 'gothick' gloom (yet, by a touch of grotesque humour, 'all gay and sprightly within') in which are commemorated those illustrious men who in war and conquest had brought the greatest number of people to death. The Duke of Marlborough, to whose memory Fielding pays a high compliment, is deliberately excepted, partly because he never sent to Death any 'subject he could keep from him, nor did he ever get a single subject by his means, but he lost 1000 others for him'. But most of Fielding's favourite conqueror-villains and imperial tyrants are there: Louis XIV, Charles XII of Sweden, Alexander the Great, Caligula. The exploits of these bad men is one of the themes of *Jonathan Wild*, as is the related theme of 'Greatness' and 'Goodness', which is given allegorical treatment in the next chapter of the *Journey* (I:v). *Jonathan Wild* was published together with the *Journey* in the *Miscellanies* (it appears in Volume III, the *Journey* in Volume II), and part of the interest of these opening chapters of the *Journey* lies in their connection with Fielding's more important works.

But the most interesting chapter in this first section, and perhaps in the work as a whole, is I:vii. It is a Lucianic judgment-piece of a kind which Fielding had already attempted in his *Champion* essay of 24 May 1740. The dead spirits seek admittance to Elysium, and are granted or refused admittance according to whether Minos approves or disapproves of their character and conduct when alive. The piece is a powerful parable, expressing some of the central tenets of Fielding's morality, and containing some fascinating parallels with, or adumbrations of, the major novels. Minos repudiates all practitioners of merely conventional or legalistic virtue: the man who regularly went to church and 'had never been once guilty of whoring, drinking, gluttony, or any other excess', but who 'had disinherited his son for getting a bastard' (this gains a special interest from the fact that Fielding was later to make his most attractive and best-known hero a bastard); the young lady who boasted of refusing many lovers, and the prude to whom Minos said 'there was not a single prude in Elysium'; the parson who testifies to the deservingness of a poverty-stricken family but who did nothing in life to relieve

their distress (the passage has a curiously tough-minded poignancy precisely because it deals with an occasion when the
clergyman *does* try to help, although at this late stage it costs him
nothing – the poor family, needless to say, are *not* turned away).

Against these examples, are those whom Minos allows in. One
is the repentant man who had been hanged for 'the robbery of
eighteen pence', but who 'had supported an aged parent' and 'had
been a very tender husband and a kind father, and . . . had ruined
himself by being bail for his friend'. This good man is related to
several figures in the major novels: the famous postilion in *Joseph
Andrews*, I:xii, who helps Joseph in distress but 'hath been since
transported for robbing a Hen-roost'; Mr Anderson, the poor
'highwayman' who attacks Tom and whom Tom later supports
(*Tom Jones*, XII:xiv; XII:x); and the very sad old prisoner in
Amelia, I:iv, who seemed 'to be giving up the Ghost', with his
head on his daughter's lap:

> These . . . were Father and Daughter; . . . the latter was
> committed for stealing a Loaf, in order to support the
> former, and the former for receiving it knowing it to be
> stolen.

A feature of these passages is that Fielding was not, in principle,
opposed to the death-penalty for small felonies, and in his late
legal-sociological writings insisted on its being severely applied.
This was not because he thought 'the life of a man and a few
shillings to be of an equal consideration', but because the deter-
rence of crime was of over-riding importance. This statement is
contemporary with *Amelia*. And what all the fictional examples
show is that Fielding's morality transcends his own explicitly
formulated socio-legal principles in contexts where the full
human situation invited a deeper and larger view.

Many of Fielding's examples in I:vii are briskly presented as
tiny parables, with an unexpected reversal, a concluding sting of
surprise, bitterness or compassion. In this too they resemble the
succession of Newgate case-histories in *Amelia*, I:iii–iv, although
the shocks and reversals in the later work are more radically
painful, less confident of the power of good to prevail in a bad
world. In the *Journey*, sharp as its satire often is, the tone is that of
the more assured Fielding of *Joseph Andrews* and *Tom Jones*, the
righteously confident moralist who is fully aware of the evils of
life but will not be overwhelmed by them. But in both the early
Journey and the later *Amelia*, the surprises and reversals often

show up the inadequacies of rules and laws (even those rules or laws which Fielding himself strongly supports) in the face of human situations and human motives which are too complex for any rules, however right in themselves, to take care of.

The best-known aspect of this is Fielding's attitude to chastity. He clearly considered chastity to be an important virtue, but was also ready to see value in those kinds of love which, though unchaste, carried a generosity of feeling, qualities of affection, tenderness and unselfishness, not to be found in some of those who observed the strict forms of virtuous conduct. The heroes of *Tom Jones* and *Amelia* exemplify this, as does the hero-narrator of the *Journey*:

> The judge then addressed himself to me, who little expected to pass this fiery trial. I confessed I had indulged myself very freely with wine and women in my youth, but had never done an injury to any man living, nor avoided an opportunity of doing good, that I pretended to very little virtue more than general philanthropy and private friendship. – I was proceeding when Minos bid me enter the gate, and not indulge myself with trumpeting forth my virtues . . .

This is clearly a glamorised self-portrait, and Fielding may be felt to be luxuriating somewhat in it (the self-undercutting in the last sentence is coy, gruffly sentimental, rather than genuinely ironic at his own expense). The passage, ironically, gave added ammunition to those accusations of personal dissoluteness which dogged the criticism of Fielding for two centuries. It is arguable that Fielding is not to be confused with his narrator, even though he made his narrator carry some overt autobiographical elements. But we are nowadays likelier to be made uncomfortable by the self-glamorising of the passage than by its revelation of libertine conduct.

Other passages of autobiographical significance in the *Journey* do not raise such problems. The reunion with his dead daughter 'on his first entrance into Elysium' at the beginning of the next chapter (I:viii) has a kind of open and freely sentimental poignancy not unlike some passages of Victorian fiction, and it is interesting that Dickens was greatly drawn to this episode, using it more than once in letters of consolation to friends who had lost a child (see especially Dickens's retelling and perhaps Victorianising of the episode in a letter to Mrs Maria Winter, 13 June 1855). A very different passage is the scene in I:ix, where dead authors meet their heroes and where (after Homer is addressed by Achilles and Ulysses, Virgil by Aeneas and Julius Caesar, and Milton by Adam) the narrator meets Thomas Thumb, hero of Fielding's early burlesque. This autobiographical tease is full of sharp wit and of fun.

The two chapters in which these scenes occur (I:viii–ix) belong to a rich literary tradition of satirical meetings with the illustrious dead which includes not only Lucian, but also Rabelais (II:xxx; V:xxxi) and Swift's Glubbdubdrib (*Gulliver's Travels*, III:vii–viii). Part of the satire, in all these authors as in Fielding, involves respected writers and philosophers. In Lucian's *True History* and in *Gulliver's Travels*, famous authors meet their commentators, who come off badly. Lucian's Homer denies the learned speculations of his biographers and editors. Swift's Homer and Aristotle are, in a characteristic piece of Swiftian uppishness, 'perfect Strangers' to the throng of their commentators, who 'always kept in the most distant Quarters from their Principals in the lower World, through a Consciousness of Shame and Guilt, because they had so horribly misrepresented the Meaning of those Authors to Posterity'. Homer appears in Fielding too, but it is to the figure of Shakespeare that Fielding transfers some of the roles played by Homer in Lucian and Swift. In particular, the Swiftian combination of lofty disdain for commentators as an ungentlemanly mob, and of impatience with their glosses, comes through when Shakespeare is asked to settle a dispute about his text between the actors Betterton and Booth:

> At last it was agreed on all sides to refer the matter to the decision of Shakespear himself, who delivered his sentiments as follows: 'Faith, gentlemen, it is so long since I wrote the line, I have forgot my meaning. This I know, could I have dreamt so much nonsense would have been talked and writ about it, I would have blotted it out of my works; for I am sure if any of these be my meaning, it doth me very little honour.'
>
> He was then interrogated concerning some other ambiguous passages in his works; but he declined any satisfactory answer: Saying, if Mr. Theobald had not writ about it sufficiently, there were three or four more new editions of his plays coming out, which he hoped would satisfy every one: Concluding, 'I marvel nothing so much as that men will gird themselves at discovering obscure beauties in an author.

Certes the greatest and most pregnant beauties are ever the plainest and most evidently striking; and when two meanings of a passage can in the least balance our judgments which to prefer, I hold it matter of unquestionable certainty, that neither of them is worth a farthing.'

The passage looks forward to the more succinct joke in *Tom Jones*, X:i, in which Fielding says to the reader: 'perhaps, thou may'st be as learned in Human Nature as *Shakespear* himself was, and, perhaps, thou may'st be no wiser than some of his Editors'. This lofty treatment of the pedants and other low creatures, thus projected by proxy, is a little-discussed feature of Augustan satire which I have noted in chapter 8.

The passage about Shakespeare in the *Journey* has a sharpness which approaches the tone of Lucian and of Swift, but on the whole Fielding is more genial. Describing a 'concert' given by Orpheus and Sappho, Fielding brings in not only Homer but two translators-and-commentators of his works:

Old Homer was present . . . and Madam Dacier sat in his lap. He asked much after Mr. Pope, and said he was very desirous of seeing him; for that he had read his Iliad in his translation with almost as much delight, as he believed he had given others in the original. I had the curiosity to enquire whether he had really writ that poem in detached pieces, and sung it about as ballads all over Greece, according to the report which went of him? He smiled at my question, and asked me, whether there appeared any connection in the poem; for if there did, he thought I might answer myself. I then importuned him to acquaint me in which of the cities, which contended for the honour of his birth, he was really born? To which he answered – 'Upon my soul I can't tell'.

Some of the details (notably the speculation about Homer's place of birth) occur in Lucian's *True History* and the general subject matter occurs in both Lucian and Swift. But Fielding's passage has a note of convivial good-temper lacking in both the earlier writers. Fielding differs in this respect even from Rabelais, whose corresponding passages of otherworldly literary satire (II:xxx and V:xxxi) do not happen to share Fielding's easy companionable way, and whose geniality elsewhere is more energetic or exuberant, less relaxed and mellow than that of the opening of Fielding's paragraph. And when in the next paragraph

Fielding reports an incident in which Addison is discomfited by some remarks made to him by Virgil, the satire is not harsh, and quickly ends when 'a very merry spirit, one Dick Steel' comes in and restores good humour all round.

The second clearly defined section of the *Journey* consists of the last sixteen chapters of Book I, beginning with chapter x. It is an incomplete story of the various transmigrations of the soul of Julian the Apostate, as has already been mentioned. The narrator is surprised in I:x to meet Julian in Elysium, 'for I had concluded, that no man ever had a better title to the bottomless pit than he. But I soon found, that this same Julian the apostate was also the very individual archbishop Latimer'. Julian tells him that even his career as the Emperor Julian had been unjustly maligned, and that he had not been 'so bad a man as he had been represented'. Minos had not originally admitted him to Elysium, but had not consigned him to the 'bottomless pit' either. Instead, he was repeatedly sent back to earth to live a new life which might earn him admittance, and experienced successively

> the different characters of a slave, a Jew, a general, an heir, a carpenter, a beau, a monk, a fiddler, a wise man, a king, a fool, a beggar, a prince, a statesman, a soldier, a tailor, an alderman, a poet, a knight, a dancing-master, and three times a bishop before his martyrdom, which, together with his other behaviour in this last character, satisfied the judge, and procured him a passage to the blessed regions.

The actual narrative as we have it stops at I:xxv with the dancing-master's career and the mention of a next stage as an English bishop, but 'Here part of the manuscript is lost . . . '

Each successive episode shows us Julian undeserving of heaven, but not actually bad enough for hell (or if bad enough, redeemed by suffering or by some other factor: if many of the incarnations are mainly disreputable, others have touches of scabrous charm or virtue). The pattern reflects an ambiguity which has often surrounded the reputation of the historical Julian, that fourth-century Roman Emperor who rejected Christianity in favour of the religious cults and the philosophy of ancient Greece, who nevertheless refused to persecute the Christians unduly and practised a measure of general toleration, and who was a very able military leader and a hardworking and controversial ruler, much loved by some, but hated by others (especially by Christians).

Julian has excited the imagination of many authors. He is an important figure in Lorenzo de' Medici's short play *La Rappresentazione di San Giovanni e Paolo*, the subject of an admiring essay by Montaigne (II:xix), and the chief character of Ibsen's massive *Emperor and Galilean*. More recently, he has been the dedicatee of Céline's unsavoury political tract, *L'Ecole des cadavres* (1938), and the hero of a long novel by Gore Vidal (*Julian*, 1964). He looms large in the history of the Roman Empire and the early Christian church, and is in particular a prominent figure in Gibbon's *Decline and Fall*.

Fielding's treatment of Julian represents a pattern of mixed feelings which may be felt to be inherent to the case. But unlike the other authors I have mentioned, he does not deal, whether historically or fictionally, with the career of the Emperor Julian. His deliberate freedoms with history are made very clear in the Preface to the *Miscellanies*:

> I have, in the relation which I have put into the mouth of Julian, whom they call the Apostate, done many violences to history, and mixed truth and falsehood with much freedom. To these I answer, I profess fiction only; and though I have chosen some facts out of history to embellish my work, and fix a chronology to it, I have not, however, confined myself to nice exactness; having often ante-dated, and sometimes post-dated, the matter I have found in the historian, particularly in the Spanish history, where I take both these liberties in one story.

Fielding mainly means that he has taken liberties with *later* historical events (i.e. between Julian's death in AD 363 and Latimer's in the sixteenth century, with which Julian's story was to end) in the course of Julian's posthumous transmigrations. As to the events of Julian's life *as Julian*, Fielding does not so much distort as ignore them altogether. The fictional method is in some ways that which Virginia Woolf was to adopt in *Orlando*, as Aurélien Digeon pointed out in an article in 1931. But Orlando's progress through history forms a continuously flowing fantasia, and is not, like Julian's, broken up into distinct, and essentially didactic, episodes. Each of Julian's transmigrations is a self-contained parable, embodying satire of particular human types and social milieux. Each is an extended version, running to chapter-length, of the kind of nutshell-morality that we get on a smaller scale in the case-histories of I:vii. The successive life-roles

329

assumed by Julian are in every case subjected to the judgment of Minos, regularly delivered as a witty or arresting pay-off. Thus, just as in I:vii the prude is refused admission to Elysium because 'there was not a single prude in Elysium', so, in I:xviii, Julian is refused a place after his scurrilous career as a court-fool: ' "Minos laughed heartily at several things in my story, and then telling me, No one played the fool in Elysium, bid me go back again" '.

The third and final section of the *Journey* leaps whimsically from Book I, ch.xxv to Book XIX, ch.vii. It is a narrative of the life of Anne Boleyn, spoken by her spirit in Elysium: a slight piece, perhaps, as Digeon suggested in 1931, written by Fielding's sister Sarah (the authorial note at the end of the previous chapter says 'this chapter is, in the original, writ in a woman's hand: and though the observations in it are . . . as excellent as any of the whole volume, there seems to be a difference in style between this and the preceding chapters; and as it is the character of a woman which is related, I am inclined to fancy it was really written by one of that sex'). At the end, as at the end of every transmigration of Julian, Minos delivers his pay-off judgment:

> On the conclusion of this history, Minos paused for a small time, and then ordered the gate to be thrown open for Anna Boleyn's admittance; on the consideration, that whoever had suffered being a queen for four years, and been sensible during all that time of the real misery which attends that exalted station ought to be forgiven whatever she had done to obtain it.

Perhaps Fielding himself wrote this final sentence, although it lacks the edge of many of the earlier conclusions. He almost certainly, however, wrote the closing footnote, which coyly proclaims the work's incompleteness and which I have already quoted: 'Here ends this curious manuscript; the rest being destroyed in rolling up pens, tobacco, & c. . . . '

1973

11

Empson's Tom Jones

William Empson's distinguished defence of *Tom Jones* (*Kenyon Review*, XX (1958), 217–49) will probably, and deservedly, remain a classic reappraisal of that novel. On one important matter, however, that of Tom's sexual morals, the essay seems to me to suffer from a misleading supererogation of critical method, of 'Empson's routine paradox' as he calls it (218). I think that Empson's conclusions are the correct ones, but that he arrives circuitously at what Fielding himself tells us plainly. The 'habitual double irony' expounded by Empson reinforces and enriches what Fielding has to say and Empson (220) is not unaware of the didactic passages which clarify Fielding's position more 'straightforwardly'. But I think the overall emphasis of the essay is misleading.

According to Empson, 'Fielding's opinions, which he seems to be expressing with bluff directness', leave the reader 'baffled to make out what [Fielding] really does think' about, among other things, 'the Christian command of chastity'. To resolve the well-known ambiguity of Fielding's attitude to Tom's sexual lapses – they are condoned on the one hand 'whereas the book makes plenty of firm assertions that Tom is doing wrong' – one must therefore turn to the 'style' of the novel, which is a 'habitual double irony'. This is a 'trick' whereby the ironist A, with 'a show of lightness and carelessness', shows that he 'understands both the positions' of persons B and C, who seem roughly to stand for opposing points of view;[1] A disingenuously pretends to support both (or rather opens himself to the interpretation of supporting either equally, so that both B and C are taken in) while in reality 'A may hold some wise balanced position between them, or contrariwise may be feeling "a plague on both your houses"'. It's a useful definition of a form of irony, but seems out of focus in stressing the obliquity or 'evasiveness' of Fielding's manner, and in suggesting that on this question he 'has a certain shyness about expressing his doctrine'. (236)

331

The famous chapter 'Of Love' (VI:i) is the important document. Fielding sarcastically 'grants' to the 'Philosophers' against whom he is arguing that, among other things,

> . . . what is commonly called Love, namely, the Desire of satisfying a voracious Appetite with a certain Quantity of delicate white human Flesh, is by no Means that Passion for which I here contend. This is indeed more properly Hunger; and as no Glutton is ashamed to apply the Word Love to his Appetite, and to say he LOVES such and such Dishes; so may the Lover of this Kind, with equal Propriety say, he HUNGERS after such and such Women.
>
> Thirdly, I will grant, which I believe will be a most acceptable Concession, that this Love for which I am an Advocate, though it satisfies itself in a much more delicate Manner, doth nevertheless seek its own Satisfaction as much as the grossest of all our Appetites.
>
> And, Lastly, That this Love when it operates towards one of a different Sex, is very apt, towards its complete Gratification, to call in the Aid of that Hunger which I have mentioned above; and which it is so far from abating, that it heightens all its Delights to a Degree scarce imaginable by those who have never been susceptible of any other Emotions, than what have proceeded from Appetite alone.
>
> In return to all these Concessions, I desire of the Philosophers to grant, that there is in some (I believe in many) human Breasts, a kind and benevolent Disposition, which is gratified by contributing to the Happiness of others. That in this Gratification alone, as in Friendship, in parental and filial Affection, as indeed in general Philanthropy, there is a great and exquisite Delight. That if we will not call such Disposition Love, we have no Name for it. That though the Pleasures arising from such pure Love may be heightened and sweetened by the Assistance of amorous Desires, yet the former can subsist alone, nor are they destroyed by the Intervention of the latter. Lastly, That Esteem and Gratitude are the proper Motives to Love, as Youth and Beauty are to Desire; and therefore though such Desire may naturally cease, when Age or Sickness overtakes its Object, yet these can have no Effect on Love, nor ever shake or remove from a good Mind, that Sensation or Passion which hath Gratitude and Esteem for its Basis.

The passage is, of course, not 'straight'. It is governed by the note of angry sarcasm, and addresses the reader not by direct statement but through the oblique tactic of 'granting' to the philosophers or 'desiring them to grant' the various propositions it is putting across. But this irony is not so much evasive as intensive. The indignant or mock-indignant business reinforces rather than attenuates or obscures the essential point, and Empson is right to call the passage a 'firm treatment of the reader' (225). The argument makes very explicit a 'doctrine' which Empson thinks of as masked by protective gestures: though what is made explicit is admittedly less simple, 'doctrinally' speaking, than the kind of feeling that Tom is 'doing wrong' which is sometimes attributed to Fielding by an opposite or neo-Christian group of apologists. (These were beginning to come to the surface in the academic study of Fielding at about the time Empson was writing: for some reflections on the phenomenon, see below, chapter 15).

The passage, as Empson says, is more than just 'healthy'. It expresses a richly moral but hardly a simplifying view of sexual passion. It distinguishes firmly between the best love (not necessarily sexual but not excluding sexuality) at one end, and 'Appetite alone' at the other, and allows for the full range of possibilities in between. It is directed at 'Philosophers' of the Hobbesian or Mandevillian cast, 'who, some Years since, very much alarmed the World, by shewing that there were no such things as Virtue or Goodness really existing in Human Nature' (though Fielding is not one of those who claim against Hobbes that *all* men are naturally good: 'there is in some . . . human Breasts', but not in all, not, for example in Blifil's, that 'benevolent Disposition' which is called 'Love'). 'Benevolence', a key-word in *Tom Jones*, had become by Fielding's time a standard term in moral discourse, both in formal philosophical contexts and in the more informal (quasi-technical or non-technical) discussion of moral issues with which I am mainly concerned here.[2] Together with closely related terms like 'Good-nature', it featured as an important element in anti-Hobbesian polemics. A condensed form of one of the traditional anti-Hobbesian arguments is that, on the premise that a man (or Man in general, according to more extreme theorists) is naturally good, the exercise of benevolence is in keeping with his spontaneous impulses and therefore directly produces pleasure in the doing. As Fielding puts it, the 'benevolent Disposition . . . is gratified by contributing to the Happiness of others' and 'in this Gratification alone . . . there is a great and exquisite Delight'. The currency of this simple doctrine during the period suggests that neither it (nor probably Fielding's application of it to sexual love) would be missed by a contemporary reader. Polemical precedent need hardly be invoked, though Fielding makes it clear that he is attacking the Hobbesians. (The harping on 'Appetite', a familiar term in Hobbesian discourse, seems further designed here to enforce the connection). Fielding is known to have been familiar with the works of seventeenth century 'benevolist' divines such as Isaac Barrow, a reading of whose works, incidentally, contributes to the conversion of Booth in *Amelia*, and whose direct expression of the doctrine is quoted by Fielding in the *Covent-Garden Journal* (No 29, 11 April 1752).[3] Fielding's novels make repeated assertions of the main psychological principle: 'Men of a benign Disposition enjoy their own Acts of Beneficence, equally with those to whom they are done'; they also are unhappy when they cause misery; indeed 'there are scarce any Natures so entirely diabolical' as not to feel in this way, though Blifil is presumably one of these. Sometimes the point is emphasised with a heightened 'sentimental' rhetoric, as when in the same chapter Jones takes over from the narrator and asks Nightingale: '"And do not the warm, rapturous Sensations, which we feel from the Consciousness of an honest, noble, generous, benevolent Action, convey more Delight to the Mind, than the undeserved Praise of Millions?"' If there is 'double irony', in a possible suggestion that Fielding himself is here dissociated from this high language, it is likely to be very faint: the excess, by the standards of the age, is not gross, and Fielding is certainly not dissociated from the thing said as distinct possibly from the way of saying (XIV:vii; see also XV:viii, citing and glossing Terence's *Homo sum : Humani nihil a me alienum puto*, a passage to which Fielding reverted more than once).

It is axiomatic in Fielding's psychology that 'to confer Benefits on each other, and to do mutual Good' is 'as agreeable to Nature, as for the right Hand to assist the left.'[4] In an immediately obvious sense, self-love and social are, to some natures, the same;[5] and whatever else Fielding might think of the unconverted Booth's inferences from his theory of the 'predominant Passion', he would certainly endorse the view that 'Where Benevolence . . . is the uppermost Passion, Self-Love directs you to gratify it by doing good, and by relieving the Distresses of others; for they are in Reality your own' (*Amelia*, X:ix). The doctrine of benevolist hedonism was sufficiently widespread in general, and insistently enough emphasised by Fielding in particular, for his refinement

334

or extension of it to the field of sex-ethics (as in *Tom Jones*, VI:i) not to be missed. Contemporaries may have disapproved, but it is unlikely that they would have misunderstood an explicitly formulated refinement of a familiar idea. The habit of referring to benevolence as analogous to sexual passion, its delights so great as to be almost sensual, seems to have become common among moralists and divines several decades before Fielding. Crane gives examples from 1676, 'There is a Delight and Joy that Accompanies doing good, there is a kind of sensuality in it' (Crane, 228), and 1704, 'doing Good' gives 'a Pleasure ... that Delights and Comforts even to the cherishing of our own Flesh, that runs along with our Affections and our Bowels so very sympathetically, that some good Men have indulged and epicuriz'd in it, till they have been tempted to call it downright *Sensuality*' (Crane, 229: 'Sensuality' may be used in a non-erotic sense, but seems unlikely here to be without some erotic connotations). Fielding sometimes spoke of the *impetuosity* of benevolence (*Works*, XIII:110: an amiable feature, but needing restraint), rather as Swift, referring to his feelings for Stella, spoke of 'violent friendship' by analogy with 'violent love' (Swift, *Correspondence*, III:145, see above, chapter 4(ii),n.56): the erotic analogy there, as in Crane's examples, suggests degrees of intensity as much as or even more than similarities of kind. But in some cases the degree of intensity is such that it converts the experience into a physical pleasure which approaches 'sensuality' beyond mere analogy. In others, similarity or relationship of kind is proposed much in the spirit of *Tom Jones*, VI:i, as when Steele, dedicating his periodical *The Lover* to Garth, praised Good-nature:

> This Propensity is the nearest akin to Love; and Good-nature is the worthiest Affection of the Mind, as Love is the noblest Passion of it: While the latter is wholly employed in endeavouring to make happy one single Object, the other diffuses Benevolence to all the World.[6]

Fielding's chapter 'Of Love' goes beyond this. Both passages use terms like 'Propensity' or 'Disposition' to describe benevolence/good-nature, and employ the term 'Passion' to describe love. In a sense, the analogy between benevolence and love is qualified by this terminological emphasis, but Fielding tends as Steele does not to collapse the difference by stressing both the active quasi-sexual gratifications of benevolence and their interaction with primary sexual pleasure. In this sense Fielding comes closer to asserting not only analogy between benevolence and love but an element of identity: an area of experience where the two converge into an undifferentiated and reciprocally reinforcing state. Thus benevolence not only seeks 'its own Satisfaction as much as the grossest of all our Appetites',[7] but its pleasures may in appropriate cases 'be heightened and sweetened by the Assistance of amorous Desires'. On this principle, genuine sexual affection, even if mainly carnal, is a form of benevolence, so long as it is a matter of real affection rather than of 'Appetite alone'. This gives status to Tom's minor sexual lapses with Molly Seagrim and others, to his easy-going unchastities and his chivalrous inability to decline the advances of female admirers. Tom's sexual indulgences are indicated as satisfying his self-love not primarily in so far as he enjoys fornication but in the more important sense connected with the benevolist rationale I have outlined. In a famous passage, Fielding comments on Tom's feelings for Molly, as contrasted with Blifil's general character:

> As there are some Minds whose Affections, like Master *Blifil's*, are solely placed on one single Person, whose Interest and Indulgence alone they consider on every Occasion; regarding the Good and Ill of all others as merely indifferent, any farther than as they contribute to the Pleasure or Advantage of that Person: So there is a different Temper of Mind which borrows a Degree of Virtue even from Self-love; such can never receive any kind of Satisfaction from another, without loving the Creature to whom that Satisfaction is owing, and without making its Well-being in some sort necessary to their own Ease.
> Of this latter Species was our Heroe.
>
> (IV:vi).[8]

Booth's liaison with Miss Matthews in *Amelia* is similarly interpreted. Booth 'was a Man of consummate Good-nature, and had formerly had much Affection for this young Lady; indeed, more than the Generality of People are capable of entertaining for any Person whatsoever' (*Amelia*, III:xii). These are pretty categorical statements, placing the minor unchastities of the two heroes within the scheme of values. As Empson says, there are 'plenty of firm assertions that Tom is doing wrong'. Fielding is undoubtedly in favour of 'the Christian command of chastity', dislikes vulgar sensuality and would scornfully repudiate any doctrine of 'free love' based on libertine or on sensibilist principles. But the unchastities of Tom and Booth cannot be identified with such things. They conform, however incompletely, to the definition of love given in *Tom Jones*, VI:i, even as the whole moral atmosphere of the novels presupposes the superiority of Tom's chaste courtship of Sophia and Booth's conjugal love of Amelia to these lesser and more transient passions. Novelistic convention would demand this, of course, but few readers would feel that the point is merely a formal or perfunctory observance of conventional expectation. The minor lapses are actively interpreted as manifestations of that same 'benevolent Disposition' of which the love for Sophia or Amelia are the full flowering. The formulations of *Tom Jones*, VI:i, and of related statements elsewhere in the novels not only make the 'doctrine' clear, but do so with an assertiveness which thrusts forthrightly through all the urbane obliquities of Fielding's ironic voice. Empson describes these obliquities with characteristic finesse and captures the essential feeling handsomely: but the emphasis on obliquity, and its suggestion of 'shyness' and stylistic subterfuge, undercuts the directness and fervour of Fielding's point and tends to that extent to mislead.

1959

Notes
1 More specifically, B is a 'tyrant', 'holding the more official or straight-faced belief', whose opposition must be circumvented. C is the 'person addressed', whose sympathies are likely to be very different from those of B.
2 For the philosophical context, see T. A. Roberts, *The Concept of Benevolence: Aspects of Eighteenth-Century Moral Philosophy* (London, 1973); see also Bernard Harrison, *Henry Fielding's Tom Jones: The Novelist as Moral Philosopher* (London, 1975), esp. 89ff.
3 On anti-Hobbesian polemics see R. S. Crane, 'Suggestions Toward a Genealogy of the "Man of Feeling"', *ELH. A Journal of English Literary History*, I (1934), 205–30, esp. 'Benevolent feelings as "natural" to man' (220ff.); 'The "Self-Approving Joy"' (227ff.); Barrow (227–28). Donald Greene's answer to Crane, 'Latitudinarianism and Sensibility: The Genealogy of the *"Man of Feeling"* Reconsidered', *Modern Philology*, LXXV (1977), 159–83, may be consulted as a rather bludgeoning confutation of some of Crane's points, but does not affect the argument here. Crane's essay seems to me on the whole to survive Greene's posthumous put-down pretty well. On Hobbesian 'Appetite' and Fielding, see my *Henry Fielding* (London and New York, 1968), 47, 142–8, 151–8; and 'Cannibalism and Fiction: Part II', *Genre*, XI (1978), 231, 313.
4 *Covent-Garden Journal*, ed. G. E. Jensen, I:354 (No. 39, 16 May 1752).
5 The background of controversy about 'self-love' and 'benevolence' has often been studied. The subject is briefly but well treated in W. R. Irwin, *The Making of Jonathan Wild* (New York, 1941), 59ff.
6 Rae Blanchard (ed.), *Richard Steele's Periodical Journalism 1714–16* (Oxford, 1959), 3.

7 See Fielding's poem 'Of Good-Nature', l.40, and the passage from John Balguy's preface to *The Law of Truth*, cited in annotation of it in Henry Knight Miller (ed.), *Miscellanies by Henry Fielding, Esq; Volume One* (Oxford, 1972), 32 and n.2. Though Balguy is cited as differing from Fielding, both authors suggest that to deny satisfaction to one's benevolence is, in Balguy's words, 'a kind of Violence and Self-denial'.

8 The fine passage about Mrs Waters's generous and unselfish sensuality at the end of IX:vi is quoted both by John Middleton Murry, *Unprofessional Essays* (London, 1956), 32–3, in an essay which provoked Empson's, and by Empson himself (244). Empson called it 'a particularly massive bit of double irony', adding 'though I take it Fielding just believed what he said, and only knew at the back of his mind that the kind of man who would otherwise complain about it would presume it was irony'!

PART IV

Others

12

Notes on 'Delicacy'

(i)

'Delicacy' is a frequent term in the vocabulary of eighteenth-century sentimentalism. It is hard to define exactly, because it has an infinite number of subtly differing usages. It is closely allied in meaning to 'sensibility' but refers particularly to fineness rather than intensity of feeling, while 'sensibility' might cover both.[1] Sentimentalists valued 'un sentiment délicat et fin' and 'sentiments ... tender and refined'[2] quite as much as violent passion and in some cases more; accordingly, 'delicacy', whatever its contextual shade of meaning, was a common term of praise during the sentimental period. Sometimes, indeed, it was synonymous with 'sensibility'. When the OED defined it as 'exquisite fineness of feeling', the definition, if it did not fully cover either word, might apply equally well to certain usages of both. Polly Honeycombe's words, when she said her father had no notion of the 'sensibility of delicate feeling',[3] were virtually tautological. And if sensibility and delicacy were not always the same thing, they were nearly always inseparable. 'There is everything to be expected from *sensibility, and delicacy*, joined; but, indeed, I have scarce ever known them separated, in a female heart.'[4]

If 'sensibility', then, is the term for that compound of qualities most cherished by the eighteenth-century woman, 'delicacy' is the term for some of sensibility's most important attributes. Closest to the meaning of 'sensibility' is the conception of delicacy as a heightened emotional susceptibility.[5] Such a susceptibility is modesty (a form of delicacy), as defined by Addison in a famous passage:

Modesty ... is a kind of quick and delicate feeling in the soul ... It is such an exquisite sensibility, as warns [the soul] to shun the first appearance of every thing which is hurtful.[6]

341

Modesty, a manifestation of delicacy, was often explicitly thought of as its equivalent. In Garrick's Epilogue to Kelly's *False Delicacy* (1768), the phrases 'False Modesty' and 'False Delicacy' are pointedly implied to be interchangeable. So also when, reviewing Hawkesworth's *Almoran and Hamet* (1761), the *Monthly Review* speaks of the 'vast indelicacy and indecorum' of the heroine Almeida in

> courting Almoran, and making him a voluntary offer of that for which she might be sure he would be forward enough to sue. In short, her behaviour, in that scene, is not answerable to that softness, and refined sensibility we might expect from her character,[7]

the word 'indelicacy' refers to a lack of punctilious modesty on Almeida's part. Her case is complex; but modesty is often concerned with checking certain feelings, or at least their display. So seen, it might appear incompatible with sensibility, which, interested in 'experiencing endless varieties of warmth', theoretically cherished the feelings as such and would give them free rein. The conception of delicacy as a restraint was moreover not restricted to those aspects of it which might be identified with modesty. Thus, in the *Nouvelle Héloïse* we read that Saint-Preux has 'plus d'amour que de délicatesse' (meaning here 'more love than tact, impetuosity than self-control'), a phrase which echoes, though it refers to other things, an earlier description of his love as consisting 'plus de transports que de sagesse'.[8] Delicacy is often a kind of regulator of sensibility, checking it when it is excessive or verges on impropriety. Interestingly, however, one of the best contemporary descriptions of delicacy as restraint uses the word 'sensibility' instead, in spite of the fact that the two are not only different but in some sense at odds – a measure of the close semantic connection between the two words, though they are not strictly interchangeable here:

> That quick sensibility to the *beautiful*, the *becoming*, in the intercourse of life; that spontaneous feeling of
> 'A grace, a manner, a decorum,'
> in morals; to which women owe half their virtue . . . .[9]

The difficulty of reconciling delicacy, which restrains the feelings, with sensibility, which indulges them, is in fact only apparent. For it was possible to see the restraint itself as a feeling in

its own right, and a 'sensibility'. The frequent interconnected use
of the two terms may be a result, or a cause, of this way of looking
at the question, insofar as it was at all conscious. Probably it was
both result and cause, though linguistic and semantic factors
cannot have been the only ones involved. If sensibility is set up as
an ideal of womanhood, and if it implies emotional libertarianism, formulas must be devised whereby the more enduring
ideals of female modesty and even chastity may be preserved.
There were several formulas for the preservation of chastity
within the sentimental code. One was that sensuality, inferior to
the pleasures of the mind, was outside the pale of sensibility.
Another was that sensibility comprised by definition a 'moral
sense', an instinctive sense of moral rectitude, which automatically kept those endowed with it in the path of virtue.[10] Later in the
century, such a novelist as Mary Wollstonecraft found less need
for such formulas, for she tended to reject, in the name of the
holiness of the heart's affections, conventional standards of chastity, thus pursuing the theoretical doctrine of sensibility a little
further towards its logical conclusion. But that, in England,
seems on the whole a late and a comparatively rare development,
and outside my present scope. Generally the restraints remained
and the formulas served to uphold them within a code which
seemingly advocated full emotional liberty.[11] Indeed, the whole
position of Mary Wollstonecraft herself was far from being a
simple one, in this matter.

The formula with which I am immediately concerned was
enlisted in the cause not of chastity but of delicacy and modesty,
insofar as they were restraints upon the feelings. By this formula
(which, as a formula, was needless to say unacknowledged and
probably unconscious) the restraints themselves became feelings.
Modesty, in Addison's phrase, was a 'delicate feeling' and an
'exquisite sensibility' and a heroine of the 1760s came to be praised
for her 'sweet *impulsive* modesty.'[12] Delicacy and modesty, thus
seen, are not merely checks to love or the improper display of
affection: they are emotions competing with them and also
requiring expression. Thus delicacy remains a part of sensibility
even in seeming opposed to it.

Another meaning of 'delicacy' is 'tact, tactful considerateness'.
This, like other kinds of delicacy, is a quality which persons of
sensibility have in great abundance. Thus in the early part of the
last volume of Frances Sheridan's *Sidney Bidulph* much is made of
the 'extreme delicacy'[13] of Lord V. towards Cecilia Arnold. But
supreme in point of delicacy, in this sense, is Richardson's Sir

Charles Grandison. His tactfulness achieved standards of benevolent subtlety seldom equalled by other heroes. It manifested itself as much in what he omitted to say or do as in what he said or did. Thus Harriet Byron, in love with Sir Charles, knows that the Italian Lady Clementina is also in love with him – literally to the point of insanity. Herself greatly endowed with delicacy, she disinterestedly approves that he should go to Italy to see what can be done for the unhappy lady. She describes Sir Charles's reaction:

> Had he praised me highly for this my address to him, it would have looked, such was the situation on both sides, as if he had thought this disinterested behaviour in me, an extraordinary piece of magnanimity and self-denial; and, of consequence, as if he had supposed I had views upon him, which he wondered I could give up. His is the most delicate of human minds.[14]

But delicacy, whether as tact, considerateness, modesty, or merely as general emotional susceptibility or refinement, did not exhaust its commendability to persons of sensibility in moral or ethical qualities. Delicacy as a *physical* attribute (and as such, it would seem, the furthest removed from sensibility's sphere of interest) was also highly commended. Many heroines were endowed with it, whether it was conceived of as a graceful slenderness ('the exquisite delicacy of Miss Arnold's figure'), a susceptibility to illness ('the slightest attack would shatter so delicate a frame'),[15] or a nervous frailty (many heroines, like Smollett's Lydia Melford, had 'delicate nerves').[16] The cult of physical delicacy may owe something to the esteem in which delicacy in general was automatically held by sentimentalists. We may also connect it with the even more general fondness of men of feeling for frailty and weakness. Hannah More complained in 1799 of the sentimental ladies who, being told 'that their strength consists in their weakness', would 'pride themselves on that very weakness, and ... become vain of their imperfections'.[17] On another level, speaking of her love for Mr Clinton, the hero's uncle in Henry Brooke's *Fool of Quality*, Matilda Golding calls the feeling a weakness, but one 'which I account my chiefest merit, and which is my chiefest pride.'[18] But whether owing more to the general cult of delicacy, or to the general cult of weakness, the fact was that physical delicacy (frailty or weakness) was at a premium. As the Rev. James Fordyce put it, 'men of sensibility desire in

344

every woman soft features, and a flowing voice, a form not robust, and demeanour delicate and gentle.'[19]

A multitude of reasons thus made delicacy, in almost any sense of the word, a highly acceptable quality to the sentimentalist, whether defined as a part of sensibility, as its near-equivalent, or as its physical attribute – even when, as we have seen, delicacy would at least superficially seem to militate against the emotional libertarianism implied by sentimentalism.

(ii)

A work which deals thematically with the concept of delicacy is Hugh Kelly's comedy, *False Delicacy* (1768). In it, 'delicacy' is a key-word, in something like the sense in which 'prudence' is a key-word in *Pamela* or 'benevolence' in *Tom Jones*. Around multiple usages of the key-word is built such moral framework as the play possesses. An examination of 'delicacy' in Kelly's comedy thus provides the two-fold opportunity of studying some connotations of the word, and of attempting a reinterpretation of a now little-read play.

Delicacy (whether or not the word itself is used in each instance) motivates the whole action of the play. Usually, here, it assumes the form of an extreme scrupulousness and considerateness. In the sub-plot, Colonel Rivers, an obstinate keeper of his word, and opposed to mercenary marriages, refuses his daughter to the rich Sir Harry, having promised her to the poorer Sidney. The couple, however, are genuinely in love, and plan to reward the Colonel's delicacy by eloping. This delicacy then displays a further refinement. The Colonel decides not to prevent the elopement by force (as a wicked antisentimental parent in a novel would), nor does he intend to hinder the lovers by withdrawing the promise of £20,000 which he had once made to his daughter for the time of her marriage. Instead, he gives her security for the money ('but never see me more'). This moves her so, that her own delicacy is brought into play, and she cancels the elopement. This sub-plot is taken fairly seriously, though it has comic elements, and is infected by the main plot, where the comic element predominates.

In the main plot, further convoluted interplay of delicacy is described by Mark Schorer: 'Lady Betty loves Winworth but rejects him because it is indelicate to accept a man's first proposal; Winworth turns therefore to Miss Marchmont, Lady Betty's companion, and asks Lady Betty to speak a word in his favour to the lady in question. Bound by honour and again, by delicacy, Lady Betty implores her friend to marry the man she herself wishes to marry. Miss Marchmont, in love with Mr Sidney, who is contracted to Miss Rivers, who in turn loves Sir Harry, feels duty bound to accept Sir George's proposal.'[20] This account is not quite as accurate as it might be (Lord Winworth, for instance, is not called Sir George), but it does convey well the atmosphere of frenzied complication created by the characters' exercise of 'false' or exaggerated 'delicacy'. The whole story, as the title suggests, is motivated by this: it is the *reductio ad absurdum* of fastidious scruple and misguided tact.

In specific instances in which the word 'delicacy' itself occurs, it is often either the equivalent of 'sensibility' or refers to qualities which would be automatically associated with it. In Act II, Lady Betty gives reasons for her initial refusal of Lord Winworth's addresses: they were ignorance of her own real fondness for him, 'my unhappiness in my first marriage', and her belief, which 'I have frequently argued, that a woman of real delicacy shou'd never admit a second impression on her heart.'[21] This latter doctrine, applicable, we are told here, to women of 'real delicacy', was a recognised standard element of the sentimental code. It is shared by the heroes and heroines of some of the novels I have cited, and by many more; and in her satire of sentimentalism, *Sense and Sensibility*, Jane Austen made a point of including it for ridicule along with the rest of her heroine's sentimental baggage. Marianne Dashwood did 'not approve of second attachments' (indeed 'she considers them impossible to exist') and her 'favourite maxim' is 'that no one can ever be in love more than once in their life.'[22] Lady Betty's 'real delicacy' in the quoted passage implies a type of emotional perfectionism directly associated with sentimentalism; the quality seems to consist partly of the strict observance of a standard sentimental rule. 'Delicacy' is here almost the equivalent of 'sensibility' and the latter word might have been used instead without perceptible change of meaning.

To continue with the story, the genial Mrs Harley, who has herself been married twice, cannot accept Lady Betty's scruples. Mrs Harley stands for good-humoured common sense, and is a cross between Jane Austen's Elinor and a sort of virtuous Pandarus. She suggests a scheme whereby she will tactfully inform Winworth that Lady Betty is not really ill-disposed towards him. Winworth would then renew his suit, and Lady Betty's happiness would be achieved. Lady Betty, invoking the 'laws of delicacy', will not hear of it at first. Mrs Harley sacrilegiously calls these laws 'trifles' and exclaims:

> ... What a work there is with you sentimental folks ... thank heav'n, my sentiments are not sufficiently refin'd to make me unhappy ... the devil take this delicacy; I don't know any thing it does besides making people miserable: – And yet somehow, foolish as it is, one can't help liking it ...[23]

Three points emerge. 'Sentimental folks' is synonymous with 'persons who obey the "laws of delicacy." ' Delicacy is associated specifically with the 'refin'd' kind of 'sentiments'. And finally, 'foolish as it is, one can't help liking it'. The latter, we may remark, is Jane Austen's attitude to Marianne, made explicit.[24]

By Act IV, Lady Betty, though herself deeply in love with Winworth, has conducted a suit to Miss Marchmont on his behalf, and at his request, though he still loves Lady Betty. Miss Marchmont, in love with another, refuses, and Lady Betty expresses her relief to Mrs Harley.[25] Mrs Harley, after a reference to the 'delicate absurdities' of the ladies' 'elevated minds', gives Lady Betty renewed assurances that it is with her and not Miss Marchmont that Winworth is still in love. Meanwhile, Miss Marchmont's delicacy leads her to imagine that she has offended Lady Betty by refusing Winworth, and she endures a conflict between the delicacy which forbids her to marry a man she does not love, and the delicacy which makes it difficult for her to cause pain to her friend. She decides to sacrifice her inclination by accepting Winworth's proposal after all.

By this time Lady Betty is convinced that Winworth is really in love with her, and Miss Marchmont's decision causes alarm. Much delicacy is exercised by both ladies. Mrs Harley is afraid lest Miss Marchmont's new decision should upset her plan for bringing Winworth and Lady Betty together ('Now will I be hang'd if she doesn't undo every thing by a fresh stroke of delicacy ... O the devil take this elevation of sentiment ... Now her delicacy is willing to be miserable').[26] Lady Betty assures Miss Marchmont that she is not hurt by her refusal of Winworth – on the contrary. Miss Marchmont takes this as a further sign of Lady Betty's considerate magnanimity, and is all the more determined to sacrifice herself by accepting Winworth ('Did ever two fools plague one another so heartily with their delicacy and sentiment?').[27]

Eventually, however, all complications are resolved and all the lovers correctly paired. Mrs Harley declares 'the triumph of good sense over delicacy', and Cecil, another character, considers it 'extremely happy for your people of refin'd sentiments to have friends with a little common understanding'.[28] It seems almost superfluous by now to note in nearly all these passages the collocation and identification of 'delicacy' with 'refined' or 'elevated sentiments'. That is, with 'sensibility' in one of its primary forms.

False Delicacy has frequently been thought of as a 'sentimental comedy' *par excellence*, of the kind which Goldsmith attacked in his famous essay of 1773, in the Preface to *The Good-Natured Man* (1768), and, in a glancing reference, in the Dedication to Dr Johnson of *She Stoops to Conquer* (1773).[29] Goldsmith may well have borne Kelly's play (of course among others) in mind when he made these attacks, for it was a much envied (and very successful) rival of his own first play on the London stage early in 1768. Goldsmith's biographer Forster, in his account of the rivalry,[30] remarks that 'Kelly had sounded the depths of sentimentalism'.[31] Mark Schorer, though he considers that Kelly's attitude towards sentimentalism was dichotomous and that even in this play there are elements critical of sentimentalism, nevertheless implies that *False Delicacy* depends 'entirely ... on the sentimental interest' and that this 'sentimental interest' overshadows everything else.[32]

This is surely a tradition which needs rectifying. The title alone should set us on our guard. Moreover, the deliberately complicated absurdity of a plot motivated entirely by 'false delicacy' does not make for a straightforwardly sentimental play.[33] Goldsmith's view of sentimental comedy as intended to draw tears rather than laughter does not apply; whether Kelly's play is funny or not, it is meant to be. Of course the action of *False Delicacy* was capable of drawing the sympathetic tear not only from its audience but even from such a character within the plot as Cecil,[34] who with Mrs Harley forms a kind of puncturing, anti-sentimental chorus to the over-delicate goings-on.[35] But if one is really disposed to weep, Honeywood's tender benevolence in *The Good-Natured Man* might be as likely to arouse tears by its extreme amiability as laughter by its absurd excess. The element of sentimentalism in Goldsmith has more than once been noticed, and on a proper sentimental calculus *The Vicar of Wakefield* would surely be found a more thoroughgoing piece than any of Kelly's three best-known comedies.[36] Arthur Sherbo notes the tendency of sentimental dramatists to satirise sentimentalism, even to make fun of their own conformity to it.[37] I think there is more than mere occasional self-deflation in *False Delicacy*. The play's sympathetic characters do not just happen to be, in the style of the time, persons of sensibility. Their extreme delicacy is isolated as their chief characteristic and as the basis for the whole absurd complication of plot; the *dénouement*, however attractive the delicate characters may be in their way, has to be brought about by those few persons who have 'a little common understanding'; it is, despite a tear and some moralising in the play's closing lines, a 'triumph of good sense over delicacy'. This surely suggests that the play is not in the same category as, say, Cumberland's *Brothers* (1769) – though that is not an extreme or pure example, and in it Cumberland made little jabs from time to time at false sentimentalism in Lady Dove. If it is objected that, to the extent that the play is satiric, it satirises delicacy, in the sense of exaggerated considerateness, and not sentimentalism in general, two points may be made in answer. First, as we have seen in the general discussion of delicacy, the quality was so closely related to sensibility that it is unlikely that the bare use of the word, in almost any sense, could escape bringing sensibility and sentimentalism to the mind of a contemporary audience. Secondly, passages from the play associating delicacy with 'elevation of sentiment' and with standard sentimental attitudes (such as Lady Betty's refusal to 'admit a second impression on her heart') indicate that Kelly was perfectly deliberate in making fun not merely of a specific kind of delicacy, but, to some degree, of the cult of sensibility in general.

There are of course qualifications. Sentimentalism included more than a cult of refined emotion: it embraced also the broad benevolence of *Tom Jones* and the intense passion of Mary Wollstonecraft's *The Wrongs of Woman: or, Maria* (1798). We have seen, on the other hand, that delicacy was associated particularly with 'refined' rather than intense (or other) sensibility, and Kelly's comedy, with its constant talk of 'refin'd' and 'elevated' sentiments, does not go beyond this limited association. As a satire of sentimentalism it does not thus cover *all* its aspects: but then it is certainly aimed at one of the most important.

A more important qualification is that obviously Kelly was far from being unsympathetic to sentimentalism. His other writings prove it, though Mark Schorer has argued some of these to be more independent of sentimentalism than is *False Delicacy*.

Hardly any writing of the period, not Smollett's novels nor the plays of Goldsmith and Sheridan, could completely avoid sympathetic treatment of things which we associate with the cult of sensibility: the melting tear, the tender sigh, the decorous fainting fit, acts of spontaneous 'good-nature', delicate heroines, highly – perhaps extravagantly – benevolent heroes. *False Delicacy* has its full share of these, and no secret is made of the amiability of it all: 'foolish as it is, one can't help liking it.' But then, in a sense (and admitting differences of merit, proportion, and emphasis), Goldsmith could not 'help liking' young Honeywood, or Jane Austen, Marianne Dashwood: their satires of sensibility are nonetheless not profitably taken to be straightforward sentimental works. In *Sense and Sensibility*, it is less sensibility that Jane Austen attacks, than *excessive* sensibility. In itself, sensibility is a desirable quality, not exclusive of, but complementary to, sense: this is clear from the first chapter. Marianne and Elinor both have sensibility as well as sense, though in different proportions. And Marianne's sensibility, whereby, for instance, she 'could never love by halves', once it has been suitably tempered with sense at the end of the novel, makes her all the better a wife to Colonel Brandon[38] and all the better a person therefore. *False Delicacy* is, similarly, less levelled against delicacy than against the excess of that quality. Jane Austen's novel is more satiric in emphasis and effectiveness than Kelly's play. But the comparison helps us to see that sustained mockery of sensibility may co-exist with a strong sympathy for it, and that, though its mockery may be mild, *False Delicacy* is rather a work of this sort than, according to the traditional view, an out-and-out sentimental comedy with a few bits of satire thrown in.[39]

Kelly was a sentimental writer, and known in his day as such. The paradox about this play is that, though a satire, it is *formally* in the sentimental medium. A note to Garrick's comic Prologue says that this Prologue is a rewriting of a 'serious one' by Kelly himself. The play is chaste, eschews ribaldry, has 'pathetic' moments, and deals in 'sentiments'. It is 'sentimental' in this sense, and people said so, in praise and blame. But its 'risible' qualities, and its ridicule, were noted too. One reviewer,[40] who thought the action a mere vehicle for 'critical situations, and noble sentiment', found the situations 'extreamly entertaining' but complained of the satire: 'the sentiments are so managed, as to destroy their merit with their use. The piece, as it stands, is more a satire on true Delicacy than false . . : .'

1962

Notes

1   According to the *Monthly Magazine*, II (1796), 706–07, a person of sensibility was 'susceptible of every impression of joy or grief' and capable of 'experiencing endless varieties of warmth'. Sensibility was thus a more inclusive quality than delicacy. It could be effusively generous, as in Henry Brooke's *Fool of Quality* (1765–70), gently melancholy, as in Mackenzie's *Man of Feeling* (1771), passionate and intense, as in the novels of Mary Hays or Mary Wollstonecraft, or more 'delicate' and 'refined', as in those of Frances Brooke or Mme Riccoboni. These are of course only rough descriptions, aiming less at exact assessment of the works mentioned, than at indicating the extreme inclusiveness of the period's conception of sensibility.

2   *Nouvelle Héloïse* (1760), Editions Garnier, I: 32; *Critical Review*, XXIV (1767), 143.

3   George Colman, *Polly Honeycombe* (1760), 2.

4   Elizabeth Griffith, *The Delicate Distress* (1769), II: 105 (quoted from B. G. MacCarthy, *The Later Women Novelists* (1947), 76). On the difficulty of distinguishing between 'delicacy' and 'sensibility', see J. M. S. Tompkins, *The Popular Novel in England 1770–1800* (1932), 93–94. This work has a number of brief discussions of 'delicacy' in scattered places (see its Index) to which I am indebted.

5   E.g., 'I have a delicacy that takes alarm at the veriest trifles' (Frances Sheridan, *Memoirs of Miss Sidney Bidulph* [1761–7], 1796 ed., I: 282).

6   *Spectator*, No. 231, 24 Nov. 1711. In the first edition of Johnson's *Dictionary* (1755), this quotation is used to illustrate 'Sensibility, 1,' defined as 'Quickness of sensation'. The definition under 'Sensibility, 2,' unsupported by quotation, was 'Quickness of perception'. In the fourth edition (1773), the word 'delicacy' was added to 'Sensibility, 2,' which now read 'Quickness of perception; delicacy,' and the Addisonian definition of modesty was transferred here from 'Sensibility, 1,' providing us with a nice lexicographical collocation of 'sensibility', 'delicacy', and 'modesty'.

7   *Monthly Review*, XXIV (1761), 435.

8   *Nouvelle Héloïse*, ed. cit., I: 207, 23.

9   Frances Brooke, *The Excursion* (1777), II: 156. Cf. the same author's *History of Emily Montague* (1769), I: 225, for a similar passage, in which the phrase 'delicacy of moral taste' *is* used.

10   Hannah More, in her poem on 'Sensibility' (1782), called it 'Unprompted moral! sudden sense of right!' (*Works* [1834], V: 336).

11   The phrases 'formula' and 'code' are misleading if they suggest any single book of rules or sentimental 'system'. But it is true to say that sentimentalists shared a large body of standardised attitudes and prejudices (of which a dislike of 'systems' was one), to which they paid great lip service, for which they were often satirised, and of which, cumulatively, the phrase 'sentimental code' seems a convenient description. Similarly with the 'formulas' outlined above. They were not thought of *as formulas*. But, for example, both anti-sensualism and the doctrine of 'moral sense' were basic to sentimentalism, and they would both obviously tend to counter any implication that the cult of sensibility, in favouring the indulgence of the feelings *per se*, might be extended to justify free sexual relations. (The argument for free love on sentimental premises in fact often occurs in novels of the mid-century, only to be met with disapproval from the truer sensibility of the author or of the 'good' characters.) It seems a not unreasonable piece of verbal shorthand to call these theoretical counter-arguments 'formulas' in such a discussion as this, as long as one bears in mind that they were qualifying assumptions rather

351

Order From Confusion Sprung

than matters of explicit ratiocination. Sentimentalists took their assumptions for granted, without always bothering to enquire into them analytically: but the literary historian can hardly hope to disentangle the lurking complications and unexpected congruences of these assumptions without bringing them out into the open with an explicitness which is in a sense factitious.

12 Frances Brooke, *The History of Lady Julia Mandeville* (1763), 5th ed. (1769), I: 213. My italics.
13 *Sidney Bidulph*, ed. cit., V: 35, *et passim*.
14 *Sir Charles Grandison* (1753–4), Shakespeare Head ed., III: 297. Sir Charles's great delicacy again shows itself (though the word in this case is not used) when, arriving late at the Selby residence, where the family is expecting him, he apologises to all, and not singly to Harriet, so as not to appear to presume her to have been 'disappointed by his absence' (V: 100). For delicacy as tactful considerateness, cf. also *Evelina* (1778), ed. F. D. MacKinnon (1930), 120: 'How grateful did I feel for a proposal so considerate, and made with so much delicacy!'
15 *Sidney Bidulph*, IV: 15, 17.
16 *Humphry Clinker* (1771), Navarre Society ed., II: 202.
17 *Works* (1834), III: 258. The words appear in the chapter 'On the Danger of an Ill-Directed Sensibility' in Hannah More's *Strictures on the Modern System of Female Education* (1799).
18 *Fool of Quality* (1765–70), III: 37.
19 Quoted in R. P. Utter and G. B. Needham, *Pamela's Daughters* (1937), 207. Quoted also are Mary Wollstonecraft's comments, in the *Vindication of the Rights of Woman* (1792), on Fordyce's description of the ideal woman, in her domestic character. 'Such a woman ought to be an angel – or she is an ass – for I discern not a trace of the human character . . . .' Mary Wollstonecraft also pours scorn on the low status of 'bodily strength' among both men and women of the day, 'the latter as it takes from their feminine graces, and from that lovely weakness, the source of their undue power; and the former, because it appears inimical with the character of a gentleman'. Burke, in his treatise on *The Sublime and Beautiful* (1757), had stated as a sober fact of aesthetics that 'The beauty of women is considerably owing to their weakness, or delicacy, and is even enhanced by their timidity, a quality of mind analogous to it'. He distinguished between the attractive sort of physical delicacy or weakness, and that caused by ill-health, but even 'the ill effect of this is not because it is weakness' (III: xvi; cf. also III: ix). The foppish Mr Lovel in *Evelina* has 'an insuperable aversion to strength, either of body or mind, in a female' (*ed. cit.*, 453).
20 Mark Schorer, 'Hugh Kelly: His Place in the Sentimental School,' *PQ*, XII (1933), 394.
21 Hugh Kelly, *Works* (1778), 16.
22 *Sense and Sensibility*, ed. R. W. Chapman, 55–6, 93. A character in Kelly's novel *Memoirs of a Magdalen* (1767) believed that 'she who can love a second time is utterly unworthy of being ever loved at all' ('Cooke's Edition' [n.d.], II: 40. The lady, oddly, has just turned down a Lord Winworth).
23 *Works*, 17–18.
24 With some differences of emphasis, it is true. The 'foolishness' is made more of in Jane Austen than in Kelly, where it is partly seen through the eyes of characters themselves comic. But there is in both an evident liking for 'sensibility' coupled with a satirical awareness of its extravagance. (I refer to *Sense and Sensibility* rather than the early burlesques, where the satire is more uncompromising.) It is no part of my argument to deny Kelly's allegiance to

352

sentimentalism; but his critics have made too much of it, and such playing down of it as there is in this paper seems to me necessary to restore a correct perspective.

25 Miss Marchmont's delicacy in refusing a prudentially acceptable proposal ranks her with many a heroine of true sensibility. The commonsensical Mrs Harley records this reflection: 'That a woman without a shilling shou'd refuse an Earl with a fine person and a great estate, is the most surprising affair I ever heard of' (*Works*, 38).

26 *Works*, 39.

27 *Works*, 40.

28 *Works*, 57.

29 In his Prologue to *She Stoops to Conquer*, Garrick (who also, incidentally, had written the Prologue and Epilogue to *False Delicacy*) attacked the muse who 'deals in sentimentals'.

30 John Forster, *The Life and Times of Oliver Goldsmith*, 2nd ed. (1854), II: 115 ff.

31 Forster, II: 116. Goldsmith's biographers usually take this view unquestioningly.

32 Schorer, 397; cf. also 392.

33 Some of the characters are given 'novelistic' names. Miss Marchmont is called Hortensia, Miss Rivers, Theodora. This was a common feature of sentimental novels, taken over from the older romances. It is mocked within the play itself: 'Theodora! – what a charming name for the romance of a circulating library! . . . ' (*Works*, 13).

34 *Works*, 34.

35 Schorer, 390–91, points out the function of this chorus, but his subsequent remarks on the play show, I think, that he undervalues the element of satire with which it is identified.

36 *False Delicacy*, *A Word to the Wise* (1770), and *The School for Wives* (1773).

37 Arthur Sherbo, *English Sentimental Drama* (1957), 147.

38 *Sense and Sensibility*, 379. Colonel Brandon is Marianne's 'second attachment'. In marrying him she has conquered a strict sentimental prejudice. Winworth, too, is Lady Betty's 'second attachment', and the end of the play sees them paired nonetheless.

39 While inheriting the traditional view about the play's essential sentimentalism, critics have often significantly felt the need to qualify it somehow. Ernest Bernbaum, *The Drama of Sensibility* (1915), 225–7, acknowledges that the title of *False Delicacy* 'and some of its conspicuous qualities are antagonistic to sentimentalism', and that it 'sometimes satirizes the very tendency it is supposed to support'. But writing of Mrs Harley he says: 'Kelly did not perceive that by admitting such a character he had placed a traitor in the sentimental camp'. This is odd. And, as he partly knows, Mrs Harley is not the only vehicle of the satire: the absurdly complicated situations in which the characters find themselves as a result of their delicacy must also be allowed to make their point. A much more extreme statement of the play's sentimentalism is to be found in G. H. Nettleton's *English Drama of the Restoration and Eighteenth Century* (1914), 268 ff., but even here 'partial alleviation of the distresses of sentimentality' is recognised; and subsequent critics such as A. H. Thorndike, Mark Schorer, and Arthur Sherbo all qualify their view of the play's sentimentalism in varying degrees by pointing to elements of comic quality within it, or to the satire embodied in the characters of Cecil and Mrs Harley. It still seems necessary, however, to stress the primary nature of the deliberate though unmalicious ridicule implied even in many apparently 'straight' sentimental passages. Arthur Sherbo's interesting recent book,

English Sentimental Drama, warns us that in reading sentimental comedies we should beware of finding deliberate ridicule where excessive sentimentalism merely 'stirs *our* sense of the ridiculous' (p. 85). This is important and true. But I think, in general and in particular, that Sherbo is also right not only in seeing that 'Kelly aligns himself with the less extreme proponents of sentimental drama' (p. 8), but also in acknowledging further the possibility of 'parody or at least deliberate exaggeration' (p. 133) in the more extreme sentimental passages, though my emphasis on this is greater than Sherbo would probably acquiesce to.

40   Hawkesworth, in *Gentleman's Magazine*, XXXVIII (1768), 78, 80 ff.

13

π-ious Boswell

Two new volumes have recently been added to the Yale Edition of the Private Papers of James Boswell: *Boswell: Laird of Auchinleck, 1778–1782*, edited by Joseph W. Reed and Frederick A. Pottle, and *Boswell: The Applause of the Jury, 1782–1785*, edited by Irma S. Lustig and Frederick A. Pottle. The papers, like those in some earlier volumes, include, in the form of day to day memoranda, some sketches towards the *Life of Johnson*, as well as the usual full reporting of Boswell's other day to day doings and viewings: drinking bouts, hangovers, amorous activities, dinners, suppers, meetings with relatives and friends of every degree of importance and unimportance. Boswell, like Johnson, suffered from a compulsive veracity, at least in his unprocessed journal-writing, and this, as in Johnson, was often introspective. Unlike Johnson's, it was trivialising and undisciplined. The need to record was unselective, the effort to understand himself undisciplined and puppyish.

(i)

The Editors of the first volume, who have provided a commentary of very high quality, write unhelpfully of Boswell's 'art'. The term, however justified in relation to Boswell's published works, is inappropriate to this welter of informal jottings. In the jargon which literary critics nowadays use when they talk about 'art', Boswell is even said to use a *persona*. But on this, Messrs. Reed and Pottle write well. For once, the critics seem to know what that word means, and they use it to convey an insight about Boswell which in fact has nothing much to do with his 'art', but everything to do with the style of his personal relationships and (we should add) his relationship with himself.

Boswell reported himself to be 'always easiest among strangers', and the Editors comment that strangers enable

Boswell freely to assume roles which he enjoys and needs for the full release of his personality. They 'permit him to use the invented, the earned persona'. It is surprising how often this comment is borne out by Boswell's way of writing himself down, as though standing outside himself and contemplating an invented or achieved role. Having been politely received by Judge Willes, he reports that 'I felt myself quite as I could wish: an agreeable Scotch gentleman creditably received by an English judge'.

There is not a single word which is not validated by the external facts as reported, even though the description is one in which the delight of self-observation is as important as what is being observed. But then, the delight of self-observation is itself one of the things to be observed. It is something which differs from Rasselas's 'complacence in his own perspicacity' and in 'the delicacy with which he felt'. The reward is in the constatation itself, rather than in any self-exalting which it may yield, and this despite the fact that Boswell is here recording an event which is satisfactory to his own ego. Another example. After reporting the complaints of the ailing Miss Cunninghame about Lady Auchinleck, he makes himself the centre piece of a *sentimental tableau*, worthy of some tender passage in Mackenzie or Henry Brooke: 'At night alone, I was tenderly sad for the amiable, distressed young creature, Miss Cunninghame'. He is not now in 'company', where according to the editors he feels free to invent his personae. But he is not 'alone' either; he is looking at himself.

Such passages show a selfconsciousness so complete and unaffected that it can only be called *un*selfconscious. William C. Dowling notes in his recent book *The Boswellian Hero* how in the course of the Hebridean tour, Boswell records not only the events which take place but the very writing up of the *Tour* and Johnson's comments on the journal as it is being written. It is, as Dowling perceives, a play of perspectives of the kind which 'we associate with certain types of fiction', as when in *Pamela* 'Squire B —— discovers Pamela's letters and has her continue them as a journal'. The selfconsciousness belongs to a mode of writing, much concerned with the process of its own composition, which underwent an accentuated development in the eighteenth century. In Richardson, and then in Sterne, this selfconsciousness is variously distanced. The authorial voice is not present in Richardson. In Sterne, where the nominally separate Tristram preserves an ambiguous authorial status, the selfconsciousness takes on a sophistication of coy indirection and posturing self-concealment which oddly resembles that of Sterne's personal letters and papers (whether or not he chooses there to call himself Tristram or Yorick) but which is far removed from Boswell's openly exhibited layers of self-observation. These are as multiple and as elaborately self-multiplying as Sterne's, without the Shandean urge simultaneously to protect the flaunted self-revelation by means of an elusive ironic guard. The display of himself playing a role exists without any impulse to disguise or falsify that fact. But surely neither the analogies, nor the difference, justify any attribution of the novelist's 'art' to Boswell's private papers, any more than the fact that he reports conversations in dialogue form can be taken to argue the dramatic self-effacement or the theatrical artistry of a playwright.

Laird of Auchinleck is also, like earlier instalments and also (if we choose to remind ourselves) like *Pamela* or *Tristram Shandy*, full of the diarist's concern for the composition and the fortunes of his diary. After reading the diary of 'the deceased Mr Bogle of Hamilton Farm', he reflects: 'Were my journal to be discovered and made public in my own lifetime, how shocking would it be to me! And after my death, would it not hurt my children?' In the face of this risk, he does not (either here, or on the inevitable later occasion when his wife stumbles on an account of his latest profligacy after he had 'left this my journal lying open in the dining-room') contemplate measures for concealing or destroying the papers, still less any cessation of the record. Instead, after a perfunctory 'I must not be so plain', he considers putting the problem to his revered mentor: 'I will write to Dr Johnson on the subject', adding immediately after that 'Lieut.-Colonel Nisbet Balfour and his sister, Mrs Boswall, supped with us'. End of entry. We sense that the writing to Dr Johnson was contemplated less as a search for guidance than as a self-exhibition in the cherished role of perturbed profligate. The editors inform us, in any case, that 'No correspondence on the subject appears to have survived', and perhaps the resolution was not carried out, any more than that of not being 'so plain'. This 'plainness' is a matter of simple factuality. The matter-of-fact reporting of who came to supper that night is as much a part of it as any scandalous revelations, and reported in much the same way.

That 'plainness' Boswell was not ready to give up. It consists of simple circumstantial frankness rather than of any marked use of unduly direct or indecently graphic language in describing his amours, although we should remember that many of his erotic confessions were later removed from the record. His amorous confessions, licit and illicit tend, in fact, in what little survives in the papers in this volume, to be reported with some slight periphrastic flourish. But what the editors call 'nuptial intercourse' Boswell often simply notes with the Greek letter π. Even this, however, is no sacrifice of 'plainness', merely shorthand for a common occurrence, and one which almost any other diarist might have thought too quotidian to be worth recording. Or perhaps not quite mere shorthand. Other common events are not similarly signalled. There is unfortunately no Greek letter for the equally frequent drinking bouts and hangovers, although in this case there are irresistible variations to be specified in the kind or quantity of liquor consumed, and in the two or three alternative symptoms of malaise. Perhaps Boswell's 'nuptial intercourse' was not blessed with the same variety. At all events, π seems so uniform and so routine, in word (or rather letter) as in deed, that it is used by Boswell as a handy anchor of ordinariness, helping him to domesticate thoughts and even actual occurrences of such untoward events as death, which have of course to be recorded like everything else, but tend to disturb the untroubled contemplation of the endless flow of experience. In this entry it is only the fear of a death which is ended by π:

> . . . at night I loved my wife warmly, though I was affected with thinking of the deplorable situation I and my children would be in if she should die, which a pretty severe cough which she now had made me fear. π

Here, deaths have actually occurred:

> I sent a note at night to Maclaurin sincerely sympathizing with him on the death of one of his sons and anxious to hear how his wife was. I got an answer from him that she was dead. Burke in his *Sublime and Beautiful* says we have some pleasure from the distress of others. There was an agitation in my mind tonight which was better than melancholy. Yet I felt for Maclaurin and his children, thinking of my own situation, should such an event happen in my family. My wife was much affected. π

A revelatory factuality of this order can only be the product of a massive self-absorption. It is hard to be sure whether this self-absorption (down to the piece of self-contemplation in the 'literary' perspective of Burke's aesthetics and the pondered judgment that his agitation was 'better' than melancholy) is more remarkable for its sheer magnitude, or for its utter guilelessness. The latter, in any case, is so total as to make any notion of egoism lose its connotations of calculated selfishness. The unconscious effrontery with which he censures poor Maclaurin a few weeks later ('Played whist and supped at Maclaurin's. There was singing too. It hurt me to see all appearance of regret for a wife so lately dead effaced') is part of the same engaging enormity, as is the afterthought, inserted two days later immediately after these words, which adds a small drama of self-debate, without deflecting Boswell from his main feeling: 'Yet (writing on Wednesday the 19 April) is it not good sense to get free of grief as soon as one can? However, there is something in doing so which shocks my feelings'.

There was no π on the night of Maclaurin's supper party, unlike that of his double bereavement. Mrs Boswell that day had a severe cough and spat blood, although such things were no less likely to lead to π than to deter from it, as his fears for her death had on an earlier date led to it. Later in the journal, one death precludes π in a way that neither those of Maclaurin's family nor the thoughts of his own wife's were able to do. It was his father's: 'Tried π, [but thought,] "What! when he who gave you being is lying a corpse?" Checked'.

These entries, with their interminable flow of self-delighted veracity, are unlikely to revise the view of Boswell of those who feel, as Thomas Gray remarked of Boswell's account of Paoli in the *Account of Corsica*, that it proved 'that any fool may write a most valuable book by chance, if he will only tell us what he heard and saw with veracity. Of Mr Boswell's truth I have not the least suspicion, because I am sure he could invent nothing of this kind. The true title of this part of his work is, "A Dialogue between a Green-goose and a Hero".' Gray's remark, as Dowling reminds us, anticipates Macaulay's stereotype of Boswell as the 'inspired idiot' whose foolishness happened to provide the right ingredients for the particular achievement of the *Life of Johnson*. These views are now unfashionable, as Dowling's eloquent attempt at refutation both reports and demonstrates, and as Boswell's editors also show when they insist on the literary 'art' of his journals.

The private papers do not, alas, have the same distinction as the published works on Paoli and Johnson, despite this insistence on their 'art'. A difference is that works about other and more interesting figures are likely *ipso facto* to be more interesting than works largely devoted to the inexhaustible unravelling of Boswell himself. The journals deal not only with (in Gray's words) 'what he heard and saw' but also with what he thought and felt, and the interest of *that*, as distinct from its quantity, is eminently exhaustible. The veracity and the enormous inclusiveness give the private papers their considerable value as a historical record. They also sometimes provide important draft versions of materials subsequently fashioned into Boswell's major finished works, notably the *Life of Johnson*, and a particularly fascinating example occurs in the next volume, *The Applause of the Jury*.

(ii)

On Easter Sunday, 20 April 1783, Boswell visited Johnson. The painter Mauritius Lowe was present and they talked about mortality rates among Londoners and Indians, about survival, parental affection and the treatment of children. 'I dined with him; the company were, Mrs Williams, Mrs Desmoulins, and Mr Lowe. He seemed not to be well, talked little, grew drowsy soon after dinner, and retired, upon which I went away'.

So ends the entry for that day in the *Life of Johnson*. What readers of the *Life* never suspected was that after Johnson had retired for his nap, a conversation took place between Boswell, Mrs Desmoulins and Lowe, which Boswell marked *Tacenda* (to be kept silent) and which is for the first time printed in full in *The Applause of the Jury*, the latest volume of the Private Papers. The two men bantered the lady with imputations that Johnson might have been impotent and that his marriage 'was quite a Platonic connexion'. Mrs Desmoulins countered by saying that Johnson had strong sexual affections, that Garrick had seen his marriage consummated by peeping through a keyhole (a highly bowdlerised account of this detail was the only part of the entry which got into the *Life*, under the year 1736), that Mrs Johnson drank heavily and kept him away from the conjugal bed. Mrs Desmoulins used to sit with him at night with her head on his pillow. Johnson would kiss and fondle her passionately and showed unmistakable signs that 'he was capable', but would stop short of the final act in a spasm of pained self-conquest. Mrs Desmoulins, though she 'never felt any inclination for him as a woman', would have yielded to him out of her 'high respect for him'.

We owe gratitude to the editors for making the account avail-

360

able. Some details of their reading of it may be questioned. It does not seem self-evident that what Mrs Desmoulins was responding to was 'the sexual attractiveness of Johnson's commanding mind'. And the nowadays habitual reference to Boswell's use 'of the novelist's skills', and the variant of it which suggests that 'the *Tacenda* could be a scene from Restoration comedy', do not set the passage in a true light. Its distinctive thing is its raw vividness, not any stylish play of dialogue or well-turned scene. In so far as the passage suggests careful plotting, it is not in the setting down of the episode, but in the instinctive management of the dialogue by Lowe and Boswell once they perceived that there was lively information to be extracted from the lady. This need not imply a prearranged strategy by the two men, only a skilled conversational opportunism once Lowe had challenged the lady with a cheeky question about Johnson's chastity. Though it probably didn't happen here, prearrangement is a recorded feature of Boswell's staging of some other social encounters. What seems clear in any case is that here as elsewhere Boswell appears less as a literary than as a social craftsman, an arranger of his experience and a creator of happenings. When, as is most usual, he is the sole arranger, and the principal spotlight falls on himself, the process is readily called self-dramatisation, though in a fuller and subtler sense than the usual one, a sense which includes plotting and deployment as well as display. The *Tacenda* dialogue turns outwards rather than inwards, but the principle remains the same. Boswell (with Lowe) composes the event rather than the account. The account seems composed, I suspect, only because it is true to the event.

This is not to deny that Boswell is often a very 'literary' author, whose writings have about them an element of stylisation, instinctive or self-conscious or both, which is fraught with novelistic reminders. He describes a meeting with George III (the willed nature of the whole event is, incidentally, reported at the outset: 'Resolved to be seen at Court . . .') in which the King appears as a royal version of Squire Allworthy ('The King with a truly benevolent, smiling countenance approached us'), while Boswell turns into a novel-heroine ('So was a little in a flutter *now*'). These effects are momentary, and probably no more designedly allusive than the *Tacenda* scene was consciously crafted as a piece of theatre. They are the work of a writer well-read in novels and plays, who easily slipped into their jargon in the course of his endless, more or less ironic, posturings before himself and others.

Boswell conversed in this volume not only with the King, and with Johnson, but with Reynolds and Paoli and Burke and the Burneys (*père et fille*) and Malone (their Johnsonian collaboration begins in this volume), with dozens of legal, political and literary personages, English and Scottish, with relatives, retainers, drinking companions and dinner-guests. He practises law in Edinburgh and is called to the English Bar. He writes some *Hypochondriack* essays, and the *Letter to the People of Scotland*, and (as an advance surrogate for the *Life of Johnson*, over which he proposes to take his time), the *Tour to the Hebrides*. The volume ends with the appearance of the *Tour* and an excellent account and sampling of its reception by reviewers. The *English Review* called Boswell 'an agreeable trifler' and hoped 'that Mrs Boswell has often given her husband more essential tokens of complaisance and affection than by changing her bed-chamber for one night to accommodate Dr Johnson'. Well, by courtesy of the Greek alphabet, posterity knows that she did. But the implied obsessiveness about Johnson annoyed Mrs Boswell and many other Boswells, then and later, as Frederick Pottle's *Pride and Negligence*, a history of the posthumous fortunes of Boswell's manuscripts, makes clear: without this obsessiveness, of course, there would almost certainly have been no Yale Editions of the Private Papers.

In the present instalment, death looms especially large. The volume's first important event is the death of Lord Kames, at a great age, soon after Boswell took notes of their last conversations, towards the biography of Kames which he never completed. The major death is Johnson's, and occurs near the end of the volume, much as the death of Boswell's father came near the end of the previous volume (a fact which suggests some artistic design on the part of the editors). Boswell was in Edinburgh when the news reached him. He had company for supper and revealed nothing: 'I received them and behaved with much ease ... I did not shed tears. I was not tenderly affected. My feeling was just one large expanse of stupor. I knew that I should afterwards have sorer sensations'.

There were other deaths, and funerals, and broodings, and nightmares and *sententiae*. And there were public executions, where Boswell could act as the stage-manager of his own emotional life without the price of direct personal loss. Burke 'alluded pleasantly to my attending executions, and said, "You have seen more life and more death than any man." "Well," said I, "and I hope I shall see immortality"': it is difficult not to see as one of the meanings of this little joke the looking forward to a ringside view of Heaven. Stage-managing his own experiences involved the setting up of an audience as well as of actors, and Boswell readily fitted into either role or even both. At executions, he sometimes 'thought of *self* as perhaps dying' or (slipping easily again into what Jane Austen was to call 'novel slang', however literally justified it might be by actual circumstances) 'imagined the feelings of a desperate highwayman'.

Sometimes Boswell was manifestly unnerved, beyond novel slang, by the results of his nurtured predilection for *sensations fortes*:

Saw some of the unhappy men's irons knocked off, and some of them pinioned. There were seven men and one woman. . . . There was a vast crowd, and a prodigious heavy rain fell. I was quite unnerved. I stayed and saw them all cut down, carried into Newgate, and stretched dead upon a table. I made Guthrie's cap be pulled up and looked at his face, which was neither black nor distorted. . . . I breakfasted at Baldwin's. Was very uneasy . . . came home dismal.

He was not always so shaken: 'Saw the nineteen pass close to me in review. Then on roof. Not shocked'. Boswell's interest in executions was a matter of public comment. The *Public Advertiser* reported on one occasion that among 'a great concourse of spectators . . . the first person who appeared upon the scaffold . . . was Mr. Boswell. *That* was nothing extraordinary, but it was surprising when he was followed by Sir Joshua Reynolds'. Boswell had taken Reynolds to see the hanging of Peter Shaw, once a servant of Burke's, who, perceiving 'two friends of his old master . . . made them a graceful bow'. Such urbanity on the gallows was worthy of Macheath, and Boswell was doubtless not unaware of literary precedents when he wrote up the scene for the very issue of the *Public Advertiser* which noted his addiction to hangings. Suspicion arises as to whether he wrote the self-rebuke as well as the report. The editors, probably rightly, think not: 'Boswell was given to advertising his own eccentricities, but he would not have accused himself of being hard-hearted'. On the other hand, Boswell *was* often openly 'hardened' to such things. Many of his comments exhibit a combination of sensationalism and apathy which is less paradoxical than it sounds, both states providing protection in circumstances where a temperamental self-centredness constantly threatens to bring the issue back to

Number One. Thus on one occasion he reports: 'Much affected, though not tenderly. Thought of *self* as perhaps dying. Then press-yard. Then Betsy, and gave good advice'. And two days later: 'George Ward struggled long. While they were yet hanging, went to Betsy just by ...'

Betsy Smith was a prostitute to whom Boswell repaired on such occasions, and not only for simple pleasure, or to 'remove' a 'shocking sight' from his mind, or to enjoy the giving of 'good advice'. Nor were executions the only deaths which precipitated Boswellian sexuality, nor prostitutes its only recipients. In the previous volume, thoughts of death and actual occurrences both stimulated what the editors like to call 'conjugal intercourse', under the sign of π. At the end of that volume, he 'tried π' after his father's death, but was 'checked'. *The Applause of the Jury* picks up where he left off. The very first paragraph reverts to his father's death and reports π on three successive nights.

Away from his wife, in London, Betsy and others consoled him. *In absentia*, Mrs Boswell became his π in the sky. 'If I was to have but *one* woman, I'd rather have her than anyone in the world', a bigger if than he was prepared seriously to contemplate, though he resolves from time to time to have 'no more *filles* while in London'. On one remarkable occasion he checks himself from visiting Mrs C. after receiving letters from Mrs B. (the occasion is remarkable also because the editors are for once unable to identify the deprived lady).

Back in Edinburgh he 'most sincerely renewed my most affectionate vows to my valuable spouse' (25 November 1783), a renewal which the editors tell us 'was followed with ironical swiftness by a relapse (see ... 14 February 1784)'. Irony or no irony, the gap is hardly 'swift' by Boswellian standards. The entry for 14 February contains a terminal dash, which the editors say 'is another private symbol for conjugal intercourse', occasionally used after May 1780 in place of π, on the principle, I suppose, that variety is the spice of life. I am not sure whether the editors regard 'conjugal intercourse' as a breach of 'conjugal vows'. At all events, the volume, like its predecessors, records a number of abstentions and of intentions to abstain, as it also records the occasions when Boswell did not drink alcohol, abstention being obviously as legitimate an object of the diarist's interest as indulgence or anything else.

(iii)

The editors of these two volumes of the private papers maintain the standards of editorial skill and the excellence of commentary characteristic of most volumes of that impressive series. It is a rueful reflection on priorities that the proper publication of Johnson's own works has been treated with less urgency and often with poorer editing than these voluminous documents whose intrinsic quality is inferior and whose importance, however great, is in many ways mainly ancillary.

One supposes that the editors' insistence on the 'art' of Boswell's papers may partly be due to a desire to convince themselves and others that their immense editorial labours have been devoted to something whose value is more than merely documentary, although apology for making such a rich record available is hardly needed and the insistence itself is misplaced. It will probably further the inevitable emergence of monographs on the rhetorical structure of the diary-entries, and lead to sober claims, lacking the editors' own tact and verbal precision, that these entries were written by a persona and not by Boswell. The publication of the private correspondence of several major authors, even without misplaced editorial claims, has already led to a number of such rhetorical studies (sometimes at book-length) of the 'genre' of the personal letter. No doubt the worst is yet to come. That the publication of Boswell's journals should have stimulated interest in the man and his works, including critical discussion of his published writings, is on the other hand welcome.

1980–1983

14

William Cowper and Christopher Smart

(i)   *William Cowper*

Cowper was born in 1731, and educated at Westminster, the school of Cowley and Prior, whose poems he pleasantly imitated in his youth. He became a man of law and letters, associating with other Westminster wits like Colman and Churchill. In 1763, his life changed radically. He experienced a spiritual crisis, attempted suicide and was converted to the Evangelical faith. In 1767, he moved with the recently widowed Mary Unwin (who was to be his cherished companion for the rest of her life) and her family to Olney, Bucks, the parish of John Newton, the slave-trader turned Evangelical preacher. With Newton he produced the *Olney Hymns* which contain some of Cowper's best religious verse.

In 1773 Cowper had a dream that God had cast him out. His religious beliefs remained unchanged, but he lost his own feeling of election: 'From that day forth Cowper never entered a church, never attended a prayer meeting, never said a prayer ... for in God's eyes ... he had already ceased to exist'. He attempted suicide again, but by the late 1770s had recovered and was writing again, some light verse, some political poems (anti-mob, and anti-French), a group of wide-ranging moral satires. The present volume of the new Oxford edition of his *Poems* contains his poems to 1782. The better-known Cowper of *The Task, Yardley Oak* and the desolate poems of his last years, after Mary Unwin became ill and then died, will appear in a second volume.

It all seems a long way from Westminster. But Cowper retained a selfconscious awareness of the school and the thread of English history that ran through it. His poems often refer, sometimes at length, to the famous poets who had been pupils there. An eloquent epigram on Warren Hastings in 1792 is woven from schoolboy memories. And in earlier days of dark religious torment it was to another Westminster poet, George Herbert, that he turned for solace.

In his autobiographical memoir, *Adelphi*, Cowper records how Herbert became for a time the 'only author I had any delight in reading'. He offered alleviation but no cure, and Cowper was then taken off him as 'more likely to nourish my melancholy than to remove it'. His value had been spiritual and therapeutic. Cowper did not think Herbert a better poet than the 'classics' he had lost pleasure in. His poems were 'gothic and uncouth', and what Cowper admired was their 'strain of piety'.

Similarly with Donne. In a late poem, Cowper spoke of the 'gold' of 'my old fav'rite bard', Homer, as 'dross, when balanc'd in the Christian scale', and added: 'Be wiser thou – like our fore-father DONNE,/Seek heav'nly wealth . . . ' Donne (from whom Cowper liked to claim descent on his mother's side) is not claimed to be a better poet, any more than Herbert was. The point is that they were better *than* poets. The Christian fundamentalism which held that Homer was mere dross compared with Christ also made Cowper feel (in some moods at least) that Sternhold and Hopkins were worth more than *any* poets, however great: 'we could shift' without poetry. Part of Cowper did not take poetry, or English poetry, very seriously, least of all his own.

In February 1770 he awoke 'with these Words',

> But what, my lovely One? and meek
> Tho' maim'd, who liv'st, with Bruises dying,

which have something of Herbert and something of Donne. He thought of them as 'plainly an Imitation' of Herbert, though their note of devotional violence is perhaps closer to Donne. It is one of the few examples in Cowper's verse where something is conveyed of the immediate grinding ache, as distinct from the sheer engulfing fact, of spiritual suffering. Cowper has been reading Herbert to his brother, and the maiming and bruising are presumably Christ's, not Cowper's, though they echo stresses in the poet: 'He knows that I am maim'd and Bruis'd'. The lines are not part of a larger poem but occur in a letter, where they are quickly defused or domesticated: 'I thought of them while at Dinner, and made a comfortable Meal upon them, while the Lord was pleased to spread my Table in the Wilderness'.

This retraction or desublimation of misery is not Cowper's invariable way of reporting spiritual suffering in his letters or autobiographical prose. Something like it is deeply characteristic of the poems, though not on the subject of spiritual suffering. But it *is* mainly in the letters that the suffering as such is charted as an achingly particularised *process*. The poems, when they deal with suffering, show it instead as an achieved and crushing state. In this sense they are unlike Donne or Herbert. The desolating late poem 'To Mary' is permeated with the single, unchanging, shattering fact of a loved one's incurable illness. *The Castaway* (1799), inspired by a page (still 'wet with Anson's tear') about a drowning sailor, and its 'semblance' to his own case, ends with an unrelieved sense of sinking and of lights going out which is beyond any particularisable self-torment:

> No voice divine the storm allay'd,
>   No light propitious shone;
> When, snatch'd from all effectual aid,
>   We perish'd, each alone;
> But I beneath a rougher sea,
> And whelm'd in deeper gulphs than he.

The bleakest terrors of *The Ancient Mariner* (published the previous year) seem almost cosy by comparison.

These are late poems. The products of his first spiritual agony are his contributions to the Olney hymns. These were written (as Cowper read Herbert) to discipline and alleviate his spiritual agony, not as expressions or renderings of it. The value of writings hymns 'for the use of plain people' was precisely that it called for a practical and simplifying state of mind which might help to silence the tortured self-complication of his own inner being. Like the reading of Herbert, the therapy seems to have ended up by exacerbating rather than allaying his anxieties. But this does not really get into the poems. If the Olney hymns are the closest Cowper gets to Herbert's devotional style, the fact will seem appropriate to those readers who feel that Herbert's accounts of spiritual conflict sometimes read like after-the-event dramatisations, written after the struggle has been resolved and peace found. Not that Cowper's hymns dramatise any struggles, or that Cowper himself found peace. But the self-torturing Cowper of the letters, who is closer to the raw unhealed anguish of his 'fore-father' Donne than to the Herbert of 'The Collar' or 'Love (III)', is largely kept out of the hymns.

The simplifying tendency of hymn-writing released a peculiar strength which Cowper was too fussily self-conscious to allow into his more overtly personal poems. The very first of his contributions, 'Oh for a closer Walk with God', expresses a Herbertian aspiration for humble self-effacement much better than do Herbert's own brilliant and energetic displays. I am more persuaded by Cowper's

> Lord, it is my chief complaint,
> That my love is weak and faint;
> Yet I love thee and adore

than I am by the eloquent pseudo-drama of God calling the erring Herbert 'Child' and Herbert replying 'My Lord'. Cowper was well aware that 'humility' could easily turn into a form of pride. He shared with Donne, Herbert and Marvell the old worry of devotional poets at the fact that self-seeking and pride in poetic accomplishment readily entered into poems expressing humility and self-effacing worship: 'I cannot make thy mercies known / But self-applause creeps in'. By comparison with Cowper's lines, Marvell's acknowledgement of the 'wreaths of Fame and Interest' coiled around his own poetic devotions has itself a kind of bravura arrogance. The devotional masters of the seventeenth century knew as Cowper did the need for the still small voice, but Cowper, I think, achieved it more often.

Humility is a fussier, more archly simpering affair in Cowper's secular poems, where it takes the form of claiming that he merely scribbles rhymes. Cowper's 'Poetical Epistle to Lady Austen', like Swift's *Epistle to a Lady*, is a poem about what sort of poem to write to a lady, and the 'I, who scribble rhyme' claims like Swift to be telling serious things in a low style. But unlike Swift's, Cowper's self-undercutting draws attention to itself because it is both insistent and half-hearted. He imitates Swift's rejection of loftiness down to using a form of sub-Swiftian Hudibrastic, but he lacks the courage of his unseriousness and quickly lapses into self-cherishing solemnities which belie the self-mockery:

> But when a Poet takes the pen,
> Far more alive than other men,
> He feels a gentle tingling come
> Down to his finger and his thumb,
> Deriv'd from nature's noblest part,
> The centre of a glowing heart!

Cowper wants to have it both ways, but the gap between merely scribbling rhyme and 'the centre of a glowing heart' is not

369

bridged. Swiftian derision has become pervaded by a Shandean tenderness for all the coy carry-on and a readiness to let the fondly egotistical slop over into a false sublime.

This uneasy see-saw between mincing gallantries and the high concerns of a poet's 'glowing heart' also informs Cowper's most ambitious poem, *The Task*, which similarly purports to be a lightheartedly gallant response to a lady's request for a poem. The lady is the same as in the 'Poetical Epistle' and had asked for a poem with 'the SOFA for a subject'. She wanted it in blank verse and so the poem is written not in Swift's Hudibrastic metre but in the domesticated Miltonics which were to provide Wordsworth with a model for the meditative blank verse of *The Prelude*. The Sofa led to other topics and 'brought forth at length, instead of the trifle which he at first intended, a serious affair – a Volume!' Now the 'serious' parts of the poem are indeed serious. They touch on many of the matters of social and spiritual life which engaged Cowper's philosophic and introspective attention. But labelling all this as 'a serious affair – a Volume' betrays a frisky loss of nerve about the seriousness, without any intention to give up the claim.

The 'unserious' dimension is mock-heroic and shows the same loss of nerve in reverse. 'I sing the SOFA' begins the poem and there is intermittent fuss throughout about adorning the sofa with 'eulogium due'. But there is also the alternative insistence that his mock-heroic is not just badinage but a responsible rejection of poetic phoniness, and that his own high styles are 'most sincere':

> Thou know'st my praise of nature most sincere,
> And that my raptures are not conjur'd up
> To serve occasions of poetic pomp,
> But genuine . . .

The undercutting of 'poetic pomp' may lead straight to a sober Wordsworthian praise of rural or domestic sights, but it is equally likely to issue in arch celebrations of such themes still 'unassay'd in song' as the humble cucumber. The mock-heroic routine, designed to express an indulgent affection for the unheroic object, succeeds only in indulging its own whimsical self. The disproportion between high style and low object is neither meant to belittle the low object nor to exalt it. It has no clear function and no meaningful relation to a primary heroic idiom, none of Pope's assured loyalty to the grandeurs he subverts, and none of Swift's assurance in the debunking of grandeurs. Cowper elsewhere quite accurately charted a retreat from both epic and satire in his

370

own day, and he himself shrank from both. But even the shrinking could not be left at that. The ceaseless twitchings of mock-heroic impulse are designed to make an amiable fuss around the very absence of a decisive position. They are a gaudy feature of stylistic loss of nerve, the 'unserious' projection or counterpart of a mind whose major experience was nervous breakdown.

The lady's request for blank verse made it more or less inevitable that he would go for the Miltonised variant which Thomson and others had adapted to serious yet less than epic themes. Cowper extended it in a way which enabled Wordsworth to turn it into an assured and consistent idiom of dignified introspection. One of the great distinctions of *The Task* is that it contains passages which read like *The Prelude*. Intermittently, Cowper had forged a medium for high informal discursive talk which was free of the pointed and lofty urbanities of those 'Horatian' epistles in couplets which had no real future after Pope. (Cowper disliked 'urbanity', especially, to his credit, its Chesterfieldian forms).

Most of Cowper's extended poems before *The Task* had been reflective 'satires' in a loosened couplet-style that seemed to look towards a more free-flowing discursive amplitude. Already within these poems, while praising Pope, he said that he had 'made poetry a mere mechanic art'. The remark referred to Pope's influence on imitators, but it is phrased ambiguously and touches the master too. Cowper later undertook to translate Homer into blank verse, feeling that Pope had tied 'bells of rhyme . . . about Homer's neck'. Even that work was in part a delayed response to a suggestion from Lady Austen, a fact which may seem amusingly emblematic of Cowper's curious reliance on 'unserious' sources for his most serious undertakings.

Unlike Pope he could not always blend his seriousness with levity, and unlike Wordsworth he often tried. Even in the sober concluding lines of *The Task*, he felt impelled to recall the triviality of its occasion. But by then a change had occurred. The coyness has largely been dropped, and the Shandean readiness to apologise and to fuss has turned into a sober idiom registering acknowledged uncertainties. If we are still conscious of a modesty nervous of its utterances, it is a modesty in its own way as genuine as that of the simple self-effacing stanzas of the Olney hymns.

1981

(ii) *Christopher Smart*

Smart was a small, fat, pot-bellied man. The portrait at Pembroke College, Cambridge, shows the drink-distended paunch protruding in almost gravid disproportion from the rest of his frame. He was conscious of physical ugliness. In 'The Author Apologizes to a Lady for His being a Little Man', he called himself 'the amorous dwarf that courts you to his arms', perhaps in a self-mythologising recollection of Pope. There's no mention of fatness here, but by the time he was paying more elderly compliments to the young Fanny Burney, that was what struck her most. His 'round and stubbed form', she wrote, seemed to belong 'to a common dealer behind a common counter, rather than to a votary of the Muses', though she also noted a 'great wildness in his . . . looks'. John Bayley says 'there was a Dylan Thomas in him – and indeed the physical resemblance is remarkable', but Fanny Burney hadn't seen Dylan Thomas. There have been fat poets, but the stereotype suggests otherwise ('Laurels on bulky bards as rarely grow, / As on the sturdy oak the virtuous mistletoe', said Smart himself, though perhaps referring as much to tallness as to fatness) and no example, other than the special case of Samuel Johnson, is reproduced in David Piper's *The Image of the Poet*. For *poètes maudits*, whose glamour or pathos came from disordered lives whereof came in the end despondency and madness, the myth seemed to prescribe a consumptive pallor, the slimness of garret-privations, the slender expiring frame of Chatterton as posthumously mythologised by Henry Wallis. So Smart's fatness came over as burgherly to Fanny Burney, and as cause for puzzlement: perhaps it was Dylan Thomas's achievement to confer bohemian appeal on the portly boozer's bulk.

Neither in appearance nor in personal character did this mixture of inebriate don and Grub Street hack, inhabitant of madhouses and debtors' prisons, pathetically caught up in excesses of both drink and devotion, conform to contemporary ideas of what a poet should be. He belongs in popular myth to that group (outsiders by dissipation or madness or misfortune) who provide proponents of an 'Age of Reason' with piquant ironies of their own devising: Savage, Collins, Churchill, Chatterton, Cowper. (The names all begin with C or S, and the Great Cryptographer seems to have made doubly sure with Christopher Smart.) Smart was seldom taken seriously in his own time, though he won the Seatonian Prize at Cambridge five times in six years and was friendly with leading figures of literary London.

When Johnson, sturdily loyal to Smart in a personal way, was asked whether 'Derrick or Smart [was] the best poet', he replied that one didn't bother to distinguish 'between a louse and a flea'. You might not readily call such a figure 'Augustan', even if you haven't yet been terrorised into abjuring that term altogether.

But Donald Davie included Smart in an anthology called *Augustan Lyric*, and his instinct was right. And Smart, the translator and imitator of Horace, admirer of Pope, practitioner of 'learned wit' in Scriblerian modes, author of georgic and mock-epic poems, and of lyrics in the line of Prior, Gay, Gray and Goldsmith, would have thought the term a compliment. In 'The Hop-Garden' he praised a dead Cambridge friend, Lycidas-like, for his 'classic sounds / In elegance Augustan cloth'd'. The historical Augustus was praised by Smart both in this poem and elsewhere, but the interesting passage shows 'Augustan' used both as a term of high cultural value and as a compliment to a contemporary of the poet's. Smart similarly complimented 'our great Augustan *Gray*'. It's true there was no love lost between Smart and Gray, whose lives intersected with some closeness at Cambridge. Gray's correspondence tinkles with spiteful elation over Smart's disreputable escapades, and Smart may once have said that 'Gray *walks* as if he had fouled his small-clothes, and *looks* as if he smelt it' (by one of those unknowing reciprocities that sometimes befall eighteenth-century gossip in an epiphany of rococo symmetry, Johnson reported that Smart was shunned for 'not lov[ing] clean linen', adding that he 'had no passion for it' himself). But the poetical compliment to Gray (part of a roll-call of admired contemporaries) was certainly straight. Any sarcasm in the subtext would be lost on readers, and the sting, if any, would be for Gray, not 'Augustan'.

Smart wore his own 'Augustanism' lightly, and was arguably the only mid-century writer (among those not obviously belonging to an alternative tradition) to do so. The urbanities and hauteurs, the witty self-consciousness, the ambiguous elevations of georgic and mock-epic come over without nervousness or ostentation. There is little of Fielding's bumptious parade of self, or Thomson's insistent Miltonising, or Cowper's coy self-depreciation. His *fêtes champêtres* have a solid unfussy elegance: 'The turf-built theatre, the boxen bow'r, / And all the sylvan scenery'. On 'lower' themes, the jars and syringes of *The Hilliad* or the processes of hop-growing, the gusto for quotidian solidities mingles with or is filtered through mock-epic or neo-georgic stylisations, but it's a world away from Cowper's fussy cele-

373

bration of themes 'unassay'd in song' like the humble cucumber and his anxiety to 'sing the SOFA' with 'eulogium due'. Cowper is an interesting paradox: distinctly cool in his feeling about Popeian styles and hostile to Chesterfieldian 'politeness', he used some of the stylistic defences we associate with their culture, in gestures of formalised nervousness which turn the old guardedness into a kind of unguarded self-exposure in itself. The early Smart, by contrast, inherited the manner with a tact of unforced assimilation and none of Cowper's half-adversarial embarrassment. When he praised his friend's wit and 'elegance Augustan', he made a point of saying these 'hardly were observ'd': the main meaning was that his 'charity of soul' was 'so rich in sweetness' that other qualities passed almost unnoticed, but there's a suggestion that the elegance is partly valued for its self-effacement.

What Norman Callan praised as Smart's 'naïve literalness' (a phrase it would be naïve to read too literally, however) was an additional guard against Cowperian fusses about the cucumber. This literalism remains as a bridge between the georgic 'realism' of 'The Hop-Garden' and the surreal elations of the *Jubilate Agno*, 'Let Nebai rejoice with the Wild Cucumber', with their unCowperian readiness to court bathos and their unembarrassed directness in apparent inconsequence or *exalté* humour: 'Let Jaalah rejoice with Moly wild garlick. / *For every thing infinitely perfect is Three . . .*'. Smart's surreal collocations have such a take-it-or-leave-it factuality as to amount to a literalism of fantasy, the very absence of connective explanation cheekily implying that none is called for. And the irrationalism even of the *Jubilate* (that baffling product of his madhouse years) should not be exaggerated. Some of the aphorisms read like condensed parables ('*For the Poorman's nosegay is an introduction to a Prince*') and we should remember that Smart's imagination worked as often through parables fully and discursively explicated as it did through visionary-aphoristic short-cuts. His *Parables of our Lord . . . Done into Familiar Verse* (1768) contain over eighty pieces, and form the largest single section of the most recent volume of the Oxford edition of his *Poetical Works*, covering his 'Religious Poetry 1763–1771' (Swift might have admired some of the brisk flat tetrameters of these narratives). Other aphorisms, superficially paradoxical, have their literal validation in a scriptural source or traditional knowledge. '*For flowers are musical in ocular harmony*' draws on old ideas of universal correspondence and more recent Newtonian theory about the harmony of colour and sound (cf. 'musick to the eye' in Hymn 12).

'*For the right names of flowers are yet in heaven. God make gard'ners better nomenclators*': the words seem almost designed to provide cover for any effect inaccessible to rational understanding. It was not outside the experience of Augustan imaginations that flower-images should defy rational expectation, though it was sometimes outside what they professed to permit, as Pope's famous couplet about 'fragrant chaplets' blowing in 'cold December' shows. Pope offered this as an example of how bad poets got it wrong, though many readers have commented on the surreal loveliness of the mimicry: a curious effect, mysteriously enhanced rather than lowered by the play of derision, and comparable to the weird lyricism of some of Smart's own satirical eruptions.

Smart's favourite image of the flower blossoming in winter is the Glastonbury thorn, and is celebrative rather than satirical. It is not, like Pope's December chaplets, a derided 'impossibility' but a botanical fact: 'the flowering of the thorn was still observed in Smart's time'. It comes into both the *Jubilate* and *A Song to David* but the finest example (where it merges, as in some other cases, with Aaron's rod) is in Hymn 32:

> Winter blossoms burst untimely
> On the blest Mosaic thorn.

The idea, traditional in English poetry, is that Christ's coming has turned winter into summer, though Smart chose an instance 'literally' true to nature. (He took the *super*natural aspect 'literally' too: 'The Lord was at Glastonbury in the body and blessed the thorn'). Swift once remarked that if Ireland flourishes, 'it must be against every Law of Nature and Reason; like the Thorn at *Glassenbury*, that blossoms in the Midst of Winter'. It's the only passage known to me whose treatment of the thorn is comparable to Smart's Hymn in spareness and power. What Smart saw as a rich fact of creation was for Swift a painful inexplicability or freakishness of nature (another instance of satirical perspectives yielding a haunting beauty).

Smart's devotion to Pope and Swift survives in the visionary strains of the *Jubilate*: 'Let Eliada rejoice with the Gier-eagle who is swift and of great penetration. / *For I bless the Lord Jesus for the memory of GAY, POPE and SWIFT.*' You would not expect to find this in Blake, who is sometimes thought to provide the closest analogue to the manner of the *Jubilate*. It differs also from Cowper, who did not find it easy to assimilate such poets into his idea of divine celebration: 'we could shift', he said, without 'Butler's wit, Pope's numbers, Prior's ease', and one 'madrigal' by Sternhold and Hopkins was 'worth them all'. 'Flow'ry stile' is how Cowper dismissed the trivialities of secular poetry, although if Religion were properly treated in poetry 'flow'rs would spring where'er she deign'd to stray'. Smart was as capable as Cowper of literal-minded devotional priorities, but in the *Jubilate* he said '*For Flowers can see, and Pope's Carnations knew him*', and the fact redounded to the glory of God rather than competing with it. The words (which may incorporate memories of a visit Smart made to Pope at Twickenham years before) have a vivid expressionist force. A few versicles earlier is a sequence whose essential burden is the rationality of flowers:

> *For there is a language of flowers.*
> *For there is a sound reasoning upon all flowers.*
> *For elegant phrases are nothing but flowers.*
> *For flowers are peculiarly the poetry of Christ.*

The association of 'elegant' with 'the poetry of Christ' is not accidental. Smart closes one of his Hymns:

> Let elegance, the flow'r
> Of words, in tune and pow'r,
>   Find some device of cleanest choice
> About that gem to place –
> 'This is my HEIR of GRACE,
>   In whose perfections I rejoice.'

'Taste and Elegance' are things we meet in the early secular poems, with their 'gardens regulated greens' which call to mind both Watteau and Marvell. They are rooted in Smart's imagination as things of substantial rather than ornamental value and enter naturally into his later devotional experience, both in intensities of worship and in spiritual peace.

So too with 'gem', a favourite image. We meet it in 'The Hop-Garden' when 'elegance Augustan' sets off 'the brighter gem' of charity. In 'The Judgment of Midas', Simplicity 'shone all ornament without a gem'. The superficial contradiction is only apparent: in one place a virtue is beautiful without the need for jewels, in the other it's a jewel beyond price. A high moral value is expressed through a metaphor which evokes worldly substance and beauty while resisting suggestions of luxury or gaudiness.

'Gems' appear again and again in the Hymns and *A Song to David*, sometimes in celebrative lists of the riches of creation, 'The jasper of the master's stamp, / The topaz blazing like a lamp / Among the mines beneath'. There are competing overtones of underground furtiveness and a hint of sumptuous excess. These are not the official meaning, which is the traditional idea, found in Ovid, Spenser and Milton, that it is sinful to rob the earth of its gems. Hymn 6 tells of 'gems' in 'caverns dark' not yet 'wrested from the mark, / To serve the turns of pride and vice'. Gems underground are still innocent, though our tainted imaginations know them mainly in their excavated state, and the fact generates a degree of unease. The *Jubilate* is more open about this unease and outfaces it:

> Let Ahimaaz rejoice with the Silver-Worm who
> is a living mineral.
> *For there is silver in my mines and I bless*
> *God that it is rather there than in my coffers.*

The Oxford editors properly cite the 'For' passage in their gloss on the Hymn. But 'the Silver-Worm who is a living mineral' is also germane, because the 'gems' in Smart's celebrative lists usually occur alongside and belong with living things, and some of his loveliest uses of 'gem' are in the word's other sense of 'bud' or 'blossom': 'fruit-trees pledge their gems'; 'a sweeter flow'r, / Which sprang and gemm'd and blossom'd'.

'*For Flowers are peculiarly the poetry of Christ*', 'elegance, the flow'r / Of words': there is no Marvellian downgrading of his devotional verse ('my fruits are only flow'rs') and none of Cowper's recoil from a secular 'flow'ry stile'. The suggestion of 'flowers of rhetoric' is even more subsidiary than the editors say. Smart's flowers are invested with properties of direct or unmediated expression. They *are* the poetry of Christ and Pope's carnations knew him. A forthright literalness is presupposed which mirrors other features of Smart's devotions. After a bout of madness in 1756, Smart 'refused to write anything which was not directly and explicitly in praise of God'. Mrs Thrale reports that he took '*au pied de la lettre* our Saviour's injunction *to pray without ceasing*' and would rouse his friends from dinner or bed. Smart's account, '*For I blessed God in St James's Park till I routed all the company*', makes it seem an orgiastic prowess, like drinking everyone under the table. Johnson said finely 'I'd as lief pray with Kit Smart as any one else' but others wanted to lock him up.

The literalness permeated critical precepts and doctrinal beliefs alike. He disliked the 'incredible prodigies' of Ovid's *Metamorphoses*: 'Poetry and nature ought never to be set at a distance, but when a writer is summoned to such a task by real miracles and divine transcendency'. When writing about miracles, Smart's verse acquires a particularly 'punching' factuality:

> At his command, ev'n Christ I Am,
> The cruse was fill'd, and iron swam;
> The floods were dry'd to make a track,
> And Jordan's wave was driven back.
>
> All these in ancient days occurr'd.

Believing in miracles is a literalism of the 'marvellous', freely given where it is due: Ovid's fictions are nonsense but there's massive scorn for the Jews who *'all the miracles atchiev'd/ By doubt stupendous disbeliev'd'*.

This literalness does not necessarily entail an avoidance of figurative style or of covert or complex meanings but rather a commitment to the literal truth contained (or concealed) within them. As Marcus Walsh says in his fine introduction to the *Hymns*, 'Smart . . . has often been considered obscure or eccentric when he is in fact being literally biblical'. This is no less true for the fact that readers then (as now) might find the meanings difficult to recover. *That* problem, even in the 1760s, was less a matter of esoteric allusion than of limited familiarity with the scriptural common stock. Plainer hymns than Smart's risked seeming 'as abstruse as if they were written in *Arabic*'. Smart's hymns, unlike Watts's or John Wesley's, were not simplified for use by congregations or to accommodate 'vulgar capacities'. They had more in common with seventeenth-century devotional poets like Donne or Herbert than with the popular hymnology of their own time: leaps of logic, puns boldly exploring 'connections of ideas', rhetorical and perhaps numerological patternings, elements of a 'wreathed garland' structure.

But within this is an assertion of the simple, perhaps simplifying, truth of scriptural teaching, 'clear and evident as light', 'the simple truth of Christ'. This plainness belongs not to a populist evangelism but to a tradition which includes Dryden, Swift and Pope. On the one hand, 'The Trinity is plain, / So David's psalms maintain', or, as Swift said, 'the whole Doctrine is short and plain, and in itself uncapable of any Controversy; since God himself hath pronounced the Fact, but wholly concealed the

Manner'. The theology is not new, but the bossy reductive lordliness is a true Augustan accent. Swift told the young gentleman lately entered into holy orders not to explain 'the Mysteries of the Christian Religion . . . If you explain them, they are Mysteries no longer; if you fail, you have laboured to no Purpose'. Or as Smart said, rewording *Deuteronomy*, xxix. 29:

> Revelation is our own,
> Secret things are God's alone.

The hauteurs of a Swift or a Pope are less starkly in evidence. Swift's bossy conception of the parson's job, 'to deliver the Doctrine as the Church holds it,' 'to tell the People what is their Duty,' softens in Smart to a more celebrative concern with practical benevolence. The difference had partly to do with changing times. Smart belonged to the kindlier and more sensibilitised generation of Fielding. Walsh relates his emphasis on practical benevolence to that expressed 'in Parson Adams or Uncle Toby or Matthew Bramble'. That he should identify Smart with these unworldly or eccentric exemplars, rather than with such official paragons of the Benevolent ethos as Allworthy or Grandison, suits Smart's somewhat fecklessly disordered character, though the analogy has its limits. But Smart was closer to the more generous anti-prudential benevolism of Fielding than he would have been to Richardson (or, in a different way, to Swift), and like Fielding he disliked the Calvinist-Evangelical insistence on salvation by faith, not works. His strongly celebrative Anglicanism frequently took a shrill jingoistic form, unlikely to be found in Swift. One precept of Horace and Pope which Smart might not invariably assent to was *nil admirari*.

This edition establishes Smart as an important religious poet independently of *A Song to David*, contrary to Browning's assertion of the miraculous uniqueness of that work; or of the *Jubilate*, not known to Smart's (or Browning's) contemporaries, who would have repudiated it, but appealing, for reasons Smart himself might not have cared for, to generations schooled in the disconnections of surrealism and of modernist poetry. Both the *Song* and (in an earlier volume edited by Karina Williamson) the *Jubilate* are now available with a better commentary than they have ever had, and one which ought finally to discredit the vulgar notion that these poems are mere products of an inspired derangement. In addition to the marvellous *Hymns*, the volume contains two oratorios, *Hannah* and *Abimelech*, and the two collections of parables and hymns for children: some contemporaries were dismissively grown-up about such things, but the parables contain some good narrative verse and the children's hymns invite 'the comparison with Blake's *Songs of Innocence*' which, as Karina Williamson says, 'has often and justly been made' (they are also 'Embellished with CUTS,' nicely reproduced here). The introductions and commentary are exceptionally full, and this is especially appropriate for a poet so readily and comprehensively misunderstood. Three further volumes are expected, including Smart's translations and all the secular verse. They should restore Smart to his proper place in the English poetic tradition.

1984

PART V

Appendix

15

More Providence than Wit: Some Recent Approaches to Eighteenth-Century Literature

This essay is concerned with some important trends in the study of eighteenth-century literature, as exemplified in a number of recent books[1]. Some of these books themselves consist in part or in whole of discussions of the trends which are my subject here. Others, especially Martin C. Battestin's *The Providence of Wit* and Max Byrd's *Visits to Bedlam*, are distinguished illustrations of tendencies and methods in recent scholarship, rather than commentaries upon them. Both, in very different ways, are important contributions to our thinking about the period, and contain new insights. They approach their topic from opposite directions. Battestin's chief interest is in the structures of order which are in his view asserted or implied in the major masterpieces of Augustan literature, whereas Byrd writes on some subversive undercurrents, on disruptive forces from within the nature of man which threatened or were felt to threaten these structures of order. Both critics deal to some extent with the same authors, and both are aware that each side of this question presupposes the other. I take Battestin's book first, and then some books which seem to me to be related to it in various ways. I then turn to Byrd's book and to others which are similarly related to it.

Fiat Lux
Battestin sets out to show

> that some at least of the salient formal features of Augustan
> literature and the arts – balance and proportion and design,

383

for example ... – are best understood in terms of the
ontological assumptions of the Christian humanist tradition,
that great coherent tradition of Western thought which
Newton at first seemed magnificently to have confirmed,
but which soon disintegrated under pressure of a new subjec-
tivism implicit in Locke's epistemology.

He argues that we have not sufficiently appreciated 'the degree to
which, during the latter half of the seventeenth century, the idea
of pure form in the arts was conditioned by a renewed theological
emphasis on design in Nature'; that Renaissance notions of
'cosmic design and providential direction,' including some
important elements of Pythagorean and neo-Platonist thought,
survived more strongly in the age of Pope than has usually been
admitted; and that the advent of Newtonian science reinvigorated
rather than hindered this continuity, if only for a time.

It is a case worth hearing. There is no doubt that it has some
truth, and that even if one does not accept (as I think one cannot)
all the implications of Battestin's argument, the information that
he brings together in pursuit of his theme is valuable. On the
other hand, I believe that Battestin has a dangerously oversimplified conception of the history of ideas, and of the relationship of the history of ideas to literary texts. He lapses very easily
into the notion that periods, centuries and generations have
thoughts and beliefs in the same way as individual human beings
have, and apparently that these thoughts and beliefs impose
themselves with a somewhat surprising consistency, coherence,
and universality of assent on individual writers of varied and
complicated character.

This is betrayed in a small way by such phrases as 'If Nature, as
Pope's generation believed, was the Art of God', which need not
in themselves be given undue significance. Our conventions of
verbal shorthand certainly make it possible for such expressions
to be less silly than they seem, although they are I believe an
invitation to lax thinking. A more radical indication is Battestin's
ubiquitous use of a whole battery of capitalised abstractions,
Nature, Art, Reality, Chance, Direction, Providence, Prudence,
Power, Reason, Time, Harmony, Order. These terms are
deployed across his pages like an occupying army, pressing every
author into service, and subjecting every literary text to a stunned
and restrictive obedience. The terms themselves are treated as
though each had the same meaning everywhere (there is some
concession to the fact that a 'good' term like Prudence could be

used in a perverted or bad sense, but very little closer discrimination than that, and very little probing of actual connotations in context);[2] and especially as though the grandest and most solemn implications of which each term is capable were necessarily evoked in all usages, however slight.

In works where Battestin's big terms naturally arise, genuinely indicating a primary concern with particular themes (e.g. the *Essay on Man*), Battestin introduces an unhealthy thematic simplification, and a tendency to equate poems with such themes as he sees in them. In works where his kind of thematic approach is not naturally applicable *as such* (e.g. Pope's *Pastorals* or Gay's *Trivia*), there is a reductive imposition of 'theme' upon text which distorts the literary work. In either case, the theme will be of the mightiest dimensions. Massive ideological and theological structures emerge whenever reference is made, whether colloquially, or jokingly, or for some small and specific local purpose, to God, or Providence, or Heaven, or creation.

An example is Battestin's treatment of the *fiat lux* theme in Pope. The motif is used, by Pope and others, in a variety of allusions, serious and comical. They are part of the natural educated language of a Christian society. But do they imply a 'theology'? Of the four examples given on p. 59 and subsequently elaborated, along with other more indirect instances, in Chapter III, one is by Belinda: '*Let Spades be Trumps!* she said, and Trumps they were' (*Rape of the Lock*, III:46). Is this to be taken as an example of 'one of the controlling motifs of Pope's poetry, implying the sacred grounds of both universal Order and artistic Form', either straightforwardly or even 'ironically to deplore its subversion'? For Battestin the answer is undoubtedly yes, and this reference to 'the sacred ideal of Order in a metaphysical, social, or moral context' should be taken 'together with similar patterns of imagery and allusion – comparing [Belinda] to the sun, for example (II: 1–14), source of light and order in the universe and emblem of divinity itself'. I think Pope's readers would have taken the comparison with the sun as primarily a playful mock-pompous application of a common image in love-poetry, in the tradition which Shakespeare guyed when he said 'My Mistress eyes are nothing like the Sunne' (Sonnet 130). And although the Sun was and still is in many contexts used to grander effect in love-poetry and elsewhere, it surely does not follow that every playful parody of sonneteering conventions brings in its train the full panoply of religious, theological and metaphysical overtones which have accumulated around that image in other places. To suggest that it does is to falsify a poem, throwing out the baby, so to speak, while keeping the bath-water.[3]

Belinda calling trumps into being is of course an example of the witty idiomatic adaptation or perversion of Genesis, I.3, perhaps the most famous of Scriptural commonplaces, which has been naturalised into the English language and which is available for many kinds of phrase-making, not necessarily in religious contexts. Belinda's speech belongs with a whole range of uses by Pope and others, some of the grandest of which are recorded in Battestin's discussion. To suggest on that basis that its major energies are located in the original and divine meaning of the terms is something else again.

Two of Battestin's four main examples ('At length great *ANNA* said – Let Discord cease!/She said, the World obey'd, and all was *Peace!*' and 'God said, *Let Newton be!* and All was *Light*'[4]) are closer to the point he makes. Both are unmocking celebrations of persons whose power to contribute to a better world order, through royal status or through genius, is respectfully asserted. But how literally are we to focus this onto the primary associations of the passage in Genesis? Is it really true that Pope literally looked forward at the time of *Windsor Forest* to 'a Golden Age for England which Anne would usher in'? Is he literally comparing Anne or Newton with God, as distinct from paying them an extravagantly witty homage whose witty extravagance, and whose limits, would be evident to all, along with the genuine praise? And, in the context of the awaited Peace of Utrecht, is there not a local and topical appositeness which would draw more attention to itself than to the general and the divine implications, just as in the lines about Newton bringing Light at his creation there is appositeness to the fact that Newton had made discoveries in the field of optics and written a famous work on that subject?

The fourth of Battestin's main examples is the reversal of *fiat lux* in the 'uncreating word' of the *Dunciad*'s ending. I think it possible to give value to this image of cultural disorder, as in some obvious ways 'a monstrous parody of the Christian system', without positing an opposite belief on Pope's part that, a few years before, in the reign of Anne or whenever, the original Divine Logos was being satisfactorily implemented, and that Pope's view of the world, positive and negative, was constantly and literally referable to the Logos's current standing on the cultural stock market.

The question of tone, or of wave-length, arises. How are we to take the *Essay on Criticism*'s '*glaring Chaos* and *wild Heap* of *Wit*' or the still more pertinently pointed remark, in a satire on Black-more (*Minor Poems*, Twickenham Edition 290–93), that Black-more 'Un-did *Creation* at a Jerk'? (Here again we should pre-sumably distinguish, in any case, between reference to the Creation as such, at whatever level, and the immediate and specific local allusion to the fact that Blackmore was the author of a long poem entitled *Creation*, which Battestin mentions only in his Index, not in the course of his argument.) I cannot believe that we are expected, in such places, to take to heart, or even to keep in mind, the full import and resonance of the story of Genesis. We cannot help recalling Genesis, of course, but less as a thematic scaffolding than as a witty ironic enrichment, a pointed allusive sting, part of a sophisticated rhetoric in which abusive hyperbole is conducted through witty exploitation of Scriptural echoes and associations. 'Allusions' to Genesis, or to ecclesiastical writers, or to Milton, are not hard to find in Pope or in his contemporaries. But their allusive status is surely open to question, and is at best gravely attenuated, when it rests mainly on terms like 'chaos' or 'creation' or their derivatives, which have passed into the lan-guage as normal idiomatic usages, increasingly independent of their specific Biblical associations. Are we not, when learnedly restoring them to these associations as Battestin does, doing as much violence to the life of the poems as any critic who wholly denied such associations?

The *Dunciad* is full of such associations, and they are deliberate: Night and Chaos, 'wild creation', 'Light dies before thy uncreat-ing word'. It is more than usually apt for Battestin to speak here of 'the *fiat nox* of annihilation'. But we should also notice that the images of cosmic upheaval are often focused elsewhere than on the cosmos. In the famous 'wild creation' passage in Book I, the lines about realms shifting their place and oceans turning to land are really about incompetent poets getting their images wrong. They look back 'at one level', as Battestin says on p. 107, to Horace's admonitions against this kind of incompetence (e.g. *Ars Poetica*, ll. 29–30). They would also be recognised as having some joking affinities with the ancient figure of *adynaton*, used by innumerable classical, Renaissance and later poets, including Horace (*Odes*, I:ii, 7–12). These affinities are complex, and include an element of true imaginative pleasure in the literary sport. Pope's passage has delighted many readers with the primary lyric power of its 'nonsense'.[5] But my main point is that the joke, whichever way one takes it, is primarily literary, not theological (just as the joke about Blackmore undoing creation is primarily literary). Battestin would doubtless answer that since the literary work is merely a reflection of the cosmos, literary aberration is by definition a reflection of chaos. This idea is, of course, far from alien to Pope. But I doubt if Pope would have accepted Battestin's solemnifying emphasis here, and Battestin almost admits as much on p. 111, as far as the 1728 version of the *Dunciad* is concerned. By p. 111, however, there has been too much Logos to unsay in this fashion, and the passages he discusses mostly occur in the final version too, so that much of what a critic might say of them, either way, applies to both versions.

Battestin goes on to discuss the passage in the light of some Miltonic parallels, and contributes useful details to what is in general terms common knowledge. But again he is determined to insist on the Creation at the expense of more immediate allusions: for example, the line about 'genial Jacob, or a warm Third-day' may carry some echo of the Third Day of the creation, but only because the creation had such a day along with five others, i.e. the First, Second, Fourth, Fifth and Sixth. Battestin thinks it is closer:

> As God on the third day divided the sea from the land, so, with reference to the productions of Grub Street, the largesse of Tonson the bookseller and the playwright's hope of a lucrative benefit 'Call forth each mass, a poem or a play.' The pun on 'Third-day' points to Genesis, but Pope's choice of adjectives (*'genial* Jacob ... a *warm* Third-day') and his earlier reference to Dulness as 'the Great Mother' (A, I:33) seem drawn from *Paradise Lost*, where on the third day of creation God causes the ocean to flow 'with warme / Prolific humour', softening the earth and fermenting 'the great Mother to conceave, / Satiate with genial moisture' (VII:279–82).

One's first inclination is to say that if the Universal Analogy, whether in its primary or its reverse forms, depended on parallels like this, the only surprising thing is that it took so many centuries to fall apart. Secondly, the Great Mother or Magna Mater is a great deal older than Milton. And thirdly, 'Third-day', in the passage as quoted on pp. 105–06 and discussed on pp. 106–07, only links up with the sequence of the days of creation if one reads Battestin's account of Miltonic and Biblical parallels (where Milton, and of course Genesis, not Pope, number the days) and then goes on to make the inference of numerical sequence. The Miltonic parallels specifically invoked here have apparently not been noticed before (p. 106). Pope says nothing about them, whether in the poem or the notes. This does not mean that Milton is not echoed in some degree, and there is no doubt that images of creation and allusions to Genesis are present in the poem. But what Pope primarily refers to is the fact that the 'Third-day' is a playwright's benefit night, and it is this, not the sequence of days of creation, that informed readers usually notice. Battestin soft-pedals the local allusion in favour of the remoter one, when it is the local one which is the main point.

The Cosmic Dance

Among examples of the re-emergence in Pope's time of 'the old ideas of cosmic design' are a number of statements about world harmony and the universal dance. They are cited from John Gilbert Cooper (1745), Bezaleel Morrice (1733), Nahum Tate (1701), and a host of odes to music which (to take those which date after 1700) include a minor poem by Congreve (1701), and poems by John Hughes (1703), Joseph Mitchell (1721), John Lockman (c.1730), John Taylor (1730).[6] Many of these come from formal celebrations of music or are prefixed to treatises on music, rather than from considered philosophical statements about the nature of the universe as such, so that an element of 'occasional' over-emphasis or special pleading should perhaps be discounted; and the formal occasion of a St Cecilia's Day celebration required certain ritual statements about the power of music to be made in the specially commissioned St Cecilia's Day odes of the kind represented by some of Battestin's examples. Besides, the statements are hardly those of major voices. To suggest, as Battestin does, that they show that the 'tradition was still very much alive' is like saying that the epic tradition was very much alive because epics by Samuel Wesley the Elder, Richard Blackmore, Thomas Ellwood, Orator Henley, Thomas Newcomb, Aaron Hill and Richard Glover kept being written.[7] Lip service was undoubtedly paid to both traditions, but the finest sensibilities of the age knew that neither was any longer viable. Pope never wrote his epic, but settled for translating Homer; and *his* 'Ode for Musick, on St Cecilia's Day' (1713) does not, contrary to the impression conveyed by Battestin on a number of occasions, proclaim the universal harmony or evoke a cosmic dance[8] (except in the very indirect sense of saying that music influences the passions, which was sometimes linked to notions of world harmony). Dryden's 'Song for St Cecilia's Day, 1687' does, as is well-known, celebrate the universal harmony, although most recent students of musical-cosmological theory believe that Dryden was really turning his back on the old 'cosmological orthodoxies' in favour of 'practical music' and its social perform-ance.[9] In the second of his St Cecilia Odes, 'Alexander's Feast' (1697), as D. T. Mace has said, 'The *harmonia mundi* and its attendant ideas do not even put in an appearance.'[10] 'The Secular Masque' (1700), written at the very end of Dryden's life, is a different kind of poem. But in so far as it too can be said to touch on notions of a cosmic dance, that dance is envisaged as nowadays taking place only, in Yeats's words, 'To the cracked tune that Chronos sings'. Dryden is a transitional figure, in this as in the epic, to which, like Pope, he paid his tribute by translating from the ancients rather than by writing one of his own; and those proponents of the universal harmony or cosmic dance whom Battestin cites from 1670 to 1700 include Thomas Mace (1676), Thomas Fletcher (1686), Thomas Shadwell (1690), Nicholas Brady (1692), and Theophilus Parsons (1693).

The 'cosmic dance' survives in solemn tributes, not as part of a live culture. The creaking badness of the examples Battestin gives (I quote from pp. 14 and 20) provide ample demonstration:

> Then all yon tuneful restless Choir
> Began their radiant Journeys to advance
> And with unerring Symphony to roll the central Dance.
>
> (John Taylor, 1730)

> Stupendous Bulk and Symmetrie,
> Cross Motion and clear Harmonie,
> Close Union and Antipathie,
> Projectile Force, and Gravitie,
> In such well pois'd Proportions Fall,
> As strike this Artfull, Mathematic Dance of All.
>
> (John Reynolds, 1709)

These illustrate the dangers of reading the history of ideas too literally, without a sufficiently sensitive regard for matters of tone and conviction, of the status of individual items of evidence, and of the relation of literary distinction to that status.[11] There is, of course, an opposite danger, which is to assume that only good poems provide accurate evidence, or to forget that it is in lesser works that typical attitudes or opinions tend to survive in a purer or less complex form.

At the risk of falling into these errors, I incline to the view that

Battestin's examples demonstrate almost the exact opposite of his view that the traditional conception of the world as a universal dance 'was still very much alive'; that the art historians and literary critics who have played down its survival into the age of Pope have not been effectively refuted; and that (I must here declare an interest) my own view, expressed in essays of 1967 and 1970,[12] that the great dance had been removed from its 'cosmic' pedestal and survived mainly in ideals of *social* harmony and of their expression in art ('True Ease in Writing comes from Art, not Chance, / As those move easiest who have learn'd to dance'),[13] makes better sense of the evidence.

Pope's formulation, which roots the harmonies of the couplet within a context of social and cultural loyalties rather than in a cosmic order, is typical of much of his imagery when he is enunciating aesthetic principles. The same might be said of a memorable passage nearly fifty years earlier in which Dryden's Neander compared dramatic repartee in good rhymed verse to a well-contrived dance.[14] Battestin's insistence on pushing the issue back to its metaphysical foundations[15] is not only in disagreement with the useful monograph on eighteenth-century prosodic theory by Paul Fussell, as Battestin admits, but would probably have seemed ill-judged and ill-focused to Pope, and preposterous to Swift. In Battestin's least cautious moods, the form of the Popeian couplet becomes a re-enactment of the divine *fiat lux*, and an expression of Pythagorean world-harmony, 'curiously like the Pythagorean *tetraktys*, . . . one of the happiest instances in literature of prosody recapitulating ontology'.

Battestin sometimes concedes that Pope may or may not have aimed 'deliberately' at this effect. Or he might pull himself up and say that Pope was 'too much a man of his times to take very seriously the "Refinements", as he called them, of those commentators who whimsically expounded the Pythagorean "Mysteries" of creation that Homer was supposedly celebrating'. But this particular concession is a rather specialised one, concerned with the history of Homeric exegesis, and is part of an argument that Pope used other than Pythagorean symbolism in rendering the 'archetypal' significance of Vulcan's forging of the shield of Achilles ('the archetypal representation of the artist's relationship to ideal Nature, the divine Artefact'). And what is one to make of 'too much a man of his times' when much of the burden of Battestin's argument is that the times *were* favourable to a Pythagorean outlook in a slightly modified or purified way, and that contemporary poems on music showed 'the ease with which

Pythagorean ideas were accommodated within the Newtonian system' (p. 9)?

Pope's loyalty to rhyme, against 'some of the most influential critics of his time', is attributed to the same causes as those given by Spitzer in explanation of 'St. Augustine's introduction of rhyme into modern poetry'. Rhyme becomes a Christian development, 'patterned on world harmony ... an acoustic and emotional phenomenon responding to the harmony of the world.' But when, in the late seventeenth and in the eighteenth centuries, rhyme is compared with dancing, it is usually (as in the examples I gave from Dryden and Pope) to the social rather than the cosmic, to persons dancing rather than to the universal order. This is true in other pronouncements comparing the couplet, or poems in general, to the dance, and in unfavourable as well as favourable applications of the image. Prior, seeking to find a good balance between regularity and irregularity in verse, including the rhymed couplet he used in *Solomon*, said in the Preface: 'He that writes in Rhimes, dances in Fetters: And as his Chain is more extended, he may certainly take larger Steps'. (Fielding used the image of dancing in chains to describe the restraints of restrictive rules upon Genius in *Tom Jones*, V:i; and see a variant comparison in *Tom Jones*, XIV:i.) Swift opens the poem for 'Stella's Birthday' of 1725 thus:

> As when a beauteous Nymph decays
> We say, she's past her Dancing Days;
> So, Poets lose their Feet by Time,
> And can no longer dance in Rhyme.

In 1767, Chesterfield said that the recitation of verse ought to be done 'in my favourite minuet time' (*Letters*, ed. B. Dobrée, VI:2800). (I have compared this passage with Valéry's description of verse-recitation as a 'danse verbale', and also with Pope's passage about 'True Ease', in *Henry Fielding and the Augustan Ideal Under Stress*, 36–7.) Fussell's *Theory of Prosody in Eighteenth-Century England*, 53, gives several similar examples from the second half of the century of comparisons between poetry or its recitation and the dance, notably, as in Chesterfield, the minuet. And when a poet failed to achieve a gentleman's 'True Ease', he might be compared to a dancing-master, on the grounds that 'Dancing Masters never make a handsome Bow, because they take too much Pains' (*An Essay on Wit*, 1748, 17): thus Percival Stockdale was to complain that Young 'is sometimes, in poetry,

392

what a dancing-master is in manners' (cited by Howard D. Wein-brot, *The Formal Strain*, Chicago and London, 1969, 128).

Poems and Big Ideas
When he is writing about interconnections among the ideas, images and forms of Order, Battestin is extremely good. His account of the traditional analogy between the artist and the Divine Creator is a powerful piece of scholarly synthesis. He offers one of the best documented explorations of the relationship between ideals of visual symmetry and those of musical and mathematical harmony, and reminds us how, in the work of Renaissance and later theoreticians of the arts, these may in turn be thought of as reflections of the universal harmony. He shows too that there was some survival of neo-Platonic and neo-Pythagorean system-making in his period. But even here he is perhaps over-inclined to suppose that because some thinkers held certain views, all their contemporaries must also be assumed to take these views for granted, and that these views must then necessarily be reflected, with an uncompromising directness, in every aspect of their art.

An interesting example occurs on p. 55, when he quotes Swift saying to Stella: 'Method is good in all things. Order governs the world. The Devil is the author of confusion.' Battestin comments:

> And the synonymous term for Order is Art, the effect of the rational mind that shapes and organizes and directs. The universe of Newton and the physico-theologians is such a work of Art; so, too, is the little world of man . . .

The suggestion in context is that these are Swift's beliefs. It ignores Swift's contempt for Newton, for physico-theologians, and for microcosmic analogy. Its feeling runs against Swift's usual inclination to deride the pretensions of 'Art' to introduce 'Order' in a disorderly world, and the notion that man's 'rational mind' often manages to 'shape and organize and direct'. The traditional comparison between the artist composing an ordered artefact and God creating the Universe is one which, as formulated by Battestin, Swift would in most moods consider to be a wild and blasphemous excess of radical self-sufficiency on the artist's part. Swift's lack of sympathy with some of the aesthetic ideals which Battestin describes is indeed noted in the chapter on Swift, but just here Swift is unquestioningly invoked as a spokesman for these ideals. And of course, Swift's attachment to Order is very strong, even though (or perhaps because) he is so often given to seeing it disrupted. But if we check on the passage Battestin quotes in its immediate context, we find that it is much less grand, and considerably undercut by comic banter:

> Here's a clutter! Well, so much for your letter, which I will now put up in my letter-partition in my cabinet, as I always do every letter as soon as I answer it. Method is good in all things. Order governs the world. The Devil is the author of confusion. A general of an army, a minister of state; to descend lower, a gardener, a weaver, &c. That may make a fine observation, if you think it worth finishing; but I have not time . . .
>
> *(Journal to Stella*, ed. Harold Williams, I:72)

It so happens that Swift has a serious version of the words Battestin quotes. It occurs in his sermon on 'Doing Good':

> All government is from God, who is the God of order, and therefore whoever attempts to breed confusion or disturbance among a people, doth his utmost to take the government of the world out of God's hands, and to put it into the hands of the Devil, who is the author of confusion. By which it is plain, that no crime, how heinous soever, committed against particular persons, can equal the guilt of him who doth injury to the public.
>
> *(Works*, ed. Davis, IX:238)

Even here, Swift is not talking of harmonious structures, except in so far as they are under stress from evil-doers. He is talking of actual society, and not of the ideal structures of poets or philosophers or theologians. His 'order' is much closer to 'law and order', and that, for Swift, is by no means a 'synonymous term' with 'Art'. Even this serious version, therefore, would have been somewhat out of place in the context of Battestin's quotation. In citing the other passage, he saw it as evidence of all the wrong things, and my point is not so much concerned with the individual content of a minor error, as with a sign of method: because Battestin believes that there is an Augustan Conception of Order, all references to Order must fit this.

Another example. 'To Pope, as to countless philosophers and divines of the Christian humanist tradition, the poet of the creation, of history, is the Deity himself, the Word who brought Form and Order out of Chaos . . .' (p. 60). It is likely that Pope thought more in those terms than did Swift. But what is interesting is that when we turn to the note which supplies documentation, it is not to Pope but to the 'general background' of the 'Christian humanist tradition' that we are referred, and there Battestin tells us that his two authorities, Patrides and Tuveson, believe that this 'general background' was no longer operative in the age of Pope. Because 'countless philosophers and divines' thought in such and such a way, Pope did so too. Now, assuming that Battestin, and not the two distinguished historians of ideas whom he cites, is right about the 'general background', and assuming even that Pope shared the ideas in question, does it follow that this is necessarily what all his poems are about? Battestin thinks yes.

Thus, the *Pastorals* 'make clear a fundamental assumption of his art and theology . . .' (p. 58). Has Pope a theology? Is that really the appropriate term? Battestin takes it for granted that it is, and this emerges in a discussion of the *Pastorals* which is in no obvious sense true or untrue, but is pitched at a level of grandiose significance which will not, I suspect, seem to belong to them in the eyes of most readers. Because Pope said that pastoral poetry deals not with present day rustics realistically described but with an idealised conception of rural life in a Golden Age, it follows that the poems comprehend 'both the Christian's conception of Time and History and, within this context, the poet's conception of the relationship of Art to Nature.' *Concordia discors* is quickly pressed into service: 'the great principle of universal Order which Pope expounds in *Windsor Forest* and the *Essay on Man* – is in "Spring" the condition of life'. The progress from 'Spring' to 'Winter' is a progress from the Golden to the Iron Age, 'from Eden to the present moment' (a notion reasonable in itself but expressed in rather extravagant terms on pp. 71–3), and 'Playing against this theme – indeed, at once containing and in a sense transcending it – are the poems themselves, the music not of time but of eternity, whose harmonies recall that ideal relationship between Art and Nature that once obtained'.

But 'playing against' all of this, there is surely the avowed slightness of the 'poems themselves', which, as Battestin notes, Pope considered a youthful 'holiday excursion in Fancy's maze'. In the light of this, Battestin's commentary seems inappropriately solemnifying, and would surely have seemed so to Pope. The poems are distorted, swollen into the wrong kind of grandeur. It remains true that ideas of the Golden Age, of Order, of Harmony, and the rest, are touched upon in some ways. But Battestin seems to me to make the mistake of equating poems with the magnitude of all and any of the metaphysical ideas which may be thought to intersect with them at any point, with whatever degree of association. In this way, Battestin can say that when Gay, in the third line of *Trivia*, speaks about the prudence required to avoid being jostled in the streets, he is ('at one level', ominous phrase) invoking that Prudence which is 'the supreme rational virtue of the Christian humanist tradition, which Cicero had called the *ars vivendi* and which Fielding and Goldsmith would consider "the Art of Life"'.

This brings us to *Tom Jones*, which 'in the present context may be taken as the consummate achievement of the Augustan mode', the 'elaborate paradigm of those correlative tenets of the Augustan world-view: the belief in the *existence of* Order in the great frame of the universe, and in the *necessity for* Order in the private soul'. Here, as in the third line of *Trivia*, Prudence reigns supreme 'within the microcosm, man', as Providence reigns in the macrocosm.

The argument rests on Cicero's distinction 'between the two kinds of wisdom, the speculative and the practical, *sophia* and *prudentia*'. Tom achieved the first by way of acquiring the second. In other (or rather, the same) words, when he finally acquires prudence, he marries Sophia, 'Wisdom herself'. As with the 'cosmic dance' and the other great themes, Battestin gives an imposing list of other authors, who, in different contexts from Fielding's, have taken a high view of prudence, and infers from this that Fielding must have thought of it as a supreme virtue. He knows that 'prudence' is often used pejoratively in *Tom Jones* (of Blifil, Mrs Western, and their ilk) and says that it appears in such cases as a nasty obverse, 'a kind of sinister parody of excellence', a reversal which may also be found in other authors who praise 'prudence'. But he does not adequately face (although he certainly realises) the fact that the majority of usages in *Tom Jones* are pejorative (a fact which critics of Battestin's persuasion often note, but seldom explain satisfactorily); or that in the main examples of non-pejorative use prudence is treated essentially as a secondary virtue or auxiliary discipline, legitimately self-protective and self-interested, and undoubtedly desirable, but 'a Guard to Virtue' rather than virtue itself, concerned with preserving 'a fair Outside':

Prudence and Circumspection are necessary even to the best of Men. They are indeed as it were a Guard to Virtue, without which she can never be safe. It is not enough that your Designs, nay that your Actions are intrinsically good, you must take Care they shall appear so. If your Inside be never so beautiful, you must preserve a fair Outside also. This must be constantly looked to, or Malice and Envy will take Care to blacken it so, that the Sagacity and Goodness of an *Allworthy* will not be able to see through it . . .

(III:vii)

It is this self-interest, distinguished explicitly from the domain of primary virtue, to which Allworthy refers when he speaks of prudence, in that phrase which Battestin makes so much of (pp. 165, 170, 191), as 'the Duty which we owe to ourselves' (XVIII:x):

You now see, *Tom*, to what Dangers Imprudence alone may subject Virtue (for Virtue, I am now convinced, you love in a great Degree.) Prudence is indeed the Duty which we owe to ourselves; and if we will be so much our own Enemies as to neglect it, we are not to wonder if the World is deficient in discharging their Duty to us . . .

In both these passages, and in others (e.g. XIV:vii, 'she hath sinned more against Prudence than Virtue'), a recurrent distinction is maintained between prudence and virtue. The linguistic usage, however deliberately, reveals Fielding's mode of thinking on the question, and the particular balance of his sympathies.

There need be no doubt that in this novel, as in other of Fielding's writings, prudence is positively recommended as a good thing. But there is a good deal of evidence that, as a form of self-interest, it has for Fielding a certain unattractiveness. Not only is it a quality which, in its nastier forms, is to be found in most of his bad characters. It is also in its good sense the quality which good people, almost by definition, will tend to lack. Being themselves good, they do not naturally think ill of others, or guard against evil designs which they would not themselves entertain. Their natural generosity tends to be unchecked by a self-regarding caution, and they are not calculating in their pursuit of their own interests. In all the novels, some of the most important and most sympathetic characters suffer from this without being shown to be stupid or earning the author's or the

397

reader's contempt. It is a regrettable fact, calling for a necessary watchfulness, although that very watchfulness risks becoming unattractive. For a degree of guileless imprudence is an occupational hazard of being generous and honest, and even the wisest and firmest of good men will tend to err in this direction when their warmth of heart and their benevolent impulses are involved. It is this which makes Allworthy so vulnerable to Blifil:

> Thus did the Affection of *Allworthy* for his Nephew, betray the superiour Understanding to be triumphed over by the inferiour; and thus is the Prudence of the best of Heads often defeated by the Tenderness of the best of Hearts.
>
> (XVI:vi)[16]

Both Allworthy and Tom are explicitly noted for their ardent nature, as well as for their instinctive benevolence (Allworthy 'had possessed much Fire in his Youth,' VI:iv., as Tom does now), and it is reasonable to suppose that this tends *a fortiori* to run against that prudence which they clearly, in their own interests and those of other good people, ought to have.

This is part of the point behind the remark at the end of the novel, when all loose ends are being tied, that Tom has 'acquired a Discretion and Prudence very uncommon in one of his lively Parts' (XVIII:xiii). It means he will no longer get into scrapes, as is right and proper now that he has married the heroine and is going to live happily ever after. We note the fact with satisfaction, as an appropriate guarantee of the stability of the happy ending, as well as a good thing in itself. A flaw in Tom's character needed rectifying. But to suggest that such a quickly dispatched rounding-up, in the novel's penultimate paragraph, conveys that a major moral deficiency has been momentously overcome does not seem justified either by the tone of the immediate context, or by the feeling of the work as a whole. The nature of Battestin's insistence on the importance of prudence here seems to me more appropriate to Richardson than to Fielding. The brief passing mention of 'Discretion and Prudence' at the end of *Tom Jones* contrasts radically with the obsessive iteration, aided by all the resources of rapturous exclamation, block capitals, and the rest, with which the story of PRUDENTIA is told at the end of *Pamela*. Nor does *Tom Jones* as a whole treat prudence with anything like the primacy and centrality with which Richardson treats it in his novel, although both novelists can be shown to explore not only good forms of prudence but evil ones too.

Fielding's acceptance of the practical necessity for prudence does not turn his novel into an 'anatomy of Prudence'. The suggestion that it does is, once again, not so much true or untrue as out of focus, an inappropriate form of thematising which distorts the nature of Fielding's fiction. But I suspect that even if this were not so, Battestin's notion of Fielding's attitude to prudence itself would still require revision. Fielding not only took a less grand view of prudence than did Richardson, but felt rather cool towards it, however valuable he considered and asserted it to be as an auxiliary virtue. And the dislike of prudential values which is evidenced in parts of *Tom Jones* and in other works was exacerbated by his well-known contempt for Richardson's first novel and the whole prudential morality with which he identified its author.

From Prudence to Providence, or the Author as God
What Prudence is in the microcosm, Providence is in the macrocosm. The 'twin themes are closely (even etymologically) related'. The 'even' almost suggests that Fielding himself had brought the etymology about. This would be fitting enough, since the narrator of *Tom Jones* is analogous to God, and there is a greater appropriateness 'than we have thought' in the fact that Fielding's example has given currency to the term 'omniscient' among students of the theory of narrative. Battestin has a way with other people's words. He likes them to signify only the grandest possible things. Thus, when Fielding creates surprising coincidences and happy resolutions to his characters' difficulties (as story-tellers have always done), Battestin takes him to be suggesting in some high sense the direct intervention of Providence. Playful or mock-pompous or merely unforced idiomatic references to 'lucky Circumstance' and 'providential Appearance' lead him to elaborate discussions of the theology of providential intervention and of the divinely ordained significance of chance events. Doubts about the appropriateness of this can apparently be silenced by the frequency with which Fielding refers to accidental or chance events, or uses the terms 'Providence' and 'Fortune'. Fielding's quasi-learned fooleries with the notion of the *deus ex machina* turn into affirmations of 'the benevolent Providence of the god *in* the machine'. Those coincidences and happy resolutions which are among the oldest and commonest features in the arts of narrative and of drama become symbols of elaborate metaphysical design.[17] It is doubtless true, and may be part of Battestin's point, that these features often have a deeper value, in

that they answer to some fundamental human aspirations (for pattern, for a satisfying close, for a sense of due rewards and punishments): but this is surely not the same thing as the sober diet of theology and water proposed here.

The mock-identification of an author and his poem with God and the creation reverses, as Battestin says, 'a familiar analogy, as old at least as Plotinus'. This is true in a way. But if the analogy is as old as Plotinus, is it always as serious or as weighty? And how much seriousness is in fact lost by Fielding's *reversal* of the ancient formula, according to which God is an Author, into his consciously cheeky comparison of himself with God? There is a world of difference between the tone of the passage by Fielding and that of the passages by Cudworth and Burnet quoted on pp. 145–6. Fielding's assertion of his Divinity is as follows:

This Work may, indeed, be considered as a great Creation of our own; and for a little Reptile of a Critic to presume to find Fault with any of its Parts, without knowing the Manner in which the Whole is connected, and before he comes to the final Catastrophe, is a most presumptuous Absurdity. The Allusion and Metaphor we have here made use of, we must acknowledge to be infinitely too great for our Occasion, but there is, indeed, no other, which is at all adequate to express the Difference between an Author of the first Rate, and a Critic of the lowest.

(X:i)

Battestin makes no allowance for irony, for playfulness, for mock-pompousness. Is God ironic, playful, mock-pompous? Does he rattle on bumptiously about his omnipotence and his 'liberty to make what Laws I please' (II:i) in the way Fielding sometimes does? Can Fielding really mean to suggest all this, or is he playfully, and for local rather than thematic purposes, risking analogies 'infinitely too great', in order to be uppishly and comically dismissive of critics and bad readers rather than to set himself up as God? And might he not be using irony in order to signal to the reader that he does *not* think of himself as God? Of course, when all the cautions are made, it remains true that Fielding exploits analogies between art and the divine creation, as do many other writers. These analogies are, in a sense, obvious and natural ones for a writer to play with. But Battestin seems to take hints and suggestions, witty glimpses, tentative moments of self-importance, and for that matter simple and genuine expressions of a sense that the order of art pays homage to God's universe, as thematic and structural armatures encasing entire novels and poems in the same unvarying and simplifying uniform.

Battestin's discussion of Fielding's burlesque introduction of Sophia is a good example of his method in close-up. He begins unexceptionably by acknowledging that the mock-sublime style is 'both playful and serious, mocking the extravagancies of romance while at the same time invoking the old values of honour and virtue which romance celebrates'. But this is almost the only concession we get that this passage contains any humour or irony, and the discussion continues as though this humour not only had no effect, but hardly existed. Battestin continues:

> By a process of allusion – to mythology, art, poetry, and his own more immediate experience – Fielding presents his heroine as the ideal woman, the representative of a beauty of form and harmony of spirit so absolute as to be a sort of divine vitalizing force in man and nature alike … Sophy Western is also the image and embodiment of '*Sophia* or the *Divine Wisdom*'.

An inattentive reader might be lulled into thinking that the last few words are quoted from Fielding. In fact, as we discover from a note at the back, they are by Jacob Boehme, an author hardly likely to be a normal part of Fielding's 'process of allusion'. Battestin does not say he is, but he seems to convince himself by his own innuendos, and may mislead unguarded readers. The allusions which Fielding *does* make, and which Battestin records, are to Flora, to the Medici Venus, to his own dead wife, and to Donne's Elizabeth Drury. One of those which Battestin does not record, although the facts have been known for some years and are now noted in his own new edition of *Tom Jones*, is to 'the rude Answer which Lord *Rochester* once gave to a Man, who had seen many Things': this was 'If you have seen all this, then kiss mine A[rs]e'.

Why is there no reference to this? Presumably because the variety of mood, and the unsolemnity, which it reveals tend to complicate the schematic neatness or simplified gravity of Battestin's reading. Few readers would dispute Fielding's tenderness either towards Sophia or towards the memory of his dead wife. But his highspirited refusal to be solemn, which gives a kind of rugged warmth and humanity to this passage, would clearly be inappropriate in the etherealised conception Battestin has of Sophia as both 'ideal woman' and ' "Divine Wisdom" '.

At the very time when he pays lip-service to the idea that Fielding sometimes demands 'to be read on more than one level', it is Battestin himself who stands most to be accused of reductive simplification. 'At one level', a phrase he falls back on in some embarrassed moments, is an ancient critical recipe in situations where the critic has chosen a 'level' which he suspects that most other readers will find inappropriate. Thus, where Fielding himself had gone out of his way, throughout the whole burlesque exercise, to stress that his heroine was not an 'ideal' but a very *real* woman, 'a middle-sized Woman; but rather inclining to tall', Battestin will assure us that 'Ultimately, her true identity is ideal, an abstraction'. A vivid, lively-tempered girl turns into 'both cynosure and avatar' of a 'paradigmatic universe', and her 'wedding dinner' becomes like (or 'in its way not unlike') 'the banquet of Socrates'. And when Tom is made to say, in the heightened jargon which is part of the standard rhetoric of fiction and drama in Fielding's time, 'To call *Sophia* mine is the greatest . . . Blessing which Heaven can bestow', Battestin finds evidence that their marriage 'is the supreme redemptive act'.

From Ontology to Plain Meaning

Mr Battestin's book has many powerful virtues. It is a monument to several years of thoughtful study. It may become a standard work of reference for its tracing of certain themes in Augustan literature and its Renaissance antecedents. Its facts, its wide-ranging quotation from creative writers and aesthetic theoreticians, both major and minor, provide us with a body of knowledge for which we should be grateful, and I am. But the interpretative use to which these facts are put seems to me wrong in both conception and method, and is likely to have a more dangerous influence on inexperienced readers, and on less gifted scholars than Battestin, precisely because of Battestin's manifest and impressive learning, and his deserved reputation among specialists in his field. For this reason, the ungrateful task of dwelling at perhaps disproportionate length on the weaknesses of the book seemed to me called for.

A book which demonstrates these dangers without the accompanying virtues is Thomas E. Maresca's *Epic to Novel*. This book appeared at about the same time as *The Providence of Wit*, and it would be absurd to blame Battestin for it. Battestin is not the only nor the first (although he is probably the best) practitioner of this style of criticism. Nevertheless, a reading of the two books together is a sobering exercise, as Maresca's book seems like a blundering parody of the bad moments of better critics. The 'divine fiat' re-emerges in Dryden and elsewhere (*fiat lux* seems to have become for the 1970s what the 'soft' interpretation of *Gulliver's Travels* was for the 1950s and 1960s; Maresca subscribes to both). 'Ontology' is rampant: 'the relationship among Fleck-noe, Shadwell, and their respective plays is totally tautological, not just literarily, but ontologically as well'; in the *Tale of a Tub*, 'ontogeny recapitulates phylogeny'; 'Dryden's, Pope's, and Swift's fears are based on an acceptance of the microcosm-macrocosm analogy as *ontologically* true: consequently, the con-ceptualisations of the human mind and the artistic cosmoses that result from them directly affect the greater world'.

'Cosmoses' are no joke to Maresca, and if he ever deviates into wit, it runs against all his sturdiest efforts. When he notes that Belinda invokes ' "the Cosmetic" – rather than cosmic – "Pow'rs," ' he is careful to ensure that this pleasant little molehill is ontogenised into a suitably metaphysical mountain, complete with an automatic Fiat careering up one of its slopes, and a Mini (or microcar?) marked 'structure of the universe' coming down the other side. (The critical tact and simplicity of Brower's comment on the same passage, in an essay on the same theme as Maresca's book and entitled 'From the Iliad to the Novel,'[18] should be contrasted with Maresca's, p. 86). And here is Maresca on the 'alternative cosmology' or 'Belindacentric universe' of *The Rape of the Lock*:

> Belinda and her attendants, both physical and metaphysical, offer an order and a corollary aesthetic; these amount, in the poem, to an alternative cosmology, a Belindacentric uni-verse competing with, and almost eclipsing, the heliocentric world of 'reality'.

Fielding and the Epic are an important part of Maresca's concerns, and we learn that Fielding

> has confronted the problems of subjectively generated signi-ficance, of the cosmos understood as flux, of pervasive corporeality, all of which overwhelmed traditional epic, and answered them with a mode of figurative narration that takes dynamic flux as its base of meaning and out of the interplay of events generates objective significance, while at

the same time wedding that meaning to the body of language.

Readers of *Tom Jones* will presumably recognise the description at once. Maresca argues that Fielding becomes increasingly epic from *Joseph Andrews* to *Amelia* (in a 52-page discussion of Fielding and the Epic, *Jonathan Wild*, in some ways Fielding's most systematically mock-heroic novel, is completely ignored); that 'the plot of *Tom Jones* forms an almost perfect paradigm of epic'; and that the process 'culminates in *Amelia*, which, simply [*sic*], *is* epic' (how's that for a fiat, then?).

Maresca's book exhibits every scholarly laxity in the business. 'World pictures' crowd his imaginary museum. Centuries have thoughts of their own, and the Renaissance was of one mighty mind ('All love, the Renaissance knew, moves toward fulfillment . . . '). Descartes wrote a book called *Traité de la Monde*. A scholar known in the real world as Lyall H. Powers is transfigured into L. H. Rowen in the (Marescacentric?) cosmos of this book. The systematic marshalling of authorities, the scrupulous accuracy of factual information, the careful transcription, the immense learning which underlie *The Providence of Wit*, whatever one may feel about its assumptions or conclusions, have turned here into a monster of freewheeling, unscholarly self-importance.

There are protests and warnings against this kind of thing in two new books concerned with recent trends and future directions in eighteenth-century studies. I have already mentioned Donald Greene's remarks about 'world pictures' in his contribution to *New Approaches to Eighteenth-Century Literature*, the recent collection of English Institute papers edited by Phillip Harth. This fine volume resists many of the simplifications and distortions that have crept into the subject. A remarkable essay by Ralph Cohen, for example, shows that the popular notion that genres were thought of in the eighteenth century as distinct and mutually exclusive literary forms is quite untrue, and that eighteenth-century authors and critics had a highly developed readiness to allow a mixture and an interpenetration of genre-features in many literary works. This essay is exceptional among those in this book in being deeply rooted in new, or newly-assembled, evidence from the period itself. It should put paid to one of the more insidious of our *idées reçues*.

But while there is an urge to desimplify, to repudiate reductiveness, whether of 'world pictures' or of 'genres', there is also a parallel reassertion of one of the old-fashioned simplicities of discourse, viz. plain literal meaning. Ralph Rader, who is also concerned with questions of genre, asserts the primacy of main meanings, determined by context, against the lures of ambiguity, tension, and the rest. One has to say that his own meanings are often other than plain, but his remark 'that the main line of contemporary literary study has gone harmfully wrong, not of course in its best practice, but in fostering a theory which permits and even encourages irresponsible critics to distort and override the native limits of significance in literary structures' deserves to be heard in many quarters.

The most powerful defence of plain meanings, however, occurs in Irvin Ehrenpreis's contribution, 'Meaning: Implicit and Explicit,' a discussion which also appears, in expanded form, in Ehrenpreis's *Literary Meaning and Augustan Values*,[19] the second of the two books which I have mentioned as reacting to recent critical excesses. Ehrenpreis's warnings are not confined to excessive critical interest in allusion (including allusions to Milton, which seem to have become a special obsession in current criticism of Augustan poets), and it might in any case be felt that Ehrenpreis is not at his best on this particular question. His attack on the pursuit of arcanely allusive subtleties has an element of hectoring reductiveness, and he risks being unjust to the extraordinary enrichment of our understanding of Pope and other poets which we owe to the best students of the 'poetry of allusion' (it should be noted, however, that Ehrenpreis pays handsome tribute to Brower's writings on Pope, and a more grudging one to Maynard Mack's).

But Ehrenpreis's note of embattled sanity becomes very valuable when he asserts the primacy of plain meaning against the various kinds of thematising superstructure ('the chain of being, the value of the contemplative life, *concordia discors*, the golden mean') imposed upon poems by critics who assert the rich survival of traditions of thought and feeling which form the background to these poems. A masterly argument distinguishes 'between the origin of a poem and its meaning'. A very telling examination of some recent work on Congreve by Aubrey Williams raises the whole question of whether it is right to see themes of Providential intervention in happy coincidences and resolutions of dramatic or fictional plots. And the sort of thinking which holds that every feature of a work contributes to ideological structures of order, and in which, for example,

the design of the action cannot be pleasingly symmetrical; its
symmetry must suggest a divine symmetry, or else it must
be ironically contrasted to social chaos,

is repudiated by Ehrenpreis as a 'kind of totalitarian analysis'
which 'debases the idea of organic form'.

Ehrenpreis's resistance to themes of order is probably matched
by a corresponding dislike of themes of misrule. In his current
mood of high common sense, he can be expected to be as sceptical
of subversive undercurrents as of orderly superstructures, and
this is healthy so far as it goes. But plain meanings have become a
bee in Ehrenpreis's normally rather subtle bonnet. That particular
bee seems uninterested either in 'Sweetness *and* Light' or in
counter-exposures of 'Dirt *and* Poison'. It has more in common
with the famous bee of one of Ehrenpreis's other authors, whose
'booming is blunt, not broken in subtleties'.[20] Its warnings are
invigorating to readers of poems, although they have their limits,
as Ehrenpreis will be the first to say if the day ever comes when
they become the academic fashion, and a flood of literal-minded
paraphrases start issuing from the learned printing-houses.

Misrule

Meanwhile, a strong interest exists in the interplay between
orthodoxy and misrule in the great Augustan writers. It is an
interest which Ehrenpreis has himself advanced in some of his
writings on Swift. It shows itself in an attenuated form in
Battestin's discussions of Swift and Sterne in *The Providence of
Wit*. And it arises very prominently in several studies of madness
as a preoccupation in eighteenth-century literature and life
published in the last twenty years by medical historians, by
historians of ideas, by Foucault in his early writings, and by
others. Lawrence Lipking, in his contribution to *New Approaches*,
briefly (and with some ambiguity) considers possible ways of
building on this, noting incidentally that 'We need good studies of
eighteenth-century madness; and more than one, I gather, is
under way'.

He was possibly referring to two new books, now actually
published, Max Byrd's *Visits to Bedlam: Madness and Literature in
the Eighteenth Century*, and Michael V. DePorte's *Nightmares and
Hobbyhorses: Swift, Sterne, and Augustan Ideas of Madness*. Both
books register the widespread obsession in the eighteenth century
with the idea of madness, 'with the nature of irrationality, and
with the relationship of madness to sanity', and both are con-

cerned with some of the same authors. Mr Byrd's book is more broadly based. It deals at some length with a larger number of major authors, and has a headier sweep with the literary history of periods before and after. Mr DePorte contributes a long first chapter on 'Abnormal Psychology in England 1660–1760' which has no direct counterpart in Byrd's book. This provides a very useful conspectus, in a book which is more soberly factual as well as somewhat narrower than Byrd's.

Byrd tells a story whose main outlines are also familiar, but in freshly observed detail, and with an unusually sharp and sophisticated commentary. His argument is that in the eighteenth century, as in the Middle Ages, 'madness' was viewed with a particular hostility, as a sign of divine disfavour, and as criminal in some sense. In the later of these periods especially, punitive incarceration and other forms of chastisement or disapproval were thought particularly appropriate. The ancient equation between madness and extraordinary insight or poetic genius, for example, had less currency in the age of Swift and Pope than at other times: Byrd notes shrewdly that Pope took a somewhat ironic view of 'the divine madness of poets', and that his own 'characteristic gesture is to "stoop to truth and moralize" his song'. It is not any good poet, but the 'slip-shod Sibyl' of *Dunciad*, III:15–16 who is shown 'In lofty madness meditating song'. Byrd astutely indicates that the remark about 'how near allied Dulness is to Madness' in the note to *Dunciad B*, I:33, is a pointed reversal of Dryden's 'Great Wits are sure to Madness near ally'd' (*Absalom and Achitophel*, I:163): strictly, it should be added that Dryden's line is itself not without irony, and that the note is not Pope's in a simple sense, but one of those 'attributed to Warburton himself in his edition of the Works, 1751' (*Dunciad*, Twickenham Edition, ed. James Sutherland, 3rd edn. 1963, lvi: 249).

Equally, later conceptions of 'madness' as radical to the artist's alienation from a bad world, or to his freedom from the confining values of a rationalist outlook, do not begin to make any powerful appearance until the end of the century. The early *poètes maudits* whom Wordsworth salutes in *Resolution and Independence*, like their later and more notorious successors, would have been relegated, in the *Tale of a Tub* or the *Dunciad*, to that lowest of all high places, the Grub Street garret: neither their 'despondency and madness', nor their pursuit of a creative 'dérèglement', would have aroused much sympathy or respect. If the later poets really lived in garrets too, that in itself became a badge of honour, and the 'poverty' which came to stand for a proud independence or

refusal of worldly approval was treated by Augustan satirists as
evidence in itself of culpable eccentricity and mediocre talent. The
twin-culpabilities of poverty and madness were, as Byrd shows,
strongly identified with one another in Pope's world (he might
have added that in 1743 Pope shifted the Cave of Poverty and
Poetry from the neighbourhood of Rag Fair to that of Bedlam)
and little compassion was granted to either. Contrast the
treatment of both poverty and madness in *King Lear*, or the later
and homelier compassion extended to both by Johnson. Later
still, both might be transformed from objects of pity to signs of
high standing. Compassion is irrelevant to the proud situation of
the *poète maudit*, who can feel more contempt for the world than
the world feels for him.

Following Foucault, Byrd notes that the 'widespread practice
of confining madmen . . . began in Europe in the mid-seventeenth
century' (perhaps slightly later in England). 'In earlier periods
madmen normally lived among relatives or upon the charity of
the community, and the devils thought to cause madness were
exorcised openly, driven out in public ceremony'. A striking
literary reflection of the transition is noted:

> The imprisoning of the insane stands in startling contrast to
> the freedom of movement of Don Quixote and King Lear,
> and even Tom o'Bedlam . . .

The new feeling that madness should be hidden ('except on
Sundays', as it were for the tourists), the madman relegated to 'a
quasi-medical prison alongside other criminals, degraded and
exiled and also punished', shows the extent to which notions of
madness as 'divinely inspired' were relegated to and replaced by a
state of opinion in which 'madness is indistinguishable from
crime'.

A reason for this shift towards an intense repudiation of
madness (a reason which presumably, later in the eighteenth
century, also paradoxically helped to introduce a new sympathy)
was a realisation that madness was a potential within ourselves:

> In earlier times men recoiled from the gods or witches who
> inflicted madness: their presence, even if it denoted super-
> natural protection, was frightening. But in the Augustan
> Age fear of the insane springs from the inescapable conclu-
> sion that it is *ourselves* who cause madness, that human beings
> possess an unpredictable self-altering, self-destructive

potential. (Present in both cases seems to be that primitive terror of ... the irrationality that destroys all order.) The alternative external explanations of human madness that had served earlier cultures held their ground poorly in the face of an advancing, skeptical science and a weary, often defensive religious establishment ... For the Augustans external explanations of the human personality no longer worked, and an *internal* mythology was not available ... until Freud. ... The Homeric gods were no longer believable, as the lifelessness of classical mythology in eighteenth-century poetry ineloquently testifies. Witchcraft was officially pronounced defunct in 1736: where else could men locate the forces of unreason except within themselves?

That force within could become the most dangerous of threats to a cherished order, felt to be precarious: it made the satirist himself a potential disruptor, along with the rest of mankind. But equally, the recognition of the wildness within could turn *either* to the compassion of fellow-feeling, *or* to a new pride in the energies of the self, challenging authority and reason:

Clearly sentimentalism in its largest sense – a passion for passions, a fascination with feeling simply for its own sake and without regard to context – begins the march from neoclassic to Romantic English literature. In two related aspects of sentimentalism, the histories of melancholy and sublimity at mid-century, we can see how the new age came to create literature deliberately out of the irrational parts of the human self that the Augustans had regarded as anarchic and insane, for melancholy and sublimity are two openly irrational experiences that transform men (temporarily) into good likenesses of madmen, into good likenesses of Cibber's manic and depressive brothers in fact. Such transformations were despised and contested by the great Augustans, but increasingly modern writers seek them out; they resemble those ecstatic moments of madness that Plato describes with so much approval; they seem not life-denying now, but life-enhancing, just as the inspiration of the gods formerly did. But one difference separates this ecstasy from the Platonic one: whatever madness comes about now, the modern tendency is to locate its source within the human personality, not outside it. Melancholy and sublimity are good examples of this new order emerging, indirect but unmistakable statements of change. In them we see the beginning of the dissolution of the Augustan fear of madness, and the modern embracing of it.

The demented grandeurs of Timon or Lear have little place in the Augustan world (I suspect that it is both the madness and the grandeur which Swift repudiated when he announced that his 'Misanthropy' was not in 'Timons manner', and not the misanthropy itself). But Byrd, exploring all too briefly some interpenetrations between tragedy and satire, reminds us that the extraordinary insights vouchsafed to the sublimer forms of madness were sometimes very close to the satirical home-truth: 'The real nature of those vital truths that Lear utters is not mysterious, not mystical: it is satirical', satirising 'human hypocrisy,' for example, in the way that 'Hamlet's "mad" speeches' also do.

This link of madness with satire places it still on the side of the satirist and not the satirised. The equation is paradoxical, and has often co-existed with an opposite equation of mad with bad, i.e. with the villains of satire (this is true not only of the Augustan period, when the mad/bad equation could be expected to be more pronounced). It has often been complicated by the two-edged paradoxes about the wisdom of folly, the folly of wisdom, the insanity of the so-called 'sane' or normal world, and the peculiarly ambiguous status of what has been called the 'medical concept'[21] in satire, in which the satirist is a surgeon curing the diseases (physical as well as mental) of immorality, open to all the imputations of quackery which satirists themselves attached to medical men, and himself mad with righteous or unrighteous indignation, with the 'folly' of thinking the world worth mending or capable of being mended, or with that worldly lucidity which assumes that cannibal proposals are natural and proper.

The main ambiguity surrounds the notion of madness as a disease. In medical history, the progress towards the understanding of madness as primarily a medical rather than a moral, or theological, or demonological matter was a slow one. Signs of shifting emphasis are evident in the seventeenth and eighteenth centuries, but there is no significant or widespread intensification of this until Johnson's lifetime. The change in outlook, the increase in the number of medical discussions of madness, did not at first produce any great advances in the pathology, but it altered attitudes, helped to improve the condition of hospitals, etc. Inmates became 'patients', and it may be that the transition from 'madhouse' to 'asylum' and then to the modern 'mental hospital' was prepared for in this period. The assumption grew that madness (hitherto often thought 'incurable', and the term 'hospital for incurables' sometimes implying some idea of 'madhouse'), once admitted to be an illness, was, like any physical illness, susceptible of cure.

The more this attitude prevails, the greater the tendency to remove madness from the domain of moral culpability, and to accord to it the sympathy to which we feel that the infirm are entitled. The age of Samuel Richardson and of Johnson is very notable for this, by contrast with the age of Swift and Pope. But the ambiguous presence of the two tendencies together seems to be constant. We still speak of the very wicked as mad, and of a world which is politically or socially immoral as a 'mad' world. Just as in the eighteenth century of Johnson and of Smollett it was the practice to incarcerate inconvenient persons in private madhouses, thus removing them from action and discrediting them in an ambiguous mixture of pitying contempt and brutal repudiation, so in our time, as Byrd notes, 'political dissidents have been silenced in mental institutions in the Soviet Union'. And although, in the reverse direction, we feel sorry for the mad and the ill, and even forgive their misdeeds if they can be attributed to 'mental illness', we have never ceased to attach a degree of moral stigma to illness and infirmity in general, and to mental diseases in particular.

Byrd takes us through a whole set of 'infirmities' which have traditionally been associated with madness, whether causally or analogically. He brings out particularly strongly the association with blindness, and with the ancient topos of the blind seer. Just as the seer deprived of sight may see more deeply than ordinary men with normal sight, so the inspired madman has powers of wisdom and understanding denied to those who have not lost their reason. The prophet or poet divinely mad, and the blind seer, have long been linked together. But blindness, like folly, can just as readily be used as an image of impercipience or obtuseness, and Byrd argues that it is the latter connotations which prevail in the satiric world of Swift and of Pope, to be overtaken later by a return of more sympathetic views, themselves stretching all the way from ascriptions of sublimity to simple pity. (By a parallel process, 'darkness' is bad in Swift and Pope, but had much to do with sublimity in earlier ages, and is strongly reinstated as potentially sublime by Burke and others.) In this regard, 'blindness' is like 'poverty': potentially sublime, or deserving of compassionate sympathy, at various times before and after the Augustan age, ignoble and more or less culpable during it.

Madness and poverty, madness and blindness: to these should be added another equation, that of madness and women. Like the others, it could show the mad as both less and more than fully human. Byrd shows that madness was often identified with the female and the obscene, and we are reminded of the etymology of the word *hysteria*. The identification survives into the compassionate phase later in the eighteenth century, when madwomen in Sterne or Mackenzie are treated tenderly and 'sentimentally' (with or without touches of irony), as pathetic victims. The assumption that women are especially remarkable for 'extraordinary delicacy, sensitivity, genius' is well-known, and the identification of refinement and sensibility with 'delicate nerves' is a familiar feature of literary history.

Byrd deals with the relationship between madness and 'refinement' in a similar way. He does his case less than justice by omitting to notice how *explicit* the link can become even in the hostile uses of the term 'refinement,' in the *Tale of a Tub* or the *Dunciad*: in the 'heads refin'd from Reason' of *Dunciad*, III:6, 'refinement' has been punned into actual synonymity with madness. But on the history of the crucial transitions, he is as good here as he is on the other related themes, and brings out how that 'melancholy' which was thought of as a peculiarly 'English malady' came to be associated with myths of British superiority (in liberty, originality, creativity), just as nervous disorders came more generally to be identified with a high civilisation.

Parallel and opposite to the notion of madness as highly civilised and 'refined' is that of madness as bestial. The history of attitudes to madness is full of examples of madmen being thought of, and actually treated, as no better than beasts, just as that other supposedly subhuman species, women, were so often considered embodiments of the most animal side of humanity. But whereas, in this paradox-ridden mythmaking, women could equally easily be seen as embodiments of extreme refinement or of extreme bestiality, beasts were in the nature of things more likely to be bestial than refined. This did not, however, prevent even that analogue of madness from acquiring a powerfully favourable symbolic status in the later eighteenth century, when animal energy and the mysterious force of such figures as Blake's Tiger may be identified with passionate forms of being, superior to or more 'authentic' than the common 'reason' of contemporary social man. Those vitalist schools of thought which, now as in the past, have rated the instinctive life of the body as wiser and better than the restraints of rational intellect are not unrelated to the story. A full consideration of this aspect would properly belong to a separate book. This is no less true of several of the other themes of this richly suggestive volume. The subject is at the very centre of the cultural history not only of England, but of the whole of European civilisation. It crosses the path of almost every subject of importance in that history, and it is Byrd's merit that he gives a vivid glimpse of this without being submerged in multiplicity of detail or imposing a false simplification.

Byrd tells a fascinating story, and gives it a fascinating commentary. It has to be said with regret that in matters of method and presentation his book lacks some of the decencies of scholarly discourse. There is some grievous misquotation, one of the earliest examples of which is the citing of one of Swift's most famous sentences as '"I saw a woman flayed the other day,"' adding to boot the mystifying suggestion that this sentence begins a 'section' of the *Tale*: the note to this quotation adds insult to injury by citing as its source the authoritative edition of Guthkelch and Nichol Smith (which of course gets it right). In other places, Byrd does not use authoritative or standard editions at all. A professional student of Augustan literature has no business to cite (pp. 180–1) Scriblerus material from Eddy's edition of Swift's *Satires and Personal Writings* when it is available in Kerby-Miller's edition of the *Memoirs*, or to quote Defoe from the introduction to an anthology of eighteenth-century literature (pp. 49, 184n). On p. 44 Byrd refers to 'The celebrated Dr. Battie (who was notorious for his own rather rambling brain and from whom I think we get our word *batty*)', but does not trouble to look up the *OED* on the point (the word is entered in the *Supplements* of 1933 and 1972, in the latter as first recorded in 1903, and as derived from *bat*, 'bats in the belfry' etc: Byrd's conjecture may or may not be right, but it is his high-handed lack of interest in the accuracy of the point he is suggesting which is disturbing). On pp. 29–30 Byrd has a good brief critique of Foucault, but here as elsewhere he uses the abridged and translated version of *Histoire de la folie à l'âge classique* known as *Madness and Civilization*, and not the full original version. And there are also misprints and a fair amount of minor looseness or imprecision of expression.

Sometimes Byrd puts his substantive points in an unhelpfully oversimplified way. For example:

One implication of the Lockean model is that all minds, since they receive the same sensory information in the same way, will perceive the same reality and come to the same conclusions about it. Hence the 'public' character of so much Augustan literature, the interest in the greater genres like epic rather than in the private meditative lyric.

It is hard not to think of the second sentence as largely a *non sequitur* to the first. No doubt, some relation exists. But *is* the epic a 'public' form in any sense of 'public' that rests heavily on Lockean ideas of the mind? Did not the epic have greater status than the lyric, whether of the 'private meditative' or any sort, at most periods before the age of Locke?

On p. 70 Byrd seems to accept Norman Brown's view that Swift anticipated 'the heart of the Freudian view of sublimation,' without the qualifications that have been made necessary by the brief critiques of Brown by Ehrenpreis and by Martin Price, and by the fact, known long before, that Swift's mockery of the disguised sexuality of the Dissenters is largely drawn from standard elements in seventeenth-century anti-Puritan satire. And Swift's comparison of 'the Notions of all Mankind' to jostling atoms has much more to do with Lucretius and Epicurean physics than with anticipating Freud or Brown.

The idea too that in the Digression on Madness 'the resonance of Renaissance "fool" has disappeared' seems to me over-simple. That a change of sympathy occurred between the attitudes to folly implied by 'Lear and his Fool' and those of Swiftian satire is not in dispute. But the Digression on Madness has an overt allusive relationship with Erasmus's *Praise of Folly*, and many of its ironies depend on some kind of reversal or part reversal of the Erasmian paradoxes about the wisdom of folly. The madness of the Digression's author is not only played off against some straightforward norm of reasonableness or sanity, but implies that his folly, which claims wisdom, lacks the wisdom which Erasmus attributed to good folly in his great prototype of the mock-encomium, from which Swift's Digression derives.

The full history of the idea of madness in eighteenth-century literature and thought, and of its relations with developments in the theory and practice of medicine, law, criminology, etc., has yet to be told. Perhaps it can only be told by the concerted work of experts in several fields, working towards a co-ordinated end. A remarkable book, which bears obliquely on this theme, may perhaps provide a model. In *The Wild Man Within: An Image in*

Western Thought from the Renaissance to Romanticism, edited by Edward Dudley and Maximillian E. Novak, experts in political science, history, and the literary and cultural history of America, England, France, Germany and Spain have come together to provide an uneven but surprisingly well-integrated study. One of its leading themes is parallel to Byrd's, namely that attitudes to, and definitions of, the wild man or savage were, like the attitudes to madness, based less on objective observation than on the inner needs of the observer. Among the contributions directly relevant to students of the seventeenth and eighteenth centuries are accounts of 'Thomas Hobbes and the Politics of Wild Men' (by Richard Ashcraft: this essay might be read as a companion-piece to the account of Hobbesian psychology in DePorte's *Nightmares and Hobbyhorses*), of Rousseau's *Discourses* (by Geoffrey Symcox), of Mozart's Papegeno (a brief piece by Ehrhard Bahr), and of some Romantic transformations of the Wild Man (by Peter Thorslev), the latter parallel in some ways to the changing conceptions of madness as traced by Byrd. The most delightful of the eighteenth-century discussions is 'The Wild Man Comes to Tea' by Maximillian E. Novak, an immensely learned chapter in the history of primitivism, and of our tendency to domesticate our conceptions of the savage. It also has the nowadays unusual distinction of throwing some real new light on *Gulliver's Travels*.

1975

Notes

1 Martin C. Battestin, *The Providence of Wit: Aspects of Form in Augustan Literature and the Arts* (Clarendon Press, 1974); Thomas E. Maresca, *Epic to Novel* (Ohio State University Press, 1974); Reuben A. Brower, *Mirror on Mirror, Translation, Imitation, Parody* (Harvard University Press, 1974); Phillip Harth, (ed.), *New Approaches to Eighteenth-Century Literature* (Columbia University Press, 1974); Irvin Ehrenpreis, *Literary Meaning and Augustan Values* (University Press of Virginia, 1974); Michael V. DePorte, *Nightmares and Hobbyhorses: Swift, Sterne, and Augustan Ideas of Madness* (Huntington Library, 1974); Max Byrd, *Visits to Bedlam: Madness and Literature in the Eighteenth Century*, (University of South Carolina Press, 1974); Edward Dudley and Maximillian E. Novak (eds), *The Wild Man Within: An Image in Western Thought from the Renaissance to Romanticism* (University of Pittsburgh Press, 1972).

2 The particular case of Prudence is discussed on p. 396 ff.

3 Maresca discusses the same passage, and does grant that 'one of the most hackneyed metaphors of love poetry' may be involved. But what he wants to emphasise is the creation of 'a Belindacentric universe competing with, and almost eclipsing, the heliocentric world of "reality"'. Belinda becomes a false god, with her own personalised *fiat-lux*-kit. But, unlike the sun, who rises and sets and rises again, Belinda 'will die,' so that, as Maresca knows the older poet said, her eyes 'are nothing like the sun' after all. But then, she picks up 'immortality' from the poem itself, rather than from 'her own miscreated

415

universe', so that if not the sun, she is at least a star, 'peripheral rather than central' (*Epic to Novel*, 82–3, 87, 95). I think I prefer the simpler version of Battestin to Maresca's jumpy and knowing sophistication.

4   *Windsor-Forest*, ll.327–28; 'Epitaph. Intended for Sir Isaac Newton'.

5   See A. D. Nuttall, 'Fishes in the Trees', *Essays in Criticism*, 24 (1974), 27–28 on this passage. The whole essay is a sharp and delightful exploration. For some studies, and lists of examples, of the *adynaton*, see my note, 'Rabelais and Horace: A Contact in *Tiers Livre*, ch. III', *French Studies*, 19 (1965), 376–77, 378 nn. 8, 11. On pp. 108–09 Battestin suggests that the dancing forests, whales sporting in woods and dolphins in the skies in *Dunciad A*, III:241–2, recall Milton, VII:324 and 410ff. These are standard *adynata*, and there seem to be no grounds for supposing that Milton was being specifically drawn attention to. Neither of Milton's two passages is an example of this very common figure. In the second Milton passage, the dolphins play and the whale sleeps or swims, but in the sea, like all real dolphins and whales, and not in woods or in the sky. Pope himself cites Horace, *Ars Poetica*, I:30, not Milton.

6   One might add another undistinguished example, in Soame Jenyns, 'The Art of Dancing' (1729), *Works*, 2nd edn. (1793), I:27.

7   For some sensitively observed notes on the decline of the heroic in literature in the lifetime of Pope, see another of the books under review, R. A. Brower, *Mirror on Mirror*, 67ff, 74–5. Brower's argument is that Pope was still 'just able to' believe 'in the heroic ideal' and 'the older unquestioning patriotism', and that this gave its particular tone, its special strengths and some limitations, to his translation of Homer. As one would expect, the conclusions are based on close and discriminating analysis of particular passages, and on a sensitive understanding of the Homeric original. Maresca's *Epic to Novel* is also concerned with aspects of the decline of traditional epic.

8   A marginal exception is part of a stanza added to the poem when it was set to music for public performance at Cambridge in 1730. This version was specially prepared for the occasion, and, according to the Twickenham editors, appears only in *Quaestiones, una cum Carminibus, in Magnis Comitiis Cantabrigiae Celebratis 1730* (1730), and in no edition of Pope's own works (*Minor Poems*, ed. Norman Ault and John Butt (London and New Haven, 1964), 31, 35–6). The argument by James Hutton, 'Some English Poems in Praise of Music', *English Miscellany*, 2 (1951), 60–61, that Dryden's and Pope's St Cecilia poems were written after the time when their conventional tributes to the power of music were any longer matters of literal belief, is rejected by Battestin: but like the studies listed in my next note, it is based on a detailed examination of a whole tradition as it developed through the Renaissance to the time of Pope.

9   John Hollander, *The Untuning of the Sky: Ideas of Music in English Poetry 1500–1700* (New York, 1970), 421–2, and see 403, 410 and 390–422 *passim*; D. T. Mace, 'Musical Humanism, the Doctrine of Rhythmus, and the Saint Cecilia Odes of Dryden', *Journal of the Warburg and Courtauld Institutes*, 27(1964), 251–92, esp. 266ff. Hollander's elaborately documented study is barely mentioned, for dismissal as erroneous, and Mace is not mentioned at all. J. A. Levine's 'Dryden's *Song for St Cecilia's Day, 1687*,' *PQ*, 44 (1965), 38–50, cited along with Earl R. Wasserman's study of Pope's 'Ode for Musick', *ELH*, 28 (1961), 163–86, in support of Battestin's general argument, seeks only to 'modify' in Dryden's special case Hollander's view of the outmodedness in Dryden's time of the 'cosmological orthodoxies': 'Dryden achieves his total ironic effect by ignoring the usual Cecilian mode of amiable

chirping and by founding his "novel" approach upon an almost outmoded body of symbolism and belief' (Levine, 48–50).

10 Mace, 271.

11 It is here that Brower's critical methods, which rely not only on the very great learning which he shares with Battestin, but on exceptionally delicate and discriminating analysis of literary texts, are particularly strong, both in his earlier writings on Pope, and in several essays in *Mirror on Mirror*, notably 'Pope's *Iliad* for Twentieth-Century Readers', 'From the *Iliad* to the Novel, via the *Rape of the Lock*', and 'Dryden's Epic Manner and Virgil'. Brower's writings, together with those of Maynard Mack, are praised by Donald Greene in an essay on 'The Study of Eighteenth-Century Literature', which is partly concerned to warn against 'the "world picture" method – the bland assumption that we can extrapolate to Dryden or Swift or Johnson what a fairly large number of their lesser contemporaries were allegedly thinking' (*New Approaches to Eighteenth-Century Literature*, ed. Harth, 23, 30, 15). I feel sure that Greene had in mind inferior practitioners, and not Battestin himself, but I think his cautions are to some extent applicable to Battestin's book too.

12 *ECS*, 1 (1967), 127–58; 3 (1970), 307–38, 491–522, reprinted as the first three chapters of my *Henry Fielding and the Augustan Ideal Under Stress* (London and Boston, 1972).

13 *Essay on Criticism*, ll.362–3.

14 George Watson (ed.), *Of Dramatic Poesy and other Critical Essays* (London and New York, 1962), I:89.

15 In some places, Brower might be thought to be doing something rather similar: 'Pope must have seen that the fixity of Homer's epithets implied a fixity in the scheme of things, an order that he naturally interpreted as the Great Show of Nature of seventeenth- and eighteenth-century philosophers. In comparison with later translators Pope thus has a further advantage in the eternal return of his rhymes. As in his original poems they lend added assurance that all is ordered for the best in the best of imagined worlds. They do this simply by being heard, and by recurring so often in company with familiar words and orders of words, and with familiar kinds of meaning' (*Mirror on Mirror*, 70–71). These words express a view which may seem superficially like Battestin's. But the unhectoring tentativeness with which he writes of Pope's rhymes as lending 'added assurance' and of the universal order as 'the best of *imagined* worlds' (my italics) contrasts with the baldness of Battestin's pronouncements. Brower is seeking to convey a reading experience, which picks up intimations or reassurances of order, and not an abstract contemplation of thematic structures. His comments emerge from the total literary fact rather than from ideological extrapolation. In all Brower's readings we are conscious of the full quality and flavour of the passages he is discussing, their eloquence and their humour, their fervour and their irony, their heroic aspirations and their touches of homeliness; and any comment which tends to the ideological or suggests a 'world picture' has visibly taken these things into account.

Two recent books, William Bowman Piper, *The Heroic Couplet*, 1969, and John A. Jones, *Pope's Couplet Art*, 1969, are among several recent works which deal with Battestin's theme, and in some ways anticipate him, but which are not mentioned here. Piper's book notes that 'Pope's metrical practice projects his faith in a metaphysical harmony' (146, 145–50), but most of the emphasis in his book is on the social rather than the metaphysical implications of Pope's couplet-rhetoric (137–45, *et passim*), as, in my view, it ought to be.

16 In the literature of 'sensibility' prudence was often thought by its very nature to be an obstacle to spontaneous benevolence. Hannah More wrote, in her poem 'Sensibility' (1782), of 'Benevolence, which seldom stays to chuse, / Lest pausing prudence tempt her to refuse' (*Works*, V (1834), 334). Fielding is by no means a typical novelist of 'sensibility', but his affinities with some aspects of that literature, and his importance as one of its precursors, are obvious and well-recognised. In any event, there is a much more compelling case for regarding 'benevolence' (or 'good nature') rather than prudence as the principal virtue celebrated in *Tom Jones*. Fielding often held that benevolence was insufficient without prudence, but never that prudence was acceptable without benevolence.

17 For a brief recent statement on prudence, providence and happy endings, which seems to me to have a much more correct critical perspective on *Tom Jones* than Battestin's long discussion, see Martin Price, 'The Fictional Contract', in Frank Brady, John Palmer and Martin Price (eds), *Literary Theory and Structure: Essays in Honor of William K. Wimsatt* (New Haven and London, 1973), 160.

18 *Mirror on Mirror*, 83. Another interesting exploration of transitions from the mock-heroic *Rape of the Lock* to the novel (in this case *Clarissa*) may be read in conjunction with Brower's essay. It is Leo Braudy's 'Penetration and Impenetrability in *Clarissa*', *New Approaches to Eighteenth-Century Literature*, 177–206. This essay is not, however, without some divagations, of which the comparison between *Gulliver's Travels* and *Clarissa* (197ff) is perhaps the chief.

19 This book reprints a number of Ehrenpreis's essays, including the magisterial 'Personae'. It also contains a newly published discussion of *Gulliver's Travels*.

20 Wallace Stevens, *Notes Toward a Supreme Fiction*, II:i.

21 The phrase is borrowed from Mary Claire Randolph, 'The Medical Concept in English Renaissance Satiric Theory: its Possible Relationships and Implications', *SP*, 38 (1941), 125–57.

Index

Index

Montaigne, Michel de 69, 73, 77, 102, 250, 328
Monthly Magazine 351
Monthly Review 342, 351
Moody, A. D. 220
Moore, Mrs 65
Moore, J. N. P. 66
Moore, Thomas 311–12
Moorehead, Alan 104
More, Hannah 344; 'Sensibility' 351, 418; *Strictures on the Modern System of Female Education* 344, 352
Morisot, J.-C. 101
Morrice, Bezaleel 389
Morris, William 204
Moryson, Fynes 142
Mozart, Wolfgang Amadeus *Magic Flute* 415
Murry, John Middleton 338
Murtuza, Athar 189
Mylne, Vivienne 302

Najder, Zdzislaw 101
Nash, Ogden 157
Needham, G. B. 352
Nero 216, 243, 252
Nerval, Gérard de 190
Nettleton, G. H. 353
New Testament 110
Newcomb, Thomas 389
Newton, Sir Isaac 317, 374, 384, 392
Newton, John 366; *Olney Hymns* 366
Nicolson, Marjorie Hope 189
Niklaus, Robert 302
Noah 106, 108
Nokes, David 141
Nordau, Max 251
Norton, Mary *Avenger* novels 113–20; *Bedknob and Broomstick* 103
Novak, Maximillian E. 415
Nussbaum, Felicity 192
Nuttall, A. D. 220, 416

Old Testament 110, 143
Oldmixon, John 248, 302
Opie, Iona and Peter 194–5
Origen 243
Orosius 244
Orwell, George 17
Osborn, James M. 219
Otway-Ruthven, A. J. 142
Ovid 211, 214, 243, 246, 378; *Metamorphoses* 378

Oxford, Edward Harley, second Earl of 137, 219
Oxford, Robert Harley, first Earl of 37, 257

Page, Norman 305, 308
Pagliaro, Harold E. 220
Palmer, John 418
Panegyric on the Author of Absalom and Achitophel (1681) 190
Paoli, Pasquale 359, 362
Parry, Benita 102
Parsons, Talcott 141
Parsons, Theophilus 390
Pascal, Roy 308
Patrides, C. A. 395
Paulson, Ronald 309
Pemberton, J. 302
Persius 245
Petronius, *Satyricon* 305
Petty, Sir William 122
Phalaris 216
Philips, Ambrose 188, 196, 305
Pichois, Claude 185
Piper, David 372
Piper, William Bowman 417
Pitt, William, the Younger 251
Plato 11, 72, 409
Plotinus 400
Plutarch 102
Pocock, Gordon 218, 235–42
Poe, Edgar Allan 202, 218
Pope, Alexander 26, 45, 61–5, 129, 147, 150–3, 158–9, 166, 180, 185–94, 196–9, 201–43, 249, 254–8, 312–13, 370–2, 375–9, 384–92, 394–6, 403, 405, 407, 411, 416–17; 'Alcander' 222; 'Brutus' 207, 223–4; *Dunciad* 22, 61, 174, 190, 196–8, 201–21, 223, 270, 313–14, 375, 386–9, 407–8, 412, 416; *Epilogue to the Satires* 62; *Epistle to Augustus* 249; *Epistle to Dr. Arbuthnot* 200, 303–4; *Essay on Criticism* 202–3, 237, 239, 253, 285, 386, 391–2, 417; *Essay on Man* 64, 224–34, 240, 307, 385, 395; *First Satire of the Second Book of Horace, Imitated* 158–9, 186, 225, 257; *Further Account of the Most Deplorable Condition of Mr. Edmund Curll* 302; *Guardian*, contributions to 201–3, 218, 305; Homer, translation of 147, 190, 203, 205, 219, 222–3, 327, 371,

Index